GW01605592

THE COMPLETE BOOK OF GOLF

This material previously appeared in *Improve Your Golf*.
This volume compiled by Steven Carr and Sally Strugnell.

CLB 2540
This edition published 1994 by Tiger Books International PLC, London in association with CLB Publishing, Godalming, Surrey

Printed and bound in Hong Kong
ISBN 1-85501-540-4

THE COMPLETE BOOK OF GOLF

TIGER BOOKS INTERNATIONAL
LONDON

CONTENTS

OPEN

Introduction

Golf is a phenomenon within the sporting world. It's not a game that people naturally turn to in their youth, and many don't try it until quite late in their lives, but once sampled and invariably they're hooked. Golf is a bug, but an extremely pleasant one.

An amazing variety of settings, a host of colourful characters, and techniques that are never totally mastered are among the pleasures that make golf unique. It begs you to find new challenges and cajoles you into aspiring to play like the greats – if only for one hole.

The Complete Book of Golf takes you on a comprehensive tour through the sometimes complicated but always fascinating world of golf. It identifies the great courses dotted around our shorelines, forests, and heaths – all thoroughbreds in their own individual way – but more than anything, this book lends a hand in your quest to conquer sport's hardest game.

The techniques section is designed to give an all-encompassing guide to the hows and whys of the golf swing.

Hopefully, the information within these pages will not only increase your knowledge of the game, but will also give you the desire and confidence to tackle any course, anywhere, come rain or shine.

1

GREAT COURSES

There is no greater thrill for a golfer than to step on to the first tee of one of the world's premier championship courses knowing that you are following in the footsteps of some of the game's greatest players. And then when you make a birdie at the difficult 12th, you can point to the time a star player made a complete hash of it during a tournament.

Imagine the sheer pleasure, if you've not already experienced it, of making a par at the dreaded Road Hole at St Andrews, or clearing the water on the Belfry's 18th. Golf seems to be the only sport where mere mortals can, for a short time, feel like top pros.

Profiled in this capter are 16 of the world's finest courses for your imagination to run riot on. Not only is it a superb pictoral account, but also a helpful playing guide to each hole, providing a detailed insight as to how four of the most challenging holes on each course should be tackled, highlighting their dangers and delights.

From America's west coast and the challenges of Pebble Beach, to the sandy wastes of Australia and Royal Melbourne, each featured course is an individual experience, and although you may never set foot on any of them, it gives you something to aspire to.

Crowds gather at the16th during the 1991 US Masters at Augusta.

Augusta

The stunningly beautiful Augusta course set in the American Deep South is the home of the famous Masters tournament. Superb design and lightning-fast greens make it one of the world's best.

Even if they've never set foot on Augusta National's lush greens, most enthusiasts are familiar with this spectacular course, the home of the US Masters. Generous fairways are set against a marvellous landscaping of trees and lakes. It's a dream course: skilfully designed, superbly laid out, impeccably maintained.

Augusta looks great, and plays brilliantly. It's strategically designed to be a real test of a player's initiative. Precise positioning of the drive is particularly vital if you are to attack the pin successfully.

The course has wide fairways, large greens and few rough areas. There aren't many bunkers – less than 50 altogether. Numerous trees along the fairways are a hazard, but an experienced player should find a path through them.

GREEN SPEED

It's the speed of the greens that makes Augusta a challenge – the putting surfaces are lightning-fast. The greens are skilfully contoured and demand extremely accurate putting. A player hoping to birdie has to place his shot precisely to avoid a downhill putt.

The Masters competitor must go for the greens with his second shot on the par 5s, where many a round is made or ruined.

▼ A display of shrubs and trees makes the precision-mown Augusta National a magnificent setting for the US Masters, played every April. The names of holes – Flowering Peach, Camellia, Juniper – are a reminder that the course was once a nursery.

HOLE BY HOLE

Championship tees: 6905 yards, par 72.

1st hole – Tea Olive
(Champ 400yd Par 4) A tee shot down the right half of the fairway leaves you well placed for your second shot.

2nd hole – Pink Dogwood
(Champ 555yd Par 5) A good tee shot should catch the downslope and shorten this long hole.

3rd hole – Flowering Peach
(Champ 360yd Par 4) Drive down the right for a shorter pitch on your second.

4th hole – Flowering Crab Apple
(Champ 205yd Par 3) Watch out for the wind – it can affect your shot to the green that slopes from back to front.

5th hole – Magnolia
(Champ 435yd Par 4) Draw your tee shot to avoid a more difficult approach from the right of the fairway.

6th hole – Juniper
(Champ 180yd Par 3) Hit your drive as far as possible to avoid the bunker.

7th hole – Pampas
(Champ 360yd Par 4) Watch out for the narrow fairway.

8th hole – Yellow Jasmine
(Champ 535yd Par 5) A long hole – play for a 6.

9th hole – Carolina Cherry
(Champ 435yd Par 4) Drive down the left for a shorter second shot.

10th hole – Camellia
(Champ 485yd Par 4) A tee shot down the left finds the downslope which gives you more distance.

11th hole – White Dogwood
(Champ 455yd Par 4) Hit your approach shot to the right to avoid the pond.

12th hole – Golden Bell
(Champ 155yd Par 3) Judge the distance carefully to avoid the bunker and water.

13th hole – Azalea
(Champ 465yd Par 5) Watch your tee shot – if you go to the right you could end up on the sidehill.

▲The Augusta clubhouse dates from the mid 19th century and symbolizes the club's traditional nature. With only 300 members, the course is never overplayed.

Augusta was the brainchild of Robert Tyre Jones Jnr, better known as the great Bobby Jones. After winning the Grand Slam, he retired early from competitive golf.

Bobby Jones was still only 28 years old and had two ambitions: to design a perfect set of clubs, which he did, and to give his home state of Georgia – and the South as a whole – a course of championship quality. The result is Augusta.

FRUITFUL COURSE

In the Fruitlands Nurseries Jones found the site for his dream course. He fell in love with the place and decided to buy it. Despite the Depression – when more courses were closing than opening – the project moved swiftly ahead.

The architect Jones chose for Augusta was Alister Mackenzie, who designed the impressive golf course at Cypress

14th hole – Chinese Fir
(Champ 405yd Par 4) Aim your second towards the back of the green for the safest putt.

15th hole – Fire Thorn
(Champ 500yd Par 5) Drive right for the best line to the green.

16th hole – Red Bud
(Champ 170yd Par 3) Don't be tempted to play too far to the left – you could end up in the pond.

17th hole – Nandina
(Champ 400yd Par 4) Although this looks like an easy hole, your second shot is blind.

18th hole – Holly
(Champ 405yd Par 4) Fade your tee shot to avoid the bunkers and for the best line to the green.

FOUR HOLES TO WATCH

◀ *12th hole – Golden Bell*

(Champ 155yd Par 3)

This is the second of three difficult holes that make up the famous Amen Corner – which has dashed many a Masters player's hopes. It's a tricky hole to play as you cannot feel the strength of the wind when you weigh up your shot on the tee.

There are two common mistakes to avoid. The first is not selecting the right club, so the ball falls short into the creek. Another problem occurs if the ball lands on the bank behind the green. From there your best bet is to leave the chip or bunker shot short – it's all too easy to run past the hole into the water.

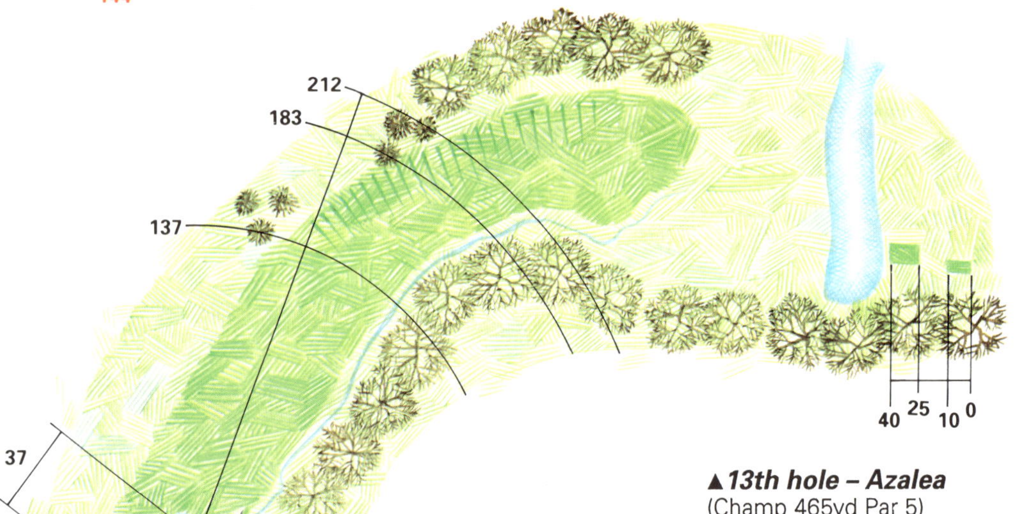

▲ *13th hole – Azalea*

(Champ 465yd Par 5)

This short par 5 is a dog-leg which turns left quite sharply. Try to follow this line with your tee shot to shorten the hole and give yourself a flat lie for your second shot. If your tee shot goes right, you have a sidehill to contend with.

With your second, either play safely short of the creek which swings across the front and right of the green, or try for a birdie by clearing Rae's Creek. Take care when the pin is at the front of the green – you have a narrow margin to clear the water.

◀ The water in front of the 15th hole makes it a tricky one to play. You must place the ball accurately to avoid the pond. Bear the wind in mind – it can catch you unawares and drive the ball over the edge of the green into the water.

►The beautiful 12th hole is the second of three that make up the feared Amen Corner – so named because players say a prayer if they get through without a problem. The swirling winds make the 12th one of the hardest holes on the course.

▼ *15th hole – Fire Thorn*

(Champ 500yd Par 5)

Your tee shot can go a long way off line without getting into trouble, but you're better off trying for a shot from the right of the fairway to find the green.

Don't go for the green in 2 – lay up short of the pond and chip in for 3.

If the wind is behind you, it's difficult to hold the green, especially when the flag is on the left where the green is shallow. It's risky to putt from the back of the green – the ball could run down the slope into the pond.

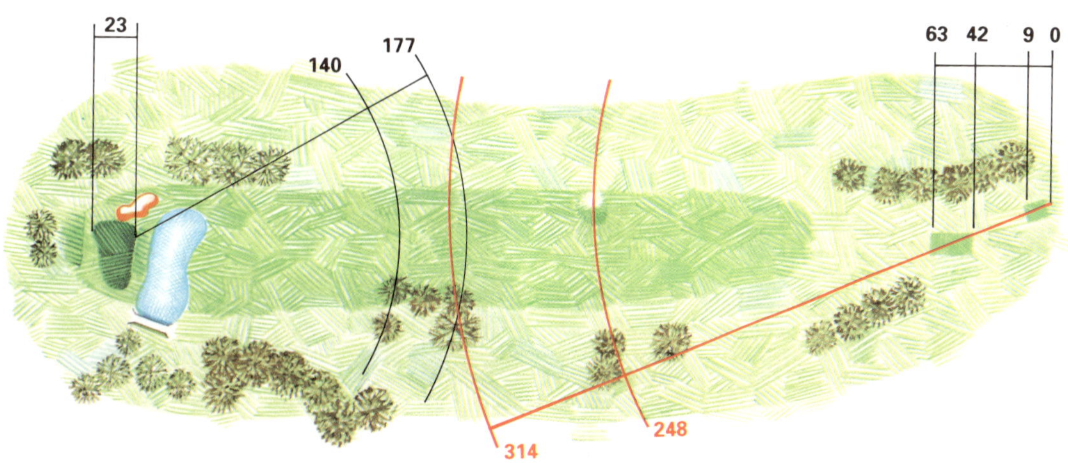

16th hole – Red Bud ►

(Champ 170yd Par 3)

Most of the fairway is covered by a lake, making it difficult to judge the distance to the green. Another danger is the three bunkers which surround the green. But the contours of the green pose the real threat on this hole.

Take your time and try to judge your shots accurately. Hit your tee shot hard to clear the lake and reach the green.

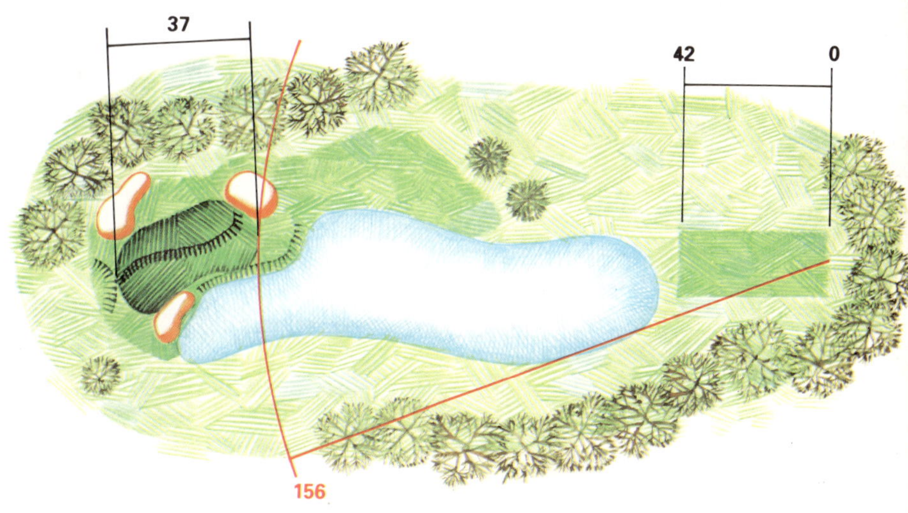

FACTFILE

Lowest score
63 – Nick Price, 1986 US Masters

Tournaments
US Masters – 1934 to present

Masters devotion
Clifford Roberts spent much of his life thinking up ways to improve the Masters. In 1960 he introduced the leader boards, with red numbers for totals under par and green for par or higher.

This helps spectators and TV viewers to see exactly what the state of play is at any given time.

Twice as nice
In 1935 Gene Sarazen played one of the greatest – and luckiest – shots ever. With four holes to play, he needed three birdies to tie with Craig Wood who had completed his round.

Sarazen faced a long shot over water to the 15th green to make his birdie 4. In his position he had to take a risk and play long. His ball hit the far bank, skipped up, ran on towards the back of the green and dropped into the hole, giving him an albatross.

With that shot Sarazen caught Wood, went on to par the last three holes and then won the play-off the following day.

Double trouble
A minor slip brought disaster to the amateur Frank Stranahan in 1948. He was thrown out of the Masters tournament for playing two balls during a practice round – it had been announced that only one could be used.

▲The 16th hole was changed after the course was completed to include a lake which covers most of the fairway. Sandy Lyle's downhill birdie putt here helped him secure the Masters title in 1988.

Point in California. Unlike many championship golfers, Jones didn't think that being a great player automatically meant he could design terrific courses. In Mackenzie he found a man who could.

Mackenzie worked out the routing of the course and the individual holes; Jones tested their playing qualities.

When the course was ready for play, Augusta was considered as a possible home for the US Open, but the Georgia summer was too hot for the championship. Instead, the Masters tournament was born and has been played at Augusta ever since.

The first event was held in March 1934 and attracted enormous attention, mainly because Jones was to play. In fact, Horton Smith was the first tournament winner and repeated his victory two years later.

Jones made a change to the course that became significant with the arrival of television in 1956. Augusta has two loops of nine holes, both returning to the clubhouse. As Mackenzie routed the course, the nine holes televised today were played first. Jones decided that they made a more dramatic finish, so they are now played last and millions of viewers can enjoy thrilling Masters climaxes.

MASTERPIECES

The last nine holes at Augusta are the most famous in the world. In 1988 the 18th hole witnessed Sandy Lyle's famous win – the first British player ever to take the title. Having hit his tee shot into the bunker – 150yd (136m) from the hole – Lyle had to get down in 3 more to tie, 2 to win. With his 7 iron, he hit the ball to within 12ft (3.5m) of the hole and then managed the straight putt to win the Masters.

Jack Nicklaus has donned the green jacket an amazing six times. His last triumph was in 1986. In spite of stiff competition from players like Langer, Ballesteros and Norman, Nicklaus played better with each round. He won the title at the age of 46 – the oldest Masters winner to date.

The US Masters has worldwide TV coverage. In Britain it's of special significance – it heralds spring and the start of a new golf season in the UK.

◄ The Masters tournament is the only event played at Augusta National. Vast crowds gather to see the world's best players fight for the honour of wearing the prestigious green jacket.

Ballybunion

Towering sand dunes, ridge after ridge of them, are formidably in play at this remote but welcoming Irish links. Situated at the edge of the Atlantic, the wind always seems to blow extra hard as you tackle the cliffside holes.

As you drive along the winding road to the clubhouse about 2 miles (3km) from the town centre your eyes feast on the opening holes. Flags flapping in the wind, plateau greens, a whole host of bunkers, rolling fairways – some generously wide – and a burn meandering across the course greet you. But there isn't a tree or a bush in sight.

Instead there are the dunes. Running at right angles to the shore, they readily catch a loose shot. You have to play the ball as it lies, and in summer the grass grows thick and tussocky to add to your trouble. But the views from these hills – both of the golf links and of the ocean and County Kerry countryside for miles around – are spectacular.

CAPTIVATING COURSE

Because of the fame it has acquired – thanks, partly, to Tom Watson's praise – and because of its onshore gales, many golfers think of Ballybunion as a particularly difficult course. Certainly it is a severe test, especially off the Championship tees, but at 6542 yards, par 71, it is not terribly long and contains five par 3s.

From the time you stand on the 1st tee you are captivated by the character of the place. It isn't everywhere that a graveyard presents the chief hazard off the opening tee – but at Ballybunion a slice is literally buried in the town cemetery.

You must also avoid two mid

▼ The 17th, like the 16th, is a left hand dog-leg. You look straight out to sea from the high tee before playing round the massive sand dune tucked into the angle of the dog-leg.

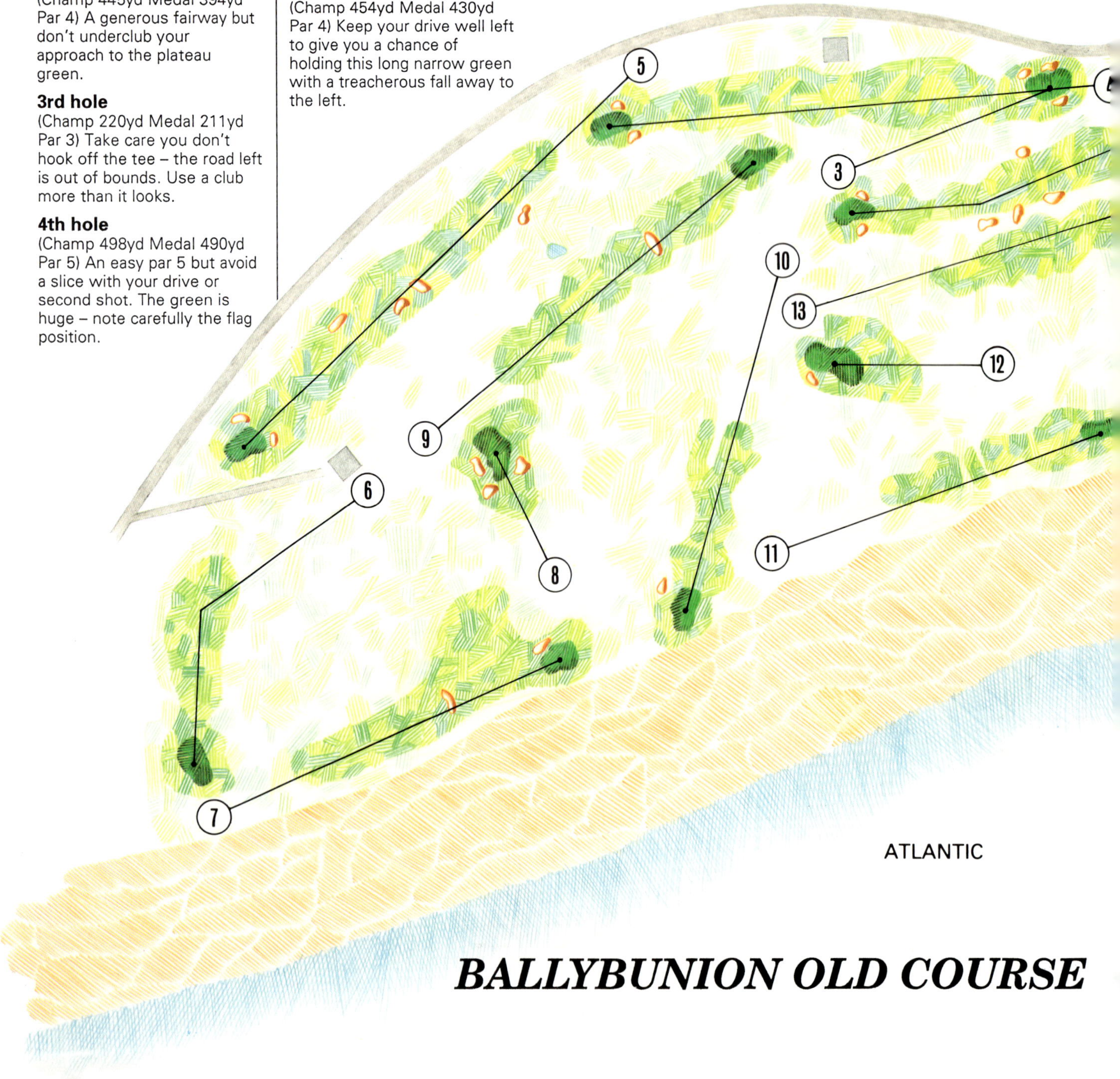

BALLYBUNION OLD COURSE

HOLE BY HOLE
Championship tees 6542yd, par 71, SSS 72. Medal tees 6201yd, par 71, SSS 70. Forward tees 5923yd, par 71, SSS 68.

1st hole
(Champ 392yd Medal 366yd Par 4) Beware the graveyard to the right of the tee and the mid fairway bunkers. Avoid missing the green to the left.

2nd hole
(Champ 445yd Medal 394yd Par 4) A generous fairway but don't underclub your approach to the plateau green.

3rd hole
(Champ 220yd Medal 211yd Par 3) Take care you don't hook off the tee – the road left is out of bounds. Use a club more than it looks.

4th hole
(Champ 498yd Medal 490yd Par 5) An easy par 5 but avoid a slice with your drive or second shot. The green is huge – note carefully the flag position.

5th hole
(Champ 508yd Medal 489yd Par 5) Keep clear of the out of bounds fence to the right and mid fairway bunkers – some are hidden.

6th hole
(Champ 364yd Medal 344yd Par 4) Play your drive as close as possible to the out of bounds wall right to give a clear shot at the 46yd (42m) long, narrow green. The ground slopes away steeply on both sides.

7th hole
(Champ 423yd Medal 400yd Par 4) Watch out – the green is on the cliff edge with trouble on the other side as well.

8th hole
(Champ 153yd Medal 134yd Par 3) There's little trouble at the back so play one more than you think.

9th hole
(Champ 454yd Medal 430yd Par 4) Keep your drive well left to give you a chance of holding this long narrow green with a treacherous fall away to the left.

10th hole
(Champ 359yd Medal 336yd Par 4) Avoid the deep gully just short of the green but don't overclub – there's out of bounds behind.

11th hole
(Champ 449yd Medal 400yd Par 4) You must hit a good drive to have any hope of getting home in 2.

12th hole
(Champ 192yd Medal 179yd Par 3) It's all carry to the plateau green so use enough club. Don't go right – a deep ravine awaits the slice.

13th hole
(Champ 484yd Medal 480yd Par 5) The burn crosses the fairway 70yd (64m) from the front of the green. Unless you can get up in 2 play short of the water.

14th hole
(Champ 131yd Medal 125yd Par 3) This requires a very precise iron, usually a 7 or 8. Again, it's advisable to be up.

15th hole
(Champ 216yd Medal 207yd Par 3) Judge the wind carefully – it can vary from a full driver to a 4 or 5 iron.

16th hole
(Champ 490yd Medal 482yd Par 5) Go for accuracy rather than distance.

17th hole
(Champ 385yd Medal 368yd Par 4) It's usually safe to play a driver from the tee – the prevailing wind is against.

18th hole
(Champ 379yd Medal 366yd Par 4) Choose your club with care – the second is entirely blind across a vast area of sand called Sahara.

ATLANTIC

How to play there

Irish golf clubs are renowned for their hearty welcome. Ballybunion stands out for its hospitality and the locals for their friendliness.

To play there, you need to produce a handicap certificate. In summer it's wise to book a month or so in advance but from November to March you can just walk on. Contact the Secretary at Ballybunion Golf Club, Ballybunion, Co Kerry, Ireland. Tel 010 353 68 27146.

There are lots of hotels and places to stay in Ballybunion – and most of them are packed with holidaymakers in summer. The town boasts an old ruined castle and there are also miles of yellow sandy beaches. Several other great courses – such as Waterville – are near by so it's worth planning your golf itinerary in advance.

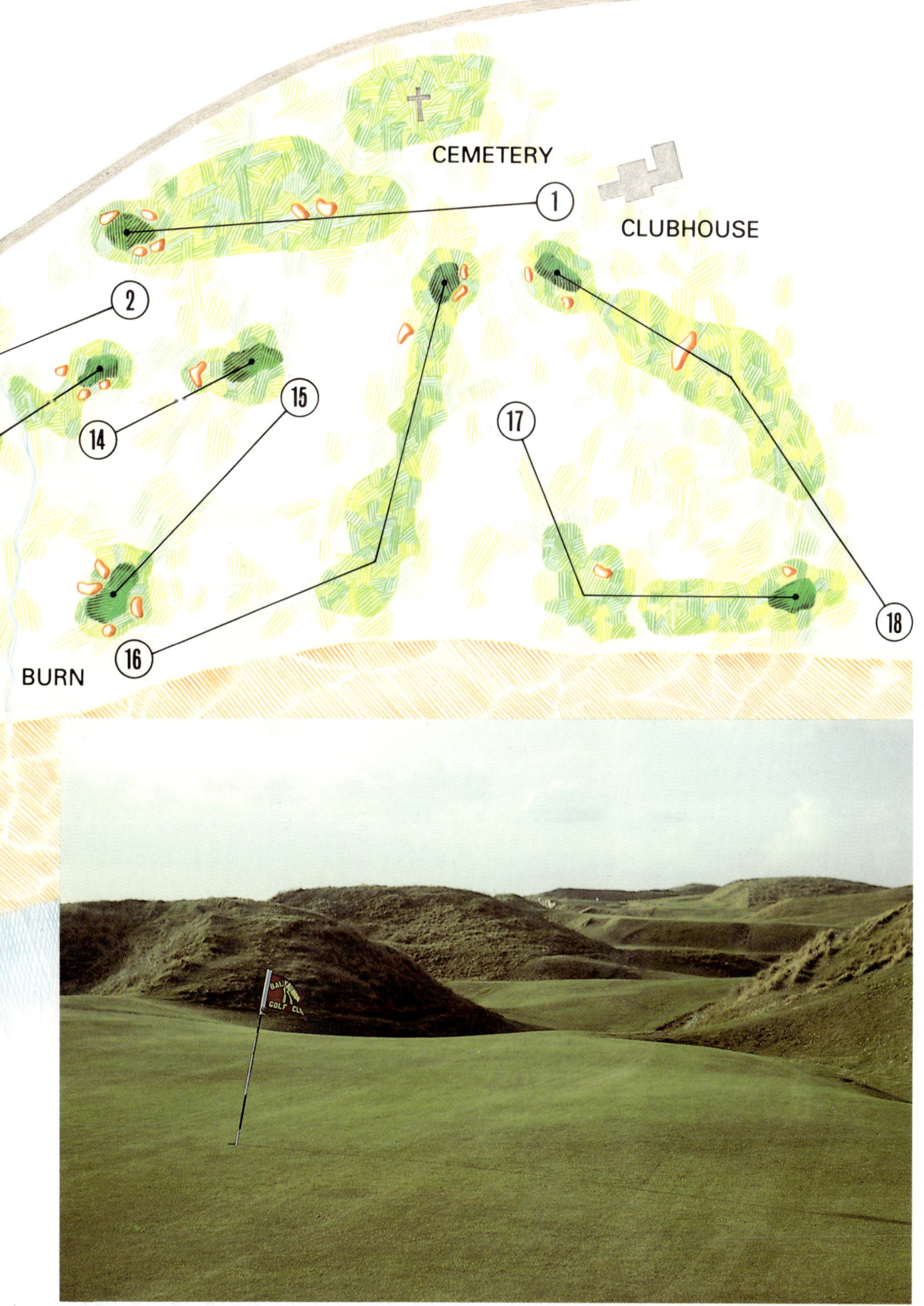

Hilly days

Before you go to Ballybunion, practise playing from sloping lies if you can. You'll have to contend with uphill, downhill and sidehill lies during your round.

The course is fair, with few blind shots, and demands accuracy. Balls that land either side of the green are punished more than straight shots hit slightly too hard or softly.

The contours don't end when you're on the greens. Remember to work on sloping putts as well as long shots when you practise.

◀ The 11th, a par 4 of 449 yards, is probably the stiffest test. Played from a tee on the cliff edge to a narrow fairway, it leaves a long iron or wood second shot to a green protected at the front on both sides by massive sandhills and thick rough.

FOUR HOLES TO WATCH

◄ *8th hole*

(Champ 153yd Par 3)
It looks so simple from the elevated tee to hit the green far below with as little as a 9 iron, especially as the prevailing wind helps. But the green is dangerously narrow, surrounded on the front and to the left by deep pot bunkers. Anything cut or pushed breaks away into a deep chasm on the right from which saving par is almost impossible.

It's best to play a club more than you think – there's little trouble at the back. Even then, it's difficult to get down in 2 putts on a green full of little borrows and undulations.

11th hole ►

(Champ 449yd Par 4)
One of the great par 4s in Irish golf, the tee is situated right on the cliff edge with the Atlantic crashing against the rocks far below. The tee shot is intimidating: a slice winds up in the sea and a hook in the dunes and thick rough. But a good drive sets up a magnificent challenge for the second, almost certainly with a wood.

The dunes continue down both sides of the fairway so thread your shot between them to reach the green – one of the few at Ballybunion that draws the ball in. There's no need for bunkers at this hole – it's tough enough without them.

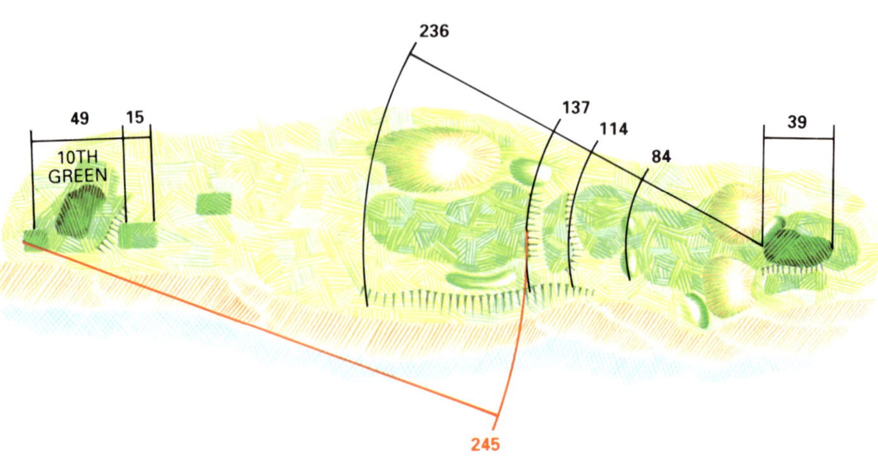

◄ *15th hole*

(Champ 216yd Par 3)
This is one of the hardest par 3s in golf. The tee shot, usually into a crosswind, often demands a perfectly struck driver that must carry all the way to the two tiered green. There are no escape routes, no safety nets at this great hole.

The green itself, located alongside the sea, is surrounded by bunkers, dunes and thick rough. If you are on the same tier as the flag the putting isn't too demanding; if you aren't you'll do well to avoid taking 3.

16th hole ►

(Champ 490yd Par 5)

A sporting par 5 where accuracy is far more important than length. Still, it takes a big drive to make it to the fairway where the hole turns sharply left away from the sea. It winds its way through the most imposing 100ft (30m) high duneland to a large back to front sloping green. The fairway gap is the narrowest on the course.

The prevailing wind helps at this hole and two straight shots get you close. Stray left or right, however, and recovery is extremely difficult.

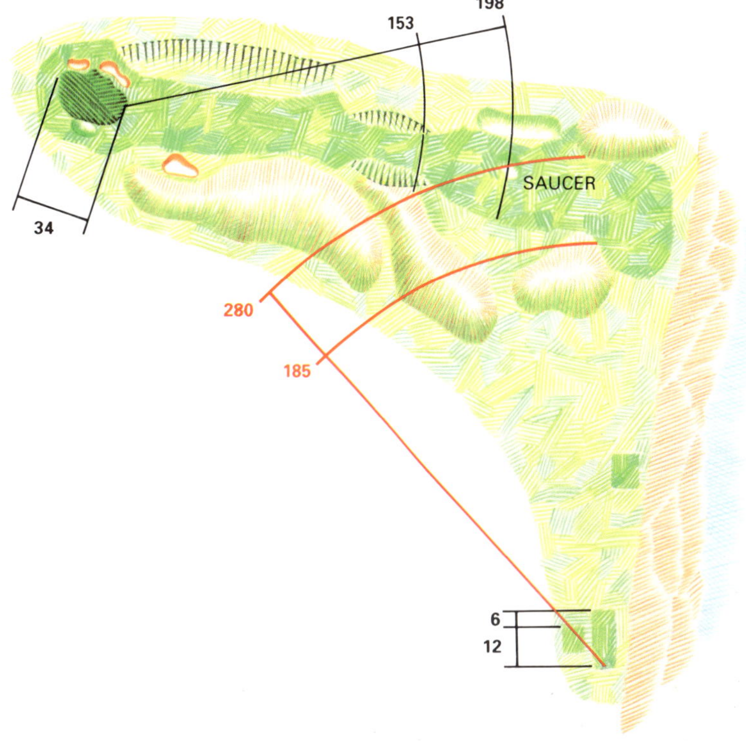

▼ The little 153 yard par 3 8th is many people's favourite. You play from a high tee to a small well guarded green far below, enjoying the best of the links – delightful springy turf, sand dune hills and gently undulating greens.

▲ **The par 3 15th is rated the best short hole on the links by former club manager Sean Walsh. Dunes take the place of trees at this wild and windswept natural course. If you're unfortunate enough to land on a dune you have to play the shot. From the steeply sloping grassy lie it's hard to play a controlled shot – just get the ball back in play.**

FACTFILE
Lowest scores
Amateur course record
67 – Pat Mulcare
Professional course record
65 – Jimmy Kinsella

Tournaments
Carrolls Irish Matchplay Championship – 1978
Carrolls No 1 professional tournament – 1967
Irish Professional Championship – 1957
Irish Close Amateur – 1937, 1958, 1971, 1979, 1991
Irish Ladies' Close Amateur – 1932, 1936, 1951, 1969, 1977, 1991

fairway bunkers, known as Mrs Simpson's after the wife of the English golf course architect who redesigned the links in 1936. Yet the 1st hole is a comfortable enough par 4 and provides a lovely start to the round.

Ballybunion really gets going at the 6th. A par 4 of only 364 yards, it requires the most precise second shot to stay on the long, narrow green. This is the favourite hole of Tom Watson. He comes back here summer after summer and adores the links: 'It is a course you will always enjoy and never tire of playing... Many golf architects should live and play [here] before they build golf courses. I consider it a true test.'

The great Christy O'Connor snr – 10 times national professional champion – has a more Irish way of describing Ballybunion: 'Anybody who breaks 70 here is playing better than he is able to play.'

Of the back nine, the 11th green is one of the few at Ballybunion that gathers in the approach shot. By now you'll have discovered that more often than not the irons must be struck with precision, otherwise the ball breaks away and leaves you with a deft pitch to salvage par. In Tom Watson's view, this is where the real difficulty of Ballybunion lies.

EARLY DAYS

Ballybunion Golf Club was originally founded in 1893 but died after only two years. The club was re-established in 1906 when a nine hole course was laid out on the instructions of Lionel Hewison, a prominent journalist of the day. It was extended to 18 holes in 1926.

When the Irish Championship of 1937 was fixed for Ballybunion, the English architect Tom Simpson was hired to give advice and make suitable alterations to the routing of the holes and the siting of the tees and greens.

He laid out the links very much as we know it today. But when the new clubhouse was built in 1970 the numbers of the holes had to be altered. The 14th (featuring Mrs Simpson's mid fairway bunkers) became the 1st and the 13th the 18th.

The course – widely accepted as one of Ireland's best – attracts visitors from all over the world. Set in the relatively remote south-west, Ballybunion has not as yet been invited to stage any international professional tournaments. But the Irish men's and ladies' championships have taken place there several times.

Cypress Point

A stone's throw from John Steinbeck's Cannery Row and Mayor Clint Eastwood's Carmel, the Monterey Peninsula is a place for hard men. Only hardened golfers need apply to take on its most fearsome course – Cypress Point.

Universally considered one of the most spectacular, Cypress Point is also certainly one of the world's most difficult golf courses.

The PGA Tour ranked the 16th and 17th as the two toughest holes the professionals played on the 1990 circuit. Of 100 holes ranked, Cypress Point was listed eight times.

DECEPTIVE RATING

At the 1990 AT&T pro-am the pros recorded 15 triple bogies at the par 3 16th, and 17 more at the par 4 17th. This is an embarrassing statistic considering Cypress Point is a par 72 layout with a USGA rating of 72.3, which suggests the degree of difficulty should not be severe. Yet it is.

The weather has much to do with how a player fares; if the winds are up, so are the scores. The beauty of Cypress is its exposed setting along the rugged coastline of California. It is this rocky, cliff strewn setting that makes Cypress such a challenge.

The course was designed by Alister Mackenzie and opened for play in 1928. The club has been male-dominated since then, but

▼ The course is one of the most spectacular spots on the secluded Monterey Peninsula about 90 miles (145km) south of San Francisco. The 16th crosses the upper bay to the green wedged into the neck of the furthest rocky outcrop while the 17th returns across the lower bay to another green hemmed in by the Pacific.

CYPRESS POINT

Hole by hole
Championship tees: 6506yd, Par 72, USGA rating 72.3.
Medal tees: 6373yd, Par 72.
Ladies' tees: 5832yd, Par 72.

15
14
16
1
17
2
18

1st hole
(Champ 418yd Medal 418yd Ladies' 404yd Par 4) A slightly elevated, sloping green tests your putting stroke.

2nd hole
(Champ 551yd Medal 551yd Ladies' 510yd Par 5) A long drive gives you a good second shot over fairway bunkers.

3rd hole
(Champ 161yd Medal 155yd Ladies' 136yd Par 3) Pin position makes all the difference on this well protected green.

4th hole
(Champ 385yd Medal 376yd Ladies' 376yd Par 4) Carry the fairway bunkers on the left and you are left with the best angle into a treacherous green.

5th hole
(Champ 491yd Medal 475yd Ladies' 417yd Par 5) Driving through a chute of trees, you are faced with a rolling dog-leg left, sprinkled with nine well placed bunkers.

6th hole
(Champ 522yd Medal 512yd Ladies' 481yd Par 5) The approach, played from a position beautifully framed by pines and six bunkers, needs to be hit from a difficult sidehill lie.

7th hole
(Champ 163yd Medal 161yd Ladies' 156yd Par 3) Only perfect length and accuracy is enough here as the green is surrounded by deep trouble.

8th hole
(Champ 355yd Medal 333yd Ladies' 311yd Par 4) The blind tee shot to a split-level fairway that dodges right leaves a dançerous second shot to a three-level, rollercoaster green surrounded by bunkers.

9th hole
(Champ 291yd Medal 291yd Ladies' 245yd Par 4) A precise second shot to a long, sloping green, surrounded by sand and tall grasses is your only hope for success.

10th hole
(Champ 491yd Medal 485yd Ladies' 470yd Par 5) This hole is reachable in 2 if you avoid the seven bunkers on the way to the green. A swift, subtle putting surface must not be taken lightly.

11th hole
(Champ 434yd Medal 422yd Ladies' 392yd Par 4) This is a long par 4, where distance off the tee is vital to provide a long to medium iron to the green.

12th hole
(Champ 409yd Medal 409yd Ladies' 315yd Par 4) This is a superb hole, protected on the point of the dog-leg by a bunker with the ever present dunes running along the entire right side. A narrow opening to the green is protected by sand and dunes grass.

▲ **Surrounded by elegant cypress trees and undeniably pretty though it is, the only weak link on the course is the par 4 18th. It's not much more than a drive and wedge back to the clubhouse, but after the exertions of the previous 17th holes few complain.**

13th hole
(Champ 362yd Medal 342yd Ladies' 342yd Par 4) After driving over a sand bar to a narrowing fairway, you have a medium to short iron remaining. The double level green is harboured among seven greenside bunkers.

14th hole
(Champ 383yd Medal 383yd Ladies' 321yd Par 4) A drive favouring the left side of the fairway opens the alley through a chute of cypress trees. The approach is protected by more cypress on both sides.

15th hole
(Champ 139yd Medal 126yd Ladies' 122yd Par 3) Yardage can be meaningless, depending on the weather. A short to medium iron must cross the inlet to a green amply guarded by six bunkers and thick pastures of ice plant.

16th hole
(Champ 233yd Medal 216yd Ladies' 205yd Par 3) Depending on the wind and the status of the match, you might elect to play for the green with a wood, or attempt the safer route left which is usually reachable with a mid iron.

17th hole
(Champ 376yd Medal 376yd Ladies' 338yd Par 4) The challenge of the second shot is enhanced by a cluster of formidable cypress in the middle of the fairway.

18th hole
(Champ 342yd Medal 342yd Ladies' 291yd Par 4) A barricade of cypress protects the corridors of this homeward hole. Normally, a short iron second is needed to a very fast green making for an exciting finish.

FOUR HOLES TO WATCH

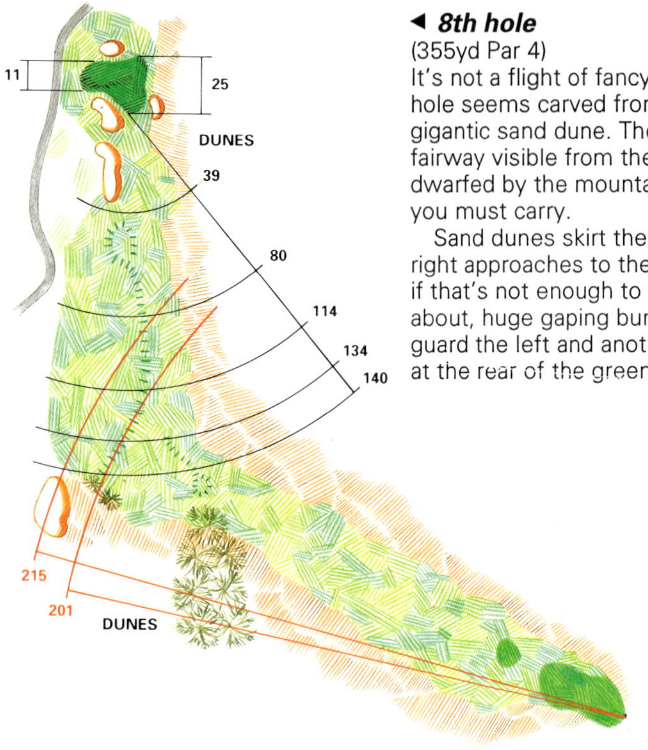

◄ 8th hole

(355yd Par 4)

It's not a flight of fancy if this hole seems carved from a gigantic sand dune. The ribbon of fairway visible from the tee is dwarfed by the mountain of sand you must carry.

Sand dunes skirt the left and right approaches to the green. As if that's not enough to worry about, huge gaping bunkers guard the left and another lurks at the rear of the green.

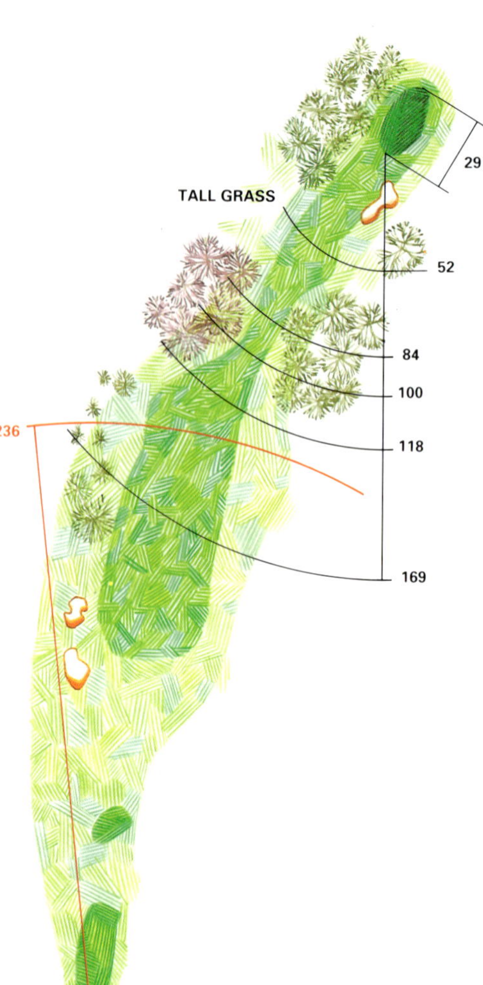

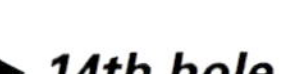

► 14th hole

(383yd Par 4)

This is a very precise hole where the weather and the direction of any winter storms make a big difference to its toughness. Pros usually hit a 1 iron off the tee, giving a view of the landing area but no hint of the green.

The length of the hole is not a factor, but the absence of a backdrop behind the green and a camouflaged bunker to the right make it very deceptive.

Hole-in-one club

Tournament lore has it that Ed 'Porky' Oliver, a colourful player at the early Crosby tournaments, once took 16 strokes to finish the 16th. But it has also been aced seven times, six of those by amateurs, including Bing Crosby himself in 1947.

The full list of aces is:
Professionals: Jerry Pate, 1982.
Amateurs: Ross Smith, 1944; Bing Crosby, 1947; A Thomas Taylor, 1972; Samuel Lindamood, 1976; George Downing, 1976; John Purchell, 1983.

► Probably the best tee shot in the world – the 16th is enough to take your breath away. There is no escape from launching a tee shot across the Pacific.

16th hole ►
(233yd Par 3)
As well as being one of the most intimidating shots in the world, this is a spellbinding hole where many matches are decided. You can't avoid hitting across an enormous expanse of crashing surf and granite rocks that separate tee from green.

Whether choosing the safe route to the left with a mid iron or going for the green with a wood, concentration on this hole is extremely difficult. The wind plays a vital role, so hope for a calm day when you arrive at one of the most hallowed spots in golf.

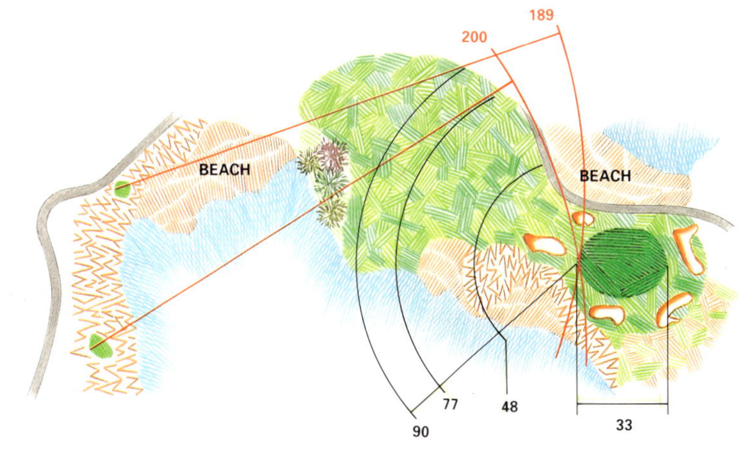

◄ ***17th hole***
(376yd Par 4)
The 17th can be the proverbial last straw. At the tip of Cypress Point, you seem to be surrounded by the Pacific Ocean and its spectacular coastline. Don't let the natural scenery entice you though.

Blocking the landing zone in the middle of the fairway is a small grove of cypress trees, which must be played over rather than through if the tee shot is errant.

Even the successful player however must deal with a green that is nestled on a precipice above the sea. Good mental and physical conditioning always help you survive this hole.

ironically it was a woman – Marion Hollins of New York – who was responsible for choosing Mackenzie as course designer.

Hollins – a real estate agent – and her partners had planned to sell 250 memberships at $2000 each, but the Wall Street Crash of 1929 changed those plans and only 40 were sold. While it has since increased to 250, it remains a very exclusive club.

Recognizing his layout could be nearly unplayable for the amateur, Mackenzie made some concessions without compromising the integrity of the design. He gave golfers the option of going for broke and being rewarded if successful, or taking the safe but longer route to the green. One of the best examples of this is the 16th itself.

The course is not all about those famous holes at the tip of the peninsula however – all of Cypress provides excellent golf.

The 1st is played down to a valley curving to the right and is a severe start. The 2nd is the longest on the course and has a demanding tee shot requiring a diagonal carry.

After the 2nd the course heads for a wooded hillside, the setting of the 5th through to the 11th. The 7th is a par 3 played from one hill to another over a valley, and the 9th shows that even a downhill par 4 of 291yd (265m) can be difficult – the small hard green can be very tricky to hold.

At the 11th tee you head back towards the rocky peninsula, with the 13th and 14th being seaside holes before the clifftops are reached.

ALL IS VANITY

It's not surprising the PGA ranked the 16th as the most difficult hole the touring pros faced in 1990. Obviously, the weather has something to do with its difficulty, but most of the disasters that happen here are caused by human vanity. What self-respecting pro would elect the easy way out and hit short and safe

Quote...unquote
Cypress Point has probably inspired more quotable quotes than any other course in the world.

The writer Cal Brown said: 'There cannot be another place on earth quite like it. It is as though every thundering emotion, every subtle line, had been withheld from creation and then dumped in one place to test our understanding of the superlative.'

OB Keeler, the biographer of Bobby Jones said the whole place resembled 'the crystallization of the dream of an artist who had been drinking gin and sobering up on absinthe.'

The best way to play the course according to actor Jack Lemmon is to 'appreciate the beauty while you can. The course is the most wonderful combination of beauty and beast.'

Sandy Tatum, a member and former president of the USGA, said it most simply. He called it 'the Sistine Chapel of golf'.

FACTFILE
Lowest Scores
Professionals:
62 – Gay Brewer, 1963
63 – Ben Hogan, 1948
63 – Jim Langley, 1973 (resident pro)
64 – Craig Stadler, 1982
Amateurs:
64 – FH Henneken, 1957

Tournaments
Bing Crosby National Pro-Am: 1947-1985
AT&T National Pro-Am: 1986-1990
Walker Cup: 1980

(Cypress Point ceased being part of the PGA Tour rotation after 1990 due to its policy towards black members.)

Rocky road
Rocco Mediate, who had been an early round leader at the 1990 AT&T, had this fate at Cypress: 'The last four holes were the hardest I ever played. You could have putted on the 16th for an hour and not made it. I simply couldn't stand still out there. My eyes were tearing. On my second shot on 17, I couldn't see at all.'

to the left?

The weather conditions are vital. When the pros played Cypress in February, 1990, the PGA reported: 'Thursday, it was mostly cloudy with rain showers. Friday, it was mostly sunny and breezy. Saturday it was overcast with winds up to 40mph. Play was suspended at 4.45pm with four groups unable to complete the round due to high wind. Golf balls would not remain still.'

The weather and the layout, or the 'beauty and the beast', make Cypress what it is. But the greens also leave an indelible impression on golfers. Tom Kite once said, 'They say everything breaks to the ocean at Cypress Point. Probably the Atlantic Ocean.'

SHORT CUT

The one serious weakness of the layout is the 18th. Nothing more than a drive and pitch with only the top of the flag visible on the second, it is little more than a short cut back to the clubhouse after the drama of the previous two holes. Indeed Cypress Point was once described as the best 17 hole course in the world.

Since it opened in 1928 only insignificant changes have been made. A few tees have been moved, a green remodelled, but nothing else.

Thought of as a course built for presidents, Cypress has hosted Dwight Eisenhower, who was a regular player, John F Kennedy and Gerald Ford. Members include Laurence Rockefeller, Leonard Firestone and local resident Clint Eastwood.

BOBBY'S BOOST

Perhaps the most lasting description of Cypress came from Bobby Jones. Back in 1929 the US Amateur was about to be played at neighbouring Pebble Beach when the great Jones was invited to play a couple of rounds at the new Cypress Point Club.

Afterwards he was asked to compare the two. 'Pebble Beach is more difficult, but Cypress is more fun,' Jones said in his typical diplomatic manner. His assessment rings true today for anyone fortunate to play this course – unless the wind is blowing at the 16th.

▼ The 15th is the shortest hole on the course but is fraught with danger. You must carry a rocky inlet to a long, narrow green completely surrounded by gaping bunkers. This is the first hole open to the ocean and can throw you into the teeth of a howling gale.

Kiawah Island

Regularly blasted by the 'inveterate rage' of the wild Atlantic, Kiawah Island is Pete Dye's American answer to the links courses of the British Isles – with a dash of southern comfort thrown in.

Although the Ocean Course at Kiawah Island only opened officially in mid 1991, it has already attracted a huge amount of attention. This is partly because of its spectacular setting on the Atlantic shore, but chiefly because it was awarded the 1991 Ryder Cup match between Europe and the USA.

The Ocean Course is built on land that golf architects dream about – a 200 acre finger of coastline on an island off South Carolina. The land is rich in wetlands, marshlands and sand dunes, with dozens of types of seaside grasses and springy sand-based turf. And, of course, it is rarely without a wind.

When Pete Dye, the American-born designer, first saw it he rubbed his eyes and said, 'If this doesn't turn out to be a good golf course, I should be shot. You don't need to do anything but build a golf course. Everything is here.'

Kiawah Island is a half hour drive south of Charleston. A soldier billeted there during the War of Independence wrote, 'The air is salubrious and rendered exceedingly soft by the salt vapour that rises from the sea. This island is divided from the mainland by a river on the north and blasted with inveterate rage by the Atlantic Ocean on the south. At low water it exhibits the finest beach in the south.'

LONG ISLAND

At Kiawah Dye has used none of the gimmicks, such as island greens, for which he has become renowned. The only railway sleepers are laid side by side to act as walkways to some tees.

Instead, Dye designed a course as similar to the British links courses as he could make and featuring the beach and the wind of the Atlantic to their best.

'This is going to be the best course anybody ever built,' Dye said once in an uncharacteristic moment of boastful enthusiasm, 'but I don't deserve any credit. God had already done 90% of the work.'

Dye's courses are long – some of the longest ever built – and the Ocean Course is no exception. Its maximum length is 7371yd (6734m) and as well as the two par 5s of between 520yd (475m) and 550yd (502m), it has two more that approach 600yd (548m).

The tees are often raised to make the tee shot more inviting and to

◄ Kiawah Island is part of that languid run of American coastline, stretching southwards from the Carolinas to Florida, which is home to alligator-infested mangrove swamps, the Kennedy space centre and world-class golf courses such as Sawgrass and Harbour Town.

13
12
14
15
16
2
3
1
9
8

◄ TO CLUBHOUSE

► **The 7th is a typical Kiawah hole with huge sandy wastes alarmingly close to the putting surface, water hazards snaking beside the fairway and deep scrub threatening to bury any wayward shot.**

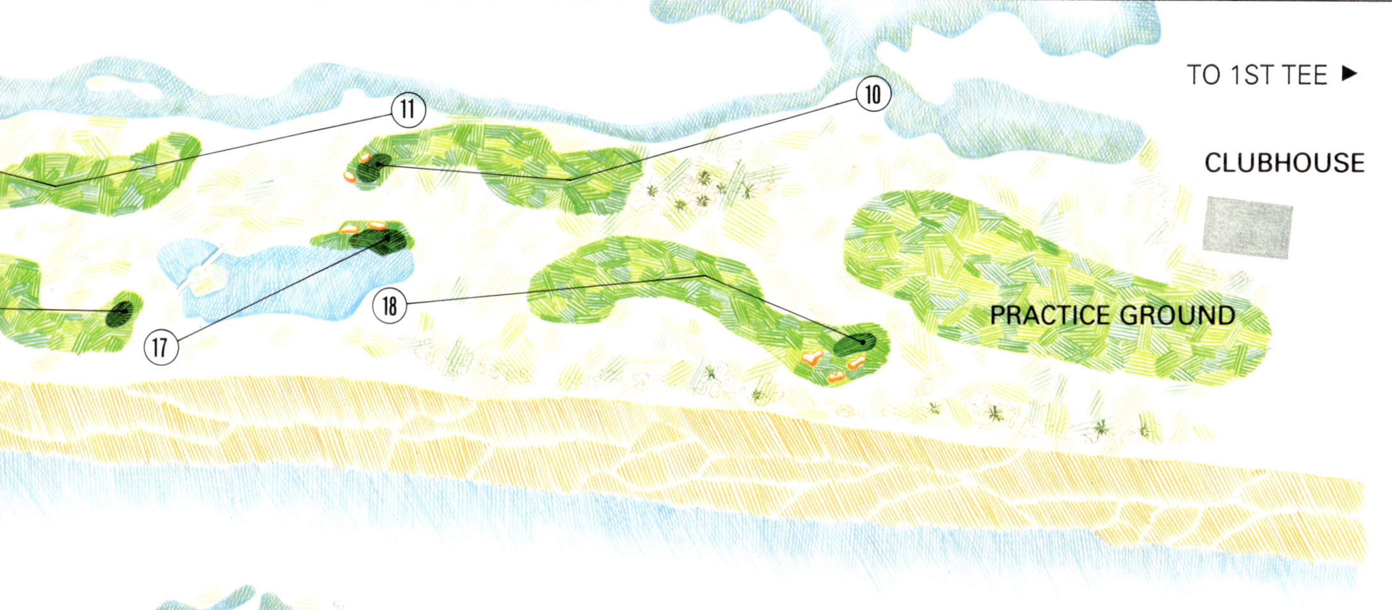

KIAWAH ISLAND OCEAN COURSE

HOLE BY HOLE
Championship tees: 7371yd. Medal tees: 6824yd. Ladies' tees 5357yd, all par 72.

1st hole
(Champ 395yd Medal 375yd Ladies' 306yd Par 4) A gentle opener. You tee off amidst a forested wetland with a prehistoric dune ridge to your left.

2nd hole
(Champ 543yd Medal 528yd Ladies' 419yd Par 5) You must hit the fairway from the tee and play an accurate second shot to stand a chance of getting home in 3.

3rd hole
(Champ 390yd Medal 367yd Ladies' 298yd Par 4) Better to be short of the green than over it and in an unplayable lie.

4th hole
(Champ 453yd Medal 432yd Ladies' 328yd Par 4) Trust your instincts – it really is as straight as it looks. Two good shots will see you home.

5th hole
(Champ 207yd Medal 185yd Ladies' 117yd Par 3) You must finish near the pin on this big green unless you want to have a very long putt.

6th hole
(Champ 455yd Medal 392yd Ladies' 299yd Par 4) At all costs avoid the long waste bunker to the left and short of the green.

7th hole
(Champ 527yd Medal 505yd Ladies' 432yd Par 5) Wetlands to the left are out of bounds and an alligator lurks in a lake to the right.

8th hole
(Champ 197yd Medal 170yd Ladies' 105yd Par 3) You should be able to hit this green – it's one of the biggest on the course.

9th hole
(Champ 464yd Medal 415yd Ladies' 344yd Par 4) Miss-hit your tee shot here and you're dead. The second shot is very difficult too.

10th hole
(Champ 439yd Medal 406yd Ladies' 310yd Par 4) Trouble lurks on both sides of the green, a steep-faced bunker on the right, a waste bunker on the left.

11th hole
(Champ 576yd Medal 562yd Ladies' 440yd Par 5) This may take 4 shots to get up. A long slog.

12th hole
(Champ 466yd Medal 410yd Ladies' 326 Par 4) A drive over water so keep your head down. Water runs all along the right of the hole too.

13th hole
(Champ 404yd Medal 371yd Ladies' 312yd Par 4) Beware three very deep bunkers seeded with sea oats which defend the left of the green.

14th hole
(Champ 219yd Medal 194yd Ladies' 132yd Par 3) Lovely short hole on which you notice the sea for the first time since the 5th at the other end of the course.

15th hole
(Champ 421yd Medal 391yd Ladies' 306yd Par 4) Don't slice from the tee – on a windy day your ball could end in the ocean and be washed up on the 17th at Ballybunion.

16th hole
(Champ 579yd Medal 540yd Ladies' 447yd Par 5) Be conservative with your drive over the lake and take the shortest carry.

17th hole
(Champ 197yd Medal 160yd Ladies' 122yd Par 3) From the elevated tee aim at the left of the green across a lake to keep your ball in play.

18th hole
(Champ 439yd Medal 421yd Ladies' 314yd Par 4) You need a good second to reach the small green but if you hit it too well you'll end up in a difficult bunker.

FOUR HOLES TO WATCH

◀ ***5th hole***
(Champ 207yd Par 3)
This is the first short hole. If you're not careful you will be entranced by the view of the Atlantic way off to the left and ahead of you, marshlands in the foreground and birds wheeling above.

Miss the proper part of the green here and you could face a putt of 30yd (27m) on a green shaped like an hour-glass.

▼ The 12th is a dice with a watery end all the way from tee to green. The drive demands a long carry over the lake while the second has to deal with the water getting closer and closer all the way to the green.

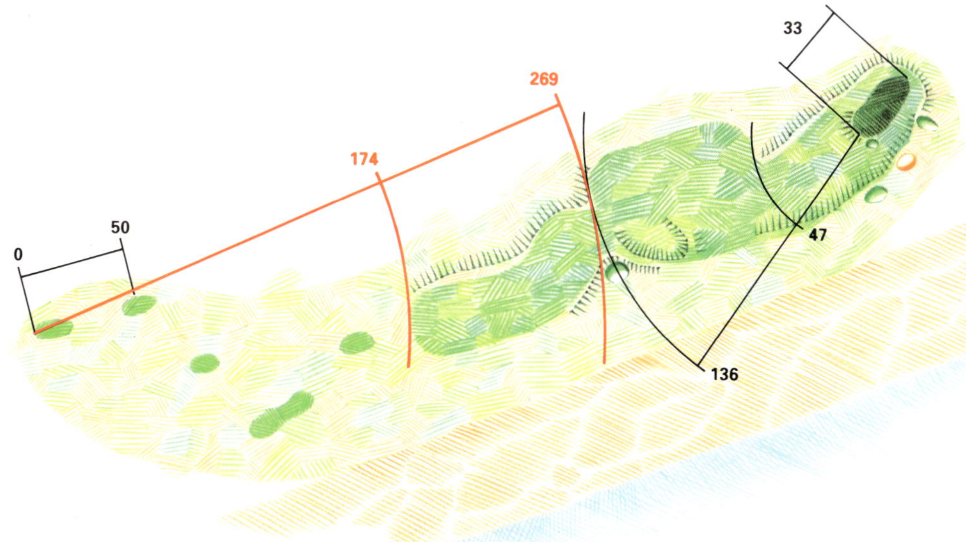

Scotland, USA

Pete Dye is probably best known for introducing carefully crafted 'stadium' courses such as the TPC layout at Ponte Vedra, Florida and PGA West in Palm Springs, California.

He has left such innovations behind at Kiawah, however. Instead, after travelling to Scotland to get a feel for links courses, he has placed a premium on inventive shot-making rather than surgical precision. Like a true links he has let the landscape itself create the challenge.

◀ *14th hole*

(Champ 219yd Par 3)
You have reached the far end of the course and now must turn, probably into the wind, to start for home.

From this raised tee the course spreads out before you. It looks magnificent but don't be distracted by this very British looking hole. It is well guarded and if you must miss the green, then miss it short and hope to bump and run a shot up close enough to single putt.

▲ *15th hole*

(Champ 421yd Par 4)
The landing area for the drive is close to the sea but don't worry, there are plenty of dunes to stop your ball being blown to perdition if you slice it. There's no room for error with your second to the green.

A large waste bunker is ready to gather almost any inaccurate shot and there is a massive bunker shaped like the open mouth of a whale at the back right of the green, which you can't see.

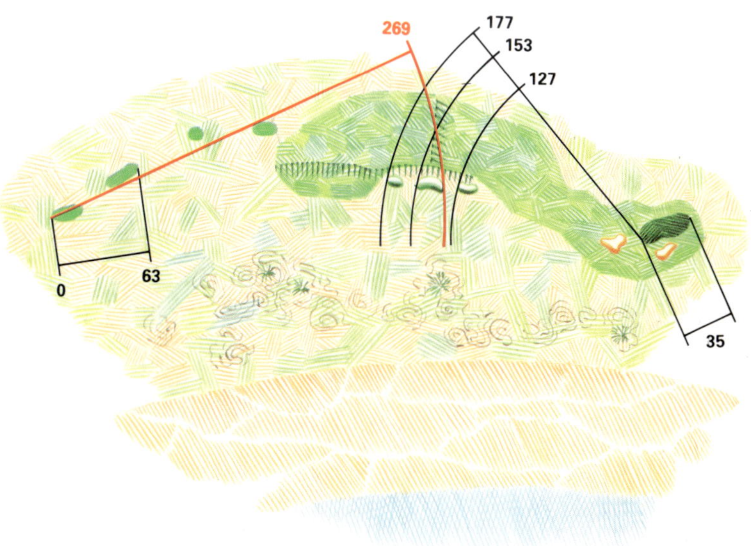

▲ *18th hole*

(Champ 439yd Par 4)
A challenging enough hole to be decisive in many matches. The drive is straightforward if it's hit long enough but the second shot poses a real problem.

The green is small and set at an awkward angle to the fairway. A tongue of meadow grass juts out before the green while a bunker adds to the fortifications. If you hit and hold the green, you deserve your par. Even downwind, it is no pushover because the putting surface is so small and hard to hold.

FACTFILE

Tournaments
Ryder Cup: 1991

take advantage of the outstanding natural beauty of the course. There isn't a house to be seen in any direction and though the sea isn't visible from every hole, it can be heard from most of them.

Long carries from the tees are a feature and when the wind is at its strongest it will be an achievement just to reach the fairway on some holes. Where possible, Dye has used the marshlands as obstacles to be driven over.

FULL SHOTS NEEDED

Dye believes that the long iron shot is becoming less important because players can hit the ball so far they rarely need more than a mid iron to reach the greens. A number of holes at the Ocean Course are designed to be reached only with a full drive and a full smash with a 2 or 3.

Yet he hasn't gone overboard about the length. From the men's medal tees, the course is 6824yd (6234m), and 5357yd (4894m) from the ladies'. Furthermore, the 13th is barely 400yd (365m) while the opening hole, even from the back tee, is only a gentle 395yd (361m).

There is a surprising amount of elevation on the course, which has been achieved by raising some greens and lowering others.

The greens, planted with a Bermuda grass variety, are likely to mature to be softer and more holding than those on traditional British links courses.

The greens have considerable movement or undulation in them and one or two are so large they wouldn't look out of place on St Andrews' double versions. Land on the wrong part of the 5th green, for example, and you could easily be facing a putt of 30yd (27m).

Though Dye has often copied the pot bunkers that are a feature of links layouts he has on many holes added his own inimitable waste bunkers.

OUTSTANDING FINISH

The two nines are quite distinctive. Wetlands, protected by law, dominate the outward half whereas much of the inward half is played along the Atlantic shore.

The sea is to the golfer's right on the stretch of holes from the 14th to the 18th and from most tees the sound is of waves breaking just behind you. The finishing holes are outstanding, containing two long par 3s, one monstrous par 5 and two long par 4s.

The Ocean Course is the nearest an American golfer can get to playing a British-style links without leaving his own country. As it matures, it promises to be a wonderful test of golf and will surely be recognized as one of the best golf courses in North America within a few years.

▼ Though relatively short, the par 4 13th is riddled with danger as you approach the green, with deep bunkers left, a lake on the right and testing slopes on the green itself. This is the last hole out before turning right round, heading towards the beach and back into the teeth of the wind.

Kingston Heath

This fiendishly bunkered course is one of Australia's greatest. It winds its way through avenues of trees just 15 miles (25km) from the heart of bustling Melbourne, and is a fine test of championship golf.

Kingston Heath is among the best of the many clubs that make up the famous Melbourne necklace of sandbelt courses. It ranks alongside Royal Melbourne and the Commonwealth in terms of history and quality of play.

The sea of sand making up the course's 118 bunkers is the most famous feature of this 6231m (6814yd) layout. It bears an uncanny likeness to its main rival in the area, Royal Melbourne. Both had their bunkering designed by the world renowned British course architect Alister Mackenzie in 1926.

The bunkers are large and clumped menacingly down the fairways and around the greens. You are often faced with a shot over five or six bunkers to the green, and any miss-hit is swallowed up.

VARDON'S VOICE

Mackenzie wasn't the only important influence in the shaping of the course – six times British Open champion Harry Vardon also left his mark. Even though he never visited Kingston Heath he was consulted at the planning stage.

▼ The championship course of Kingston Heath severely tests your accuracy from tee to green. The 14th is a long, tight, snaking par 5 of 502m (549yd) needing all your concentration and skill. You must avoid two clusters of bunkers and the mass of trees and shrubs if you are to make your par.

The free form of the huge bunkers is a trademark of the great course architect Alister Mackenzie. His touch helped create a course that you must always concentrate on if you're to score well.

HOLE BY HOLE

Championship tees: 6231m, Par 72. Ladies' tees: 5426m, Par 74.

1st hole
(Champ 419m Par 4 Ladies 393m Par 5) Avoid slicing your tee shot – a clump of traps awaits your ball.

2nd hole
(Champ 334m Ladies 297m Par 4) Play a long iron or fairway wood to the dog-leg.

3rd hole
(Champ 271m Ladies 214m Par 4) Hit your tee shot left of centre with a long iron or fairway wood.

4th hole
(Champ 356m Ladies 324m Par 4) Drive down the left for the best approach to the green.

5th hole
(Champ 173m Ladies 145m Par 3) Beware of the five bunkers on the right that catch a sliced shot.

6th hole
(Champ 397m Ladies 352m Par 4) Hit your tee shot straight. Nine bunkers catch the off line drive.

7th hole
(Champ 459m Ladies 443m Par 5) Stick to the right side of the fairway. Danger lurks all down the left.

2
12
6
5
3
7
1
CLUBHOUSE

Open summons

Kingston Heath has been the scene of many great championships. But one of the oddest incidents happened in the 1957 Australian Open.

The eventual winner Frank Phillips had to be summoned back to the course to collect his cheque and trophy. He had headed off well before the finish believing he hadn't a chance of winning with his score of 1 under par 287. But then Gary Player took 7 at the 13th, Ossie Pickworth a 6 at the 17th and Peter Thomson 4 putted the 16th. The biggest prize in Australian golf fell into Phillips' lap.

KINGSTON HEATH

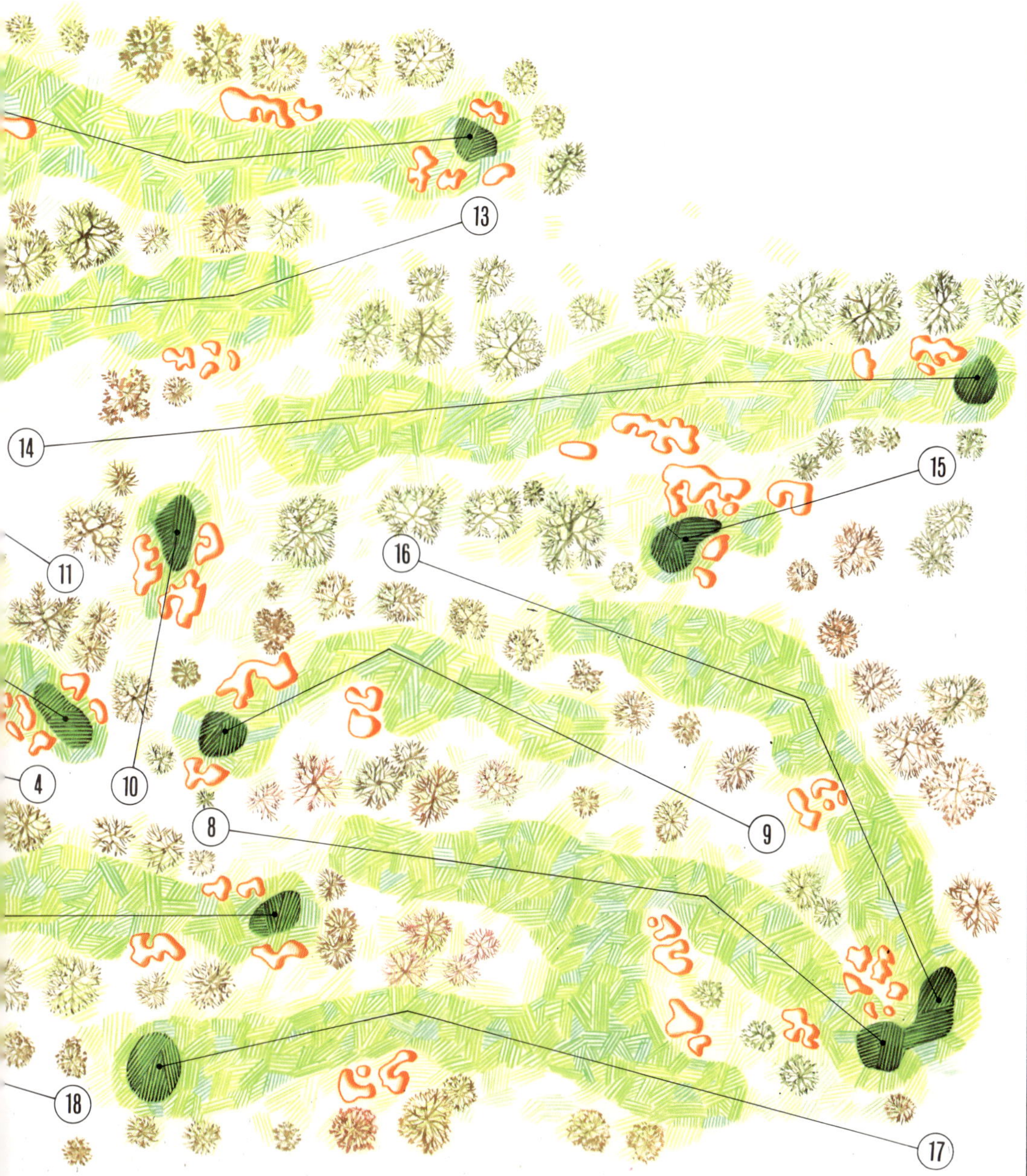

8th hole
(Champ 394m Ladies 319m Par 4) A blind tee shot – hit down the right for the shortest route home.

9th hole
(Champ 324m Ladies 269m Par 4) Avoid the left side.

10th hole
(Champ 131m Ladies 106m Par 3) Your short iron must be spot on to avoid three large bunkers.

11th hole
(Champ 368m Ladies 321m Par 4) The best line from the tee is just left of the fairway traps on the right.

12th hole
(Champ 442m Ladies 380m Par 5) Hit a long tee shot over the bunkers in the middle of the fairway.

13th hole
(Champ 324m Ladies 259m Par 4) The perfect tee shot is a long drive up the left to open up the green.

14th hole
(Champ 502m Ladies 434m Par 5) Aim your second shot down the right as the fairway falls away to the left.

15th hole
(Champ 142m Ladies 113m Par 3) Assess the wind – the ball is affected when it climbs above the trees.

16th hole
(Champ 386m Ladies 340m Par 4) Don't go right as trees and ten bunkers await any wayward shot.

17th hole
(Champ 418m Par 4 Ladies 393m Par 5) Be careful not to underclub with your second to the blind green.

18th hole
(Champ 391m Ladies 324m Par 4) Avoid going left or you're in trouble.

◄ The course lies on sandy soil in the southern suburbs of Melbourne. The majestic setting has been a backdrop to many top-flight events since the opening in 1925. The holes constantly change direction, making judgement of the wind a problem.

► The elegant, spacious clubhouse – with its many verandas – is a peaceful retreat for the weary golfer. It overlooks the subtly sloping 6th and 18th greens and the 1st tee.

FOUR HOLES TO WATCH

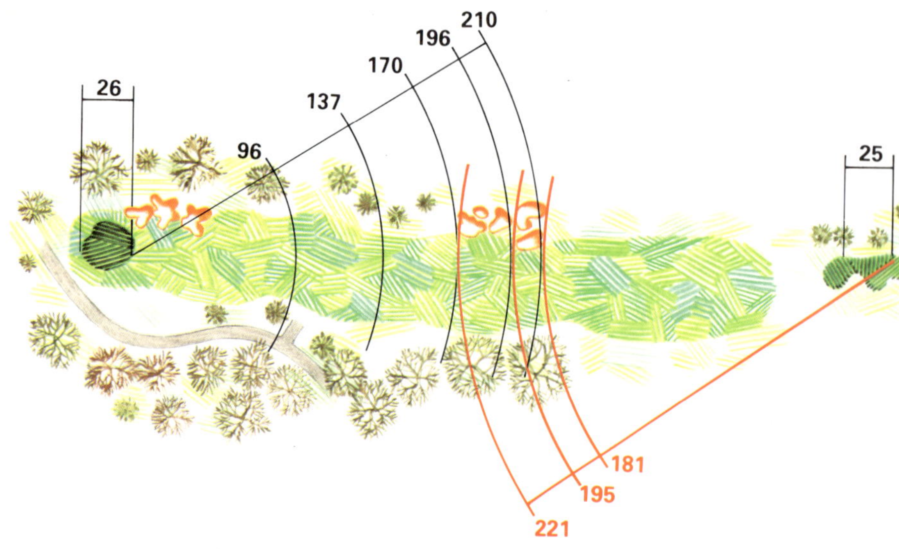

◄ ***1st hole***
(Champ 419m Par 4)
Very few courses open with a tough par 4, but this hole could easily fit the demands of a testing 18th.

You must first drive to the top of a hill. If you manage to avoid the classic bunch of yawning traps on the right, you're left with 200yd (180m) to go over gentle bumps and hollows to a large, haphazardly undulating green. Getting your par here is like opening up with a birdie.

► If you don't hit the fairways or greens at Kingston Heath you are faced with a shot from sand, tough scrubby rough or from the towering trees that line the course. The 3rd is a very short par 4 but is fraught with danger.

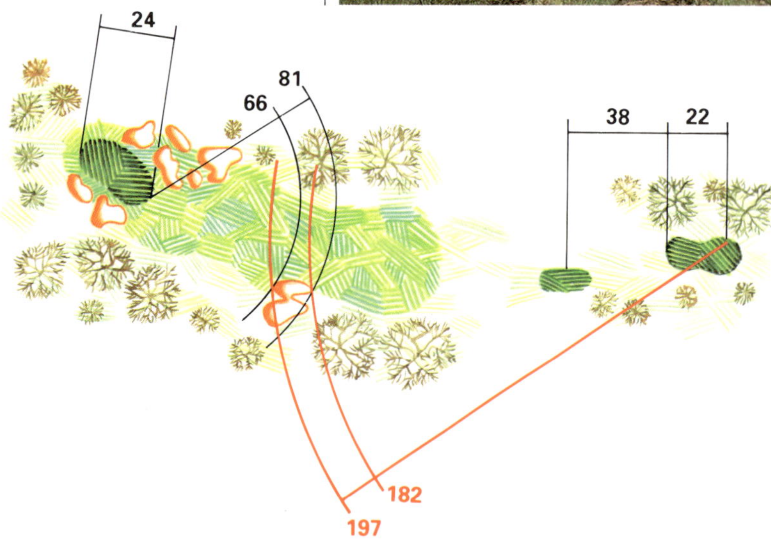

◄ ***3rd hole***
(Champ 271m Par 4)
This little gem disproves the theory that a par 4 needs to be at least 400yd (360m) to provide a decent challenge. In certain conditions it's driveable, but is a very risky shot to play.

The safer option is to hit a 3 wood from the tee and then to throw up a wedge to the small, heavily bunkered green. If you miss the green and land on either the left or right you face a difficult task to get your next close to the flag. Big trouble also lurks at the back if you overshoot.

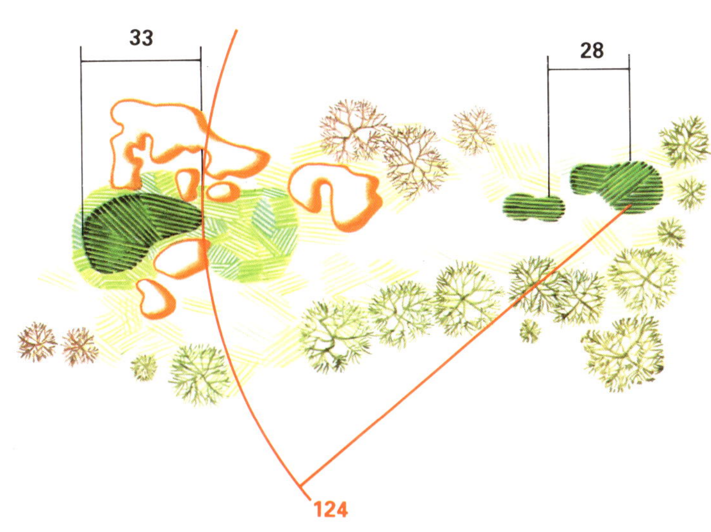

◄ *15th hole*

(Champ 142m Par 3)
This hole has solid claims to being Australia's finest par 3. You must hit a medium iron uphill to a rolling green guarded by cavernous bunkers.

One of the main surprises is the false feeling of shelter from the wind. The trees that line the hole are high enough to shelter the player on the tee, but the well struck drive climbs above the tree line, and can be severely affected.

◄ The view from the 15th tee is frightening. You must carry your tee shot over a large expanse of sand and scrub to a well guarded green. Even if you hit the green, putting is made difficult by severe slopes.

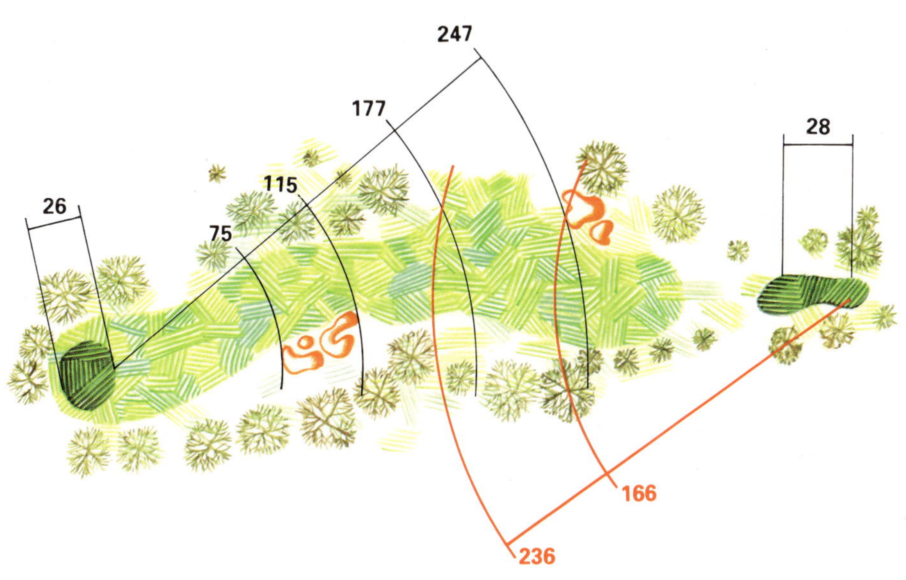

◄ *17th hole*

(Champ 418m Par 4)
The five times British Open champion Peter Thomson calls this hole 'superb and a penultimate prizewinner'. There's an element of luck as to whether your second stroke finishes close to the hole or not, because the shot is blind.

Unusually the green has none of the fearsome Mackenzie bunkering that is such a feature on the rest of the course, but relies on length and tightness for its defence.

▲ Often the setting for the Australian Open, Kingston Heath is an excellent test of all round ability. One of the greatest skills needed to tame the course is a sure putting touch – demonstrated here by Sam Torrance – on fast greens that rise and fall alarmingly.

FACTFILE
Lowest scores
Professional course record: 65 – Gary Player, Ronan Rafferty, Curtis Strange, Colin Montgomerie

Tournaments
Australian Open: 1948, 1957, 1970, 1983, 1989
Australian Matchplay: 1986, 1987, 1988, 1989, 1990, 1991, 1992

He told the breakaway group of members of Elsternwick GC who bought the land to 'construct a course of sufficient length to stand the test of time'. It says much for the strength of character of the men who founded the club that they stuck rigidly to his plan, despite much criticism.

Former Australian Open champion Dan Souter designed the layout in 1925 and the course became the longest in the country. It has been lengthened only slightly in 65 years, a testament to Vardon's foresight. In those days the par was a phenomenal 82. There were 12 par 5s and only two par 3s.

MANICURED HEATHLAND

The condition of the course is equal to any in the world. The magnificent couch fairways ensure perfect lies, and the bent grass rollercoaster greens are true and terrifyingly fast. The fairways rise and dip gently through narrow avenues of gums and wattle trees and wiegelia shrubs.

The fairways and greens may be beautifully manicured, but if you stray from them you're in trouble. The natural state of the surroundings is untouched, and the scrubby heathland grass punishes the wayward shot. Only accurate tee shots are rewarded. The deep classical Mackenzie bunkering and hard, fast greens also demand deft iron play and putting.

Kingston Heath is one of the few great courses to start with one of its hardest holes. You are thrown straight into the fire at the 419m (458yd) 1st, and there is little respite after that. The finishing stretch of 16, 17 and 18 is one of the toughest in Australia. All the holes measure over 385m (420yd) and require long, precise striking.

But power is not as important as control if you are to tame this tiger of a course. The three par 3s are short by modern standards but are heavily bunkered, needing pinpoint accuracy to keep your score down.

The course was officially recognized as a true championship test in 1938, when the Australian Golf Union approved Kingston Heath as a venue for the Australian Open. It has staged the Open five times since. Kingston Heath has always thrown up a worthy winner – a player who combines steady, accurate play down the fairways with a steely nerve on the pacy greens.

The course remains a joyful experience for high handicappers as well as a searching test for the professionals. Staying true to Harry Vardon's words, Kingston Heath continues to stand the test of time.

Muirfield

Many leading players see Muirfield as a stern but fair test of a golfer's true ability – every shot you play is rewarded or penalized accurately.

Laid out on the East Lothian coast in Scotland, Muirfield is flatter than most championship links – a feature which pleases many American visitors who aren't used to playing on Britain's typically up and down coastal courses.

Muirfield is a true test of golf. It gives you the chance to play to your handicap – so often courses are designed with only the most skilful and powerful in mind.

There are few humps and hollows to slew your ball off line. Only one tee shot is blind and most bunkers are visible from the tee. There are no great carries between tee and fairway, no water hazards and few trees.

On the other hand, your drives need to be accurate: avoiding the many bunkers – 151 in all – is the key to a good score. And when you reach the greens – small by links standards – you need to be wary of subtle contours.

The course is relentless. There's practically no let up between the 1st tee and 18th green. Tony Jacklin considers the start at Muirfield to be 'one of the scariest opening holes in golf'.

With its flat fairways and few blind shots, Muirfield is one of Britain's finest and most popular championship courses. Opened in 1892, its layout is unusual for a links course.

▲ 'One of the best anywhere in the world' is Jack Nicklaus' verdict on the final hole, which is notable for its island bunkers. Nicklaus fell in love with the course the first time he played it – during the 1959 Walker Cup match – and has always performed well here.

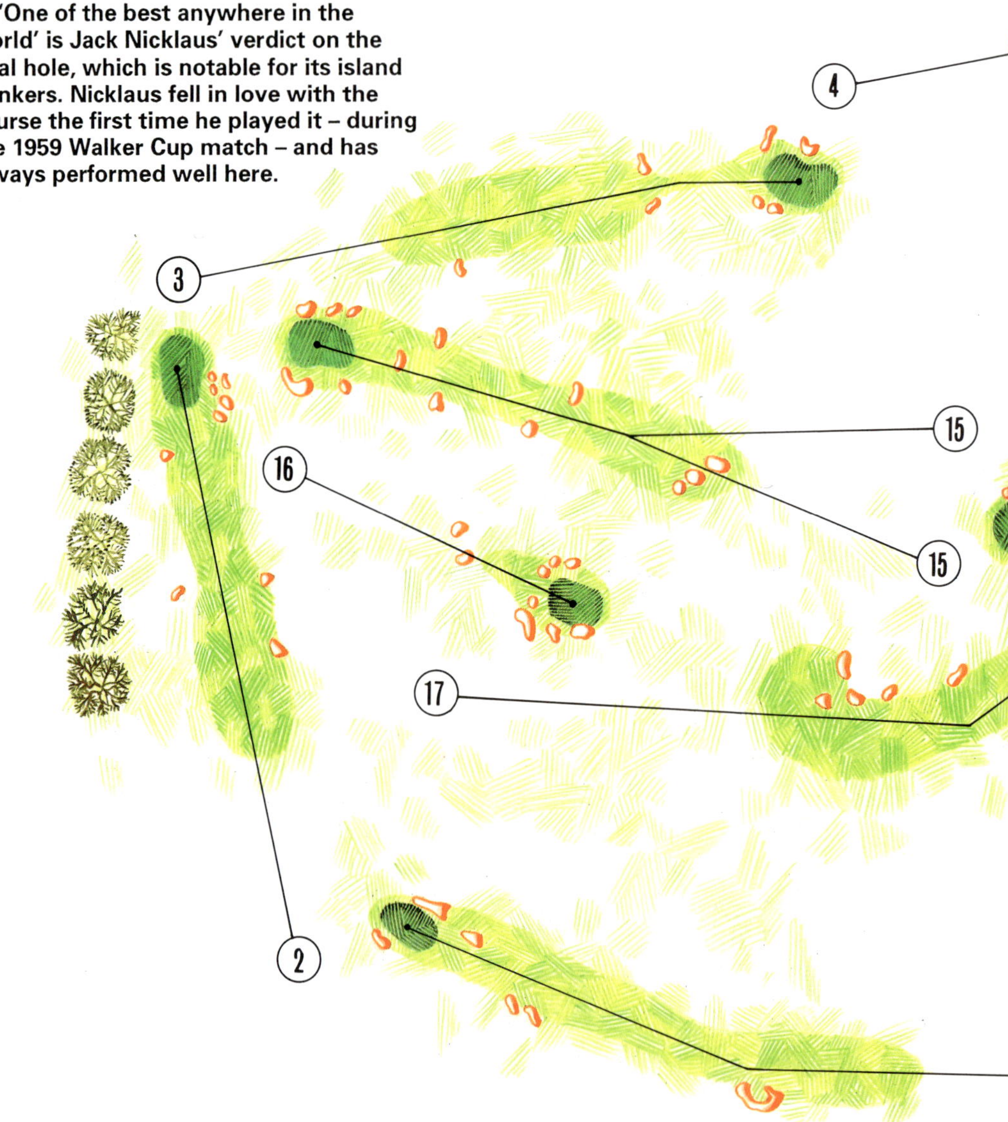

HOLE BY HOLE

Championship tees: 6963 yards, par 71. Medal tees 6601 yards, par 70.

1st hole
(Champ 447yd Medal 444yd Par 4) Drive as close as you can to the horseshoe bunker down the left.

2nd hole
(Champ 351yd Medal 345yd Par 4) Drive down the left half of the fairway for the easiest approach to a tricky green.

3rd hole
(Champ 379yd Medal 374yd Par 4) Keep left for the best view between two giant sand hills 70yd (63m) from the green.

4th hole
(Champ 180yd Medal 174yd Par 3) Better to be long than short with four bunkers fronting the green.

5th hole
(Champ 559yd Medal 506yd Par 5) Use the slope on the right to run your second shot into the centre of the fairway.

6th hole
(Champ 469yd Medal 436yd Par 4) The second is one more club than you think because of the dip near the green.

7th hole
(Champ 185yd Medal 151yd Par 3) Take enough club to clear the two bunkers at the front of the green.

8th hole
(Champ 444yd Medal 439yd Par 4) Drive down the left for a clear view of the pin across the dog-leg.

9th hole
(Champ 504yd Par 5, Medal 460yd Par 4) Play your second short of the five bunkers on the right.

10th hole
(Champ 475yd Medal 471 Par 4) Play it as a Par 5.

11th hole
(Champ 385yd Medal 350yd Par 4) Drive down the left on this blind tee shot.

MUIRFIELD CHAMPIONSHIP COURSE

12th hole
(Champ 381yd Medal 376yd Par 4) Aim your drive at the huge fairway bunker on the left for the best line.

13th hole
(Champ 152yd Medal 146yd Par 3) Take one more club than you think to clear the slope leading up to the green.

14th hole
(Champ 449yd Medal 442yd Par 4) Aim your second at the left half of the green.

15th hole
(Champ 417yd Medal 391yd Par 4) Keep right for the best line past the big central bunker about 30yd (27m) from the green.

16th hole
(Champ 188yd Medal 181yd Par 3) Aim at the right half of the green to avoid the slope on the left.

17th hole
(Champ 550yd Medal 501yd Par 5) Play your second towards the left edge of the green for the best line on your third.

18th hole
(Champ 448yd Medal 414yd Par 4) Play short to avoid the two central fairway bunkers with your second.

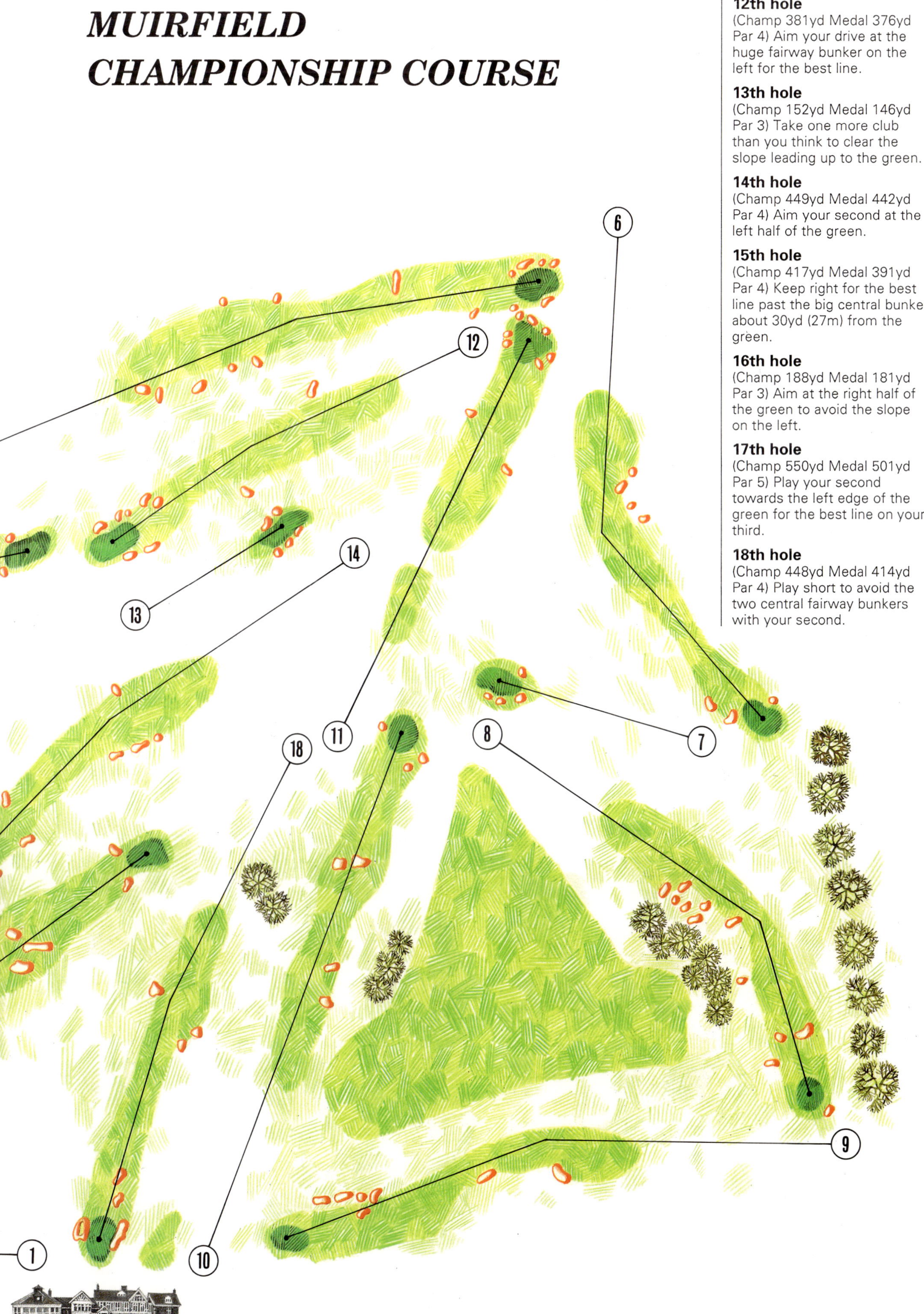

FOUR HOLES TO WATCH

9th hole ►

(Champ 504yd Par 5, Medal 460yd Par 4)
According to the stroke index this is the third hardest hole on the course. Aim your drive to the right of the huge sand hill – though the landing area is narrow.

There is even less margin for error on your second shot, with five bunkers just short of the pin on the right, and an out-of-bounds wall that runs from tee to green on the left.

Unless you're confident of avoiding these hazards, play safe by hitting to the wider part of the fairway – short and left of the five bunkers. If the wind is against you play for one over par.

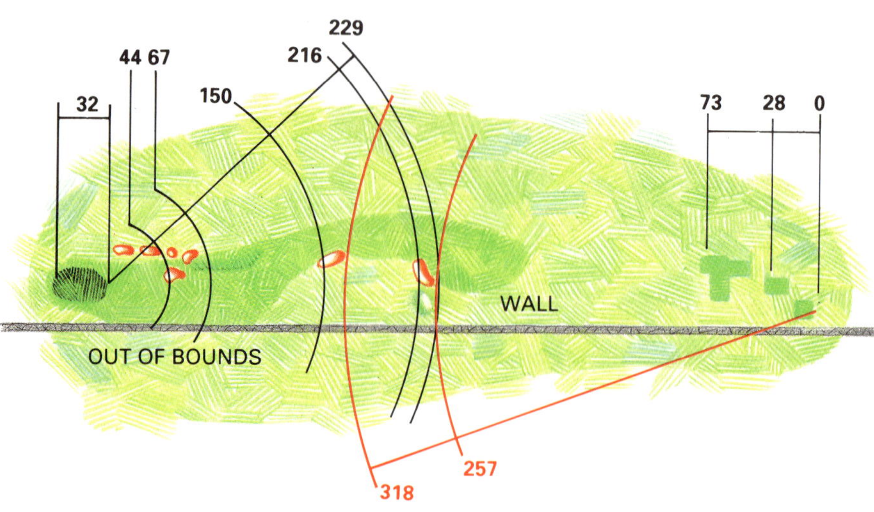

◄ *16th hole*

(Champ 188yd Medal 181yd Par 3)
There are nine bunkers on this short hole – seven of them around the green. Only the back is not guarded by sand so it's better to be long than short.

A small dip in front of the green makes the pin look closer than it is. The green breaks gently from left to right.

Muirfield the monster
Muirfield has more bunkers than most courses – 151 in total. But this is less than in 1980, when 14 were removed because technical advances in equipment meant they hardly came into play.

► The distinctive Greywalls Hotel overlooks the difficult 9th hole from behind the out-of-bounds wall. Five pot bunkers lie in wait on the right side of the fairway for any ball that strays off line. To score par 5 at this 504-yard hole, every shot needs to be planned and played with precision.

◄ The small, slightly raised green at the short par-3 16th is surrounded by seven bunkers. Muirfield is famous for its bunkers – the course has 151 altogether.

Jack high

At the 1966 Open, Jack Nicklaus demonstrated his immense power by reaching the green at the par-5 17th – then measuring 542 yards – in 2 shots (a 3 iron and 5 iron). He won the title by a single stroke.

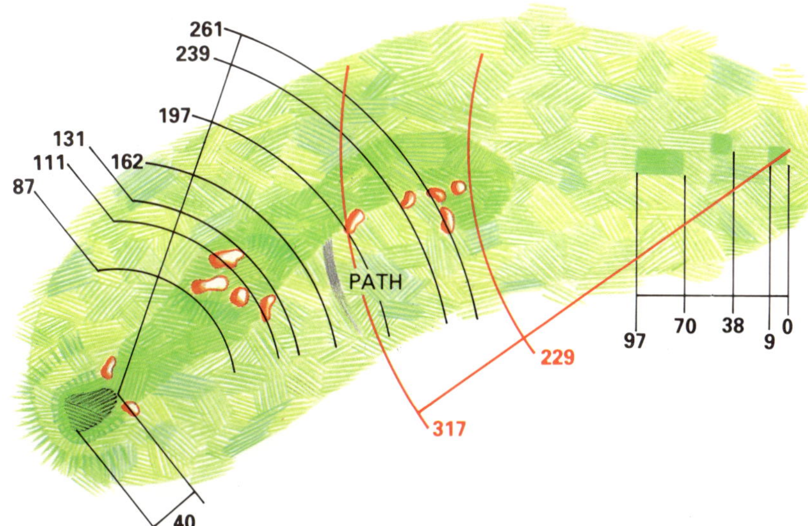

◄ *17th hole*

(Champ 550yd Medal 501yd Par 5)
This is another tight driving hole. Play down the right for the best line to the green and to avoid four pot bunkers on the left.

Your second must clear broken ground and more sand – which shouldn't be a problem unless the wind is against you. Your short third has to thread its way between two massive bunkers at the entrance to the green. Although over 500yd (456m) away, the green is reachable in 2 with a following wind.

18th hole ►

(Champ 448yd Medal 414yd Par 4)
For the best line to the green your drive should finish just right of centre. Watch out for bunkers on both edges of the fairway.

It's difficult to judge the uphill second – your view is obscured by two centrally placed bunkers some 40yd (36m) in front of the green. If you can't clear them, play short and aim to save par with a chip and putt. The green falls away sharply into deep bunkers on both sides.

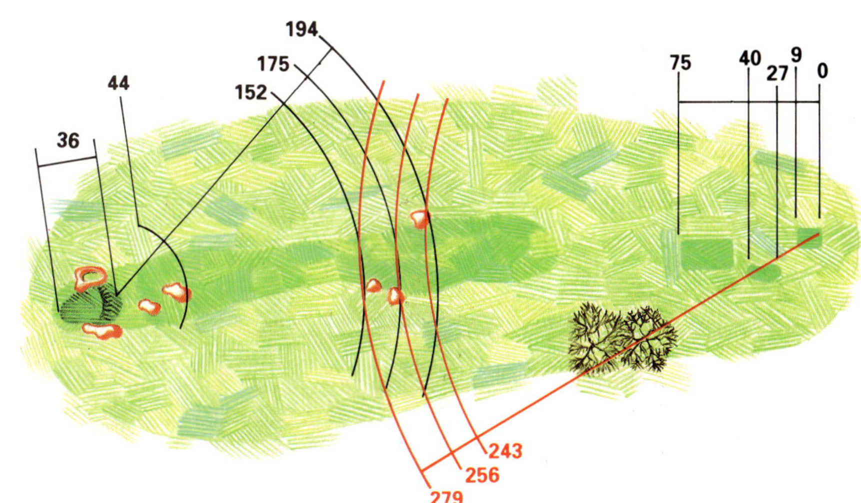

FACTFILE
Lowest score
Isao Aoki – 63, 1980 Open Championship

Tournaments
Open Championship – 1892, 1896, 1901, 1906, 1912, 1929, 1935, 1948, 1959, 1966, 1972, 1980, 1987, 1992

Ryder Cup – 1973

British Amateur Championship – 1897, 1903, 1909, 1920, 1926, 1932, 1964, 1974, 1990

Walker Cup – 1959, 1979

Curtis Cup – 1952, 1984

How to play
You can play at Muirfield on certain mornings. Your handicap must be not more than 18 if you're a man and not more than 24 if you're a woman. Your application to play should be accompanied by a letter from your club.

Write to Major Vanreenen, Honourable company of Edinburgh Golfers, Muirfield, Gullane, East Lothian EH31 2EG.

Troubled Tony
Tony Jacklin suffered the worst moment of his career in the 1972 Open at Muirfield. Walking on to the 71st green the Briton looked all set to win the title.

He was about 15ft (4.5m) away from the pin in 3 shots, while playing partner and co-leader Lee Trevino was off the green in 4.

It seemed Jacklin was going to take at least a 1-shot lead down the final hole. But to his dismay Lucky Lee chipped in for a par 5. A shaken Jacklin 3 putted for a 6.

Demoralized, Jacklin dropped another stroke at the 18th and finished 2 strokes behind Trevino. He was never in contention for a major title again.

WINDS OF CHANGE

For a course built in 1891, Muirfield has an unusual – and modern – layout. The first nine holes form a clockwise circle, outside the back nine which run in an anti-clockwise direction.

This means that the wind at Muirfield never blows at the same angle for long, so great concentration and skill are demanded of the players.

The 9th green is near the 1st tee, unlike many links where the 9th is at the furthest point from the clubhouse.

The course is also further from the sea than most championship links – but still has a wonderful view of the Firth of Forth and the distant Kingdom of Fife hills.

THREE HOMES

The course is owned by the Honourable Company of Edinburgh Gentlemen. The exact date of the club's formation is generally accepted to be 1744 – it's reckoned to be the world's oldest golf club.

In its early days the Honourable Gentlemen played over the 5-hole Leith Links. But the course and its facilities became so congested with other clubs and societies that the Honourable Gentlemen moved to Musselburgh. When in 1891 Musselburgh also became overcrowded the club bought land further east, at Muirfield, 18 miles from Edinburgh.

Although former British Open Champion Tom Morris snr was credited with the imaginative design of the course, most of the planning and building was the result of a collection of minds. A number of structural changes were made in the 1920s but the basic layout remains the same.

GREAT CHAMPIONS

Within its first year, in 1892, Muirfield staged the Open. In all, 14 Opens have been held here. Its champions equal those of any course in Britain – Gary Player, Jack Nicklaus, Lee Trevino, Tom Watson and Nick Faldo are among the more recent great players to triumph here.

Only the very best win at Muirfield. Jack Nicklaus' record is particularly impressive. As well as winning the Open in 1966, he lost only one of the eight Ryder Cup and Walker Cup matches he played here. Nicklaus also finished runner-up and fourth in the 1972 and 1980 Opens.

His love of the course is so great that he named his own Muirfield Village complex in Ohio after it.

Muirfield has witnessed a number of Open firsts. In 1892 it was the first held over 72 holes and the first to charge an entrance fee. In 1966 the Open was played over four days for the first time and the Royal and Ancient allowed advertising banners on the course – a practice short lived as it was felt that the Championship was becoming too commercial.

▼ Nick Faldo chips on to the 18th green during the third round of the 1987 Open Championship. The following day he won the title by a single stroke.

Pebble Beach

One of the greatest courses in the world, Pebble is awesome. Located south of San Fransisco, it hugs the rocky Californian coastline and is a monstrous challenge in a high wind.

Deceptive in the early holes, Pebble Beach gives the impression that it's easily conquered. But any golfer who believes that is in for a long day. This links course is set so hard against the Pacific Ocean that the waves crash on to the cliffs just paces away from some of the fairways and greens.

Eight holes run beside the ocean, which is very much in play. Bluffs and cliffs dominate the right side going out, and they reappear at the finish for the 17th and 18th. Any waywardness is severely punished as the ball plummets down the rocks and is swallowed up by the swirling waters.

Pebble is a public course that anyone can play at a price, but it plays no favourites. You need long, accurate striking, hard concentration and shots of often Herculean proportions to succeed on this masterpiece.

The course was the brainchild of Samuel Morse – a relative of the telegraph inventor – back in 1919. His dream was to create a course on his land fronting Carmel Bay and the ocean. He hired Jack

▼ The course has been the scene of extraordinary drama, with the 18th having its fair share of action. The 548yd par 5 – with its green perched precariously next to cliffs and the fairway sweeping round a small rocky bay – is a dangerous hole in any weather. Beware of the strong winds which are hurled in from the Pacific Ocean – they can play havoc with your score.

PEBBLE BEACH GOLF LINKS

HOLE BY HOLE
Championship tees: 6799 yards, Par 72, USGA rating 75.

1st hole
(Champ 373yd Par 4)
Watch out for the subtly sloping green. Like all the greens it falls towards the sea.

2nd hole
(Champ 502yd Par 5)
Make sure you clear the large gorge in front of the green.

3rd hole
(Champ 388yd Par 4)
Don't overshoot the green because it slopes down into thick rough.

4th hole
(Champ 327yd Par 4)
You mustn't go right as there is a sheer drop to the beach.

5th hole
(Champ 166yd Par 3)
Leave your approach shot short of the flag – the green slopes severely from back to front.

6th hole
(Champ 516yd Par 5)
Play up the left side all the way to the hole, as the fairway slopes right towards the cliffs.

Neville – a Californian amateur champion and Walker Cup international – as his architect.

HIGHLY RANKED

Neville had never designed a course before, but with the help of Douglas Grant – who did the bunkering – he fashioned one of the world's finest championship tests. The present course has recently been rated second in the world, behind only Pine Valley, by a panel of US golf writers and players.

Jack Nicklaus – a consistent winner here – said of the course, 'If I had only one more round of golf to play, I would choose to play it at Pebble Beach. My hat is off to the two men who designed Pebble – they did everything right. After all these years with no major revisions Pebble Beach still stands up. It's a superb championship test.'

The inland holes burst through cypresses, oaks, eucalyptus and pines and are fine holes in their own right. But the course wouldn't be the classic it is without the holes perched on top of the cliffs. Over the years Pebble has drawn varying comments from those who have challenged it, but no golfer goes away with hatred in his heart.

It's a hospitable course through the first five holes, and gives no hint of the terrors to come. Lee Trevino once quipped with the gallery as he stood on

◀ **The 13th green slopes heavily towards the sea, and is a devil to putt on. The local Pebble secret is to think hard about your approach shots before you play them. All the greens slope towards the Pacific and this knowledge helps you decide where to place the ball and how your putt breaks.**

7th hole
(Champ 107yd Par 3)
You must hit the green, as sand and the ocean await any miss-hit.

8th hole
(Champ 431yd Par 4)
Keep away from the cliffs on the right.

9th hole
(Champ 464yd Par 4)
Beware of the ocean on the right and the bunkers on the left.

10th hole
(Champ 426yd Par 4)
Be content if you're in the bunker on the left as the Pacific awaits your ball on the right.

11th hole
(Champ 384yd Par 4)
Don't slice – there's out of bounds down the right.

12th hole
(Champ 202yd Par 3)
Aim for the right half of the green as it slopes away to the left.

13th hole
(Champ 392yd Par 4)
Play your approach to a spot below the hole, because the green slopes viciously.

14th hole
(Champ 565yd Par 5)
The key to this hole is club selection. An approach shot plays about a club longer than it appears.

15th hole
(Champ 397yd Par 4)
Play straight as trees line the fairway on both sides.

16th hole
(Champ 402yd Par 4)
To avoid an undesirable downhill-sidehill lie, don't be too long off the tee.

17th hole
(Champ 209yd Par 3)
The green stands on a small peninsula so watch out for the swirling wind.

18th hole
(Champ 548yd Par 5)
Beware of the drop into the ocean all down the left.

FOUR HOLES TO WATCH

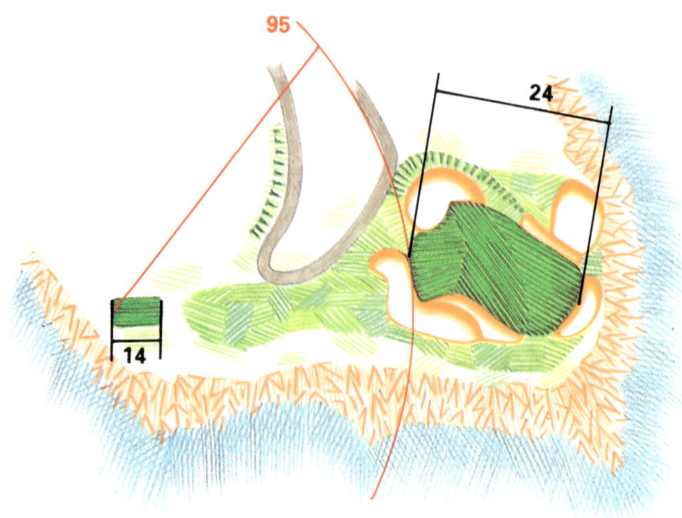

◀ 7th hole
(Champ 107yd Par 3)
A little wedge shot does the trick most of the time – as long as your nerves hold up – but pray you hit the green. If you miss, just hope that you're in one of the bunkers around the green, because the Pacific is on three sides. The green is very small and even if you manage to hit it putting is tricky.

Beware of the wind. If it's coming off the sea, your ball can be blown back considerably. The hole needs to be played with a long iron into a really strong wind.

8th hole ▶
(Champ 431yd Par 4)
With the ocean on the right and 60ft (18m) cliffs at the end of a long tee shot, this hole plays havoc with the slicer. You must hit a blind tee shot on to a plateau, from where you need to carry the ball about 180yd (165m) to clear a huge ravine.

If you're not feeling brave hit your tee shot down the left and play round the dog-leg rather than go for the carry.

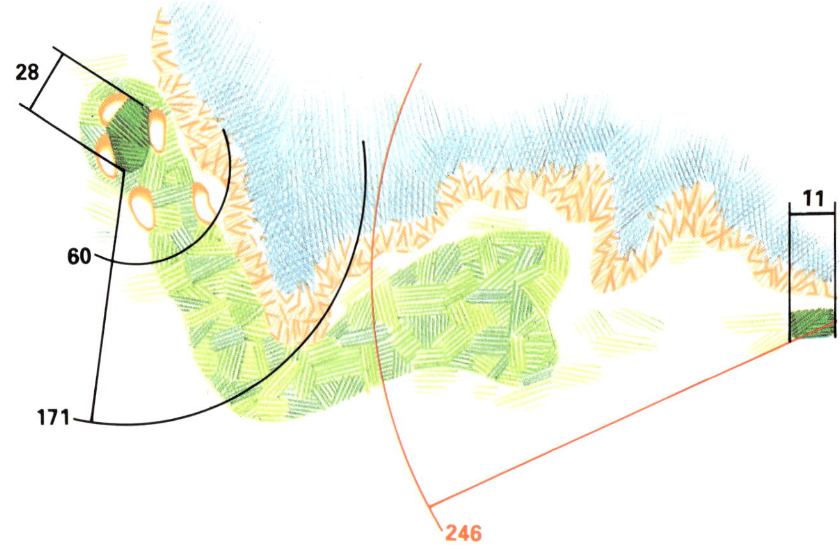

▶ Spectacularly beautiful but extremely hazardous, the 8th needs power and courage if you are to make par. Countless balls have plunged down the cliffs from those attempting the carry from the first half of the fairway.

Stormy revenge
Arnold Palmer found fame but never success at Pebble. Playing in Bing Crosby's 1967 Pro-Am, he crashed to a 9 on the 14th while going for the green in 2. His approach shot hit a towering pine on the right and landed out of bounds. On his next try he hit the same tree with the same disastrous results.

That night came sweet revenge. During a tremendous storm the tree fell.

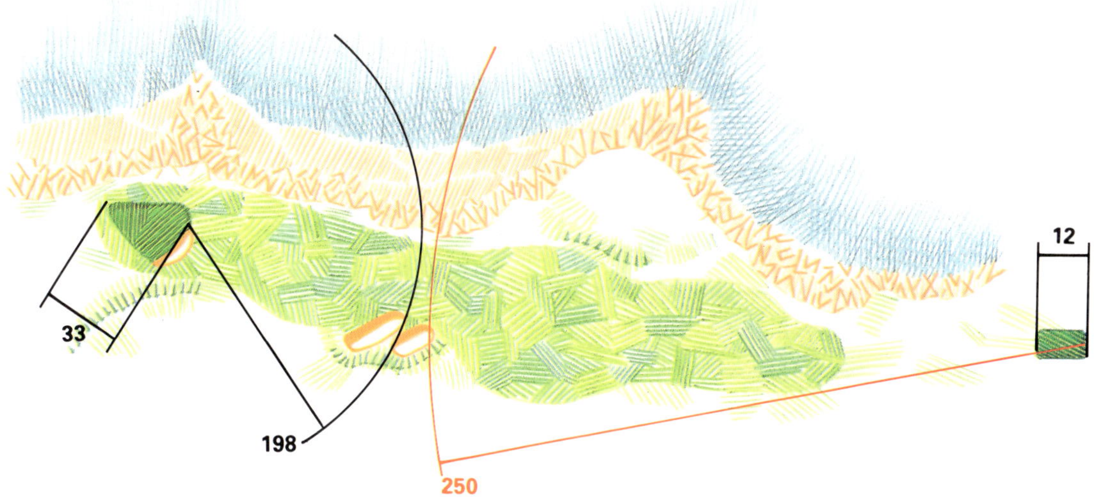

▲ ***9th hole***
(Champ 464yd Par 4)
Beautiful but awesome, this is the terror of Pebble Beach. The fairway slants dangerously from left to right towards the ocean, and bunkers guard the left. Aim your tee shot just right of these bunkers and you are set up for your second.

But it takes two massive blows to reach in 2. To be safe aim up the left as the green is sited very close to the cliffs on the right. Even the pros find it a severe challenge.

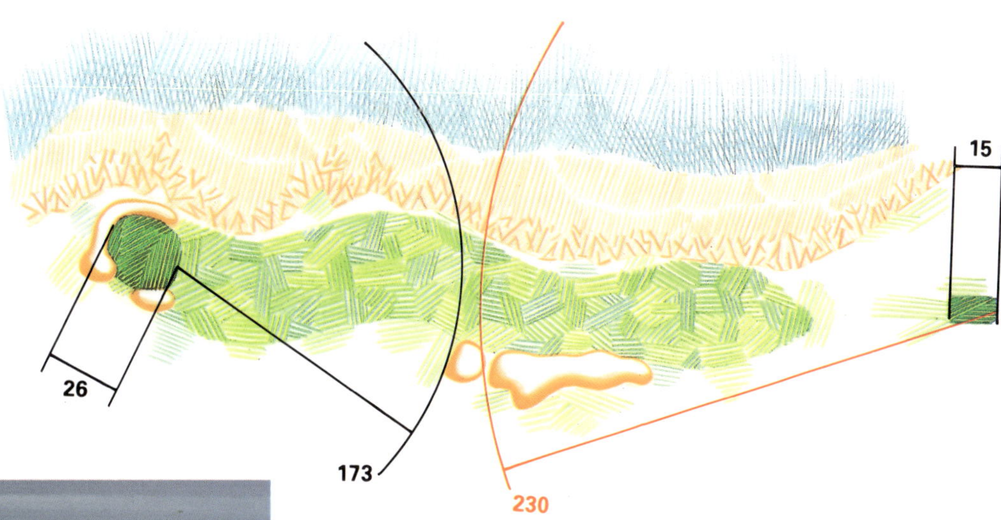

▲ ***10th hole***
(Champ 426yd Par 4)
This is the last of what's generally considered the hardest four hole sequence in golf.

You must stay left because of the cliffs on the right. Aim at the fairway bunker to be safe with your tee shot. If the ball goes into the sand be thankful. It is a far better fate than a watery grave on the right. If you come off with a par here it's a bonus.

Watson's wizardry
Standing on the tee at the 71st hole of the 1982 US Open, Tom Watson was level with Jack Nicklaus who was already in the clubhouse. Watson's chances of winning dimmed when he hit his tee shot into the forest-high rough beside the green on the left, leaving him an almost impossible shot.

'I'm going to make it,' he whispered to his caddie, and make it he did. He went on to birdie the 18th to clinch the title. That chip from the rough at 17 became known as, 'The shot that was heard around the world.'

▲ **The notorious 107yd 7th can be a card wrecker. Though it's short by championship standards, the penalties around the green are vicious. The pounding Pacific is a constant menace to the wayward golfer.**

FACTFILE
Lowest scores
Professional course record: 62 – Tom Kite 1983

Tournaments
US Open: 1972, 1982, 1992
USPGA Championship: 1977
US Amateur: 1929, 1947, 1961
Pebble Beach National Pro-Am: 1947 to 1985, sponsored by Bing Crosby. 1986, 1987, 1988, 1989, 1990, sponsored by AT&T
US Women's Amateur: 1940, 1948

the forbidding 6th tee, 'If you're 5 over when you hit this tee it's the best place in the world to commit suicide.' Trevino knew that ahead of him lay the toughest four hole sequence in golf.

FEARSOME FOUR

The 7th, 8th, 9th and 10th are consistently ranked by the USPGA as some of the hardest on the tour. Depending on the weather they can range from being very difficult to nigh on impossible. Heroism is needed at every corner. The three longest par 4s are to be found in this stretch and are all knee knockers.

The back nine is a bear in terms of length. At 3525yd (3220m) it's made all the more difficult by the raging wind that often sweeps in from the sea. The two par 3s measure over 200yd (183m), with the 17th perilously close to the cliffs. And both the par 5s are over 545yd (498m) – you need immense power and courage to reach the green in 2 shots.

PEBBLE TREBLE

Pebble has become a regular tournament venue, and has held many major championships. It staged the US Open for a third time in 1992, and as countless players failed to break 80, Tom Kite came through a last day storm with a famous 72 to win his first Major.

Even if some players have a disaster, let there be hope that they come a way thinking along similar lines to American pro Dave Marr the first time he ventured out on to Pebble Beach's famous links.

The former USPGA champion and now TV commentator said, 'I was stunned. There is nothing like it. As a golfer, my career wouldn't be complete without knowing the beauty and the grandeur of Pebble Beach.'

Pinehurst No.2

No false landscaping, no shimmering water hazards, no glitz or glamour – Pinehurst No.2 in North Carolina is traditional golf at its very best.

The No.2 course at Pinehurst Country Club is bereft of many of the popular trappings that adorn modern golf architecture. There are no sweeping seaside vistas. There are no azalea-banked streams fronting par 5s. There are no man-made waterfalls.

First-time players often wonder what all the fuss is about, and the resort's advertising counsellors fret that the look of the course doesn't yield picture-book photographs.

Yet the pinnacle of Donald Ross' design portfolio is listed among most great players' top five courses. It's what the golf course *doesn't* have that makes it so good. A good golf course doesn't need glitz and glitter.

CONSTANT REWORKING

No.2 began as a 9 hole layout in 1903, three years after Ross arrived at Pinehurst and four after he moved to America from his native Scotland. Nine holes were completed in 1907, and Ross eworked and improved the design until it reached its current configuration in 1935.

The course stretched nearly 7000yd (6395m) at that time and has remained basically the same length ever since, though a number of holes have been stretched in response to improvements in equipment. With 16yd (14.5m) added to the 5th and 20yd (18m) to the 11th holes during the

▼ The ideal line into the green on the par 4 2nd is from the left hand side of the fairway. However, the further left you go the more you flirt with a string of bunkers which are lined up perilously close to the fairway.

PINEHURST No.2

HOLE BY HOLE

Championship tees: 7056yd, Par 71, USGA rating 74.1. Medal tees: 6369yd, Par 71, USGA rating 71.0. Ladies' tees: 5934yd, Par 74, USGA rating 73.5.

1st hole
(Champ 396yd Medal 378yd Ladies' 361yd Par 4) This is a relatively simple starting hole. The fairway slopes downhill and a good drive leaves only a short iron.

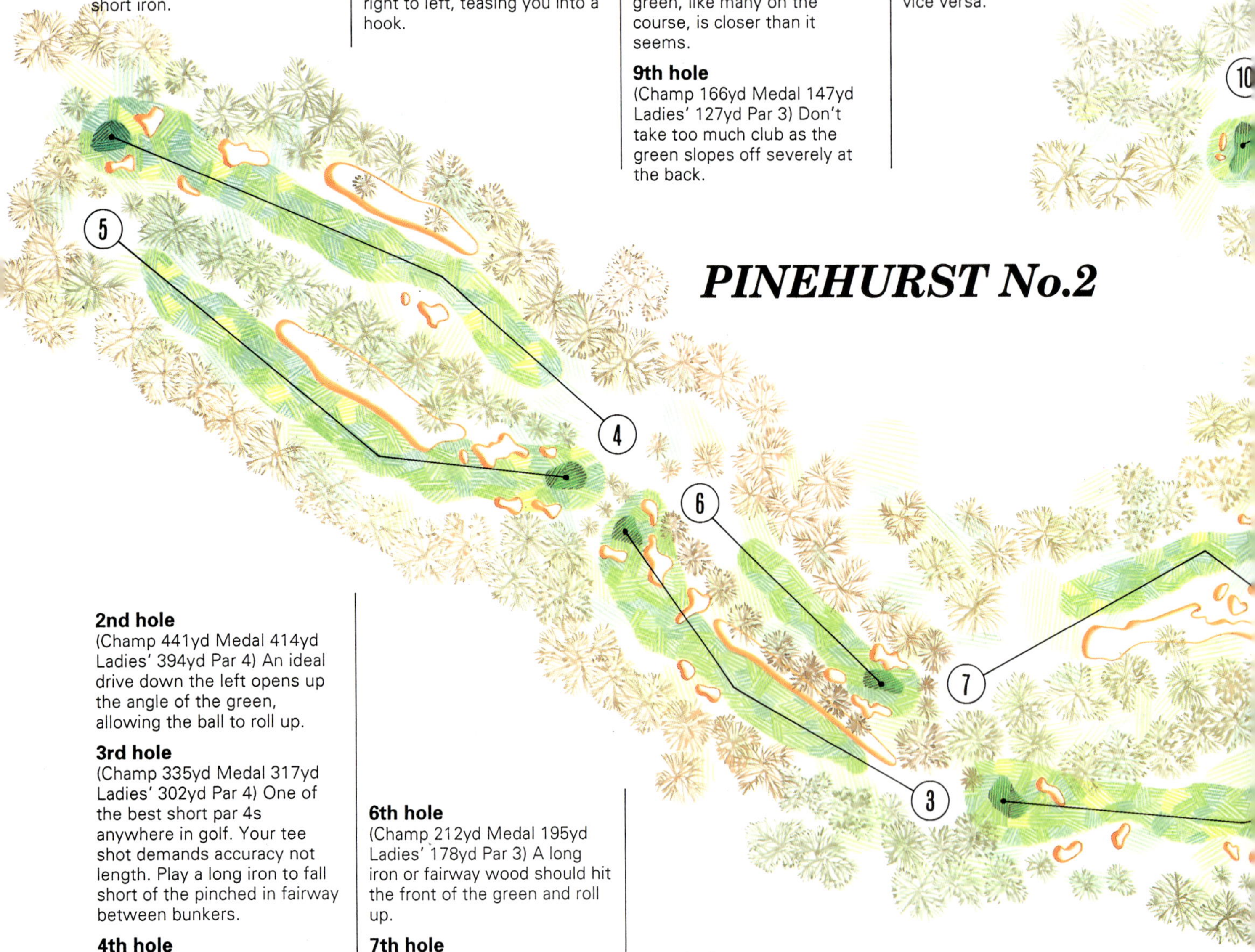

2nd hole
(Champ 441yd Medal 414yd Ladies' 394yd Par 4) An ideal drive down the left opens up the angle of the green, allowing the ball to roll up.

3rd hole
(Champ 335yd Medal 317yd Ladies' 302yd Par 4) One of the best short par 4s anywhere in golf. Your tee shot demands accuracy not length. Play a long iron to fall short of the pinched in fairway between bunkers.

4th hole
(Champ 547yd Medal 477yd Ladies' 449yd Par 5) Be careful on the long approach to avoid the fairway bunkers on both sides.

5th hole
(Champ 461yd Medal 427yd Par 4 Ladies' 417yd Par 5) This is the hardest hole on the course. You play the second shot from a fairway sloping right to left, teasing you into a hook.

6th hole
(Champ 212yd Medal 195yd Ladies' 178yd Par 3) A long iron or fairway wood should hit the front of the green and roll up.

7th hole
(Champ 401yd Medal 372yd Ladies' 320yd Par 4) Smart play is left of the fairway bunkers, leaving a short iron to the green.

8th hole
(Champ 487yd Medal 455yd Par 4 Ladies' 429yd Par 5) This is an outdated par 5 now played as a par 4. The bunker on the front right of the green, like many on the course, is closer than it seems.

9th hole
(Champ 166yd Medal 147yd Ladies' 127yd Par 3) Don't take too much club as the green slopes off severely at the back.

10th hole
(Champ 578yd Medal 459yd Ladies' 443yd Par 5) A sharply crowned green makes the exacting third shot the key.

11th hole
(Champ 453yd Medal 410yd Ladies' 363yd Par 4) Position off the tee is crucial to open up the pin on the approach. If the pin is left, drive right and vice versa.

◀ The elegant clubhouse is just one of the many facilities at the Pinehurst Resort and Country Club. The resort was the dream of the Tufts family who built the first of seven courses at the turn of the century. It remained in the same family for over 70 years.

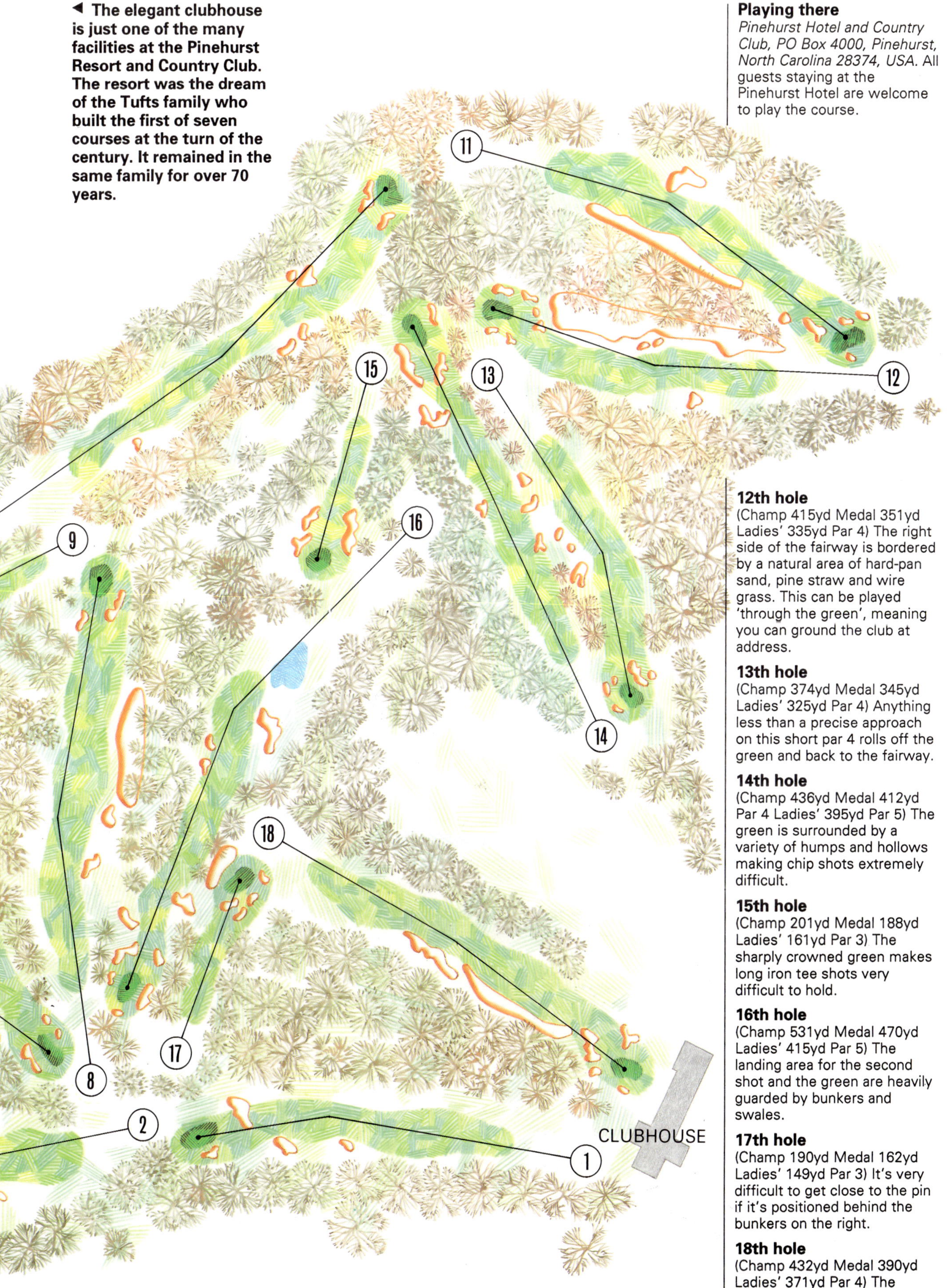

Playing there

Pinehurst Hotel and Country Club, PO Box 4000, Pinehurst, North Carolina 28374, USA. All guests staying at the Pinehurst Hotel are welcome to play the course.

12th hole

(Champ 415yd Medal 351yd Ladies' 335yd Par 4) The right side of the fairway is bordered by a natural area of hard-pan sand, pine straw and wire grass. This can be played 'through the green', meaning you can ground the club at address.

13th hole

(Champ 374yd Medal 345yd Ladies' 325yd Par 4) Anything less than a precise approach on this short par 4 rolls off the green and back to the fairway.

14th hole

(Champ 436yd Medal 412yd Par 4 Ladies' 395yd Par 5) The green is surrounded by a variety of humps and hollows making chip shots extremely difficult.

15th hole

(Champ 201yd Medal 188yd Ladies' 161yd Par 3) The sharply crowned green makes long iron tee shots very difficult to hold.

16th hole

(Champ 531yd Medal 470yd Ladies' 415yd Par 5) The landing area for the second shot and the green are heavily guarded by bunkers and swales.

17th hole

(Champ 190yd Medal 162yd Ladies' 149yd Par 3) It's very difficult to get close to the pin if it's positioned behind the bunkers on the right.

18th hole

(Champ 432yd Medal 390yd Ladies' 371yd Par 4) The approach shot needs to be accurate as the green features a deep swale through the middle.

FOUR HOLES TO WATCH

5th hole

(Champ 461yd Par 4) ►

This is the only blind shot off a tee on No.2 – there's a crown in the fairway between the tee and landing area, forcing you to pick a tree on the horizon to aim for. That sets up one of the hardest shots in golf – a long iron from a sidehill lie. But that's exactly the challenge – provided you've hit a good tee shot leaving you in the 220yd (201m) range.

The green is angled from right to left, making the right side of the fairway the better from which to play your second shot. Bear in mind that the hole plays longer from that side. Beware the sharp fall on the left side of the green into a pair of bunkers.

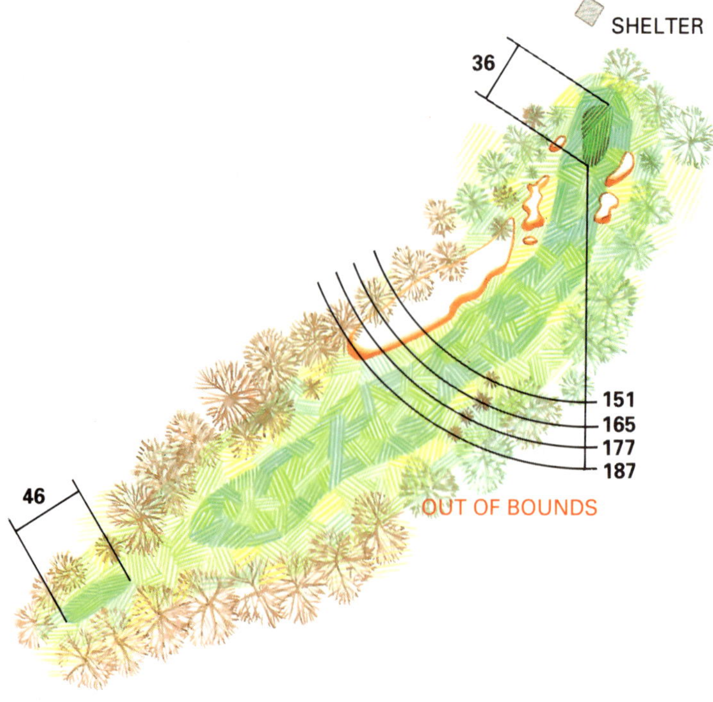

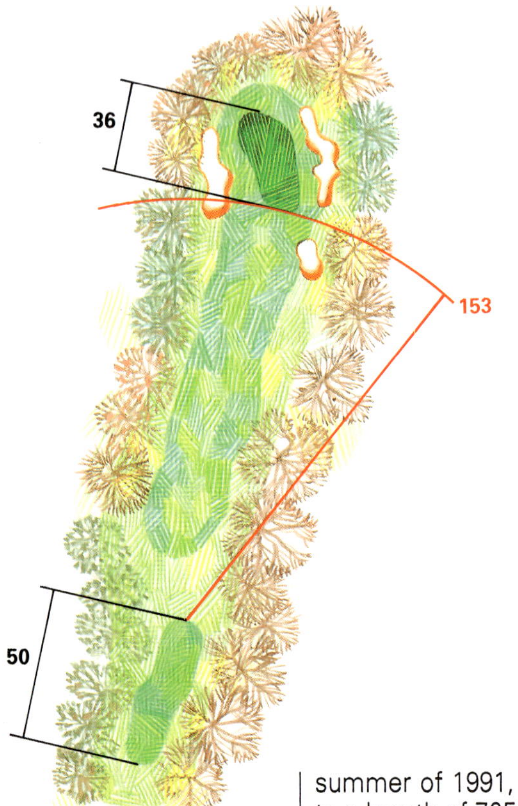

◄ *6th hole*

(Champ 212yd Par 3)

This hole is long enough at 212yd (193m), but it also plays into the prevailing wind. There's a subtle downslope from the fairway to the front of the green. Often the best play is to knock the ball under the wind, let it catch the downslope and roll on to the green.

Like all greens at No.2, this one is crowned and falls off around the edges. It is also quite deep – the pin position can mean the difference of a couple of clubs.

The 5th and 6th holes back to back comprise the toughest two holes on the course. The golfer who can get through this stretch in par is generally headed for a good round.

summer of 1991, the course now plays to a length of 7056yd (6446m) and a par of 71.

No.2 (now one of seven courses at Pinehurst Resort and Country Club and one of four Ross built during his time there) was hailed from its inception as one of the finest layouts in a nation that had become quickly enamoured with the old game.

The North and South Amateur – played from 1901 to the present – and the North and South Open – contested among professionals from 1903 to 1951 – brought to Pinehurst all the finest: Walter Hagen, Francis Ouimet, Ben Hogan, Sam Snead, Jack Nicklaus and Tom Watson span the generations of champions at Pinehurst.

Pinehurst provides a thorough examination in course management, driving skills, iron play, putting and, perhaps more than anything, chipping. Ben Crenshaw says it 'may be the finest chipping golf course in the world'.

FLYING SAUCERS

The difficult, crowned greens are Ross trademarks – they're shaped like upside-down saucers, falling off gradually around the edges. The aprons are mowed tight and maintained much like the greens themselves.

◄ **The 16th is a long par 5 on which both the landing area and the green are heavily guarded by bunkers. Ross himself described the difficulties on the green: 'The slope rises gently on the front part of the green and faces slightly away at the rear. Regardless of where a pin may be placed, a player whose approach is either short or strong will be faced with the problem of putting across the ridge formed by this change in slope'.**

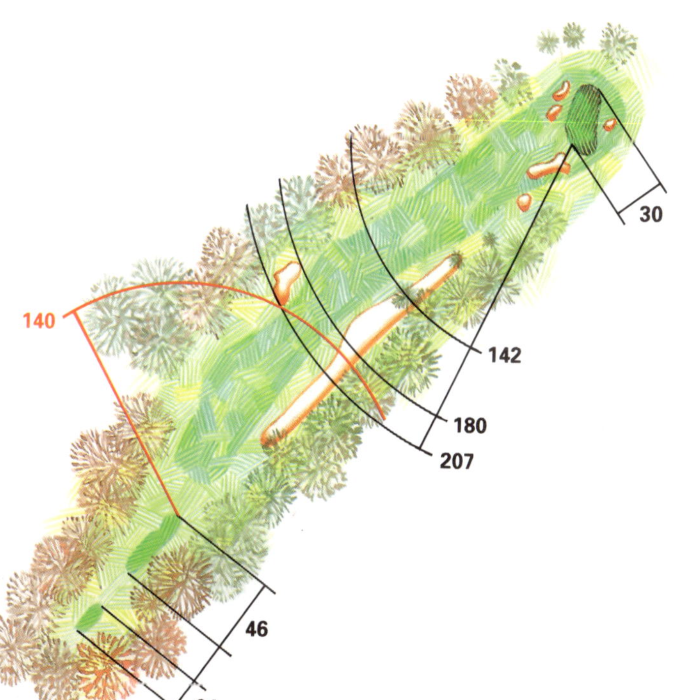

◄ ***11th hole***
(Champ 453yd Par 4)
Ben Hogan holed out from a greenside bunker for a birdie en route to winning the 1940 North and South Open, his first pro tournament win after seven years of frustration. The right side of the fairway is bordered by the trademark Pinehurst 'natural area' – pine trees, pine straw, hard pan sand, wire grass and scrub oaks.

The fairway appears wide from the tee, but you need precise position to open up the best angle of approach to the pin. If the flag is just beyond the bunker on the right and the greens are firm, it's next to impossible to hit an approach from the right side, carry the bunker and get the ball to stop close to the hole.

16th hole ►
(Champ 531yd Par 5)
This hole features the only water hazard on the course, which only comes into play if you're hitting off the back tees and top the ball.

The fairway is very wide at the landing area but narrows sharply as you approach the green. Long hitters can reach the green in 2, but a miss-hit gamble is likely to find one of a number of bunkers around the green. Most players elect to lay up, just beyond one bunker on the left and short of the greenside bunkers. That leaves a wedge into a deep, narrow green.

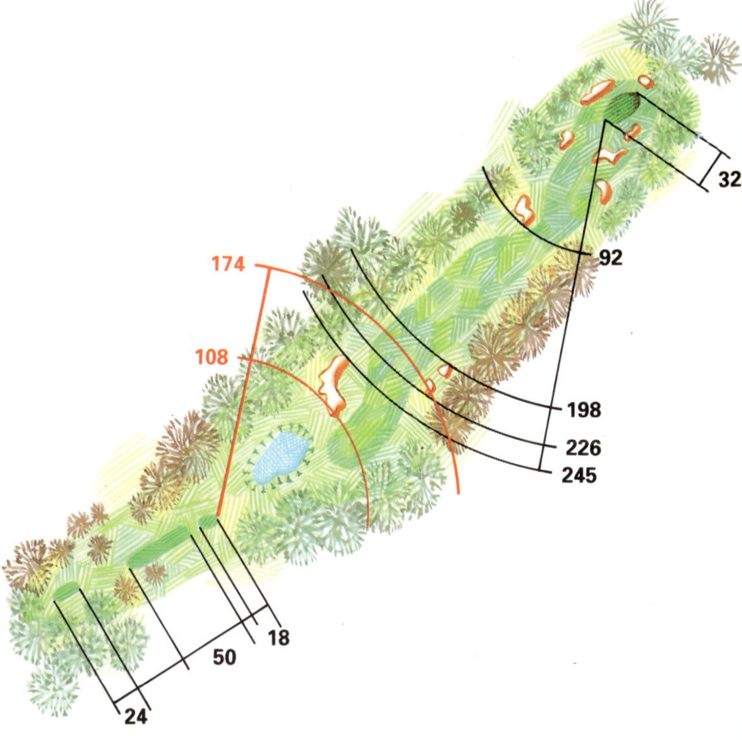

▲ **The short 17th is the easiest hole on the course, although it can be difficult to master if the pin is tucked in behind the right hand bunkers. One of the most delightful features of Pinehurst is that despite the heavy tree cover, it's almost impossible to lose a ball.**

FACTFILE
Course record:
62 – Gibby Gilbert

Tournaments
USPGA Championship: 1936
Ryder Cup: 1951
US Amateur: 1962
Eisenhower Trophy (world men's amateur team championship): 1980
Espirito Santo Trophy (world women's amateur team championship): 1980
North and South Open: 1903 to 1951
North and South Amateur: 1901 to present
US Ladies Amateur: 1989

Surrounding the greens are a variety of mounds, dips and hollows. They repel and/or collect slightly miss-hit balls that strike the edges of the greens and, with no thick grass to catch them, roll and roll. Because of the sandy nature of the soil, Ross constructed the indentations around the greens without fear they'd stagnate with run-off water during rainy periods.

The golfer facing one of these shots has three options: he can lob the ball with a wedge, hit a bump and run with a mid or short iron, or even putt the ball. It is this variety of challenges that keeps the golfer on edge and wondering, each time he addresses one of these short monsters, if his strategy is correct.

There are no water hazards on No.2, although a pond sits in front of the 16th tee without coming into play. It's difficult to hit a ball out of bounds, and because there are no thickly wooded areas on the course – the fairways are lined with huge areas of pine trees, pine straw and native wire grass – it's next to impossible to lose a golf ball.

Fans of No.2 resist naming favourite holes. Indeed, part of the course's charm is that, unlike many others, there are no signature holes that cut through the rank and file and define the golf course.

WELL KNIT LAYOUT

All the holes on No.2 are excellent, and each fits with the one before it and the one after it like hand-in-glove. There's an ebb and flow to the test that can lull you into a feeling of comfort one moment and a state of nervousness the next.

The first three holes, for example, are all par 4s, the 1st requiring a good drive and mid or short iron; the 2nd a massive drive and long iron; the 3rd a gingerly placed lay-up and a short iron. It's a varied start.

Best of all, Pinehurst No.2 is a course anyone can play. The course is open to members and all guests of the Pinehurst Hotel in the resort.

Pine Valley

For toughness, character and sheer beauty, this magnificent course in the sandy, pine covered wastelands of New Jersey is hard to surpass. Many golfers go home broken but thrilled they sampled its delights.

Rated the best in the US – and some say the world – Pine Valley is awesome. At 6765yd (6186m) it may not seem long for such a brute of a course, but as soon as you venture out you realize why it's so demanding.

The setting is unique. The holes cut a swathe through dense pines which form an intimidating corridor. There is no rough – just sandy scrub. The impeccably lush fairways and greens are the only sanctuary in an otherwise sandy wilderness. At Pine Valley there is no margin for error – you're either safe or in deep trouble.

ISLAND CARRIES

The fairways form island oases surrounded by a desert scrub which is designated as one big bunker. Every tee shot involves a carry of " at least 120yd (110m), and many of the holes need another good hit to clear more wasteland to find the green.

The penalties for missing the fairways or greens are severe. Miss a fairway and you must contend with the unraked natural bunker – and a really wild shot is lost in the thick woods.

The sand runs right up to the greens – many of which are slightly raised – and is shaped into the more usual manicured bunkers. A fraction off line and the ball is gathered into trouble. It's green or nothing.

Pine Valley doesn't stage professional tournaments – the trees and scrub make the course so tight

▶ Pine Valley's major hazards are the mass of sandy scrub and trees, but water also plays its part. To find the fairway at the monster 603yd 15th your drive must clear a large stretch of lake. Even if you do hit a long straight shot, the rest of the hole is fraught with danger. No one has ever reached the green in 2, so a par here is a good score.

HOLE BY HOLE

Championship tees: 6765yd, Par 70, USGA Rating 73.

1st hole
(Champ 427yd Par 4)
You must hit a long drive to the corner of the dog-leg to leave yourself a decent approach to the green.

2nd hole
(Champ 367yd Par 4)
Nothing but your best tee shot will do – the carry over scrub to the fairway is almost 180yd (165m).

3rd hole
(Champ 185yd Par 4)
Aim to the right half of the green as it slopes sharply from right to left.

4th hole
(Champ 461yd Par 4)
Hit a big drive to make certain of clearing the sandy patch of waste ground short of the green with your second.

5th hole
(Champ 226yd Par 3)
Be straight or a big score stares you in the face.

6th hole
(Champ 391yd Par 4)
Don't bite off more than you can manage from the tee at this sharp dog-leg right – if you miss the fairway your second is very difficult.

7th hole
(Champ 585yd Par 5)
If you hit a poor drive you must lay up short of Hell's Half Acre – you have no chance of clearing the mass of scrub with your second.

8th hole
(Champ 327yd Par 4)
Make sure your approach is below the flag – the green slopes alarmingly from back to front.

9th hole
(Champ 432yd Par 4)
Don't overshoot the green – whichever one the flag is on – as there is a large drop at the back.

10th hole
(Champ 145yd Par 3)
Your tee shot has to be accurate – trees at the back and bunkers all round swallow any wayward shot.

11th hole
(Champ 399yd Par 4)
Aim down the left for the best line into the green.

12th hole
(Champ 382yd Par 4)
Drive down the right to leave a clear path for your second.

▲ **The 10th is the shortest hole on the course but needs a precise short iron to hit the green. With slopes dropping into sand all the way round, there is no room for manoeuvre. One tiny pot bunker at the front catches many shots – often you must play out backwards to recover.**

PINE VALLEY

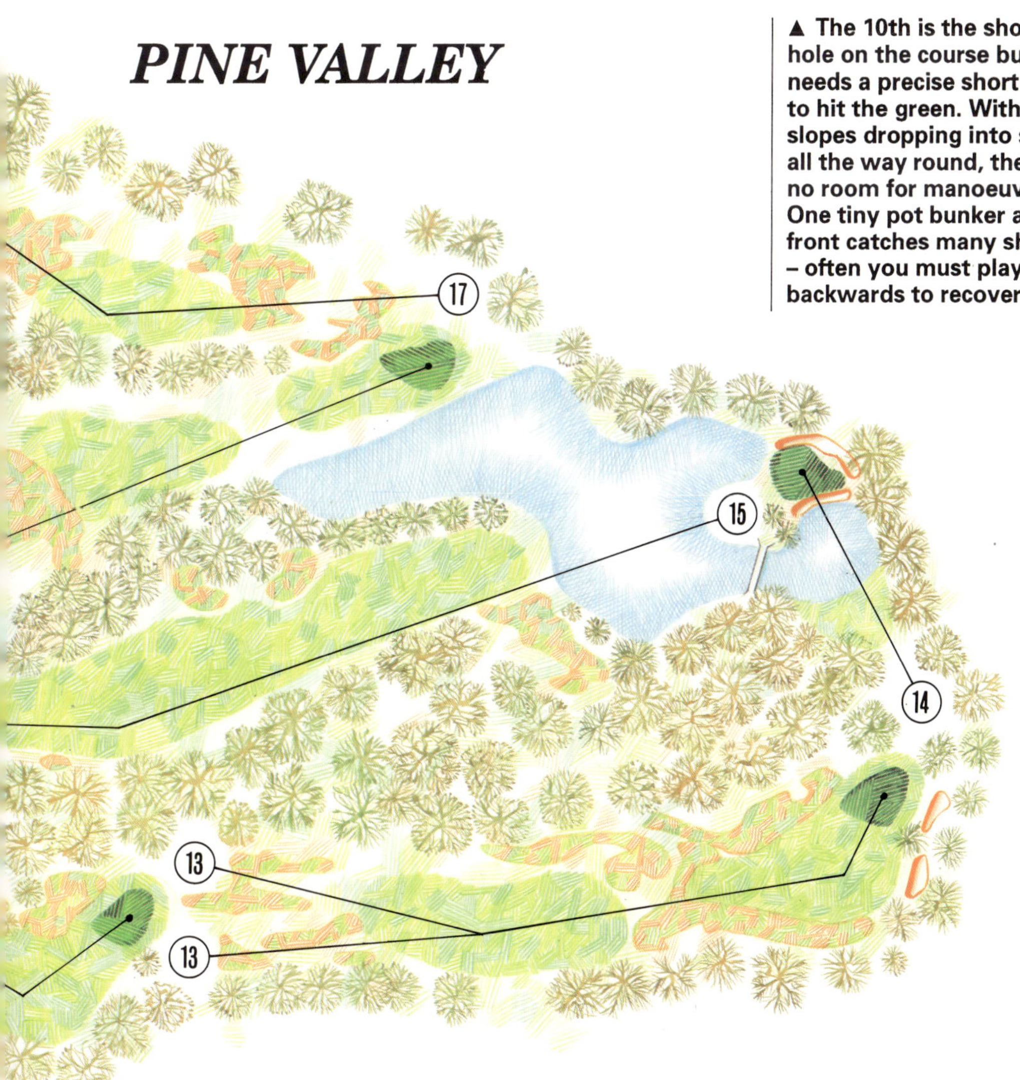

13th hole
(Champ 446yd Par 4)
Because the green is tucked away behind a patch of dead ground, your approach must carry all the way if you're to reach in 2.

14th hole
(Champ 185yd Par 3)
Choose enough club – there are no prizes for being short. Thick scrub, water and sand are the dangers.

15th hole
(Champ 603yd Par 5)
Don't be intimidated by the water in front of the tee. Once you've cleared the lake settle for a steady par at this monster hole.

16th hole
(Champ 436yd Par 4)
Hit your best drive – the carry is long to the small island fairway.

17th hole
(Champ 344yd Par 4)
Check your yardages for the second shot – the sandy stretch of ground in front of the green can be deceiving to the eye.

18th hole
(Champ 424yd Par 4)
Even though the carry from the tee is about 170yd (155m), the hardest part of playing this hole is negotiating the subtle slopes of the massive green.

FOUR HOLES TO WATCH

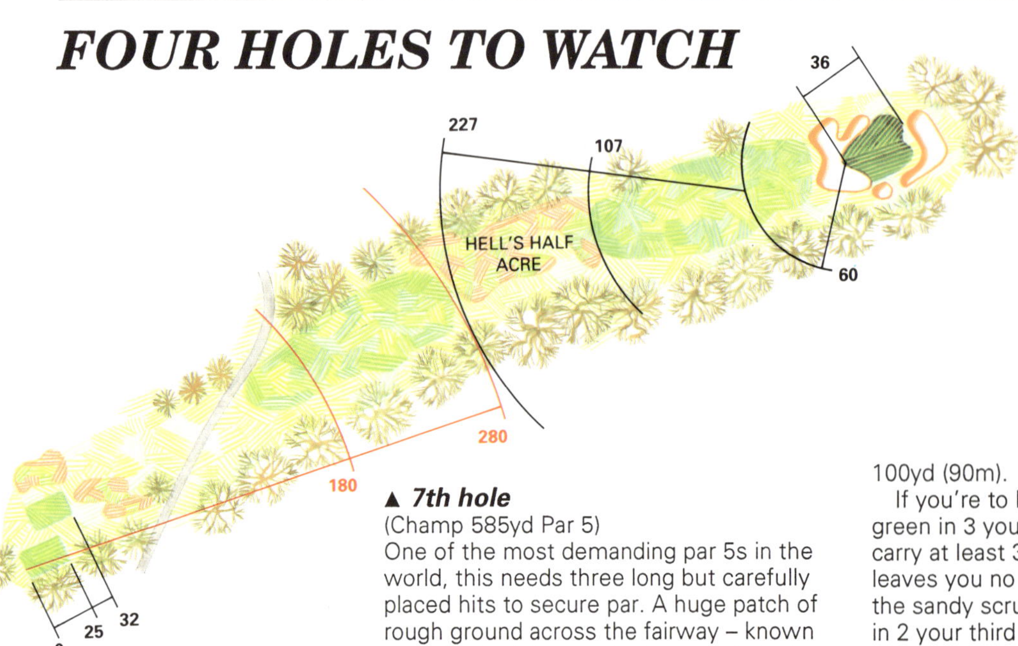

▲ *7th hole*

(Champ 585yd Par 5)
One of the most demanding par 5s in the world, this needs three long but carefully placed hits to secure par. A huge patch of rough ground across the fairway – known as Hell's Half Acre – starts some 280yd (256m) from the tee and stretches for over 100yd (90m).

If you're to have any chance of hitting the green in 3 you must play two shots that carry at least 380yd (347m). A poor drive leaves you no option but to lay up short of the sandy scrub. Even if you do clear Hell's in 2 your third has to be played over more sand to an elevated green. No one has ever reached this green in 2.

► The daunting carry – a familiar feature at Pine Valley – from back tee to 14th green is 161yd (147m). Crossing sand and scrub, water and front bunker, it is definitely one of the most challenging par 3s in the world.

Woody works wonders

Talented US amateur Woody Platt once had a miracle start to his round. He played a superb approach to the 1st to make a birdie, and followed it up at the 2nd by holing a 7 iron for an eagle 2. He could have been forgiven for thinking that his bubble might burst at the extremely difficult 185yd (169m) 3rd, but instead he ignored the dangers and holed in one.

Not believing his luck he walked to the 4th tee and struck a huge driver, followed by a 4 wood into the heart of the green. Amazingly he holed out for birdie – and he now stood 6 under.

Not altogether happy about tackling the terrifying 5th, Woody walked into the nearby clubhouse for a celebration drink. He never reappeared to finish the round.

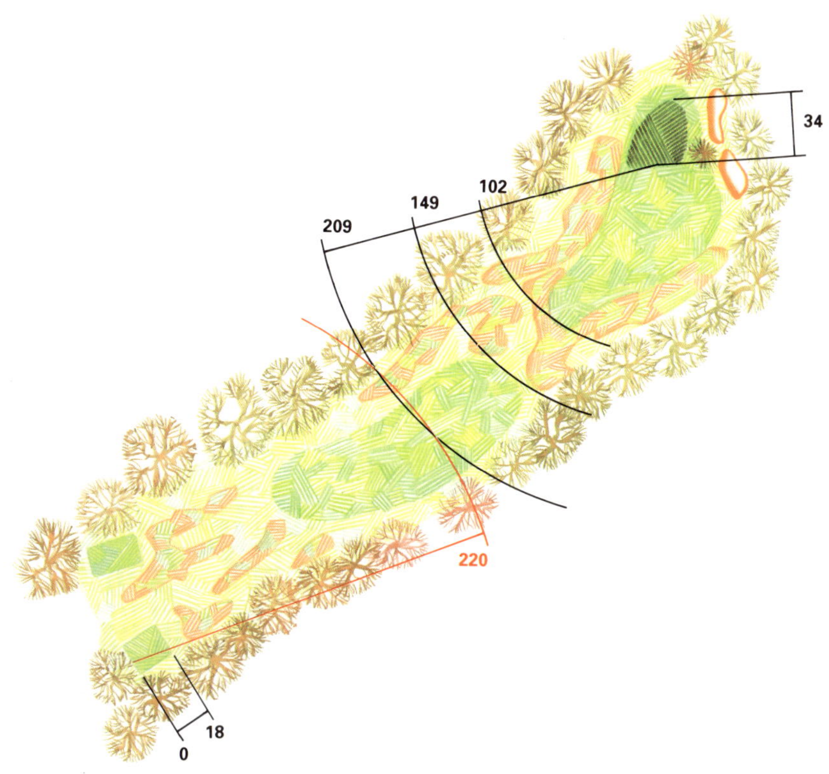

◄ *13th hole*

(Champ 446yd Par 4)

To play this hole as a genuine 2 shotter you must first hit a long tee shot that finds the island fairway then a brave all carry second to the green. If you're unsure of making the carry it's best to play for the second stretch of fairway to the right of the green and hope to pitch and putt.

To go for the green you usually need a long iron or wood that must fly a mass of sand to pitch on the putting surface. But the problem is holding the ball to avoid overshooting into the sand or trees.

14th hole ►

(Champ 185yd Par 3)

Possibly the most intimidating hole on the course, this par 3 is all or nothing. It plays slightly shorter than the yardage suggests because you drive from an elevated tee downhill to the green. But this doesn't diminish its dangers.

The ball must clear a mass of shrubs then a large stretch of water and a strip of sand before it finds the green. But if you think that going long is better than being short, think again. Beyond the green more sand awaits, and pines, oaks and birches can easily ruin your score.

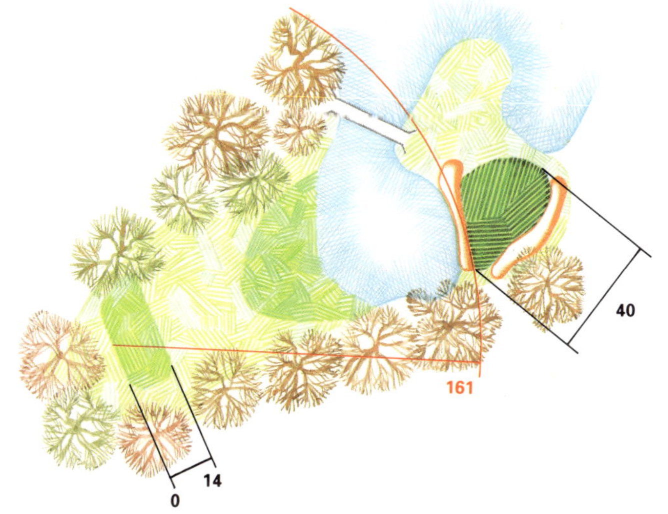

◄ *18th hole*

(Champ 424yd Par 4)

This stunning finishing hole is a fitting climax for such a great course – it tests your skill right to the last stroke. Luckily the fairway is generous but you must still carry the ball over 150yd (137m) to find it.

The second shot is critical. You play off a downhill lie over 100yd (91m) of sand and water to an elevated green, and placement is vital.

The putting surface is huge – unless your approach is good a 3 putt is always a possibility.

▲ Looking down the 5th you realize why the course is so demanding. The dense woods encroach on the holes leaving no margin for error – there is nowhere to bale out. If you hit the right distance to the flag you're either in good shape on the green or in severe trouble – these swings of fortune are typical of the course.

FACTFILE
Lowest scores
Course record:
64 – Robert Lewis jnr

Tournaments
Walker Cup: 1936, 1985

that it can't cope with the large galleries that accompany an event. But the Walker Cup has been held here twice, in 1936 and 1985, as the spectators are allowed to walk the fairways while following the matches.

GAMBLING GOLFERS

It's a pity that no one ever gets to see the world's top players fighting it out at Pine Valley as the course brings out the best. But the golf greats have all played here. Some have gambled and taken up the club members' challenge of shooting below 80 on their first attempt. Many have failed.

One notable exception was Arnold Palmer fresh from his 1954 US Amateur win. He took up far more bets than he could afford, but salvaged the day with a sparkling 68.

It takes more than mere talent to conquer Pine Valley – hard concentration and thought are essential. Every shot must be calculated, placed correctly and struck precisely if you're to avoid the double and triple bogeys that can easily jump up and grab you.

This demanding layout is testament to the design skills of two men, club founder George Crump and H S Colt. Opened in 1919 after seven years' work, Pine Valley has a superb array of holes, and each hole has its own special character.

SHORT HOLE SNAGS

Pine Valley's most distinctive holes are the brilliant par 3s. Every one is all carry – whether you must shoot over the wasteland and pot bunkers of the short 10th, or fly 226yd (207m) over water and scrub to find the 5th green. You need steely nerves and an exacting strike.

It's not only the par 3s that provide danger – the 5s are a monstrous challenge too. Neither par 5 has been reached in 2. You must contend with a 120yd (110m) stretch of dead ground across the fairway – known as Hell's Half Acre – at the 7th, while the 15th is a gruelling 603yd (551m). To add insult to injury the 15th gradually narrows and is uphill at the end.

An undoubtedly tricky nature is not the only difficulty you must overcome. Psychologically the course is a nightmare. Even before a golfer sets foot on the luxuriant turf his mind is awash with tales of woe.

If your game is on song and you're feeling up to the formidable test, Pine Valley *can* be played well. But win or lose you're presented with one of the most exhilarating challenges of all.

Royal Birkdale

At Birkdale it is easy to believe that you're on your own when you play the course. Hemmed in by sand dunes, the outside world seems a long way away.

Among the British links courses to have staged the Open, Royal Birkdale is unusual in being relatively smooth and flat. From fairway positions there are few blind shots to the green. It does not have the undulating fairways, difficult sloping lies, humps and hollows, and uneven bounces common on links courses.

It is also different in that Birkdale is as much man-made as sculptured by the elements. This is in stark contrast with St Andrews and most other British links which have been shaped mainly by the elements.

FAIR FAIRWAYS

Birkdale's flat fairways make it one of the favourite British courses among American professionals. Many Americans dislike traditional links because they believe it is unfair when a perfectly good shot kicks at right angles off a bump or hollow into the rough or a bunker. But on the level fairways of Birkdale the punishment fits the crime.

However, if your shots do stray from the fairway, you are almost certain to find yourself among the many sand hills that surround and separate most holes. These sandhills turn each hole into an arena. Birkdale's greens are also friendlier than those on most of Britain's championship links, even though the putting surface speeds up considerably in dry conditions. South African Bobby Cole fell victim to the greens at the 1976 Open during the very dry weather of that year's drought. He five-putted the opening green.

▼ The 13th hole is typical of Royal Birkdale with its lush green fairways, surrounded by sand dunes, with the Irish Sea in the distance.

HOLE BY HOLE
Championship tees: 7022 yards, par 71. Medal tees 6711 yards, Standard Scratch Score (SSS) 73. Men's Tees: white 6703 yards, SSS 73; yellow 6305 yards, SSS 71. Ladies' Tees: 5777 yards, SSS 75.

1st hole
(Champ 450yd Medal 447yd Par 4) Don't go too far right from the tee or you're out of bounds.

2nd hole
(Champ 419yd Medal 416yd Par 4) Don't be long with your second shot because danger lurks just beyond the green.

3rd hole
(Champ 411yd Medal 407yd Par 4) Take one more club than you think for your second.

4th hole
(Champ 205yd Medal 202yd Par 3) You usually have to allow for the left-to-right wind – and you can't feel it from the tee.

5th hole
(Champ 348yd Medal 341yd Par 4) Don't be tempted to cut the corner of the fairway from the tee or you could end up in the pond.

6th hole
(Champ 492yd Medal 488yd Par 5) Play left from the tee for the best approach to the green.

7th hole
(Champ 156yd Medal 150yd Par 3) Check for wind strength, because the plateau tee is surprisingly sheltered.

8th hole
(Champ 460yd Medal 414yd Par 4) Stay clear of the dunes on the left and don't be short with your second.

9th hole
(Champ 416yd Medal 413yd Par 4) You can't see the fairway off the back tee. It's better to be right.

10th hole
(Champ 397yd Medal 372yd Par 4) Don't be tempted to play left. The scrub is extremely thick on this side.

▲ If you drive across the corner of the dog-leg at the short par-4 5th, you'll probably end up in this pond.

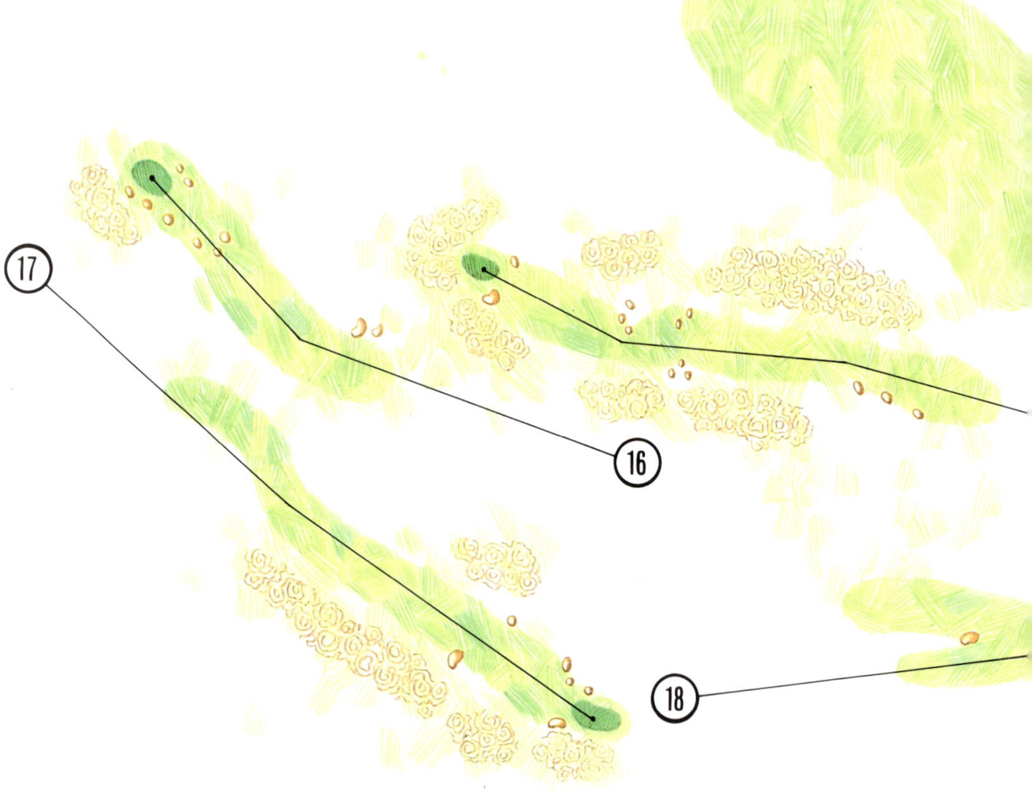

CHANGE OF SITE

The club was founded as a 9-hole links in 1889, a short way down the coast from its current site. Eight years later it moved to its present position.

Its layout has changed a few times in the intervening years. Five-times Open Champion J H Taylor, and course architect Charles Hawtree, supervised Birkdale's first major reconstruction between 1931 and 1933.

In the early 1960s Birkdale built a new par 3 (12th hole) to replace the short 17th. It meant the course had three par 5s over the final four holes, which gave even championship players a long and demanding finishing stretch.

By The 1983 Open, however, this had changed, as the 18th was shortened from a par 5 to a 472-yard par 4.

For the 1987 Lawrence Batley International, the championship course increased its yardage from 6986 to 7022, as a result of R and A recommendations. The 4th green was turned lengthways to the tee, the 6th was remodelled as a par 5 (it was previously a par 4), and new championship tees were built at the 7th and 16th.

POPULAR TOURNAMENT VENUE

The various reconstructions over the years have developed the dunes to form

ROYAL BIRKDALE CHAMPIONSHIP COURSE

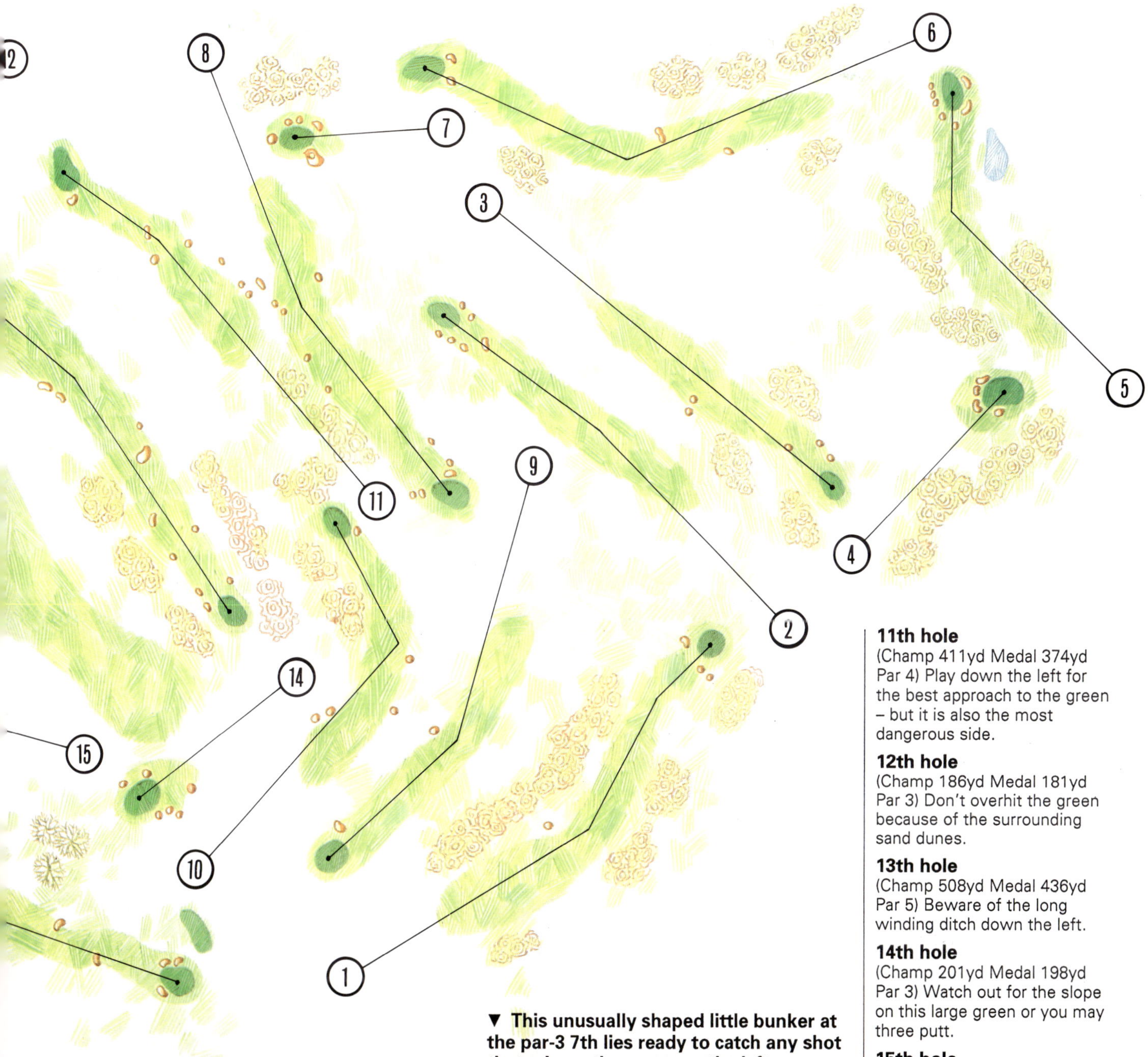

▼ **This unusually shaped little bunker at the par-3 7th lies ready to catch any shot that misses the green on the left.**

11th hole
(Champ 411yd Medal 374yd Par 4) Play down the left for the best approach to the green – but it is also the most dangerous side.

12th hole
(Champ 186yd Medal 181yd Par 3) Don't overhit the green because of the surrounding sand dunes.

13th hole
(Champ 508yd Medal 436yd Par 5) Beware of the long winding ditch down the left.

14th hole
(Champ 201yd Medal 198yd Par 3) Watch out for the slope on this large green or you may three putt.

15th hole
(Champ 545yd Medal 542yd Par 5) Beware of bunkers that are ready to catch your ball on tee shots.

16th hole
(Champ 416yd Medal 344yd Par 4) Play down the left from the tee for the best line at this hole.

17th hole
(Champ 527yd Medal 502yd Par 5) You mustn't hook your tee shot on this extremely tight driving hole.

18th hole
(Champ 474yd Medal 476yd Par 4) Your second shot is probably one more club than you think.

FOUR HOLES TO WATCH

1st hole ►
(Champ 450yd Medal 447yd Par 4)
This opening dog-leg is a formidable hole. A short hitter may be troubled by the ditch on the right, while a long hitter must guard against the out of bounds on the same side – particularly if the wind is blowing off the sea.

Even when the fairways are dry and hard and the ball is running long, you need a couple of mighty thumps to reach the green in two. Accuracy is vital because of the narrow entrance to the green which is guarded by three bunkers and a number of mounds.

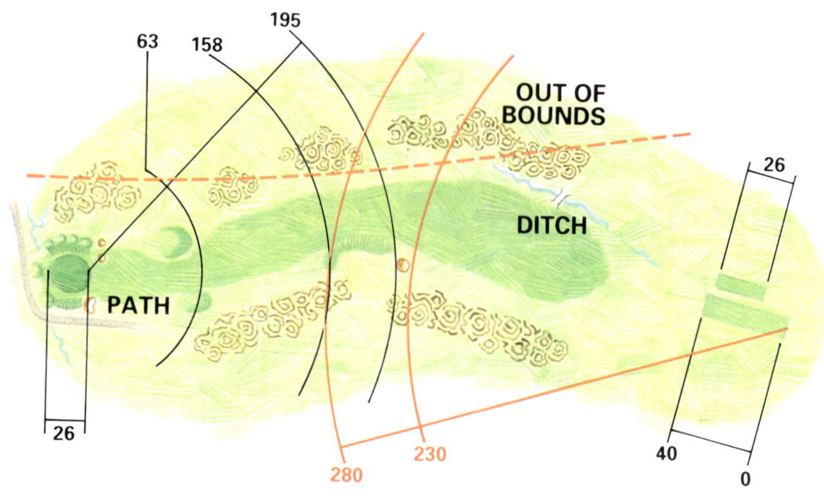

◄ ***6th hole***
(Champ 492yd Medal 488yd Par 5)
Whatever your standard this dog-leg is always a challenge. If you drive the ball more than 250yd (228m) you can reach the dog-leg from the tee, but watch out for the big bunker on the right side of the fairway.

If you're a short hitter you face a more difficult second shot across the angle of the dog-leg. There is trouble everywhere: three ditches, dangerous slopes, extensive rough and a plateau green that is closely surrounded by mounds and bushes. Best to take a safe three shots to reach the green.

► Trouble awaits any golfer who strays from the fairway at the difficult 6th hole. Before 1987, this par 5 was a monster par 4. Typically for Royal Birkdale, the green (in the centre of the picture) is surrounded by sandhills.

▶ **The green at the beautiful par-4 8th hole is very hazardous. Unplayable lies await anyone whose ball fails to find the fairway at this long hole.**

Head hunting
At the final hole of The 1971 Open Championship, runner-up Mr Lu injured a woman spectator when a bunker shot struck her on the head.

Battling Butler
The severity of Birkdale in stormy conditions was underlined at the 1963 PGA Championship when only Peter Butler and Bernard Hunt broke 80 in all four rounds. Butler won the event with a four-round total of 306 – the highest winning score for any British PGA event.

Dynamic Davies
Britain's Laura Davies shot a remarkable 17 under par to win The 1987 Women's British Open.

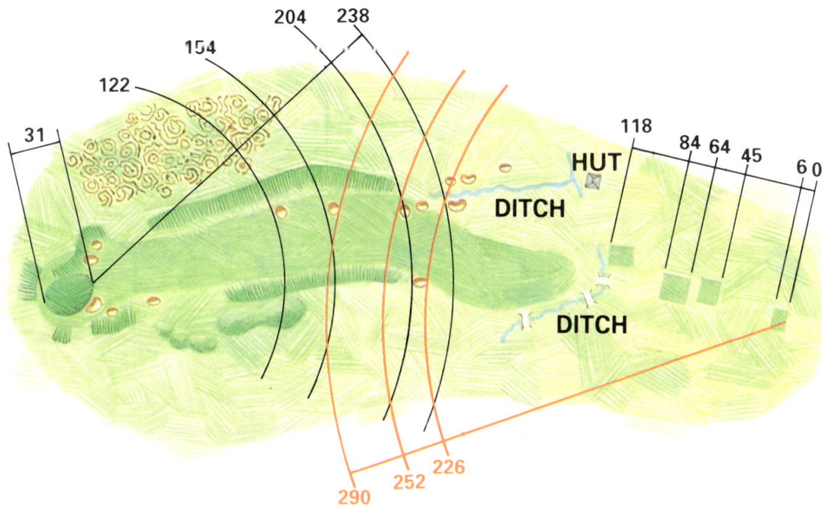

◀ ***8th hole***
(Champ 460yd Medal 414yd Par 4)
For the best line to the green on this dog-leg, play down the right side of the fairway from the tee. But be careful – if you stray too far to the right there is a group of bunkers ready to catch your ball. Although the right is the more dangerous side, don't play safe down the left because you may leave yourself a blind second shot to the green. Take one more club than you think for your shot to the raised green.

12th hole ▶
(Champ 186yd Medal 159yd Par 3)
You can't see the green from the hole's elevated tee because of the sand dunes that closely guard the putting surface. Don't be short off the tee or your ball is likely to finish in one of the four greenside bunkers. Anything wide or overhit leaves a difficult chip.

This hole is the newest on the course; it was introduced in time for the 1965 Open Championship.

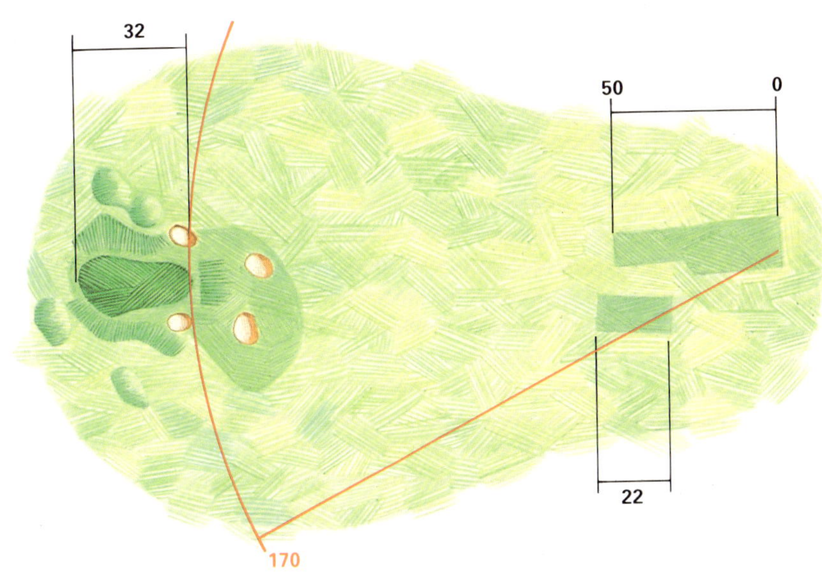

FACTFILE

Professional course record (pre-1987) – 64: Craig Stadler (USA), 1983 Open Championship (first round). Professional course record (post-1987) – 64: Mark O'Meara (USA), 1987 Lawrence Batley International (second round).

Open Championship – 1954, 1961, 1965, 1971, 1976, 1983, 1991

Ryder Cup – 1965, 1969

Amateur Championship – 1946, 1989

Walker Cup – 1951

English Amateur Championship – 1939, 1953, 1970

Brabazon Trophy – 1947, 1950, 1958, 1963

Women's British Open – *1986*

Women's British Open Amateur Championship – 1909, 1962

Women's British Open Amateur Stroke Play Championship – 1970

Curtis Cup – 1948

English Women's Amateur Championship – 1935

Dunlop-Southport Professional Tournament – 1930, 1935

Schweppes PGA Closed Championship – 1963

Dunlop Masters – 1964

Carling World Championship – 1966

Alcan International – 1968

PGA Championship – 1978

Lawrence Batley International – 1987

English Open – 1988

Lord Derby's Under-25 Championship – 1972

PGA Club Professionals Championship – 1986

▲ This plaque, at the 16th, was erected to commemorate Arnold Palmer's championship-winning 6-iron shot in The 1961 Open.

▲ Vandals damaged the 6th green during The 1983 Open Championship. The Birkdale greenkeepers made a valiant attempt to repair the damage on the morning of the third round.

natural viewing points for spectators. Birkdale is also popular with tournament organizers. Not only is its on-course viewing better than most, but Birkdale can also take huge crowds and is not far from Southport – with many hotels.

Since the Second World War it has staged more championships than any other British course. Although Birkdale did not host an Open Championship until the 1950s, the Ladies' Golf Union recognized its potential as early as 1909, when it staged their Amateur Championship.

OPEN CHAMPIONS

Birkdale is the second youngest recruit to the British Open rota, hosting its first in 1954. Victory went to 24-year-old Australian Peter Thomson, who became Champion again at these Lancashire links in 1965.

The course has staged seven Opens, but is yet to crown a British champion – although Welshman Dai Rees came close in both 1954 and 1961. At the first Birkdale Open, Rees needed a four at the final hole to force a play-off.

Unfortunately he overhit his second shot to the green and scored five. Rees again finished one stroke too many seven years later after American Arnold Palmer pulled off a series of miraculous shots. One such stroke was at the 15th hole (now the 16th), when he demolished a bush with a 6 iron. The ball landed on the green 140yd (128m) away. That stroke is commemorated by a plaque, close to the spot where he played it.

Lee Trevino won in 1971, despite taking a 7 at the 71st hole where he drove into sand dunes on the left. He beat the popular Mr Lu of Taiwan by a single stroke.

Using a 1 iron off many tees for accuracy, Johnny Miller shot a final round 66 to win by six shots in 1976. Putting well on greens, made difficult by that summer's drought, Miller was helped by chipping in at the 13th.

Ian Baker-Finch is the most recent Birkdale Open Champion, winning his first title in 1991.

STARMAKER

Seve Ballesteros and Nick Faldo both made their professional names at Birkdale. In 1976, Seve led The Open by three strokes with 17 holes left. He eventually finished equal second.

Despite hosting seven Opens, Birkdale's greatest moment was the climax to the 1969 Ryder Cup match. With the teams tied at 15 points all, American Jack Nicklaus and Great Britain's Tony Jacklin were also level after both reached the 18th green in two shots. The destiny of the cup hinged on their final strokes. Both players missed with their first putts, which left Nicklaus about 4ft (1.3m) away and Jacklin half that.

The American coolly sunk his putt and nobly conceded Jacklin's putt for a half. It was a generous gesture by the greatest player of the last 30 years.

Royal Melbourne

World-famous for its fast greens, the beautiful West Course at Royal Melbourne demands unusual accuracy. It's hosted more international events than any other Australian course.

Royal Melbourne is Australia's best-known club. It has two courses, an East and a West, which are laid on excellent golfing turf in the district of Sandringham.

Built on a sandy sub-soil, the ground drains easily to provide superb playing conditions the whole year round. The West is the more famous of the two courses although both are of high quality.

VARIETY OF SHOT

There is plenty of roll on the dry sand-based fairways of the West Course – which at 6,009m is not long by any means. But don't be deceived by its lack of length.

Although not a slogger's course, it is a challenge to any golfer's skill and nerve. To score well you must have a wide repertoire of shots. You need good placement from the tee, accurate approach work and skill at stopping the ball quickly on the green.

An outstanding feature of the course is its fast putting surface. For the average putter it is difficult to avoid three stabs from long range. The key to low scores is to leave yourself an uphill first putt.

LEADING ARCHITECT

Founded as Melbourne Golf Club in May 1891, the prefix Royal was approved by Queen Victoria in 1895. The club moved to its present site in 1931, when the West Course was opened.

Alister Mackenzie, a leading architect of his generation, was commissioned to design the West Course in 1926. He was helped by former Australian Open Champion Alex Russell who designed the East Course.

Mackenzie had a series of principles which he always tried to follow when designing a course – and Melbourne was no exception. His code was:

- Greens and subsequent tees should be close together.
- Two loops of nine holes should start and finish near the clubhouse.
- The character of each hole ought to vary.

▼ Large bunkers are a typical feature of the West Course. Hugging the green at the short par-3 5th, they leave you no margin for error with your tee shot.

ROYAL MELBOURNE, WEST COURSE

HOLE BY HOLE

Championship tees: 6009 metres, Par 72. Ladies tees: 5231 metres, Par 73.

1st hole
(Champ 392m Ladies 326m Par 4) Try to avoid a long first putt – or you may take 3 on the fast green.

2nd hole
(Champ 439m Ladies 388m Par 5) Hit your tee shot down the left to avoid bunkers.

3rd hole
(Champ 324m Ladies 283m Par 4) Take care to judge the run on your second.

4th hole
(Champ 430m Ladies 360m Par 5) Blot from your mind the many fairway bunkers when teeing off.

5th hole
(Champ 161m Ladies 131m Par 3) Hit a strong tee shot or you face a tough second.

6th hole
(Champ 391m Ladies 340m Par 4) Shorten the hole by carrying the dog-leg angle.

7th hole
(Champ 135m Ladies 118m Par 3) Play to the left half of the green to avoid the sand.

8th hole
(Champ 346m Ladies 311m Par 4) Aim left from the tee for best angle to green.

9th hole
(Champ 370m Ladies 358m Par 4) Keep right for the best view of the green.

10th hole
(Champ 279m Ladies 242m Par 4) Play safe from the tee down the right-hand side.

11th hole
(Champ 402m Ladies 359m Par 4) Drive down the left for a short second shot.

12th hole
(Champ 430m Ladies 359m Par 5) Play your second shot down the right-hand side.

13th hole
(Champ 139m Ladies 115m Par 3) Take enough club – better to be long than short.

14th hole
(Champ 335m Ladies 290m Par 4) Play left from the tee for a straight second.

15th hole
(Champ 427m Ladies 311m Par 5) Hit your second down the right side of the fairway.

16th hole
(Champ 197m Ladies 165m Par 3) Drive straight to avoid the sand.

17th hole
(Champ 416m Ladies 389m Par 4) Play down the right side from the tee.

18th hole
(Champ 396m Ladies 348m Par 4) Keep left from the tee or you're blocked by trees.

▲ Course architect Alister Mackenzie succeeded in blending natural vegetation with the specially prepared greens and fairways. The 6th hole, a dog-leg right from a high tee, is rated one of the best.

- •All constructed features must look natural.
- •Avoid blind shots to the green.
- •Give the long hitter a number of challenges but provide alternative routes for lesser players.
- •Test the ability to use every club in the bag.
- •Test golfers with long par 4s but include a few drive-and-pitch holes and four par 3s.

Apart from only one drive-and-pitch hole – the 10th – you can see these principles applied to the West Course.

CHAMPIONS AND COMPLIMENTS

The West Course has received many compliments over the years. The late Henry Longhurst, distinguished golf writer, described it as one 'that sifts champions from mediocre players'.

Peter Thomson, five-time British Open Champion, said 'Royal Melbourne was in many ways Mackenzie's masterpiece. By any judgment it must have strong claim to equal anything on earth'.

Mind you, not everyone praises it. Lee Trevino was particularly discourteous – although his opinion of the course did change with his form. Before playing in the 1974 Chrysler Classic he noted, 'It would be hard to name a better course anywhere in the world than Royal Melbourne'.

However, after taking a 9 on the 4th hole during the final round he snorted, 'The people of Royal Melbourne are proud of their greens – they can have them'. Trevino continued to fume, 'The greens are the biggest joke since

FOUR HOLES TO WATCH

Measurements at Royal Melbourne are in metres, not yards. To work out the yardage add 10% on to the metric figure. For instance, 410 metres is about 451 yards – 410 + 41.

4th hole ►
(Champ 430m Ladies 360m Par 5)
From the tee you're faced with an upslope, set with a number of threatening bunkers. Drive down the left side from the tee or you'll be blocked by the dog-leg. Unless you are long from the tee, hit your second short of the rough that lies just in front of the green.

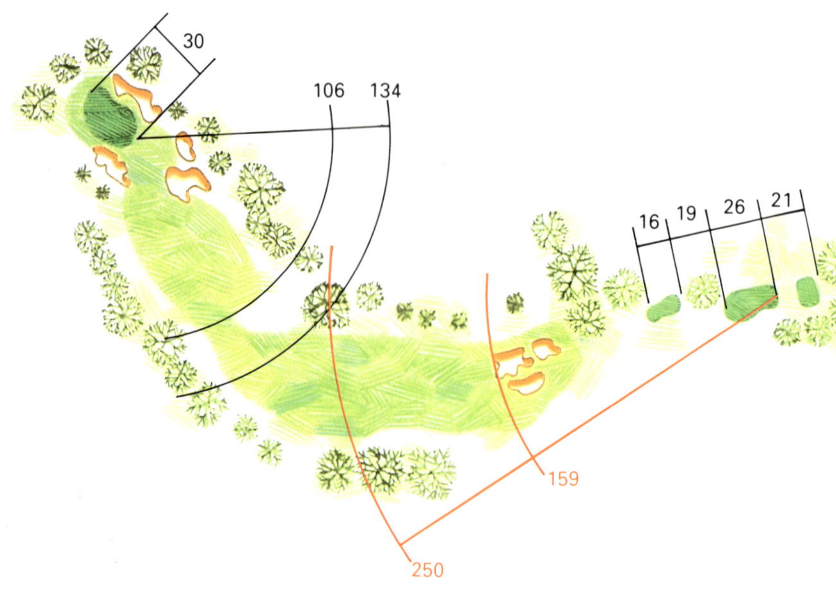

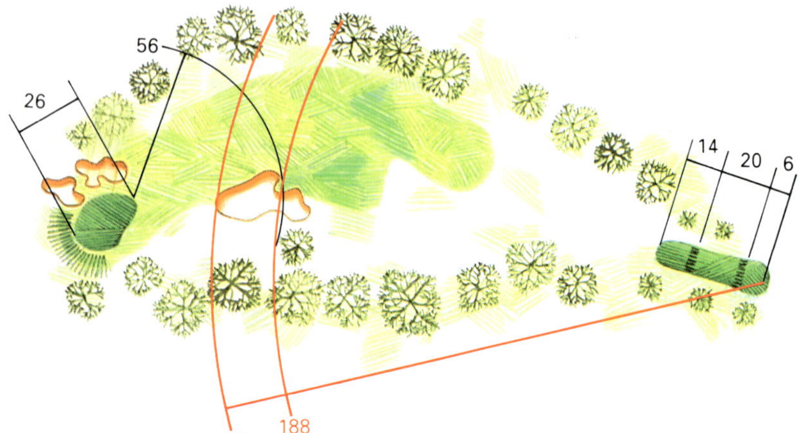

◄ ***10th hole***
(Champ 279m Ladies 242m Par 4)
A classic short par 4. If you can clear the large bunker that blocks the shortest route to the green – across the dog-leg – you may be rewarded with an eagle 2 for your bravery. If you're confident of getting down in no more than 3 from the sand then you might as well go for it! The alternative is to play safe by knocking a 5 iron short and to the right. Then chip on.

▼ Like all good championship courses, the last few holes are fraught with danger. If you aim to cut across the dog-leg at the par-4 17th make certain that you clear this giant fairway bunker.

▲ **The 10th may be a short par 4, but it takes confidence to reach the green with your drive – on the way you have to carry the large bunker guarding the angle of the dog-leg.**

16th hole ▶

(Champ 197m Ladies 165m Par 3)
An uncompromising hole that requires a long, straight tee shot. If you aim at the left-hand side of the green be sure to take enough club. The green is virtually an island in a sea of sand. Getting the ball to stop quickly on this green is no mean achievement.

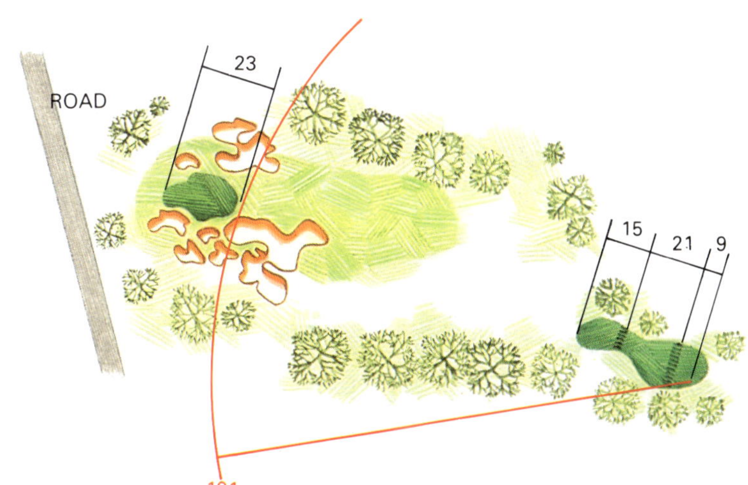

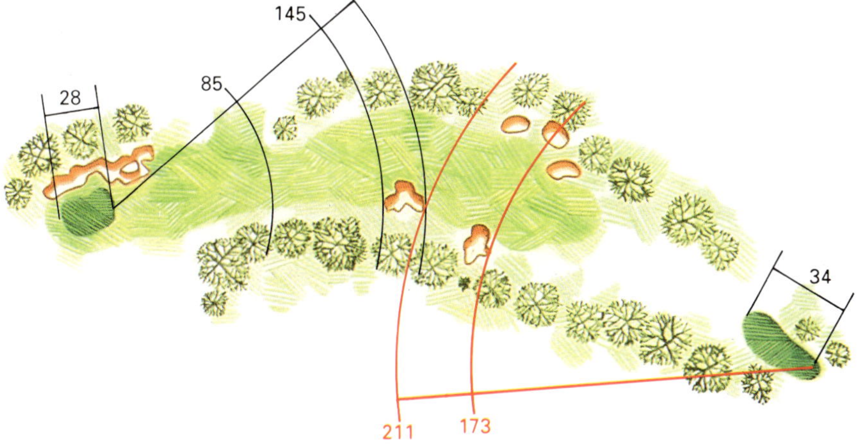

◀ ***17th hole***

(Champ 416m Ladies 389m Par 4)
A blind tee shot. Beware of the large bunker that lurks at the left-hand edge of the fairway. However, if you play safe down the right your second is both longer and more tricky. Don't underhit your second or you might be in sand. Your troubles don't stop on the treacherously fast putting surface.

FACTFILE
Lowest scores
63 – Tom Crow, 1956 (West Course)

64 – Hale Irwin, 1978 Australian PGA Championship (Composite Course)

Tournaments
WEST COURSE
Australian Open – 1933, 1939

COMPOSITE COURSE
Australian Open – 1984, 1985, 1987, 1991

Australian PGA Championship – 1978, 1979, 1980, 1981, 1982

World Cup – 1959, 1972, 1988

Bicentennial Classic – 1988

Chrysler Classic – 1974, 1975, 1976

World Amateur Team Championship – 1968

Pay day
In winning the 1988 Bicentennial Classic, Rodger Davis collected A$500,000, the largest amount of money earned in Australian golf.

Watergate. You'd better get a picture of me going out through these gates because I won't be coming back'. And he hasn't.

JOINING FORCES

The West Course hosted its first big professional tournament – the Australian Open – in 1933. It continued to hold major events until 1959, when a composite championship course, using 12 holes from the West and 6 from the East, staged the World Cup.

The West Course is challenging enough to host important championships on its own. But the problem is that public roads intersect parts of the course. Modern tournament golf demands above all that spectators can easily move around.

The composite layout is compact and efficient and there are no roads to restrict the crowd flow. This course is only used during tournament weeks.

Melbourne remains the only club to have hosted three World Cup tournaments. It is Australia's foremost club, hosting the National Open on most occasions. Most of the world's top players have competed here.

Australia's finest golfing hour happened at Melbourne in 1959, when Peter Thomson and Kel Nagle demolished the United States by 10 shots to win the World Cup.

▲ The tight approach to the 6th green, made even more tricky by the upward slope, makes typically strong demands on your strategy and play.

▼ Australia's number one player, Greg Norman, blasts his way out of a treacherous sandy lie.

Royal St George's

To score well at Sandwich your driving must be long and accurate, as you plot your route around and between the giant sand hills. Even some of the professionals consider this links course a real challenge.

Sandwich is as tough a test as there is in golf. The Kent course, owned by Royal St George's Golf Club, has undulating fairways, blind shots and massive sand hills. Every stroke is a severe test of skill and strategy.

Even the world's best struggle to tame the course. At the 1981 Open Championship only American Bill Rogers finished under par, while four years later Sandy Lyle won at 2 over par.

The game's greatest player, Jack Nicklaus, also had problems at Sandwich. In 1981 he recorded his highest ever Open round of 83 and four years later missed the

▼ Scattered with pot bunkers, humps and hollows, many professionals think the course at Sandwich is one of the hardest in tournament golf. Before the number of blind shots was reduced, the links was called the St Andrews of the South.

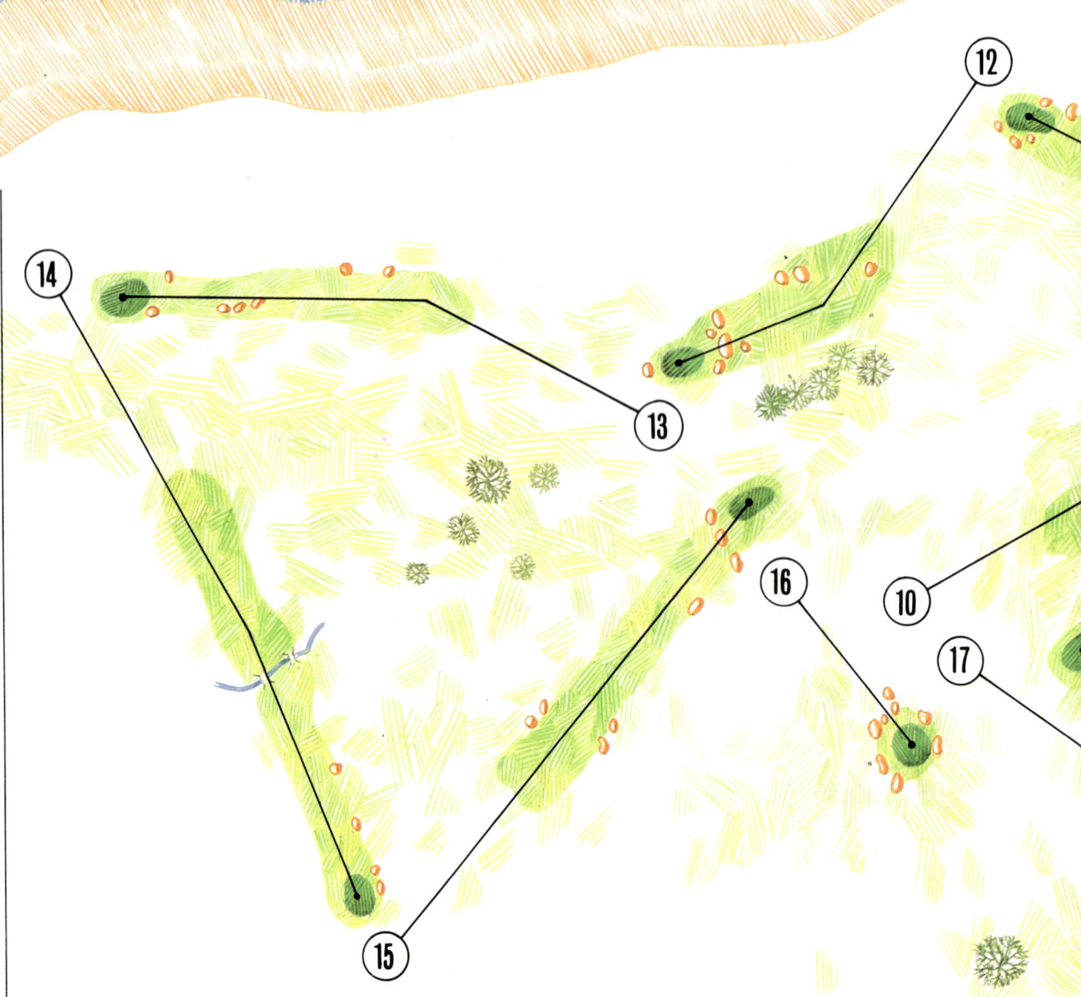

HOLE BY HOLE
Championship tees: 6857 yards, par 70. Medal tees: 6534 yards, par 70.

1st hole
(Champ 445yd Medal 400yd Par 4) Play your second short of the bunkers fronting the green.

2nd hole
(Champ 376yd Medal 341yd Par 4) Drive down the right for the best angle across the dog-leg.

3rd hole
(Champ 214yd Medal 200yd Par 3) Take one more club than you think you need to clear the front slope.

4th hole
(Champ 470yd Medal 420yd Par 4) Drive down the left to avoid two huge bunkers.

5th hole
(Champ 422yd Medal 422yd Par 4) Drive down the right for the easiest angle over the sand dunes.

6th hole
(Champ 156yd Medal 156yd Par 3) Take enough club to clear the huge bunker at the front of the green.

7th hole
(Champ 529yd Medal 475yd Par 5) Drive down the left and play an iron across the angle of the dog-leg.

8th hole
(Champ 415yd Medal 410yd Par 4) Play your second short of the rough that cuts the fairway in two.

9th hole
(Champ 387yd Medal 376yd Par 4) Drive down the right for the best view of the green.

10th hole
(Champ 399yd Medal 377yd Par 4) Take enough club to clear the slope by the green.

11th hole
(Champ 216yd Medal 216yd Par 3) Take care to read the links' most difficult green.

12th hole
(Champ 362yd Medal 343yd Par 4) Play down the left and don't try to cut the corner of the dog-leg.

36-hole cut for the first time in his career. Many professionals believe Sandwich to be the most difficult course on the Open rota.

ACCURACY FROM THE TEE

From most tees your ball has to carry long stretches of rough to reach the fairway. The rough is usually between 160yd (146m) and 200yd (182m) long, and there are no fairway lies to follow a topped or badly hit drive – even if you're straight down the middle.

But you need more than just a long drive. You also have to choose the perfect line over and between all the sandy mounds, humps and hollows, so that you can find the best position for attacking the green. Long, accurate driving doesn't guarantee a low score, but without it you stand little chance.

The layout hasn't changed much since it was built in 1887, although a few holes were redesigned in the 1970s to reduce the number of blind shots. In the early 1900s blind shots were considered both fun and a challenge. But today's tournament pros – with their yardage charts and scientific approach to the game – want to see the flag from a good fairway position.

In the mid 70s changes were made so that the Open could be played at Sandwich again. Golf architect Frank Pennink was responsible for some of these improvements, which included a major new design for the 3rd. This short hole runs the same way as the former blind hole, but the different green is clearly seen from a new tee.

After the 1981 Open two bunkers just short and left of the putting surface were removed and the upward slope from the front edge of the green was eased. At 214 yards this par 3 now has a long, narrow green with grassy hollows and hillocks at the back and on both sides.

To increase the length of the course to today's Open standards, Pennink's partner Donald Steel laid out six new

▼ **The short 156-yard 6th has a two-tier green, which makes reading the slopes difficult. The surrounding sand hills provide excellent natural vantage points for spectators.**

13th hole
(Champ 443yd Medal 438yd Par 4) Best to approach the green from the right side of the fairway.

14th hole
(Champ 508yd Medal 497yd Par 5) If you try to clear the stream with your second, aim down the right.

15th hole
(Champ 467yd Medal 439yd Par 4) If you can't reach the green in 2, play your second short and left.

16th hole
(Champ 165yd Medal 165yd Par 3) Play safe and aim at the centre of the green regardless of pin position.

17th hole
(Champ 425yd Medal 422yd Par 4) Take at least one more club than you think.

18th hole
(Champ 458yd Medal 437yd Par 4) Play down the left for the best line to the green.

FOUR HOLES TO WATCH

1st hole ►
(Champ 445yd Medal 400yd Par 4)
You need a long, accurate drive to avoid the grassy ridges between 200yd (182m) and 247yd (225m) from the tee.

Your second is almost as long – if the wind is against you, you won't reach the green in 2. Unless you're confident of clearing the trio of bunkers in front of the green, don't try. Lay up short and aim to save par with a pitch and putt.

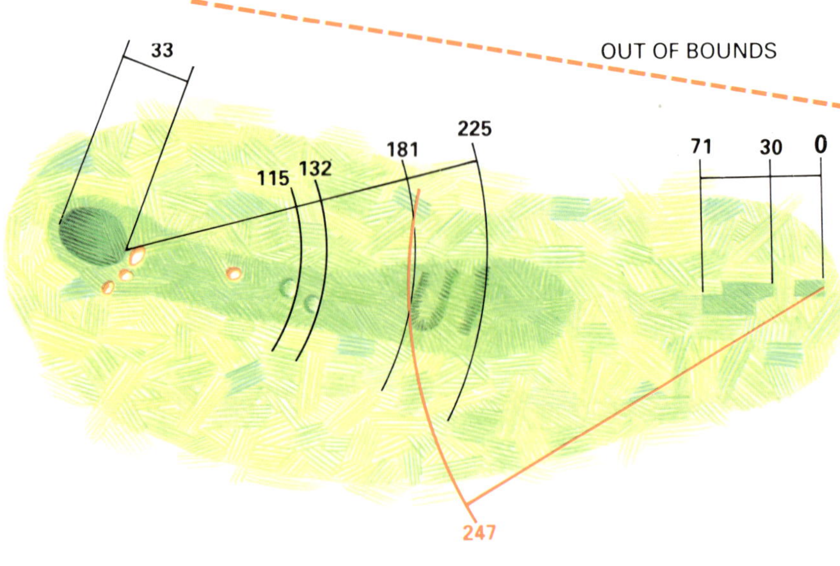

◄ ***4th hole***
(Champ 470yd Medal 420yd Par 4)
Aim your drive left of the huge sand hill which blocks your passage down the right side of the fairway. Unless you're a low handicapper, play it as a par 5 and hit your second down the right for the best line to the green.

Use the left-to-right slope to run your ball up to the flag, but don't overhit your approach with out of bounds just beyond the back of the green.

Master Tony
Tony Jacklin made history when he scored the first hole in one to be screened live on British television – in the final round of the 1967 Dunlop Masters. His 7-iron shot at the short 165-yard 16th helped win him the tournament.

► Get out of here if you can. If you hit your drive into this massive bunker to the right of the fairway at the par-4 4th, you stand no chance of reaching the green – 260yd (240m) away – with your next shot.

▲ **The Suez Canal, which winds its way across the 14th fairway, should not come into play on your second shot unless you drive into the rough.**

Walter's win
American Walter Travis dismayed spectators at Sandwich by using what seemed at the time a bizarre centre-shaft putter to win the 1904 British Amateur Championship.

Five years later the Royal and Ancient banned his revolutionary putter in Britain. The ban was lifted in 1952.

Caddie's payment
At the presentation ceremony of the 1922 Open at Sandwich, American Walter Hagen gave his £75 winner's cheque to his caddie.

This flamboyant gesture underlined Hagen's concern at the low prize money for the winner. Hagen continued to come to the Open for another 15 years – though the reward was only £100 in 1939 – as he recognized the prestige value to the winner.

14th hole ►
(Champ 508yd Medal 497yd Par 5)
Drive down the left to avoid the out of bounds which runs from tee to green on the right. But don't over compensate. If your ball runs off the fairway, you'll find it difficult to clear the Suez Canal – a stream that runs across the fairway – from a rough lie.

Hit your second to the right of the four bunkers that skirt the left edge of the fairway. The green is fairly flat.

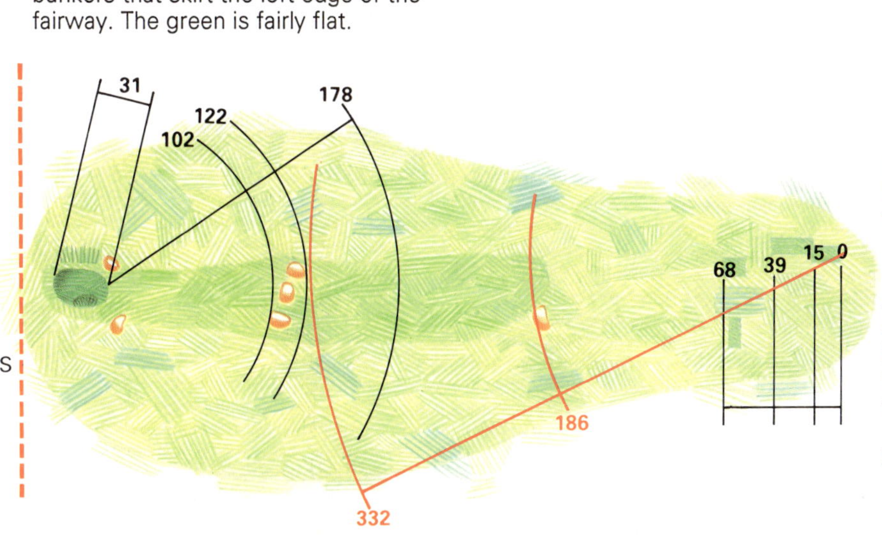

◄ ***18th hole***
(Champ 458yd Medal 437yd Par 4)
Drive down the left for the best line to the green on this long par 4.

Your second is usually either a long iron or a wood – you must avoid tricky slopes on either side of the putting surface. Go too far to the right and your ball is gathered by a deep bunker. Too far to the left and a small hollow runs your ball off the green.

There is out of bounds a few yards beyond the back of the green.

FACTFILE

Lowest Score

Course record – 63 by Nick Faldo, Payne, Stewart, 1993 Open Championship

Tournaments

Open Championship – 1894, 1899, 1904, 1911, 1922, 1928, 1934, 1938, 1949, 1981, 1985, 1993

British Amateur Championship – 1892, 1896, 1900, 1904, 1908, 1914, 1929, 1937, 1948, 1959, 1972

English Amateur Championship – 1932, 1954, 1969, 1979, 1989

Walker Cup – 1930, 1967

Curtis Cup – 1988

Dunlop Masters – 1967

PGA Championship – 1975, 1976, 1977, 1980, 1983

Golffinger

Ian Fleming, creator of James Bond, was a member of Royal St George's Golf Club. The description of the course on which Bond beat Goldfinger could be no other than Royal St George's.

back tees. The drive from the 14th, formerly a blind shot, has a view of the distant green.

Previously, three of the four par 3s were on the front nine. Pennink balanced the two halves, with two par 3s on each. The front half is marginally easier than the back nine, and most low scores are recorded over the opening holes. When the wind blows – which it often does – low totals are rare.

THE FIRST OPEN

Laid out on dunes and salt marshes on the Kent coast, Sandwich is one of only two courses south of Liverpool to have hosted the Open Championship – the other is Deal just a few miles away. Eleven Opens have been held here, including the first ever to be played in England in 1894.

After staging its ninth Open in 1949, the event didn't return to Sandwich until 1981 – a gap of 32 years. This was no reflection on the standard or playing conditions of the course, but was the result of transport problems.

Even on a normal weekday the roads in and around the medieval town of Sandwich became badly congested. Better roads eased the traffic in the 1970s. These improvements persuaded the Royal and Ancient to take the Open to Sandwich again in 1981.

Record crowds were able to travel to the course. The event was such a success that the Open returned to Sandwich in 1985 and 1993. Because of south-east England's huge population, Sandwich is always likely to be a well supported tournament venue.

IN SEARCH OF GOLF

Royal St George's Golf Club was founded by Edinburgh doctor Laidlaw Purves. Purves chose Sandwich after travelling east from Bournemouth in search of a suitable coastal site for golf that was within reasonable distance of London.

It's reputed that he instantly recognized the potential of the area when he viewed giant sand hills from a church tower. Purves designed the layout, which remained almost untouched until Pennink's alterations. The course was opened in 1887 and was an immediate success. Within five years it held the British Amateur Championship.

Most of the world's top golfers have played Sandwich. Two of the Great Triumvirate – James Braid in 1894 and Harry Vardon in 1899 and 1911 – won the Open here. Walter Hagen was also a double Open Champion at Sandwich, in 1922 and 1928.

Since the First World War, three Britons have delighted the crowds by lifting the Open trophy at Sandwich. Henry Cotton won in 1934, opening with rounds of 67 and 65 – this 36-hole total of 132 is so far still an Open record.

Reg Whitcombe won in 1938 and Sandy Lyle in 1985 – the first British winner of the Open Championship for 16 years.

▼ Drama thrills the crowd at the 72nd hole of the 1985 Open, as David Graham plays from a greenside bunker. He needed to sink the shot to force a play-off with Sandy Lyle. He failed, finishing 2 strokes adrift in a tie for third place.

St Andrews Old Course

St Andrews is the oldest golf course in the world. Its layout and natural hazards make it as challenging today as when it was first played – possibly as early as the 1300s.

Today, St Andrews has five 18-hole courses and a beginners' 9-hole course, all owned by the district council. The most famous of these is the Old Course on which are played some of the important tournaments.

The Old Course is laid out on true links land (the 'link' between the shore and the farm land). It is mainly level, but full of humps and hollows. Unlike today's carefully designed inland courses, the wind, sea, sand and other natural forces created the famous layout of St Andrews.

The links came about when the sea moved back from the land leaving banks of sand and salt-water gullies. With time the sand-banks became dunes covered with marram grass and the gullies were colonized with other grasses. With the vegetation came rabbits that cropped the grass to make the turf suitable for golf.

COURSE DEVELOPMENT

The links land has been played on for many centuries. It started with just five holes, in the 14th century, later expanded to seven, then 12 and finally 22 with 11 going out and 11 coming back. This was reduced to 18 in 1764 with nine out and nine back. The double green feature of the Old Course is unique, born out of limited space 500 years ago. In parts the course

▼ Dominating the scene at the start of the Old Course is the clubhouse of the Royal and Ancient Golf Club of St Andrews. The clubhouse is closed to the public but the course itself is owned by the local authorities and anyone can play it.

HOLE BY HOLE

6933 yards, par 72 (for the Open Championship, 1984). Otherwise 6578 yards, Standard Scratch Score (SSS) 72.

1st hole – Burn
(Champ & Medal 370yd Par 4)
Off the tee, lots of room on the left. Judge your distance carefully for the shot to the green, just beyond the Swilcan Burn.

2nd hole – Dyke
(Champ & Medal 411yd Par 4)
Long hitters beware Cheape's Bunker on the left. Hit long with the second.

3rd hole – Cartgate (out)
(Champ 371yd Medal 352yd Par 4)
Safe to drive to the left, but hard to get near the flag from there.

4th hole – Ginger Beer
(Champ 463yd Medal 419yd Par 4)
Safest to be left off the tee, leaving a second over the rough and bunkers.

5th hole – Hole o' Cross (out)
(Champ 564yd Medal 514yd Par 5)
Once more, drive left as there are seven bunkers on the right.

▲ **The oldest and most famous course in the world is laid out along a narrow strip of links land on the Eden Estuary.**

◄ **At Open Championship time the crowds flock to the Old Course. Stands are put up round the 1st (centre), 18th (right) and 17th (bottom right) holes, and at many other points on the course.**

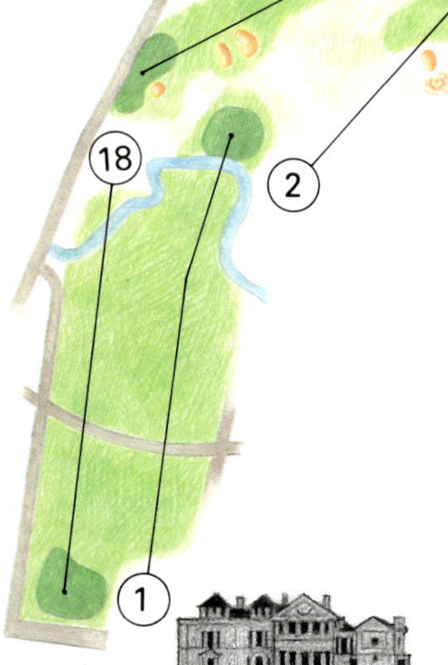

► **This bunker – made by layering strips of turf – is typical of St Andrews' intimidating hazards. The natural bunkers are thought to have been created by sheep sheltering from the wind.**

◄ **Shrouded in mist, the Swilcan Burn Bridge – believed to have been built by the Romans – is situated on the 18th fairway. The bridge is so famous that an exact copy of it has been built at the Old Course at New St Andrews, Tokyo.**

THE OLD COURSE AT ST ANDREWS

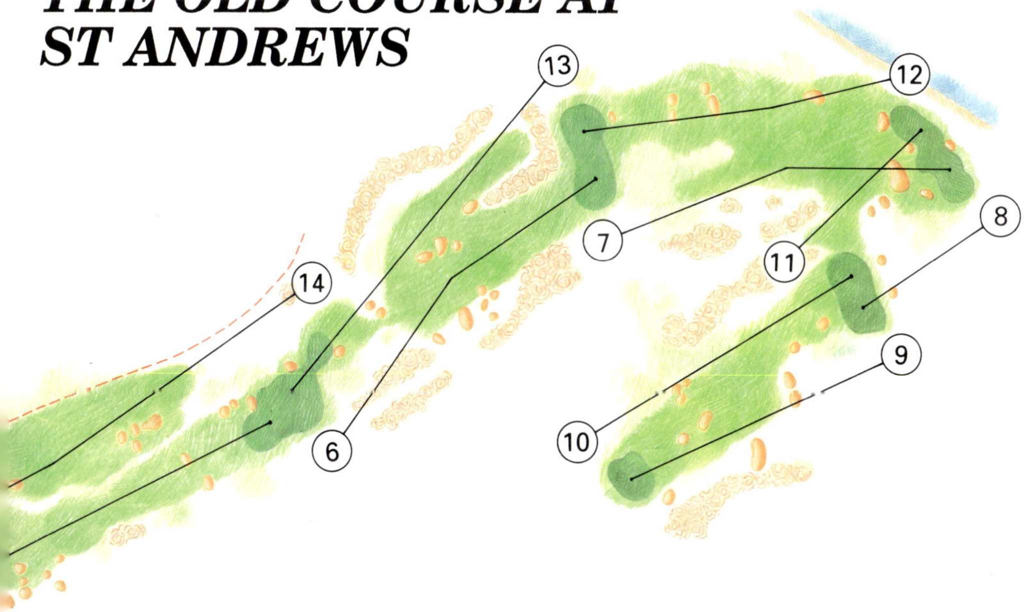

is less than 40yd (36.5m) wide. This meant using the same green going out and coming back.

In 1764 there were 18 holes but only nine flags. Even today only the 1st, 9th, 17th and 18th are single greens; the others are huge double greens. The east side of each green is used for the outward holes while the west side carries the flags of the homeward holes. The famous shape of the course was largely fixed by 1842.

PLAYING THE OLD COURSE

Until the late 1800s, play was the other way round. The modern 1st tee led to the 17th green, and so on. Occasionally, the course is still played the 'wrong' way round.

The west side of the course was originally flanked by railway lines, with a number of railway sheds obstructing the view of the 17th green from the tee. Although these have long since been knocked down, a similar building erected in the mid 1980s re-creates the sheds' profile.

Television gives a false impression of St Andrews. The cameras are mounted high, allowing the viewer to see all the trouble at a glance. At a golfer's eye level, very little of it is visible and the line to play is seldom obvious.

The general rule is: 'when in doubt, play to the left – and do keep out of the whins (gorse)!' For golfers playing the Old Course for the first time, even this maxim does not guarantee full protection from its subtle hazards. Rises and falls in the ground, some slight, some hillocks up to 8ft (2.4m) high, make it hard to judge both distance and line. Many shots are blind. The broken ground makes it impossible to see the base of the flags and shots often appear shorter than they really are.

There is no substitute for experience when tackling the Old Course. From the tee many bunkers are not visible and plenty of 'good' drives unwittingly find sand. All the bunkers have an apt name – some have won labels that match their character, like Hell on the 15th. Others are memorials to members who spent much time in them, as did Mr

6th hole – Heathery (out)
(Champ 416yd Medal 374yd Par 4)
Hard to see the fairway so hit towards the Leuchars airfield hangars.

7th hole – High (out)
(Champ 372yd Medal 359yd Par 4)
If you can knock it over the hill, do so. Otherwise go left.

8th hole – Short
(Champ 178yd Medal 166yd Par 3)
Better to leave a long putt from the back than risk the deep left-hand bunker.

9th hole – End
(Champ 356yd Medal 307yd Par 4)
Avoid the fairway bunkers and you have a clear second shot to a flat green.

10th hole – Bobby Jones
(Champ 342yd Medal 318yd Par 4)
Drive towards the mound.

11th hole – High (in)
(Champ & Medal 172yd Par 3)
Avoid the Hill bunker at all costs as you could take three to escape.

12th hole – Heathery (in)
(Champ & Medal 316yd Par 4)
Four bunkers lurk unseen in the centre of the fairway. The green is very shallow.

13th hole – Hole o' Cross (in)
(Champ 425yd Medal 398yd Par 4)
Drive on to the 6th fairway, so you can see where to go next.

14th hole – Long
(Champ 567yd Medal 523yd Par 5)
Drive towards the church spire on the right. That way, you miss the Beardies. Watch out for Hell, too.

15th hole – Cartgate (in)
(Champ 413yd Medal 401yd Par 4)
Again, you have the church spire to guide you. The second is one more club than you think.

16th hole – Corner of the Dyke
(Champ 382yd Medal 351yd Par 4)
Best to be left off the tee as too far right puts you out of bounds.

17th hole – Road
(Champ & Medal 461yd Par 4)
Very few professionals try to hit this green in two. Play it as a par 5.

18th hole – Tom Morris
(Champ & Medal 354yd Par 4)
An easy hole if you stay out of the Valley of Sin, a deep dip at the front of the green.

FOUR HOLES TO WATCH

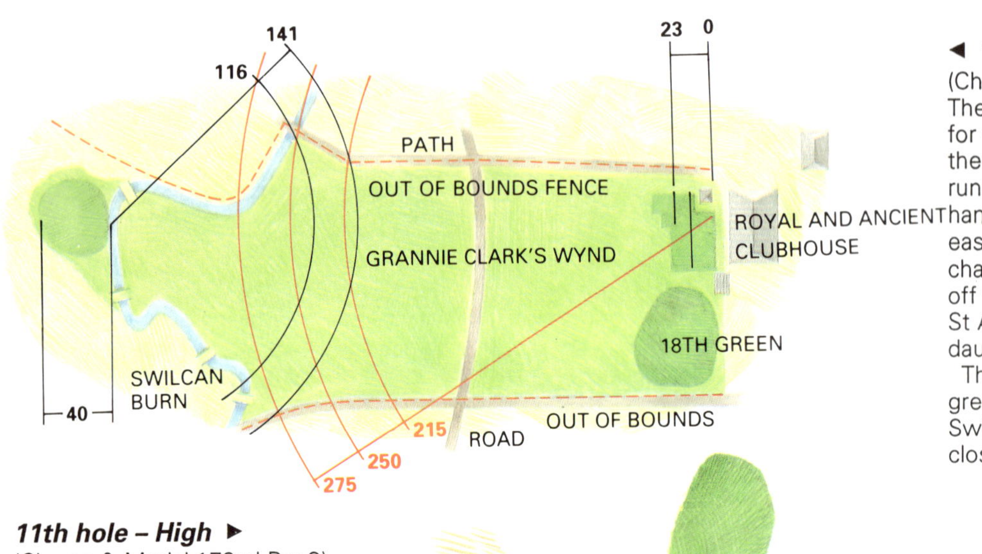

◀ *1st hole – Burn*

(Champ & Medal 370yd Par 4)
There's acres of room on the left for your drive. The only danger is the out-of-bounds fence which runs all the way down the right-hand side. It is arguably the easiest opening hole in championship golf, although teeing off with the history and tradition of St Andrews all around is a daunting prospect.

The second shot is tricky. The green starts on the bank of the Swilcan Burn, and the pin is often close to it.

11th hole – High ▶

(Champ & Medal 172yd Par 3)
The green is on the edge of the River Eden and exposed to the wind, making club selection a problem.

Anything short is likely to run into the large, deep Hill bunker on the left, or the small, deep Strath bunker on the right. If you land in either, consider playing out backwards. Make sure you don't go over the back – you're in thick rough playing to a downslope.

The putting surface is always very quick, with a great deal of borrow.

Train of thought
The railway once played a large part in Old Course life. In the 1929 Ladies' Championship, Joyce Wethered had a critical putt against Glenna Collett on the 16th. After sinking it, she was asked why she had not waited until the train had passed. She replied: 'What train?' Miss Wethered, for whom competition was a traumatic experience, won 3 and 1 – but fainted when she returned to the clubhouse.

First class reply
Most of the great names of golf have been associated with St Andrews. Andrew Kirkaldy, the Royal and Ancient's professional from 1910 until his death in 1934, was one of the best players never to win the Open. Asked by someone buried in Hell bunker 'What do I take out of here?' he is said to have replied in typical forthright style, 'How about the 9.40 train out of St Andrews?'

▲ Masahiro Kuramoto of Japan successfully plays on to the green from the deep Strath bunker at the 11th. High handicappers are often advised to play backwards out of the bunker, rather than risk hitting over the back of the green and into heavy rough or even the Eden Estuary.

▲ Hell bunker on the long and difficult 14th. The choice for the average golfer is whether to play up short of the bunker with the second shot or risk going into it. Once in Hell you are almost certain to drop a stroke. From Hell there is another 100yd (90m) to the green.

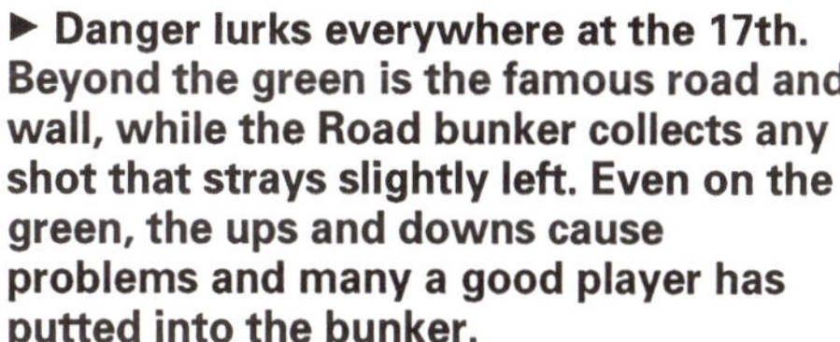

► Danger lurks everywhere at the 17th. Beyond the green is the famous road and wall, while the Road bunker collects any shot that strays slightly left. Even on the green, the ups and downs cause problems and many a good player has putted into the bunker.

◄ 14th hole – Long

(Champ 567yd Medal 523yd Par 5)

The ideal shot passes to the right of the four Beardies bunkers – which are hard to see from the tee – but avoid the out-of-bounds wall on the right. This is especially difficult if the wind is coming off the sea.

The next main problem is Hell bunker, which is huge. Middle-handicap players who have hit their best drives still cannot carry this bunker in a head wind. Good players who can carry Hell may end up in Grave or Ginger Beer.

However, you can hit left on to the 5th fairway, leaving maybe a 5-iron to the double green.

17th hole – Road ►

(Champ & Medal 461yd Par 4)

Your strength and the wind determine how much of the Old Course Hotel grounds you overfly.

If you have avoided Cheape's bunker, you probably have 200yd (180m) to go. Don't try it – it's too dangerous. Hit the ball 190yd (170m), up the right of the fairway, then pitch on – very carefully.

The green is raised, wide and shallow, and is set at an angle to the fairway. The road runs behind the green, inviting disaster. The Road bunker is cut into the front of the green, which is contoured towards it. If you avoid pitching into it, you can always putt into it. Many do so.

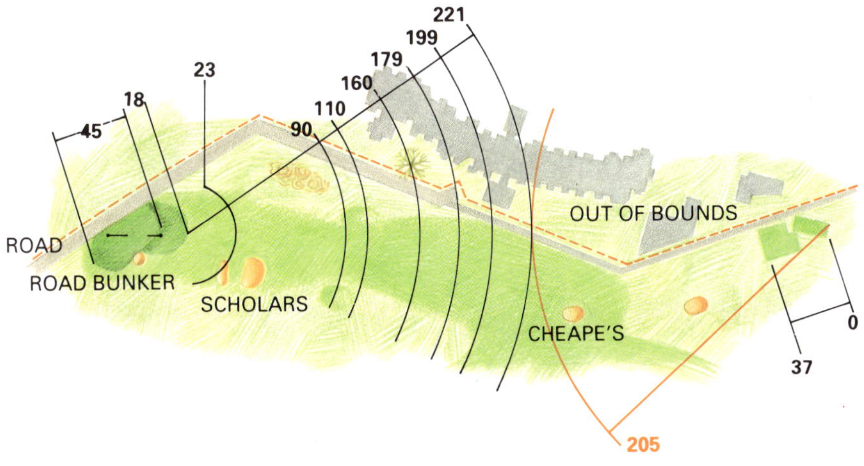

FACTFILE

Lowest score

Professional Course record – 62 by Curtis Strange, Dunhill Cup, 1987

Tournaments

Open Championship (36 holes) – 1873, 1876, 1879, 1882, 1885, 1888, 1891. (Low total – 166 by Hugh Kirkaldy, 1891)

Open Championship (72 holes) – 1895, 1900, 1905, 1910, 1921, 1927, 1933, 1939, 1946, 1955, 1957, 1960, 1964, 1970, 1978, 1984, 1990. (Low total – 270 by Nick Faldo, 1990)

Amateur Championship – 1886, 1889, 1891, 1895, 1901, 1907, 1913, 1924, 1930, 1936, 1950, 1958, 1963, 1976, 1981

Walker Cup – 1923, 1926, 1934, 1938, 1947, 1955, 1971, 1975

Eisenhower Trophy – 1958

European Amateur Team Championship – 1981

St Andrews Trophy – 1976

Ladies' Amateur Championship – 1908, 1929, 1965, 1975

Commonwealth Tournament (Men) – 1954, *(Ladies)* – 1959

Daily Mail Tournament – 1919, 1922, 1926

Spalding Tournament – 1947, 1948

Dunlop Masters – 1949

PGA Match Play Championship – 1954

Martini International – 1962

Alcan Golfer of the Year Championship – 1967

Alcan International – 1967

Scottish Open Championship – 1973

PGA Championship – 1979

Dunhill Cup – 1985, 1986, 1987, 1988, 1989, 1990, 1991, 1992, 1993

How to play

Because of the popularity of the Old Course, unreserved tee times are decided by a daily ballot. For further information on playing, contact: Secretary, Links Management Committee of St Andrews, Golf Place, St Andrews, Fife KY16 9JA.

▲ **Bobby Jones, the greatest player of his era, drives from the first tee while practising for the 1927 Open Championship – which he won. Even during practice rounds, he attracted the crowds.**

◀ **All but four holes are on large double greens. This one belongs to the 7th (right) and 11th (left) holes, the fairways of which cross over each other.**

Sutherland (16th).

Many seaside courses suffer from winds that veer alarmingly, often with the tide. St Andrews is no exception. The so-called Guardbridge wind which comes from the north west can turn the shorter outward holes into monsters.

The trouble doesn't end when you approach the greens. Because of their size, club selection is difficult, and it is easy to underestimate the distance from the front of the green to the pin.

FAMOUS HOLE

The most famous hole on the Old Course is the Road – the 17th. It is a long par 4 that can be shortened by driving up and over the out-of-bounds building – if you dare. The green is backed by a road and wall, with a deep bunker guarding the front of a treacherous putting surface. Every shot requires precision play.

With only one hole to follow, many a major championship has been decided here. In the 1984 Open, Seve Ballesteros stood on the 17th tee tied with defending champion Tom Watson – who was playing the 16th. The Spaniard had taken five shots at the 17th in each of his first three rounds and desperately needed a four this time.

He made it by hitting a 200yd (180m) 6-iron, out of the left rough, to the front of the green. Then he knocked an enormous putt dead. Ten minutes later Watson bounced his second shot on the dreaded road and his ball ended up inches from the wall. He could only manage a five. Ballesteros made certain of the title with a birdie on the last to win by two strokes with a St Andrews low Open total of 276.

During the 1930 British Amateur Championship, Bobby Jones was battling with Cyril Tolley. Jones struck a spectator with his second shot to the Road Hole. Many thought this luckily prevented the ball running into the road, saving Jones from terrible trouble. But the hole was halved – and Jones went on to win the Championship and the Grand Slam.

Sunningdale

The Old Course stretches out over sandy soil and through wooded, heathery glades. It's the finest example of inland golf in Britain, and is a magnet for golfers the world over.

If St Andrews is the supreme example of links golf, then Sunningdale is the king of heathland courses. This excellent layout is set in the heart of glorious wooded Berkshire. It winds its way through what was once wild and barren wasteland but is now a forest of pines, birches and oaks.

Enclosed among the trees, each hole is played as if in its own private world – the course dips and dives over the gently rolling countryside.

Heather and gorse flourish everywhere in the sour soil. The superb drainage of sandy soil creates conditions similar to the open coastal stretches of Scotland, with tough but smooth and springy turf that's ideal for golf.

PRECISION AND POWER

Sunningdale is short by modern standards – at times the pros burn up the 6607yd (6042m) championship course. Yet it isn't a course that can be easily overpowered – it also needs great judgement and precise striking.

Sunningdale is almost completely tree lined, but it's never claustrophobic. Most holes offer generous driving areas, but your tee shots must be positioned well if your approach is to finish close to the pin. Often the second shot is nothing more than a pitch or run-up shot. But par is usually tough – contours are subtle and many greenside bunkers make the target small.

▼ From the tee of the short 13th you look out over Sunningdale's beautiful woods. Although a wonderful sight, the mature trees and mass of heather can play havoc with your scoring. Well placed bunkers are also a constant threat.

HOLE BY HOLE
Championship tees: 6607 yards, Par 70. Medal tees: 6341 yards, Par 70.

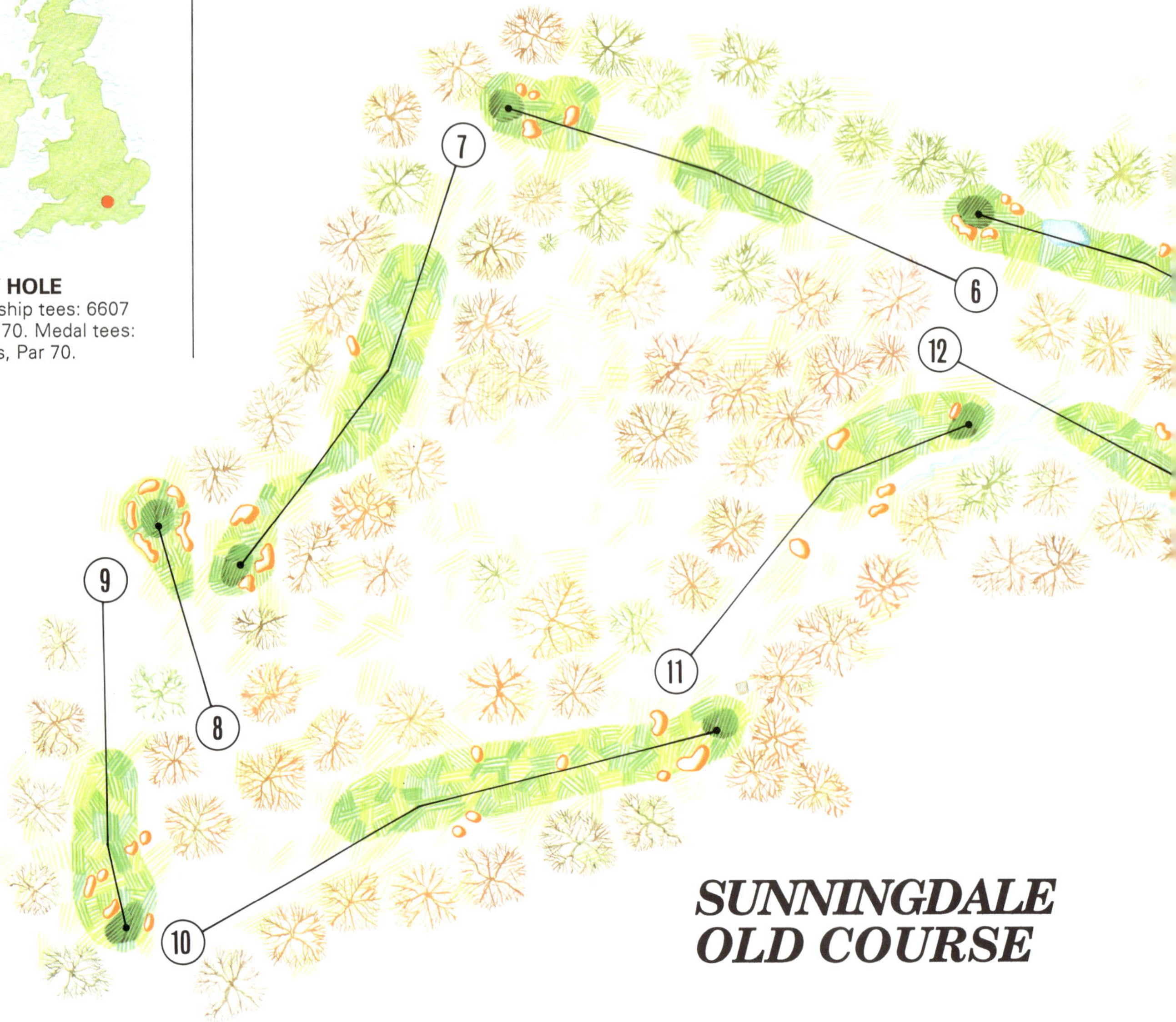

SUNNINGDALE OLD COURSE

1st hole
(Champ and Medal 494yd Par 5) Keep your second shot to the right of the pin – the slope brings the ball in.

2nd hole
(Champ 471yd Medal 456yd Par 4) Hit your tee shot down the left so you can see the bottom of the flag.

3rd hole
(Champ 323yd Medal 296yd Par 4) The green slopes away to the back and right and needs the most delicate of chips to get the ball close.

4th hole
(Champ and Medal 161yd Par 3) Played uphill, you may well need one more club than the distance suggests.

5th hole
(Champ 410yd Medal 400yd Par 4) Aim your tee shot at the lake to gain the best line into the green.

6th hole
(Champ 415yd Medal 388yd Par 4) Take care with your approach shot to this well guarded tricky green.

7th hole
(Champ 409yd Medal 383yd Par 4) The best line to the green is from the right side. But beware of the out of bounds.

8th hole
(Champ 182yd Medal 172yd Par 3) Concentrate hard while putting – the green is fast and has subtle borrows.

9th hole
(Champ 280yd Medal 267yd Par 4) Aim at the left half of the green to avoid the three bunkers on the right.

10th hole
(Champ 473yd Medal 463yd Par 4) Make sure you play straight – three well placed bunkers threaten your drive.

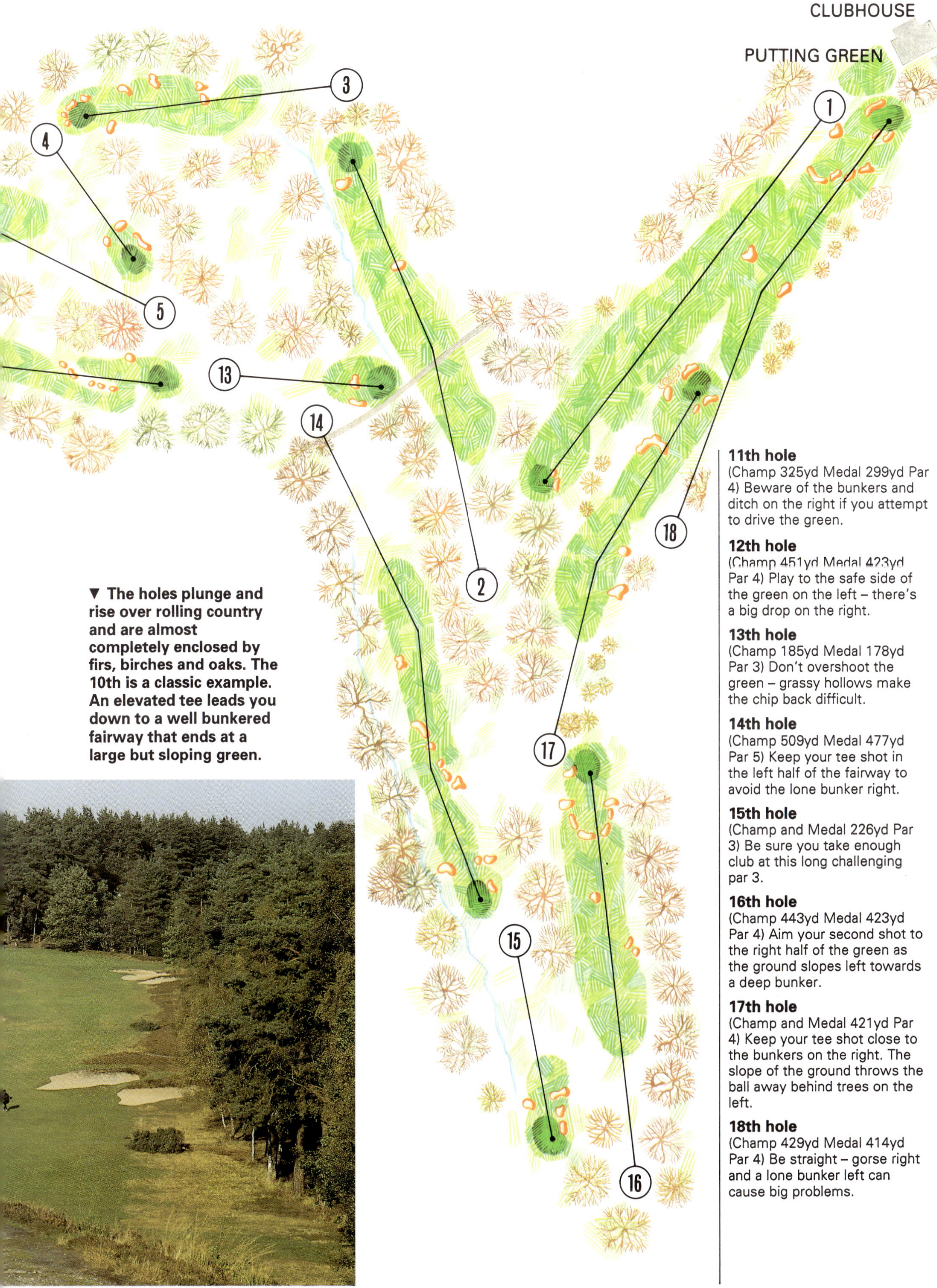

▼ **The holes plunge and rise over rolling country and are almost completely enclosed by firs, birches and oaks. The 10th is a classic example. An elevated tee leads you down to a well bunkered fairway that ends at a large but sloping green.**

11th hole
(Champ 325yd Medal 299yd Par 4) Beware of the bunkers and ditch on the right if you attempt to drive the green.

12th hole
(Champ 451yd Medal 423yd Par 4) Play to the safe side of the green on the left – there's a big drop on the right.

13th hole
(Champ 185yd Medal 178yd Par 3) Don't overshoot the green – grassy hollows make the chip back difficult.

14th hole
(Champ 509yd Medal 477yd Par 5) Keep your tee shot in the left half of the fairway to avoid the lone bunker right.

15th hole
(Champ and Medal 226yd Par 3) Be sure you take enough club at this long challenging par 3.

16th hole
(Champ 443yd Medal 423yd Par 4) Aim your second shot to the right half of the green as the ground slopes left towards a deep bunker.

17th hole
(Champ and Medal 421yd Par 4) Keep your tee shot close to the bunkers on the right. The slope of the ground throws the ball away behind trees on the left.

18th hole
(Champ 429yd Medal 414yd Par 4) Be straight – gorse right and a lone bunker left can cause big problems.

FOUR HOLES TO WATCH

◄ 7th hole

(Champ 409yd Par 4)
Like many at Sunningdale this hole calls for accuracy rather than power. The fairway is completely hidden by a ridge in front of the tee. Driving down the right leaves the best line into the gently sloping green.

Take care with your alignment on the second shot – the fairway slopes from right to left and you're usually left with an awkward hanging lie. You should favour the right half of the green as slopes gather the ball in, and there are bunkers left.

12th hole ►

(Champ 451yd Par 4)
The tee shot has to go through a narrow gap between bunkers as there is plenty of trouble should you miss the fairway. The green is set off to the left on raised ground beyond a nest of five bunkers which intimidate your second shot.

You normally have to play a long iron approach over sand to the green. Trees crowding in from the left and a steep bank which drops away on the right protect the putting surface.

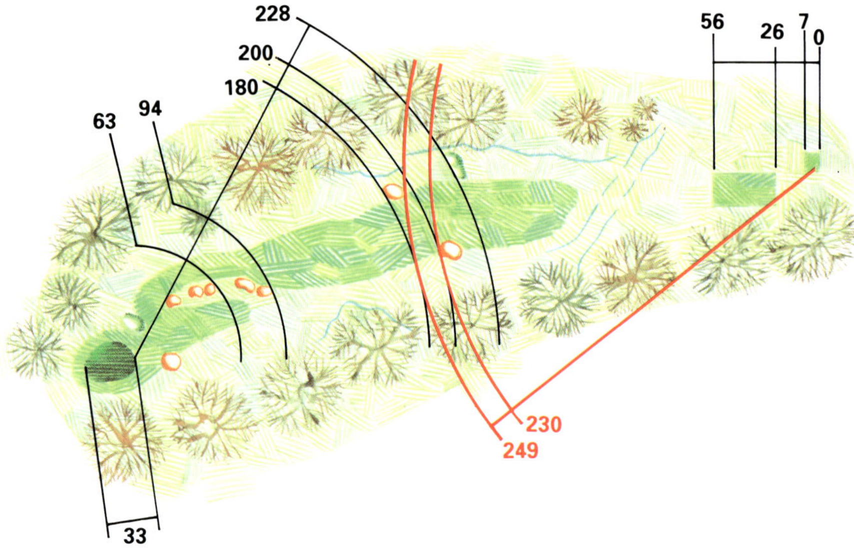

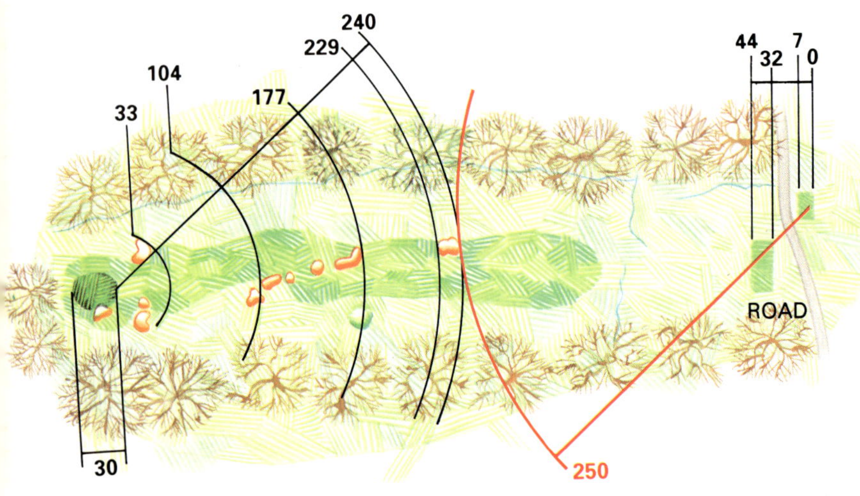

◄ 14th hole

(Champ 509yd Par 5)
There is ample room for the tee shot but from that point on the hole becomes increasingly difficult. A diagonal string of bunkers across the fairway – a trademark of Willie Park jnr – plays havoc with short hitters or anyone in trouble from the tee.

From a long drive these bunkers pose no problems, but beware of a further three up near the green over the brow of a hill. If in doubt play short and leave yourself a pitch into the green.

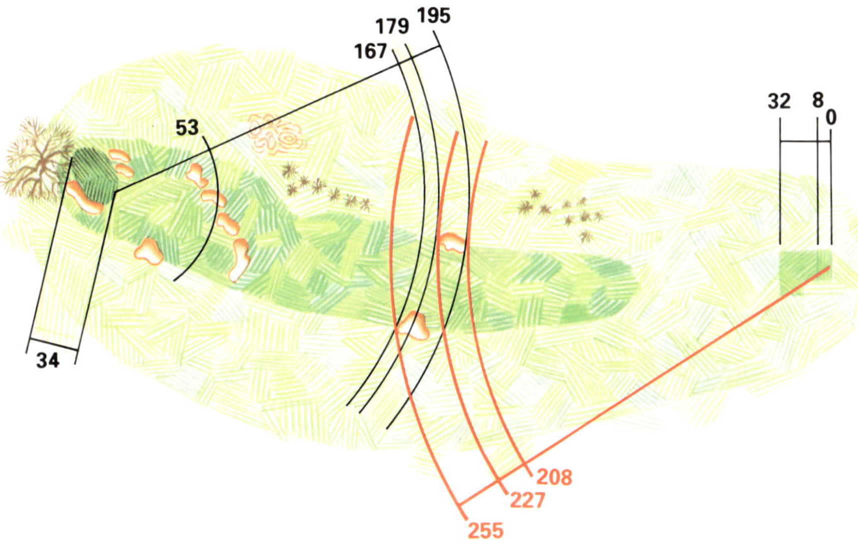

◀ *18th hole*

(Champ 429yd Par 4)
This fine finishing hole climbs gently uphill towards the imposing clubhouse. You need an accurate drive to fire between the two fairway bunkers. Knocking the ball into one of the traps leaves you a difficult decision of whether or not to go for the carry over cross bunkers just short of the green.

The usual second shot is deceptive because you can't see the bottom of the pin. The best way in is to aim for the right of the huge oak tree as the green slopes from the left.

▼ The sloping fairway on the par-4 7th makes your approach shot into this well guarded green harder than usual. The trouble on this hole is typical of Sunningdale. Banks of heather and gorse, deep bunkers, trees and fast greens test your skills.

Bobby's dazzler

In the regional qualifying event for the 1926 Open Championship, the great US golfer Bobby Jones was acclaimed as having played the perfect round of golf at Sunningdale. He completed every hole in either 3 or 4 to shoot a 66. Missing only one green in regulation, he had 33 shots and 33 putts.

What made his feat more remarkable was that the man from Georgia used hickory shafted clubs, and had to play a driver followed by a 2 iron seven times. Jones went on to win the Open at Royal Lytham.

▲ **The superb clubhouse stands next to the practice putting green. The building sits well in the landscape to complement the course that has set worldclass standards.**

FACTFILE
Lowest Scores
Professional course record: 62 – Nick Faldo
Amateur course record: 66 – Mike Hughesdon

Tournaments
Walker Cup: 1987
European Open: 1982, 1983, 1984, 1985, 1986, 1988, 1990, 1992
PGA Matchplay Championship: 1903, 1907, 1910, 1912, 1922
Dunlop Masters: 1948, 1953, 1960, 1968
European Women's PGA Championship: 1974 – 1979
British Youths': 1983
British Boys': 1956, 1976
English Amateur Strokeplay: 1953
English Ladies' Amateur: 1956

Visitors are welcome on weekdays with a handicap certificate or letter of introduction.

Though Sunningdale needs mostly precise striking, there is still plenty of scope for power play. Three of the par 4s – the 3rd, 9th and 11th – are driveable in dry summer conditions or downwind.

If you stray from the fairways the trouble is fearsome. Bunkers are a major part of Sunningdale's defences. There are around 100 traps – some appear in clusters across the fairways and around the greens, or as singles that threaten your tee shot. Knocking your ball into a bunker is sometimes a blessing – playing from the tough, clumpy heather and gorse can be far worse. The heather is so thick in parts that the only option is to hit a wedge out sideways to regain position on the fairway.

UNEXPLORED PARK

The course was created in 1900 by Willie Park jnr and has been altered only slightly since. Park combined the classic features of established courses with his own ideas, to develop a unique style for inland golf.

Up to that time all the great courses were on linksland, and inland golf – often no more than playing over a series of fields – was something of a joke. But Park changed all that by setting totally new standards of playing quality and beauty.

Many of the game's greats have walked the famous fairways. A regular venue for amateur and professional tournaments, it was entirely fitting that Sunningdale was chosen as the first non links course to stage the Walker Cup in 1987. The Old Course is now ranked as the top inland layout in the British Isles.

Sunningdale also stages its own unusual tournament at the start of every season – the Sunningdale Foursomes. Both amateurs and professionals, men and women battle it out off fixed handicaps, trying to win this prestigious title that has been going for over 50 years.

The club has two courses – the Old and the tougher New – just like its well known neighbours Wentworth and the Berkshire. Sunningdale is one of the most famous clubs in the world, and both courses are superb. But it's the Old that has become the blueprint for hundreds of heathland courses all over the globe.

► **Although Sunningdale isn't long for the professionals who play here regularly in the European Open there are still nine par 4s over 400yd (366m) from the championship tees. The 5th at 410yd is a beauty. It takes 2 good shots to hit the smallish green.**

Turnberry

The Ailsa Course is a true links set hard against the often ferocious Irish Sea on Scotland's Ayrshire coast. With craggy rocks and sweeping dunes, this Open Championship course is spectacularly challenging.

Most links courses run along close to the sea but are separated from the coast by a line of dunes. The golfer is protected from the full vigour of winds off the sea. But Turnberry is a links in the true sense of the word.

From the 4th to the 11th the Ailsa holes hug a shoreline exposed to the full force of the waves and winds. The long sweeping sands of Turnberry Bay suddenly turn into the rugged craggy coastline of the Firth of Clyde.

The air is fresh and invigorating, and the scenery is breathtaking. This is one of the great coastal walks of the British Isles – it would be hard to find a more magnificent setting for a golf course.

▼ The precariously placed 9th tee fills golfers with fear as they have to drive over the rugged shore of the Irish Sea to a blind fairway. Turnberry's most famous hole runs by a well known landmark, the lighthouse near the remains of Robert the Bruce's castle. The disused runways are a reminder of the part Turnberry played in two World Wars.

▲ **The 6th hole at 222yd is a very demanding par 3 made more so when the wind blows. Three bunkers on the left of the green await a pulled shot, while the large trap on the right tends to catch any short ball.**

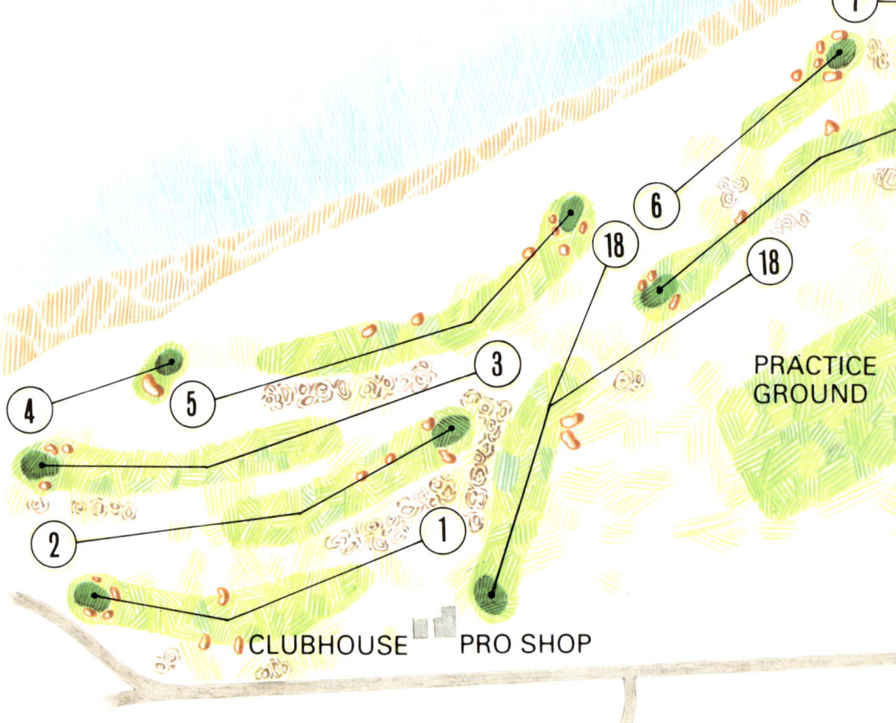

BOMBER LINKS

The golf itself is majestic. Both the Ailsa Course, used for the Open, and the neighbouring Arran are stiff tests. A host of elevated tees guides you to narrow fairways flanked by wild, thick rough and gorse. Deep bunkers and tricky greens mean you have to play with thought and use the full range of iron shots to work your way round.

Although the first holes were laid down in 1903 for a private course owned by the Marquess of Ailsa, the course was extensively remodelled after World War 2. Some fairways had been bulldozed level, with concrete runways laid for RAF planes in both World Wars. Golf at Turnberry was almost abandoned – only the efforts of hotel chairman Frank Hole saved the course from extinction.

Course architect Mackenzie Ross had the unusual task of making what had once been natural linksland look natural again. In 1951, after two years of

▶ **Turnberry is one of the foremost golf resorts in the world. The elegant hotel – a haven for golfers who have just braved the elements – stands proud on a hill overlooking Turnberry Bay and both courses.**
Ailsa and Arran are open to the public – with reduced green fees for hotel residents – but you do need either a handicap certificate or letter of introduction.

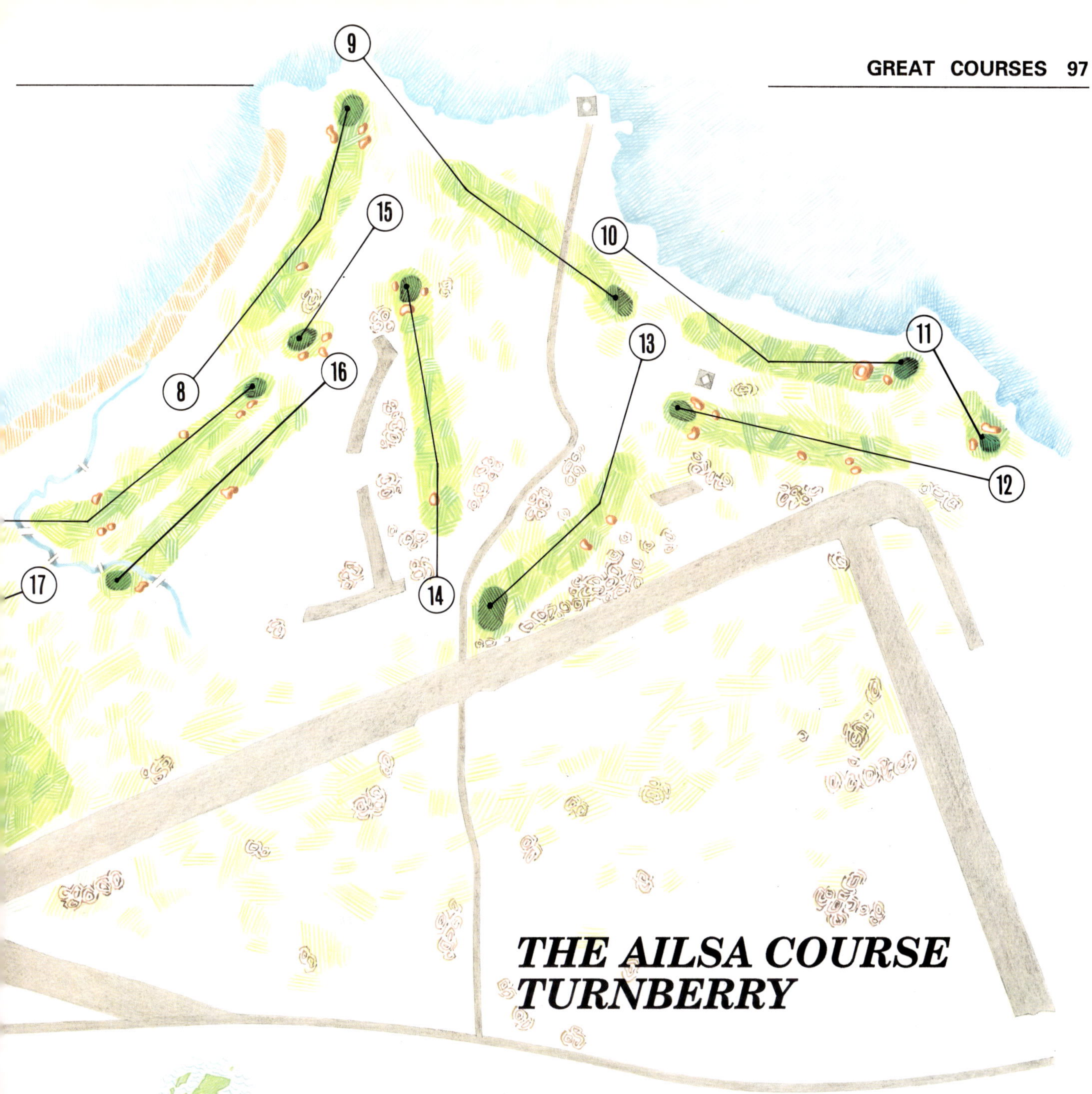

THE AILSA COURSE TURNBERRY

HOLE BY HOLE
Championship tees: 6957 yards Par 70. Medal tees: 6408 yards Par 69.

1st hole – Ailsa Craig
(Champ 350yd Medal 362yd Par 4) Beware of the out of bounds on the left.

2nd hole – Mak Siccar
(Champ 428yd Medal 378yd Par 4) Play straight as there's trouble on both sides.

3rd hole – Blaw Wearie
(Champ 462yd Medal 393yd Par 4) Watch out for the bunkers on both sides of the green.

4th hole – Woe-be-Tide
(Champ and Medal 167yd Par 3) Make sure you take enough club to clear the big bunker on the right.

5th hole – Fin' me oot
(Champ 441yd Medal 411yd Par 4) Watch out for the bunkers set short of the green.

6th hole – Tappie Toorie
(Champ and Medal 222yd Par 3) Take enough club – it can be as much as a driver.

7th hole – Roon the Ben
(Champ 528yd Par 5 Medal 465yd Par 4) Beware of Wilson's Burn which you have to carry off the tee.

8th hole – Goat Fell
(Champ and Medal 427yd Par 4) Play your tee shot down the left to avoid a fairway bunker on the right.

9th hole – Bruce's Castle
(Champ 455yd Medal 413yd Par 4) Aim for the stone cairn on the fairway.

10th hole – Dinna Fouter
(Champ 452yd Medal 430yd Par 4) Don't hook your tee shot as the rocky shoreline awaits your ball.

11th hole – Maidens
(Champ 177yd Medal 157yd Par 3) Beware of the waiting sea on the left of the hole.

12th hole – Monument
(Champ 448yd Medal 391yd Par 4) Play down the right side of the fairway to avoid bunkers on the left.

13th hole – Tickly Tap
(Champ 411yd Medal 379yd Par 4) Be careful when playing to the green – there are slopes all around it.

14th hole – Risk-an-Hope
(Champ 440yd Medal 400yd Par 4) Take time to select your club into this slightly elevated green.

15th hole – Ca Canny
(Champ 209yd Medal 168yd Par 3) Be brave and aim just right of the left side bunkers.

16th hole – Wee Burn
(Champ 409yd Medal 381yd Par 4) Be sure to take enough club to the green to avoid rolling back into the burn.

17th hole – Lang Whang
(Champ 500yd Medal 487yd Par 5) Hit a long drive and you may get home in 2 shots.

18th hole – Ailsa Hame
(Champ 431yd Medal 377yd Par 4) Aim to miss the two fairway bunkers on the left.

FOUR HOLES TO WATCH

6th hole – Tappie Tourie ▶

(Champ 222yd Par 3)
This is an all or nothing tee shot but at least there isn't the ultimate disaster of water if you're short. For the good hitter it can play as little as a 5 iron with a strong breeze at your back. With wind against it's everything you've got, and more.

Because the green is set at the top of a rise, there's no chance of a shot running on to it. A short ball topples back down the slope. If you go left you can end up in one of three traps. Go right and your ball bounces down a big bank.

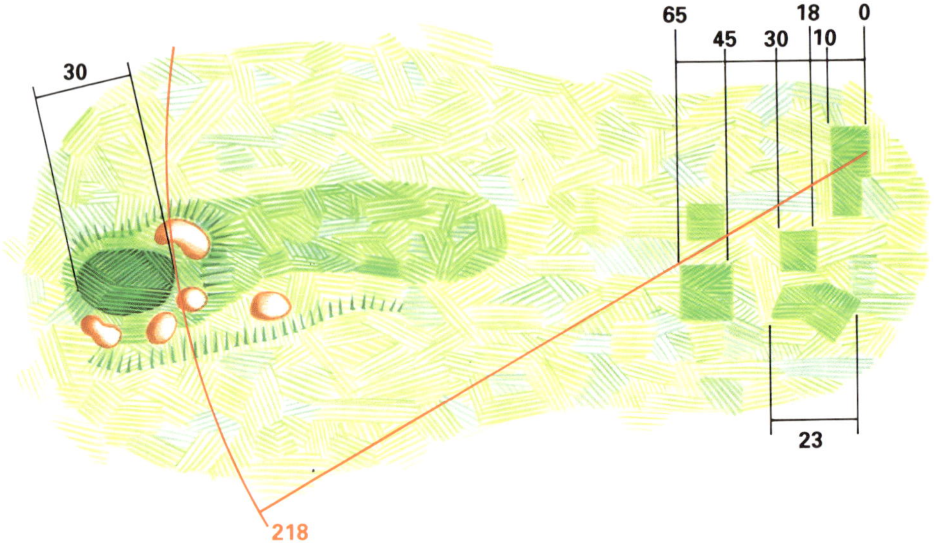

▶ The sweeping 441yd 5th features all the hazards typical of Turnberry's holes: length, narrow fairways, banks of penal rough and deep devious bunkering. The hole is difficult in normal conditions but when the wind blows the dangers are really severe.

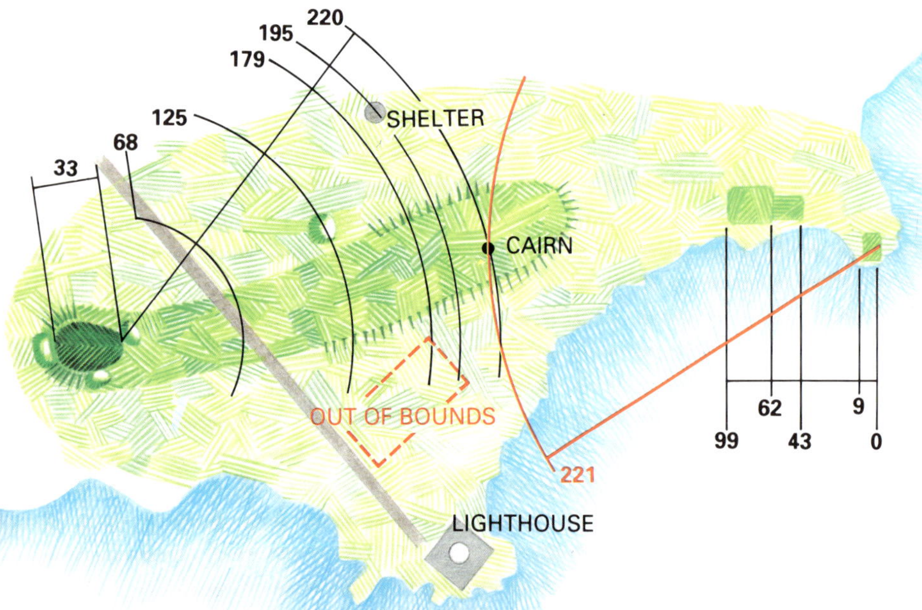

◀ *9th hole – Bruce's Castle*

(Champ 455yd Par 4)
This is the most photographed tee shot in British golf. You must fire over a craggy shore towards a stone cairn and the blind fairway beyond. The fairway is hogbacked so even a good shot tends to fall away to either side into semi-rough.

If you do find the rough, your long second shot is far more difficult. Though the green is not protected by bunkers, the ground falls away quite sharply to either side and a hump at the front on the right diverts many balls into the rough.

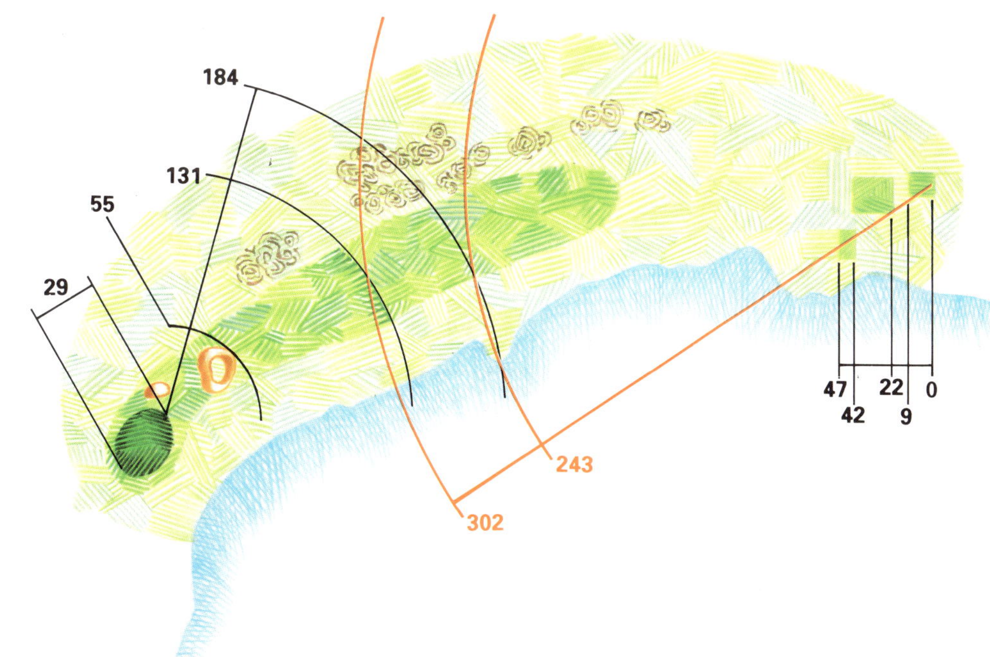

◄ *10th hole – Dinna Fouter*

(Champ 452yd Par 4)
The prospect which lies before you on the tee is every bit as dramatic as on the 9th – but this time you can see all of the hole before you. Humpy ground in front of the tee catches any really poor shot, while a hook almost certainly lands among the rocks on the left.

Safety suggests a tee shot along the right but the rough is often severe. The green isn't heavily protected, but a large circular island bunker set 50yd (45m) short catches the miss-hit second.

16th hole – Wee Burn ►

(Champ 409yd Par 4)
On the face of it this isn't a demanding hole – a par 4 of just over 400yd (364m) and a gently sloping fairway to give you a little extra run. But the lone bunker on the left of the fairway catches plenty of tee shots.

The most difficult feature is Wilson's Burn which runs in front and to the right of the green. The ground gathers your ball in towards the burn, and it catches most miss-hit or under clubbed second shots.

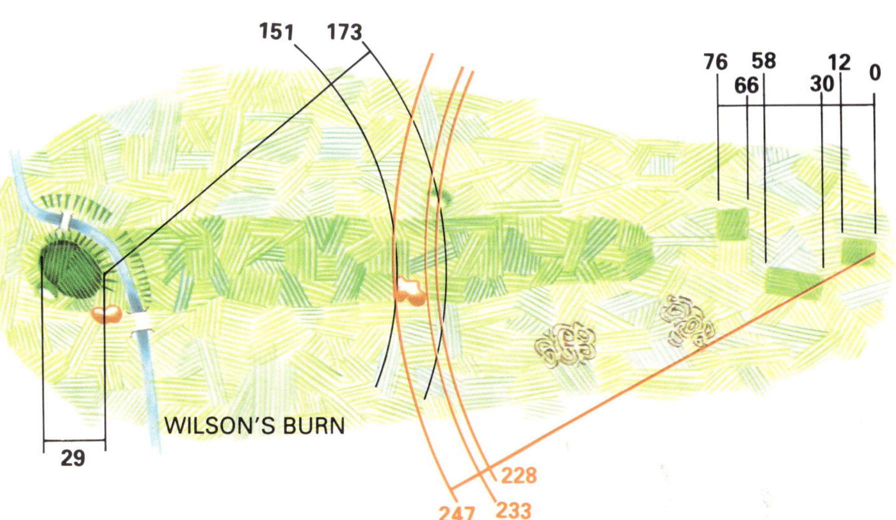

Auld Scottish names

Turnberry's holes are aptly described by their Scottish names. The 2nd – Mak Siccar – means 'make sure', and that is exactly what you have to do with every shot. The 6th – Tappie Tourie – tells you to 'hit to the top' as you have to play to an elevated green.

Dinna Fouter – 'don't mess about' – on the 10th or you are in trouble. At the 17th you need a Lang Whang, or 'good whack', as the hole is 500yd (455m).

◄ Wilson's Burn on the 16th is the ruin of many a round. The ground slopes towards the burn from every angle, catching any poor second shot. The difference between a good shot and disaster is only a short distance.

Greg Norman holes out at the 8th on the final day of the 1986 Open Championship. He went on to shoot 69 and won his first major title by 5 clear strokes.

intensive work, Turnberry was reopened. The course created by Mackenzie Ross has no gimmicks and is fair to all departments of the game.

After some relatively gentle sparring on the first three Ailsa holes, there is no let up. You set off to shadow the rocky shoreline until the 12th. From there you turn for home and some crafty finishing holes.

JUST REWARDS

When the wind blows, the 6957 yard championship course is a stern test. The first day of the 1986 Open was one of the coldest and windiest of modern times. Ian Woosnam was the only player to match the par of 70, and over 40 players could not break 80. But whatever the weather the course rewards good play.

Scoring at times has been brilliant. Turnberry staged its first Open in 1977 and records were shattered. American Mark Hayes shot an amazing 63, which was equalled by Greg Norman in 1986. And Tom Watson, the '77 winner, set a 72 hole record of 12 under par 268. These three records still stand.

Greg Norman's round was remarkable in that it contained three bogies, and was played in testing conditions. It is arguably the best round ever played in any championship, and set Norman up for his first win in a major.

HEAD TO HEAD BATTLE

Turnberry was also the setting for perhaps the greatest man to man duel the Open Championship has ever seen. In 1977 Tom Watson and Jack Nicklaus entered the last round neck and neck, and by halfway they were the only two left in it.

On the back nine Nicklaus pulled away slightly only to see Watson hole out from well off the 15th green to draw level. A birdie at the 17th let Watson go ahead. At the 18th he lashed an iron to an ideal position, while Nicklaus went all out for length and carved a driver dangerously close to the gorse.

Watson played a fine second to within 3ft (1m) of the hole and it all seemed over. Then Jack kept the tension going when he holed a long and difficult putt for his birdie. But Watson coolly knocked in his ball to win. They were an amazing 10 and 11 shots ahead of the rest of the field.

FACTFILE
Lowest scores
Professional course record:
63 – Mark Hayes 1977
63 – Greg Norman 1986

Tournaments
The Open – 1977, 1986
British Seniors Open – 1987, 1988, 1989
Amateur Championship – 1961, 1983
Walker Cup – 1963
PGA Matchplay – 1957, 1960, 1963
PGA Cup Match – 1984
European Open – 1979
British Club Professionals – 1980
John Player Classic – 1972, 1973

Valderrama

With breathtaking views of the mountains and the Mediterranean, Spain's Valderrama is an ideal setting for one of the world's great championship courses. Don't let its elegance fool you: any wayward shot is soon punished.

Robert Trent Jones, the world's most famous course architect, believes Valderrama to be one of his finest. Opened in its present form in 1985, the course is a masterpiece that severely tests the professionals yet provides enjoyable golf for all standards. The guiding principle is flexibility: difficult pars for the pros but easy bogies for the average golfer.

The course is set against the backdrop of the Sierra Blanca mountains in Spain ten miles east of Gibraltar. Gently undulating fairways lead to slick, subtly sloping greens. Cork and olive trees grace every corner and are an ever present hazard.

LUSH CONDITION

You are unlikely ever to play on better fairways. The turf is manicured and magnificent and the Bermuda grass thrives on the hot Andalucian summers and frost-free winters.

But while the grass is lush it's also very tough. The rough is cut to a height of only 2in (5cm) but is long enough to cause problems. Your ball settles down in the grass and is difficult to move. Because the rough lines the fairways, there is no margin for error.

The greens are a generous size and receptive but many large bunkers await any loose shot. These bunkers aren't filled with sand but with finely crushed marble from local quarries - they present a dazzling picture when the sun is shining.

▼ The 12th is a very challenging par 3 of 200m (219yd). Its dangers lie in the four bunkers and the twisted cork trees that surround the green. The carry over the valley means a long accurate strike is needed.

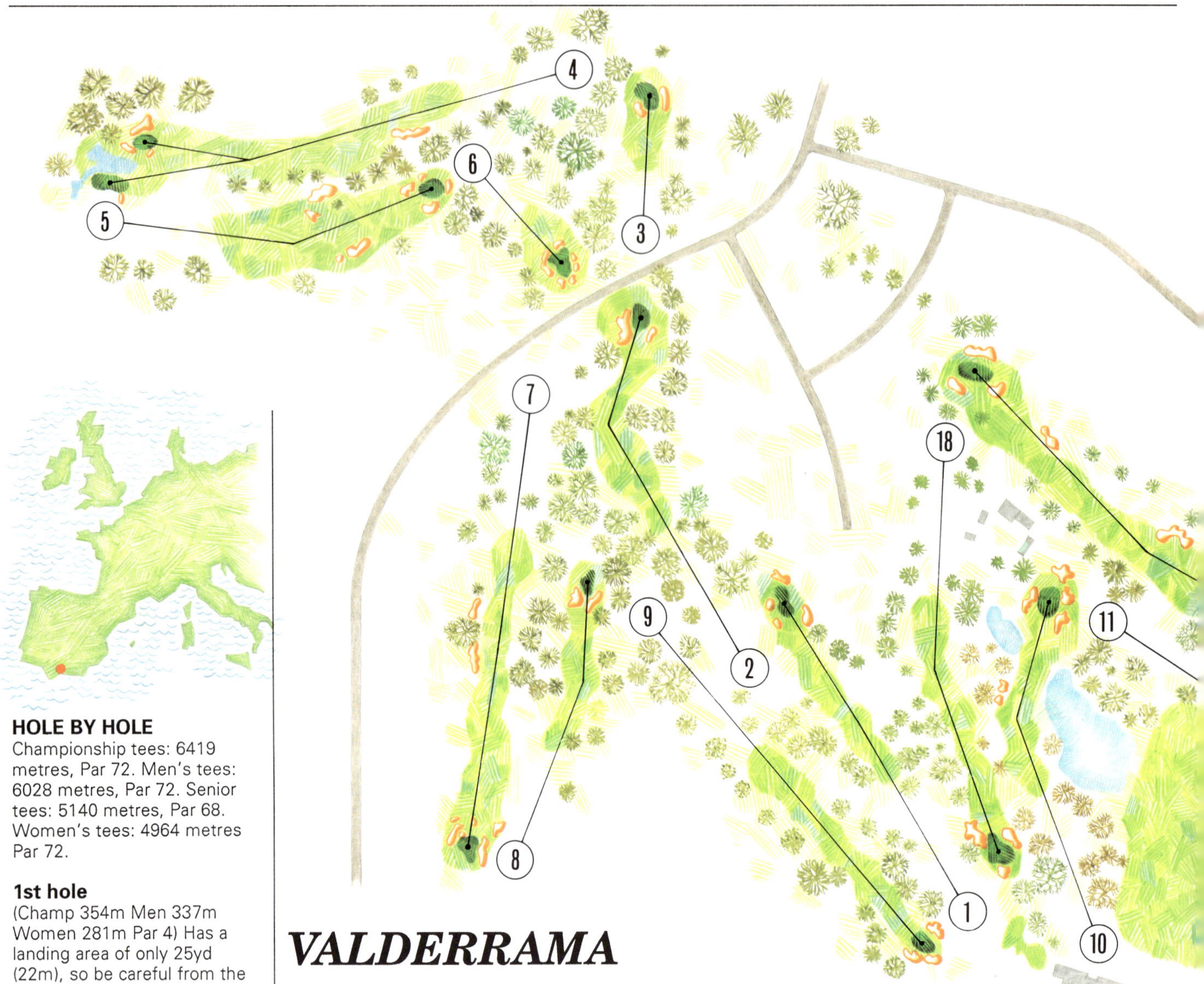

VALDERRAMA

▼ **Valderrama's clubhouse is cool, spacious and typically Andalucian – it makes a welcome refuge from summer heat. Large terraces beside the course mean you can enjoy a drink while watching the golf.**

HOLE BY HOLE

Championship tees: 6419 metres, Par 72. Men's tees: 6028 metres, Par 72. Senior tees: 5140 metres, Par 68. Women's tees: 4964 metres Par 72.

1st hole
(Champ 354m Men 337m Women 281m Par 4) Has a landing area of only 25yd (22m), so be careful from the tee.

2nd hole
(Champ 375m Men 355m Women 295m Par 4) Play your tee shot down the left to avoid a large tree.

3rd hole
(Champ 156m Men 141m Women 100m Par 3) Check the wind direction before you choose your club.

4th hole
(Champ 515m Men 490m Women 421m Par 5) Hit your tee shot to avoid a large bunker on the left.

5th hole
(Champ 344m Men 330m Women 255m Par 4) Aim your tee shot to miss the trap on the left, but beware of the out of bounds on the right.

6th hole
(Champ 150m Men 139m Women 111m Par 3) Watch out for the subtle humps and hollows on the green.

7th hole
(Champ 486m Men 445m Women 375m Par 5) Beware of the six bunkers that surround the green.

▶ **The location of the course is a major factor in how it plays. Sea breezes waft in from the nearby Mediterranean to provide testing conditions and a cooling effect in midsummer. The trees that cover the area are one of Valderrama's main hazards.**

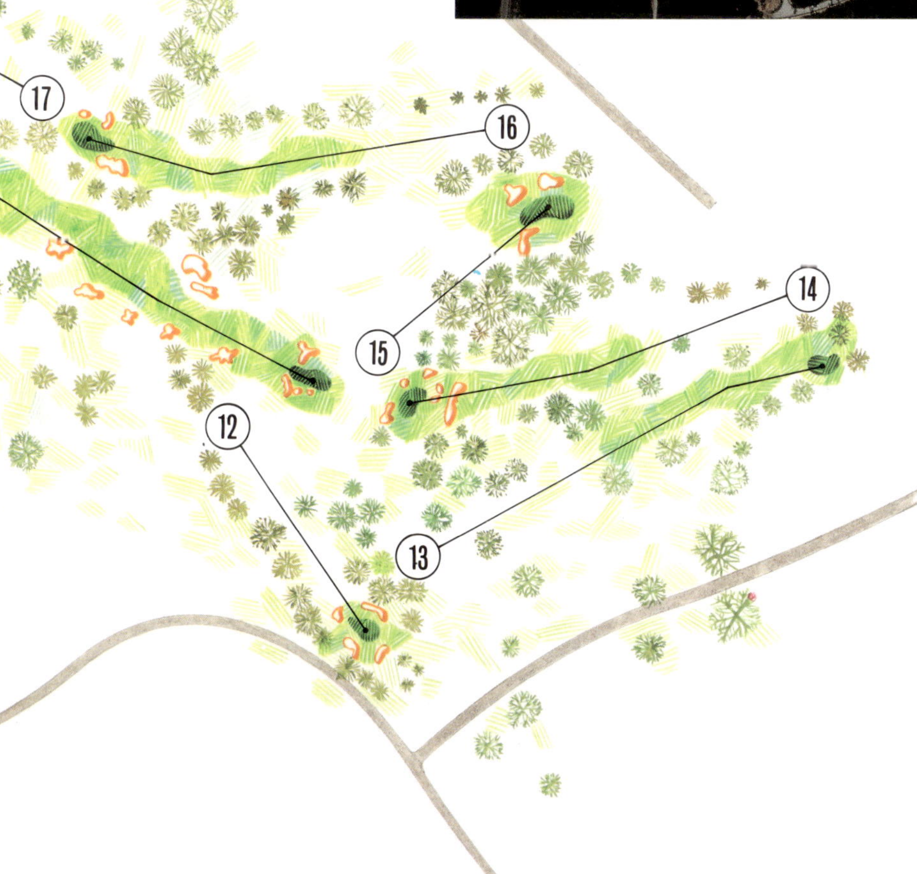

8th hole
(Champ 319m Men 293m Women 229m Par 4) Hit a 3 wood or long iron for position on this very narrow fairway.

9th hole
(Champ 415m Men 400m Women 348m Par 4) Make sure your second is accurate as the massive green has a narrow entrance.

10th hole
(Champ 369m Men 346m Women 275m Par 4) Don't slice as you may find yourself in the lake on the right.

11th hole
(Champ 504m Men 484m Women 420m Par 5) Aim your tee shot down the left side as the ground falls from left to right.

12th hole
(Champ 200m Men 188m Women 122m Par 3) Make sure that you hit your best shot as four bunkers are awaiting any miss-hit.

13th hole
(Champ 367m Men 340m Women 280m Par 4) Hit your tee shot down the left to avoid a tree in the fairway.

14th hole
(Champ 337m Men 314m Women 272m Par 4) Beware of the well guarded and undulating green.

15th hole
(Champ 207m Men 184m Women 148m Par 3) Land your tee shot short of the hole as the green slopes away.

16th hole
(Champ 385m Men 354m Women 285m Par 4) Aim at the right side of the fairway over the crest of a hill.

17th hole
(Champ 519m Men 491m Women 405m Par 5) Hit your second down the left to avoid leaving a blind third shot to the green.

18th hole
(Champ 417m Men 397m Women 342m Par 4) You must hit a long drive to have a clear view of the green round the dog-leg.

Each hole has four different tees that vary the length considerably. On some holes the championship tees are over 100yd (90m) behind the women's tees. From the championship tees the total length is over 6350m (7000yd), and plays all of it because of the lack of run on the fairways.

But the flexible siting of tees means the club player can enjoy the same course that the top pros find so taxing. A cluster of gnarled old cork trees seems less daunting from the men's tees than from the championship tees.

FAMOUS FIVES

One of the features of the course is the par 5s. There are four and as a set are difficult. They are all long - precise striking is essential to keep the ball in play and make par. From the back tees the shortest is the 486m (531yd) 7th. Even with the distance the pros hit the ball, two big shots are needed to get home in 2. And you must be brave if you are to go for it in 2 as the green is surrounded by six bunkers.

There are four excellent par 3s that

FOUR HOLES TO WATCH

4th hole ▶

(Champ 515m Par 5)
This is one of the most beautiful holes on the course. Aim from the tee to avoid the bunker on the left side of the fairway just short of the landing area. From there you can see the green.

Your next shot should reach a second rise on the right, setting up a pitch over the water hazard to a three-tiered green. It can be a very tough hole when the local Poniente wind from the mountains is blowing.

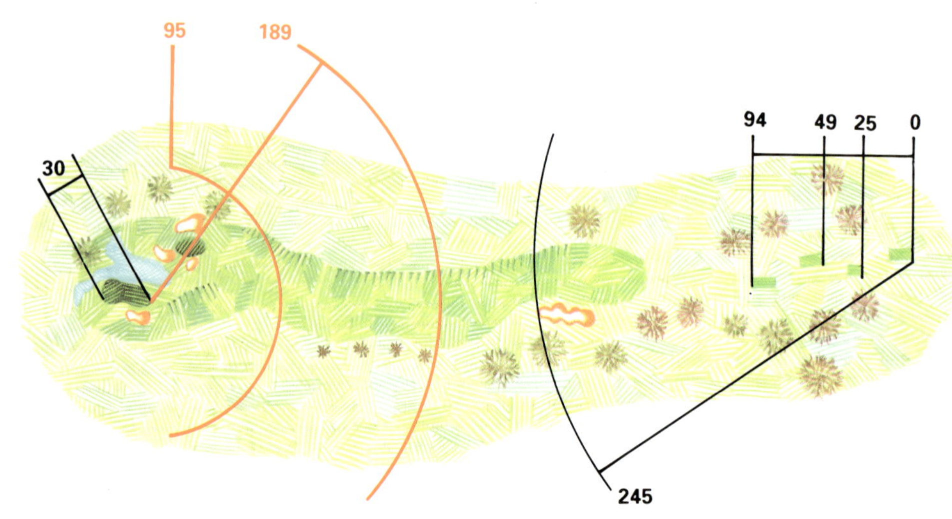

◀ *5th hole*

(Champ 344m Par 4)
This heavily bunkered hole requires two accurate shots to hit the green. Stay slightly right off the tee because the two bunkers on the left are in range. But be careful not to go too far right as there are bunkers which can be reached by long hitters on that side.

The green is protected by an overhanging cork tree on the right and by four tricky bunkers. Play your second to the left side of the green to avoid too much trouble.

▶ A completely tree-lined hole, the 9th provides the golfer with enough fairway problems to contend with – bunkers are saved for the green. The main clump of trees starts at 235m (257yd) from the tee, just in the driving area of the professionals.

Rafferty rules

When Ronan Rafferty beat José-Maria Olazabal to win the 1989 Volvo Masters, he also clinched the title of Europe's leading money-winner. His cheque for £66,660 helped him to amass over £400,000 for the season.

◄ **Many holes at Valderrama have trees that guard the fronts of the greens. They don't totally obscure the way in but encroach just enough to be a problem. The approach to the 5th green is protected by two bunkers on its left side as well as a group of cork trees.**

Scoring tough

In the 1988 Volvo Masters – featuring the cream of the European Tour – the par-72 course proved to be so difficult that there were only six scores in the 60s during the whole tournament.

In 1989 scoring improved slightly with ten scores in the 60s being returned. Winner Ronan Rafferty's best score was a 69. David Feherty said of the course, 'It is so difficult that I dropped a shot walking from the 18th green to the recorder's tent.'

11th hole ►

(Champ 504m Par 5)

Drive the ball down the left side, to hold a fairway that has a natural left-to-right fall. Make sure you play a precise second shot – the landing area is small because of bunkers on both sides of the fairway.

From here you see the flag on the skyline. Your third must be played between two bunkers that guard the hole. From the green you get great views of the Rock of Gibraltar, the sea and the mountains.

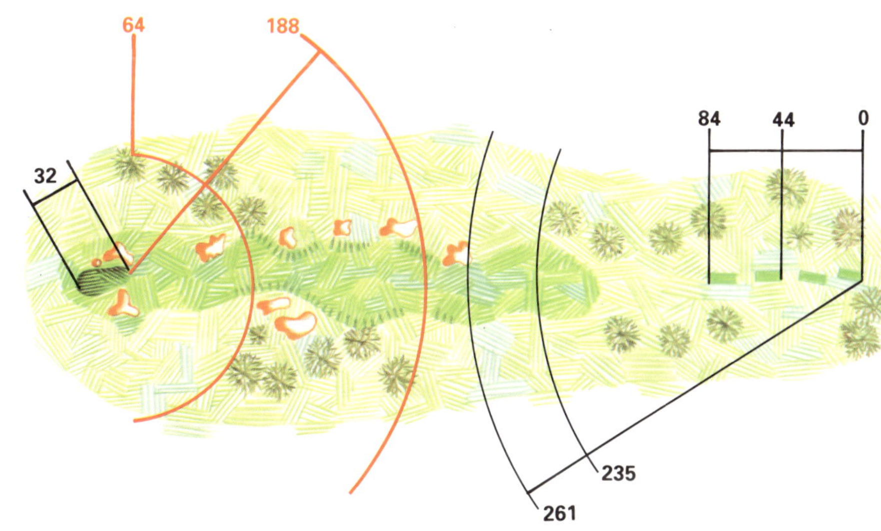

◄ ***16th hole***

(Champ 385m Par 4)

The tee shot is blind on this very tough dog-leg. Hit to the crest of the hill and on to a narrow landing area which slopes from right to left. Only then do you see the green, with its king-size bunker on the left and a lesser trap on the right.

The green is strongly influenced by a diagonal ridge, and can be very tricky to putt on. It is part of the long and difficult finish to the championship course.

▶ **In 1989 the 18th green was the scene of a magnificent triumph by Ronan Rafferty of Ireland. In the Volvo Masters his chip and putt from just off the green secured victory beating Nick Faldo into second.**

▲ **Jaime Ortiz-Patino (right), together with architect Robert Trent Jones, has created a masterpiece fit to hold major championships.**

FACTFILE
Lowest scores
Professional course record - 67 – José-Maria Canizares, 1988
67 – Anders Sorensen, 1988

Tournaments
Volvo Masters - 1988, 1989

test your ability to play the full range of shots. The short 6th of 150m (164yd) is a medium iron, but the 207m (226yd) 15th can be as much as a driver when the wind is against.

Whether the holes are short or long, they all have one thing in common: none is a giveaway. Where most courses have some holes that are definite birdie chances, Valderrama hasn't one.

When the first Volvo Masters was played in 1988, even the pros found birdies hard to come by. Of the 80 starters only two - the winner Nick Faldo and Seve Ballesteros - were under par for the 72 holes.

On the eve of the tournament, Trent Jones said to the players, 'Gentlemen, take your best shots with you.' And with mean pin placements and clutching grass to contend with, they needed to.

PRESIDENT'S PRIDE

The conditioning of the course, and the lofty position the club holds in European golf, are mainly thanks to the owner, president and head greenkeeper Jaime Ortiz-Patino.

Valderrama is his pride and joy. Unlike at other Spanish courses no villas line the fairways. Patino aims to keep it that way. He wants the course to stay as a haven for serious golfers, and a venue fit for the world's best.

▶ **The 15th may be relatively open around the green but at 207m (226yd) it causes problems for any standard of player. It can be as much as a driver.**

2

TECHNIQUES

There is something compelling about golf that makes you want to come back for more, whether you're playing well or suffering from a persistent problem. When your game is infuriatingly poor, it's a challenge; when you're scorching the fairways, it's a drug – you want to play on and on. But whatever stage you are at – a relative beginner or a seasoned professional – there is always room for improvement. Not one of the world's finest players would ever claim to having completely mastered this game. Some have come close, but just around the corner there's a double bogey staring them in the face.

This section will help players of all levels to build up a sound knowledge of the golf swing as well as an understanding of the strategies that can make such a startling difference to a score.

Through concisely written instruction, tell-tale photographs and simple illustrations, golf becomes less of a puzzle. Have you ever wondered how to play a pitch and run, or a high lob over a bunker? Do you ever crave to be able to hit a draw off the tee or consistently hole those awkward six footers? Well, every detail is covered, and with practice and patience, the tips and drills will help you achieve your goals and make you a much more complete golfer.

Sam Snead demonstrates his distinctive putting style during the 1991 US Masters at Augusta.

Aim and grip

Before you can even think about hitting the ball you have to know where you want the ball to go and how to hold the club. Aim and grip are the first two of the fundamentals that must be correct or your shots will be off target. Even the most experienced golfer should constantly check that both his aim and grip are right. It is only too easy for a simple fault to creep into a good golfer's play at the most basic stage.

The concept behind aim applies to whatever type of stroke you are playing. You must have your clubface square to the ball-to-target line to hit the ball straight.

The grip described here is the standard grip – called the overlapping, or Vardon, grip – that you use on every club apart from the putter.

When you've mastered aim and grip you can then go on to think about alignment of your body and club, the ball position in relation to body position, and the posture needed to attain the correct swing. These pre-swing essentials are part of the pre-shot routine that gets you to the right address position – the position from which you can produce a good swing.

AIM THE CLUBFACE

Before you think about the grip, look at the ball and the target – whether it is the flagstick, or some point on the fairway – and imagine a line joining them. This is your ball-to-target line and is the line you want the ball to travel along. Look at your target two or three times to ensure that you see the line clearly in your mind's eye.

You aim the club simply by setting the leading edge of the clubface precisely at right angles to the line from your target to the ball. Rest the sole of the clubhead on the ground behind the ball, hold the shaft in one hand and set the aim. It doesn't matter too much which club you use but a 6 or 7 iron is a good one to start off with. Stand so that your feet are about as far apart as your shoulders with your toes pointing outwards. The ball is about 1 ft (45cm) from the centre of your toe line.

When you go through the process of adjusting the grip, check every so often that the clubface is square to the ball-to-target line.

GRIP KNOW-HOW

The correct grip is vital and it is easy to adopt. It's important to remember that in the golf swing the hands play different roles and these roles are reflected in the way

ON TARGET
The correct aim and grip are essential if you want to hit the ball accurately and powerfully towards your target. At all times, while assuming the grip, the clubface should be square on to the imaginary line from the ball to the target.

TAKING UP THE OVERLAPPING GRIP

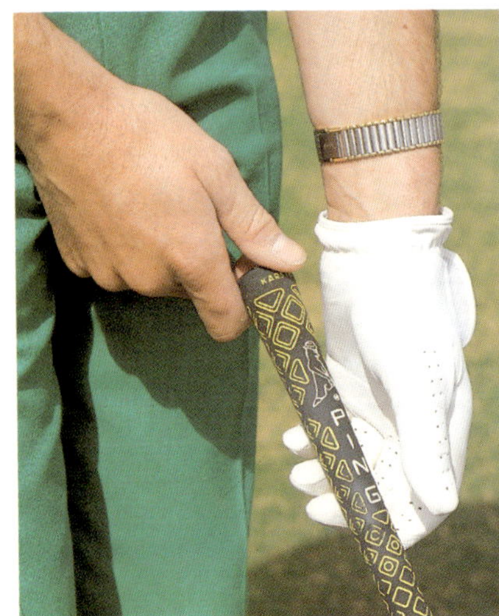

1 BEFORE YOU GRIP
Rest the clubhead on the ground and support the club with your right forefinger and thumb. Let your left arm hang naturally beside the club. Make sure the clubface is properly aimed.

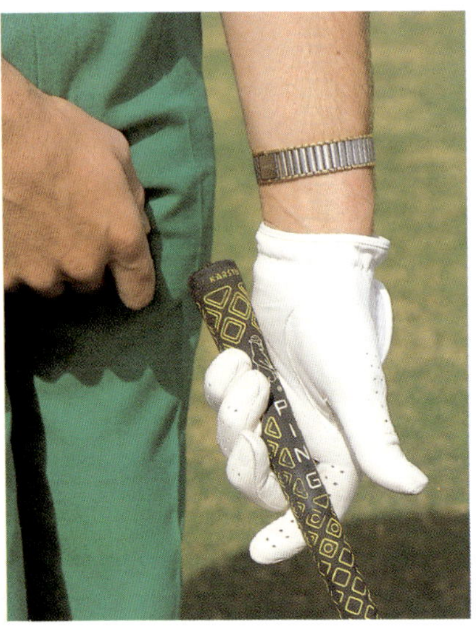

2 THE LEFT HAND
Move your left hand on to the club and position the grip diagonally across the 'meat' of your hand. Close your third and little fingers – vital pressure points.

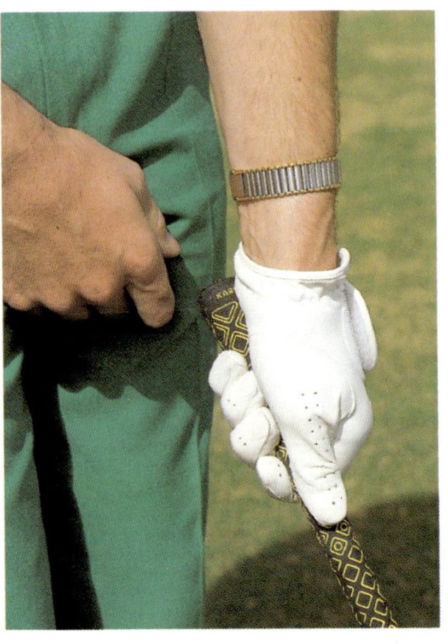

3 THUMB POSITION
Completely close your left hand, allowing your thumb to rest to the right of centre. Make sure your grip is not too tight.

TAKING AIM

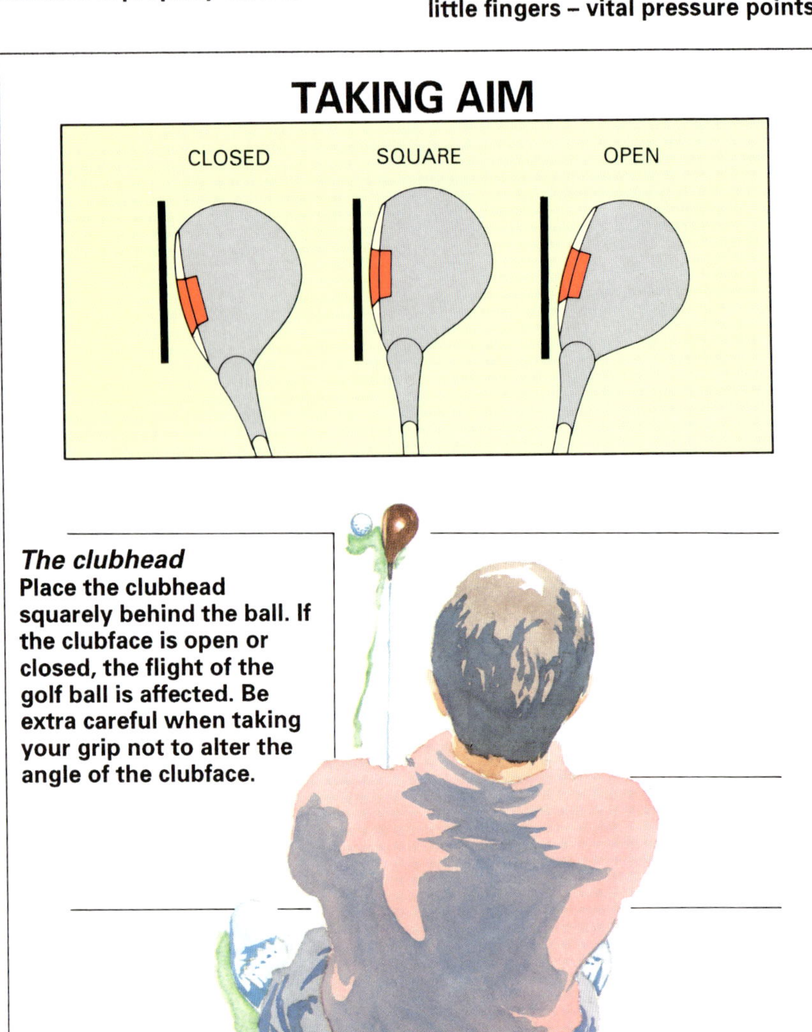

The clubhead
Place the clubhead squarely behind the ball. If the clubface is open or closed, the flight of the golf ball is affected. Be extra careful when taking your grip not to alter the angle of the clubface.

they are used in the grip. The hands are placed in different positions and work together during the swing.

Your left hand supports the club and maintains the clubhead in the correct position through impact with the ball. It can be described as the 'strong hand' in the grip. The club is positioned diagonally across the palm, resting against the 'meat' of your hand.

Your right hand, however, is going to 'release' the clubhead just before impact. This release gives the clubhead the power and speed to get maximum distance.

Releasing the clubhead is similar to the action of throwing a golf ball or skimming stones across water. When you do this you instinctively hold the stone somewhere between the forefinger and middle finger, with the thumb resting lightly on it as a support.

The release comes from the 'trigger finger' or, to be more precise, the middle joint of your forefinger.

When you hold the club with your right hand the grip should run through these fingers. By holding it this way you can be sure of a good release of power at the correct time.

When taking your grip, start by placing the sole of the club on the

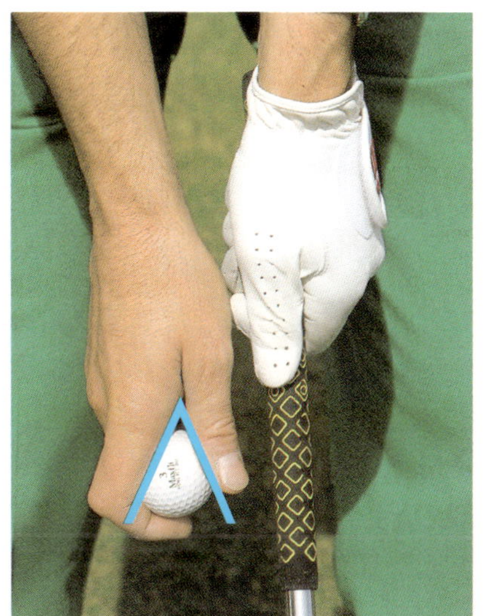

4 FORMING THE 'V'
Create the 'V', between thumb and forefinger, by holding a golf ball between the forefinger, middle finger and thumb of your right hand. Drop the ball by slightly releasing the pressure but keep your hand in the same position.

pro tip

Not so tight a squeeze
There's a simple way to get your grip pressure correct. Take a large tube of toothpaste and unscrew the cap. Hold the tube with the nozzle pointing down and grip the tube as you would your club. The pressure you exert should be just hard enough to hold the tube securely without squeezing the toothpaste out.

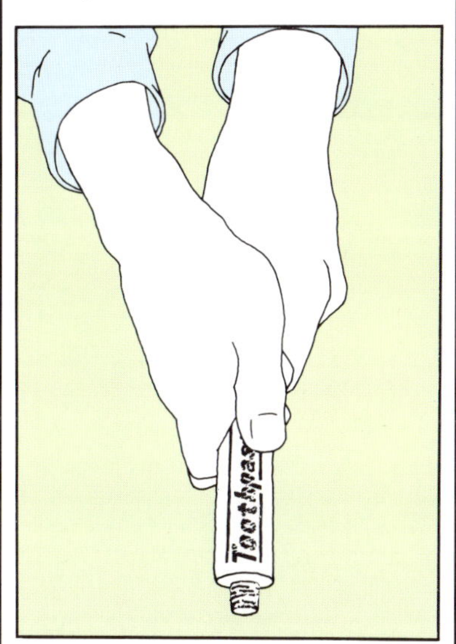

5 THE RIGHT HAND
Move your right hand on to the grip and hold the club with your two middle fingers and forefinger. Let your little finger overlap with the forefinger of your left hand and your right thumb rest to the left of centre of the shaft. Raise the club up to eye level. You should see two knuckles showing on each hand and a 'V' made by the thumb and forefinger of your right hand.

ground – preferably up against the ball on a tee peg as this helps you keep the clubhead square. Support the club using the tip of your right forefinger and thumb placed on the top of the grip.

THE LEFT HAND

Let your left arm hang naturally by the side of the grip before bringing it across to the club to take hold. About -1in (1.5-2.5cm) of the grip protrudes above where it rests across your hand. Your thumb should fall slightly to the right of centre and your third and little fingers should grip hardest. These are important pressure points. The club must rest diagonally across your palm, in the 'meat' of your hand.

THE RIGHT HAND

When you have the club correctly positioned in your left hand let go with your right hand and let it hang naturally by your side. The grip formed by your right hand should take up the form of a 'V' between your thumb and forefinger.

To get an idea of how the 'V' should look, hold a golf ball as if you are about to throw it. Drop the ball by slightly relaxing your grip and, with the grip still in place, bring your hand across to the club.

Grip the club below your left hand with the middle two fingers and forefinger of your right hand. Let the little finger of your right hand overlap with the forefinger of your left hand. The thumb of yourright hand should rest lightly on the grip pointing down the shaft and slightly to the left of centre. Check that the clubface is square.

When you have both hands on the club, lift it up to chest height. Take a good look at your hands – you should see two knuckles on each of your hands and a very pronounced 'V' in your right hand, pointing towards your chin. The hands are now completely moulded into one unit.

Why one glove ?

Most golfers wear a glove on their left hand (right hand for left handers). This is because the left hand supports the club, maintaining correct clubhead position through impact, and the glove gives you a more secure hold with the stronger hand.

OVERLAPPING GRIP
In the finished grip, the little finger of your right hand is over the forefinger of your left hand. It is the standard grip (also called Vardon grip) for all shots except putts. It is the best grip for most golfers.

INTERLOCKING GRIP
If you have small hands or fingers try the interlocking grip. This is the same as the overlapping grip except that the little finger of your right hand interlocks with the forefinger of your left hand.

BASEBALL GRIP
This is an unusual grip in which all ten fingers are in contact with the grip. It is mainly used by players who are physically weak, such as youngsters and those suffering from arthritis.

pro tip

Leave a space

When taking your grip leave -1in (1.5-2.5cm) of the grip showing above your left hand. This secures your hold and prevents you straining the back two tendons of the left hand. It also prevents overswinging.

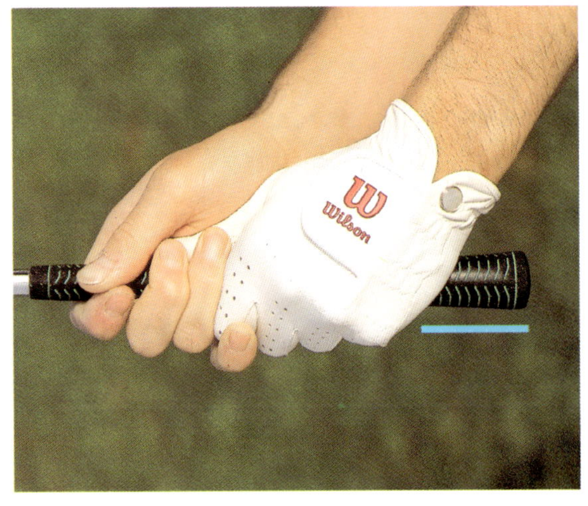

Posture and alignment

The right posture sets up your body in the correct position for the swing and proper alignment ensures that you hit the ball straight along the imaginary ball-to-target line.

Body position and alignment of the body are two of the five essentials necessary for a good swing, along with aim of the clubface, grip and ball placement. You need to know these basics and practise them regularly until you don't have to think about them before you make your swing.

POSTURE

Correct posture is vital. Just watch the top players on TV. Although the world's great golfers may swing the club differently, they all have identical posture at address when they are preparing to strike the ball.

Before you take up your posture, hold your club in your right hand and place the clubhead behind the ball, check that you are aiming the clubhead correctly and take your grip on the club. Use a 6, 7 or 8 iron as these three clubs are all easy to swing.

There are three stages on the path to correct posture. The first is your stance – where you place your feet when you address the ball. The two other stages involve your knees and back.

POSTURE AT ADDRESS
Flex your knees and stick your bottom out slightly. Your hands should lie directly below your chin. The angle of your back allows your shoulders to rotate easily. Keep your chin up so it is clear of your left shoulder during the backswing.

FROM THE FRONT
Your left arm, your hands and the clubhead can be joined by an imaginary straight line. The ball is in the centre of your stance and your hands are slightly ahead of the ball.

THE RIGHT STANCE

Your feet should be as far apart as your shoulders are wide. In other words you take up a shoulder-width stance. They should also be at a slight outwards angle. The best way to get your feet at the correct angle is to imagine you are standing on the centre of a big clockface. Your right foot should point to 1 o'clock and your left to 11 o'clock.

Once your feet are in the right place, lift the club off the ground, and stand upright and at ease, with your legs straight. Now go on to the next stage.

Keeping your legs straight, bend your torso so that you are leaning forwards with your weight on the balls of your feet.

Finally, bend your knees slightly and let your bottom stick out. This should straighten your back. A straight back at the correct angle to the vertical allows your body to rotate properly when you make your swing.

This final stage also moves your body weight back from the balls of your feet to a more central position. You should always be comfortable and balanced when you have correct posture.

ALIGNMENT

Correct alignment means lining up your body parallel to the ball-to-target line. This may sound easy, but very few golfers achieve it or realize its importance in making sure the ball goes straight and accurately to the target.

Too many golfers take up what they feel is the ideal grip and posture without understanding the correct alignment procedure. Preparation for a shot is as vital as making the stroke itself.

BALL-TO-TARGET LINE

Before aligning yourself for a shot, you must first re-check your aim so that your clubface is square on

Hands below your chin

To check your hand position, try tying a small weight to the end of a piece of string, about 2ft (60cm) long. Grip the other end between your teeth and let the weight hang freely. The string should pass along the same line as your grip.

THE CORRECT POSTURE

1 POSITION OF FEET
Your feet at address must be the same width apart as your shoulders. They should also point slightly outwards.

2 LEAN FORWARD
Stand at ease with your legs straight then lean forward so that your weight is on the balls of your feet. Place the clubhead squarely behind the ball.

TRAINING ALIGNMENT

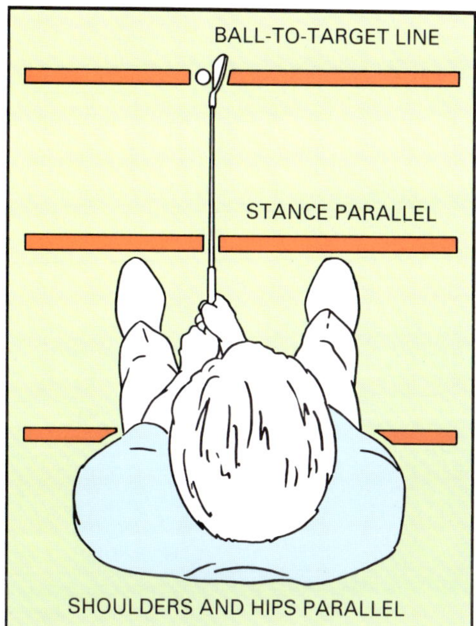

ALIGN YOUR BODY
Alignment can be surprisingly hard to get right. Your shoulders, especially, must not point at the target but must be parallel to the ball-to-target line.

3 BEND YOUR KNEES
Bend your knees and stick your bottom out slightly. This straightens your back. Add the correct grip. The club should rest firmly on the ground.

ON TRACK
One tried and tested way to achieve perfect alignment is to imagine a railway track between your ball and the target. The ball and clubhead are on the far rail, which runs to the base of the target, while the tips of your toes touch the nearside rail. Align your shoulders, hips and knees so that they are parallel to this nearside rail.

RAILWAY FORMATION
You can make the imaginary railway line idea clearer by placing a number of clubs on the ground in railway line formation. Line up your clubface square on to the club furthest away from you, while taking a stance parallel to the near line. Although your feet and body point left of target, they are in fact correctly placed: parallel to the ball-to-target line.

to the ball-to-target line. It's essential to remember that your body must be parallel to this line. To help do this, imagine another line running between the tips of your big toes.

This line should run parallel to the ball-to-target line. Your knees, hips and shoulders must also be parallel to this new line running from toe to toe.

It might feel as if your shoulders are aiming left of the target but remember you strike the ball with the clubface. Aligning your shoulders *parallel* to the ball-to-target line is vital for creating the perfect swing.

Aligning your shoulders so they point *at* the target is a common fault which makes the club aim too far right. It often occurs when a golfer lines up a shot by looking at the target over the left shoulder. Avoid it by rotating – rather than lifting – your head to check that your clubface is aimed properly. Check your aim several times before you play a stroke that is square to the ball-to-target line.

PRACTISING AIM AND ALIGNMENT

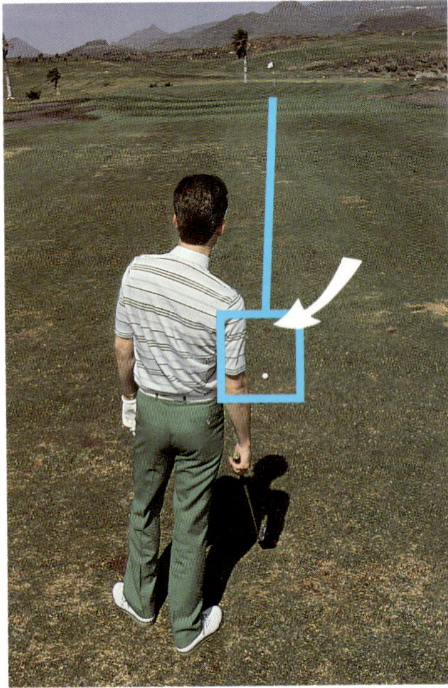

1 VIEW FROM BEHIND
First, view the shot from behind – it's easier to find the intended line of flight. Pick out a marker such as a divot 3ft (1m) beyond the ball on the target line.

2 AIM THE CLUBFACE
Holding the club in your right hand, place the clubhead on the ground behind the ball and aim it square on to the selected marker.

3 TAKE A PARALLEL STANCE
Take a stance parallel to the ball-to-marker line, and grip the club correctly using both hands. Keep the ball central in your stance.

Practise this routine regularly until it becomes as natural as walking. Remember, you must always find the correct alignment before you consider playing the shot.

Ball position and the swing

The last of the five pre-swing essentials to know before learning about the swing is where you place the ball in relation to your feet when you are using the various clubs.

In the normal golf swing, the clubface must be square on to the ball-to-target line at impact. Knowing what goes on during the swing and what happens to the clubface during the swing helps you to get your clubface square on to the ball-to-target line at impact.

CLUB AND STANCE

Depending on the type of club, you stand with your feet further or closer apart. Once you've decided how far apart your feet should be you can then go on and accurately position your ball.

The longer the shaft of your club, the wider apart you have your feet. So your stance is wider for the longer irons such as a 2 or 3 iron and a driver and is narrower for the shorter clubs such as the 8 or 9 irons and the wedges. With a 2 iron, for instance, your stance should be about as wide as a normal walking pace is long. With a short iron such as a sand wedge you stand with your feet about half as far apart as for a long iron. With a 6 or 7 iron your feet are about shoulder width apart.

PLACING THE BALL

The general rule is: the shorter the shaft, the more central the ball should be in your stance. If you are using a 9 iron, position the ball in the centre of your stance. With a 2 iron, place the ball opposite the inside of your left heel.

For the clubs in between, place the ball between these two positions. When using a medium iron, for instance, place the ball midway between the centre of your stance and the inside of your left heel.

The length of each club's shaft

PLACEMENT AND STANCE
Correct placement is determined by the club you are using. With a medium iron such as a 7 iron, the ball should be placed on a line midway between the inside of your left heel and the centre of your stance. The width of a 7-iron stance is just over half the length of a normal walking stride.

also determines how far away from the ball that you stand. For a long-shafted club such as a 2 iron the ball is further away from you than for a shorter-shafted, high-numbered club.

POSTURE AND SWING PLANE

The ball is placed in these different positions because of the changes to posture brought about by the length of the differing clubs. The shorter the shaft, the nearer you are to the ball, the narrower your stance and the more your back is bent.

It is the angle of your back at address that influences swing plane. The more bent it is the steeper your swing plane. With a longer-shafted club, such as a 2 iron, the ball is further from your feet than with a 9 iron. Your hands are higher and your back is more upright. This automatically creates a flatter swing plane around your body.

The shape of your swing affects the angle at which the clubhead hits the ball, and dictates the amount and type of spin. The steep swing plane of the 9 iron creates backspin, while the flatter plane of the 2 iron produces overspin. Backspin prevents the ball running as far as normal on landing, while overspin increases roll.

SWING PATH

During a correct swing the clubhead travels in a path from the inside of the ball-to-target line, briefly along the ball-to-target line at impact and then back inside the ball-to-target line after impact. It

THE SWING

1 TAKEAWAY
In the first 6-9in (15-23cm) of the backswing, the club moves in a straight line. It has yet to be influenced by your upper body.

CLUBS, POSTURE AND PLACEMENT

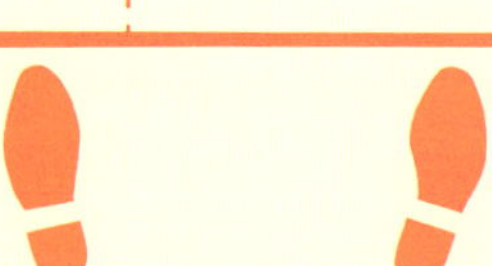

3 IRON (LONG IRON)
Your back is slightly bent at address and the width of your stance is equal to the length of a normal walking stride. Place the ball opposite the inside of your left heel.

7 IRON (MEDIUM IRON)
The shaft is shorter so your feet are closer together and your back is more bent. The ball is placed closer to your feet and positioned midway between the centre of your stance and opposite your inside left heel.

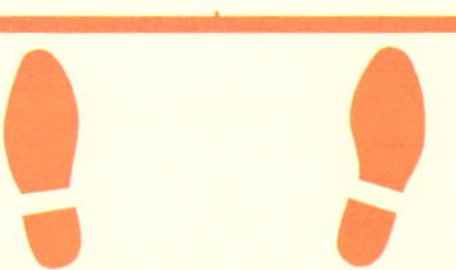

SAND WEDGE (SHORT IRON)
At address, your back is more bent than it is with either a long or medium iron. The ball is closer to your feet and is placed in the centre of your stance.

2 NATURAL ROTATION
By the mid-point of the backswing the body rotation moves the club inside the ball-to-target line. This also opens the clubface.

3 THE HIGHEST POINT
Near the top of the backswing, the club continues its path around the body. At the top, the shaft of the club should be parallel with the target.

4 DOWNSWING
The downswing is almost identical to the backswing. The club follows a path inside the ball-to-target line and the clubface closes.

5 SQUARE CONTACT
The clubface gradually returns, from being open at the start of the downswing, to being perfectly square to the ball-to-target line at impact. The club travels briefly along the ball-to-target line at impact.

6 THROUGHSWING
On the throughswing, the club continues along its path and moves back inside the ball-to-target line. The clubface continues to rotate and gradually closes as the throughswing continues.

never goes outside the ball-to-target line.

At the start of the backswing, turning your body moves the clubhead inside the ball-to-target line. It also causes the clubface to open and, at the mid-point of the backswing, its face has opened so that it is at an angle of 90° to the ball-to-target line.

CLUBFACE AT IMPACT

During the downswing and right up to impact the clubhead gradually closes and only at one brief moment – impact – is the clubface square to the ball-to-target line. On the throughswing the face continues to rotate and closes.

A perfect in-to-in swing path alone does not guarantee square contact. The ball must also be correctly placed in relation to your stance. Golf is often said to be a game of inches. One inch off target on the tee can mean 10-15 yards off line down the fairway.

When the ball is too far back in the stance, the club meets it too early on the downswing. The clubface is still open and, even with the correct in-to-in swing path, the ball goes to the right of target.

If the ball is too far forward in the stance, the club makes contact too late (on the throughswing). The clubface has closed slightly and the ball lands left of target.

pro tip

Toeing the line

To help understand the opening and closing of the clubface during the swing path, slowly swing the club back and through the normal swing plane. At the mid-point on both the backswing and the throughswing, the toe of the club should point directly at the sky. At these points, the face should also be open by 90° and closed by 90° respectively.

SWING PLANES

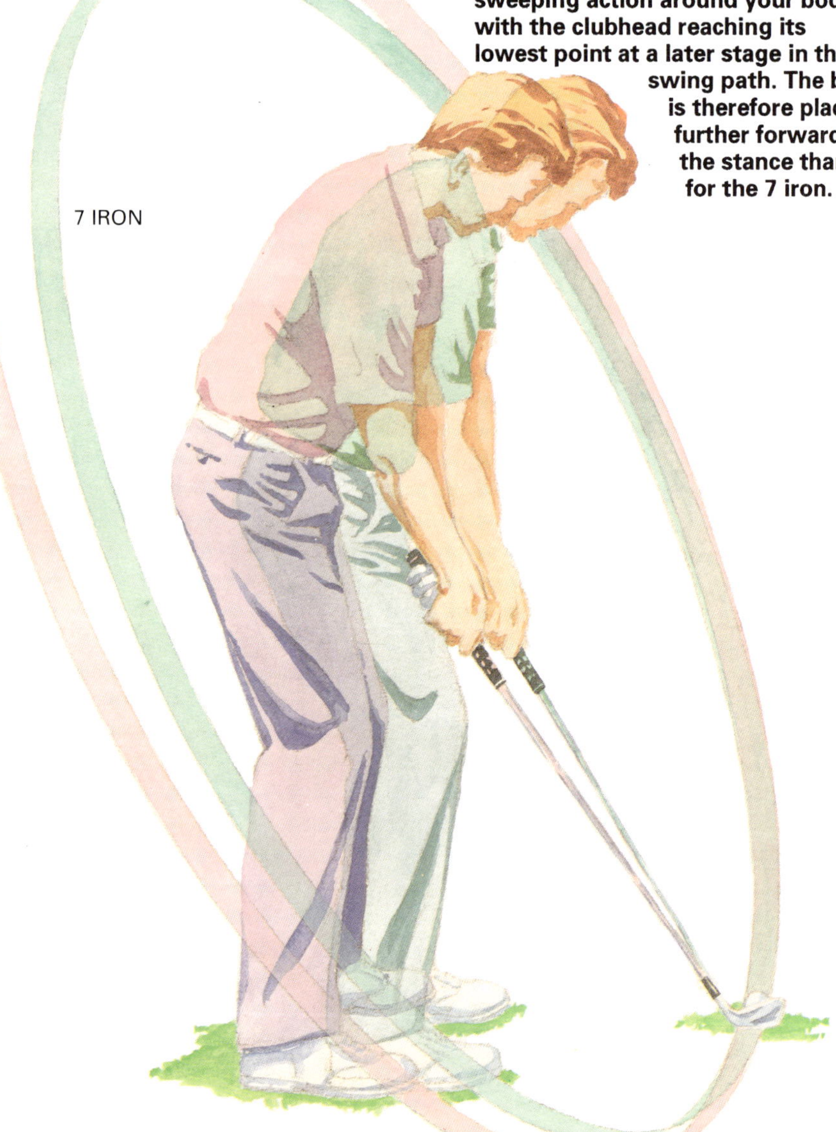

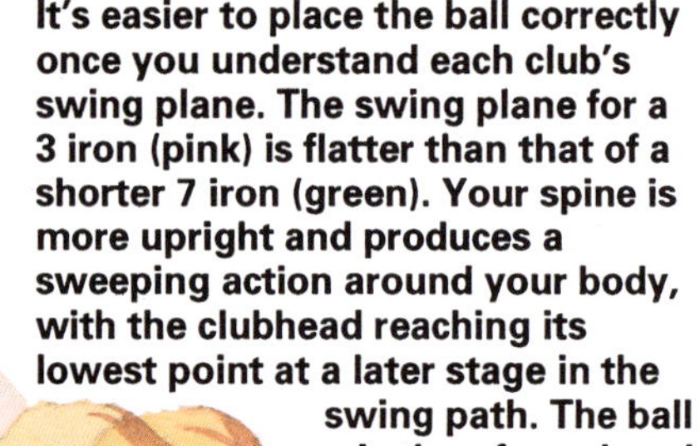

It's easier to place the ball correctly once you understand each club's swing plane. The swing plane for a 3 iron (pink) is flatter than that of a shorter 7 iron (green). Your spine is more upright and produces a sweeping action around your body, with the clubhead reaching its lowest point at a later stage in the swing path. The ball is therefore placed further forward in the stance than for the 7 iron.

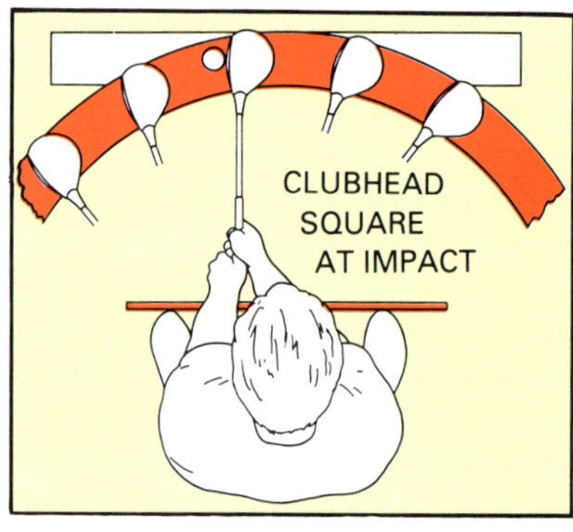

IN-TO-IN CLUBHEAD
During the correct in-to-in swing path, the clubhead should never move outside the ball-to-target line. Note how the clubface is square to the target at one point only – impact.

Shaping the swing

The aim of all golfers is to develop a simple, repeatable swing. The fewer individual movements there are in your swing, the less parts there are to go wrong and the better chance you have of repeating it.

When building a swing it is vital to understand how different parts of the body work together. Your head, shoulders, arms, hands, hips, knees and feet, must interact correctly if you are to swing efficiently. A good swing is the result of co-ordinated body rotation, and not a collection of separate movements.

SWING EXERCISE

Practise this exercise several times a week to help you develop correct body rotation, flexibility and freedom of movement. Hold the club behind your shoulders with both hands, and take up a normal middle-iron address position. Make sure your feet are the correct distance apart.

KEEP YOUR HEAD CENTRAL

Your head is the centre of any swing, and influences the movement of every other part of the body. By keeping a central position throughout, your head helps you to return the clubhead to its precise starting point. Your shoulders turn around your head. This sparks off hip rotation, which in turn begins leg movement.

TAKEAWAY AND BACKSWING

From the address position, where you have set your aim, taken grip, adopted the right posture, aligned your body and placed the ball correctly, you can start the take-away – the beginning of the backswing.

For the first 6-9in (15-23cm) of the takeaway, the club moves in a straight line as the left arm triggers the backswing. The base of the clubhead keeps quite close to the ground. Your left arm pulls the left shoulder under your chin. From here, body rotation begins to shape the swing as it coils up the power.

Your right arm must stay relaxed, so it can fold under the influence of your rotating left shoulder. This shoulder continues to be pulled around – although it stays on the same plane. It must stay level and not dip or rise during any part of the swing.

Move your head

The old saying, 'keep your head still', should not be taken literally. Although your head mustn't sway, the natural movement of your body means it has to revolve slightly during backswing and downswing, and more on the throughswing. Head rotation should co-ordinate with shoulder action. Holding your head rigid prevents correct body rotation and could even injure you.

ROTATE TO THE RIGHT
Rotate your body to the right, making sure your shoulders stay on the same plane (level). From an even distribution at the start, your weight transfers to the inside of your right foot. At this point your back should face the target. Your right knee stays flexed throughout the backswing.

RETURN TO CENTRE
Your left hip starts the movement that returns the body to a central position. The rotating hip triggers your left shoulder, which also revolves to the left. You are now in a position similar to your starting point. When you begin your followthrough, think of it as a reversal of your backswing.

CHEST FACES TARGET
Your shoulders continue to rotate to the left. By the end of the exercise your chest and head should face the target, with your weight on the outside of your left foot. Your left knee stays flexed on the throughswing. This exercise trains the various parts of the body to work together.

BUILDING YOUR SWING

1 **STARTING THE BACKSWING**
From address (inset) the club moves in a straight line for the first 6-9in (15-23cm) of the takeaway – staying close to the ground. This action pulls your left shoulder to the right, as you begin your backswing.

2 **LEFT SHOULDER PULLED UNDER CHIN**
Your left shoulder continues to be pulled under your chin and at the two-thirds point of the backswing is almost directly under your chin. Your wrists hinge naturally, caused by the passage of the club.

3 **TOP OF THE BACKSWING**
At the top of the backswing your shoulders have rotated 90° and your hips 45°. The shaft points at the target and is parallel to the ground. Your left knee is flexed and most of your weight is on the inside of your right foot.

4 **STARTING THE DOWNSWING**
Your left hip starts the downswing by turning to the left. This action must be smooth, pulling your arms and hands into the proper striking position. Don't turn your hip too soon or the club moves outside the in-to-in path.

As your shoulders rotate, they pull your hips in the same direction. The hips must also remain on the same plane. But they must be flexible enough to let your body weight shift from an even distribution at address, over to the right foot by the mid-point on the backswing.

By the top of the backswing, your shoulders should have turned 90° and your hips 45°. The shaft of the club points towards the target and is parallel to the ground. Most of your weight is on the inside of your right foot, with the right leg flexed.

DOWNSWING AND IMPACT

The start of the downswing must be smooth and unhurried. It is triggered by the left hip which starts rotating back to its original address position. This action pulls your hands and arms into a position where they can swing freely through the ball.

After impact, your right shoulder continues to pull the hips to the left, which in turn rotates the right leg. As your right shoulder rotates to its final followthrough position, it turns your head around. This is a natural movement. If you force your head to stay still after impact, you prevent your body completing the correct followthrough movement.

By the completion of the swing, your body should have rotated to face the target, with the weight transferred to your left foot.

YOUR ARMS AND HANDS

Let your arms and hands swing naturally. They should be passive during the stroke and influenced only by the rotation of the swing. They do not shape the swing.

Many beginners wrongly believe that as the arms and hands are in direct contact with the club, they alone control the swing.

If you move your hands and arms independently from the rest of your body, they swing back and through impact in various directions and it is difficult to develop the correct in-to-in swingpath. You must have co-ordinated body rotation so that you'll be able to develop a consistent, repeatable and accurate swing.

THE HALF SWING

To help you build your full swing, try practising the half swing, in which you finish the backswing and throughswing at the two-thirds position of the full swing.

Feel these key movements: your left shoulder being pulled under your chin; the clubhead's weight pulling your right shoulder and hands into impact; your face and chest turning to the target after impact; correct weight transfer.

pro tip

Mirror image
Looking in a mirror is an excellent way to check your swing – but make sure you are out of reach of furniture, glass and lights. If you have a large mirror at home, you can watch yourself build a swing and compare the way you are moving to the sequence on these pages. This way you can check that you are building your swing properly. Alternatively, use the reflection from a large window.

5 IMPACT AND FOLLOWTHROUGH
At impact your left arm, hands and the clubhead form a straight line and your weight moves on to your left foot. On the followthrough your right shoulder is pulled to the left.

6 THE END OF THE SWING
Most of your weight is transferred on to the outside of your left foot by the end of the swing. Your left knee remains slightly flexed and your chest is square to the target. Your head has revolved to face the target.

HOW YOUR HEAD MOVES

1 BACKSWING
Your neck muscles must be relaxed enough to let your head revolve. Your head turns slightly to the right, affected by shoulder turn, but it mustn't tilt up or down.

2 IMPACT
As the club moves back to impact, your head returns to the same position it was in at address. This occurs naturally with the movement of the swing.

3 THROUGHSWING
As your right shoulder continues to turn to the left after impact, your head automatically comes up. Head movement must be natural or it restricts followthrough.

HALF SWING

To help you build a complete swing, it is often best to practise the half swing. From a normal address position, swing the club to the two-thirds point on the backswing (1), down through impact (2) to finish at the two-thirds point on the follow-through (3).

The half swing concentrates on the basics. It increases clubhead feel at impact and improves your timing. It also helps you understand body movement, in particular weight transference and rotation.

The nine strikes

Finding out the cause of a fault in your swing is much easier if you develop an understanding of how the clubface strikes the ball.

If you spray the ball to all points of the compass, don't simply curse your luck and move on. Ask yourself why your shots fly off target.

You can strike a golf ball in nine different ways – some desirable, others disastrous. Whatever you intend with your shot, one of those nine is sure to dictate its flight path.

When you can assess precisely which one of the nine is responsible for each shot, you find the root of any swing problem more quickly.

The two vital factors in deciding the ball's fate after impact are your swing path and the clubface position at impact – assuming that you strike with the centre of the clubface.

The immediate direction of the ball is caused by the swing path of the club. Its direction for the rest of the shot is determined by the angle of the clubface at impact – open, closed or square – in relation to the ball-to-target line.

HIT STRAIGHT FIRST

The greatest golfers play with different styles, but they all agree on one point: the hardest shot in golf is the straight one.

For this reason, some draw the ball, others prefer to fade – but very few set out to play straight. To rely on consistent straight hitting is risky.

Straight hitting is hard because golf balls are designed to take up spin – it helps them to rise, to stop and to roll. Sidespin is also easy to apply. If you apply the correct amount of sidespin – by changing your alignment – you fade and draw the ball. Too much sidespin causes a slice or a hook.

Set your mind on hitting the ball straight before you start working on draws and fades. Concentrate on achieving an in-to-in path with a square clubface at impact by setting up parallel to the ball-to-target line.

There's a small margin of difference between a deliberate fade and a damaging slice. Only when you know how to take sidespin off the ball can you add it intentionally.

NINE POSSIBLE PATHS

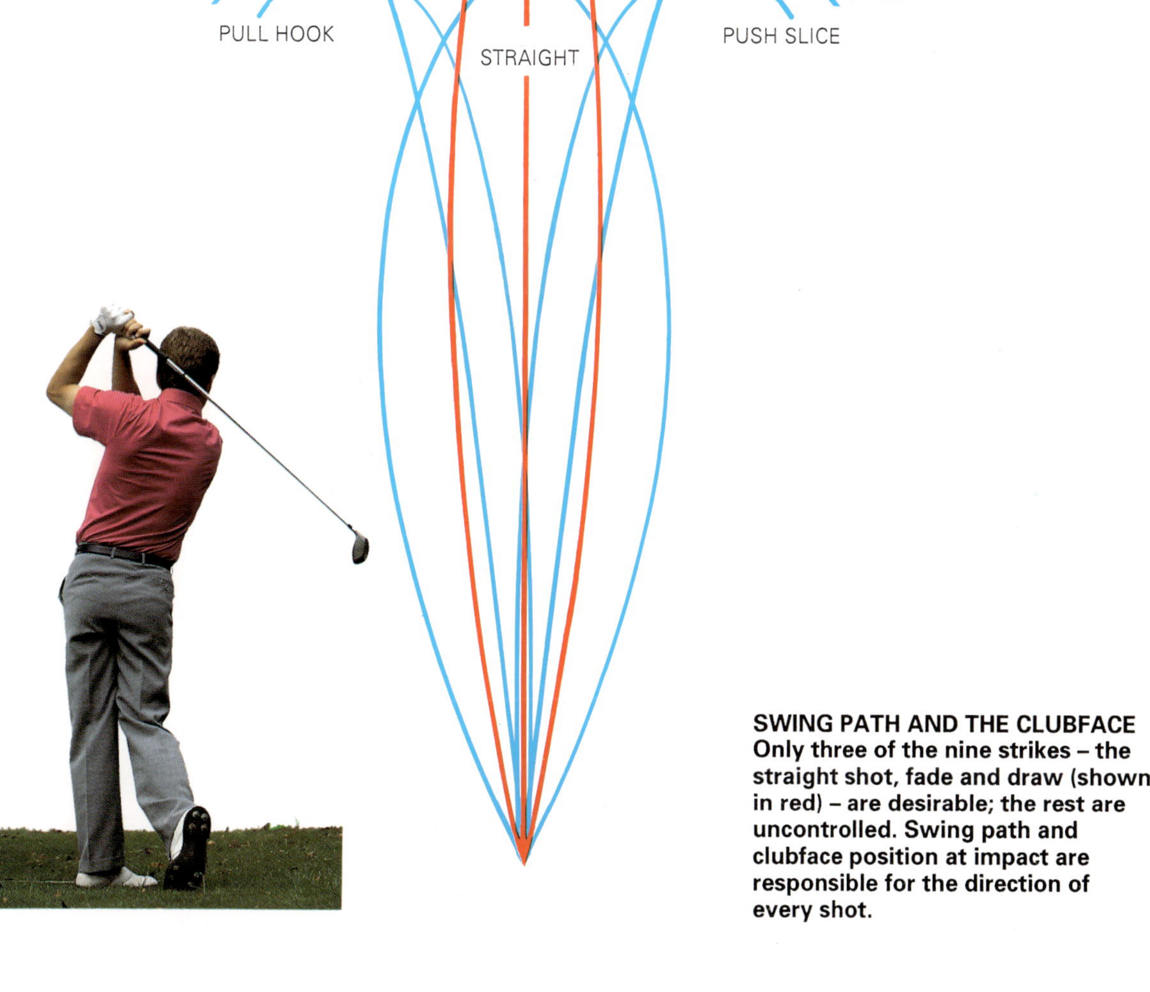

SWING PATH AND THE CLUBFACE
Only three of the nine strikes – the straight shot, fade and draw (shown in red) – are desirable; the rest are uncontrolled. Swing path and clubface position at impact are responsible for the direction of every shot.

IN-TO-OUT SWING PATH

OUT TO IN

PATH OF BALL

BALL-TO-TARGET LINE

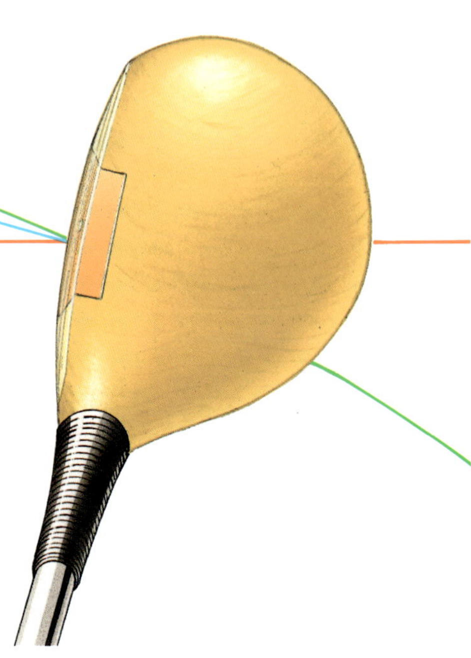

OPEN CLUBFACE

✗ **PUSH**
The club travels from inside the ball-to-target line to outside, and the clubface is open at impact. The ball travels immediately right of target in a straight line.

✗ **SLICE**
The clubhead comes from outside to inside the line, with an open clubface at impact. The ball starts left of target before curving sharply to the right.

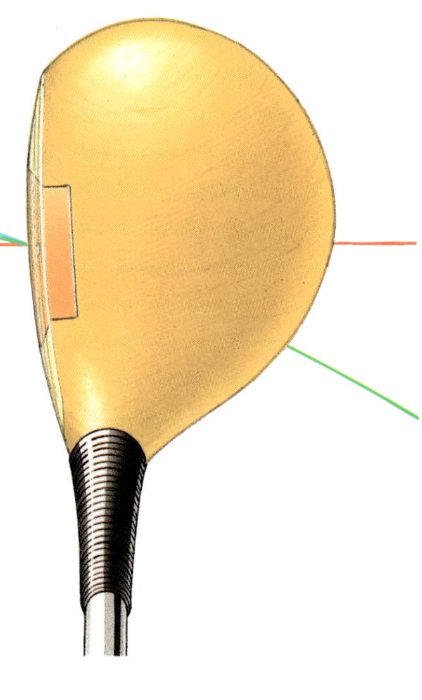

SQUARE CLUBFACE

✓ **DRAW**
Widely regarded as the ideal golf shot – because it combines distance and accuracy – the draw flies slightly right before returning to centre. It happens when the clubface meets the ball square to the ball-to-target line on an in-to-out path.

✓ **FADE**
The fade starts left of target and returns to centre, stopping quickly. The clubface is square at impact, travelling on an out-to-in path.

✗ **HOOK**
The ball starts straight – or slightly right – and curves violently left, because the clubhead has passed along an in-to-out path with the clubface closed at impact.

✗ **PULL**
The out-to-in swing path combines with the closed clubface to send the ball immediately left of target in a straight line.

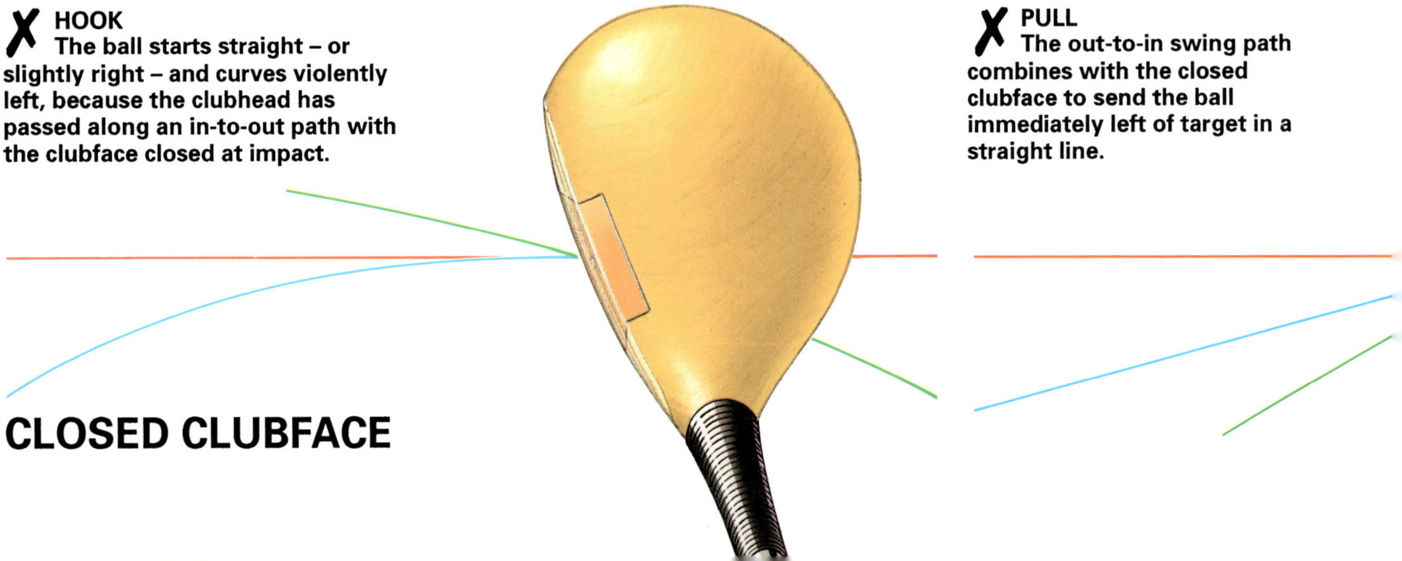

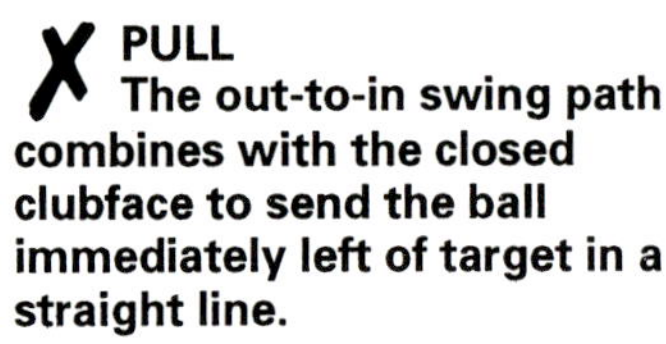

CLOSED CLUBFACE

IN TO IN

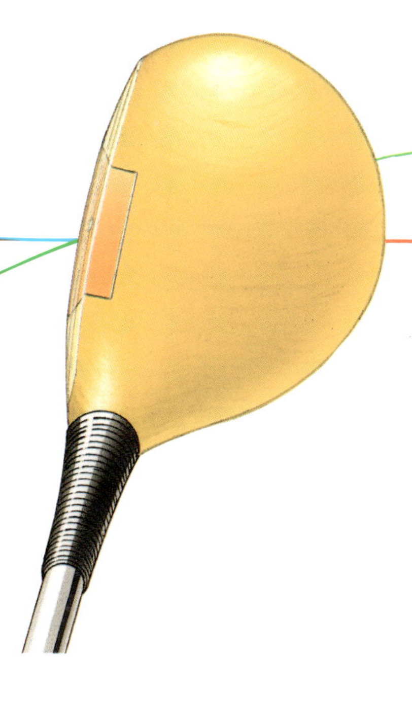

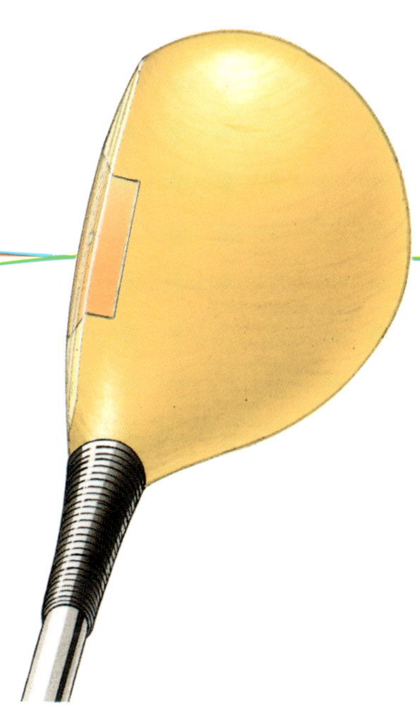

✗ **PUSH SLICE**
When the clubhead passes on an in-to-in path but the clubface is open at impact, the ball starts straight before drifting right of target.

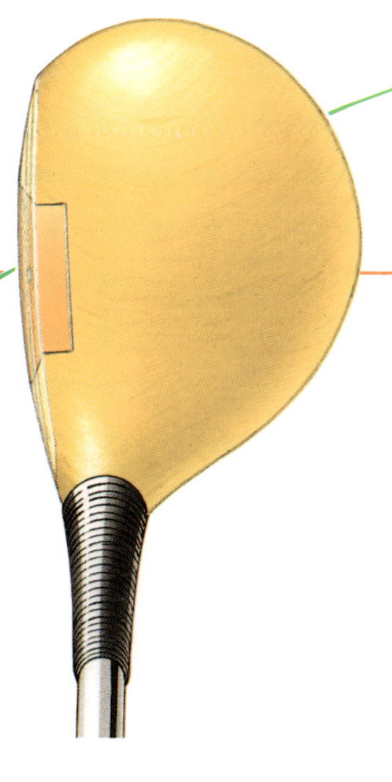

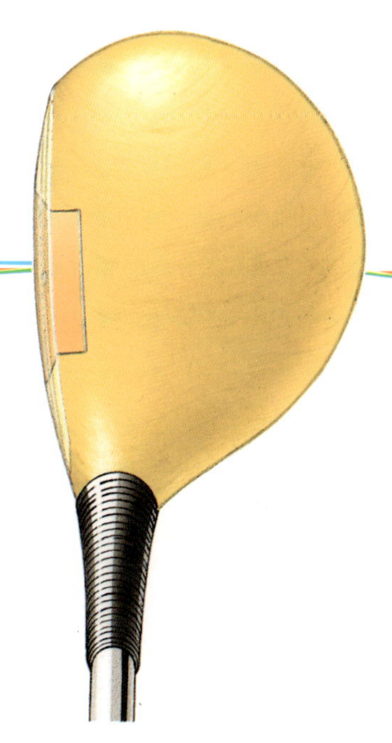

✓ **STRAIGHT SHOT**
You hit the ball straight when the clubhead travels on an in-to-in path and the clubface meets the ball square to the ball-to-target line. The ball carries no sidespin.

✗ **PULL HOOK**
The pull hook – when the ball starts left before curving further left – results if the clubhead travels on an in-to-in path and the clubface is closed at impact.

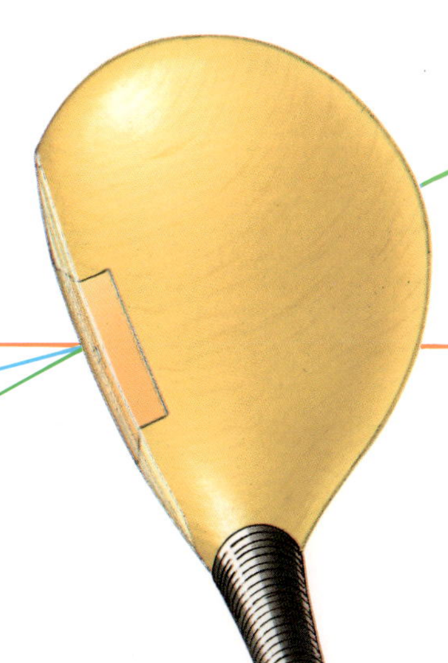

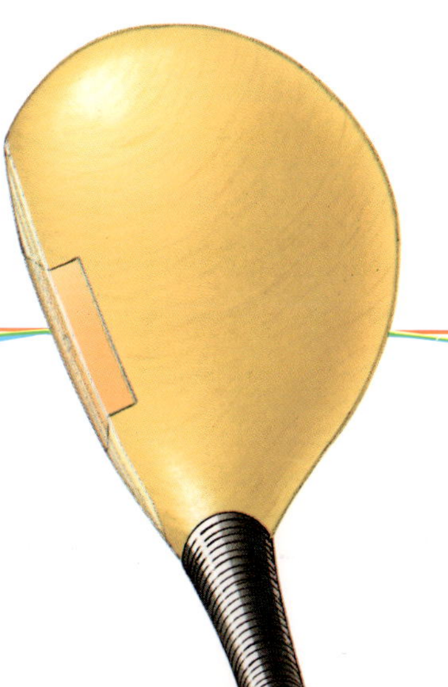

Out to in for sand play

Although you should normally try to achieve an in-to-in swing path with your straight tee, fairway and green shots, accurate greenside bunker play requires an out-to-in swing path.

The ball must normally gain height and stop quickly. Square the blade to the ball-to-target line and open your stance – this provides the extra loft you need. Your stance creates an out-to-in swing path, and the clubface is square at impact.

Keep it square when putting

If you ever struggle for accuracy on the green, always remember to return to the basics – the swing path and position of the clubface should be consistent when you're putting.

All putts are straight – the clubhead should always travel straight along the line of your putt. The clubface must be square to that line at impact, and on shorter putts should be square to it throughout the stroke.

Because of the extra backswing and throughswing needed for long putts, the path of your pendulum swing can be slightly in to in.

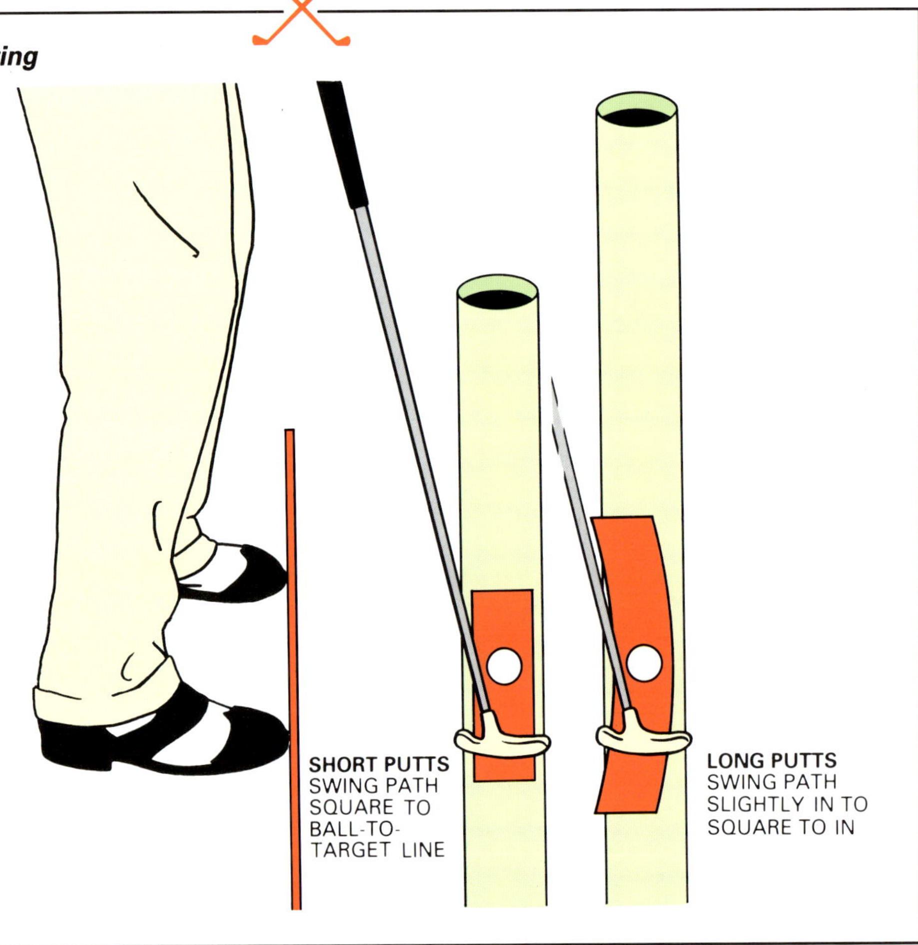

Pre-shot routine

Learn and use a good pre-shot routine to eliminate the faults that can occur before you make any strike. Correct preparation helps you to become more consistent, which in turn lowers your score.

The pre-shot routine is a blend of mental and physical stages that leads you to the right position and frame of mind to hit the ball where you want it to go. You should build a consistent pre-shot routine into your game at an early stage.

The physical aspects of it – where you achieve the correct address position through a series of actions – are usually quite easy to pick up and perform.

The mental aspects – visualizing where you want the ball to go and then deciding on the type of stroke you want to play – can be a bit hard at first. But visualizing does improve with experience and in the long run is the key to lower scores.

The visualizing aspect of your pre-shot routine begins the moment you walk on to the tee, or

ASSESSING THE SHOT

Pre-shot routine starts as you approach the ball or teeing off area and assess the factors involved in making the shot.

DISTANCE
Try to judge the distance between your ball and the target – use a distance chart if there is one.

HAZARDS
Make a mental note of the hazards that lie between your ball and the target, such as the bunker and rough here. Check the position of the pin, and look for any slopes.

WEATHER AND COURSE CONDITIONS
Find out the direction and strength of the wind – if there is any – and assess the condition of both the fairway and green. Are they damp, dry or even bone hard? The state of the ground affects the amount of roll on the ball.

CHOOSE YOUR CLUB
Choose the best club for the stroke from your knowledge of distance, hazards, and the probable effect of weather and course conditions.

SHAPE THE SHOT
Decide on the best line to the target. Is it right, left, or centre? Your choice of club might affect the decision. A high shot can clear hazards, while a low running shot doesn't. Visualize the ball's path.

FEEL THE SWING
Picture and feel the stroke in your mind before making a few practice swings.

PREPARING TO HIT

1 **STAND BEHIND THE BALL**
Stand behind the ball and select your ball-to-target line. Pick a small mark (such as a divot hole, leaf or twig) on that line, no more than a club's length from your ball.

2 **AIM THE CLUBFACE**
Hold the club in your right hand and place the clubhead behind the ball. Aim the clubface square on to the ball-to-mark-to-target line.

when you reach your ball on the fairway.

PREPARING TO VISUALIZE

Visualizing is a two-part process: assessing the difficulty of the shot by studying the hazards and course conditions, and deciding on the type of stroke you want to play so that you can set about shaping the shot in your mind.

If you are new to golf, you may find it difficult to visualize. Although assessment of hazards and course conditions is quite easy to grasp, deciding on the shape of your shot takes a little longer to perfect.

ASSESS THE PROBLEMS

You have to assess a number of factors. You can't just walk up to the ball, take a swipe at it and hope it goes the correct distance and in the right direction.

First, judge the distance your ball is from the target – whether this is a flag on the green or a

3 **TAKE A PARALLEL STANCE**
Align your feet and body parallel to the ball-to-mark-to-target line, and adopt the ideal posture. Take the correct grip with your left hand.

4 **COMPLETE THE GRIP**
Add your right hand to the club to complete the grip. Check that the clubface is still aimed square on to the ball-to-mark-to-target line.

position on the fairway. Make a mental note of the hazards that come into play, such as out-of-bounds posts, ditches, trees, bunkers and streams. Also note exactly where the pin is and any fairway slopes.

Second, assess weather and course conditions as these dictate which club you should use. Check for wind, its direction and strength. Is the fairway or green damp or dry and how is the ball likely to run? Even when playing from familiar tees and fairways, you need to re-assess club selection because of changing conditions.

When you have analysed hazards and conditions, select your club.

SHAPING THE SHOT

Now decide on the type of shot you want to play, and imagine the intended flight path of the ball. To visualize the path of the ball, you must shape the shot. For example, if all the trouble is on the right side of the fairway, it is best to play down the left. If the fairway is narrow, you might want to use an iron, not a wood, from the tee for accuracy.

Visualize the ball travelling through the air, landing on the green or fairway, and rolling towards the target.

The key to shaping your shot is knowing your capabilities. You must know the distance you can hit with each club and understand the flight path of the ball in each shot. The average player hits a wedge shot between 100 and 110yd (90 and 100m), with a 10yd (9m) difference between each successive club.

As your swing develops and your timing improves, your game becomes more consistent and it is easier to judge the distance you achieve with each club. Your swing must be repeatable. Inconsistency creeps in if your tempo varies from shot to shot.

Your tempo has to remain the same before you can develop a feel for distance. Only when you know the level of your own ability can you attempt to shape the shot.

Once you have shaped your shot, 'feel' the swing in your mind before removing the chosen club from your bag. Then take a couple of practice swings.

Learning to visualize your shots takes experience, so don't worry if

Don't be rushed

Never rush your pre-shot routine. Hurrying your preparation leads to a quick, jerky stroke. Stay relaxed and calm at all times. Then you can maintain a smooth rhythm and tempo from the moment you start visualizing your shot, through to pre-shot routine and to making the stroke itself. Be deliberate and remember there is no time limit for playing a shot. If you feel tension creeping into your grip, lift the club off the ground and jiggle it.

5 REMOVE TENSION
Lift the club off the ground and waggle it in your hands. Move your feet at the same time to release tension. Check your aim by looking at the target.

6 FINAL ADDRESS POSITION
The pre-shot routine is now complete and you're in a position to play the shot. Careful preparation is the key to a correct swing and successful shot.

on the first few occasions it is very much a case of trial and error.

PREPARING TO HIT

Having selected your club and decided on the type of shot you want to play, you now have to adopt the correct address position by following a number of stages.

This routine builds up the correct grip, posture and alignment and puts you in a relaxed and confident frame of mind. It gives you the best possible chance of making a good stroke. As with the visualizing stages of the pre-shot routine, you must go through these physical stages every time you play a shot, whether on tee or fairway.

BALL-TO-TARGET LINE

Stand behind the ball and select your intended ball-to-target line. Choose a small mark, such as a twig, leaf or divot hole, about a club's length in front of the ball and on that same ball-to-target line.

Hold the club in your right hand, and place the sole of the clubhead behind the ball, aiming the clubface square on to the mark. Then stand parallel to the ball-to-marker line and adopt the correct posture. Your knees, hips and shoulders must also be parallel to this line. Add the correct grip, before checking that the clubface is still aimed properly.

Rid yourself of any tension by lifting the club off the ground and waggling it in your hands. Move your feet up and down in sympathy. This relaxes your body and muscles, and allows you to swing freely and correctly. Tension creeps in at address when the body becomes rigid. You have to remove it before you make any stroke.

A consistent pre-shot routine is as important as the swing itself.

How much wind?
To detect the amount of wind, throw a few blades of grass into the air above your head and see where and how fast they are blown. You may need to repeat this action to confirm wind strength and direction. Club selection varies considerably in windy conditions.

Imagine the ball's path
Try to imagine the ball's flight, where you expect it to land and how it might run. This golfer's ball is 160yd (146m) from the flag, there are no hazards, but there is a right-to-left slope. There is no wind and the surface of the fairway is hard and dry.

He chooses a 7 iron for the shot, as he intends to land the ball about 20yd (18m) from the green. Because the slope is from right to left, he aims his shot about 15yd (14m) right of the pin. The slope will then carry his ball towards the flag. He completes his final practice swing and is now ready to make the stroke.

Swing Triggers

Too many amateurs are scared of starting their swing for fear of making poor moves and hitting a bad shot. Much of this fear stems from too stiff and static an address that's full of tension.

Starting the swing from a totally motionless position makes it hard to take the club away smoothly and find good rhythm. Standing too still can lead you to freeze over the ball. There should always be some part of your body moving slightly to avoid freezing – even if it's just a tiny shift of weight from foot to foot. This relieves tension.

HABIT FORMING

To help start the swing in a confident and repeatable fashion every time, you can develop a habit of moving the same part of your body just before you take the club away. If this trigger is harnessed to a good takeaway your whole swing becomes more consistent. It's encouraging to know that when you make this trigger move your backswing should start properly.

Many of the world's top players have some little manoeuvre that starts their swing, but there is no hard and fast rule of what it should be – it's personal taste. It can be with your hands, legs or head, and may be a tiny or quite noticeable movement. But it must be natural.

Jack Nicklaus gives the club a quick squeeze, while others push their hands forward just before they start. Both Gary Player and

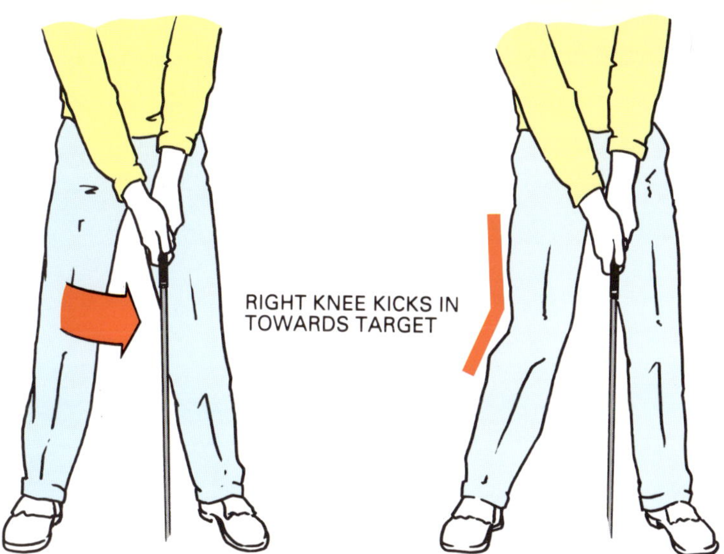

KNEE KICK
Take note of Australian Rodger Davis' swing, particularly the deliberate pushing of his right knee towards the target just before he starts his stroke. At an easy pace his knee moves about 2in (5cm), giving him the stimulus to start his swing. His right leg is then set and acts as a brace, around which he can turn fully into a powerful backswing position.

Rodger Davis kick the right knee in towards the left but in different ways. Player's knee action is fast and looks almost involuntary, while Davis' is slower and even appears calculated. It shows that there's no proper or correct way of performing it – both players do what works for them.

Nick Faldo flexes his knees immediately before his takeaway, triggering the most consistent swing in golf. Because his swing is based on such a solid stance the movement is slight.

But a word of caution. Whatever you try, be sure not to become too reliant on it. Having a helping hand to start your swing with rhythm doesn't mean you can neglect your full swing. Go on working on perfecting your swing, using a starting trigger as an effective grooving aid.

pro tip

PUSH HANDS FORWARD SLIGHTLY JUST BEFORE STROKE

Forward press

The forward press technique can be used as a swing starter with all clubs from tee to green, and also with the putter. Many golfers find it difficult to take the putter back with assurance. If you suffer from a jittery takeaway try the forward press – it helps relieve tension.

Just before you start the stroke push your hands towards the target a fraction, making sure the blade stays square. This gives you the momentum to make a smooth stroke.

FALDO'S FLEX

Since Nick Faldo has been working with David Leadbetter, his swing has changed dramatically. Nick's willowy action has been transformed into a solid, compact swing. He now starts his stroke with a small flex of the knees. This creates the momentum to move easily and smoothly into his backswing with a free leg action and the club on perfect plane.

McNulty's move

Zimbabwe's Mark McNulty is one of the few top golfers who activates the swing with a move of his head. After setting up he makes a slow deliberate turn of his head to the right, and then starts his swing.

This not only gives McNulty the impetus to begin his swing but also provides a pivot around which he can turn fully and still keep a steady head throughout the stroke.

One of the most consistent golfers in the world, Mark also uses the forward press when putting. Both the head move and his press have helped him develop an excellent swing and putting touch.

Using woods

You use the woods for maximum distance both on the tee and the fairway. Although woods are usually harder to control than irons, especially when you are new to the game, you should learn how to use them as soon as possible. Using woods to hit the ball long distances is an ability you must learn at an early stage to lower your scores.

A well-struck wood shot sets you up in the best possible way for the remainder of the hole.

The most commonly used woods are the 1, 3 and 5. They are designed to increase your distance and power without any extra effort.

While the size and shape of the clubhead provides the most obvious visual difference between woods and irons, it is the length of their shafts that helps you achieve the extra distance.

Shape, material and length combine with your technique to extract power from the club.

MORE POWER

When you swing a wood, the longer shaft gives a wider arc and this means that the clubhead has a greater distance to travel. If you swing a wood with the same rhythm and tempo as an iron, the clubhead travels around the arc in the same time, but it has to cover much more distance and this raises its speed. It is this increase in clubhead speed that provides you with the additional power to hit the ball longer dis-

WOOD AND IRON SWINGPLANES

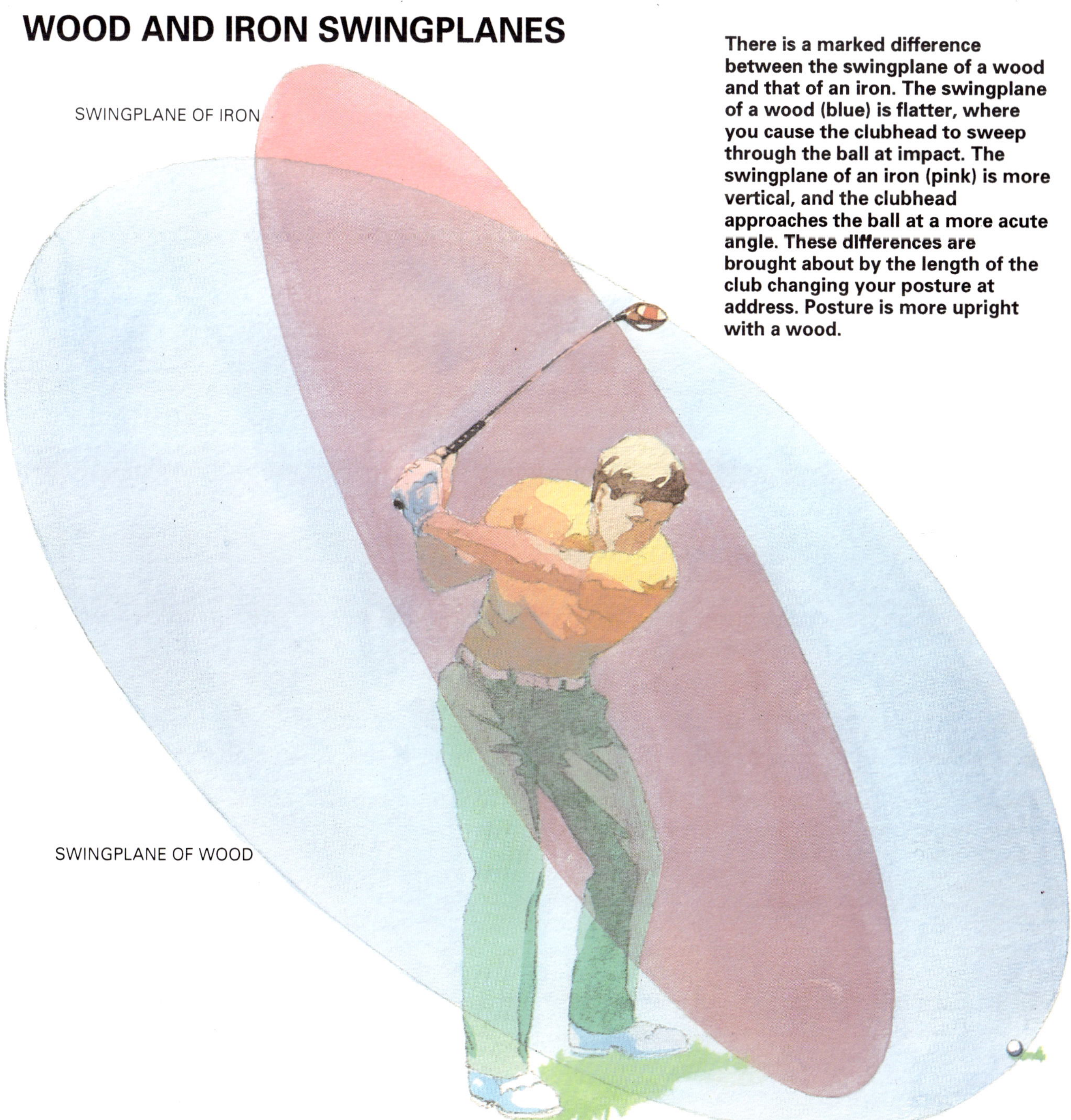

There is a marked difference between the swingplane of a wood and that of an iron. The swingplane of a wood (blue) is flatter, where you cause the clubhead to sweep through the ball at impact. The swingplane of an iron (pink) is more vertical, and the clubhead approaches the ball at a more acute angle. These differences are brought about by the length of the club changing your posture at address. Posture is more upright with a wood.

SWINGING WITH WOODS

1 ADDRESS & TAKEAWAY
At address the ball is opposite the inside of your left heel. Take the club away slowly keeping the clubhead low to the ground.

2 ROTATE TO THE RIGHT
Allow your upper body to rotate freely as your left arm swings the club back. By the two-thirds point in your backswing your weight has transferred from a central position at address to the inside of your right foot.

tances. You do not have to speed up your swing and tempo to make the clubhead go faster. Your tempo should be the same for every 'full' shot from driving to pitching.

While the longer shaft of the wood should not affect your timing, it does lead to changes in your address including stance, posture and ball position. It also affects your swingplane.

ADDRESS AND SWINGPLANE

With a wood, you stand further away from the ball than you would with an iron because the shaft is longer. Your stance is wider so that you can maintain your balance. Your posture changes so that you address the ball with your back more upright and you position the ball opposite the inside of your left heel.

This upright posture triggers a number of other differences between woods and irons. Your swingplane is flatter, so the clubhead approaches the ball at a shallower angle. You sweep through the ball, which is struck at a later point in your swing. This is why the ball is placed opposite the inside of your left heel.

3 TOP OF THE BACKSWING
At the top of the backswing your shoulders have rotated 90° and your hips 45°. Make sure you complete the backswing before starting the downswing – a slight pause before the downswing helps. At the top of the backswing the shaft should point at the target.

4 STARTING THE DOWNSWING
Rotate your left hip to the left to start the downswing. This pulls your arms and hands into an ideal striking position.

5 FOLLOWTHROUGH
After impact, allow your weight to move across to the outside of your left foot. The left side of your body controls the entire swing – from takeaway to followthrough – while your right side remains passive.

6 THE COMPLETED POSITION
Allow the momentum of your club to pull your right shoulder and your head to face the target. Your whole body should also face the target. At the finish you should be balanced with most of your weight on your left foot.

Pick your wood

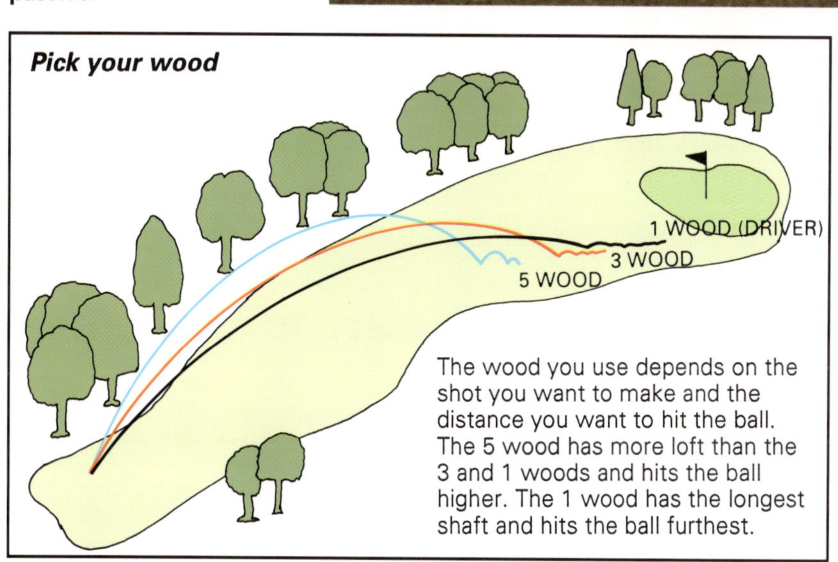

The wood you use depends on the shot you want to make and the distance you want to hit the ball. The 5 wood has more loft than the 3 and 1 woods and hits the ball higher. The 1 wood has the longest shaft and hits the ball furthest.

BALL POSITION AT ADDRESS

FORWARD IN THE STANCE
With a wood, place the ball opposite the inside of your left heel and stand with your feet about as far apart as a normal walking pace is long. With a medium iron the ball is near the middle of your stance.

DISTANCE FROM FEET
Stand further away from the ball when you use a wood than you do with an iron. You have to do this because the shaft of a wood is longer.

THE BACKSWING

Once you have understood the changes to your stance, posture, ball position and swingplane, the basic technique for using woods is similar to using irons. Your tempo remains the same, as do your grip, aim and alignment procedures.

From address, take the club away slowly, keeping the clubhead close to the ground for the first 6-9in (15-23cm). Your left shoulder is pulled across and your weight transfers from an even distribution at address to the inside of your right foot by the completion of the backswing.

PAUSE AT THE TOP

When you reach the top of your backswing, allow for a slight pause before starting the downswing. This pause helps create rhythm and improves timing by separating the backswing from the downswing. Many golfers believe that the backswing and downswing are one continuous movement. This is wrong, and to treat them as one movement only leads to a rushed swing and a poor strike.

THE DOWNSWING

Begin the downswing by smoothly rotating your left hip to the left. This pulls your hands, arms and the clubhead down to the halfway position where your arms and hands swing the clubhead through the ball. The momentum of the clubhead pulls your right shoulder under your chin. Your head rotates to face the target and your weight moves across to your left foot.

TEEING UP THE BALL

When playing a wood shot from a tee peg you have to place the peg at the correct height. The height varies from club to club, but the general rule is that the centre of the ball should be level with the top of the clubface when the club is resting on the ground and the ball is on the tee.

Clubfaces on woods vary in depth, although within any one set, the lower the number of the wood then the deeper its clubface and bigger its clubhead. The 1 wood has the deepest clubface of all woods. The tee peg for a 1 wood should be higher than for a 3 wood, which in turn is higher than for a 5-wood. A ball teed at the correct height is easy to sweep off the top of the tee peg.

If you don't tee your ball at the correct height you lose both distance and accuracy or even mis-hit the shot.

TEEING HEIGHTS

When teeing up, half the ball should be above the top of the clubface at address. So, the deeper the clubface, the higher the tee peg should be set in the ground. Because the 1 wood has a deeper clubface than both the 3 and 5 wood, its tee peg should be higher. The 5 wood has a shallower clubface so the ball is teed lower.

If you tee-up too high you might hit the ball with the top of the clubhead and send it into the sky. If you tee up too low you might hit the top of the ball and send it a short distance along the ground.

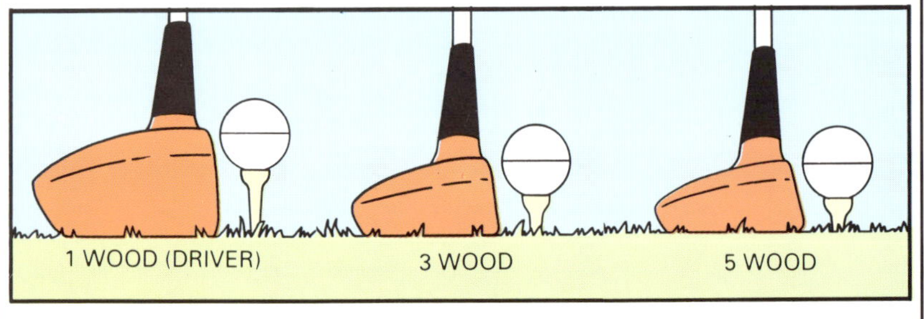

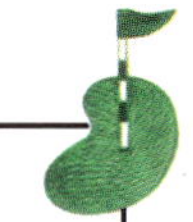

Practise your driving

It's vital to build a repeatable and consistent stroke with your woods. A long hit with your driver gives you the best possible chance of reaching the green of a long hole in few strokes. Practise with your woods until you are confident that you can hit long distances accurately. If you neglect any part of your game, the whole of your game is bound to suffer.

Fairway woods

Fairway woods – used for distance – are commonly referred to as numbers 2, 3, 4 and 5. Most players carry two – usually a 3 and 5.

There are similarities between a fairway wood and a driver (1 wood). Both hit the ball a long way. The clubhead on both is made from wood, metal or graphite. But fairway woods are designed to hit the ball off the ground and are ideal for your second shot on long par 4s and par 5s.

The clubhead on a fairway wood has a low centre of gravity so that most of its weight hits below the middle of the ball, which helps to propel it upwards.

This is not the case with a driver,

MAXIMUM FAIRWAY DISTANCE
If you need top distance from the fairway take a wood. It is easier to use than a long iron because of its bigger clubface loft and rounded clubhead – which sweeps through impact more smoothly than an iron.

SWINGING A FAIRWAY WOOD

1 ADDRESS POSITION
At address the ball is opposite the inside of your left heel and your posture is more upright than normal.

2 MID BACKSWING
Rotate your upper body to the right, keeping the clubhead close to the ground for the first 6-9in (15-22cm). Your left arm remains straight for the takeaway.

3 TOP OF BACKSWING
At the top of the backswing your upper body has rotated halfway – about 90° – and your lower body about 45°. The club's shaft points at the target.

pro tip

Clearing a hazard close to the pin

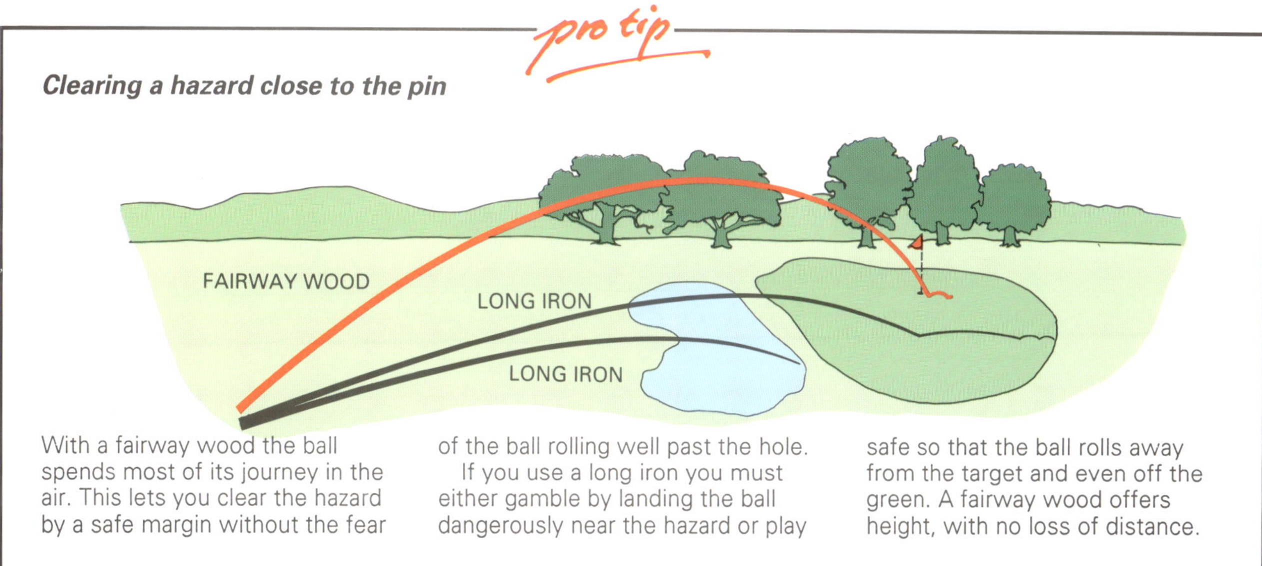

With a fairway wood the ball spends most of its journey in the air. This lets you clear the hazard by a safe margin without the fear of the ball rolling well past the hole.

If you use a long iron you must either gamble by landing the ball dangerously near the hazard or play safe so that the ball rolls away from the target and even off the green. A fairway wood offers height, with no loss of distance.

4 THE DOWNSWING On the downswing your body starts to uncoil, led by your left hip which rotates to the left. The downswing must be smooth and unhurried.

5 THROUGH IMPACT The clubhead is swept through the ball by power generated on the downswing. Don't let your head lift up too early on the followthrough.

6 FINAL POSITION At the end of the swing your upper body and head face the target, with most of your weight on your left foot. Your finish should be balanced and relaxed.

which has a clubhead with a high centre of gravity and is designed to play a raised ball from a tee peg. Don't take a driver from the fairway because most of its weight is above the centre of the ball.

EASY TO USE

The 3 and 5 woods hit the ball about the same distance as the 1 and 2 irons. When faced with a long shot, the high handicap player should choose a wood.

A fairway wood gives much better height than an iron – it has a lower centre of gravity and a bigger clubface loft. The rounded clubhead also sweeps through impact more smoothly than a long iron, especially in the rough.

While long irons give slightly more control when struck perfectly, they are so difficult to use that only low handicap golfers and professionals are skilful enough to play with them. An average player achieves a consistently better strike with a fairway wood.

HEIGHT AND LENGTH

A fairway wood is one of the most versatile clubs in your bag, combining height with length. Not only does it hit the ball as far as a long iron, it also hits it higher.

If your path is blocked by a tall obstacle, such as a tree, hedge or wall, a fairway wood often provides quick enough lift for your ball to clear any problems. A long iron is unlikely to give you a successful shot.

PLAYING THE SHOT

Grip the club normally and stand with the ball opposite the inside of your left heel. Aim the clubface square to the target and align your body parallel to the ball-to-target line. Make sure that the sole of the clubhead rests flat on the ground at address.

Because of the long shaft, your posture is more upright than normal. This creates a flat swing plane. Take the club away slowly, keeping a smooth tempo during the entire swing. The clubface sweeps the ball cleanly off the turf without taking a divot.

Remember you don't have to increase the speed of your swing to find extra distance. Power and clubhead speed are created by the long shaft, which in turn produces a wider arc.

The fairway woods

2 WOOD
3 WOOD
4 WOOD
5 WOOD

There are four fairway woods – a 2, 3, 4 and 5 – although most players carry only a 3 and 5 wood. The lower the number, the steeper the clubface and bigger the clubhead. Low numbers give you most distance; high numbers give you most height.

Do's and don'ts

- DO use a 2, 3, 4 or 5 wood for distance from fairway or rough, and for height to clear an obstacle.
- DO check that the ball is opposite the inside of your left heel, and further away from your feet than for an iron to allow for the longer shaft.
- DO keep an even tempo.
- DON'T increase the speed of your swing.
- DON'T use a driver from the fairway.
- DON'T take a gamble – in a tricky lie choose your most lofted wood.

Which wood?

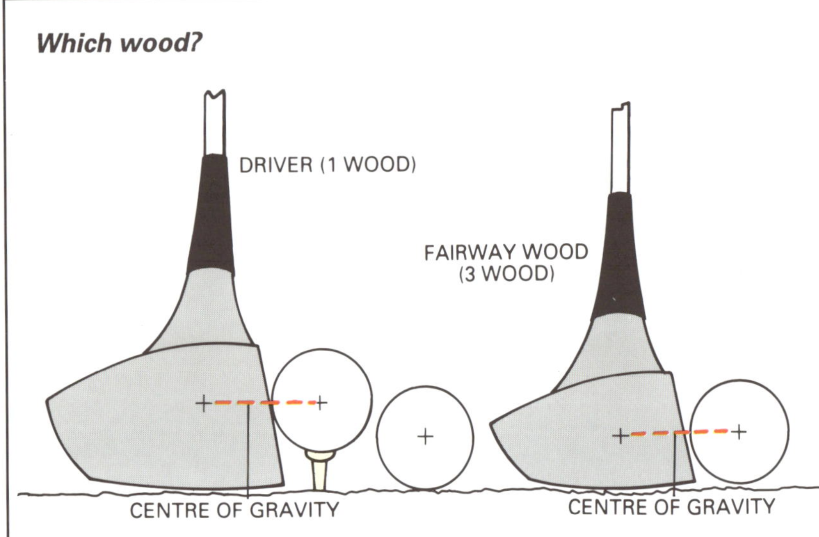

It's difficult to achieve height when the clubhead's centre of gravity is above the middle of the ball at impact. A driver has a high centre of gravity and is designed for striking a ball off a tee peg.

With a fairway wood most of the weight is near the bottom of the clubhead. It strikes below the centre of a ball on the ground, propelling it upwards without sacrificing distance.

Long iron approach

Fear strikes deep into the hearts of far too many golfers as they set up for a long iron to a green. But there's no need to be nervous. Though an approach with a long iron is more difficult than with a short iron, it's only slightly more so.

Negative thoughts affect your technique, so wayward or mis-struck long irons are usually a result of a poor mental state. Expecting a poor shot before you play is bound to hinder the stroke.

Often, negative thinkers take little care over their set-up and aim because they are used to trusting to luck rather than their method.

Most also change their swing. They seem to have an inbuilt mechanism that makes them hit the ball harder, believing that the further you have to hit it, the faster you must swing. This combinations of a sloppy set-up and rapid rhythm can only lead to disaster.

To produce consistently good results, you must unite a positive attitude with sound basics and a smooth, even tempo. Let the club do the work – a long iron is designed to hit the ball further than a short iron so you don't have to force the shot.

SET SQUARE

Take time to aim and set up properly. Set your blade square to the target and then move your body in to position. Make sure you're aligned perfectly parallel to the ball to target line, and the ball is placed correctly just inside your left heel.

For the best chance of returning the blade square at impact a solid set-up and a controlled, rhythmical swing are essential. A square

LONG SUFFERING
There is no need to be afraid to hit a long iron – remember that the difference in technique between playing a 7 iron and a 2 iron is very small. The only changes are the ball position – slightly more forward for a long iron – and a fractionally wider stance. If you realize this – so that your swing stays the same – and think positively, the ball should sear at the flag from long distance.

LONG RANGE ATTACK

1 **CRUCIAL ADDRESS**
A sound set-up is critical for long iron success, as any mistake is accentuated with a straighter faced club. Make sure you align perfectly parallel to the target line and the ball is placed correctly. It's also vital for your blade to be set square to the target. Your posture should be relaxed but not sloppy.

2 **ON LINE TAKEAWAY**
Be sure your takeaway is in one piece – don't just use your arms. At the full extent of the takeaway your shaft should be parallel to your feet and the ground. Taking the club back too far on the inside or the outside has a knock on effect and makes it hard to get the club back on plane for the downswing.

3 **HALFWAY BACK**
A good takeaway position should naturally lead your backswing into the correct plane. Halfway to the top, your shoulder turn should be already quite full. And if you're on perfect plane, the angle of your shaft to the ground should be the same as at address.

4 **POINTING PARALLEL**
Good moves on the backswing mean you can put the club in the correct position at the top of the backswing – pointing parallel to the target line and the ground. There should be no hint of overswing as this leads to getting ahead of the ball at impact.

5 CONTROLLED DOWN
The first move on the downswing is a pull down with the hands but the club should stay on plane even if the path is steeper than on the backswing. Keep the action smooth, rhythmical and controlled.

6 INTO IMPACT
If your backswing is good and the initial stages of the downswing on plane, your club should attack the ball from slightly inside the line, so the blade returns square at impact. Don't thrash at the ball – keep the swing simple and fluid.

7 FREELY THROUGH
Swing through freely, letting your hands release naturally after impact. A tell-tale sign of a correct down and through swing is if the angle of the shaft halfway to the finish position is the same as at address and halfway back.

8 BALANCED FINISH
Provided you have swung with an even tempo and kept the club on plane, your finish position should be balanced with your body facing the target. Your weight should be firmly on your left side.

Top draw

So often a handicap golfer struggles to reach a long distance target – particularly into wind – because they either play the wrong shot or choose the wrong club.

Because a 3 wood flies further than a 1 iron in normal conditions, it shouldn't be an automatic choice when shooting into a wind. The 3 wood can balloon and land short, but you can keep the long iron low and running by playing a draw.

It is possible to hit the draw with a wood, but because of it's design a long iron is easier to manipulate. Aim the blade square and align a fraction to the right. Swing normally – don't force the shot – let the combination of the closed stance and square blade do the work.

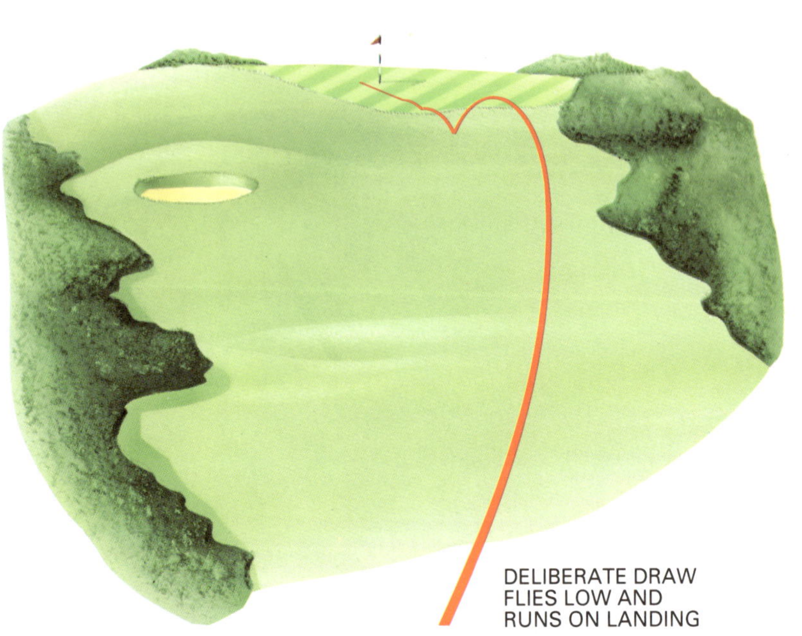

DELIBERATE DRAW FLIES LOW AND RUNS ON LANDING

clubface is critical to long iron success, as sidespin is accentuated by a straight faced club. The ball veers off line more than when you hit a short iron, because lofted clubs produce more backspin than sidespin.

LONG MANOEUVRES

Often you can gain an advantage if you shape a shot to a green – perhaps to land a ball softly or to avoid trouble. So the way a long iron is able to move the ball in the air can work in your favour.

Sometimes it's hard to stop a long iron on a green – especially if the ground is firm. But you can easily play a controlled fade that flies higher and has more backspin than normal by just changing your set-up slightly. With the blade still square, align a fraction to the left and swing as normal along the line of your feet.

It's also easy to draw the ball with a long iron, which is particularly useful when firing into a wind. You can hit a long raking runner that flies low and moves from right to left. The ball can go surprising distances, and is more likely to find the target than a high flying wood.

Too many golfers overlook long irons when practising. But if you're to be totally competent with all aspects of your play, you must work hard on them – never spurn long iron practice.

Faldo's finale

Nick Faldo's confidence and prowess with the long irons have helped him win many championships. But one exacting strike thrilled thousands at Wentworth in 1989

In the 36 hole final of the World Matchplay, Nick reached the last hole and had never been in front. His opponent Ian Woosnam had set the pace and played scintillating golf throughout the final. But Faldo had all but matched him.

The double Open Champion played from the 28th to the 35th in 5 under to claw his way back to all square standing on the last tee.

After a perfectly positioned drive on the 502yd (459m) par 5, Faldo unleashed a 1 iron that drilled straight at the flag. It rolled past the pin and finished about 20ft (6m) behind the hole. After Woosie failed with an eagle putt from over 30ft (9m), Nick rolled his in for an incredible victory.

Faldo showed everyone watching exactly how a long iron to a green should be played. There seemed to be no strain involved at all. With a solid set-up and an even tempo swing, Nick had faith that the club would do what it was designed for.

Play the draw

The draw is a shot which starts to the right of the target and moves left in flight back towards the target. It's a useful shot for playing around a hazard. It also increases the distance of your shot because the ball rolls on landing more than it does for a straight shot or a fade. This makes it an effective shot to play with woods and long irons.

The draw is a feel shot so it's not easy. Persevere with it and it will give great flexibility to your game.

When playing the draw, the first principle to understand is precisely how the ball spins from right to left in the air.

If you have a table tennis bat handy, try spinning a ping pong ball from right to left across a table. You soon realize that you need to brush the bat across the ball from *left* to *right* to achieve the spin you want.

Playing a draw in golf is exactly

THE ADVANTAGES OF A DRAW
The draw shot is a great asset when you want to hit the ball around a hazard or a tree. Also play a draw to increase your distance – the ball rolls further on landing.

Aim and align right

Aim the club right of the target to allow for the draw spin and to help you visualize an in-to-out swing path. Align your body right of the ball-to-target line, by bringing your right foot back slightly.

FEEL THE SHOT

The draw is a feel shot. To improve your feeling for the in-to-out swing path required imagine you're standing in the centre of a clockface. The ball is positioned exactly in the middle and your ball-to-target line stretches from 6 o'clock to 12 o'clock. Now feel as if you're swinging to 7 o'clock on your backswing and to 1 o'clock on your throughswing.

When you hit the draw shot your swing automatically becomes slightly flatter on the backswing. This is because your club is swinging more to the inside. On the throughswing, your left arm is more extended than normal as the club swings outside the ball-to-target line. The ball-to-target line remains the same as usual.

the same. You produce an in-to-out swing path, which takes the clubhead inside the ball-to-target line and then outside it after impact. The clubhead brushes left to right through the ball, like the table tennis bat.

AIM AND ALIGNMENT

Aim the clubface slightly to the right of the ball-to-target line. This helps you to visualize the in-to-out swing path and also allows for the draw spin. Now align your body parallel to the clubface, by bringing your right foot back a little.

Your body should now be aligned just to the right of target. Correct aim and alignment are essential if you are to start the ball to the right.

Because the draw is a feel shot, first try it with a club you're comfortable with – a 6 or 7 iron. As your confidence grows, move on to the more difficult longer clubs.

masterclass

Tom Watson's winning draw

Many of the world's top players use the draw to give them extra control. Tom Watson, who dominated world golf in the late 70s and early 80s, plays a draw as an important part of his game.

Watson has won the US Masters on two occasions, 1977 and 1981. He can thank his draw for these successes, because Augusta is laid out to suit players who have mastered the draw. It's no coincidence that Lee Trevino, the greatest player of the fade, has never triumphed at Augusta.

A well-played draw is a penetrating shot. This makes it a handy shot for windy courses, where you can fight or use a strong wind to your advantage. Watson's record on the windy, links courses of the Open Championship proves the point. He has won five times.

How to fade

When you hit a fade shot, the ball is struck left of the target but travels right during flight. Your most likely use for it is when there is an obstacle such as a large tree between you and your target.

The fade is an advanced, controlled shot – unlike the slice, a poor hit that also moves the ball from left to right during flight.

You achieve the fade by changing your body alignment at address. This alters your swing path – not the swing itself – and puts sidespin on the ball.

The ball flies higher and runs shorter than a normal shot. You may have to take a slightly less lofted club than usual (for instance, a 5 iron instead of a 6 iron).

ALIGN LEFT OF TARGET

Your body should align left of the ball-to-target line, while you keep the clubface aimed square on to it. Slightly open your hips and shoulders by turning them left and swing normally. Your swing follows an out-to-in path: the clubhead travels from right to left across the standard swing path, causing it to brush through the ball and giving it sidespin. There is no need to change your grip.

You must have confidence in your set-up and your swing to achieve a successful fade, so rehearse the shot on the practice range. It is a 'feel' shot – you must be able to see the shot in your mind if you are to play it well.

Once you have developed a consistent routine, you are ready to attempt the shot on the course.

WHAT HAPPENS WHEN YOU FADE

Fade swing path (out to in)
By aligning your body left of the ball-to-target line, in an open position, you automatically shift your swing path. Compared with a normal swing path, the fade produces a path that travels outside the normal line on the backswing and downswing, but moves inside that same line on the throughswing. You alter only your address position to achieve a fade. You do not change your swing to change your swing path.

Clock golf
To help you see your fade swing path in your mind, imagine you are teed up on the centre of a clockface, facing 3 o'clock. When you hit a straight shot, you hit along a ball-to-target line stretching from 6 o'clock to 12 o'clock. When you fade correctly, that ball-to-target line remains the same – but you in fact hit along a line from 5 o'clock to 11 o'clock.

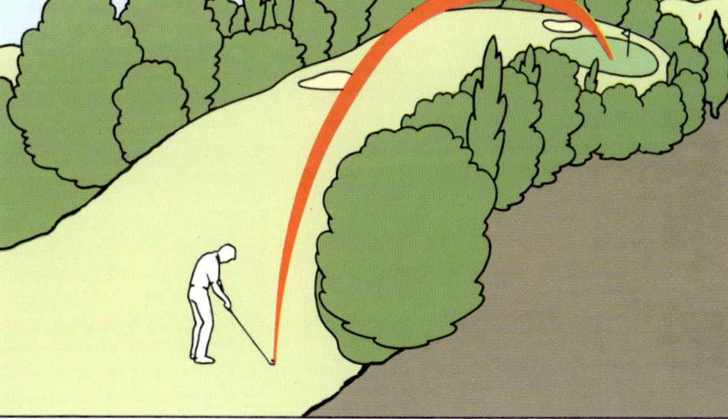

Path of ball
The fade shot is ideal for playing around obstacles such as a row of trees. A faded ball starts out on a line which is left of the intended target. During its flight the spinning ball returns to a more central position by moving right in the air.

CHANGING YOUR SWING PATH

NORMAL SET-UP
In normal set-up, your feet, hips and shoulders are parallel to the imaginary ball-to-target line. During normal takeaway and backswing, the club travels on a straight path inside and parallel to the ball-to-target line. Throughout the swing, the club remains inside this line.

FADE SET-UP
Move your left foot about 6in (15cm) away from the club closest to your feet. This aligns you left of target. Keep the clubface square to the ball-to-target line, even if this imaginary line passes through the obstacle. Although you swing normally, adjustment at address produces an out-to-in swing path, which gives sidespin.

masterclass

Nicklaus' percentage fade

At the 18th tee at Augusta, Nicklaus fades the ball around the right-hand dog-leg, avoiding the bunker on the left. The ball is shown in mid-air, just about to drop.

Nicklaus also uses the fade to reduce his margin for error in a straight shot. Imagine you are 160yd (145m) from the green with a centrally positioned flag and 30ft (9m) either side. If you aim straight at the flag but slice it 20ft (6m) wide, you have a long putt.

Nicklaus' tactic is to aim the shot 10ft (3m) left of the pin and fade the ball. Should he over-fade it by 20ft (6m), he is only 10ft (3m) right of the pin. Should he hit it straight by mistake he is still only 10ft (3m) from the hole, this time on the left. If he hits well he is closer still.

Tackling sloping approaches

Far too many golfers become frustrated and nervous when they have to play a shot from a sloping lie. Negative thoughts take over – even if the target is a short iron away – and trusting to luck becomes the order of the day.

This lack of confidence stems from a hazy knowledge of the techniques needed to pull off an approach from a slope. An understanding of the different set-ups for the various lies is essential to your success.

FLIGHT PLAN

For every shot you face from a slope – it could be an uphill, downhill, sidehill or combination lie – you must also know the shape of flight that's produced.

The flight varies markedly – low and slightly left to right from a downhill lie, or turning right to left when the ball is above your feet. Working out the flight path and setting up to compensate for it are the keys to accurate approaches.

A blend of a subtly changed set-up and technique isn't enough – club selection is critical. Because the flights vary so much, you have to hit a different club from your normal choice for a certain distance. From the same yardage, the club you hit can vary by as much as four depending on the type and severity of slope.

On a steep downslope you can sometimes hit as little as a 9 iron even from a distance of 150yd (137m). But from an upslope you could play a 5 iron for the same length.

Finally, after taking time to plan your shot, play the stroke with authority. Have the conviction that your preparations and a smooth, balanced swing send the ball searing at the flag.

BANK MANAGER
A balanced and stable stance gives you the base to tackle awkward sloping lies. Combined with simple alignment and aim changes and an easy rhythm, your body positioning holds the key to success. With the ball below your feet, it's critical to stay still when firing into a green – a smooth swing with a steady head and body guards against the thin.

BEAT THE SLOPES

DOWNHILL

From a downslope the ball flies low, slightly left to right and runs on landing. The steeper the slope and the longer the distance, the more the ball curves. Because of this flight, choose less club than the yardage suggests and aim left of the target. Put more weight than usual on your left side to move with the slope, and position the ball back in your stance. Both these moves ensure you strike the ball before the ground yet guard against the thin.

UPSLOPE

The ball flies high and slightly right to left and stops quickly from an uphill lie. To compensate for this flight take more club than the yardage suggests and align and aim right of target. Your weight should favour your right side to counter the slope. Position the ball forward in your stance. This set-up helps you to swing along the slope and catch the ball crisply. If the ball's too far back you strike down and can stab the shot.

SIDEHILL – BALL BELOW FEET

As your plane naturally becomes more upright than normal when the ball is below your feet, the shot flies from left to right. You must align and aim left of target to compensate for this fading flight. When the slope is quite severe aim well left of your target – especially as the ball kicks right on landing. Because the ball fades you have to take more club than the yardage suggests. You may find that you have to stoop a little more than usual to reach the ball, but try not to become too crouched. Gripping at the end of the club helps keep your posture as normal as possible.

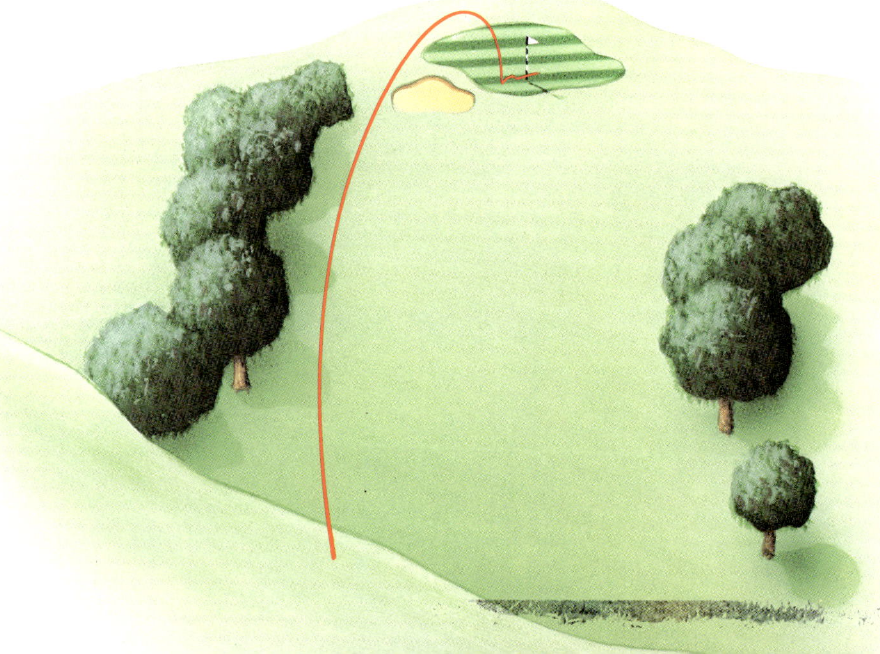

1 LEAN WITH THE SLOPE
Position the ball back in the stance and move your weight on to your left side to help a balanced swing.

2 SHORT TO THE TOP
Keep your backswing short so you don't overbalance. As you swing down resist moving your weight back on to the right side – stay on the left.

3 FOLLOW THE LEVEL
Swing into and through impact keeping the club close to the level of the slope. This ensures against the thin or top and leads you into a slightly crouched throughswing position.

Distance: 140yd (128m)
Grip: normal
Stance: align and aim slightly left of target
Ball position: back in stance
Weight distribution: favour your left side
Swing: short of normal
Swing path: normal
Club: 9 iron

1 FORWARD PLACEMENT
Move the ball forward in your stance and position more weight than usual on your right side to encourage a sweeping strike.

2 STAY BALANCED
Follow the line of the slope into and through impact and resist moving your weight on to the left side too soon. This action helps you to strike the ball crisply and avoid the stab.

3 THROUGH CONTROL
Lead through the stroke with the left hand to lessen the draw on the ball, and move on to your left side for a balanced finish.

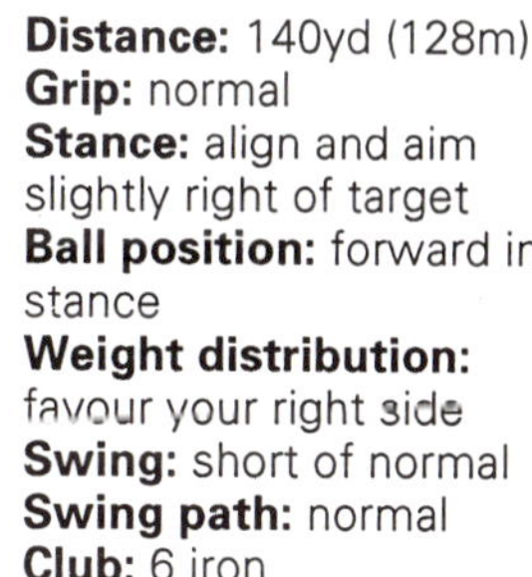

Distance: 140yd (128m)
Grip: normal
Stance: align and aim slightly right of target
Ball position: forward in stance
Weight distribution: favour your right side
Swing: short of normal
Swing path: normal
Club: 6 iron

1 COMFORTABLE ADDRESS
The key to this shot is to have a balanced and stable stance. Grip up the club and bend the knees to help you reach the ball. If it's well below your feet, try spreading your legs.

2 STEADY HEAD
It's very important to keep your head perfectly level and still throughout the backswing, to help stay balanced and improve your chances of swinging down on the correct path.

3 LEVEL ATTACK
Attack the ball with your head steady and the same amount of flex in the knees as at address. This helps you avoid rising up and coming off the shot. If you don't, a thin or top is likely.

Distance: 140yd (128m)
Grip: further up than normal
Stance: align and aim left of target
Ball position: normal
Weight distribution: normal
Swing: full
Swing path: slightly more upright than usual
Club: 6 iron

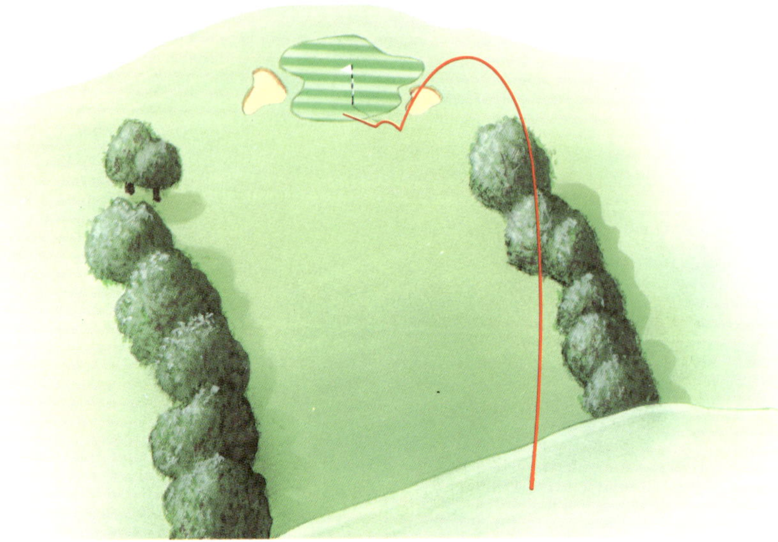

Choke down to help posture and control.

Distance: 140yd (128m)
Grip: choke down
Stance: align and aim right of target
Ball position: normal
Weight distribution: normal
Swing: full
Swing path: slightly flatter than usual
Club: 8 iron

BALL ABOVE FEET

When the ball is above your feet your swing naturally becomes flatter and the shot draws and runs to the left on landing. Because of this flight you have to aim well right of the target – especially off a steep slope – and take less club than the yardage suggests. It's important you judge the shot so that the ball pitches short and right of the target as the drawspin makes it difficult to stop the ball. Choke down the club to help keep your posture and swing as normal as possible.

Hill training

To bolster confidence of sloping approach shots, it's essential to practise them and gain an understanding of the techniques.

There is no real substitute for working on these shots outside on the range or on the course. When you can't find a suitable spot on the practice ground try to seek an alternative way to fine tune your skills.

Increasingly, slope trainers can be found at driving ranges and are a valuable aid. The platform moves hydraulically and you can set it to the slope and angle you prefer. A few sessions on the trainer should give you confidence to play accurate shots out on the course.

Practice becomes even more vital if you're to play on a links – especially if you usually play on a flat course. Links ground is dune ridden and even the fairways undulate severely in places.

Royal Birkdale is a classic example of links golf and almost all the fairways are lined with huge grassy sandhills. If you're not practised and proficient an encounter with a steep slope can lead to more trouble. Notice how US pro Rica Comstock stays perfectly balanced during the shot – something you must practise for slope success.

Control in the wind

PLAYING IN THE WIND
Assess the wind carefully and keep the ball low. If you're using an iron, play the shot with the ball slightly nearer your right foot than normal to deloft the clubface. Maintaining good tempo and rhythm is vital for playing well in the wind.

A shot struck perfectly into the wind should stay straight. But if you're a high handicapper, wind from any direction is likely to blow your ball off-line unless you adjust your technique. To play well in the wind you must understand the effect it has on the ball so you can reduce the damage.

Wind exaggerates spin. You have to strike cleanly because even a small miss-hit can be heavily penalized. For example, if you slice into a left-to-right wind the ball travels even further off-line than in normal conditions.

In windy weather you must prepare thoroughly for each shot

Grip down
Because you need as much control in the wind as possible, grip about 2in (5cm) further down the club than normal. The closer your hands are to the clubhead and the ball, the greater clubface feel you have through impact.

LEFT-TO-RIGHT WIND

Imagine a flag to the left of the real target and aim the clubface at that. Align your body parallel to this substitute ball-to-target line and let the wind blow the ball to the real pin.

RIGHT-TO-LEFT WIND

Aim the clubface and align your body right of the real flag. Because your upper body now faces away from the target this set-up feels strange but have confidence in your aim and don't rush your swing.

INTO THE WIND

Stand parallel to the ball-to-target line with the ball slightly nearer your right heel than normal. Keep your head still through impact, making sure your tempo stays smooth and even.

DOWNWIND

You can make a smooth swing because the wind does the work for you. Beware of the bunkers and other obstacles you can't normally reach – they may be now in range.

or your game will be blown apart. You need to assess the wind's strength and direction, select the most suitable club for the stroke and make changes to your set-up and technique.

ASSESS THE WIND

The simplest way of assessing the strength and direction of the wind is to throw a few blades of grass into the air and notice how they are blown. Check how the flag on the green is flying – if you're in a sheltered position, see if the tops of the trees or bushes are moving and how strongly.

Whatever the direction of the wind, it's often a good idea to play the ball low. If the land is flat and the lie is good, try to run the ball along the ground for as long as possible. The higher you hit the ball the more it's affected by the wind. Wind currents are stronger higher up, and hedges, bushes and trees give shelter at ground level.

If the wind is against you, a low stroke travels further and straighter than a high shot because of the reduced wind resistance nearer the ground.

With a following wind, your ball is certain to fly further than usual. Make sure that hazards such as bunkers you can't normally reach are not now in range – if they are, club down to play safe and keep control.

CROSS WINDS

Make adjustments in your alignment to use the wind to your advantage. For example, with a right-to-left wind, aim your shot right of the target and let the ball move back towards the flag on the currents. How far left or right you aim depends on the wind's strength.

Because most players slice, a left-to-right wind causes extra problems for a right-hander. A left-

PLAY SAFE TO LIMIT SLICE

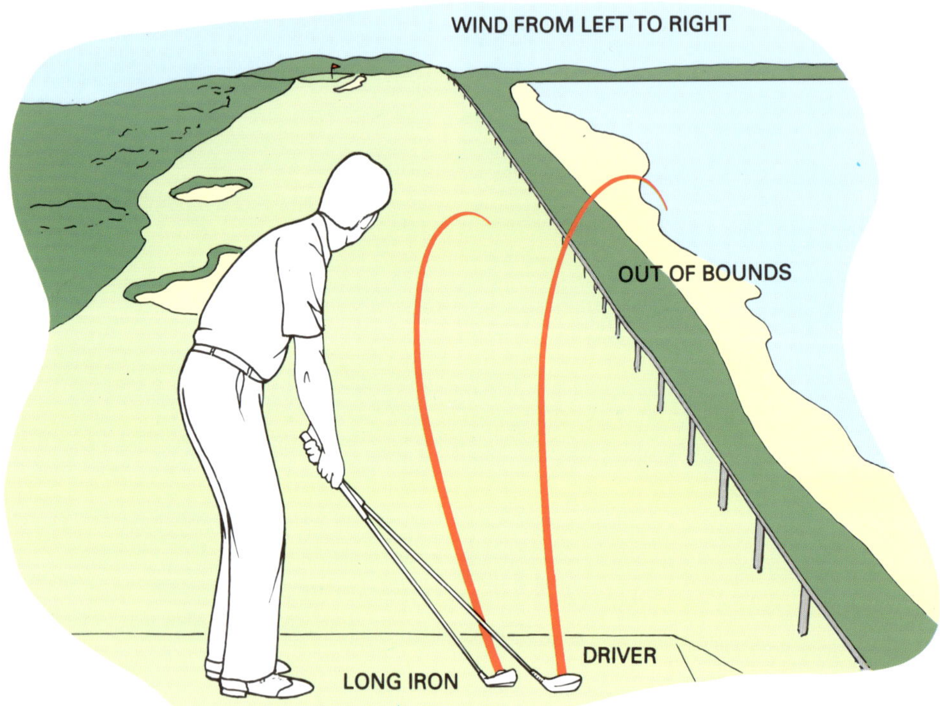

When a strong wind is blowing from the left and there is out of bounds on the right, take an iron off the tee for safety.

A slice is the most common fault in the game and a left-to-right wind exaggerates any clockwise spin on the ball, blowing it further to the right and into trouble.

Because an iron doesn't hit the ball as far as a wood – and is also easier to control – the ball is more likely to stay on course.

Accept that your next shot will be longer than usual – but at least you'll be hitting from the fairway, which gives you much more chance of keeping control.

Stay warm to concentrate
If the wind is very strong a woollen hat helps you concentrate on your game as well as keeping you warm. Pull the hat right over your ears to block out the cold and muffle distractions while you play a stroke.

hander finds wind blowing from the right more difficult.

HITTING THE SHOT

Take care over club selection. Depending on the strength of a wind that's against you, you may have to take up to three clubs more than normal to make up the distance.

Make sure you strike cleanly by reducing the length of your swing to three-quarter or even half – but again be guided by the wind's strength. Don't try to gain extra distance by hitting harder – it severely reduces your chances of playing a good shot.

If you decide to hit the ball low under the wind, you must make changes to your set-up and swing. Grip the club about 2in (5cm) further down the shaft than usual to increase your control and feel of the clubface.

Take up a slightly narrower stance than normal. This automatically reduces the length and power of your swing and helps you to make a clean strike. Stay calm and think positive before you start your swing.

There's no need to change your regular ball position when using a wood. But with an iron place the ball slightly nearer your right foot than usual. This ensures impact is on the downstroke which lessens the loft and keeps the ball low. Keep your head still through impact and concentrate on shifting your weight to your left side as you swing through.

MENTAL APPROACH

Try to keep good tempo and rhythm at all times. Because the game is more difficult in the wind and scores get higher, many golfers increase the speed of their swing in a vain attempt to hit the ball harder and further. This only makes matters worse. You must keep a cool head and accept that your total will be higher than average.

Concentrate on making a smooth swing and have confidence in your game plan. Take your time when selecting your club and don't rush your set-up and stroke.

Using the wind

Get the wind to help you lower your scores – use it rather than fight it. If you are confident in your approach, you can turn both tailwinds and headwinds to your advantage.

A tailwind can help you increase your distance and improve your tempo, and a headwind can help you stop your ball quickly on the green. Playing these positive shots brings greater confidence to your all-round play.

USING A TAILWIND

The key to playing downwind is to concentrate on keeping a smooth rhythm and staying relaxed – the same as in other wind situations. Do not let the wind disturb your timing. Your club and the wind combine to do the work for you, and your ball soars further down the fairway than usual.

When you stand on the tee with the wind behind you, consider the options, as a tailwind has more uses than simply gaining extra distance.

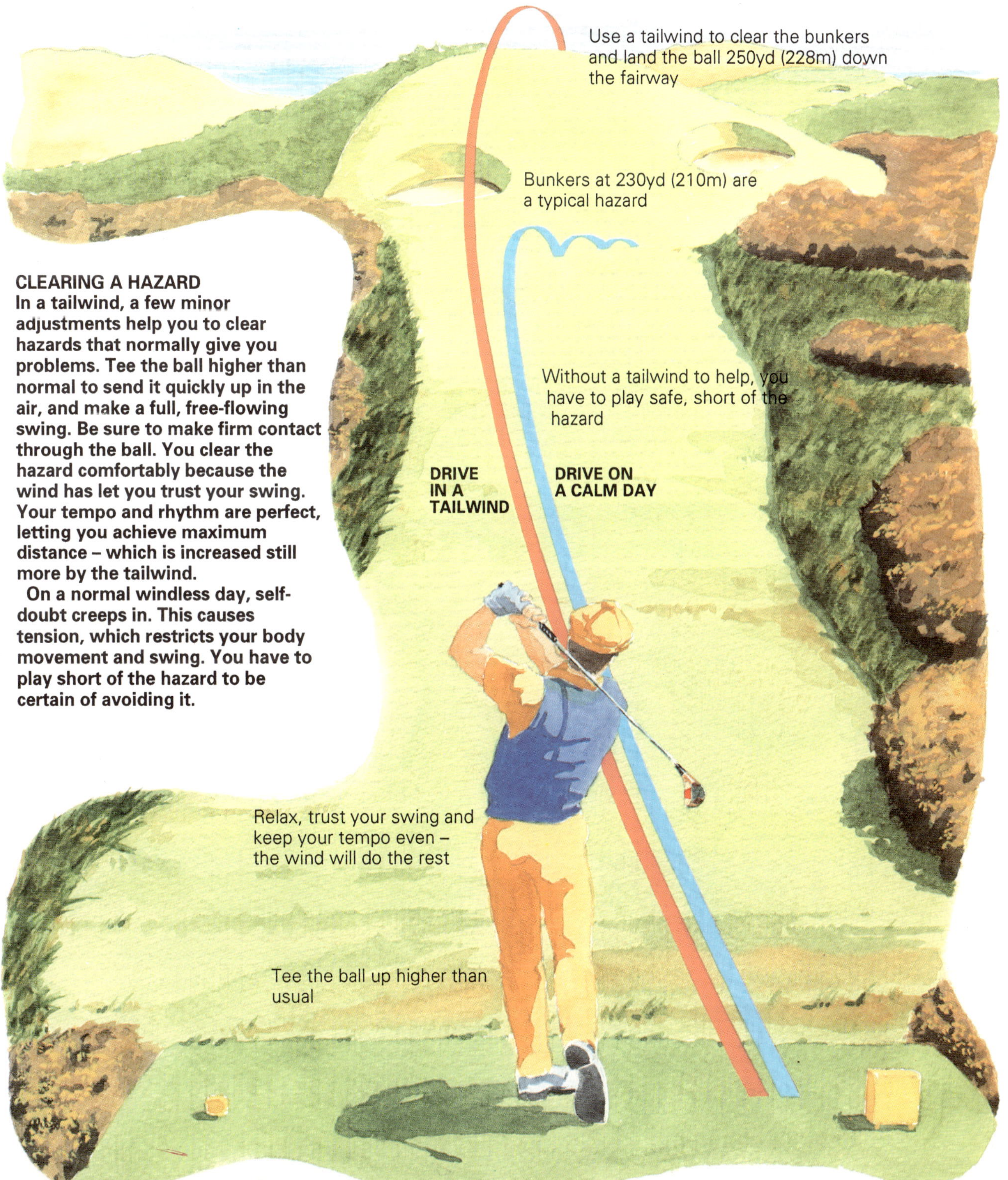

CLEARING A HAZARD
In a tailwind, a few minor adjustments help you to clear hazards that normally give you problems. Tee the ball higher than normal to send it quickly up in the air, and make a full, free-flowing swing. Be sure to make firm contact through the ball. You clear the hazard comfortably because the wind has let you trust your swing. Your tempo and rhythm are perfect, letting you achieve maximum distance – which is increased still more by the tailwind.

On a normal windless day, self-doubt creeps in. This causes tension, which restricts your body movement and swing. You have to play short of the hazard to be certain of avoiding it.

Play safe without losing distance

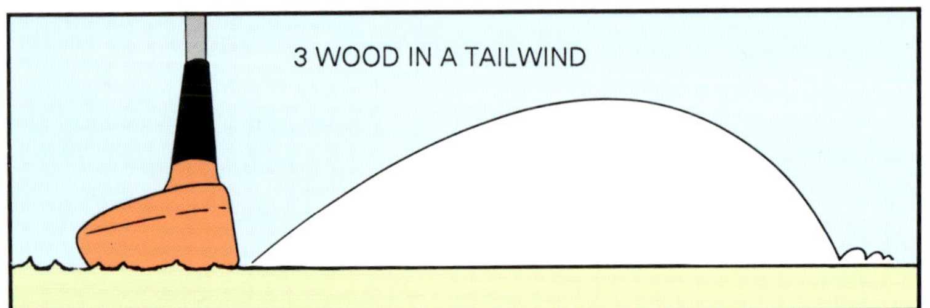

If you are nervous with your driver, a 3 wood hit with no extra effort in a tailwind gives you as much distance as a driver would on a windless day.

Your more composed attitude helps you to swing correctly and keep your rhythm. The greater loft of the 3 wood sends the ball up and it is then taken by the wind.

A huge drive can make your second shot easier, but it can also send your ball into the trees or out of bounds. If you want to play safe, and do not feel confident with your driver, club down to a 3 wood.

Tee the ball higher than normal and set up with your weight slightly favouring (about 60% of your body weight) your right side. Although you make a full swing, your set-up ensures that you hit the ball on the upswing. The ball should rise quickly into the air and be taken by the wind.

The ball travels just as far as it does with a full drive in windless conditions. You also have the advantage of more ball control because the extra loft of the 3 wood makes your shot easier to play, increasing your confidence.

USING A HEADWIND

A headwind is a huge asset in stopping your ball quickly on the green, which lets you fire your ball straight at the pin.

You must be confident and keep your rhythm. Trust your swing to take care of the shot. Don't let the wind in your face disturb your concentration by causing you to swing more quickly than normal.

Whatever the distance is to the green, take more club than normal (for example, a 7 iron when you would normally use a 9 iron) and be sure to make a firm hit. Do not be afraid of overshooting the green with the extra club – the strong headwind causes the ball to hang in the air longer than you expect before it falls softly to the green.

As you strike through the ball, make a positive weight shift to your left side into a balanced followthrough position.

Using headwind to stop your ball

A headwind helps you to stop your ball quickly on the green (red line). Take more club and concentrate on making a firm hit. The wind makes up for the lack of loft in the club and takes your ball into the air. The headwind then 'stops' the ball as it hangs in the air, before dropping to the green. If you play a club with too much loft, your ball may 'balloon', landing short (black line).

Woosnam in the wind

Ian Woosnam is one of the shortest players in the world – and also one of the longest hitters. The stocky Welshman is perfectly comfortable in the wind because he concentrates on weight transfer to give good balance. He gains maximum roll on his long shots by using the wind to favour his natural draw as much as possible.

Choke down for control

The best and safest way to keep the ball under control – especially in a wind – is to grip down the club a little and use a shorter swing than normal.

Choking down naturally shortens the swing arc – you stand closer to the ball so you feel compact which leads to greater confidence. Your wrists also become stiffer, helping to keep the ball lower than usual.

TACKLING THE WIND

Because you hit the ball low, the grip down shot is mainly used for playing in a wind. Most amateur golfers think of choking down only when firing into the wind, but it also has crucial uses in both a cross and downwind.

If you hit your usual club for the distance in a **headwind** the shot towers and falls well short of the target. Take more club – up to four clubs in a strong wind – and grip down. Play the ball from further back in your stance. This produces much backspin and gives you greater control.

With your hands pushed ahead of the ball, make a three-quarter swing. Keep your hands ahead of the ball at impact and finish short. The ball flies low, boring through the wind, but still lands softly as it's held on the air.

When you're on the fairway and face a shot of 3 wood distance into wind it's sometimes best to hit a choked down driver with a shorter swing. The ball stays low and under the wind and reaches the target – a 3 wood climbs too high and falls short.

In a **crosswind** you can use the same iron technique. The ball doesn't drift as far on the wind as a normal stroke – this is most useful if there's trouble around the green. But you do have to aim either slightly to the left or right of the target – depending on the direction of the wind – as the ball still drifts a little.

If you feel confident, try to hold the ball on the crosswind. Use a faint draw into a left to right wind, or a soft fade into a breeze coming in from the right.

Downwind, too, the choke down shot has its advantages. When faced with an awkward length pitch – when you can't hit a full shot that stops – you have to play a pitch and run.

Instead of hitting a wedge you should play a straighter faced club – perhaps an 8 iron. Grip down and use a firm wristed, half shot action. The ball flies low and pitches well short of the target but runs on landing.

It's surprising how much control and finesse you can apply when you play this shot. The type of action is also very useful for playing

SECURITY SHOT
Learning the skills to play the choke down shot – and knowing you can pull it off with ease – gives you a great feeling of security. You needn't be worried by a left to right wind – even if there's trouble on the right. An easy rhythm punch shot under the wind – with a 7 iron from about 125yd (115m), for example – has a much better chance of going close to the target than a normal high flyer.

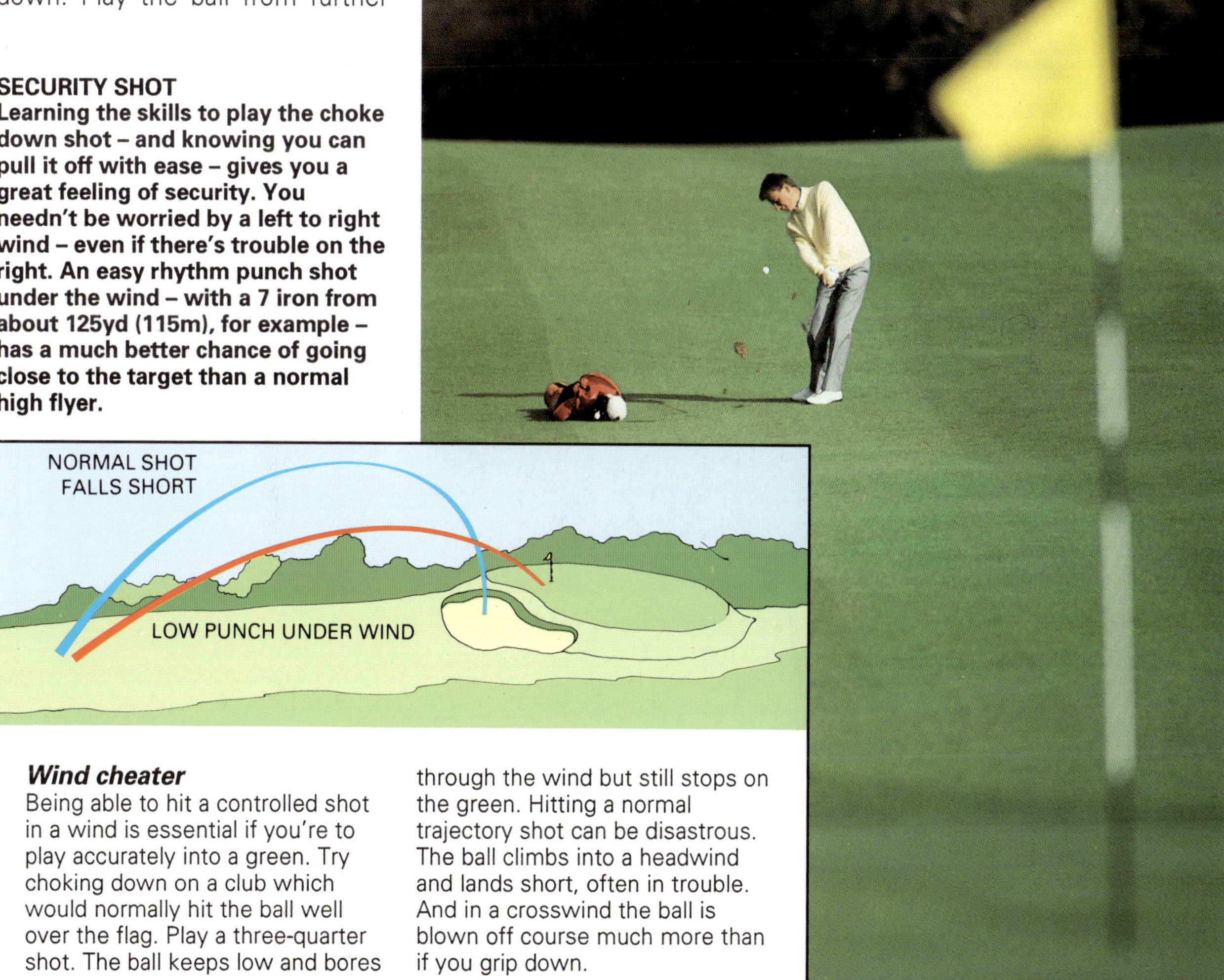

Wind cheater
Being able to hit a controlled shot in a wind is essential if you're to play accurately into a green. Try choking down on a club which would normally hit the ball well over the flag. Play a three-quarter shot. The ball keeps low and bores through the wind but still stops on the green. Hitting a normal trajectory shot can be disastrous. The ball climbs into a headwind and lands short, often in trouble. And in a crosswind the ball is blown off course much more than if you grip down.

CONTROLLED PUNCH

BACK IN THE STANCE/SHORT AT THE TOP
Choose more club than the yardage suggests. Align parallel to the ball-to-target line and position the ball just inside your right heel. Choke down the club and square up the blade. Your hands must be ahead of the ball. With a smooth unhurried action and little wrist break take the club back on a wide path. Move up into a three-quarter length backswing position and turn fully.

HANDS AHEAD AT IMPACT/STOP SHORT
Swing down smoothly and lead the stroke with your left hand. Keep your hands ahead of the clubface through impact to ensure the ball flies low. Concentrate on striking the ball before the ground. Swing through into a short yet balanced finish. This is natural if you extend fully through the ball on a wide arc – the ball climbs too high if you release the hands.

delicate chips round the green – the more you go down the grip the easier it is to control the clubhead and the more your touch is refined.

The choke down shot is a valuable asset when recovering **from trouble**. Often after driving into trees you have to play a low shot **out under branches**. Going down the grip on a long iron lets you keep the ball low and – most importantly – under control.

You can also choke down when the **ball is above your feet**. This helps you adopt a balanced stance and use your normal swing, and reduces the often damaging drawspin.

When playing from a **fairway bunker** it's easier to strike the ball cleanly with the stiffer wristed and shorter swing of a choked down shot. This is essential when you must play safe, and an escape from the trap is the priority. Hitting a normal shot increases the risk of either thinning or fatting the stroke.

masterclass

Tom Watson: links champion

The amiable American, one of the all time greats, has an unsurpassed record at the Open Championship in modern day golf. Watson's control and shotmaking ability on links courses are amazing – and the way he manipulates the ball in the wind is one key to his success.

A links course like Turnberry needs subtle and delicate handling as well as power. Watson has shown over the years that his touch approaching the greens is excellent. The choked down pitch and run from close in is a valuable weapon in Tom's armoury. Brilliant control helped him win five Open titles, three other top ten finishes and the Championship scoring record of 268 at Turnberry in 1977.

Driver off the fairway

The driver off the fairway is an extremely effective weapon when used in the correct way. But it should only be played when you can gain a definite advantage.

The shot produces a low-boring trajectory – ideal when hitting into wind, or for a long running ball to a distant target – but it's also difficult to play perfectly. Only advanced players should attempt this shot – it's not for high handicappers.

WEIGH UP THE RISKS

Use the shot to reach a long par 4 into the wind or to get home in 2 on a par 5. Yet if there is only a small chance of success and trouble looms near the green, it's wiser to play a long iron and then

pro tip

Short for control

When confronted by a shot into wind of roughly 3 wood distance, it's sometimes better to go down the grip on your driver and shorten your backswing.

The three-quarter backswing means the ball doesn't go as far as a normal driver but you have more control over the shot. The ball flies low and runs towards the target, while a full 3 wood shot is more affected by the wind as the ball climbs higher than with a driver.

You may be pleasantly surprised how far the ball goes using this method, especially on a firm, dry fairway.

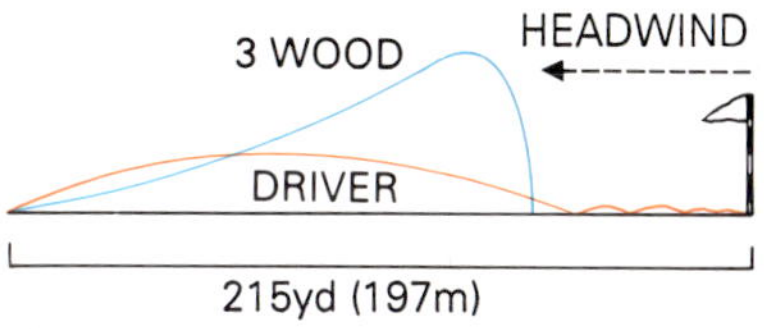

3 WOOD
HEADWIND
DRIVER
215yd (197m)

THOUGHT AND TEMPO
The secret of success is positive and careful thinking, while maintaining good rhythm with a normal swing. With the feet slightly open the ball starts fractionally left and slides back to the right during flight. The ball flies low and can run long distances, perfect for playing into wind.

hit a short iron in.

The lie must be flat or slightly uphill – to act as a launching pad – and the ball must be sitting well, preferably on dry ground. When the ball is lying badly always think hard about hitting the shot even if there is a chance of reaching the green. It's a tricky enough shot to play well without added problems.

Many regard the driver off the fairway as the hardest of all shots, but as long as the lie is good the risks are mainly in the mind. The fact that most good golfers happily hit a 3 wood off the fairway makes their fear all the more unnecessary.

There is only a slight difference in the degree of loft, the centre of gravity and length of shaft from a 3 wood to a driver. The driver is just a bit more difficult to play.

THE TECHNIQUE

The basic technique of hitting the driver from the fairway is the same as from a tee peg. At address, position the ball opposite or slightly in front of your left heel and aim the clubface at the target as normal.

Your feet should be fractionally open – this slightly increases the loft on the driver to help get the ball airborne and to guard against the snap hook. Because you are aligning slightly left and your clubface is square, the ball starts left and moves gently to the right in the flight.

Think positively – imagine you are hitting a 3 wood – and swing as normal. Don't overhit the ball – rhythm is far more important when applying power.

The key difference between hitting off the fairway and from a tee peg is timing. It needs to be spot on to achieve good results from the fairway. It's important to strike the ball at the bottom of your swing arc, and to sweep it off the turf.

TIMING IS VITAL

✔ ***Just right***
You must catch the ball at the same time as you brush the turf to get a good result. Sweep the ball off the fairway with a smooth shallow arc.

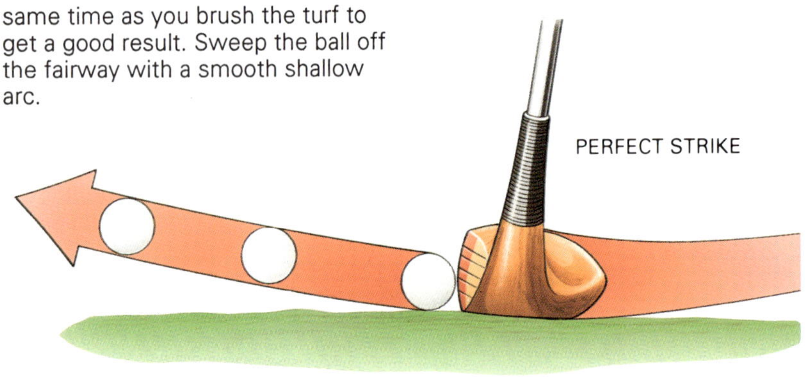

PERFECT STRIKE

✘ ***Too late***
Beware of catching the ball on the upswing – it's easy to thin or top the shot. Make sure you position the ball properly in your stance.

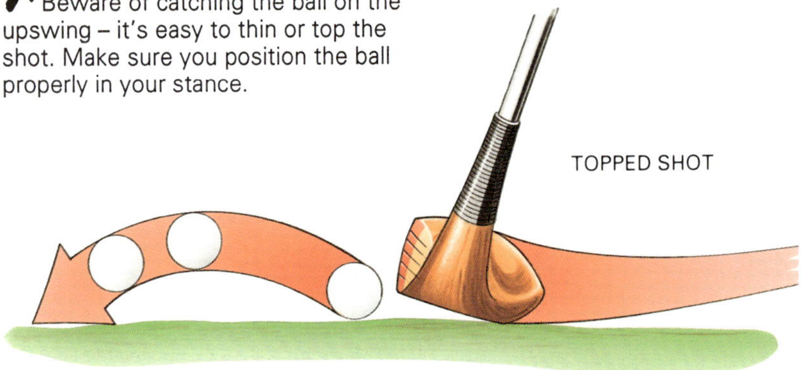

TOPPED SHOT

✘ ***Too early***
Don't swing down on a steep plane as it's difficult to time and control the ball. The tendency is to chop at the ball and hit behind it. The result – a fat shot.

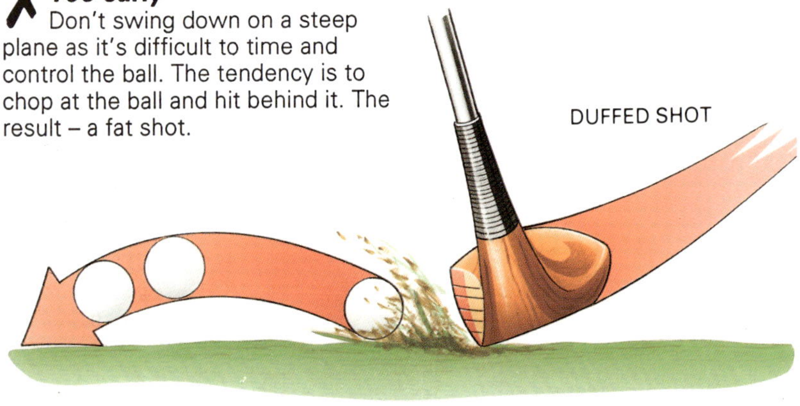

DUFFED SHOT

Ian's killer blow

The driver from the fairway presents Ian Woosnam with few problems because he is such a great timer of the ball. Combined with his power he can reach greens that are out of range for most golfers.

In the 1989 Irish Open at Portmarnock, the little Welshman came to the 514yd par-5 16th neck and neck with Philip Walton. But Woosie struck two drivers one after the other – the second off the fairway – to within 15ft (5m) of the hole to make birdie. He went on to win the title.

Low under the trees

Every golfer – no matter how good – ends up in trouble at some time, often among trees. What most amateurs see as a no hope situation can be turned into a positive result. Instead of chipping out sideways or bunting the ball only slightly further up the fairway, it's possible to play an attacking shot at the green.

Being able to hit the low drilling shot – often bending round trouble as well – is a valuable addition to your list of recovery shots.

The technique for hitting the low shot differs from a normal stroke in both set-up and swing, but the changes are simple. The ball is further back in the stance, the swing shorter and with less wrist break. But the most vital difference is in your club selection.

To keep the ball low you must use a straight faced iron – anything above a 7 iron climbs too high off the clubface and can easily tangle in the branches. If you use a 6 iron for a normal shot of 165yd (150m), you probably need either a 3 or 4 iron to hit a low shot under trees the same distance.

WHICH SHOT?

The club you choose also depends on what shape of shot you have to hit. If you need to play a deliberate hook or draw as well as keeping the ball low, a 6 iron might be enough to reach the green. Your changed set-up naturally takes loft off the clubface and makes it play like a 4 iron. The ball also runs on landing as the draw spin gains extra yardage.

When you cut the ball low and left to right, you must take more club than the yardage suggests. To play this shot you have to open up the blade – increasing its loft – so that a 5 iron becomes like a 7. The 5 then runs the risk of crashing into the branches. You must play a straighter faced club – perhaps even a 1 iron if you need to hit the ball a long way.

PUNCHING POWER
Too many golfers try to hit a full shot out under trees, with disastrous results – the ball crashes into the branches. A simple change in set-up and swing means you play an attacking and controlled long punch shot at the green.

RUNNING LOW

1 ADDRESS
For the low running fade, aim your clubface at the target and align left. Position the ball back in your stance. Grip down the club slightly for better control, and push your hands forward. For the straight shot only your alignment should alter – you must stand parallel to the ball-to-target line. Align right to draw the ball.

2 SHORT CONTROLLED BACKSWING
Your swing should be exactly the same whether you are playing a low fade, draw or straight shot. Take the club away on a shallow path with little wrist break. The backswing should be three-quarter length, and your left arm almost straight. You must still make a full shoulder turn.

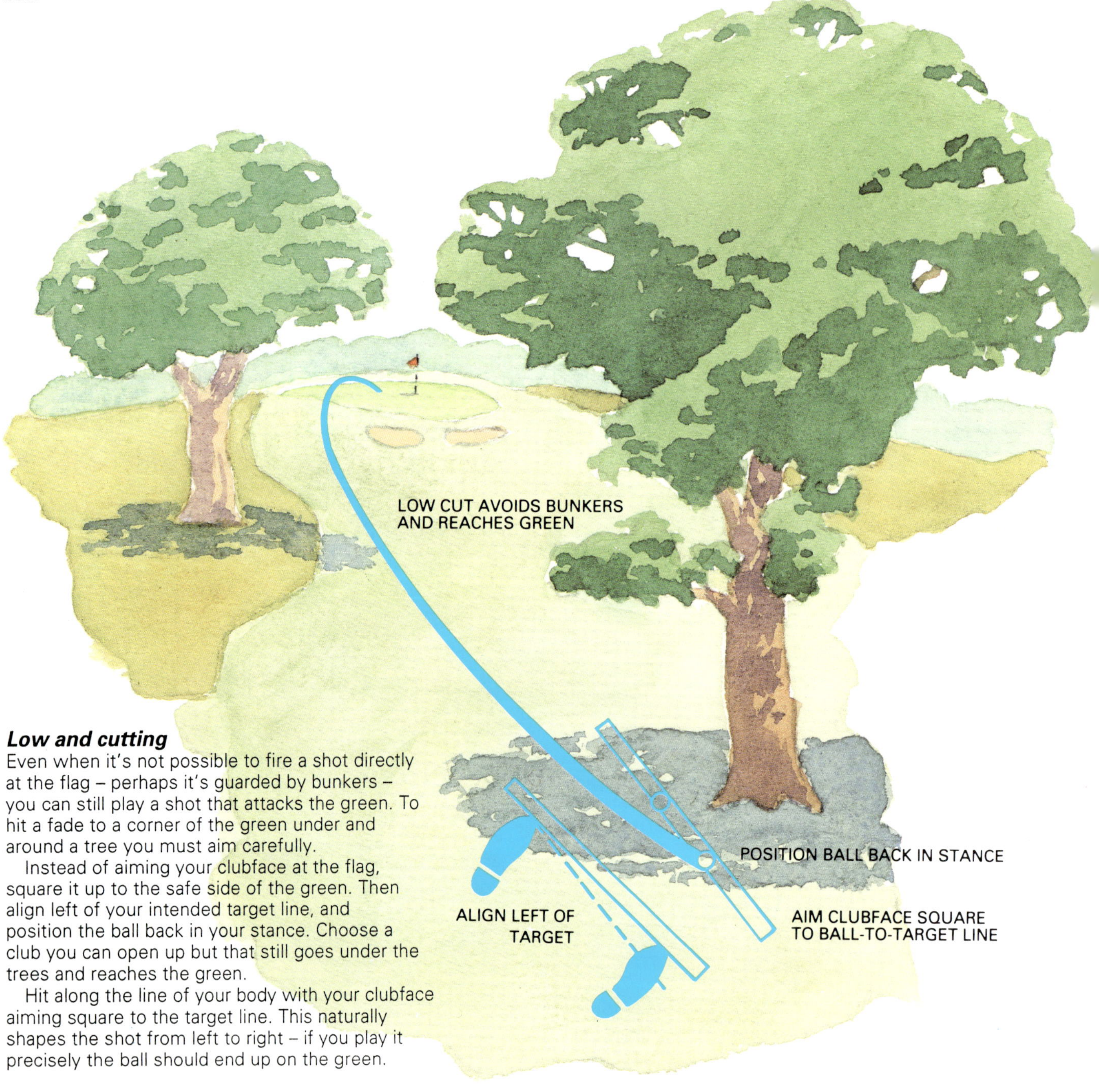

Low and cutting
Even when it's not possible to fire a shot directly at the flag – perhaps it's guarded by bunkers – you can still play a shot that attacks the green. To hit a fade to a corner of the green under and around a tree you must aim carefully.

Instead of aiming your clubface at the flag, square it up to the safe side of the green. Then align left of your intended target line, and position the ball back in your stance. Choose a club you can open up but that still goes under the trees and reaches the green.

Hit along the line of your body with your clubface aiming square to the target line. This naturally shapes the shot from left to right – if you play it precisely the ball should end up on the green.

3 DOWN TO IMPACT
Swing down with a smooth unhurried action – the harder you swing down the higher the ball flies which is dangerous. The combination of a sweeping downswing and the ball position makes for a crisp strike and the ball flies low. The ball starts left of target when you hit the fade.

4 EXTEND THROUGH AND STOP SHORT
Your extension through the ball should be as full as possible and your finish should be short – ensuring the ball drills low. But make sure you don't stop your followthrough too short as this leads to a stabbed shot. The combination of your alignment and aim sends the ball moving from left to right.

LOW DELIBERATE DRAW ATTACKS FLAG

POSITION BALL BACK IN STANCE

ALIGN RIGHT OF TARGET

AIM CLUBFACE SQUARE TO BALL-TO-TARGET LINE

Low and hooking

The normal draw around trees is simple to play, but having to go underneath branches as well needs a more precise execution. Select your club carefully. Look for one that can reach the green and keep low to go under branches but is lofted enough to fly a good distance and not snap hook and dribble along the ground.

Aim your club at the target but align your feet, hips and shoulders to the right – how much depends on how far you have to move the ball from right to left. Position the ball slightly further back than normal to help keep the ball low.

Your swing should be the same as for a straight low shot – the combination of your alignment and aim sends the ball curling right to left.

Use some ingenuity

A good imagination is essential for tackling tricky situations. When faced with a problem shot think through all possible options and try to be creative – there may be five or six strokes you could play. Trees give great scope for invention when there is some room to manoeuvre.

If you have to negotiate a series of trees, it may be possible to keep the ball low under all the branches, but reaching the green could be difficult. The stock option of hitting a low cutting shot round the second tree is on, but flirting with the greenside bunker is a danger.

A more imaginative shot – such as a cut up under the first tree but over the second that lands quite softly – could be the best choice. To play this shot you need a good understanding of technique, but above all trust in your own ability.

Confidence and conviction come from experimenting with various shots. The practice ground is the perfect arena for developing your imagination, but never be afraid to attempt the unusual at any time. Playing the creative shot bolsters your golf and adds to your enjoyment.

THOUGHTFUL ATTACK

One of the keys to playing this stroke well is good visualization.

Combine your thoughts on the shape of shot and clubbing with a keen awareness of the weather and state of the ground – bearing in mind that a low shot always runs on landing whatever the conditions. A low draw should usually run more than a fade – the ball has topspin on it as well as sidespin.

Your lie and other hazards between you and the green also affect your choice of shot.

Even if there are bunkers in front of the green and the flag is guarded by sand, you may be able to hit an attacking shot. There may be a way of avoiding the traps yet still reaching a corner of the green with deadly accurate aim.

But don't be over ambitious. Unless you have a realistic chance it's probably best to lay up short of the trouble and hope to pitch and putt.

King James conquers the Dukes

The Dukes Course at Woburn – home of the Dunhill British Masters – is completely treelined, which causes many golfers severe problems. But in 1990 England's Mark James negotiated the woods brilliantly to win with an 18 under par total.

His feat wasn't without a scare. At the 16th on the last day – only 2 strokes ahead of his nearest rival – his drive finished close to the large pine at the corner of the dog-leg, blocking him out from the green.

Using superb technique and imagination he created a low drawing 5 iron under and round the tree on to the green. He salvaged his par and held on over the final holes to beat David Feherty.

Positive rough play

Taking the safe option of playing a short iron back on to the fairway from rough, rather than going for the green, is usually wise. But with their sound technique most advanced players can usually play in a positive way even from thick rough. It sometimes pays to be brave so long as you're not over ambitious.

You must balance a positive attitude with careful thought. Learn when you can go for the green, and when you must play safe. If you desperately need birdies or have to reach the green for a chance to save the hole in matchplay, it's a good idea to be positive and take on the adventurous shot.

If trouble looms near the green or you have to clear bunkers or water, think again. The penalties for a bad shot are severe and outweigh the advantage gained if the shot comes off. But by using the correct technique it is still possible to play a positive stroke even if there is some trouble near the green.

FROM LIGHT ROUGH

The only changes you make to conventional technique are to attack the ball from a steeper angle and to play it from slightly further back in your stance. Your aim and alignment should stay the same as normal.

Be aware that the ball runs further from rough than from the fairway because of lack of backspin. Choose less club than normal to gain the same distance – perhaps an 8 iron instead of a 7.

STEEP ATTACK
A slight change in your technique can turn defensive play into positive when tackling a shot from rough grass. If you attack the ball with a steep downswing – by breaking your wrists early on the backswing – there is less grass between the clubface and the ball than with a normal stroke. This helps you to gain some control over the shot – you can go for the flag instead of playing safe.

The action of hitting down on the ball gains height on the shot. This means you can still go for the flag even if there's a bunker in the way – providing the distance between the trap and the hole is large enough.

From long range it's often a good idea to hit a smooth, sweeping, running 4 or 5 wood rather than a long iron. But because the ball runs a long way, it's better not to aim for the flag if there's a bunker in your path. Often you can take a line to miss the trouble and still make it to the edge of a green.

FROM HEAVY ROUGH

When playing aggressively the clubface tends to close at impact. If you play the shot with a square blade you can easily hook the ball. To compensate for the club turning, lay the blade slightly open at address – this is one of the rare times the clubface isn't square to the ball-to-target line.

How much you open the club face depends on how tough and thick the grass is. Also take into account the amount of trouble there is around. Don't open the blade too much when the right hand side is packed with trouble – if the club doesn't turn the ball flies off right. When there's a lot on the left, make sure you open your blade enough to avoid going into it even if you do hit a slight hook.

Your downswing path is again steep which allows as little grass as possible between the clubface and the ball. But even if you hit the shot well, you can't apply any backspin on the ball from thick rough. Allow for a lot of run on the shot.

When playing from either light or heavy rough, strike firmly at the ball and never quit on the shot.

AVOID THE HOOK

Beware of the clubhead turning in your hands when playing from thick rough. If you lay the clubface square to the target the blade closes at impact and the result is a hook. To stop the hook, open the clubface at address. Opening the blade returns the face to a square position at impact. This is especially important when playing from wiry bermuda grass.

CLOSED CLUBFACE LEADS TO SNAP HOOK

SLIGHTLY OPEN BLADE FOR STRAIGHT SHOT

THICK ROUGH

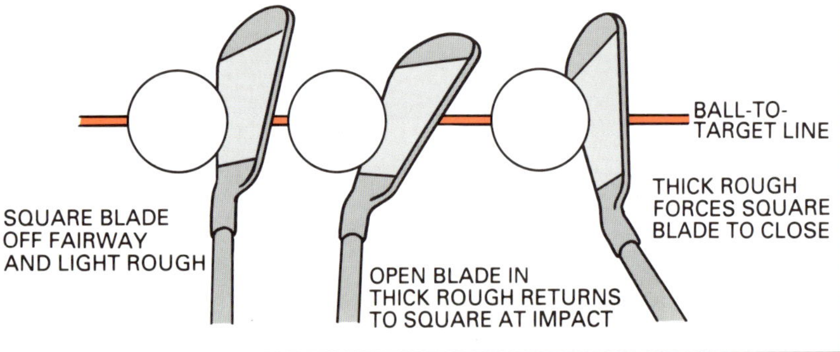

BALL-TO-TARGET LINE

SQUARE BLADE OFF FAIRWAY AND LIGHT ROUGH

OPEN BLADE IN THICK ROUGH RETURNS TO SQUARE AT IMPACT

THICK ROUGH FORCES SQUARE BLADE TO CLOSE

Lyle's power play

The burly Scot Sandy Lyle has few problems with the rough. He manages to attack the flag even from heavy grass. With a steep attack his awesome power and excellent clubhead control mean he can cut through the rough without the fear of hitting a really bad shot. He used all his strength to cope with the grass at the 1989 Scottish Open, and finish as top placed Scot.

Exploring the fade

Many top players – including Nick Faldo, Lee Trevino and Jack Nicklaus – use the fade as their stock shot. Although you can't hit the ball quite as far with a fade as you can with a draw, you have greater control over the shot – as the ball has a high flight path and lands softly.

Hitting the fade for control and accuracy is not the only way to play this shape of shot. Make full use of the fade to set up birdie chances on awkward holes.

FADING FAVOURITES

You can play the fade to counter the effects of both slope and wind. If the fairway slopes from right to left and is hard and running, a straight shot or draw is likely to roll too far left and end up in the rough. But if you hit the fade the ball moves from left to right and runs slightly uphill on landing, which holds the ball on the slope.

Aim the clubface square to a target on the left of the fairway and align left of the ball-to-target line so that when the shot cuts back it has plenty of room to work with. Even if the ball doesn't fade it shouldn't run too far into the left rough.

The fade is also useful to hold the ball in a right to left wind. Instead of aiming right of the target and letting the wind drift the ball back, set it off on a line just left of the flag and cut it back on to the target. The ball lands softly – especially helpful if the green is firm.

Play one or two clubs more than usual – depending on the strength of the wind – as the ball doesn't fly as far when cutting into it.

TARGET RIGHT

Hitting the left to right shot is also very useful for getting at a hidden target on the right.

Some dog-legs right are angled so sharply that you can hit only a long iron to the corner before running out of fairway. But if you hit a driver and move the ball from left to right you can slide a shot around the corner, leaving you with a much shorter second.

CONTROLLED SLICE

Exaggerate the fade – so it becomes a controlled slice – to hit a shot around trouble, usually trees. The technique of the swing is almost the same as normal. The only difference is that your body aligns well left of the target but the clubface is still square to the ball-to-target line. The ball sets off well to the left of the target and cuts back a long way.

▼ Playing the exaggerated fade is very useful when you haven't a clear shot to the target. By aligning left and aiming your clubface squarely at the flag the ball starts left of the trees and cuts back through the air towards the green.

Hold the slope

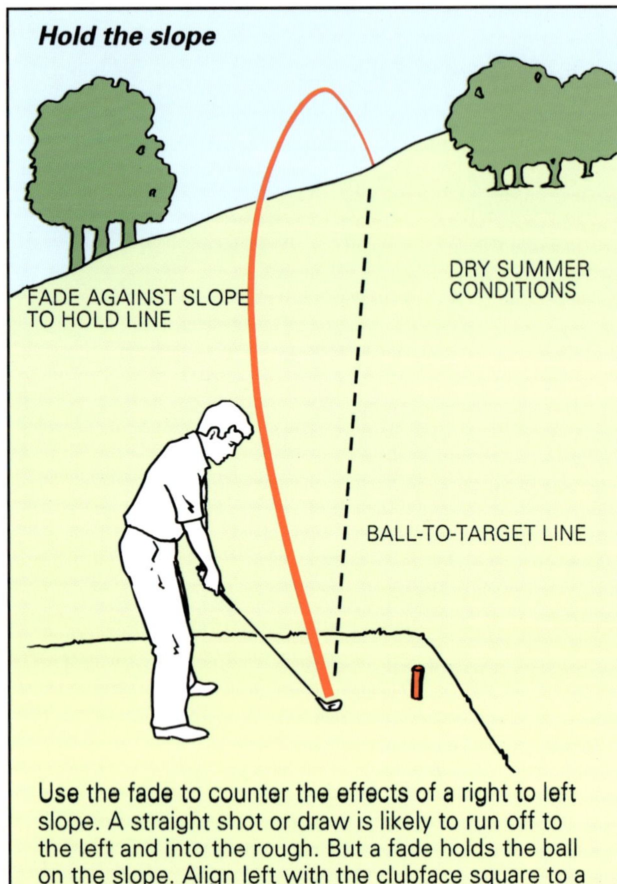

Use the fade to counter the effects of a right to left slope. A straight shot or draw is likely to run off to the left and into the rough. But a fade holds the ball on the slope. Align left with the clubface square to a target on the left of the fairway.

Counter crosswind

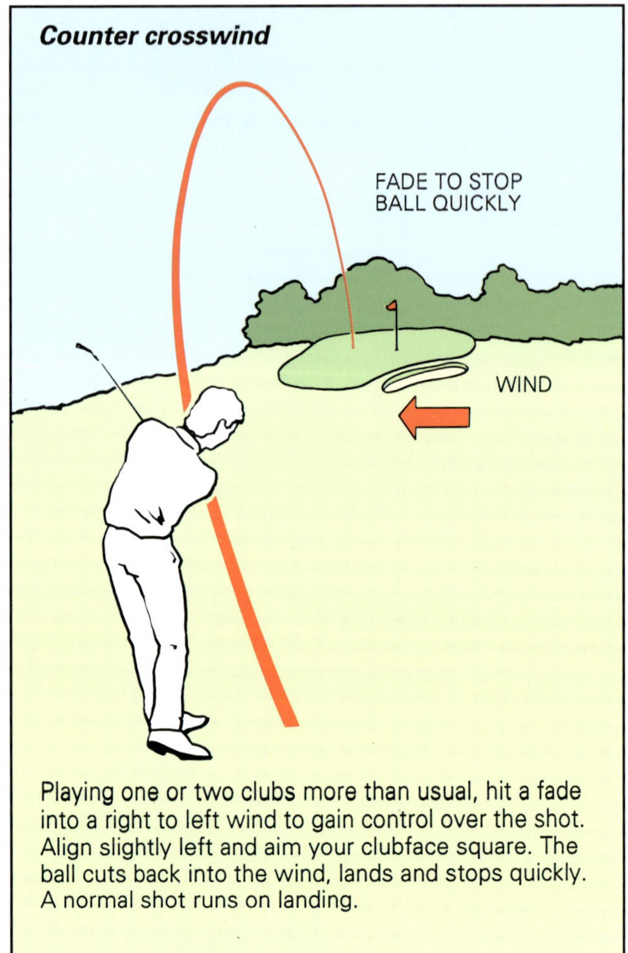

Playing one or two clubs more than usual, hit a fade into a right to left wind to gain control over the shot. Align slightly left and aim your clubface square. The ball cuts back into the wind, lands and stops quickly. A normal shot runs on landing.

Dog-leg driver

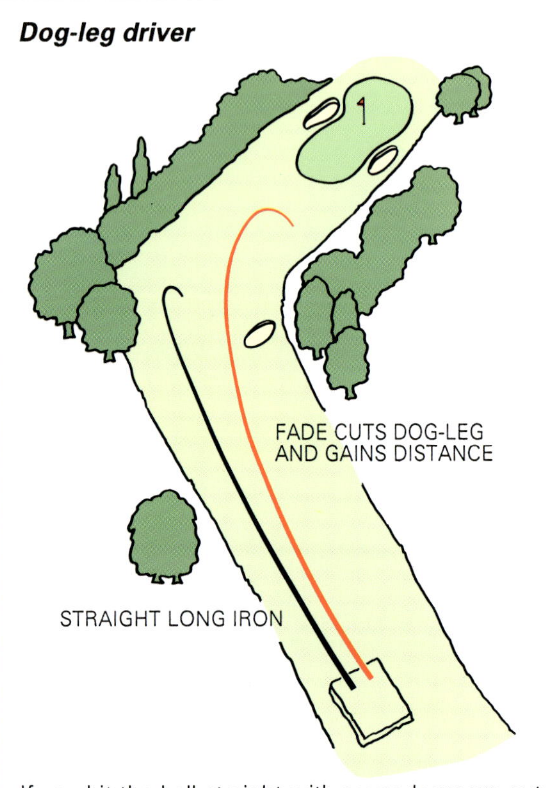

If you hit the ball straight with a wood you run out of fairway on the dog-leg. You must either play a long iron to the corner or a long fade with a wood. Fading left with the wood leaves you with a much shorter second to the green.

Faldo's fabulous fade

In the 1989 PGA Championship at Wentworth, Nick Faldo played a magical shot at the 15th hole to secure the title. After driving to the right he found he was blocked out from the green by trees. He had to aim about 60yd (55m) left of the green as he took his stance.

Using a 3 iron he hit a low cut shot some 200yd (183m) to within a few feet of the flag. A possible bogey became a birdie and he went on to win by 2 shots from Ian Woosnam.

Pitching

For a pitch shot, the ball is hit high and travels further in the air than along the ground. A pitch is an extension of both the medium and high chip shots and is played between 35yd (32m) and 100yd (91m) from the green.

The aim of a pitch is to play the ball close enough to the hole so that your next shot is a short putt. To play it well requires a lot of practice as well as a fine touch, but once you've mastered it you could save yourself several shots per round.

The pitch is a feel shot played with no more than a three-quarter swing and with any one of a number of clubs. The most common are the sand wedge, pitching wedge and 9 iron.

CHOOSING YOUR CLUB

The club you use depends on the distance of the shot. The sand wedge, with a clubface loft of about 56°, is for shots of 35-60yd (32-55m) while a pitching wedge (with a loft of about 50°) is for 61-80yd (56-73m) strikes. A 9 iron (about 46° loft) hits the ball 81-100yd (74-91m) with a three-quarter swing.

These distances increase as you improve. But whatever the distance of the shot and whichever club you use, your tempo must stay the same.

The technique is the same for

PITCHING TO YOUR TARGET
The pitch is a high shot played with a lofted club – the ball spends more time in the air than rolling along the ground. The key to a successful pitch is to keep your left hand, wrist and arm firm at impact.

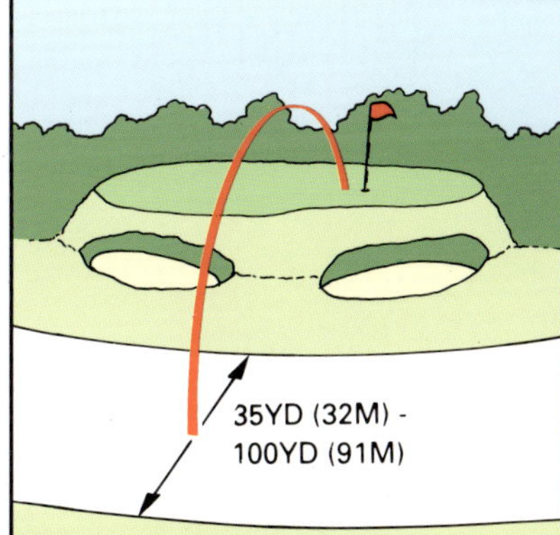

The pitching zone
The pitch shot is played to a target between 35yd (32m) and 100yd (91m) away – and even further as your game improves. You have to hit the ball high from this distance because you are too far away to play the chip and run – even if there are no hazards between your ball and the target.

Vary your swing length

Providing you keep the same tempo for all shots, the length of your swing determines how far you hit the ball. To develop a feel for distance, vary your swing from half to two-thirds to three-quarters when practising – but keep the same tempo for each stroke.

each club – although the swing plane changes slightly according to the length of the shaft. The shorter the shaft the more your back is bent and the more upright the swing plane is. The sand wedge has a steeper swing plane than either the pitching wedge or the 9 iron.

ADDRESS AND SWING

Hold the club about 2in (5cm) down the shaft with the standard overlap grip. Take a slightly open stance with your left foot about 2in (5cm) behind your right, so that your hands and arms can swing freely through impact. However, your hips, chest and shoulders remain parallel to the ball-to-target line.

Your stance is slightly wider than if playing a chip and run. The ball is midway between your feet.

Let your left wrist break immediately you start the takeaway. This helps create a steep backswing and moves your hands and arms into the correct position to start the downswing.

Your left hand must stay ahead of the clubface on the downswing, and pull it into the ball. Keep both hands, your wrists and arms firm as you hit the ball. At impact, both hands are still slightly ahead of the clubface – it is only after impact that it moves level with your hands. Your right hand stays behind the left for as long as possible.

It's vital to remember that your left hand dominates the swing,

The three wedges

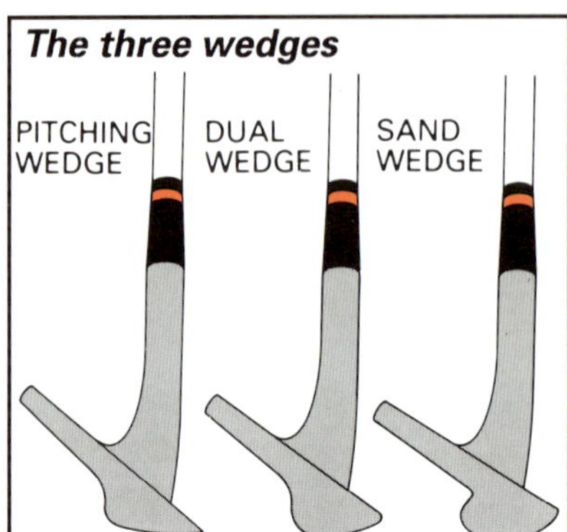

In addition to the sand wedge and pitching wedge, there is a dual wedge which combines the qualities of both. Its loft angle is midway between the two – and it has a rounded sole for bunker play. If you have all three clubs in your bag, practise pitching with each to feel the differences you achieve in height and length.

REDUCED BACKSPIN FROM ROUGH

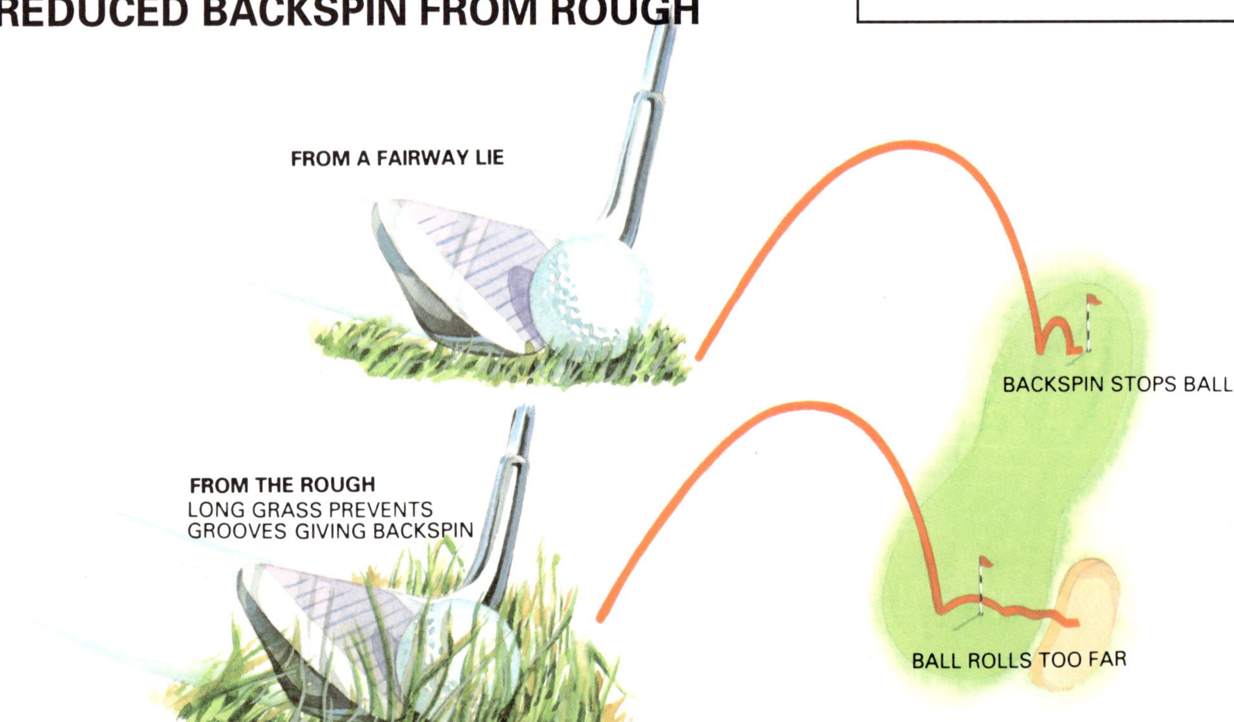

You can't generate much backspin when playing from the rough. This is because blades of grass become trapped between the clubface and the ball and stop the clubface grooves from imparting spin. This results in a 'flier' and the ball doesn't stop quickly on landing.

Keep this in mind when pitching from thick grass. Try to land your ball a few yards further back than normal and let it run up to the flag. Remember to visualize your shot carefully when playing from the rough.

PLAYING A PITCH SHOT

1 ADDRESS POSITION
Open your stance by sliding your left foot back about 2in (5cm) but keep your shoulders, chest and hips parallel to the ball-to-target line.

2 TOP OF BACKSWING
Make about a three-quarter backswing. The exact length depends on the distance of the shot. Your weight moves from an even distribution at address to your right foot.

3 THROUGH IMPACT
Keep your left wrist firm and focus on striking the back of the ball. Don't scoop it. Just after impact the clubhead moves level with your hands for the first time.

4 COMPLETION OF SWING
Your weight transfers on to your left side which lets your upper body rotate to the left to face the target. The throughswing is the same length as the backswing.

> *pro tip*
>
> ***Maintain hand speed at impact***
>
> When pitching from a difficult or rough lie be sure to hit through the ball at an even tempo. Don't shy away from difficult shots. Be aggressive at impact – if your hands slow down you fail to strike through the ball correctly. This leads to a poor hit and you will be lucky if your ball reaches even halfway.

while your right remains passive. This is the single most important point in pitching because your left arm and hand pull the clubface through the ball and so control its speed and path.

Let your body rotate to the left on the throughswing and allow your left shoulder to rise. From an even distribution at address your weight moves on to your right foot on the backswing, and on to the outside of your left foot by the completion of the swing.

A FIRM IMPACT

Your hands must be firm at impact to give you clubface control, direction and feel. Many golfers flick at the ball in an effort to gain height. Not only is this bad technique, it is also unnecessary. It's the loft of the clubface that gives your ball height.

As you practise, note that the s and wedge imparts more backspin than either the pitching wedge or the 9 iron. It has the most loft and creates a steep swing plane with its short shaft.

However, when learning to pitch, concentrate on selecting the club that hits your ball the necessary distance with a three-quarter swing. If the pin is close to a hazard don't risk forcing a sand wedge up to a full swing just because it imparts more backspin and stops the ball quickly. Take a longer club and accept that your ball will roll further on landing.

At this stage concentrate on developing a repeatable swing with all three clubs. Your backswing and followthrough must be of equal length.

OUT OF THE ROUGH

Pitching from long grass (rough) provides its own special problems, although the basic technique remains the same.

As the clubface passes through the rough, the tall, thick grass acts as a barrier and tries to twist the club in your hand to the left (clubface closes). Your left hand feels a greater strain at impact than if playing a pitch from the fairway.

You must counter the extra pressure exerted on the clubhead – and your left hand – by gripping the club a little more firmly and opening the clubface slightly at address. Be sure to keep an even tempo throughout the swing.

Grass gets entangled between the ball and the clubface. This is unavoidable, so concentrate on hitting down on the ball and making as clean a strike as possible. Your swing path, stance, and ball position do not change when playing from the rough.

PLAYING FROM THE ROUGH

1 OPEN CLUBFACE AT ADDRESS **Open the clubface slightly at address and grip the club firmly. This limits the amount it slips in your hands as the clubhead cuts through the rough.**

2 FOCUS ON BACK OF BALL **Take the club away smoothly and break your wrists immediately to steepen the angle of the swing plane. Focus on cleanly striking the back of the ball.**

3 LEFT HAND FIRM IN ROUGH **Your left hand takes the strain at impact as the rough gets entangled with the clubface, which turns to the left. This is why you open the clubface at address. Keep your head down through impact.**

4 WEIGHT MOVES ON TO LEFT SIDE **Your weight transfers on to your left foot on the followthrough and your body rotates to face the target. Try to maintain your tempo throughout the stroke.**

Punch Pitch

GREEN CONTROL
The punch pitch – one of the pros' favourites – is easy to control as your action produces a lot of backspin and the ball pulls up quickly on the green. Learning and being confident with this shot greatly increases your chances of getting up and down in 2 with your wedge – especially in a wind.

Controlling a wedge from the awkward distance of 50-90yd (45-80m) is a great asset. The punched pitch is the perfect shot to manoeuvre the ball through a wind from this range, but is by no means it's only use. All top golfers regularly hit this type of pitch both in windy and calm conditions to gain control.

The technique is simple and easily repeatable, which helps you play the stroke consistently well, provided you practise it. When hit properly the ball flies lower than a

PRECISE PUNCHING

1 **BACK ADDRESS**
Grip down the club slightly for more control. Align parallel to the target line. Position the ball back in your stance – just inside the right foot for a very low punch. Aim the blade square to the target, and push your hands ahead of the ball. Distribute your weight evenly.

2 **FIRM WRIST TAKEAWAY**
Take the club away smoothly with little wrist break. Though the shot is mainly a hands and arms stroke you must still turn you hips and shoulders during the backswing.

normal wedge and stops quickly on the green, as the way you strike the shot naturally creates much back-spin.

FAVOURABLE FLIGHT

The boring, penetrative flight is invaluable when firing into a head or crosswind, but is equally useful with the wind at your back.

Instead of hitting a pitch and run or a high floating shot – both trusting a little to luck – you can afford to attack the flag by playing the punch pitch. Even though you're hitting downwind the ball should pull up quite sharply, but allow for some run depending on the firmness of the green.

The spin comes from a sharp downward blow on a ball that's placed slightly further back in the stance than normal. The action of striking the ball before the turf is important for the shot to succeed. A touch fat and the ball runs on landing – as little spin is produced – and control is lost.

The ball stays low because it is placed back in the stance with your

Wedge comfort
However good your technique is, you must also feel positive for the punched pitch to come off. For your confidence to be high it's vital to be comfortable with your wedge. There is no way that you can play the punch pitch well if your wedge doesn't suit you.

Knowing you have a club in your hand that you consistently strike out the middle of the face puts you in a positive frame of mind.

You may already have a favourite wedge – often bought years ago – but if you don't, there are plenty of specialist wedges on the market. Finding a suitable one-off wedge means you needn't part with it when you change your set of irons.

3 SHORT AT THE TOP
Still keeping the wrists firm stop your backswing well short of parallel. Though the position at the top is not as long as usual, try to turn fully. Poor shoulder turn leads to an out-to-in downswing and a wayward shot.

4 SMOOTHLY DOWN
Swing down smoothly and keep your wrists firm. Too steep and wristy an attack makes the ball fly too high. Make sure your hands stay ahead of the clubface all the way to impact.

5 CRISP STRIKE
Lead the strike with your left hand and be sure to hit the ball before the turf. Keep your hands ahead of the clubface through impact and resist releasing, so the blade stays square for as long as possible.

6 SHORT AND BALANCED
Because you resist releasing your hands your extension is full and the followthrough short, which helps to keep the ball low and firing at the target. Don't stop too sharply as it leads to a stabbed shot. The finish should be balanced, with your weight fully on the left side.

hands forward, which delofts the clubface. The less wristy action than normal also helps to produce penetrative flight.

The punch pitch shot helps eliminate a miss-hit when playing under pressure, as the chances of hitting a thin or fat are less than with a straightforward pitch.

Reduced wrist action and having the ball placed further back in the stance both encourage crisp striking, so long as you don't dip too sharply on the downswing.

But for the shot to be accurate you must also be controlled on the followthrough. Lead with the left hand through the shot and avoid releasing too early. Try to keep the blade square to the target for as long as possible – this lessens the risk of a pull. Your finish position is much shorter than normal, but your whole action should be smooth.

WORK THE WIND

If you feel confident with this shot you can also shape the ball slightly to counter a crosswind. To produce a slight draw that holds on a left to right wind, stand a touch closed with the blade still square. But be sure not to use too much right hand as you could easily hit a hook.

If you open up your stance a fraction and keep the blade square the ball naturally fades slightly, which is useful in a right to left wind. The ball climbs a touch higher than the straight punch pitch and lands very softly – improving your control.

pro tip

Practice pitch
If you haven't tried to play the punch pitch before, it's sometimes hard to resist breaking your wrists on the backswing and through impact. One drill that is quick and easy to perform helps you naturally to keep the ball low and drilling.

Stick an umbrella into the practice ground, and pace out about 60yd (55m). From there, try to pitch balls – without bouncing – on to the umbrella and knock it over. This breeds an attacking and positive approach and helps you to hit the ball crisp and low – vital for punch pitch success.

José-Maria's wedge mastery
The brilliant Spaniard José-Maria Olazabal has worked his way to the top of world golf very quickly. His superb all-round game is capped by complete mastery of the wedge. He has tremendous natural flair and combines it with outstanding technique.

The punch pitch is an important weapon in Olazabal's armoury and makes him a deadly short game player. The dry, running fairways of Gleneagles in mid summer are the perfect surfaces for Chema to show off his prowess with the wedge. The short, controlled finish is a tell-tale sign of a low, spinning punched pitch shot that bites on the slick greens.

Chipping around the green

A chip is a stroke played from between 5yd (4 m) and 30yd (27m) of the green. The aim of a chip is to get your ball close enough to the hole so that your next shot is simply a tap-in with the putter. Good chipping can save you at least half-a-dozen strokes per round. With regular practice you'll find your chipping improves dramatically.

The chip is a short shot you play with two-thirds swing or less and it needs a deft touch to do it well. Although you can chip with any iron from a 5 down to a sand wedge – depending on the length of the shot and the obstacles to clear – this chapter concentrates on three of the most common types of chip using the 7 iron; 9 iron; and sand wedge.

WHICH CHIP?

Before choosing your chip, you must consider three factors: how high the ball needs to fly; how far it has to fly; and how far it can roll.

As a general rule you should always try to run the ball along the ground for as great a distance as the terrain permits, since there is less chance of the shot going wrong on the ground than in the air.

If the ground is relatively flat and even and there are no obstacles to clear, then a low-flying chip and run is best. Play this shot using a clubface with little loft, such as a medium iron, so that the ball travels in a low trajectory (curving flight path through the air). The ball spends one-third of its journey in the air and the remaining two-thirds rolling along the ground.

If there is an obstacle to clear between you and the green but there is still quite a way for the ball to roll, play a medium height chip using a short iron. With this shot the ball spends roughly equal parts of its journey in the air and on the ground.

The ground between your ball and the green may be uneven with humps, bunkers or an irregular surface, and with not much level ground to the pin for the ball to roll over. In this case you want the ball to spend nearly all its time in

PICKING THE SHOT

The type of chip you play depends on the situation you find yourself in. Assess the lie of the land for how far the ball can fly and how far you want it to roll. As a general rule always try to run the ball along the ground for as far as possible. This is easier and safer than trying to stop the ball quickly with a more lofted club.

When the first part of the surface between your ball and the pin is relatively flat, but not smooth enough to use a putter, use a 7 iron for a low chip and run.

When the flag is close to the edge of a hazard such as a bunker, you have to get the ball over the bunker then stop it quickly on landing. In this case use a sand wedge for a high chip and stop.

To clear a bumpy bank and reach the top level of a sloping green, you have to send the ball over the bank and then let it run along the green. Use a 9 iron for a medium chip and run.

7 IRON CHIP AND RUN

1 AT ADDRESS Use a putting grip down the handle. Move your left foot about 2in (5cm) back to open your stance but align your upper body parallel. Clubface aim is square to target. Your weight favours the left.

2 BACKSWING AND IMPACT Do not break your wrists on the backswing. The clubhead reaches no higher than knee level at the top of the backswing. The swing is a pendulum movement similar to a crisp putting stroke.

3 THROUGHSWING Your shoulders, arms and hands move as one during the whole stroke. Do not break your wrists on the throughswing which is as long as the backswing. Your left shoulder rises after impact.

the air before stopping quickly. Play a shot – commonly known as the chip and stop – where you send the ball high with a club that has a big loft angle, such as a sand wedge. With this shot the ball is in the air for at least two-thirds of its route.

Chip tip

When you are playing a short chip and run, the stroke is crisp and firm and your wrists must not move forward of the clubhead. Lift your left shoulder on the throughswing.

CHIPPING BASICS

Regardless of the stroke you play and the club you use there are a few basics that apply to all chipping strokes. For a start, your back and throughswing are the same length. At the same time you need a longer back and throughswing the further you have to chip. The slightest change in clubhead speed makes a great difference to the result of the shot. Practice will help you learn a feel for the ball and teach you how far you have to swing.

Another common feature of all chip shots is aligning your lower body left of the ball-to-target line. An open (aligned left) lower body prevents your hips from obstructing your hands at impact. For proper chip alignment take a normal parallel stance, and then slide your left foot back about 2in (5cm) to open your stance and align left.

However, you must still align your upper body parallel to the ball-to-target line. Also, the aim of the clubhead is always square on to the ball-to-target line.

THREE USEFUL CHIPS

Around the green there are three common situations you might find yourself in. Each calls for a different chip. The first is where your ball is lying just off the green beyond the apron. Here you use a 7 iron and a low chip and run. Where your ball is slightly further away, with perhaps a bank in the way you can chip with a 9 iron. Finally, where

9 IRON MEDIUM CHIP

1 AT ADDRESS Hold the club with a normal grip but still down the handle. Otherwise address the ball the same as for a 7 iron chip and run.

your ball is lying with a bunker or some other hazard in the way and the hole is close to the hazard, use a sand wedge to play a high chip and stop to bring your ball close to the hole.

7 IRON LOW CHIP

Use this shot when there are no obstacles to clear and there is a large area of even ground for the ball to roll along. The ball travels two-thirds of its distance on the ground and only one-third of it in the air.

To play this shot, hold the club with a putting grip and grip down the handle. Aim the clubface square on to the ball-to-target line and adopt an open stance. Position the ball in the centre of your stance.

Do not break your wrists on the backswing, and let your shoulders, arms and hands move in unison during the whole movement. This produces a smooth action which should be short and crisp.

The swing is, in effect, like a crisper version of the putting stroke. By using the putting grip you eliminate wrist action. Try to imagine your swing as a pendulum motion with an equal length back and throughswing.

Your shoulders, arms and hands move as one unit from start to finish and the clubhead stays square to the ball-to-target line during most of the stroke, only moving inside this line at the furthest point in both backswing and throughswing.

After impact allow your left shoulder to lift up. This stops your wrist from breaking and keeps the clubface square to the ball-to-target line for most of the followthrough.

The clubhead approaches the ball at a shallow angle, crisply sweeping it off the turf. This puts top spin on to maximize roll.

IN THE AIR AND ON THE GROUND

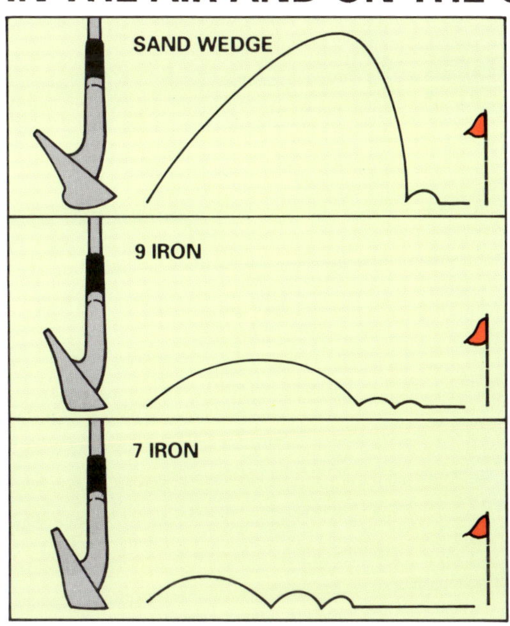

To help you select the right club for the chip remember that in a 7 iron chip the ball travels about two thirds of its journey rolling along the ground; with a 9 iron chip the ball is on the ground for half its journey; with a sand wedge chip and stop it is on the ground only for the last third of its journey.

9 IRON MEDIUM CHIP

Use a 9 iron to produce a medium chip when the ball needs to be hit high enough to clear an obstacle, but doesn't need to stop quickly on landing. The curve of the ball is higher than that of a 7 iron – although it doesn't run as far along the ground.

With this chip use your normal grip but still grip down the handle. Set the clubface and address the ball in the same way as for the 7 iron chip.

2 BACKSWING
Break your wrists a little on the backswing and swing the clubhead to about waist height. Backswing is equal length to throughswing.

3 IMPACT AND ON
Allow your left shoulder to rise after impact so as not to let your clubhead overtake your hands. Hold your followthrough position.

pro tip

Grip down for greater feel

You can improve your feel, and achieve greater clubhead control and awareness, by gripping down the handle. The closer your hands are to the clubhead, the better touch you have, and the more accurate your shot.

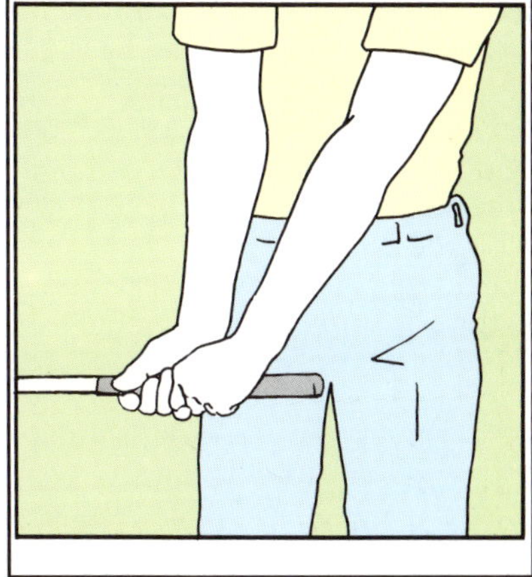

SAND WEDGE HIGH CHIP AND STOP

1 AT ADDRESS
Adopt the same grip and stance as you would for a 9 iron chip. Distribute your body weight evenly over both feet.

2 BACK AND DOWN
Allow your wrists to break at the start of the backswing which should be about two-thirds the length of your normal full swing.

3 IMPACT AND THROUGH
Your right hand must stay underneath the shaft to prevent any wrist roll. As you follow through, rotate to face the target.

This time let your wrists break a little during the backswing. At the top of the backswing your clubhead should reach no higher than hip level. The clubface attacks the ball at a steeper angle than the 7 iron and the clubhead follows a normal in-to-in swingpath.

Hold your followthrough and don't allow your wrists to break after impact. Let your left shoulder rise on the followthrough. As you complete the throughswing allow your upper body to rotate towards the target.

SAND WEDGE HIGH CHIP

Use the sand wedge to play the chip and stop. Select this club when the nearest landing point beyond a hazard is very close to the target – and when there is very little room for the ball to run. The sand wedge produces a high curve and creates backspin to stop the ball quickly. However, it is the least easy chip to perform because you have only a small area in which to land and stop the ball.

Grip the club and address the ball in the same way as you would for a 9 iron chip.

Let your left wrist break almost immediately as you start the swing. Your backswing is about two-thirds of the length of your normal swing. On the downswing the clubhead approaches impact at an acute angle, but don't let your hands overtake the clubface at any time.

Do not break your wrists through impact. Feel that your right hand is a passenger staying underneath the shaft as you strike. Your upper body turns to face the target at the completion of the followthrough.

CHIPPING PRACTICE

If you want to develop a good short game you must practise these strokes regularly. Not only do you need to learn the different techniques involved, but you have to acquire a feel for the shots. It is a general rule in golf that the shorter the shot, the more precise you must be and the greater feel you must have.

One good practice routine is to chip into an umbrella. Place the umbrella at the point where you want the ball to land. Position it at different distances and practise with different clubs – especially the sand wedge.

Another useful chipping practice aid is a chipping net. Use it in the same way as you would an umbrella, changing the distance away from you so you build up feel for the amount of swing needed.

When you become consistent at landing the ball in the umbrella or net, you are halfway to being a good chipper. The other half is achieved by correctly visualizing the shot – knowing where to land the ball and how it runs.

pro tip

Clubface control

To ensure that you do not flick at the ball through impact, your right hand stays under the shaft during impact and followthrough.

To pitch – or to chip

Pitches and chips are the shots that can make all the difference to your score by the end of the round. While both are played from anywhere between 40-100yd (35-90m), that is where the similarity ends.

A pitch is a high trajectory shot, usually played with a wedge, which lands the ball softly on the green. It's a useful shot for flying high over trouble. In wet conditions when the ground is soggy underfoot you can land the ball close to the flag and be confident of stopping it quickly.

A chip is the complete opposite and often played from closer range. A low flight means the ball is on the ground for about the same distance it's in the air. It's a good links shot – ideal when the wind is blowing or the greens aren't holding. A 7 or 8 iron is usually the best club for the job.

Choosing the right shot at the right time is one of the keys to successful scoring – it helps keep you out of trouble and can turn three shots into two. The factors which should make up your mind are the hazards and ground conditions between you and the green, and the strength and direction of the wind. Only when you've taken stock of the situation should you consider techniques.

HIGH FLYING PITCH

An approach shot over some form of hazard – whether bunkers, water or deep rough – is a situation you face on all types of course. Whatever the wind conditions, there's really only one way you can hope to finish close to the flag and that's to play a high pitch.

Think of the positive aspects of the shot to boost your confidence. The major benefit of pitching the ball on the green is that you can predict the bounce. This helps you attack the flag and removes any guesswork from the shot.

Remember, accuracy is all important – you must feel in control of the shot. Swing smoothly and strike with authority. There's seldom a call for hitting a wedge with all the force you can muster.

If there is trouble immediately beyond the green, play a high pitch to land the ball softly. The less run on the shot the slimmer the chance of the ball bouncing

KNOWING WHAT'S BEST
There's more than one way to tackle almost every situation in golf. You can master the art of choosing the right one – just as the professionals do – providing you're aware of the conditions around you. When you're close to the green, the right approach can make all the difference between leaving you a holeable putt or a recovery chip.

CLEAR PATH: LOW CHIP AND RUN

1 ADDRESS PRECISION
There are no hazards in the 60yd (55m) between you and the flag. When the wind blows, the safest shot is usually the low chip and run – this is the stroke that gives you the greatest margin for error. Using a 7 or 8 iron, grip down the club and position your hands ahead of the ball. Bring your feet closer together than for a full shot, with the ball back in your stance. Use your imagination to picture the path of the ball all the way up to the hole.

2 HANDS AND ARMS SHOT
Swing your arms back and through with very little wrist movement. Pull the clubhead down and strike crisply into the bottom of the ball, pushing the back of your left hand low towards the target. Make sure your backswing is the same length as your followthrough to help you accelerate down into impact. The shallow angle of descent creates a tiny divot as the ball flies low, lands short of the green and runs up towards the flag.

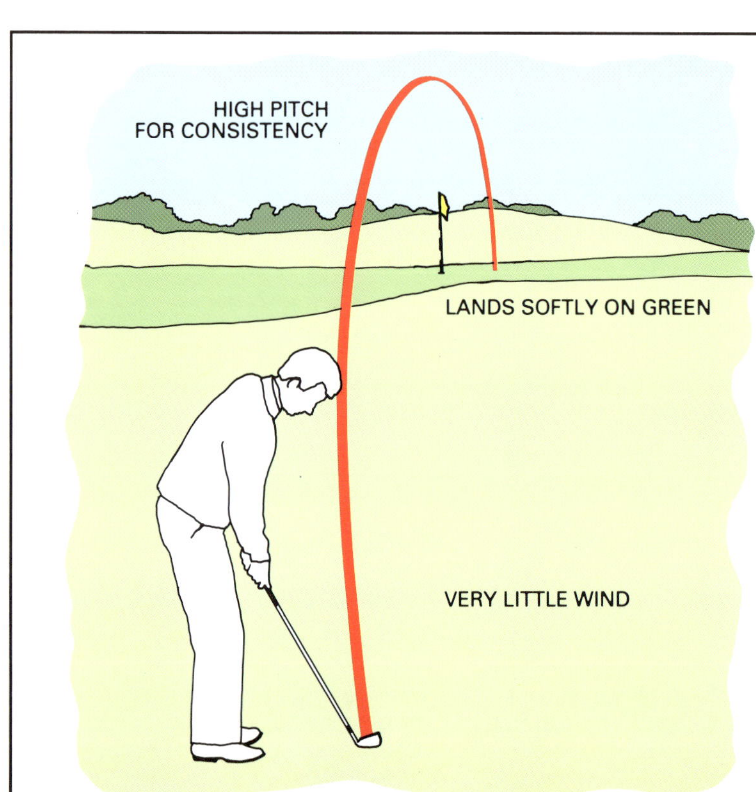

Second choice

If the wind isn't blowing, a high pitch is an effective shot on any hole. You can accurately judge the flight of the ball and how it reacts on landing. Though the ground ahead is flat, there's no rule stating you must play a chip and run.

A great deal depends on how you visualize the shot. If you're under pressure – perhaps on a good score in a competition – it's crucial you play the shot you're most confident with. When a mistake might cost you dearly is no time for experimenting.

OVER TROUBLE: THE HIGH PITCH

1 WEDGE TO BETTER SCORES
The best shot to play in this situation is the high pitch – you can safely avoid flirting with the crater on the right. A chip and run may put you on the green, but it's a risky shot and difficult to judge when there's light rough ahead. Use your sand or pitching wedge depending on the distance you want to carry the ball. Stand square to the ball-to-target line and make a three-quarter backswing, breaking the wrists earlier than you would for a full shot.

2 FIRM STRIKE
Strike down firmly into the bottom of the ball, leading the clubhead with the back of your left hand to promote a steep angle of descent. Transfer your weight gradually on to the left side – driving your right knee towards the target helps you achieve this. Maintain a smooth tempo on the downswing – remember you should never force any shot, particularly an approach from close range. The clubhead strikes first the ball and then turf to create quite a large divot.

through the green into serious danger.

PERCENTAGE PLAY

When there are no hazards lying in wait you have the luxury of choice. In these situations it's important to play the percentages – choosing the shot that is least likely to go wrong.

In a strong crosswind your ball can easily be buffeted off line, particularly if you play a high pitch. With a stiff breeze behind or into your face distance can be difficult to judge accurately. The lower to the ground you keep the ball the less likely it is to be affected. A low chip and run is often the safest shot, but you need to be a little more creative than for a pitch shot.

Reach for a 7 or 8 iron and keep your swing simple. Visualize the ball landing on the fairway and running up towards the hole. Predict how humps, hollows or slopes are likely to affect the path of your ball.

You may have to accept the occasional bad bounce which kicks your ball slightly off line. But it's unlikely to be one so severe that it makes the difference between hitting and missing the green.

TAKING CHARGE

If you learn to make the right decisions about when to pitch and when to chip, you're bound to see an improvement in your scores. This course management ability has you thinking *before* you reach for a club. You find yourself hitting the ball close to the target more often and missing the green less.

But even the best golfers in the world – with experienced caddies alongside – make errors of judgement from time to time. Don't be hard on yourself if you make the same mistake twice, but include those specific points in your practice routine.

Shrewd swap for pitching

You can increase your short game repertoire by carrying a 60° wedge as well as your pitching and sand wedges. This extremely lofted club is ideal when you need to lob the ball high into the air and stop it quickly.

If you already have 14 clubs in your bag you're likely to benefit from dropping one – perhaps your 2 iron – in favour of a third wedge.

HIGH ROLLER

1 ADDRESS POSITION
There's a hump in front of you and a two tiered green to negotiate, so you need to play a shot with a little height and plenty of run. An attempt to pitch the ball close to the flag is fraught with danger. From a fluffy lie, a sand wedge is the ideal club. Stand slightly open with your hands forward and the ball back in your stance.

2 SHORT BACKSWING
Pick the club up quickly on the backswing by breaking the wrists early. Tuck in your right elbow close to your side to increase your control over the club. Keep your backswing short – this encourages you to accelerate on the downswing. A little more than half your weight remains on the left side.

3 STRIKE WITH AUTHORITY
Pull the clubhead down with your left hand to position your hands ahead of the clubhead at impact – this effectively reduces the loft of the club to ensure a lower flight. Focus your eyes on the back of the ball – you should strike firmly and with purpose. Stay down until the ball is well on its way.

4 THE RIGHT RESULT
Push the back of your left hand through towards the target to keep the clubface travelling in the right direction. Resist any temptation to let your right hand take charge of the swing. The ball pitches halfway to the flag and runs down the step in the green towards the hole.

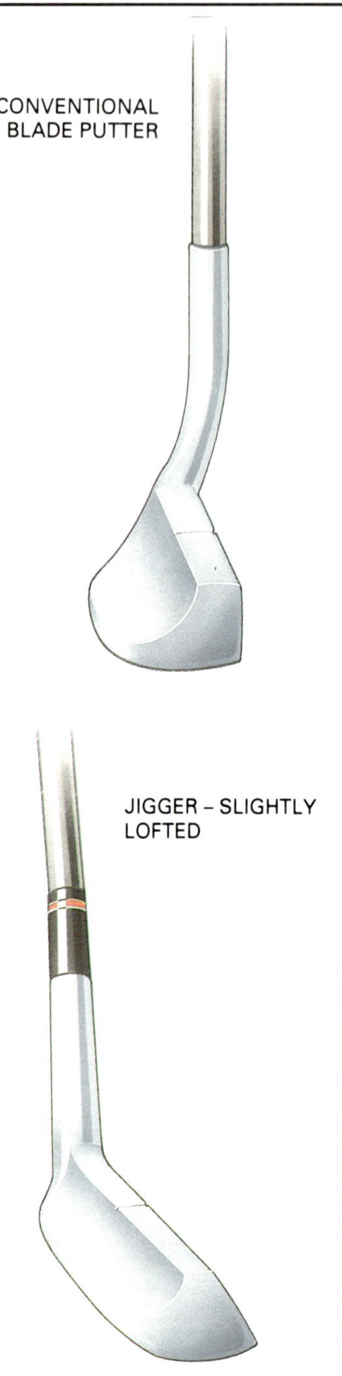

Gentle loft for chipping
If you have problems with your chipping a jigger can give good results and restore your confidence at the same time.

Similar to the look of a blade putter, the jigger has a loft about the same as a 1 iron. Over closely mown grass you can use the club to play a low chip and run shot. The swing is simply an extension of your putting stroke – your grip and stance should be the same.

You may find you use this club more than one of the longer clubs in your bag, so weigh up the options and decide which is more beneficial to your golf.

Wedge off hard pan

During a dry summer the ground can become hard and bare – especially around the greens where golfers have trampled. Links courses are particularly prone to this problem.

The patches worn by the weather often cause problems for the inexperienced golfer when chipping. But as skills develop you should be able to play off hard pan without fear by using the correct techniques.

Whether you are faced with a bunker to go over or just a straightforward chip to the flag, your striking must be exact. Unless you nip the ball off the ground you can easily thin or fluff the shot.

LOB OFF BARE GROUND

If there's a bunker in the way, play the stroke with a pitching wedge to be safe. A sand wedge has a wide sole and may bounce into the ball. But you must still push your hands forward to lessen the risk of the pitching wedge doing the same. The club must strike the ball fractionally before the ground for a crisp strike.

Play the shot with very little wrist break – making timing easier – and from a central position to give the club as much loft as is safe.

If you hit slightly behind the ball the club may bounce into the back of it and you scull the shot. Quitting on the stroke usually means a duffed shot. Be confident

CRISP STRIKE
Playing from a hard, bare and awkward lie frightens many golfers – especially if you have to chip over a bunker. But by making a simple set-up change, and with sensible club selection, the shot can be played confidently and precisely.

Position the ball centrally in your stance to gain enough loft to take you safely over sand. Align slightly left and strike crisply. If your path to the flag is clear, place the ball back in your stance (below) and strike down firmly.

NORMAL CHIP FROM A BARE LIE

1 BACK FOOT ADDRESS
Position the ball opposite your right foot and square up the blade. Align slightly left of target and push your weight on to your left side. Grip lightly.

2 PUTTING BACKSWING
Play the stroke with a putting action. The backswing is short and controlled, and your wrists must remain firm. Keep your weight on the left side.

LOB OVER A BUNKER

1 CENTRAL POSITION
Place the ball centrally in your stance. This creates as much loft on the club as is safe. Square the blade and push your hands and weight forward. Align left.

2 WRIST BREAK FOR GREATER HEIGHT
Breaking your wrists a little on the backswing helps the ball gain height. But avoid too much wrist action as this makes timing difficult.

3 DOWNWARD BLOW
Strike down on the ball firmly, ensuring you hit it before the ground. Make sure you keep your hands ahead of the ball at impact, and don't break your wrists.

4 STIFF ARMED FOLLOWTHROUGH
Because you're chipping with a long putt action your followthrough should be short and your wrists still rigid. Your swing length varies with distance of shot.

3 LEAD WITH THE HANDS
Don't flick at the ball even though you need loft on the shot – you run the risk of thinning it. Keep your hands ahead of the ball and strike firmly.

4 FULLER FINISH
Make sure you don't quit on the shot. Follow through firmly and positively. The length of your throughswing should be the same as your backswing.

and strike firmly.

Never try to be too cute with the shot. Make sure you clear the bunker – a putt from 20ft (6m) behind the hole is far better than having to play from the sand.

CLEAR PATH

Even if the shot is free from obstacles, the dangers of thinning and fluffing remain. These problems can be ironed out by playing the shot with a pitching wedge from the back of your stance. Use a firm wristed putting action. Placing the ball back in the stance means you strike it with a firm downward blow – essential if you're to play the shot successfully.

Both shots need to be played with crisp confidence and poise – adopt a positive attitude rather than worrying over what could go wrong.

Safer shots
You can sometimes reduce the risk of fluffing or thinning the shot when playing from hard pan. With a lot of green to work with and a trouble free path to the flag, try running the ball along with a putter or a straighter faced iron. Use a putter only if there isn't much fringe to go over and the flag is quite a distance away. Play a 7 or 8 iron off the back foot if you need to clear a thick fringe.

Putter

7 iron

Beware the scull
Laying the blade too far open or catching the ground before the ball can lead to you hitting it thin. This sculled shot is destructive. The ball shoots past the flag, through the green and possibly into severe trouble.

Always play the wedge off hard pan by striking down on the ball and catching it first – then the ground. Trapping the ball between the ground and the clubface eliminates the danger of the thin or duff. Be firm – never try to be too delicate.

Watson's wonder wedge
Tom Watson is the master of links golf. His control and accuracy from the hardened, dusty ground are brilliant. Notice the controlled finish – his hands have stayed ahead of the clubhead throughout the stroke. The amount of dust thrown up shows how firmly he played the shot. He never quits on the stroke.

Watson's mastery helped him win five Open titles – he nearly equalled the Open record of winning a sixth in 1989.

Rough recovery play

On every course you can find different types of rough – dense and sparse, long and short, fairway and greenside. Alas, so can your ball.

If you're lucky, rough is no more difficult than playing from the fairway. But introduce a hazard or two, add a more challenging lie, and a recovery shot from rough is a demanding test.

Common sense is often more important than being a master magician at shot making. Know what you can do and resist the temptation to try any more. Don't risk turning a minor mistake into a potential disaster – landing in even the most severe rough need never cause you to run up a high score.

Even Seve Ballesteros – a genius at recovery play – confesses he'd have more trophies on display in his living room if he'd known when to exercise a little self control earlier in his career.

OUT OF THE ROUGH STUFF
It's impossible to rehearse every recovery shot out of rough, because now and then you come across a totally unfamiliar lie. Your main thought must always be to find a safe route back to the closer mown grass – this is the first step away from disaster. By applying common sense to every situation, you can achieve a satisfactory result first time – and perhaps an even better outcome when you're next faced with a similar shot.

LIE MATTERS

Study the lie carefully – this has a tremendous bearing on how ambitious you can afford to be with your recovery. A vital point is that it's harder to control the ball from rough. Backspin is almost impossible to achieve and shaping the ball through the air is difficult.

Look at which direction the grass is growing around your ball. If the grass is with you (leaning towards the target) it's easier to strike the ball cleanly without making adjustments to your swing.

If the grass is against you a more precise strike is required. The clubhead must come down at a steep angle to prevent too much grass coming between the clubface and ball at impact.

Don't rule out the possibility of a flyer, particularly if the rough is wet. This can add yards to the flight of your shots.

A ROUGH RIDE

When you hit a tee shot into **rough lining the fairway**, survey the entire hole as you approach your ball. You then have a clearer picture of the situation when you come to prepare for the shot.

If the ball is sitting down, you may have to accept that the green is out of reach. Decide on a club you're confident with – one that guarantees a comfortable escape from the rough and puts you in a good position for your next shot.

If the green is in range, don't forget it's hard to apply spin from

Keeping watch
Make sure you keep an eye on your ball when it's heading for the rough. Don't turn away in disgust even though bad shots can be upsetting – your ball may prove very difficult to find in thick rough if you fail to watch it all the way.

Try to pick out a mark where the ball eventually comes to rest – perhaps a lighter patch of grass, a small tree or a different coloured bush. You can then walk straight to it and avoid holding up play.

FIRING THROUGH THE GAP

DECIDE ON THE SHOT
There's not much green to work with here, so concentrate on finding the putting surface rather than trying to place the ball close. When you size up the shot there are two points to consider – you must keep the ball low to avoid the overhanging branches but have enough height to carry the rough in front of you. Be careful – it's usually better to flight your ball too low than too high. If there's one stray branch jutting down lower than the others, a ball often has an uncanny knack of hitting it. You may then finish in an even worse spot.

1 SET UP TO HIT LOW
Choose a 9 iron for this shot and position the ball back in your stance opposite the right heel. With your hands pressed forward in front of the ball and the clubface aiming at the flag, you effectively decrease the loft of the club (above). This address position and the poor lie mean the ball comes out lower than normal.

rough, so pitch the ball short and allow for a little run on the shot. From a good lie you can almost afford to play your normal game, but you must still allow for less backspin. Don't expect to stop the ball quickly, even if it's lying cleanly.

SALVAGING SHOTS

In **greenside rough** the first concern is the lie. You should have a fair idea long before you reach the green – if you can see your ball from a distance you can expect a reasonable lie.

You immediately have a greater choice of shots open to you. Hazards shouldn't present you with a problem – you can safely negotiate your way around every form of obstacle.

If you can't see your ball as you approach it, prepare for the worst. A bad lie limits your options, so resign yourself to salvaging what you can without taking a big gamble.

2 SMOOTH PICK UP
Swing back smoothly along the ball-to-target line and allow your wrists to hinge (above). Don't take the club back outside the line – there's no need to cut across the ball with this shot. Stop the backswing when your hands are about waist high (below) – this is the perfect length to enable you to accelerate down into impact.

ON TO THE GREEN

3 STEEP ATTACK
You need to be extra firm from this lie or you risk moving the ball no distance at all. Strike down with your hands ahead of the clubhead (above). Even though you're using a lofted club, the slight variation in your technique ensures the ball flies fairly low. From behind, your impact position looks almost identical to address (below).

Check how much green you have to work with – if you're not sure of the exact distance, try standing to the side of your ball for a better view.

FLYING HIGH OR LOW

If there are bunkers to carry, a **high float shot** with a soft landing is called for, particularly if there's not much green to work with. Treat the shot much as you would if you were in the bunker – the same techniques in a different situation serve you well.

Adopt an open stance with the ball central, or slightly towards your back foot if the rough is very thick. Swing back steeply by breaking the wrists early and strike down firmly into the bottom of the ball. The clubhead cuts through the grass from out to in and the ball pops up high in the air.

You may have to play a **low trajectory shot** at any time – perhaps to avoid overhanging branches. Depending on the lie,

4 COMFORTABLE FINISH
Your left hand dominates before impact and it should continue to do so after the ball is on its way. Make sure the back of your left hand faces the target for as long as possible (above). This serves a double purpose – it prevents the clubface closing and guards against you scooping at the ball.

your club selection may vary from a long iron down to as little as an 8.

Judge the height and the amount of run you want on the ball and match the club best suited to the shot. Play the ball back in your stance and grip down the club for extra control. Strike down crisply, leading the clubhead into impact with your hands.

CALCULATED RISK

Much depends on the situation when you decide how ambitious you are with your recovery. If you're on a good score in a competition it usually pays to play cautiously. You can then limit the damage and move on to the next hole with your card intact.

In a relaxed game there's less at stake so you can afford to be more adventurous when you make your decision. You learn a valuable lesson whichever option you decide to take, and whether it's a success or not.

CLEAN THROUGH
As you look up you're greeted with the sight of your ball flying low towards the target – safely avoiding the overhanging branches. You're likely to take no more than 3 shots from an awkward predicament.

Occasionally you take one less – it's then you start to notice how the ability to recover makes a difference to your score. It's also a tremendous boost to your confidence.

On closer inspection
Identifying your ball in long or dense rough is sometimes a bit of a problem – thick grass easily conceals the manufacturer's name or number. If you're at all uncertain the rules allow you to lift the ball, check if it's yours and carefully replace it.

You must first announce your intention to someone in your playing group. This gives the player an opportunity to observe the correct lifting and replacement of the ball. If you fail to do so you incur a one stroke penalty.

THRASHING AWAY TO SAFETY

1 ◄ **OPEN UP**
You can find some pretty wild rough on most courses. It's difficult to escape from but you can do better than hit and hope. Stand open with your shoulders, hips and feet aligning left of target. Aim the clubface at the flag. Grip firmly and further down than normal – hover the club above the ground to prevent the ball moving.

2 ► **LEFT AT THE TOP**
Make a full backswing along the line of your body to create an out-to-in swing path. Make sure your right elbow points down at the ground to help keep the backswing compact at the top. The club should point well left of target. Maintain a firm grip – particularly with the left hand – to prevent the club twisting when you swing down through the grass.

3 ◄ **CUTTING EDGE**
Generate plenty of clubhead speed coming down – you want to remove as much grass around the ball as possible. The out-to-in swing path combined with the cushion effect of the grass means the ball is unlikely to travel very far.

4 ▼ **WRAP AROUND**
Concentrate on completing your followthrough, even though you may feel some resistance from the wiry grass. Some of the dense rough is still tangled around the hosel of the club – this emphasizes the need to grip tightly throughout the swing.

The greenside bunker shot

The key to playing from a greenside bunker is to be positive – forget about the dangers of playing a bad shot. Don't be scared to attack the ball, even if the flag is only a few club lengths away. Most bad bunker shots are caused by being too hesitant – so the ball just trickles along the sand.

At first it's difficult to grasp a technique that moves the ball without a direct hit – the clubhead strikes sand. The shot takes courage, but you'll be surprised how easy and enjoyable it is when you've learnt the knack.

HITTING THROUGH SAND

Once you understand the mechanics and feel of hitting through sand, you're halfway there. The rest – as for every other shot in golf – is a question of addressing the ball properly and swinging the club correctly.

To get out of a bunker successfully, you have to gain enough height to clear the lip of the bunker and then stop the ball quickly on landing. For this, the sand wedge is ideal. Its rounded sole allows for an easy passage through the

LIFTED ON SAND

The greenside bunker shot is unlike any other in golf. At no time during the stroke does the clubface make contact with the ball itself. The clubface hits behind and underneath the ball, which is lifted by the momentum transferred through the sand from the clubhead to the ball.

Address and swing path
Open the clubface to give the ball height. Align your body left to compensate for the open clubface at address. Otherwise you would send the ball in the same direction as the clubface is pointing – to the right. The ball is opposite the inside of your left heel. Your alignment and the ball position create the correct out-to-in swing path.

PLAYING OUT OF A BUNKER

1 SETTING UP
Open the clubface, grip down the shaft and take an open stance. At address, lines passing through your toes, knees, hips, chest and shoulders point left of target.

2 TAKE CLUB OUTSIDE BALL-TO-TARGET LINE
With the clubhead 1 in (4cm) behind the ball, take the club away outside the ball-to-target line – but don't touch sand. Break your wrists early on the backswing.

3 TWO-THIRDS SWING
At the top of the backswing your hands are no higher than shoulder height and your wrists are fully hinged. Rotate your body less than for a standard full swing.

4 OUT-TO-IN DOWNSWING
On the downswing let your arms and hands pull the clubhead from out to in. Keep your left wrist ahead of the clubhead to prevent the clubface from closing.

sand. Its loft angle – the greatest in the bag at 56-60° – puts height on the ball.

HOW THE SHOT WORKS

Instead of striking the ball, the clubface hits the sand behind the ball. It then passes through the sand under the ball. The momentum of the clubhead is transferred through the sand to the ball, which is lifted into the air.

The ball doesn't travel as far as if struck directly by the clubface. The sand between the clubface and ball acts as a cushion and by the time the power of the stroke reaches the ball it is greatly reduced. Despite the fact that the ball might travel a few club lengths only, this is still an attacking stroke.

ADDRESSING THE BALL

To play a greenside bunker shot, you set up with an open clubface and an open stance and body alignment. You then make a two-thirds swing with your club travelling in an out-to-in (right-to-left) swing path.

Hold the sand wedge in your right hand and open the clubface, so it aims right of target. The open clubface gives greater height to the ball, a softer landing and little roll.

When you've set your aim open, add the correct left-hand grip – slightly lower than usual to improve feel of the clubhead – and remove your right hand. Then add the correct right-hand grip. Always open the clubface before adding the correct grip.

You mustn't ground the clubface at address, so hold it just above the sand. The clubface should be about 1 in (4cm) behind the ball. Stand so that your feet are shoulder-width apart, with the ball opposite the inside of your left heel.

SWING AND SWING PATH

Adopt an open stance by standing with your left foot dropped back from the normal parallel alignment position. The rest of your body is also aligned left so that lines passing through your toes, knees, hips, chest and shoulder all point left of the ball-to-target line. Stand so that just over half of your weight (60%) is on your left foot. This set-up automatically produces the correct out-to-in swing path.

Smoothly take the club away outside the ball-to-target line. For the controlled two-thirds swing, swing the clubhead back until

Which wedge?

The sand wedge, with its rounded sole, slides through sand, making it the best club for bunker play. If you don't have one, use the next most lofted club – the pitching wedge. The sharper-edged pitching wedge meets with more resistance from the sand, which reduces clubhead speed, but its loft should give you the height to lift the ball over the lip of the bunker.

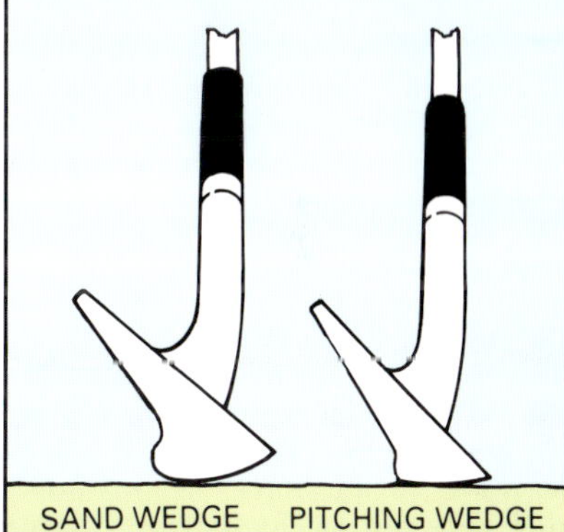
SAND WEDGE PITCHING WEDGE

5 STRIKE UNDERNEATH AND BEHIND BALL
Strike 1 in (4cm) behind the ball so that it explodes out on a wedge of sand. Your weight favours your left foot throughout the stroke.

6 MAKE FULL FOLLOWTHROUGH
After impact the club continues to move inside the ball-to-target line. Make a full followthrough to prevent stopping on the stroke.

your hands reach shoulder height at the top of the backswing. The precise length of the swing varies with the distance of the pin from the bunker. Practice will help you develop the feel for how long your swing should be.

Bring the club down on an out-to-in line so that the clubface travels from right to left through impact, entering the sand about 1 in (4cm) behind the ball. The clubface travels under the ball and re-emerges in front of the point where the ball was at address.

It is vital to keep the clubface moving through the sand at the same tempo as the rest of the swing. Exaggerate the through-swing to begin with to make certain that you don't stop on the shot – sand resistance slows down club-head speed. Keep your weight on your left side throughout. Practise hitting through the sand until you become confident.

SPLASHOUT ON THE SAND
The most important rule in bunker play is to hit sand not the ball. It is the force of the clubface as it passes through the sand that creates the power to splash the ball out – amid a shower of sand. The clubhead travels faster than the ball. Note how the clubhead is ahead of the ball.

HIT UNDERNEATH THE BALL AND AT LEAST 1½IN (4 CM) BEHIND IT

pro tip

Undercut your scorecard

One way to learn the technique is to place a ball in the centre of a scorecard in a bunker. Then swing the clubface under the card. This ensures you hit sand not the ball.

HIT UNDER THE SCORECARD

Testing the sand depth

Always test the depth and texture of the sand before playing a shot. Do this by wriggling your feet as you take your stance. If there's only a shallow layer of sand – a crust of solid mud, clay or hardened sand might exist just below the surface – your spikes don't move freely.

This test tells you how far under the ball your clubhead can pass.

Sloping bunker lies

Level greenside bunker lies present a tricky problem – upslopes and downslopes in the sand are often worse. You have to take exactly the correct amount of sand if you're to clear the face of the bunker and pitch the ball in the best place on the green.

UPSLOPES

When your ball is resting on the upslope of a bunker, the main point to remember is that the shot travels higher but covers less distance than from a level lie.

To fight this, change your technique by striking with a fuller swing than usual. Confidence is vital – many players are too cautious from an upslope, so the ball finishes a long way short of the hole.

DOWNSLOPES

If your ball rests on a downslope, the chances are that it has just trickled in. This makes your shot harder because the edge of the bunker – just behind the ball – impedes your backswing and downswing.

The ball is sure to have a reduced angle of flight path, and rolls on landing. This is because downhill lies deloft the clubface. It's vital to remember this – and adjust your technique accordingly – when you play this shot.

JUDGE IT CAREFULLY
When your ball is lying on a slope near the front or back edge of the bunker it's an awkward shot to play. Tackle an upslope by opening your stance and body alignment but aim square to the target.

UPHILL SLOPE IN A BUNKER

1 SLIGHTLY OPEN STANCE
Set up with the clubface square to the target and an open stance. The ball should be on the inside of your left heel – this helps create extra loft so that you are confident of clearing the bank. Keep your hands just ahead of the clubhead. Good tempo is vital. A longer, even swing applies power – a hurried stab at the ball does not.

2 WEIGHT ON RIGHT
Take the club away smoothly. Stand at 90° to the slope – this helps you feel as if you're playing from a flat lie. Don't lean into the slope or you dig the clubhead deep into the sand on the followthrough.

3 KEEP YOUR TEMPO
The ball flies higher but covers less distance than a level bunker shot, so compensate by making a fuller backswing than normal. As the downswing begins, keep a steady tempo. Let your left wrist and arm lead the club.

4 CONSTANT CLUBHEAD SPEED
Maintain momentum through the ball – your aim is to let a wedge of sand lift the ball up and out. Don't let the clubhead slow down. Make contact with the sand about 1½in (3cm) behind the ball.

5 OBSTRUCTED FOLLOWTHROUGH
The upslope helps your ball gain height so the shot should not be ruined if the upslope or the bank prevents a full followthrough. Your weight still just favours your right side.

DOWNHILL SLOPE

1 OPEN CLUBFACE
Open the clubface as much as possible – this helps the ball to gain maximum height so that it clears the face of the bunker and stops more quickly. Align left to compensate for the clubface position and lift the club up sharply.

2 STEEP BACKSWING
Your immediate wrist break produces a steep swing path and guarantees that you don't incur a penalty by touching the hazard. It also helps you make a steep attack down on the ball so that it's forced up. The ball must be well back in your stance.

Don't hit the hazard

If you ground the club in the hazard, or hit the sand on your backswing or downswing, you incur a 2 stroke penalty. Play out of the bunker sideways – or backwards – if you're in any doubt at all about the club's path. Striking the grassy bank – above the border with the sand – does not incur a penalty.

Be extra careful not to touch the surface with your club if you fail to free your ball from the sand at the first attempt. Your ball is still in the hazard, so the rule still applies – even after impact.

The best of players sometimes forget this. Top pro Howard Clark once had a nasty bunker lie and failed to escape in one. In disgust, he stabbed his club into the sand – and had 2 strokes added to his steadily increasing score.

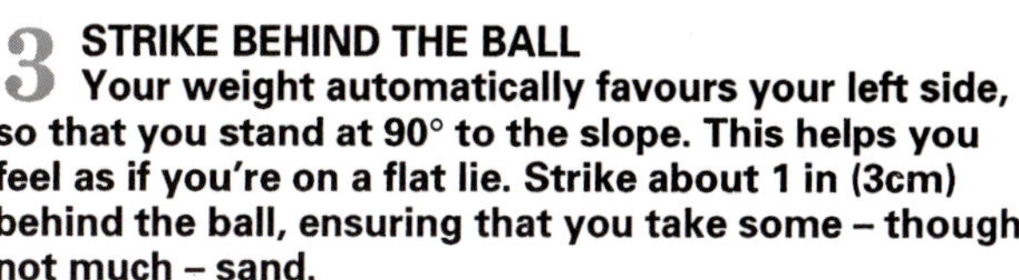

3 STRIKE BEHIND THE BALL
Your weight automatically favours your left side, so that you stand at 90° to the slope. This helps you feel as if you're on a flat lie. Strike about 1 in (3cm) behind the ball, ensuring that you take some – though not much – sand.

4 FULL FOLLOWTHROUGH
Make a full followthrough – you need to do everything possible to lift the ball up and over the face of the bunker. Because of the downslope the ball is sure to run on landing – take this factor into account when you prepare for the shot.

LOOK AT YOUR SHOT FIRST
From a bunker's downslope, the ball is certain to roll on landing. Spend a few seconds – no more or you delay play – visualizing the shot in your mind. Pitching the ball to a precise spot is tricky – you need as much green as possible to roll the ball on, but you must also strike with enough power to clear the bunker. Keep a firm mental image of the shot in your mind as you play.

Grip down for clubhead feel

Make sure that your hands take up their position lower down the grip than usual. This promotes your feel for the clubhead as you swing through the ball – vital if you're to take the proper amount of sand.

Hitting thin means that the ball either stays in the bunker or skims through the green. If you strike fat you may not even move the ball. Good clubhead feel reduces the likelihood of these disasters.

pro tip

Firm footing

As you take your stance to play the shot, make sure that your feet are firmly embedded in the sand. This helps you to keep your balance through the stroke, which is made harder than usual by the slopes. You must be comfortable, standing at 90° to the slope to give the feel of playing from a flat lie.

Planting your feet solidly also serves as a gauge for sand texture – use it to judge how the clubface will pass through the sand.

The fairway bunker shot

A fairway bunker shot is the most varied in the game. A fairway bunker is separated from the green by fairway or rough, and can be anything between 20yd (18m) from the target to 300yd (274m) or more away.

The wide range of distances is reflected in the clubs you can use – any one from a fairway wood to a sand wedge. However, the technique stays the same.

The club you choose depends on the position of the ball in the bunker and the distance between the ball and the target.

CLEAN STRIKE FOR LENGTH
To hit the ball a long way from a fairway bunker – a difficult shot – you must nip it off the top of the sand as cleanly as possible. It's a precision stroke with a lot at stake – success lands you on the green but failure leaves you still in the bunker and even worse off.

CHOOSING YOUR CLUB

Before choosing a club, assess how high the ball must fly to clear the front lip of the bunker. Visualize a straight line between the ball and the highest point on the lip. The nearer the ball is to the front of the bunker, the higher the lift it needs, and the greater loft the club must have.

Shifting your weight

Practise hitting fairway bunker shots with most of your weight on your right side by keeping your right foot firmly planted on the ground on the backswing and downswing. Don't let your right heel lift until after impact.

This routine delays the natural forward leg movement on the downswing, stops your weight shifting from right to left too soon and prevents the clubface striking sand.

5 IRON

If you're, say, a 7-iron distance from the green but need an 8 iron to clear the lip, don't gamble with the lower numbered club. You won't get enough elevation and the ball will strike the front face of the bunker – ending up in a worse position than before.

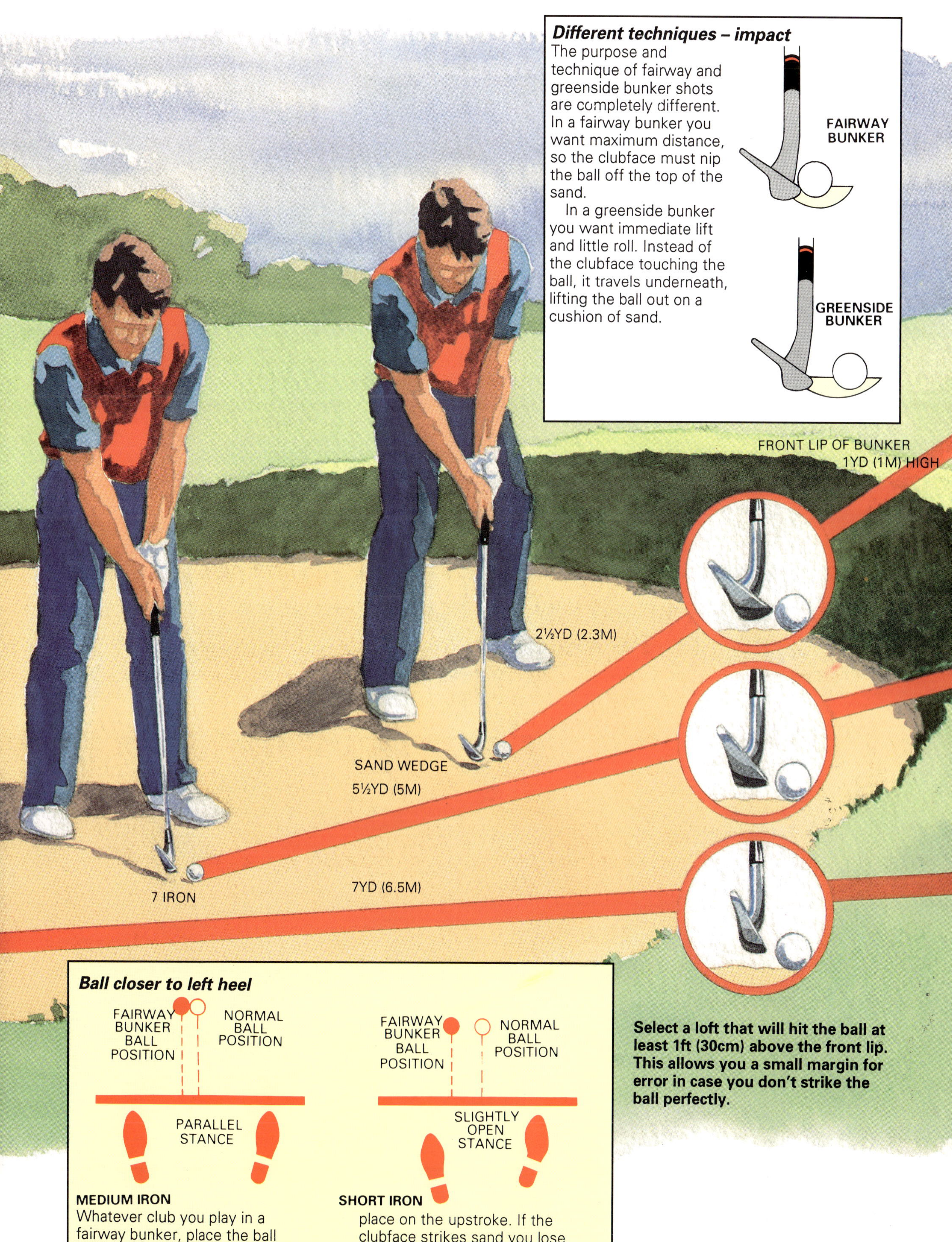

Different techniques – impact

The purpose and technique of fairway and greenside bunker shots are completely different. In a fairway bunker you want maximum distance, so the clubface must nip the ball off the top of the sand.

In a greenside bunker you want immediate lift and little roll. Instead of the clubface touching the ball, it travels underneath, lifting the ball out on a cushion of sand.

Select a loft that will hit the ball at least 1ft (30cm) above the front lip. This allows you a small margin for error in case you don't strike the ball perfectly.

Ball closer to left heel

Whatever club you play in a fairway bunker, place the ball slightly nearer your left heel than normal. This reduces the risk of taking sand, because impact takes place on the upstroke. If the clubface strikes sand you lose power and strength.

Align your feet as if using the same club from the fairway.

HITTING FROM A FAIRWAY BUNKER

1 ADDRESS
Grip down the club and aim square. Adopt a normal stance for the club with the ball nearer your left heel than usual and with just over half your weight on your right side. Keep the clubhead above and behind the ball.

2 TAKEAWAY
Be careful the clubhead doesn't brush the sand on the takeaway. To create a wide swing plane, avoid breaking your wrists too early. Your hands, arms, shoulders and chest move together.

WHICH CLUB TO PLAY?

When assessing a fairway bunker shot, you must work out the height needed to clear the front lip of the bunker and the distance that your ball has to travel to reach the target.

First you need to consider clearing the bunker lip. The closer the ball is to the front of the bunker the greater height it needs to clear the lip. Work out which clubs have enough loft to hit the ball above the lip. Then choose your club.

If you can reach the target from your position, select the club with the most loft that also gives the perfect distance. Using the *highest* numbered club gives you the best chance of clearing the front lip of the bunker.

If you can't reach the target, maximum distance is usually your priority. Choose the *lowest* numbered club that gives your ball enough height to clear the front lip of the bunker.

Club selection is as important as making the correct swing. Assess the facts coolly before making a fairway bunker shot. Don't be greedy – a gamble rarely succeeds. Your ball usually stays in the bunker but in a worse position than before.

3 THREE-QUARTER BACKSWING
Make a controlled three-quarter backswing, turning your upper body 90°. At the top of the backswing your wrists are fully hinged. Don't be tempted to make a full swing or you may lose rhythm.

4 WEIGHT STAYS ON RIGHT SIDE
As your hands, wrists, arms and the clubhead approach the ball, more than half your weight is still on your right side. This stops the clubface from hitting too far behind the ball and taking sand.

5 IMPACT ON UPSTROKE
Impact is on the upstroke. This gives you a cleaner strike than normal, as well as full benefit from the clubface loft for height to clear the bunker lip.

6 WEIGHT SHIFT
Only after impact does your weight transfer to your left side. Your upper body and head rotate to face the target. Maintain your normal tempo throughout the swing.

A CLEAN STRIKE

The fairway bunker technique is the same for every club. The aim of the stroke is to pick the ball cleanly off the top of the ground – without the clubface touching the sand.

If sand gets trapped between the clubface and the ball it acts as a cushion, slowing the clubface down at impact, and loses you power and distance. There is also a 2-shot penalty if any part of the club touches the sand before impact.

For a clean strike, have the ball slightly nearer your left heel than normal. This means that impact is on the upstroke, so the clubface is moving up and away from the sand when it meets the ball. You also gain maximum benefit from clubface loft.

If you position the ball normally the clubface moves into the ball on the downstroke, increasing the risk of striking sand.

ADDRESS AND WEIGHT SHIFT

Having chosen the club, grip about 1in (2.5cm) further down the shaft than normal for greater clubhead control. Aim the clubface square to the ball-to-target line.

Align your body normally for the club but with the ball slightly nearer your left heel. Address the ball with just over half your weight on your right side, to help you strike the ball on the upstroke. This prevents your weight shifting on to your left side too early on the downswing and stops the clubface striking the ball on the downstroke.

Although your upper body turns fully during the swing, leg action is restricted because of your weight distribution at address.

If your weight is distributed evenly at address, the natural forward movement of the swing and your body brings the clubhead into the ball too steeply and too early – and you take sand.

How ever far from the green you are, always make a three-quarter swing. This helps you maintain a good tempo, and makes it easier to achieve a clean contact.

PLAYING SAFE

Never force a full shot. For instance, a 7 iron may have the least loft available to clear the front lip but would still leave your ball short of the green. Don't lengthen or increase the speed of your swing in an attempt to make up those extra yards. Accept that you'll be short and aim to save par with a chip and putt.

Playing safe is particularly important when your ball is very close to the lip – possibly so close that even the loft on a sand wedge won't give you quick enough lift to clear it. In this case, you must give up all thought of sending the ball far and instead use the greenside bunker technique to play out.

Using the same club – a sand wedge – the greenside bunker shot provides almost vertical elevation, floating your ball out on a wedge of sand.

Playing from wet sand

Surprisingly, you get a cleaner strike from wet sand than from dry sand. This is because wet sand is firmer and the ball perches on top of the surface – just as it does on the fairway. The ball is easier to hit because you see more of it, and there's less risk of taking sand at impact – and of touching sand at address or takeaway.

INCREASE CLUBHEAD AWARENESS

GRIP DOWN
For better clubface control, grip about 1in (2.5cm) further down the shaft than normal. The closer your hands are to the ball, the greater your feel for the clubface is.

PENALTY POINT
Don't let any part of the club touch the sand before you hit the ball – or you face a 2-stroke penalty. This rule applies to all sand bunker shots.

A wood from the bunker

It's frustrating when your ball lands in a fairway bunker, particularly if you've notched up a good score. But be positive – all is not lost.

A well negotiated strike could land you in a position to save shots. Most fairway bunkers are shallower than those beside the green – and are often less difficult than they first appear.

Be flexible over your choice of club – an inspired shot is often the result of creative club selection. If the ball is sitting up well a fair distance away from the front of the bunker, it is much easier to get out using a utility wood rather than the more usual iron.

The small head and low centre of gravity of the wood allow more weight to pass underneath the ball and so lift it up quickly. And the smooth rounded shape of the head prevents snagging in the sand which often happens with the long irons.

CLUB CHOICE

One of the keys to success with a fairway bunker shot is choosing the right club. An iron is the obvious choice – but in many situations the wood may give a better combination of lift and distance.

Weigh up the facts carefully – enter the bunker, take your stance to the ball and visualize the shot coming out. You must decide which club is best for getting over the lip of the bunker *and* reaching the green. To work out the lift, consider how far the ball is from the front of the hazard.

The 5 wood lifts the ball higher and sends it further than a 2 iron, because it has more loft and a longer shaft. But if you feel that a wood is not going to clear the bunker, play safe – take a lofted iron instead.

ASSESS THE LIE

It's important to study the lie of the ball carefully. If the ball is sitting down or partly buried in the bunker, choose a lofted iron club and play a safe shot. But if the lie

FAIRWAY BUNKER WOOD
Use a utility wood to good effect to lift the ball up and over the lip from a fairway bunker lie. Grip down the club to compensate for the lower position of your body. A shorter swing and lower grip reduce distance but give greater control. To avoid a 2-stroke penalty remember not to ground the club at address or on the backswing.

MAKE A CLEAN STRIKE

1 SET-UP
Take a normal stance – wriggle your feet for a firm footing in sand. To hit cleanly focus your eyes on top of the ball before taking the club away slowly and surely.

2 CONTROLLED CONTACT
Make a three-quarter back and throughswing to increase your control. Keep a smooth rhythm to help you swing firmly down and through the ball.

3 BALANCED FINISH
After you've swept the ball cleanly from the sand, aim for a balanced finish. Keep your head still until your right shoulder forces it to turn and watch the ball's flight.

is reasonable and you have a good distance between the ball and the front of the bunker, pick a 5 wood – or even a 7 if you normally carry one.

POSITIVE APPROACH

After you select your club and take your set-up, be single minded in your approach – block out distractions and focus purely on your objective. Set aside thoughts of failure – a positive approach gives a better chance of achieving your target.

Take a firm footing in the sand – to avoid a 2-stroke penalty, remember not to ground the club at address. Grip down the club for extra control and sweep the ball cleanly off the sand with a smooth and purposeful three-quarter swing.

masterclass

Bunker courage
One of the most memorable shots of all time was played at the 1983 Ryder Cup. By the 18th hole the singles match between Seve Ballesteros and Fuzzy Zoeller looked as if it could go either way.

On this final hole, Seve played his drive to the left of the fairway to avoid water – only to find the fairway bunker. He needed to carry the ball some 250yd (230m) over water to reach the green. The risk was high.

Coolly assessing the situation, Seve chose a 3 wood and sent the ball searing over the face of the bunker. As it landed on the green the crowd roared in appreciation. Jack Nicklaus said it was one of the finest shots he'd ever seen.

LONG IRON

UTILITY WOOD

Off the sand
With its rounded head and low centre of gravity, a lofted utility wood lifts the ball quickly and provides the necessary distance for a fairway bunker shot to reach the green.

The long irons have narrow soles which may dig into the sand – the ball is likely to end up at the side of the bunker.

Plugged lies

When your ball is sitting up in a bunker, you have a relatively simple shot. Plugged lies are another matter – extracting a buried ball from the sand is a tricky prospect.

Your ball could plug for a number of reasons. The texture of the sand is critical – newly laid sand can give you problems because it hasn't had a chance to settle.

Thick sand is likely to absorb your ball before the sand has time to thin out. When it does become finer, it acts as a cushion.

STUN SHOT

It's always the power of the club through the sand that blasts your ball out of the bunker – never try to play the ball itself.

With a ball that's lying well, you open the face, align left and use a fairly long swing. This provides height and backspin, so that the ball stops quickly.

The opposite happens when your ball is plugged. You set up parallel to the ball-to-target line with a slightly closed clubface.

That's why you can't expect height – the closed clubface digs

LESS HEIGHT THAN USUAL
Hitting successfully from a plugged lie is awkward because you don't get as much height and backspin as with a standard splash shot. Play a stun shot with a closed clubface to check the roll.

ESCAPING FROM A PLUGGED LIE

1 CLOSE THE CLUBFACE Stand parallel to the ball-to-target line with the ball central. Close the clubface – this helps dig out the ball. Set up differently from your normal splash shot address – for a good lie – when you align left with the ball forwards and open the clubface.

GOOD LIE

2 HALF BACKSWING Swing back about halfway, breaking your wrists straight away. You need a steep angle of attack into the sand – the wrist break ensures it. When you play from a good bunker lie, your backswing is longer.

Don't hit yourself

You incur a 2-stroke penalty if the ball touches you at any time – so be on the lookout for rebounds.

If the ball is plugged in the lip of the bunker, consider playing out sideways. It's better to escape anywhere than to attempt too hard a shot – you might be looking down at yet another bunker lie, which leaves you in an even worse situation.

out the ball effectively, but with very little lift. The ball emerges with top-spin and runs on landing to reduce further your chances of landing close to the flag.

To compensate for the strong roll, you must play a stun shot. This means having the confidence to cut short your throughswing, so that the clubhead does not pass your hands at any time.

Carefully assess the situation before you take up your stance, because the ball doesn't rise as well as from a good sand lie. You may not escape if the bunker has a steep face. If the face does look forbidding, play out sideways – at least you'll be out of the trap in one.

Strike firmly if you want plenty of roll. Trying for hardly any run on the ball is a riskier shot because you need to hit more softly – but

3 HANDS LEAD THE CLUBFACE
Let your hands lead the clubface – exactly as you do when you're splashing out normally – and keep your left wrist dominant throughout the downswing.

4 KEEP LEFT WRIST FIRM
Strike about 3in (7cm) behind the ball. At impact your hands should still be ahead of the clubhead with the left wrist – which mustn't collapse – taking the force of the shot. With a normal shot (right), the clubhead catches up with your hands at impact, but the role of the left hand is again vital.

not so softly that the club slows down, leaving your ball in the sand.

Although you strike with less power for the short hit, keep your left wrist firm. This helps to prevent slowing down the club as it enters the sand. When tempo is erratic, so is timing – and your shot is certain to suffer.

FIRM HOLD

Grip pressure is important. It should be firm for a long shot and more relaxed – though still solid – for a shorter shot.

It's worthwhile to spend some time in the bunker rehearsing strokes from a plugged lie. The more confident you are the more daring you can afford to be – but your top priority is to escape in one shot.

5 LOW CLUB AFTER IMPACT
Shorten the throughswing. This stunning action reduces the roll of the ball when it lands. From a good lie you don't need to lessen the followthrough, as the ball's height stops roll.

HOW'S IT LYING?

ASSESS THE SITUATION
When you enter the bunker, visualize your shot carefully. You can move man-made obstructions, but natural impediments must be left as they are. It's possible that you can move stones without penalty – check your scorecard for local rules. When you've played, leave the bunker as you'd wish to find it – litter free, raked and smooth.

CIGARETTE ENDS
You can move cigarette ends, sweet wrappers and the like – they're man-made objects.

FOOTPRINTS
You must play from footprints even though your ball can plug in them. Unfortunately you're paying for the lack of etiquette shown by another player.

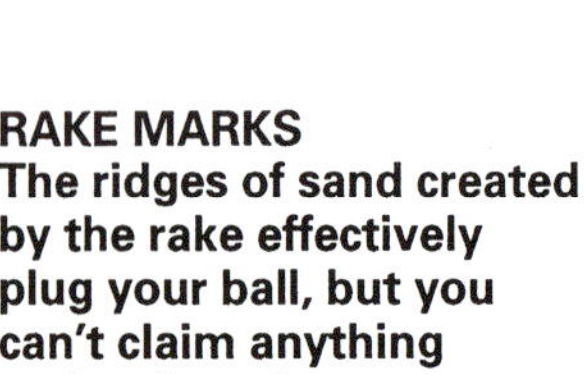

RAKE MARKS
The ridges of sand created by the rake effectively plug your ball, but you can't claim anything under the rules.

LEAVES
If a stray leaf is lying next to your ball, you can't move it because the leaf is a natural object.

Putting

Almost half your shots in any round are putts so it is vital to develop a good stroke. If you putt well you are halfway to recording a decent score. Good putting is so important that just a handful of missed putts per round can mean the difference between a 19 and a 24 handicap.

The object of every putt is to hole the ball. If you don't, try to ensure that the ball is past the hole but near enough so that your next shot is from close range. Anything more than two putts per green is a waste of strokes.

After hitting tee and fairway shots 200yd (182m) or more, you finish every hole by putting the ball into the cup. Putts vary in distance from a 90ft (27m) one from the edge of a large green to a mere tap-in from the edge of the hole. However, most putts are between 2-30ft (0.5-9m).

Because a putt is normally quite short, it needs the shortest swing and least energy of any shot. Yet good putting requires precise stroke-making.

ROLLING THE BALL

Putting requires a unique technique – rolling the ball along the ground. It is the only shot where the ball does not travel through the air. The ball travels over a special surface – the green – and you use a specially designed club – the putter.

The putter has the least loft of any club – between 2° and 4° – so you cannot use it for gaining height on the ball. It is also the shortest club in the bag and the most upright. It has a small club-head and is not built for distance.

Head start

You should keep your head still while you putt. You can practise this indoors, by resting your head against a wall while putting on a carpet. Stand close to the wall and touch it gently with your head. Keep your head there so it can't move as you putt along the side of the wall.

PUTT IT RIGHT

Although the putting stroke is the shortest of all, it is vital to get it right. Stand parallel to the line of the putt with your left eye directly over the ball. The clubhead travels along this same line for most of the stroke.

Your shoulders, hips and toes are parallel to the line of the putt.

SHOULDERS, HIPS AND TOES PARALLEL TO LINE OF PUTT

LINE OF THE PUTT

LEFT EYE OVER BALL

STANCE PARALLEL TO LINE OF PUTT

LINE OF THE PUTT

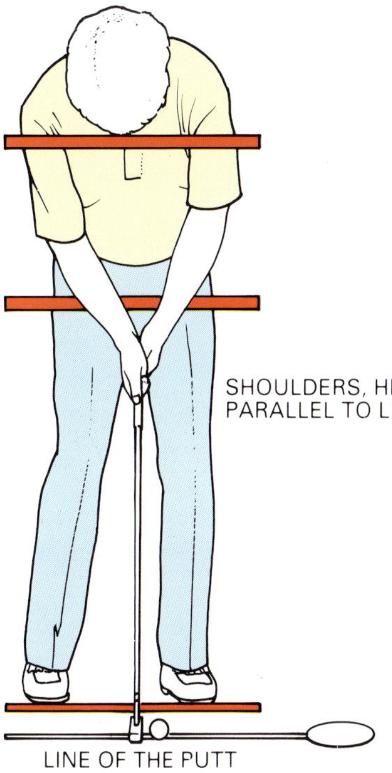

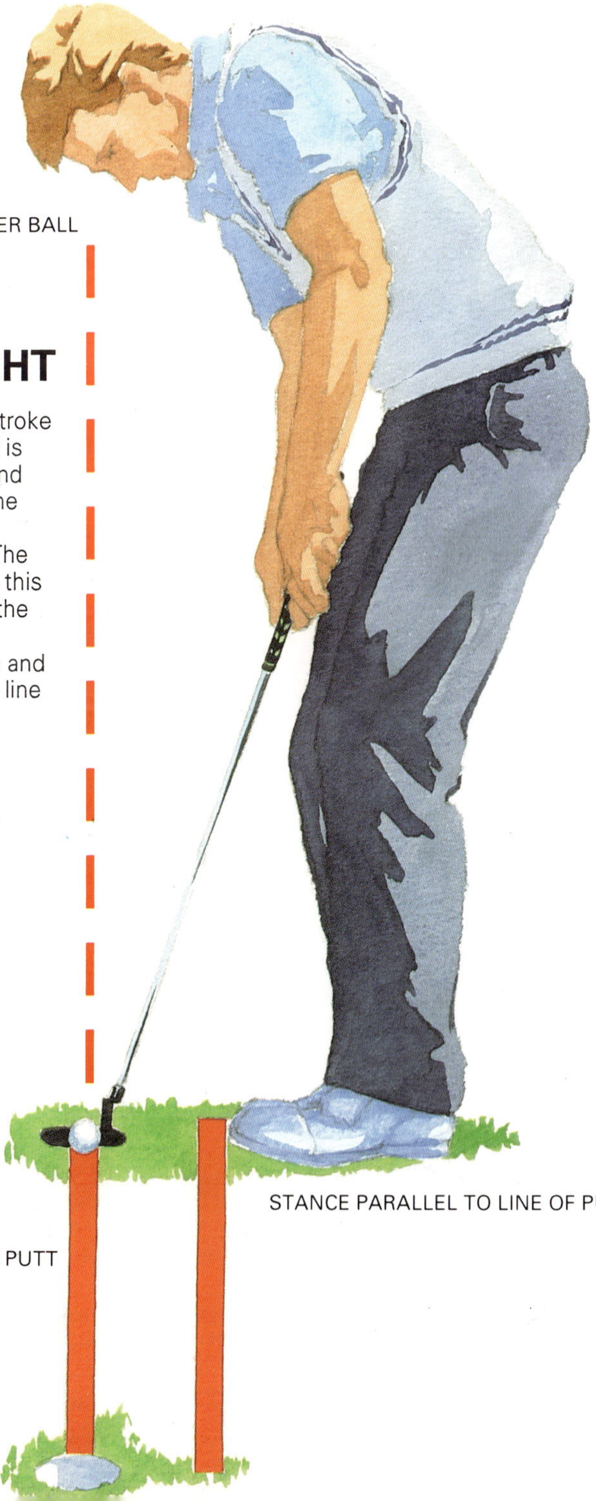

GETTING TO GRIPS

1 **PLACE LEFT HAND ON GRIP**
Leaving a gap at the top, grip the club lightly with the middle, third and little fingers of your left hand. Point your forefinger down the shaft and hold your thumb above the flat front side.

2 **ADD RIGHT HAND**
Slide the little, third and middle fingers of your right hand against your middle left finger. Rest your left thumb against the centre of the shaft. Point both forefingers down the shaft.

3 **COMPLETE THE GRIP**
Wrap the forefinger of your right hand round the grip and rest your right thumb down the shaft. Let your left forefinger lie across your right hand. A straight line runs through wrist, hand and shaft.

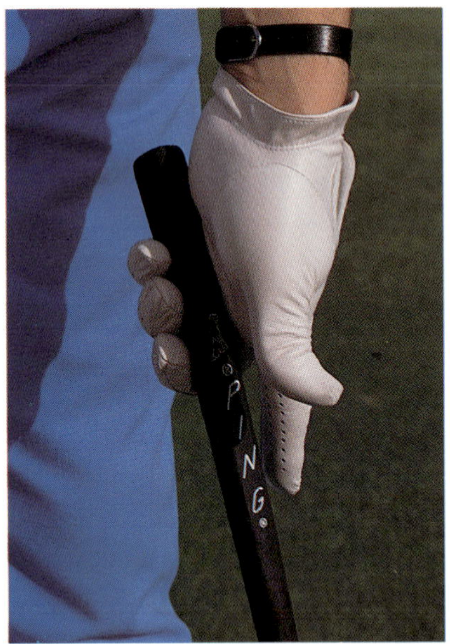

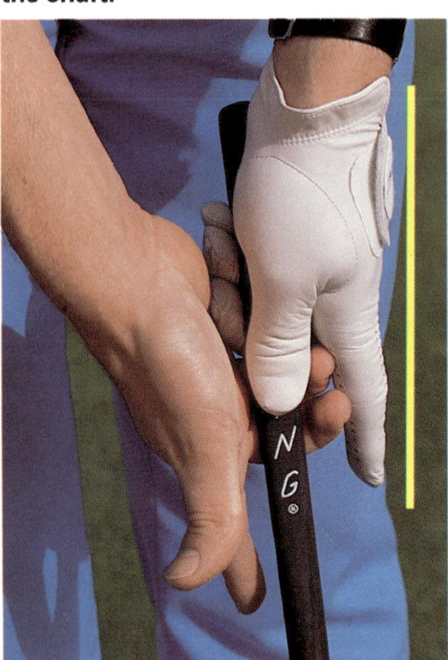

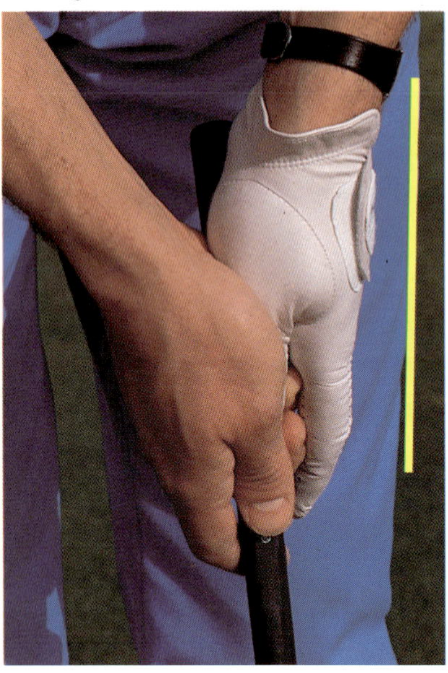

THE PUTTING STROKE

1 **YOUR ADDRESS POSITION**
The ball is opposite the inside of your left heel and your left eye is directly over the ball. Stand parallel to the line of the putt.

2 **THE BACKSTROKE**
Take the clubhead back straight. Your hands, arms and shoulders form one unit – a triangle which moves but never changes shape. Keep your head and lower body still.

pro tip

Feel the pendulum action

You can achieve the correct putting motion by practising the stroke with an object such as a short strip of wood trapped between your elbows. This makes your hands, arms and shoulders move as one and helps create an even pendulum action. Practise this until it feels natural.

LINE OF THE PUTT

Before you make your stroke you must decide on the line of the putt. This is not necessarily a straight line between ball and target – the ball-to-target line – because the roll of the ball will be affected by slopes.

To find the line of the putt try to visualize the path of your ball between its start position and the hole. If the green slopes from left down to right, the ball travels in the same direction, so compensate by selecting a point left of the hole at which to aim your putt. A straight line between the ball and this imaginary hole is called the line of the putt. A ball putted towards the imaginary hole curves with the slope and into the actual hole.

The exact point at which you aim depends on the severity of the slope and the length of the shot. The longer the putt and the greater the slope, the further away from the actual hole you should aim. This is because the more extreme conditions make the ball break further from the original line of the putt.

As well as assessing cross-slopes, you must take into account up and down slopes. An uphill putt needs a firmer strike than a downhill stroke.

Much of visualization is common sense, but to be really good at it requires practice and experience. The more you putt, the easier you'll find it to judge the pace and direction.

AIM AND GRIP

Once you have established the line of the putt, aim the clubface square on to it. Some putters have a mark on the clubhead to help you aim correctly. Then you take up your grip.

There are almost as many putting grips as there are individual players but the reverse overlap is the most popular putting grip in today's game. It is similar to the standard overlap grip, with one difference: the forefinger of the left

3 THROUGH IMPACT
The throughstroke follows the same straight line as the backstroke. Keep your left wrist firm through impact to ensure the clubhead is pulled smoothly through the ball.

4 ENDING THE STROKE
The clubhead continues to the same height as the top of the backstroke. Your hands, arms and shoulders still move as one. Let your head rotate slightly to the left after impact.

hand changes places with the little finger of the right hand. This change helps to keep your left hand, arm and shoulder moving correctly through the ball.

POSTURE AND ALIGNMENT

The key point about putting posture is that you stand so that your eyes are directly over the ball at address. This gives you a clear view of the line of the putt and makes aiming easier. It usually means that you have to stand with your knees slightly bent and your back bent from the waist.

Because the putter is the shortest, most upright, club in the bag you stand close to the ball. With your feet about 12in (30cm) apart, stand so that the ball is opposite the inside of your left heel. By placing the ball forward in your stance you hit it on the upstroke. This produces topspin and gives a consistent roll. Your weight is evenly spread throughout.

As with all golf strokes, alignment is crucial. when putting you align your feet, knees, hips and shoulders parallel to line of putt.

Stand parallel to line of putt

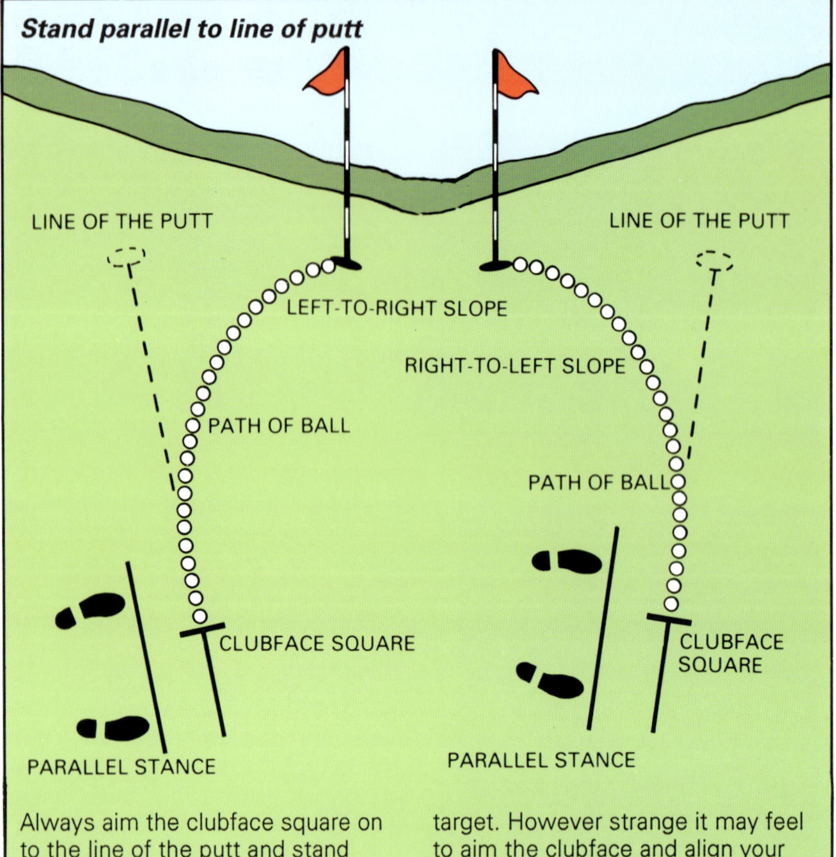

Always aim the clubface square on to the line of the putt and stand parallel to this line. Depending on the type and severity of the slope, this line may point left or right of the target. However strange it may feel to aim the clubface and align your body away from the target, it is the correct method – otherwise you hit a poor, badly aimed shot.

Judging pace and distance

To help you develop a feel for length, practise this simple routine. Place five balls in a line at 12in (30cm) intervals from the hole. Starting with the one nearest the hole, try to sink each ball in turn.

For each putt set yourself up carefully and assess the length of the stroke. Repeat until your back and throughstrokes are automatically the correct length to hole the ball.

THE STROKE

The putting stroke is dictated by your hands, arms and shoulders – which move as one unit. There is no body rotation, unlike full iron and wood shots. This is why it is vital to align your shoulders correctly at address.

Take the clubhead back with your hands, arms and shoulders moving together. The length of the backstroke is determined by the length of the putt. The clubhead travels in a straight line for most of the stroke, and only briefly moves inside the line of the putt as it nears the top of the backstroke.

Follow the same path into impact, keeping your left wrist firm. This allows the clubhead to be pulled through the ball on the correct line and prevents your right hand from flicking at it. Accelerate the clubhead through impact. Keep your head and lower body still, while allowing the clubhead to swing in a pendulum motion. The back and throughstrokes are of equal length.

Long putts

Many golfers spend hours on the practice range trying to improve their wood and long iron play – but neglect their putting stroke. That's why putting is the most underrated part of the game – but you strike almost half your shots on the green.

You shouldn't take more than two putts on any green. Yet most players waste more shots here than anywhere else on the course. A 3 putt is damaging to your confidence as well as your score – usually it's the result of a poor first putt. It's vital to work on a repeat-

PUTT TO A LARGER TARGET
When faced with a long putt try to roll your ball into an imaginary 3-4ft (1-1.5m) circle around the hole. Don't attempt to sink the shot. By setting an easier target you stand more chance of getting the ball close to the pin – expecting to hole it increases the pressure on you. If you try to sink a long putt you focus your attention on the hole rather than the stroke needed to combat the speed and slopes of the green. Widening the target is a psychological trick that works.

THE PENDULUM ACTION

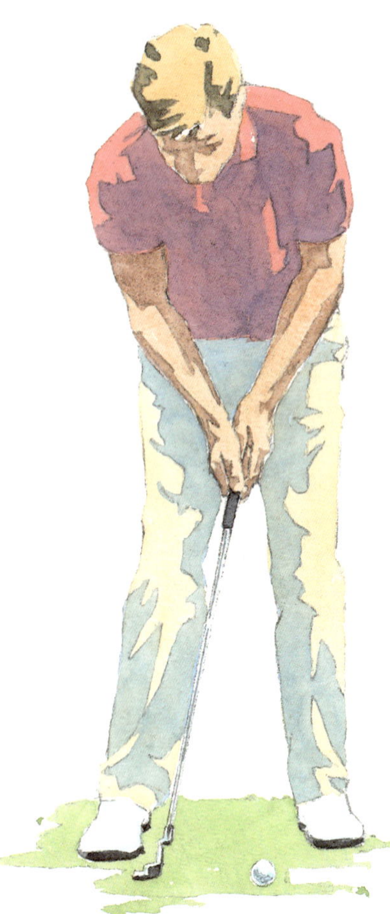

1 BALL OPPOSITE INSIDE OF LEFT HEEL
Stand with the ball opposite the inside of your left heel and your left eye directly over the ball. Your address position must be relaxed. Use the reverse overlap grip to help your feel for the shot.

2 SQUARE CLUBFACE
Keep the sole of the clubhead close to the ground for the first 12in (30cm) of the takeaway. To create the pendulum action of hands, arms and shoulders, keep the clubface and the back of your left hand square to the line of the putt for as long as possible on the backswing.

Late strike for smooth roll

For an even roll, place the ball opposite the inside of your left heel. Impact occurs late – on the upstroke – with the clubhead smoothly striking the ball forward.

If the ball is central in your stance impact is at the lowest point of the stroke. The clubhead hits down on the ball, pressing it slightly into the ground and causing it to bobble off line.

able putting stroke so that you can putt well from long distances.

Putting is the one area of the game where the high handicapper can perform as well as the low handicapper. This is because the stroke doesn't rely on power or an athletic swing. You can even practise putting in your own home.

Long putts are precision strokes. You must develop feel, intense concentration and an ability to read the green correctly.

ROLL THE BALL CLOSE

Although many players try to sink every putt – whatever the distance from the hole – they fail to hole most putts over 20ft (6m). This is true of even the most legendary players.

From beyond this distance you should try to stop your ball within 3ft (1m) of the hole. Don't expect

3 UPPER BODY MOVES AS ONE
To ensure a firm, smooth stroke, your hands, wrists, arms and shoulders move as one throughout the swing. This stops your wrists breaking. Impact occurs on the upstroke to produce an even roll. Your left eye remains directly above the ball and your head stays still through impact.

4 KEEP YOUR HEAD STILL
Even as the clubhead lifts up on the followthrough the clubface stays square to the line of the putt. As you complete the stroke – and not before – your head turns to face the hole. Your backswing and followthrough should be of equal length.

to sink it – if you hole a long putt accept it as a bonus. When you're a lengthy distance from the hole it's more important that you don't take 3 to get down.

READING THE GREEN

To assess your stroke accurately you must analyse two factors – the speed of the green and the lie of the land. Never be complacent – no two greens are the same.

Green speeds vary from course to course, season to season and at times even hole to hole. This happens for many reasons – mainly the soil type, its drainage and the type and length of the grass. The weather conditions are also important.

Bear in mind that the faster the green the more precisely you need to judge the speed and line of a putt, as the ball breaks more acutely on fast greens.

You must also assess the lie of the land between your ball and the hole. The slope of the green affects the line of the putt. Will the ball travel straight or curve left to right?

SPEED AND LINE

The steeper the slope the greater the curve and further left or right of the hole you must aim.

To putt well, both speed and slope must be judged correctly. Checking for slopes is fairly obvious to the eye, but speed is a mixture of experience and trial and error. Most 3 putts are caused by misjudging the pace. Try to get a feel for pace early in your round and learn from it.

For longer putts, assessing speed is more important than gauging the line as distance from the hole gets bigger. This is because there is less margin for error over long distances.

You should not be more than 3ft (1m) off line from wherever you putt. A slight miscalculation in pace can result in your ball finishing 10-12ft (3-4m) away. Some greens are so fast that even the smallest boost in putter head speed means a difference of 10-15 ft (3-5m).

To become an accurate long putter you must combine correct green reading with a repeatable stroke.

REVERSE OVERLAP GRIP

Remember that the putting grip is similar to the standard overlapping grip – with one small difference. The forefinger of your left hand rests along two fingers of your right hand. This reverse overlap grip gives you greater feel and reduces the chances of left wrist break.

MOVE AS ONE

1 BACKSWING
Hold a club lengthways between your chest and upper arms before adopting your putting stance and starting your backswing.

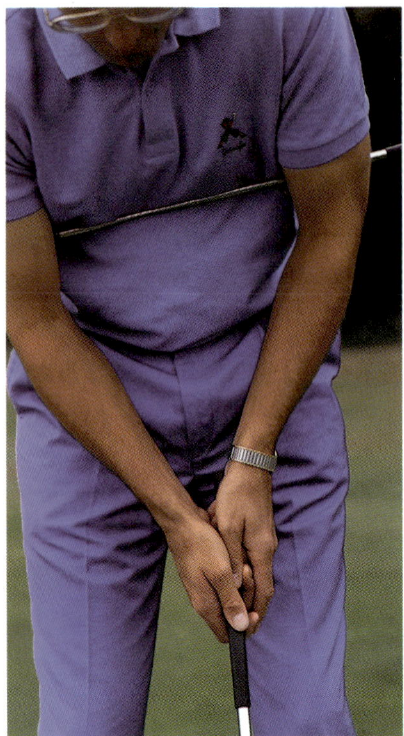

2 IMPACT
The club under your arms forces your shoulders, hands and arms to move as one unit through impact – if they don't, you drop the club.

3 THROUGHSWING
Your hands are still passive as your upper body – which moves as one unit throughout – completes the throughswing.

Take an open stance – it helps you to see the line – and make sure your hands are square to the line of the putt. The ball should be opposite the inside of your left heel. This is slightly further forward in your stance than normal.

Impact occurs later than usual – on the upstroke – to help produce a smooth, even roll.

Stand with your left eye over the ball. This lets you look directly along the line of the putt. If it feels uncomfortable, your putter must be either too long or too short for your height and needs changing.

Aim the clubface square to the line of the putt. Take the club a way with both hands – everything must work together – keeping the back of your left hand and the clubface square to the line of the putt. Keep the sole of the clubhead close to the ground, without letting it touch.

Play it with a sand wedge

To get the feel of striking the ball on the upstroke, practise putting with a sand wedge. With the ball opposite the inside of your left heel, try to strike so that the leading clubface edge makes contact with the middle of the ball.

Unless impact is perfect, the ball jumps and bobbles towards the hole. Only when the roll is smooth and even is your putting stroke correct. Don't practise this on the course – you should not take divots on the green.

PENDULUM ACTION

Imagine the clubhead as a pendulum – moving back and through impact on the same line. Your hands should be passive – let your hands, wrists, arms and shoulders move as one to create a smooth, unhurried stroke.

The length of the putt determines how far back you take the clubhead. The backswing and throughswing should be the same length. This promotes even clubhead speed as you swing through. Don't speed up or slow down the club through impact – it affects the putt's pace.

Practise your putting regularly to develop a consistent technique and a feel for the shot.

Steep slope putting

Judging pace is critical if you are to avoid three putting on steeply sloping greens. But a fine judgement of speed must be linked with good reading of the line. The pace determines the line. You must first gauge the weight of the putt, then concentrate on the line and balance the two considerations.

DIFFERING APPROACHES

Aim to hole your first putt only when it's close to the pin. From long range think of two putting, as three putts are always a danger and holing out must be seen as a bonus.

Straight uphill: This is easily the simplest putt on a steeply sloping green. You can afford to hit the ball firmly and it still should drop because of the angle of the hole. But be wary of overhitting the ball on a long putt – you could leave yourself a very awkward downhill putt.

From short range, make a smooth stroke and hit the ball firmly at the back of the hole.

Straight downhill: The pace is all important. Any putt going at even slightly more than perfect speed has little chance of dropping.

To help you judge the pace from long range, pick a point – perhaps an old hole or small mark on the green – between you and the hole. Choose a spot just a few inches away on a very steep green. Then play a normal putt to your spot – the slope carries the ball the rest of the way.

Always make sure you hit the ball with enough pace to send it past the hole should you miss. A putt from 6ft (2m) straight back up the hill is far better than facing a tricky downhiller of 3ft (1m).

From short range concentrate on the line. Take time to set the blade exactly square to the target line because a downhill putt that catches the lip spins out unless going very slowly. Never leave a putt short from close range – it's a waste of a stroke.

Long putt across the slope: The ideal putt across a steep green is for the ball to topple in from the

EXPLORE ALL ANGLES
There is an art to balancing the line and pace on a steeply sloping green – an understanding of how the ball behaves from all angles makes putting much easier. From long range aim to knock your ball just past the hole to leave an uphill second. Holing out is a bonus.

top side. For this you judge the weight of the shot so the ball comes almost to a standstill above but nearly level with the hole. The ball then rolls down the slope and comes in from almost 90°.

But be realistic – aim to two putt on most occasions. Your main thought should be to lag the ball and regard holing out first time as a bonus.

Pace and line are vital. If you under or overhit the ball – even if you've chosen a good line – you're left with the same awkward type of putt but from a slightly shorter distance. Hit the ball too low and it gathers speed down the slope and runs well by. Hit too high and the ball stays up on the top side and you're left with a tricky downhill breaking putt.

Short putt across the slope: Aim at a point level with the hole. Again almost stop the ball on the top side so that it rolls slowly down towards the hole.

Always allow more break than you think – it's better to be on the top side (known as the pro side) because the ball has a chance of dropping in as it trickles slowly down the hill. Once the ball falls below the line of the hole it can't break back up the hill.

Die the ball into the hole rather than play an aggressive stroke. This eliminates any risk of the putt lipping out and running away down the slope.

Combination putt: When you're faced with a putt across the slope, but also either up or down the green, there is one vital point to bear in mind. The slower the ball is travelling the more it breaks.

A downhill putt across a slope needs to be given a much wider berth than an uphill putt with the same amount of break.

A downhiller has to played with caution – unless it's definitely holeable be content to two putt. An uphill putt can be hit firmly on a narrow line – the ball breaks near the hole, and you can afford to be aggressive.

pro tip

Toe tip

An excellent way to gain more control over a downhill putt is to hit the ball off the toe of the putter. This deadens the strike – the ball doesn't come off the clubface as fast as it would if struck in the middle of the blade.

It's especially useful when you need just to set the ball rolling on a very steep slope or down lightning fast greens.

Pace pointer

If you find difficulty in judging the pace of a downhill putt – particularly with break – hit a normal putt at a chosen point between you and the hole. It may be an old hole, a small leaf or patch on the green.

If you have judged the slope properly the ball is carried past this point and breaks naturally down towards the hole. The faster the putt the nearer your imaginary point should be.

This method helps you focus on your putting stroke rather than worrying about the putt itself.

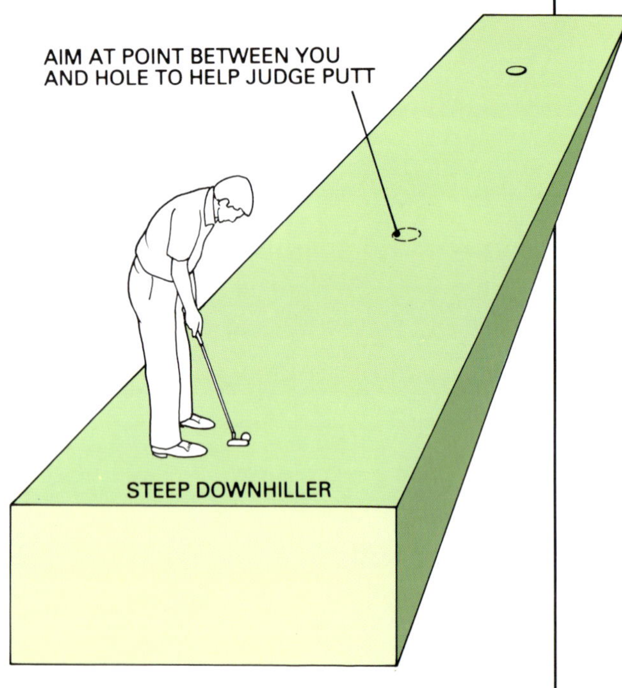

The Crenshaw touch

Ben Crenshaw is regarded by his fellow pros as one of the greatest putters of modern times. He combines a rock solid stroke with his natural ability to read greens. The American's understanding of how a steeply sloping green affects putts has helped him gain this reputation.

Crenshaw accurately judges the pace and line of even the fastest and most steeply sloping greens. His touch was at its best when he conquered the world's hardest greens at Augusta and won the 1984 Masters.

Holing six footers

Being able to hole out consistently from the awkward range of about 6ft (1.8m) is vital for good scoring. It's a confidence booster to know that even if you miss the green and your chip finishes that tricky distance away you have a very good chance of saving par.

Problems with this shot are mainly mental – a negative attitude can hinder your technique. The length of swing is so short that it's hard for a proper technique to go drastically wrong on its own.

STRAIGHT BACK

Although the club naturally moves inside the line on the backswing of a long putt, the path should be almost straight back along the ball-to-target line on a short putt. There is only a very slight move inside – if at all – on a six footer.

The crucial points are at impact and the followthrough. The blade should always return square at impact, and you must follow through along the ball-to-target line on a straight putt. This reduces the risk of pushing or pulling the ball and missing the putt.

If you swing a putter along the target line on a straight putt, only the pace or a bad kick can keep the ball out. Your stance should be sturdy but relaxed, and your action free of tension and smooth

CONFIDENCE AND TECHNIQUE
Six footers are awkward. While you expect to hole a short putt, and finding the cup from afar is a bonus, holing out from about a flag's length away is puttable – just. Be bold – all you need is confidence and a sound technique.

SIX FOOTER SUCCESS

1 TARGET LINE TAKEAWAY
Your takeaway must be smooth with no wrist break – you should be conscious of the club moving back along the ball-to-target line. The clubhead moves naturally inside on the backswing (below), but the movement should be only very slight.

2 DOWN THE LINE
The blade must be square at impact. Make sure the club follows through along the target line – it mustn't move to the inside. The proper line keeps the clubface square to the target for as long as possible, reducing the risk of a pull or a push.

3 CONTROLLED FINISH
Hold the club at the finish position. Resist the tendency to jerk the putter back to the address position after impact – this leads to a jabbing stroke. Notice how the head has remained still throughout the stroke. Don't look up until you hear the putt drop, or your body can turn at impact and pull the ball off line.

yet controlled. Keep your grip light, and make sure you never break your wrists.

Stay perfectly still throughout the stroke. To help you achieve this, never look up to watch the ball rolling towards the hole. Wait until you hear the putt drop. This helps keep the putter swinging on the proper path.

On a breaking putt the technique remains the same but you must now judge the line and pace carefully. Don't be tempted to guide the ball at the hole – once you have chosen your line, putt straight along it letting the slope – not your putter blade – turn the ball back towards the target.

Confidence is the key – build it up by going out to practice. A positive attitude helps you relax and make a good stroke when it matters. Having negative thoughts on the greens can destroy even the best putting technique. Always try to be positive and assume you're going to hole out every six footer.

pro tip

Eye drops

It is a great help to be able to turn your head while standing over a putt to see straight down the line to the hole. For this your eyes should be directly over the ball. To find the position, hold a ball on the bridge of your nose and then drop it. Where the ball lands is where you should place it in your stance.

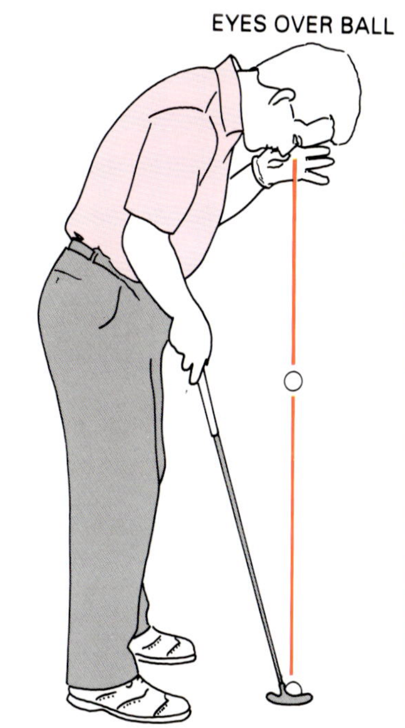

pro tip

Tee peg training

Placing two sets of tee pegs in the practice green to channel your club is an excellent way to ingrain the proper stroke into your game. The sets should be about 10in (25cm) apart, and just wide enough for your clubhead to pass through.

Place a ball in the middle of the rectangle formed by the tees. Swing the putter away and through the back two pegs without touching either one. Hitting a peg means you have taken the club away on the wrong line.

Swing through smoothly making sure the putter blade travels between the front tees. This ensures the blade follows through along the target line.

Hold the finish position. Notice how a straight line can be drawn from the centre of the rectangle through clubhead, ball and to the hole.

Fearless Faldo

Double Open champion Nick Faldo is cool under pressure and expects to hole six footers. Because his technique is excellent – straight back and through – and his temperament ideal, the awkward length putt holds no fear for him. With an extremely smooth and confident stroke he misses very few putts of a flag's length.

Faldo's stroke held up under the severest of pressure from about 5ft (1.5m) in the final round of the 1987 Open at Muirfield. He had to hole out several times from this tricky length to save his par. Incredibly, the man from Hertfordshire parred all 18 holes – at the last, this missable one clinched the title.

Charge or die putting

To achieve a consistent putting game on sloping greens, it is important to know when to attack and when to defend. A firmly struck, aggressive putt aimed at the back of the hole is called a charge. For a die putt you need a more calculating, cautious approach – the aim being to roll the ball gently up to the hole so it just topples into the cup.

Your technique for hitting either a charge or die putt remains exactly the same as normal. The difference between the shots is how firmly the putt is struck and the line taken. Across a slope, a charge putt travels to the hole along a straighter path than a die, which is given a wider berth.

As you hit the charge putt fairly straight, you must also strike the ball firmly to counter the effect of the slope. You have to hit a die putt on a wider line because it needs a softer strike, so the slope has more time to affect the ball's path.

AGGRESSION OR DEFENCE

The perfect time to hit a charge putt is on an uphill slope – even if the ball breaks. Coming down the green across the same slope, hit a die putt to limit the risk of the ball racing past the hole if you miss.

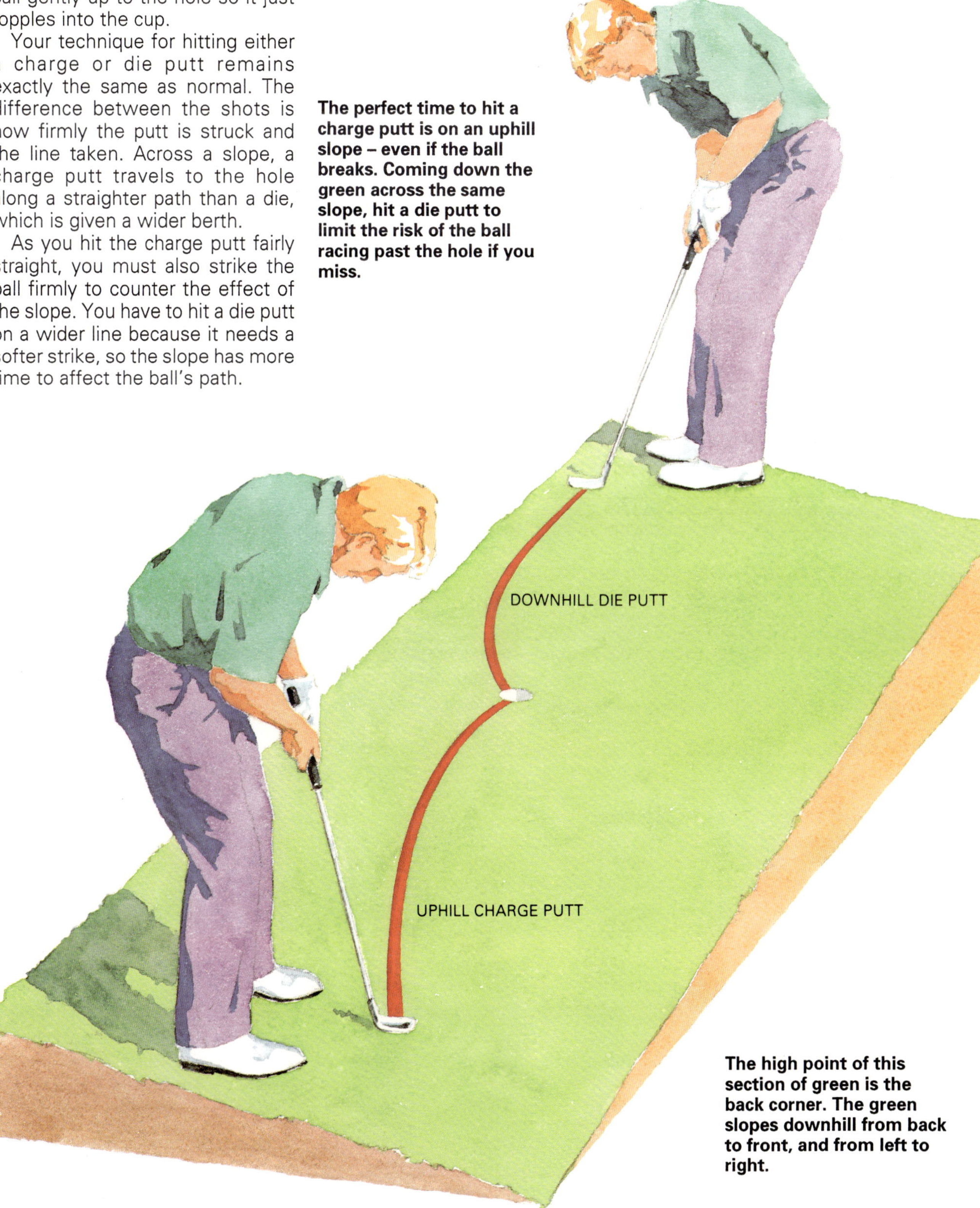

The high point of this section of green is the back corner. The green slopes downhill from back to front, and from left to right.

SPEED AND LINE

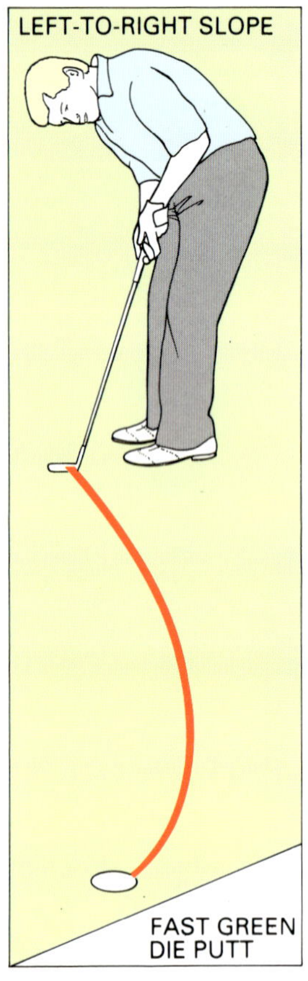

SLICK GREEN
When a green has been newly mown for a competition it's usually very fast. You should give the ball more width and try to die the ball into the hole, reducing the risk of three putting.

MEDIUM PACED
On the same-sloped green of normal speed your decision to charge or die depends on how confident you feel, and whether you need to attack or defend your score. It's foolish to charge if a two putt wins you the hole.

SLOW AND GRASSY
When the same green hasn't been cut for a few days and is slow, the ball doesn't break as much as normal so you can afford to charge most of your putts. Even if you miss, the ball shouldn't run too far by.

masterclass

Palmer's charging
In his heyday one of the great trademarks of Arnold Palmer's game was the way he used to attack the hole with his putts. He was never afraid of aiming for the back of the hole and giving the ball a good rap. Even if he missed, he was such a fine putter that the return was always holeable. The famous Palmer charging putts helped him win seven major titles.

DO OR DIE

The decision whether to play a charge or die comes with experience. Think about the slope, the state of play and the speed of the green.

Slope: Any uphill putt is a potential charge. You can afford to be bold with the shot if you know that – should you miss – the ball would not go too far past. But there is little point in charging a downhill putt, because if you miss the ball rolls well past the hole. One downhill exception is when the green is so slow that the ball can't go too far past the hole.

Hit the die instead of the charge if you have to putt across a very steep slope. A charge gathers pace on the slope and unless you hole out the ball runs by.

State of play: You can take an aggressive approach to a downhill putt if you need a birdie to avoid losing a hole or the match. But there is no point in hitting a charge when you have the luxury of two putts to win a hole or competition, even if it's uphill. Be content to take the two putts by dying the ball at the hole.

Speed: When a green is lightning fast you should aim to die the ball at the hole. On a very slow green you can charge most putts unless it's severely downhill.

PACE AND PRACTICE

Whatever your choice, judging the pace of the putt is all important. Knowing how firmly to hit a putt along different lines comes with experience. You should experiment on the practice putting green.

For both types of putt you must pick a spot to aim at. With a die putt it's best to pinpoint a spot you want the ball to roll over between you and the hole. With a charge, choose a point level with the hole and aim to hit the ball at it. If you read the break properly the ball hits the back of the hole and drops in.

When you're deciding how hard and how wide you need to hit the ball towards the hole, it's essential to visualize the path and how the slope affects it.

Being able to weigh up the facts quickly and make the right decision on the putting green – do you want to charge or die? – is vital to protect your score. Often it's a decision that must be made under pressure in a match – prepare yourself by brushing up these putting skills.

Perfect your putting

It's the most talked and written about aspect of golf, and it's often the most frustrating. None of this is pure coincidence – putting is the most crucial area in any round of golf.

A look at the 1990 European Tour statistics is proof in itself. Bernhard Langer averaged less than 29 putts per round having played in 17 tournaments and finished fourth in the Order of Merit with prize money of over £420,000.

The putting stroke requires less movement than any other shot – yet a sound technique on the greens eludes golfers the world over. Lack of ability is rarely to blame – not enough practice is often the culprit.

There are endless opportunities to practise your putting. You don't need much space and you can putt indoors as well as outdoors – even if it's only putting to a chair leg.

Whether it's on the carpet or on

STATISTICAL EVIDENCE

When you're next in a competition at your home club, talk to a golfer with a good score – he's likely to be someone who putted well. When that happens, every long putt tends to finish close and the short ones drop with monotonous regularity. It's seldom down to luck – hard work on the practice putting green is usually the only way to achieve this type of success.

A FEEL FOR DISTANCE

1 COMFORTABLE ADDRESS
Above all you must feel comfortable and relaxed at address on the greens. Think of grip pressure – it must remain consistent throughout the stroke. Check the alignment of the putter head – it should be square to the line you want the ball to roll along.

2 INSIDE TAKEAWAY
On a longish putt, sweep the putter back slightly inside the ball-to-target line. The distance you are from the hole determines the length of your backswing. Whatever style of putting stroke you adopt, there should be no movement from the waist down.

pro tip

Trial and error

Every golfer loses confidence on the greens from time to time – it usually only needs a couple of putts to drop for your state of mind to be transformed. But sometimes it pays to search for an alternative cure.

Most club professionals are happy to let you on to the practice green with a variety of putters. The face is usually taped up for protection, but you soon develop an overall feel for the club.

Take about half a dozen balls and stroke putts across the green swapping different clubs. It doesn't take long to discover which of the putters you like and which are totally unsuitable.

More often than not, practising with a variety of putters makes you realize that the old faithful you were about to dispense with is not quite as bad as you thought. Either way, you stand an excellent chance of restoring lost confidence.

3 RETURN TO SQUARE
With a fundamentally sound putting stroke the position at impact mirrors that at address. The putter face returns square to the ball with the hands leading the clubhead through impact. Strike the ball slightly on the up to generate the necessary overspin.

4 SET THE PACE
Smoothly accelerate the putter head through impact – it should travel slightly inside the line again to complete the in-to-in path of the clubhead. Only now should you look up. Repeat the same putt several times to test your ability to judge pace consistently.

the putting green, there's just one factor that should remain the same – always introduce variety into your practice to ensure your interest level remains high.

FREEDOM OF CHOICE

There's no right or wrong way to putt – it's very much a case of finding a system that works for you. Nick Faldo is a shoulders and arms putter. Gary Player has a wristy, stabbing type putting stroke. The only similarity is that their techniques are awesomely effective.

There are certain fundamentals which are consistent with most great putters – hands directly above the ball at address; a constant grip pressure throughout the stroke and the putter blade square to the intended line.

Once you have a comfortable style based on sound technique, the next step is to build into your game a method that works over and over again even under severe pressure. The practice putting green is the place to groove a repeatable stroke.

Place several balls in a circle around a hole to sharpen your short range putts. Attempt to knock in each ball and only move on to another drill when each one is in the hole. If you miss one, start all over again – this adds an exciting element of pressure into the exercise.

To improve your feel for distance, stroke a ball from one side of the putting green to the other. Then attempt to stop another dozen balls on precisely the same spot – the tighter the grouping the better your judgment of line and weight.

COMPETITIVE EDGE

It's always a good idea to set aside a few minutes for pre-round preparation, particularly if you're in a competition.

An excellent way to brush up on your stroke is to hit several long putts. Concentrate on making a smooth swing – note how the ball comes off the putter face. You should be looking to sharpen your judgment of distance.

It's seldom advisable to practise short putts just before a competitive round. It only needs a couple to slip by the hole and your confidence takes a dive. This is unlikely to have you stepping on to the 1st green in a very positive frame of mind.

Always use the same ball on the practice putting green as you would on the course. Don't carelessly pluck a two piece solid ball from your bag if you intend playing a balata out on the course. The difference in feel between the two is enormous.

COPY SLAMMIN' SAM

As soon as you walk on to the 1st green, take a close look at the length and texture of the grass. It may differ slightly from the type found on the practice green and have an effect on the roll of your ball.

If you find you're having a bad day on the greens – and it happens to everyone from time to time – try adopting the Sam Snead philosophy. He was once quoted as saying about short putts, 'if you're going to miss one, miss it quick'. You may be pleasantly surprised – a carefree approach might make the putts start to drop again.

Blind spot

Putting is such a precision art that it's easy to tie yourself up in knots over technique. Do you crouch over the ball or stand upright? Is an open or square stance best? How do you grip the club? The permutations are seemingly endless.

Sometimes it's a good idea to forget about the text book and rely solely on feel. Putting with your eyes closed can help you achieve this – it relieves tension in your body and places the emphasis on your stroke.

Address the ball with your eyes open. When you feel comfortable, close your eyes and putt the ball towards the hole. Before you open them again, try to predict where the ball has finished – short or long, pulled left, pushed right or dead straight.This exercise increases your control over the putter head and develops your feel for line and length on the greens.

Listen – don't look

One of the keys to Nick Faldo's 1990 Open victory at St Andrews was his impeccable holing out. His only 3 putt of the entire championship was from long range at the treacherous Road hole. That was in the final round and by then the tournament was his.

Copying a technique practised by Nick Faldo may help you to hole out more regularly – but it's something you need to experiment with on the practice putting green before you carry it out in a competition.

On short putts wait for the sound of the ball dropping into the hole before you look up. This encourages you to concentrate on the stroke rather than ball direction.

Looking up before striking the ball causes miss-hits and is one of the major causes of missing short putts.

Playing in the rain

Few golfers relish the prospect of playing in the rain. Wet weather affects the playing conditions of the course, and may lower morale – there's nothing more miserable than struggling through a round feeling the damp seep through clothes and shoes.

But with careful planning, playing in the rain needn't be a washout. To play your best, learn to adapt your game with a few simple techniques, and always set out properly equipped for a sudden shower.

Modern wet-weather clothing is light and waterproof, and does much to keep you comfortably dry. Buy the best you can afford, and look after it carefully, so that you continue to enjoy your game whatever the weather. Have it with you whenever you play a round.

READY FOR THE RAIN

A few well chosen wet-weather basics should give good service for years.

A men's golf **umbrella** is larger and stronger than a normal one. For extra protection on an exposed course, choose one with a sturdy frame – a weak-framed umbrella is likely to collapse when the wind picks up.

There's a smaller golf umbrella for women and junior players which is robust and easy to hold on to in high winds.

Keep two large **towels** in your bag. Use one to dry and clean your clubface before and after every shot. Grass, mud and water clog up the grooves so that you don't make firm contact with the ball at impact, and your control over the shot is reduced.

Dry and clean your ball on the same towel after every hole and before you putt.

You can't lift and clean the ball between the tee and the green, so when you're playing from a wet fairway there's likely to be water on the ball at impact. This reduces control and the amount of spin you put on the ball, which ends in a flier – the ball doesn't stop as quickly as it should on landing. Also, when you strike a wet ball a certain amount of spray is thrown

KEEP YOUR HANDS AND GRIPS DRY
Before every shot, dry your hands and the grip with a towel to give you a firm hold on the club. If either are wet the club is likely to slip in your hands – especially at impact.

Clean the clubhead for control

Always dry and clean the clubface before hitting the ball. Mud, grass or moisture that gets trapped between the clubface and the ball cushions the power, reducing length as well as control. You can waste shots needlessly if you try to ignore the problem.

Remove mud from spikes

To keep a firm footing on wet ground, check your spikes every few holes and remove mud and grass. If too much dirt builds up on the bottom of your shoes it stops the spikes digging into the ground and gripping on a slippery surface.

Secure your grip

Wear a rubber rain glove for a secure grip in the wet. Rubber gives a firmer hold than leather or any other material, and reduces the risk of the club slipping in your hands – which ruins your shot.

COPING WITH CASUAL WATER

IN THE BUNKER
If you land in a bunker area flooded with casual water you can lift and drop your ball on the nearest dry section without penalty – but the ball must stay in the same bunker.

ON THE GREEN
When your path to the pin is obstructed by an area of casual water you can place your ball on the nearest dry point the same distance away from the hole – the rules don't let you move closer to the hole.

Beware the flier
When playing a shot from wet rough you get even less backspin than if hitting from dry rough. Moisture trapped between the clubface and the ball stops the grooves making clean contact and imparting backspin. This creates a flier, with the ball running further than normal on landing.

When you visualize the shot, aim to land the ball shorter than you normally would to allow for the lack of backspin.

up, slowing the ball down as it travels through the air or along the ground.

Take the effects of water into account, and allow for less backspin, when visualizing shots in the rain.

Use the second towel to dry your hands and the grip as thoroughly as possible. If they're wet the club is likely to slip in your hands during the swing, and the clubface won't strike the ball squarely.

KEEPING DRY

A good **waterproof suit** makes all the difference to a round in the rain – keep one in your bag at all times so you're always prepared for a sudden shower. The best type of wet-weather suit lets air pass through, keeping you cool and dry. Beware of buying a cheap airtight suit which traps the moisture in, leaving you hot and sticky.

As well as keeping your head dry, a peaked **golf hat** stops water running down your face. A hat makes for greater comfort and concentration – rain trickling down your face may blur your vision and put you off your shot.

A **rain glove** helps you grip a club firmly in the rain. This type of glove is made from rubber – it's similar to a washing-up glove. In damp conditions rubber gives a firmer hold than other materials, and stops the club from turning in your hands.

If it starts to rain during a round replace your normal glove with a rain glove immediately. Never use a leather glove in the rain. Not only is it more liable to slip in your grip, but moisture ruins the glove.

Keep your clubs dry under a waterproof **bag hood.** This stops water running down inside the bag and making your clubs wet. Most new bags have hoods, or you can buy one separately from some pro shops.

If you play most of your golf in a damp climate ask your club pro to fit your clubs with **half-cord grips**. This type of rubber grip fits over your regular grip to give a more secure hold when it rains.

Waterproof shoes, also made from rubber, stop water seeping through so you can avoid the dismal experience of playing a round with wet feet. For a firm footing in slippery conditions, check after every few holes that your studs aren't clogged up – remove excess mud and grass with a tee-peg.

SWINGING IN THE RAIN

As well as having the correct wet-weather equipment you must also be aware of swing problems caused by wet conditions.

A normal swing is difficult in a wet-weather suit. The extra weight and additional layers restrict body movement. Don't try to overcome the problem by forcing your swing. Keep your normal tempo and make a three-quarter swing if it feels easier.

The key is to maintain your concentration and tempo in the rain. This may be harder than you think. A wet fairway slows down the roll of the ball, so many players wrongly increase the speed of their swing to compensate for reduced length. This is often disastrous.

When the course plays long, take one more club than usual and concentrate on keeping the same tempo as always. It's particularly important to play within your limits in damp conditions. Never gamble.

KNOW THE RULES

It's vital to understand the rules that apply to rain-affected areas of the course.

Excessive rain can cause small areas of the green, fairway and bunker to become flooded. These areas are described as 'casual water' in the Royal and Ancient rules book.

If there's casual water directly between your ball and the pin when you're putting, you can re-position the ball – but not move it nearer the hole in the process.

If your ball lands in casual water you can lift it out and drop it on the nearest dry area without penalty. In a bunker the nearest point of relief must be in that same bunker – and not the nearest dry point on the fairway or green.

If you lose your ball in casual water you can drop another one without penalty near to the point where you think it landed – providing your partners agree. You pick up a 1-stroke penalty, as with a normal lost ball, if your partners don't agree that the ball finished in casual water.

STAY DRY IN A WATERPROOF SUIT
Wear a wet-weather suit in the rain. If you don't, your clothes become damp and uncomfortable which may upset your concentration.

Checklist
Be prepared for rain whenever you play a round. Keep wet-weather equipment in your golf bag at all times.

- You need a strong and sturdy umbrella, specially built to withstand high winds.
- Carry two towels – one to keep your clubface and ball dry, the other to dry your hands and grip.
- A bag hood stops water getting inside your bag and making the clubs wet.
- Made from rubber, a rain glove gives a firmer grip than leather in the wet.
- A good waterproof suit is light and keeps out the rain while letting air through.
- A peaked hat or cap stops water running down your face and into your eyes, which is uncomfortable and puts you off your stroke.

Playing a parkland course

Successfully making your way round a parkland course demands a particular approach to golf – it's not like playing any other type of course. The conditions are completely different from links and heathland – as are the hazards which confront you. The ground tends to be flat and there are always plenty of trees, so you must form your strategy accordingly.

Correct club selection is all important if you want to give yourself the best chance of hitting a good shot. Don't make life difficult for yourself. Learn to understand what clubs are best suited to certain situations.

Lush grass on the fairways can cause you to hit a flyer on any full shot. Grass comes between the clubface and ball at impact, so less spin is applied causing the ball to fly further than you might expect.

HARD OR SOFT

As well as being flat, parkland courses are usually built on a clay base. Drainage is always a problem and conditions vary from one extreme to the other.

In summer the ground is often very hard - let the ball run when you pitch. For the rest of the year it is usually soft with plenty of grass all over. Conditions in the winter months may become unpleasant underfoot with wet, muddy fairways and greens. The ball pitches and stops quickly wherever you hit it. In these conditions you can afford to be more forceful with your shots.

It's no use playing a links type pitch and run shot along winter parkland fairways. The ball simply comes up short. Instead, hit the ball high into the air and pitch it all the way on to the green.

PARKLAND SHOTS
Parkland fairways are soft except in high summer. When they're soft, hit a high approach shot that pitches all the way to the green. Where bunkers guard the flag, aim to the safe part of the green. If you learn to understand the conditions around you, you perform well on all types of golf course, not just your home club.

pro tip

Practise pitching

Encouraging good feel in your short game is a sure way to lower your scores out on the course. Feel for distance is something that cannot be taught though – it is achieved only through hard work.

Place a target – perhaps a towel or bag – about 50yd (45m) away and practise pitching balls to it with your wedge. Remember, greens on parkland courses are nearly always soft so aim to hit a high shot, landing the ball as near to the target as possible. If you make good contact the ball should stop quickly.

Go through this practice drill as often as you can.

CLUB SELECTION
Parkland grass is often quite lush. When your ball is sitting down in this type of grass and you are faced with a long shot, hit a wooden club. The clubhead slides through the grass for a better strike on the ball. An iron becomes tangled, causing the clubhead to twist at impact and the ball to fly off line.

Judging the wind

It is difficult to judge the strength and direction of the wind on a parkland course – you tend to be sheltered by the trees. Throw grass high into the air and note which way it blows. Study the tree tops and clouds if you are still not sure. Play a low shot if it is very windy.

SUMMER SAFETY

Concentrate on accuracy off the tee in the summer. A drive that pitches and stops on soft winter fairways may run into trouble when the clay soil of parkland fairways is baked hard. A lofted wood or long iron is the safer bet – length takes care of itself in dry conditions. Use a driver only when the fairway is wide.

What shoes to wear

✓ Think carefully about what shoes to wear before stepping out on to a damp, soggy golf course. Leather golf shoes with a manmade sole and spikes are good in wet conditions. They are comfortable and stop you from slipping around when you swing. Some rubber waterproof shoes are also excellent.

✗ Moulded studs provide very little grip in wet weather. In any case, many clubs ban them in winter because of the damage they cause to soft greens.

LOOSE OR LIVING
On a parkland course you come across many fluffy lies where there's fairly long grass around the ball. Think carefully before you move anything lying near. If something is growing, like the buttercups here, don't move it. This is a good maxim to keep you within the rules. You are allowed to move loose impediments – dead twigs or scraps of paper – but only if the lie of your ball is not improved.

Sculled shot
Bunker sand on a parkland course is often hard packed, making the splash shot impossible to play. The clubhead bounces off the sand into the back of the ball sending it shooting across the green – a sculled (thin) shot.

Nip the ball cleanly taking as little sand as possible with a pitching wedge instead of a sand wedge. The ball flies lower and runs further than a normal bunker shot, so consider where you want to pitch the ball.

Once you've decided on the shot to play, don't change your mind. Second thoughts in golf usually result in disaster.

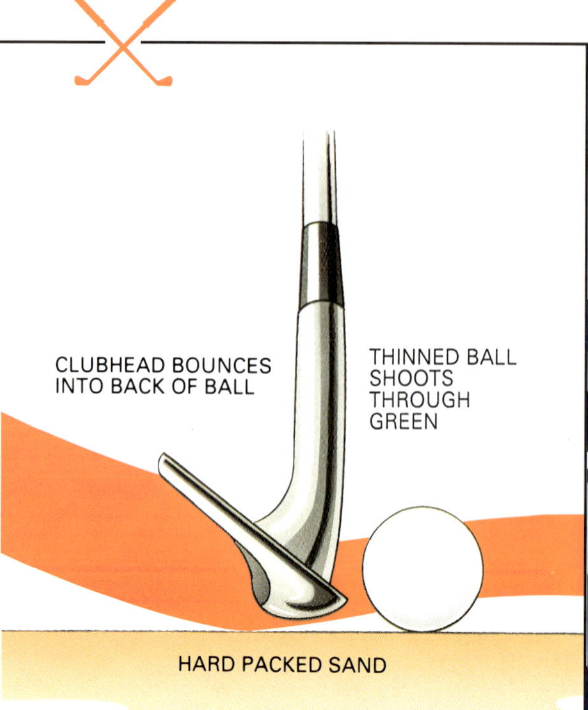

FAT SHOTS

The fat (heavy) shot happens when the clubhead makes contact with the turf before the ball. It's the most destructive shot you can hit in wet conditions if the ground is soft. You lose all clubhead speed and the ball travels no distance at all. When the ground is wet and spongy it's vital that you strike the ball cleanly.

HEAVY CONTACT LOSES DISTANCE

SOFT GROUND

Playing a heathland course

A combination of heather, gorse and tree lined fairways based on firm well drained soil makes heathland courses a delight to play. But don't be deceived by the beauty – danger lurks on every hole.

Heathland fairways aren't just skirted with trees – punishing heather and gorse bushes are ready to gather your ball. When you stray into heather it usually costs you at least a shot – all you can hope to do is hack out back on to the fairway.

Hit your ball into a gorse bush and the penalty is likely to be more severe. Forget trying to play a recovery shot – you'll be lucky if you can even retrieve your ball from the prickly branches.

HARD AND FAST

It's important when you tee up on a heathland course to think of accuracy more than distance. Your number one priority must be to keep the ball in play. You'll have the opportunity to hit irons off the tee for safety on a lot of holes, so brush up on your iron play if you're not confident with it.

The sandy well drained fairways can be used to good effect as they are invariably fast running. Your tee shots travel further so use a lofted wood or an iron if you're confident you can reach the green in regulation.

You often find yourself on bare, unforgiving lies on the closely mown fairways – it's essential you don't hit the ground before the ball. Grip the club slightly shorter to help you strike the ball cleanly with your iron shots. As an extra precaution, place the ball further towards the centre of your stance for clean contact.

PUNISHING IN PINK
Heather is an attractive feature of every heathland course but it's tough on your wrists. Many accomplished golfers come unstuck trying to do too much when they hit out of heather. If the ball is sitting down, play the shot with a wedge. Grip tightly to stop tangled heather closing the clubface at impact.

WOOD FROM HEATHER

1 FIRM GRIP
Risk an aggressive shot from heather only if you're confident the lie is good enough. Stand slightly closer to the ball and place it towards the centre of your stance – about the position you take with a mid iron. Grip more tightly than normal to prevent the clubhead twisting in the heather.

Splashing out

Greenside bunkers on a heathland course tend to be deep with soft sand – they are ideal for the high splash shot.

Open your stance so your shoulders, hips and feet align left of target – aim the clubface at the flag. Make a full backswing from out to in and pull the clubhead down with the left hand into the sand behind the ball. The clubhead cuts through the sand and the ball floats high, landing softly on the green.

2 UPRIGHT PLANE
Pick the club up more steeply on the backswing by breaking the wrists early in the swing. Your stance should help you swing on a more upright plane. Don't hit the ball hard out of the poor lie – maintain your control throughout the shot. Never go past horizontal at the top of the backswing.

3 STAY DOWN
Pull the butt of the club down with the back of the left hand – don't lunge forward with your upper body. The clubhead must strike the ball with a descending blow, cutting through the grass and heather. Watch the clubhead make contact with the ball to help you stay down on the shot through impact.

Grass roots
All heathland courses have one advantage in common – firm, fast running fairways. The sandy soil is typical of heathland in damp climates such as in the UK. The ground drains extremely well which means you can play golf in firm conditions all year round. Very seldom is a heathland course damp and soggy.

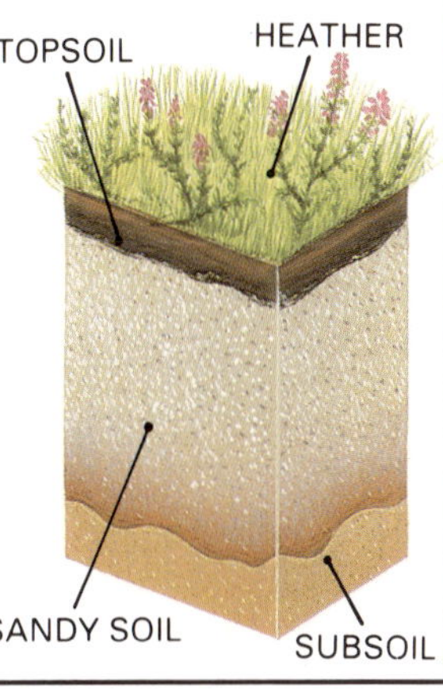

4 FREE FLOWING
The clubhead speed you generate at impact pulls your arms up into the followthrough position with your body facing the target. Your swing should flow freely at this stage. The control is maintained throughout the swing – there's no loss of balance as you watch the ball fly straight down the middle of the fairway.

ESCAPE TO SAFETY

From a poor lie in heather, reach for your wedge and look for the shortest route back to the fairway. Don't ground the club – heather is springy and could move the ball, costing you a 1 stroke penalty. Grip firmly, make a steep backswing and hit sharply down into the bottom of the ball.

pro tip

Sleeper shot

On many heathland courses railway sleepers are used to stop soil drift. For distance off a sleeper use a similar technique to a long bunker shot. Place the ball in the centre of your stance and grip well down. Make a three-quarter backswing and aim to nip the ball cleanly off the wooden surface. The ball flies low with almost no backspin and runs a long way. Take care – you might damage the clubhead and your wrists if you catch the shot heavy.

Use a mid iron to chip from a sleeper close to the green. Treat the shot very much like a long putt. Swing your arms back and through without breaking your wrists. Try to pitch the ball on the green so you can rely on a more even bounce.

THE RIGHT APPROACH

Let the course help you whenever possible. You don't have to pitch your approach shots on the green – particularly if you're playing downwind.

Look at the ground in front of you and assess what is the safest shot. With wise club selection you can achieve a good result without taking unnecessary risks. When the ground is hard use the natural contours of the fairway. Bounce the ball short of the target and let it run on to the green. A 5 iron may pitch all the way to the flag but most golfers find a 7 iron is the easier club to hit straight.

WEATHER WATCH

Heathland courses are often situated on high ground and exposed to the elements. When it's windy let the breeze work for you – don't fight it.

Hitting a draw into a left to right wind is difficult and risky. Aim slightly left of target and let the wind bring the ball back on line. When you feel on top of your game try lower trajectory shots to keep the ball under the wind.

Playing a links

Links golf courses lie on often remote stretches of land close to the sea. Playing a links is an exhilarating but demanding experience. You're exposed to extreme weather conditions and usually play in winds far stronger than you ever experience inland.

From a distance such a course looks flat and quite featureless. But once you set foot on a links you discover that the ground is a mass of humps and hollows – many of the tee shots you face are semi-blind.

Hard, fast running fairways can cause the occasional unpredictable bounce. Your ball may shoot forward on the first bounce, while the same shot pitching into a hump stops quickly. If you're very unfortunate a ball flying straight down the middle of the fairway kicks into the rough.

The short grass and closely mown fairways on a links course can remove some of the fear from your mid range approach shots to the green. A crisply struck iron shot generates a great deal of backspin because very little grass comes between the clubface and the ball at impact.

WATCH THE WIND

Strong wind is an important feature of links golf, so make sure you use it to your advantage whenever possible. Try to forget the distance you usually hit the ball – wind drastically alters your normal club selection.

Into the wind demands a precise strike. Always take plenty of club and swing shorter than normal. A three-quarter shot helps you hit the ball lower to give you

TOTAL EXPOSURE
Links courses such as Troon in Scotland provide the purest, most natural form of golf in the world. Strong winds stretch every department of your game – you need control from the tee, accuracy with your irons and a delicate touch on undulating greens. An all round test for even the most accomplished golfer, links courses have staged the British Open since the first tournament in 1860.

PUNCHING LOW INTO WIND

1 SOLID AT ADDRESS
A bunker guards the flag so aim at the right edge of the green. Set up parallel to the target line with the ball central in your stance. Grip down and stand slightly closer to the ball than normal. Your left arm and the club shaft form a straight line.

2 CONTROLLED BACKSWING
Swing smoothly away from the ball, breaking the wrists halfway back. Concentrate on a full shoulder turn and stop the backswing short of horizontal – this helps you stay in complete control of the clubhead. The position at the top should feel solid and compact.

3 SMOOTH DOWNSWING
Gradually transfer your weight to the left on the downswing. Keep it smooth – many golfers mistakenly try to hit the ball harder into the wind. This only makes you swing more quickly and you risk losing control – remember the saying: don't hit it harder, hit it better.

4 PURE STRIKE
Keep your hands ahead of the ball at impact – if you scoop in the hitting area you rule out any hope of a low penetrating flight. The clubhead makes crisp contact first with the ball and then the turf. Notice how still the head remains until impact.

PUNCHING LOW THROUGH IMPACT

5 FLOWING FOLLOWTHROUGH
Allow your forearms to roll through impact. Stay down on the shot until you feel your arms pulling the body up into the followthrough position. Almost all of your weight is supported on the left foot – don't topple on to your right side or you miss-hit the shot.

6 PERFECT BALANCE
The swing looks and feels effortless. Clubhead speed has been generated by making the correct moves – not by sheer force and muscle power. The balance achieved earlier in the swing is maintained as you watch the ball fly quite low towards the green.

Fairway fallacy
Links fairways are undulating with lots of humps and hollows. They're also very fast running – a ball rolling on the fairway tends to be gathered in by the hollows.

You may have to cope with some wild bounces on a links, but the ball often finds level ground – you play from fewer uneven lies on the fairway than you might expect.

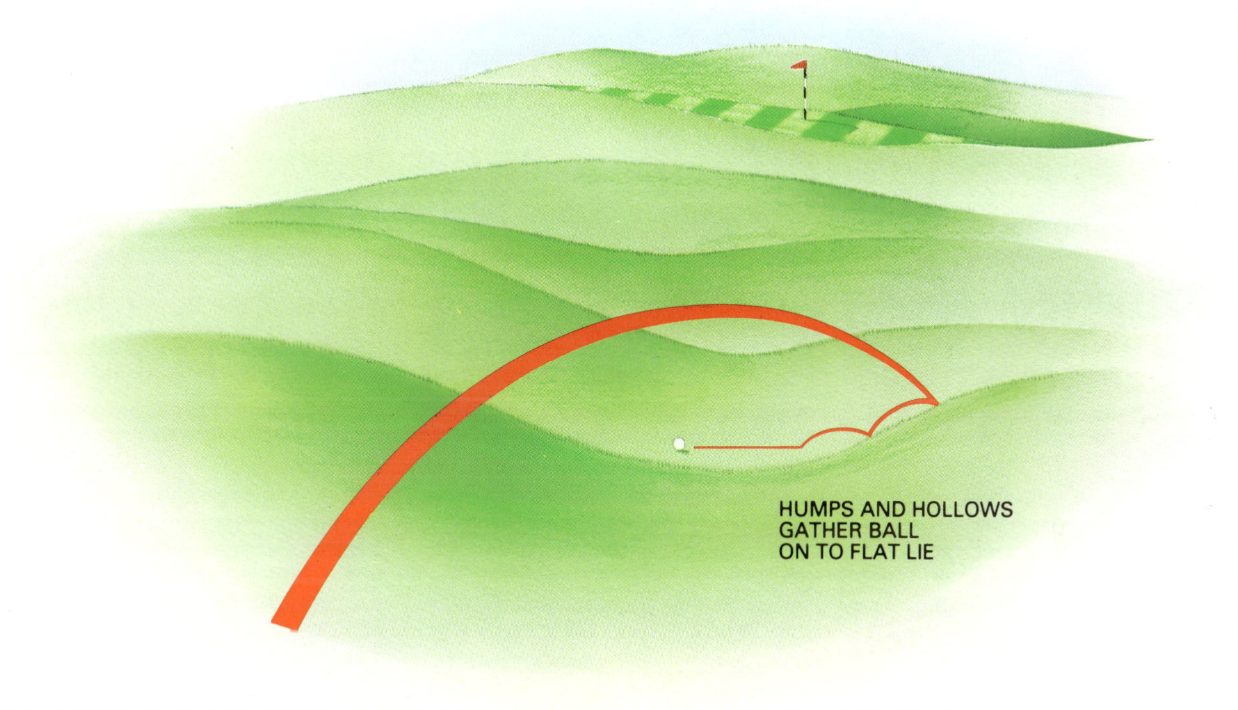

Better safe than sorry
Bunkers on a links are invariably deep – often the front edge is above head height. Even the best golfers can't play towards the flag from every bunker – as anyone who's watched top pros go through the 17th at St Andrews can testify.

Be content to escape from an awkward bunker away from the flag if necessary. Resist the temptation to try a miraculous recovery. You record fewer high scores on your card and playing a links becomes an enjoyable rather than frustrating experience.

more control in the wind.

Remember that playing into the wind exaggerates the spin off links turf and you can stop the ball even on firm greens.

Wind behind should encourage you to hit the ball higher to gain maximum distance on the shot. With luck you can reduce long par 5s to a comfortable 4 strokes and look for birdies on par 4s.

Downwind it's difficult to put enough backspin on the ball to pitch and stop it neatly on the green. Take less club, swing smoothly and let the wind carry the ball towards the target. Aim to pitch the ball well short of the green and expect plenty of run on the shot.

Cross winds force you to aim way off line and allow the ball to be blown back on target. Depending on the strength and direction of the wind, select a spot to one side and set up to hit the ball straight at it. Swing normally and let the wind do the rest.

SHORT GAME STRATEGY

Many golfers forget that wind affects the short game as well as the longer shots. This is especially true on a links course.

When you chip from close to the green your main thought must be to keep the ball near the ground. A low pitch and run is always a safer shot in wind than a high lob.

A 7 iron is the ideal club for the shot. The ball runs twice the distance it travels in the air, so select an area to pitch the ball on and visualize it running up towards the hole.

Grip down the club and position the ball towards the centre of your stance. Swing the club as you do with a long putt – the arms moving back and through together with very little wrist break. Make sure you keep your hands ahead of the ball throughout to promote a crisp strike.

Bear in mind that a long putt on a large sloping links green can often take two or three different breaks. It's important to study the slope of the green carefully. Look at a putt along the ball-to-target line and then from side on to give you a better perspective. Wind also affects the roll of the ball.

Set yourself realistic goals – occasionally a long putt drops but you should never be disappointed to get down in 2 strokes.

ROUGH STUFF

1 FIRM GRIP
The rough on the sandy dunes of a links is left largely untouched. You often find yourself in dense, wiry grass. Reach for a lofted club and choose a direct route to safety. Grip tightly and stand open.

2 STEEP BACKSWING
Pick the club up sharply on the backswing, breaking the wrists early. A steep backswing is essential because it helps you swing the club down into the ball. Aim to strike down on a patch of grass just behind the ball.

3 SAFELY OUT
Swing down steeply as hard as you can without losing control. Cut through as much grass around the ball as possible – this is no time for delicacy. The shot is tough on wrists so keep a firm grip on the club.

DEEP TROUBLE

Bunkers are hard to spot in the humps and hollows of a links course and devilishly difficult to escape from. A yardage chart comes in useful if you're not familiar with the course – it can perform the role of an experienced caddie.

Study the chart and lay up short of bunkers if necessary. Don't take risks – it's fine to sacrifice distance, particularly if it keeps you on the fairway.

When you land in a fairway pot bunker it's unlikely you have a direct route to the green – concentrate on making sure your next shot isn't from the same spot. The powdery fine sand is perfect for the high splash shot. Open your stance and keep the clubface open. Swing long and smooth on an out-to-in path.

Huge sandy dunes are punishing hazards that surround many fairways and greens. You're bound to be faced with an awkward stance and the thick, wiry grass doesn't let go of your ball easily.

Play your recovery with a sand wedge and grip the club tight. It's difficult to achieve any distance, so don't be too ambitious with your escape.

Run of the green

In a strong wind adopt a wider putting stance to give you more stability – it's extremely distracting to feel the wind buffeting you when you're trying to hole a putt.

Wind has a minimal effect on the line of short putts – but the run of your ball on a long putt is greatly affected by strong winds.

When you study the line of a long putt, take note of the wind direction as well as the slope on the green.

A ball stroked towards the hole in calm conditions leaves you with a simple tap in. But if you hit an identical putt into the wind, the ball pulls up well short. A crosswind sends the putt off line. It can also exaggerate the break on a putt – or cause the ball to run on a straighter line than it would in calm conditions.

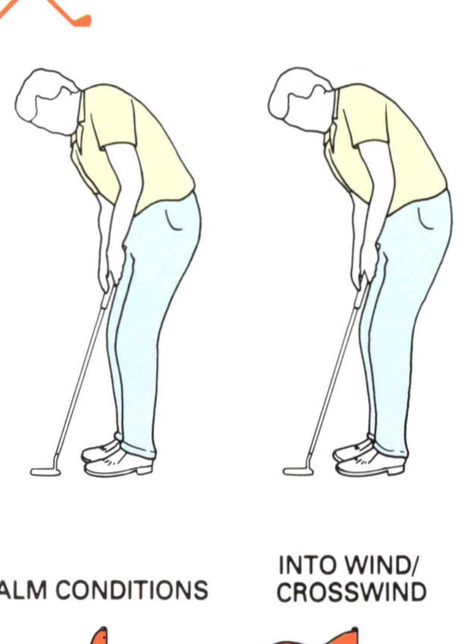

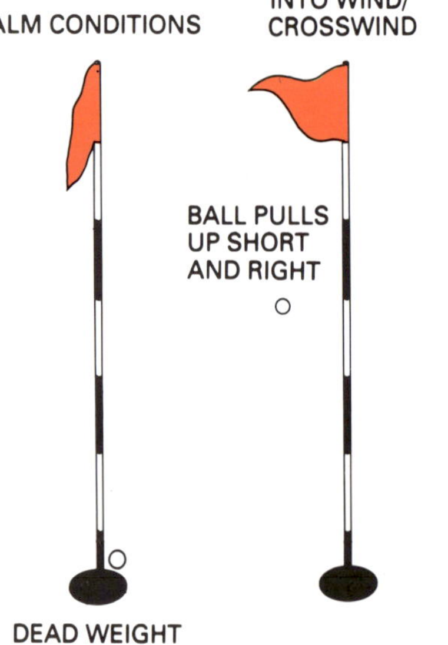

Playing a US type course

Often superbly landscaped and impeccably maintained, US style courses are a delight to behold – but take care: their charms conceal some wicked ways. Plenty of water, rolling fairways, huge bunkers and slick running greens make the courses tough, but with the right technique they offer a fair test to your golf.

Ask any golfer to picture a US course and Augusta National, home of the US Masters, usually springs to mind. One of the best known in the world, this dream course is typical of American design. But you needn't be in the USA to have the opportunity of playing one of these magnificent monsters. This type of course architecture is becoming popular all over the world.

Water hazards are a prominent feature of US style courses and help to create some fearsome penal holes. Often there can be as much water as dry land – a snaking fairway or sculptured green provide the only safe haven. If your judgement and technique are sound, you can accurately predict how the ball behaves on landing. But you're never more severely punished for a mistake than you are on a water hole.

TROUBLED WATERS

While you have the luxury of a bridge over the water, your ball must take an aerial route. But it's not just the physical presence of water that has an effect on your golf – it's the psychological factor

▼ DREAM COURSE

US style courses are a dream to play, with impressive views at every turn. Dramatic water hazards, usually manmade, test your nerve and skill to the full. It's essential you adopt a positive mental attitude if you are to stay out of trouble. Seldom are you confronted by blind shots into greens – but water is everywhere, and shallow, sculptured bunkers are cleverly placed to gather your ball if a shot strays off line.

Unlike the traditional links course, the US style owes little to its natural setting. Artificial slopes are thrown up by massive earthmoving operations, and dense plantings of trees and shrubs overhang lakes and rolling fairways to form a perfectly manicured golf landscape.

as well.

Once you know the distance of the shot, have confidence in your club selection. If the green is very close to the water's edge, take one more club to allow for a slight miss-hit. Concentrate on making a smooth swing – just because there is water ahead, you don't have to hit the ball hard.

FINDING THE FAIRWAY

Plentiful supplies of water help keep the undulating fairways green all year round. Take a good look at the roll of each fairway before you tee off – aiming down the middle is not always the best option. Even a gentle slope may kick your ball off line, so predict the path of your

▼ MENTAL BLOCK
Faced with a shot over water the mind can often become awash with negative thoughts. The water looms large and the target almost fades into the background. This mental block is the making of a bad shot – it's usually followed by the depressing sight of ripples as your ball descends into a watery grave.

▼ OPEN MIND
The same hole without the hazards paints an entirely different picture. This is what you should visualize as you approach your ball. Block out the water from your mind as though it doesn't exist. Concentrate on your technique and play a positive shot to the green – confidence helps form a good swing.

shot along the ground as well as in the air.

If you're confident of reaching the green in regulation, look ahead and judge which is the best line into the flag. Concentrate on intelligent placement off the tee to blot out hazards from your mind and make ticklish approach shots less dangerous.

Because the grass is quite lush the ball often stops on slopes on the fairways. Remember, when the ball lies below your feet it has a tendency to fly to the right – align slightly left of target to compensate. With the ball above your feet it's easy to pull the shot to the left, so make sure you adjust your alignment accordingly.

The rough lining the fairways is always well defined and perfectly manicured. But it's often quite dense which makes it hard to judge how far the ball flies. Your control is reduced and a fade or draw is difficult to achieve. Weigh up your shot carefully and avoid ambitious carries – even the slightest miss-hit may end in disaster.

HAZARD PLAY

Large fairway bunkers are common on US type courses. Often a daunting sight from the tee, the bunkers are less punishing than they look. The traps are usually shallow and offer an escape route – and from a reasonable lie distance is seldom a problem.

Take one or two clubs more than you would from the same range on the fairway. Position the ball in the middle of your stance and grip down the club. Make a three-quarter backswing to give you maximum control and reduce the risk of hitting sand before the ball.

SLIPPERY SLOPES

This style of green is invariably quick and some of the slopes and undulations may be quite severe. Like every part of the course, the greens are heavily watered and ideal for target golf.

They look inviting and attractive to the eye, but if your approach shot lacks accuracy you are often faced with a treacherous chip or putt.

You must think of the pin position before you decide where to hit your ball. On receptive greens a high shot lands softly, so pitch the ball all the way to the flag and you can be confident of it stopping quickly.

Always aim to leave your ball below the hole – a 20ft (6.5m) putt uphill is far easier than half that distance down a slippery slope. Use this tactic with your approach shot, too. If you miss a green it's better to stray on the low side of the hole to give you a more straightforward chip back up the slope to the pin.

American style greens are so fast and contoured it can often feel as if you're putting across a tilted table top. A long putt downhill requires a gentle touch and you may want to lag some putts rather than attack the hole.

The slopes of the green, variety of grass and direction of cut all determine the grain of the putting surface. Look closely at the grain and judge the likely effect on the roll of your ball.

When you're putting *with* the grain (grass growing away from you) the green appears light in colour and the putt is faster. The reverse is true when you putt *into* the grain (grass growing towards you) – the green looks relatively dark and the putt meets more resistance and is slower.

Read the break of the putt and picture the ball dying towards the hole. Don't be too aggressive or you risk racing the ball past. Always be grateful for two putting from long range.

pro tip

Practice opportunities

A great benefit of the US style of golf course design is the emphasis on practice facilities. Whenever you visit a course with a good practice ground, take a ead from the professionals and warm up before your round.

It's the perfect opportunity to check the basic fundamentals such as set-up and alignment. You also loosen up your golfing muscles and avoid the often destructive 1st tee stiffness.

Sight and sand

Greenside bunkers are often regarded with dread by the average golfer. But they can have a positive side – when several are knitted together on a hole they accentuate the shape and contours of the green. When you're some distance from the flag, this visual aid helps you place your approach shot.

Jack Nicklaus finds bunker clusters a great help, and uses them to good effect in his own designs. The course at St Mellion in Cornwall is a fine example, with bunkers hugging many of the greens. While it's hard to appreciate if your ball lands in one, intelligently placed bunkers are an integral and attractive feature of a hole.

Types of play

Golf involves a greater variety of competition than any other sport. You can tread the fairways on a wide range of courses and there are several types of game you can try.

Those who only play one form of golf week after week deny themselves the change of pace and strategy offered by other forms of competition. Each game produces excitement and a whole new range of challenges.

Probably the game most played around British courses at the weekend is **fourball best ball**. Usually arranged between groups of friends, this is one of the most enjoyable forms of matchplay.

It often produces quality golf because your partner is usually there to help out should you find trouble. This relieves pressure and encourages you to play more attacking golf.

Foursomes is the closest golf comes to becoming a team game. Partners share the same golf ball

MULTIPLE CHOICE
Most types of play appeal to every golfer – there's certainly plenty to choose from. Being aware of every one helps make your time on the course more enjoyable. Variety is also extremely good for your game – a head to head singles match provides the perfect opportunity to sharpen your competitive edge.

TYPES OF PLAY

FORMAT	RULES AND CONDITIONS
MATCHPLAY SINGLES	Doing enough to beat your opponent is all that matters in matchplay. Many titles have been won with scores that would look quite ordinary in a strokeplay competition. Three-quarters of the difference in handicaps determines the number of strokes given or received over 18 holes. For example, if you have a handicap of 10 and your opponent plays off 19 you give 7 strokes (three-quarters of the 9 stroke difference = 6.75). Your opponent receives a shot on the holes where the stroke index is 7 or less. The winner is the golfer who manages to be up by more holes than there are left to play. For example the term 4 and 3 describes a victory where a player is 4 holes up on an opponent with only 3 holes to play – winning the remaining 3 holes is still not enough to get back on level terms. When you're dormie up on an opponent you're ahead by as many holes as there are to play – 3 up with 3 to play for instance. If a match is all square after 18, the winner is decided by playing extra holes. If a player wins on the first extra hole, it's described as a victory on the 19th.
 STROKEPLAY	In a medal strokeplay event you compete with the best golfers in the club on an even footing, because all players receive their full handicap allowance. Usually played in threes, the person with the lowest net score (number of shots less handicap) wins the competition. In the event of a tie, a system known as a countback usually decides the outcome. The score for the back nine holes on each card is taken and half the relevant handicap deducted to arrive at the lowest score. If this fails to break the deadlock, the back six holes are looked at with a third of each handicap deducted. This process continues – right down to the last hole if necessary – until a winner is found. Play-offs in strokeplay events are not unheard of, but because it's hard to arrange a mutually suitable date, they're far less common than countbacks.
 FOURSOMES	In this format you and your partner share the same ball and play alternate strokes. It's officially matchplay, but this form of golf can also be used for stableford and strokeplay events. Each partnership decides in advance who tees off on the even holes and who tees off on the odds. You keep to this format no matter who knocks in the putt on any given hole. To work out the number of strokes you give or receive in a matchplay competition, add together the handicaps of the two pairs and take three-eighths of the difference. Seldom do a great deal of shots change hands in a game of foursomes. In strokeplay foursomes the pair add together their handicaps and divide the total by two – this figure is then deducted from the final gross score.
 FOURBALL BEST BALL	This form of golf is played in pairs with each golfer playing his own ball. The lowest score recorded by a pair on each hole is the one that counts. Strokes given or received in a matchplay competition are worked out as three-quarters of the difference in handicaps. The golfer with the lowest handicap gives strokes to the other three members of the fourball. In a strokeplay competition players receive three-quarters of their individual handicap. For example, if you play off 18 you receive 13.5 shots – this is rounded up to 14. So, on the holes where the stroke index is 14 or less the course effectively gives you a stroke. The fairest way to decide on partners in a fourball best ball is to throw up four golf balls – one belonging to each member of the group. The two balls which come down closest together determine who plays with who. This helps ensure there's a fair mix of handicaps. It also means you're not partnered with the same golfer every time.

FORMAT	RULES AND CONDITIONS
 GREENSOMES	There's one big difference between this game and foursomes. With greensomes every player tees off and each pairing decides which of their two drives is in the best position. Then the pair take alternate shots until the hole is completed. The handicap system for this form of play is the most complicated in golf, so it's a good idea to calculate it before you reach the 1st tee. The player with the lowest handicap in a pairing takes three-fifths of his handicap and the higher handicap player two-fifths of his handicap. The two figures are added together to arrive at the allowance for that pair in a strokeplay event. For example: Player A with a handicap of 12: three-fifths of 12 equals 7.2. Player B with a handicap of 16: two-fifths of 16 equals 6.4. Added together the strokes received equal 13.6 – this is rounded up to 14. In matchplay greensomes the calculation of handicaps is the same as for strokeplay. Three-quarters of the difference between the two pairs' total handicaps determines the number of shots given or received.
 MIXED FOURSOMES	Mixed foursomes are a familiar sight on most courses. This form of golf is identical to normal foursomes except for one important difference – each pairing consists of a male and female. The handicap allowances and rules of play don't differ in any way. It often gives the gents an opportunity to play longer shots into greens – and the ladies shorter ones – than they're used to.
 JUNIOR SENIOR	Most clubs organize challenge matches between teams of junior and adult golfers. As many clubs impose restrictions on the times young members may play, it gives juniors a rare opportunity to match their skills with the older members. Often a very competitive day, the format is usually matchplay singles, with the occasional fourball best ball. There are no allowances for age – handicaps are all that matter. Normal matchplay rules apply.
 SINGLE PLAYER	One of the great benefits of golf is that you only need yourself and a set of clubs to make up a game. As a single player one of the best games you can play is a competition with the course. Basically it's a game of matchplay against an invisible opponent in the form of par. Give yourself three-quarters of your handicap to determine how many shots you receive. From there on it's the same as any other game of matchplay – though you can't give yourself putts! As a single player you have no standing on the course. As a matter of etiquette you have to wave through other groups when necessary.

and play alternate shots. There's a certain camaraderie in foursomes, because the end result depends as much on your partner's performance as yours.

Greensomes is closely related to foursomes. This form of golf is very popular on society days and club invitation events – both of which usually involve 36 holes. Having had a refreshing lunch, it's a light-hearted and enjoyable way to spend the afternoon. The more serious competitions usually take place in the morning.

DREAM SCORES

Texas scramble is similar to an advanced form of greensomes. Partnerships can be made up of groups of two, three or four players.

Every player in the group tees off on every hole and they choose the best drive. From that spot each player hits a second shot. The partnerships then decide on the best position from which to play their third shots, and so on until one player holes out.

With each golfer having a go at every shot the handicap allowance is far from generous – one eighth of the combined handicaps being the number of strokes received.

Texas scramble is played in a strokeplay format. It gives club golfers an opportunity to record the sort of scores they often see on television, but only dream about achieving themselves.

Mutual concession
In a friendly knock with nothing at stake there's no rule stating you have to hole out every putt. Many golfers agree on the 1st tee that a ball coming to rest inside the grip of your putter is conceded.

This is ideal if you're playing an evening game and the light is fading fast. It's also a good idea when the greens are in poor condition and you want to preserve your silky smooth putting stroke.

However, before you agree to this change in the rules, make sure your opponent doesn't have a broom handle putter similar to the one used by Sam Torrance!

PLAY YOUR OWN GAME

Most clubs organize competitions on a regular basis, particularly in summer. The most popular is **medal strokeplay** – you're on your own here, with no partner to blame or rely on. In many ways, success is that much more satisfying in a strokeplay event because you know it's all down to you.

The **stableford** system was invented in 1931 and is one of the more recent introductions to the selection of golf games. You record points according to your score on each hole – one point for a bogey, two for a par, three for a birdie and so on.

You receive seven-eighths of your full handicap in a stableford competition. For example if you play off 16, the course gives you a shot on each of the holes with a stroke index of 14 or less – shoot par on one of these holes and you notch up three points for a net birdie.

A high handicap golfer may receive more than one stroke on some of the harder holes on the course. If you're a low handicapper and this makes you feel a little hard done by, think again – golfers with handicaps better than scratch find themselves in the unenviable situation of giving strokes to the course. To them a birdie may be worth only two points.

The beauty of the stableford format is that you can have a complete disaster on one hole and still not ruin your chances of winning. If you drop two shots on a hole or comfortably run into double figures, the result is the same – zero points for that hole.

Singles matchplay is competitive head to head stuff. As with all matchplay games you may not have to hole out every time – short putts can be conceded. However, don't be too quick to give your opponent a short putt early in the round – on the 1st green they're easily missed.

Eclectic competitions are run over a pre-determined number of rounds and require several strokeplay cards to be returned. At the end of the allotted period the cards for each competitor are sorted. The lowest score returned for each of the 18 holes is taken to arrive at the final total.

Over a period of years it can be a great morale boost for the club golfer. Scores in the 40s are quite realistic – and for someone who seldom breaks 80 this can be a very comforting thought.

KEEP IT COMPETITIVE

As for gambling in private matches there's no one to tell you what stakes you should or shouldn't play for, except perhaps your dependants.

As long as you're fully aware of the stakes, and you understand the rules of the game, you have the recipe for enjoying every one of the many forms of golf.

Using your course planner

Used on the professional tour for decades, course planners – also known as yardage charts – are quite a recent introduction to the amateur game. They started to become popular with club players in the early '80s.

There's little doubt that a yardage chart can prove useful, particularly when you're on a strange course. It tells you the exact distance to the flag – wherever you are – and also helps you steer clear of any trouble that might be waiting for you along the way.

However, there are several points you need to bear in mind if you intend making the most of the information contained in your course planner. If you don't fully understand a yardage chart it can be a totally useless pocket filler – it may even land you in more trouble than you deserve.

TEE TO GREEN

Distances to each green are marked in black on most charts. Your first job should be to check whether they are measured to the front or to the centre of the green. You can usually find this information on the inside front cover of the booklet.

You must be clear on this point – there's almost no end to the number of disasters that might befall you if you get it wrong.

The figures printed in red describe distances from the tee. Bear in mind that there is more than one teeing area on almost every course – there can be up to three or four on some championship venues.

This means you may have to work out a few sums in your head before you decide on a club to use. Make a note of the tee you're playing from and take into account the difference in yardages. A bunker that's out of reach from the back marker may gladly welcome your

BETTER SAFE THAN SORRY

Many golfers fail to make the most of course planners when they tee up on par 3s. The numbers on the tee marker tell you how far it is to the centre of the green, but you need to take other important factors into account.

The 17th on the Old Course at Walton Heath is a good example. On a huge green like this it's not enough simply to know the distance to the centre of the green. You need to be aware of exactly how far it is to the flag if you're to hit your ball close. The putting surface spans the best part of 40yd (36m) from front to back. This probably represents a difference of as much as three or four clubs, so a careless choice here can leave you with a monster of a putt.

Your main priority is to clear the bunker that eats into the front of the green – leaving your ball short is almost unforgivable when there's more trouble at the front than there is at the back. Use your course planner to make sure you give yourself some margin for error – with this much green to work with, only your worst duff should land in the bunker. There may be holes on your home course where you can apply this theory too – you don't have to be at Walton Heath.

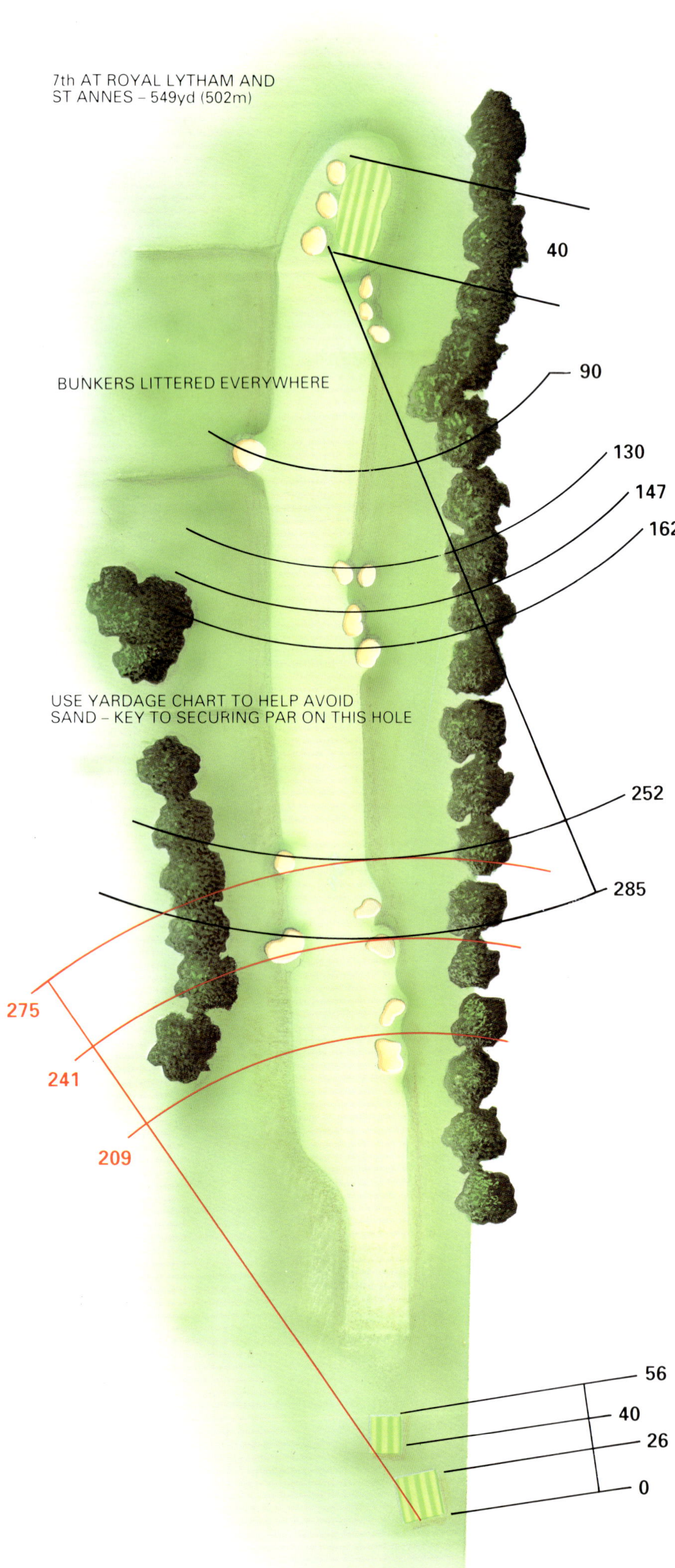

PATH FINDER
The 7th at Royal Lytham and St Anne's is a real monster of a hole – 549yd (502m), well out of reach in 2, and littered with bunkers, ditches and gorse bushes. A sensible frame of mind is the key to securing your par on holes as long as this. A go for broke attitude is unlikely to do wonders for your score.

Make your passage down this fairway as smooth and as easy as possible. This means identifying hazards, finding out how far they are from your ball, and then selecting the club that enables you to give them a wide berth. This is where your yardage chart comes in.

A group of bunkers comes into play around the 200yd (180m) mark, so the first job is to stay out of the sand with your drive. Don't be afraid to take a lofted wood off the tee to achieve this – even on a long hole. If it means your next shot can be played from a good lie on the fairway, you've made the right decision.

The next stage is to give yourself the best possible chance of hitting the green with your third shot – once again this means finding a position on the fairway and not in the sand.

All the way along this hole your overall strategy should be position, not power. Remember, the less pressure you put on yourself in a round of golf the better – use the course planner to help you achieve just that.

ball from the front tee. Equally, you may be able to carry hazards you wouldn't dream of firing over from the back tee.

GREEN CARD

The length of a green is often neglected when looking at a course planner. However, it's a valuable nugget of information – particularly on a flat hole where it's difficult to grasp the overall perspective, or on a hole with a raised green where you can't see the putting surface.

From a long way out, greens tend to look shorter than they really are, so a yardage chart can help you judge how far on to the putting surface a hole is cut.

OVER THE HILL
The 3rd on the Kings Course at Gleneagles is a picturesque hole in keeping with the beautiful surroundings. It's not long either – only 374yd (342m). But nothing can hide the degree of difficulty on this unique hole.

The drive isn't a problem. A lone bunker lurks on the left of the fairway – while it's around the distance you hit your tee shot, you should still be able to avoid it without too much trouble.

It's when you approach the second shot that your yardage chart comes in very handy. The hump in the middle of the fairway could almost be a mountain – the flag would need to be at least 50ft (15m) high for you to see it from the level of the fairway. It's as blind a shot as you could ever imagine on a golf course.

There's nothing to stop you wandering up to take a look at the green, but because you're at such a high level, judging distance is extremely difficult. Your eyes tell you what lies in wait over the hill, but you need your course planner to gauge the exact distance to the flag. This is the main problem on blind holes – the severity of some slopes upsets your ability to judge distance accurately. In these situations more than any other a yardage chart justifies the money you spend on it.

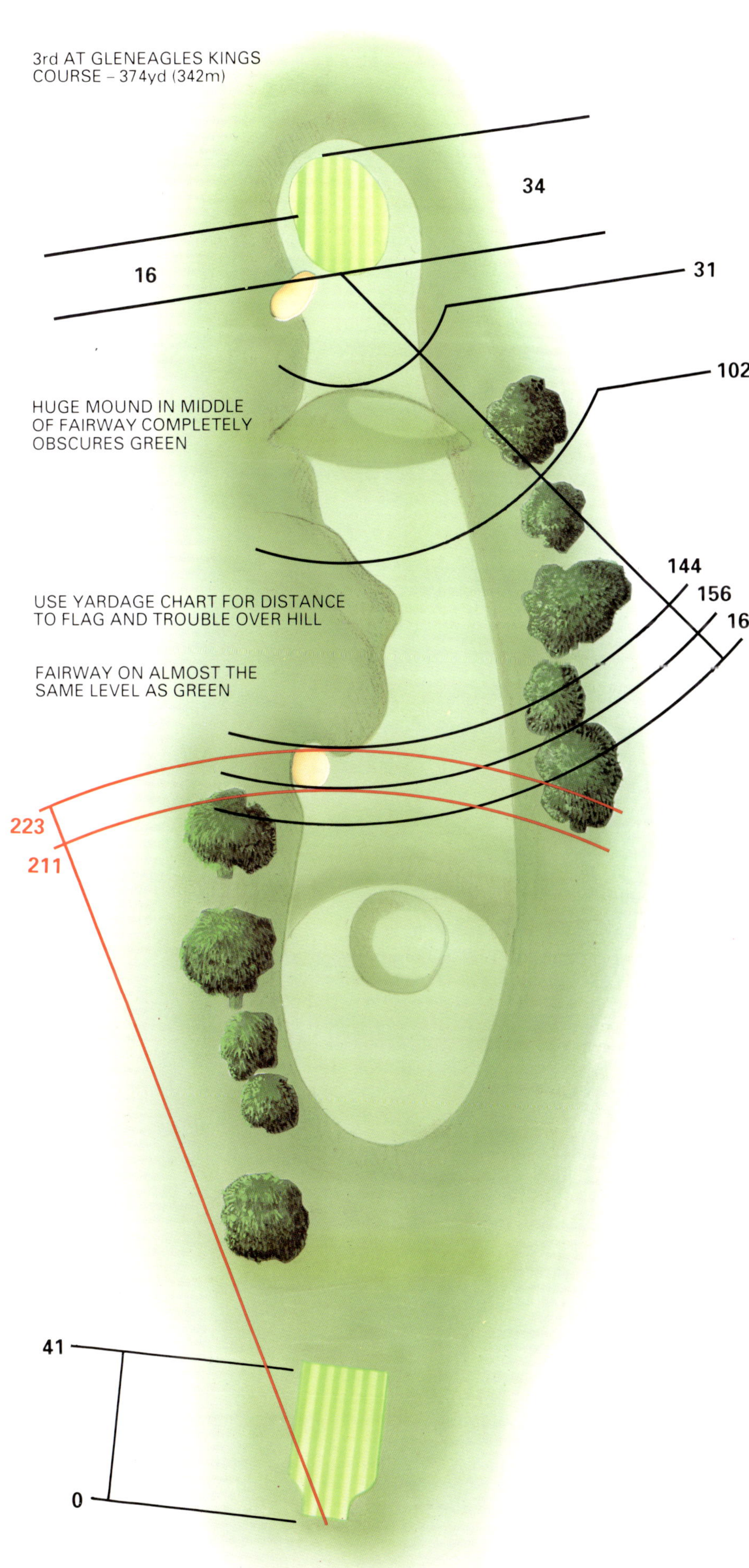

While yardage charts have a valuable role to play in negotiating your way round a course, you must not become totally dependent on them. Your eyes are an equally integral part of the process, giving you information in three dimensions, not just two.

EXTRA PAIR OF EYES

However, one task the human eye cannot perform is detecting hidden danger. On undulating ground it's easy for ditches and bunkers to be all but invisible from the tee. A quick glance at the yardage chart can help you pick your way through unknown territory. This is perhaps the most valuable function a course planner can perform.

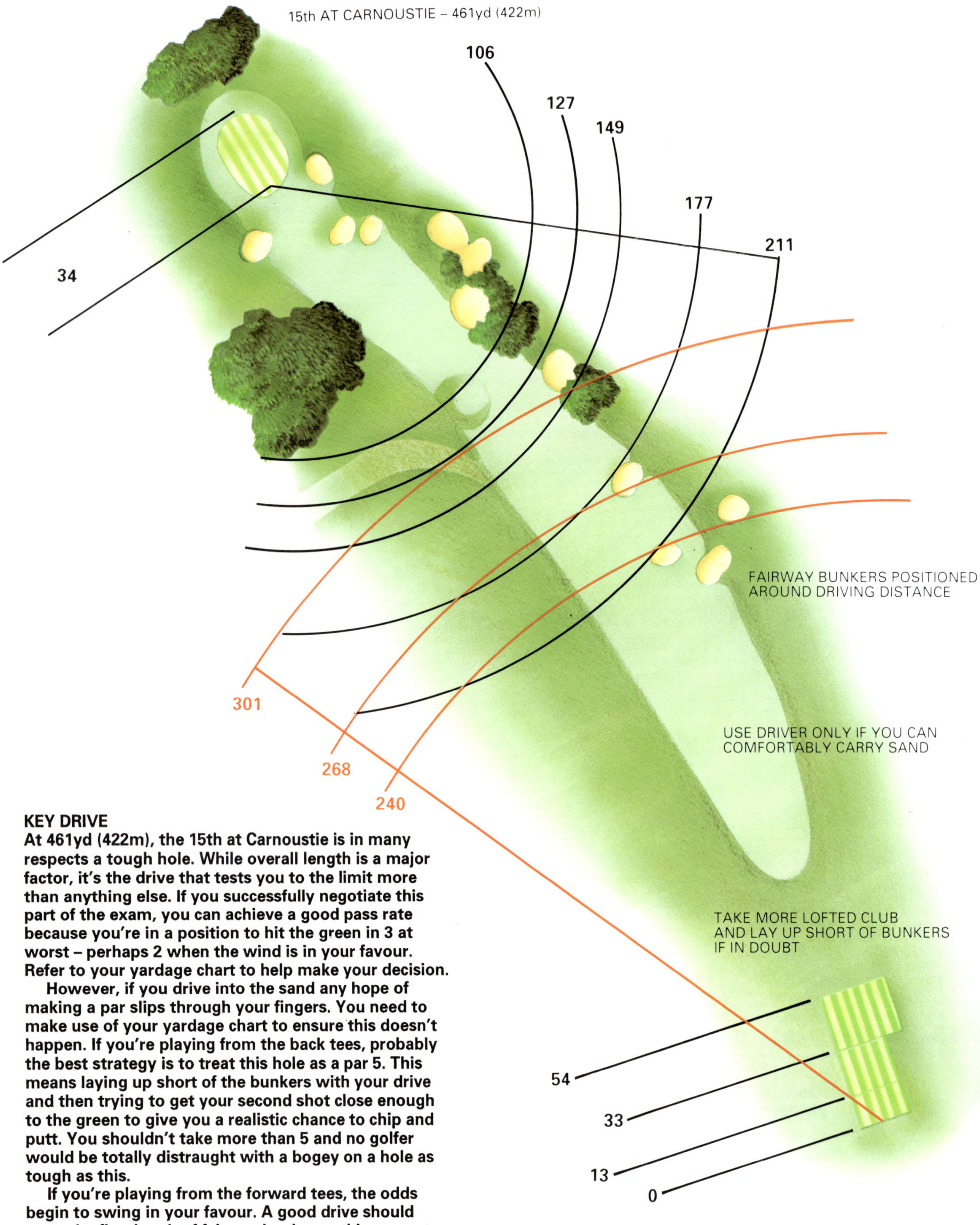

15th AT CARNOUSTIE – 461yd (422m)

106
127
149
177
211
34

FAIRWAY BUNKERS POSITIONED AROUND DRIVING DISTANCE

301
268
240

USE DRIVER ONLY IF YOU CAN COMFORTABLY CARRY SAND

TAKE MORE LOFTED CLUB AND LAY UP SHORT OF BUNKERS IF IN DOUBT

54
33
13
0

KEY DRIVE

At 461yd (422m), the 15th at Carnoustie is in many respects a tough hole. While overall length is a major factor, it's the drive that tests you to the limit more than anything else. If you successfully negotiate this part of the exam, you can achieve a good pass rate because you're in a position to hit the green in 3 at worst – perhaps 2 when the wind is in your favour. Refer to your yardage chart to help make your decision.

However, if you drive into the sand any hope of making a par slips through your fingers. You need to make use of your yardage chart to ensure this doesn't happen. If you're playing from the back tees, probably the best strategy is to treat this hole as a par 5. This means laying up short of the bunkers with your drive and then trying to get your second shot close enough to the green to give you a realistic chance to chip and putt. You shouldn't take more than 5 and no golfer would be totally distraught with a bogey on a hole as tough as this.

If you're playing from the forward tees, the odds begin to swing in your favour. A good drive should carry the first batch of fairway bunkers – this presents a great opportunity to hit the green in regulation. Look at your course planner and calculate whether you can fly the sand with your drive. You should be able to do this comfortably – if clearing the sand relies on you hitting your best ever drive, the gamble is probably not worth taking.

Raised and sunken greens

Many golfers are baffled by why they can't hit the ball close to the flag on elevated or sunken greens. Even though their striking and direction may be good the result can be disappointing because of poor club selection.

Understand the flight of the ball when hit up or downhill, and how the ball behaves when it pitches – these are the keys to playing to different green levels.

UPHILL STRUGGLE

When playing to a raised green a ball pitches on the putting surface before it can fly its full normal distance. To combat the effect of the slope you must play more club than the yardage suggests.

Too often you see players struggling to reach the green when firing uphill. They choose too little club and fall short of the target – the ball frequently rolls back down the slope.

The more elevated the green is, the more club you must hit. But however steep the slope you should never need to go up more than two clubs in calm conditions.

You must also take flight path into account. The ball comes in on a lower path than normal, and it runs on landing – more so as the green is likely to be well drained and firm.

UP AND DOWN DALE

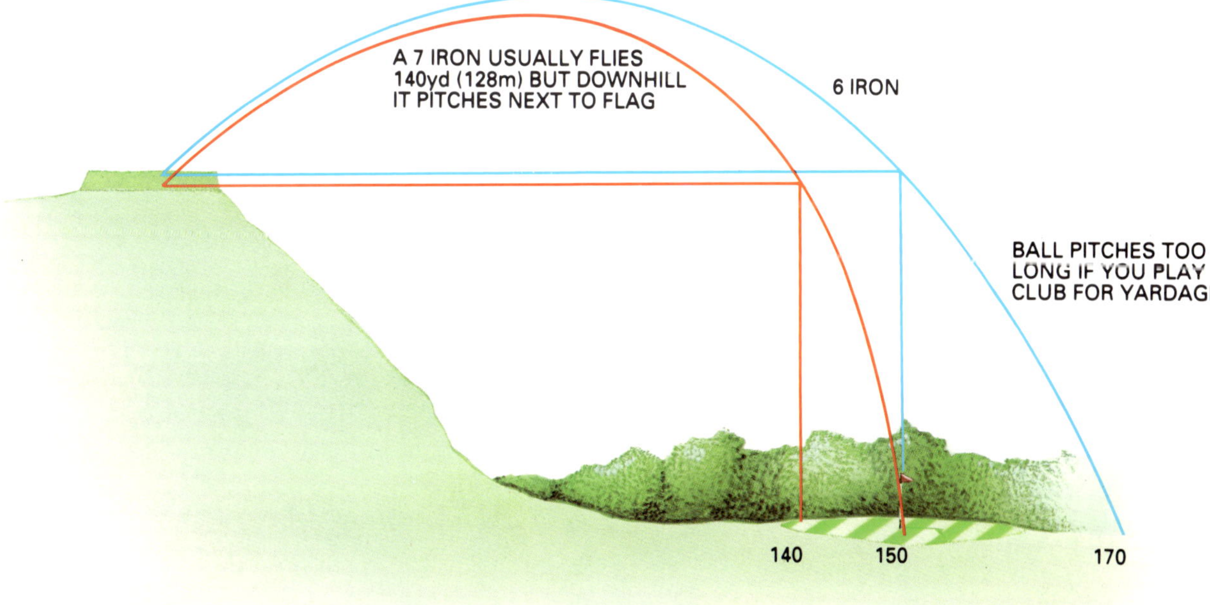

▲ When firing downhill to a sunken green, select one club less than the yardage suggests. The ball crosses a point level with the tee, then drops further until it pitches close to the flag. Even though you hit only one less club the distance between where the shots land is considerable.

Choosing the club you normally hit for the distance lands you in trouble – the ball pitches beyond the green.

▼ The opposite applies when shooting up to an elevated green. To play a shot to the target you must select a club that would pitch beyond the flag on level ground. If you rely on just the yardage and choose your usual club for the distance, the ball falls short.

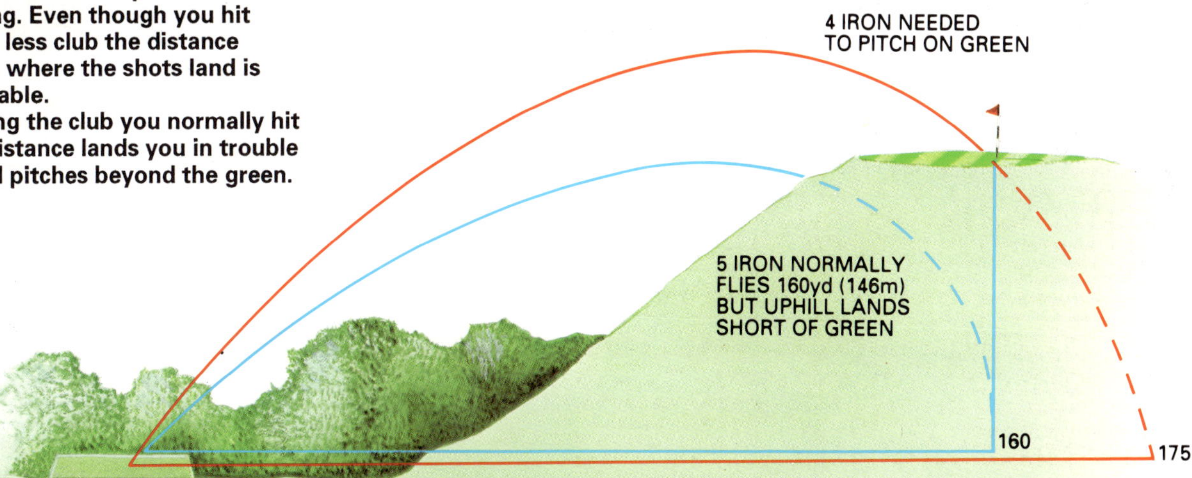

Try to hit the shot slightly higher than usual to help you stop on the putting surface. Aim to pitch the ball on the green but short of the hole.

DOWNHILL DEADEYE

When played downhill to a green the ball is in the air longer than usual so it flies further. Play less club than the yardage suggests – hitting your usual club could mean the ball pitching in trouble over the back of the green. But beware of playing *too* little club as the ball may land on the downslope and shoot through the green and into trouble.

You can afford to be bold and pitch the ball right up to the flag. The shot stops quickly as sunken greens are usually softer than normal and the ball drops from a steep angle.

The most your clubbing should vary is by two on a still day. In a head or cross wind, take more club and play a three-quarter shot to keep the ball low – this gives you greater control.

SHORT AND RUNNING

If you are faced with a downhill shot which is also downwind you may find that you can't pitch the ball on the green without it bounding through the back, leaving you a tricky shot back.

Provided there is no trouble between you and the green and the ground is firm, it's best to play a shot that lands short and bounces on. But make sure you reach the green – or your next shot could be equally tricky.

pro tip

Down and upslope lies

When firing down to a sunken green you often have to play off a downhill lie. Position the ball slightly further back in your stance – lessening the chance of a thin – and flex your right knee more than usual to compensate for the slope. The ball flies low and from left to right, so choose your club, and aim, carefully.

On an upslope, push the ball forward in your stance, flex your left knee and remember the ball flies high and right to left.

Langer's thoughtful clubbing

Bernhard Langer is one of the world's most accurate iron players. He knocks both long and short irons close to the flag with amazing regularity.

The sinewy German is also a great strategist and prepares for each stroke thoroughly. He fully understands how a ball behaves when going either up or downhill, and can choose a club which he knows should go close provided he hits it solidly and straight.

If the 134yd (123m) 2nd at Woburn was on the level instead of being set in a deep dell, Langer would probably hit an 8 iron. But because the hole is so far below his feet a pitching wedge is the sensible choice.

Even though Bernhard usually hits a 5 iron about 180yd (165m), he would choose more club to tackle the famous uphill 179yd (164m) 14th at Wentworth to combat the effect of the upslope. He relies on crowd reaction to tell him if the shot finishes close.

Langer tees off at Woburn's 2nd, with its sunken green.

Think like a pro

You can shave vital strokes off your score by taking a sensible and calculated approach to every shot you play. Thinking strategically is just as important as confidence. All top professionals carefully weigh up each shot to decide which option is the best for the situation.

KNOW YOUR LIMITS

It's vital to know the distance you hit each club for any strategies to work. A yardage chart is extremely helpful when used in the right way, but is useless if you don't know how far you hit the ball.

Most club players use a chart only for their second shots – if at all – but pros consult it on the tee. They look at what trouble there is and how far off the tee it is. They don't automatically take a driver at a reachable par 5 hole when they know that some cross bunkers are in range. A long iron is shorter and safe but still means they can reach the green in 2.

Use yardages in a positive way.

pro tip

Use your eyes

Take every opportunity to learn about a course you're going to play – do some reading or ask the pro questions.

Even in mid round you can pick up useful information. Take note of the pin position as you walk past the green of a hole that you're to play later on. This helps you decide what shot to hit when you reach that hole.

THOUGHT PROCESS

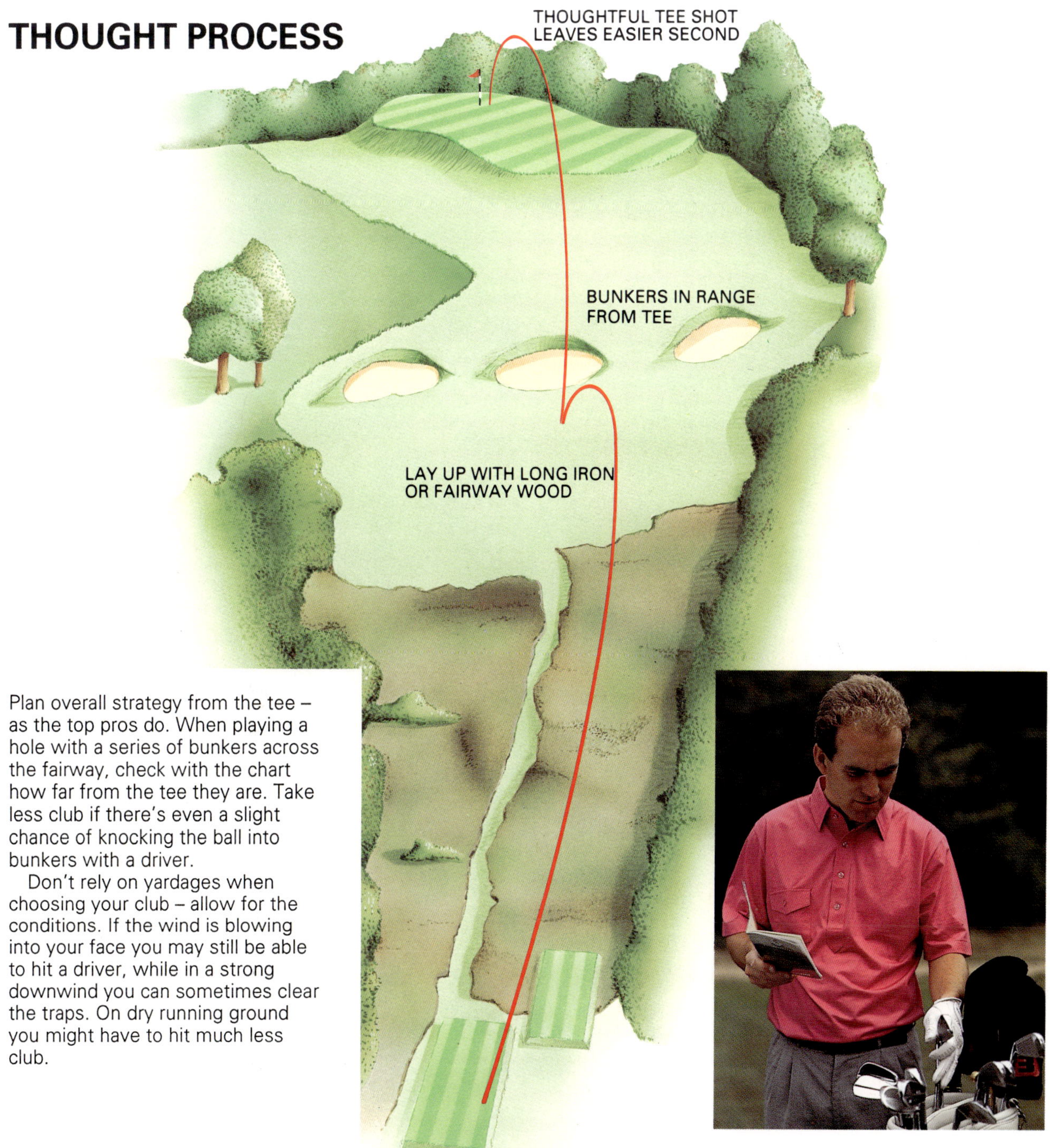

Plan overall strategy from the tee – as the top pros do. When playing a hole with a series of bunkers across the fairway, check with the chart how far from the tee they are. Take less club if there's even a slight chance of knocking the ball into bunkers with a driver.

Don't rely on yardages when choosing your club – allow for the conditions. If the wind is blowing into your face you may still be able to hit a driver, while in a strong downwind you can sometimes clear the traps. On dry running ground you might have to hit much less club.

Check the carry you need to clear bunkers at the corner of a dog-leg. Judge the wind and see if you can carry the trap with a driver. You may be able to make the hole a lot shorter. But never try to shorten the hole if the trouble around is too severe. A pro is content to take an iron to the corner of the dog-leg to be safe.

TWO SHOTS AHEAD

Being clever with your placement from the tee is an asset to your game. You should always think two shots ahead when deciding what club to play and where to aim. Unless a short par 4 is driveable, it's often wise to hit a long iron from the tee to leave yourself a full shot in with a wedge. A driver can leave you an awkward length pitch that's difficult to judge – a full wedge is easier to control.

When possible look at the green in the distance and try to see which side the flag is on. If the hole is cut behind a bunker on the left try to fire your tee shot down the right to leave yourself an easier approach shot.

Always assess the profile of the hole. Most pros shape the ball from the tee away from trouble, or along the contours of the hole – a ploy you should try to copy.

With bunkers down the left it's best to fade the ball away from them. Aim slightly inside the bunkers and hit the ball left to right. Even if you hit the ball straight you shouldn't land in sand. On a sweeping dog-leg right hit a draw to hug the contours of the fairway.

The shape of the hole also dictates which side of the tee you should play from. Don't just play from the middle of the tee – you can make your second shot easier by teeing up in the right place. You should play from the left side of the tee on a dog-leg right.

GATHER KNOWLEDGE

Don't think ahead just from the tee – approach shots need mapping out too. If a green is sloping you must aim to the high side so that the ball runs round to the flag. On a very steeply sloping green, choose a club that keeps the ball below the hole for easier uphill putting.

Every time you go out on to a course you should try to learn the subtleties of each hole. Look to see where the trouble is and how the green slopes, and work out the best way to play the hole for future reference. Gather as much information as possible, and in all types of weather – strategies must change to suit the conditions if they're to pay off.

Concentrate hard and use this knowledge to work your way down the holes. Take your time to assess the situation on every shot you play. Never rush – but don't dwell on the shot. Once you have made up your mind what's needed play promptly. Try not to think of the trouble – top pros nurture only positive thoughts.

Shot preparation

Playing golf well has a lot to do with how you approach each shot. Choosing the right club and imagining the shape of shot is critical. You should take into account the weather, character of hole, ground conditions and the yardage.

The top pros – such as Colin Montgomerie – use their caddies to give an accurate yardage and also to help them work out what type of shot is needed to get a good result. Work together with a friend on a practice round. Always prepare thoroughly but be quick – never stew over the stroke.

masterclass

Faldo's game plan

Nick Faldo is the master strategist. He has total confidence in his game and never asks too much of himself. At the 1990 US Open he needed a birdie at the 72nd to go into the play-off. Though the hole was a long tricky par 4, Faldo still hit an iron off the tee. To stand any chance of achieving the 3 he needed he had to hit the fairway, as the rough was thick.

A driver was risky even though he would have had a shorter second shot, so he was content to hit an iron and then a 3 iron into the green. Nick's approach ended up 15ft (5m) away so his strategy paid off – but sadly his putt just missed.

Dog-leg strategy

Golf courses would be very dull if all the holes were straight. A major part of a player's enjoyment is to be able to manoeuvre the ball down and around varying shapes of hole using their skill and judgment. Tricky dog-legs are the ultimate challenge for the strategist.

Never take on a dog-leg hole before you have worked out exactly how you should play it. Look to see what you can gain by playing a particular shot off the tee – perhaps a draw to shape the

TIGHT AND TRAUMATIC

The 18th at Valderrama in Spain is a classic finishing hole. It severely tests your drive and approach, and to play it well both must be spot on. The hole is tight and unless your drive finds the fairway at the corner of the dog-leg, you're blocked out from the green by trees.

There are two strategies you can use to tackle this corking right-to-left hole. One is to calculate the distance to the corner – 220yd (200m) from the yellow tees – and settle for a positional shot with a touch of draw to leave a clear view of the green. The other is a brave drive with draw down the edge of the trees on the left that bounds around the corner. This leaves a much shorter approach to the green.

But there is no need to be frightened by it or any other dog-leg holes – they needn't be a traumatic experience if your strategy and striking are good. Concentrate on the basics of the set-up and swing, and choose your club and type of shot wisely, to conquer even the trickiest of dog-legs.

417m (456yd) 18th VALDERRAMA

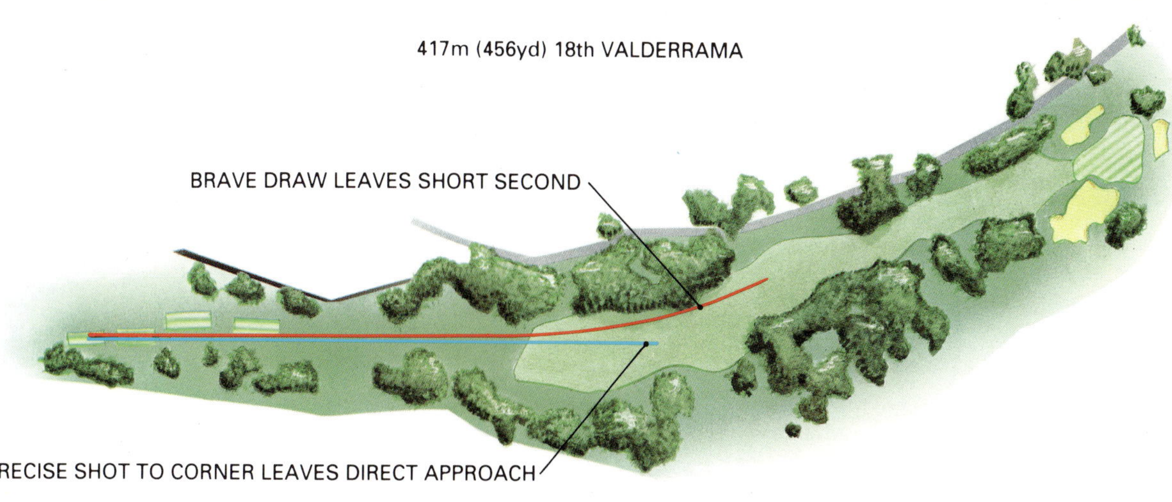

TEMPTING CARRY

Often a dog-leg hole presents you with an inviting challenge – an opportunity to cut the corner. In the right conditions the 18th on the Duke's course at Woburn (the 17th for a championship) is driveable for long hitters by carrying the tall trees on the right. Though the hole is listed at 356yd (325m) from the back, the tee is brought forward slightly for a tournament to tempt the pros to go for it.

This strategy of hitting over the corner instead of laying up with an iron can be a match winner. But never let your heart rule your head and attempt something out of your scope – there are only a few times when you should go for it.

Whenever you have a chance of taking on a big carry over a corner, you must weigh up the situation. Ask yourself what you gain. It may be that the risks outweigh the advantages and you should settle for the sensible lay-up.

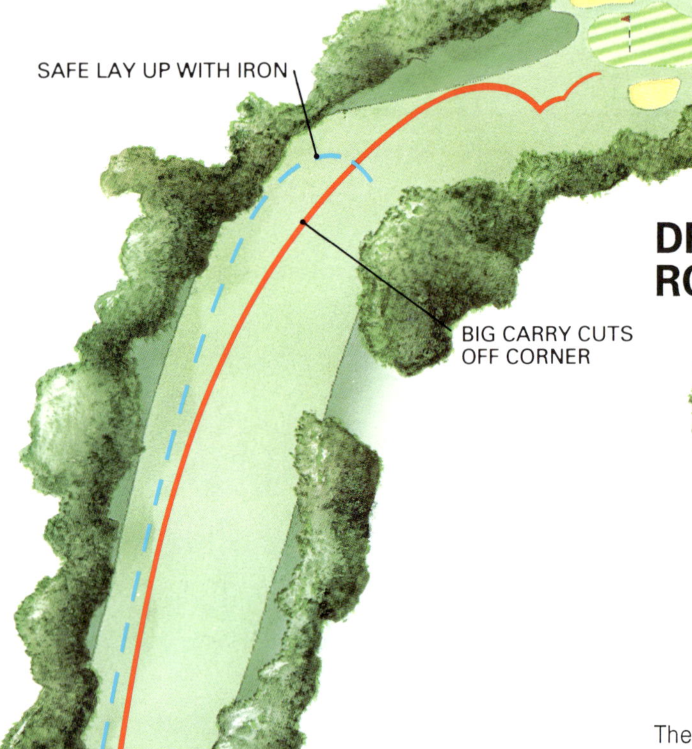

DRIVING DOWN THE BURMA ROAD

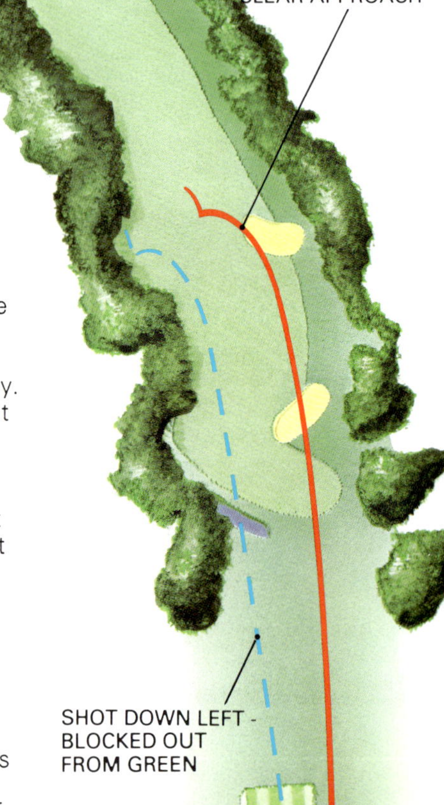

The West Course at Wentworth – nicknamed the Burma Road – is littered with classic dog-legs each needing a separate plan to negotiate it successfully.

At the 441yd (403m) 13th, placement is the key. If you're to have a straight shot into the green you must hit your drive down the right side of the fairway. Going too far left means you're blocked out from firing straight at the flag by trees. Even if you hit the left side of the fairway you still have to draw the ball to hit the green.

On every dog-leg try to assess where the green is and decide whether it's best to favour one side of the fairway. Life is made much simpler when you can hit direct approaches.

SHAPE YOUR COURSE

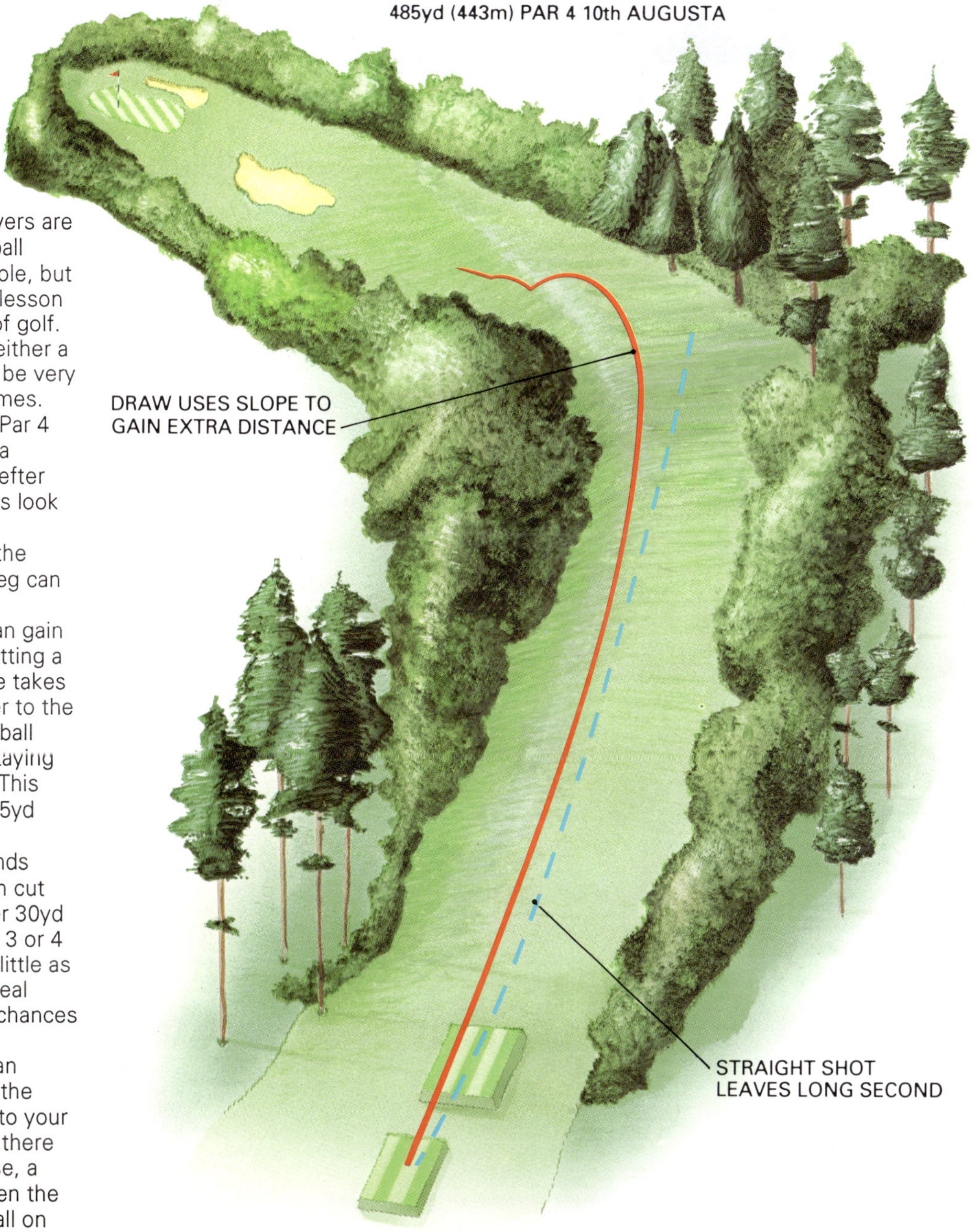

485yd (443m) PAR 4 10th AUGUSTA

DRAW USES SLOPE TO GAIN EXTRA DISTANCE

STRAIGHT SHOT LEAVES LONG SECOND

Most handicap players are content to hit the ball straight on every hole, but you should learn a lesson from the masters of golf. Shaping the ball – either a draw or fade – can be very advantageous at times. The 485yd (443m) Par 4 10th at Augusta is a sweeping right-to-lefter and the pros always look to hit a draw.

Steep slopes at the corner of the dog-leg can be used to their advantage. They can gain extra yardage by hitting a draw – as the slope takes the ball away closer to the hole. If you hit the ball straight, you risk staying up on the plateau. This leaves you over 215yd (195m) to the flag.

A draw that bounds down the slope can cut the yardage by over 30yd (27m). Instead of a 3 or 4 iron you can hit as little as a 6. This makes a real difference to your chances of making par.

Always look for an opportunity to use the contours of a hole to your advantage. Even if there are no slopes to use, a shaped drive is often the shot to keep the ball on the fairways.

ball round a long gradual right-to-left hole.

You may find that you need to hit an iron so you don't run out of fairway at the corner. Or you may have to play down one side or the other to leave yourself the best approach into the green. But what is certain is that no two dog-legs are exactly alike and need to be treated as individuals.

Weigh up all the dangers and check the yardages. One crucial yardage is the distance to the corner of the dog-leg if the angle is sharp, so you know what club to hit from the tee.

You may sometimes be tempted to cut the corner, so check how large the carry is. Be happy to play the percentage shot – don't attempt to clear a distance you know is on the edge of your limit.

CONTOUR HUGGING

Be prepared to shape your shots to gain an advantage. Often if you hit a straight shot – even on a gradual dog-leg – you can miss the fairway and find trouble. You may also leave yourself a longer next shot than if you shape the ball.

You can make a dog-leg easier just by standing in the proper place on the tee. When faced with a gradual left-to-right hole it's best to tee up on the left side of the hole. You don't have to shape the ball as much as you do from the right so it becomes a safer shot.

But if there is trouble down the right side – perhaps out of bounds – you should tee up on the right to play away from the danger.

Woosnam's alternative way

The 18th at Augusta has ruined many players' dreams of pulling on the Master's green jacket. The 405yd (370m) hole dog-legs right, and under pressure it can be hard to hit the fairway.

The perfect tee shot is a fade, but you run the risk of letting it go into the trees on the right – especially when the nerves are tingling. But the main danger is the two gaping bunkers on the left.

In the 1991 Masters Ian Woosnam showed how you can use your imagination to conquer certain dog-legs.

Tied with Tom Watson coming to the final hole, he knew that if he tried to hit a cultured fade around the corner he might have come unstuck. After watching his rival cut a 3 wood into the trees, Woosie decided attack was the answer.

He blasted a driver straight over the fairway traps – a carry of 275yd (251m) on to the member's practice ground, which left him only an 8 iron into the green. He had trusted his power and avoided trying to be too clever by playing the conventional way.

Ian played up to the green, two putted and par was enough to beat off the challenge of Watson and the clubhouse leader Olazabal. Imagination secured his victory.

Practising on the range

The purpose of practising is to build up a repeatable swing *before* playing a round. Practice shots warm up your muscles and make you feel confident of swinging the club correctly from the first shot through to the last.

Practice sessions are also worthwhile in themselves; they don't have to be the prelude to playing a game. At a practice session you can concentrate on a part of your game that's giving you trouble or a part you want to improve.

But practice is especially useful just before a game – look at the way tournament professionals practise before each game. None of them would dream of playing a competitive round without practising beforehand.

Far too often golfers stand on the first tee having not hit a ball since their last game. It usually takes four or five holes to loosen up and develop a repeatable swing, by which time the score is ruined.

To give yourself the best chance of recording a low score you must feel 'in the groove' before you reach the first tee – ready to face any situation on the course.

Don't practise a fault

It's important to get the details right during a practice session. Spend time on the preliminaries. Make quite certain that your aim, grip, alignment, posture and address position are correct when practising. If they are not, you'll start practising a fault – and once a fault develops into a habit it becomes increasingly difficult to get rid of it.

PREPARING TO PLAY
The practice range is where you prepare to play a round by warming up your muscles and finding a repeatable swing. Take your time over each shot, and remember not to stand in front of anyone else on the range or you might get hit.

This practice session works well just before you play but it's also effective when you want to hone up your technique between games.

CHECK THE BASICS

As with any sport, loosen up first. When you arrive at the practice range, do a few warm-up or stretching exercises before even picking up a club.

Then make sure your basics are sound. Carefully check your clubface aim, grip, posture, body alignment and ball position. These must be correct if you want to hit a good shot.

Next, work on your swing. Break

Practice net
If you have a reasonably sized garden or back yard, you could buy a practice net for use at home. This is a convenient way of allowing you to hit balls and perfect your swing in between visits to the practice range. To save your lawn from too much wear and tear, move the practice net from time to time and hit all of your shots off a mat.

TARGET YOUR SHOTS

Every shot must have a target. How far away this is changes from club to club. If the range at your club has distance markers, use these to guide you. Once you can achieve a consistent distance with every club, you'll find it easier to choose the right club when out on the course.

it into sections. Practise the takeaway, the backswing and the downswing into the impact position. All three must be correct before you make a complete swing movement.

Practise the half swing to start with. This increases your awareness of the clubhead, your hands and shoulders moving through impact. It also helps you develop a smooth rhythm and tempo. Hit your first ball only when you feel confident you've shaped your swing correctly.

Get into the habit of preparing for each practice shot just as you would for one during a round. Set yourself targets and take time to prepare properly for each shot. Visualize the path of the ball and follow your pre-shot routine to adopt the correct set-up position.

PRACTICE SHOTS

HALF SWING: WEDGE
Using a sand wedge, place the ball centrally in your stance and aim at a target 30-50yd (27-46m) away. Make a half swing, swinging across and to the left to give backspin.

FULL SWING: MID-IRON
Place the ball midway between the centre of your stance and the inside of your left heel. With near upright posture make a full swing at a target 150yd (136m) away.

THREE-QUARTER SWING: SHORT IRON
Position the ball in the centre of your stance. Your posture is more upright than with the sand wedge. Aim at a target 140yd (128m) down the range. Make a three-quarter swing both back and through.

FULL SWING: 3 WOOD
Tee the ball low and opposite the inside of your left heel. Adopt an upright posture. Try to hit the ball about 200yd (182m) with a full swing. Good rhythm and balance are essential for hitting long shots.

USING YOUR CLUBS

During a session practise every type of shot you expect to face on the course. Hit the ball high, low, long and short, with full, three-quarter and half swings. This doesn't necessarily mean using every club in the bag. In total hit about 40 to 50 balls.

Start all sessions with a short-shafted club, such as a pitching or sand wedge. Short clubs are easiest to use as they have the most loft. They help you swing properly and hit the ball well, so giving you the confidence to move on to a longer club and get the most out of the session.

Using your wedge, select a target about 90yd (82m) away and hit 10 balls at it. Then move on to a longer-shafted club, such as a 7 iron; hit another ten balls at a target. Do the same with a 5 iron and a 3 wood. Each successive change is to a longer-shafted club. Always end with a wood or long iron.

Then go to the practice putting green to build a confident stroke. Spend about ten minutes putting various distances to acquire a

pro tip

Take your time
To prepare properly for each shot keep your balls a club's length behind you. This slows you down – for every stroke you play, you must step away, pick up another ball and follow your pre-shot routine before hitting your next shot. If the balls are close, it speeds up the rate at which you collect, address and hit them – your preparation is rushed.

CHIP TIP
To improve feel on short shots, chip into an umbrella. This makes you focus on a target and helps you visualize the flight path. Try to land the ball on a precise point – aiming in a general direction is rarely successful.

feeling for putts of all lengths. If no practice green exists, finish a session with ten chip shots.

End every practice period with a stroke that needs no more than a half swing. This helps you unwind and allows your muscles to relax in readiness for the round itself.

A typical session should last between 45 minutes and an hour. Spend an equal time on each club. If you can't set aside a one-hour practice period before every round, try to spare at least 15 minutes. Some practice is better than none. Go through the same clubs but reduce the number of shots accordingly.

Follow a similar pattern every time you practice.

Winding down

End all sessions on the practice putting green. This helps you calm down and relaxes your muscles. After making half, three-quarter and full swings on the range, the shorter, slower putting stroke gives you the chance to unwind. This is especially useful if you are practising before a round.

Lowering your handicap

It's the aim of all golfers to reduce their handicap. Whatever standard you play to, you wouldn't be alone if you wished you could boast a lower handicap than your current one.

Most juniors starting out have dreams of playing off scratch – and many seniors discover that with more time on their hands there's a golden opportunity to creep closer to that elusive single figure handicap.

The way to lower your handicap is the same whether you're going from 28 to 18 or 8 to 4. However, as you get lower, you soon realize that it does become harder to shave strokes off your handicap.

There are also times when your handicap comes to a standstill for months on end, or even goes up a shot or two. This is true for all but the exceptionally talented, so don't be overly concerned if it happens to you.

All golfers have the ability to improve, but many fail because they simply don't know how best to go about it. A lot depends on how you make use of your time

PLAY AWAY
At most clubs there are plenty of competitions to enter, particularly in the summer months. But don't forget about open tournaments at other courses in your area – they provide an extra opportunity to lower your handicap. Your local club secretary should be able to give you dates and venues. Playing away from home is good for your game – unfamiliar holes make you think more and the overall test on a strange course gives you a fair idea of how realistic your current handicap is.

PROBLEM HOLES

PAR 3S	LENGTH OF HOLE	R1	R2	R3	R4	R5	R6	R7	R8	AVG
3 RD	132 YD (120 M)	3	4	3	3	2	4	3	4	3.25
8 TH	208 YD (190 M)	4	4	3	4	5	3	4	4	3.88
12 TH	187 YD (170 M)	4	2	4	4	4	3	3	4	3.50
14 TH	158 YD (145 M)	3	3	4	4	3	3	4	3	3.38
18 TH	210 YD (190 M)	4	5	4	3	4	5	3	4	4.00

SUMMARY:
Poor stroke average on long par 3s – probably room for improvement in your long iron play. Also indicates slight weakness at getting up and down in two.

PAR 4S										
1 ST	410 YD (375 M)	6	4	5	5	7	4	5	4	5.00
2 ND	324 YD (296 M)	4	5	4	3	4	4	5	3	4.00
4 TH	392 YD (360 M)	4	4	5	4	4	5	4	4	4.25
5 TH	460 YD (420 M)	5	4	5	6	5	4	7	4	5.00
7 TH	295 YD (270 M)	3	4	4	4	5	3	4	4	4.00
10 TH	320 YD (290 M)	4	4	4	3	4	4	5	5	4.13
11 TH	447 YD (405 M)	5	4	6	4	7	5	5	5	5.13
13 TH	342 YD (313 M)	4	4	4	4	5	5	4	4	4.25
16 TH	421 YD (385 M)	5	5	4	5	5	6	4	4	4.75
17 TH	338 YD (309 M)	4	3	4	4	5	4	4	5	4.13

SUMMARY:
Good performance on short and medium length par 4s almost certainly proves major strength is with the pitching wedge and 9 iron.

PAR 5S										
6 TH	510 YD (466 M)	6	5	5	4	7	5	5	4	5.13
9 TH	495 YD (453 M)	4	5	5	6	4	5	5	5	4.88
15 TH	524 YD (479 M)	6	5	7	5	5	6	4	5	5.38

SUMMARY:
Average on par 5s as good as the long par 4s indicates poor strategy on par 4s. Treat all long holes as par 5s, don't force shots and stroke average improves.

GOOD AND BAD HOLES
Take a look at every one of your competitive rounds over the last few months to see how well you scored on the par 3s, 4s and 5s. This helps to highlight your strengths and weaknesses.

If you tend to score badly on the long par 3s, you need to sharpen up on your long iron play. Continually missing greens places too much strain on your chipping and putting. It's a typical example of an unbalanced game and is a prime reason why golfers fail to lower their handicaps.

If you score a lot of bogies or worse on the long par 4s, the problem is probably with the driver – trying to hit the ball too hard in an effort to reach the green in 2. Treat these holes as par 5s and concentrate on keeping your ball on the straight and narrow. The number of disasters drops dramatically and you'll be surprised how many opportunities you have to make par.

If you fare badly on the par 5s there's every chance you land yourself in poor position with your drive. Be honest with yourself and assess how good you are off the tee. Decide what needs improving most – accuracy, distance or both. Then set out to raise that part of your game to a higher level.

It may not even be a serious technical flaw in your swing – perhaps you're trying to do too much. There's no rule stating you have to smash the ball as close to the green in 2 as possible. Par 5s are meant to be hit in 3, so play them the way they were designed to be played.

on the practice ground.

If your spare time is limited only to weekends and the occasional evening after work, make sure that you spend wisely every minute on the practice ground. If you have lots of free time then so much the better – you have a distinct advantage over most other golfers. But don't waste time when you're there.

TARGET AREAS

All players have their strengths and it's important to play to them whenever possible. Equally there are chinks in all golfing armouries – even those of the top professional.

But no one is naturally poor in a particular department. For instance many players are too quick to accept that they are bad chippers. An expression of near terror comes over them as they approach a delicate shot over a bunker – the result is almost a foregone conclusion and the problem continues to plague them.

Try not to let this happen to you. Identify the parts of your game that cause anguish and misery, because they prevent you from reducing your handicap more than anything else.

REGULAR CHECK-UP

If you play in lots of competitions, keep a watchful eye on the handicap board in the clubhouse. Your playing handicap may differ from one week to the next and you are ultimately responsible for making sure you play off the correct handicap at all times.

Also be careful that the committee hasn't cut you for standard of play. This generally happens to high handicappers, new members who are improving rapidly, and in particular junior golfers who have a habit of coming down extremely

Winter freeze

Everyone likes to see their handicap plummet to new lows, and there are periods when it does seem quite easy. Winter is not one of these times, so don't expect too much.

The weather seems always to work against you as you try to grind out a good score. The greens are generally in poorer condition than in summer which adds to the problem by making it difficult to hole out.

Many clubs also move the tees forward. This might seem an advantage at first, but you soon discover the downside to forward tees. The standard scratch score for the course is likely to drop by a shot or two. Therefore, you have to reduce your score by the same amount just to play to your handicap.

Given the poor condition of the course and the cold air – which means the ball doesn't fly as far – it's easy to see why many handicaps freeze along with the wintery conditions.

Fluctuating figures

It can be hard to get used to the system by which handicaps are adjusted. Try to make sure you know it virtually inside out.

There are four categories of golfer: those with a handicap of 5 and below; 6 to 12 inclusive; 13 to 20 inclusive; and 21 to 28 inclusive. Your handicap is adjusted by varying degrees depending on which category you fall into. Handicaps which end in .5 or above are rounded up, and .4 or below are rounded down.

The lower your handicap goes, the harder it becomes to reduce it further because a smaller fraction is deducted for each shot under the competition scratch score (CSS). The CSS can differ from the standard scratch score of the course by 1, 2, or no strokes at all, depending on the average performance of the competitors.

There is also a buffer zone that includes scores up to 2 strokes above the CSS. If your net score is equal to the CSS or falls into the buffer zone your handicap remains the same.

HANDICAP CHART

CATEGORY	HANDICAP BAND	ADJUSTMENT FOR EACH SHOT BELOW CSS	ADD ONCE FOR SCORES ABOVE BUFFER ZONE
1	up to 5	0.1	0.1
2	6 to 12	0.2	0.1
3	13 to 20	0.3	0.1
4	21 to 28	0.4	0.1

Example Player A: Gross 74 less handicap of 5 equals nett 69. CSS of 72 means exact handicap lowered by 0.3 (ie 0.1 for each stroke below CSS)

Example Player B: Gross 88 less handicap of 23 equals nett 65. CSS of 72 means exact handicap lowered by 2.1 (ie 0.3 for each stroke below CSS)

Example Player C: Gross 89 less handicap of 13 equals nett 76. CSS of 72 means exact handicap increased by 0.1 for a net score above the buffer zone.

PERFORMANCE ANALYSIS – AUGUST MEDAL

ALAN WICKES – HANDICAP 15

Mixed bag

It's easy to walk off the course after a competition not really knowing what went right or wrong. This can be frustrating if you're looking for a marked improvement in one department of your game.

A simple exercise can help you analyse a round from the first drive to the last putt. Grade each shot in one of three categories – good, average or poor. Be honest and resist the temptation to expect too much.

The class you describe as good should include shots that find the middle of the fairway or leave you a holeable putt. Average probably represents tee shots that just drift into the light rough or land on the fringe of the green. Poor shots include those that put you in trouble – deep rough, trees or worse!

This report presents figures in a clear and easily digestible format. You can see at a glance where you excelled and where you didn't.

CLUB	GOOD	AVERAGE	POOR
DRIVER	II	III	~~IIII~~
3 WOOD	I		I
5 WOOD		I	
2 IRON			I
3 IRON		I	I
4 IRON	I		
5 IRON		III	I
6 IRON	I		
7 IRON	II	II	I
8 IRON		I	III
9 IRON	I	II	II
PITCHING WEDGE	I	IIII	II
SAND WEDGE	III	II	I

TOTAL SHOTS	49
TOTAL PUTTS	35
GROSS SCORE	84
HANDICAP	15
	69

quickly. Although standard of play reductions are quite rare, you need to avoid being caught unawares.

Cutting your handicap is no easy task, so make sure you don't fall victim to the most soul destroying experience in golf – posting an incorrectly marked card.

DOUBLE CHECK

Always compare the scores for each hole on the player's card with those of the marker – never just look at the total and take it for granted that the rest is correct. A thorough check only takes a few minutes and it's time well spent if your handicap comes down a notch or two.

No matter how high your spirits soar as you walk from the 18th green, if you've made a basic error you'll be brought down to earth with a painful bump when you see the results board.

Card inspection

The biggest and most important step towards lowering your handicap is to identify your weaknesses. The easiest way to discover what you're worst at is to analyse your most recent competitive rounds.

Make a precise job of the study – you need to find out about every aspect of your game. Some of the more crucial points are:

- number of fairways hit;
- average putts per round;
- times you get up and down;
- percentage of sand saves.

The results of your survey give you hard facts. Some of them may please you, other figures you might find disturbing. Either way it shows that you must improve some parts of your game if you want to knock strokes off your handicap.

COMPETITION STATISTICS FOR DAVID RICHARDS – HANDICAP 9

(Number in brackets indicates figure you should strive for)

1 Fairways hit: 48% (60%)

2 Average putts per round: 35 (32)

3 Successful up and downs from just off the green: 48% (65%)

4 Sand saves: 24% (50%)

Revive a stale game

Have your firepower, touch and feel deserted you? Is your enjoyment dwindling? If so, it's time to shake yourself out of your slump.

There is usually nothing seriously wrong but just a staleness running through your game. A complete lay off is the most drastic measure – yet probably one of the most effective. A few weeks off can give you back the thirst for golf and you should be raring to get back on the course. But there are several on course adjustments that can also help.

REFRESHER COURSE

Staleness usually creeps in over a period of time, until your actions and thinking become almost robotic. You seem to be just going through the motions and the same faults keep cropping up. What you need to do is break this mould by

PROFESSIONAL HELP
All golfers go through bad patches, however accomplished. The will to play is weakened usually through minor yet persistent faults that creep into your game. If your play just isn't firing on all cylinders and nagging inconsistencies plague you, seek professional help. It may take only half an hour for a qualified pro to sort you out. He can spot a minor fault very quickly and this can transform your game, and renew any lost enthusiasm.

BREAK THE MONOTONY

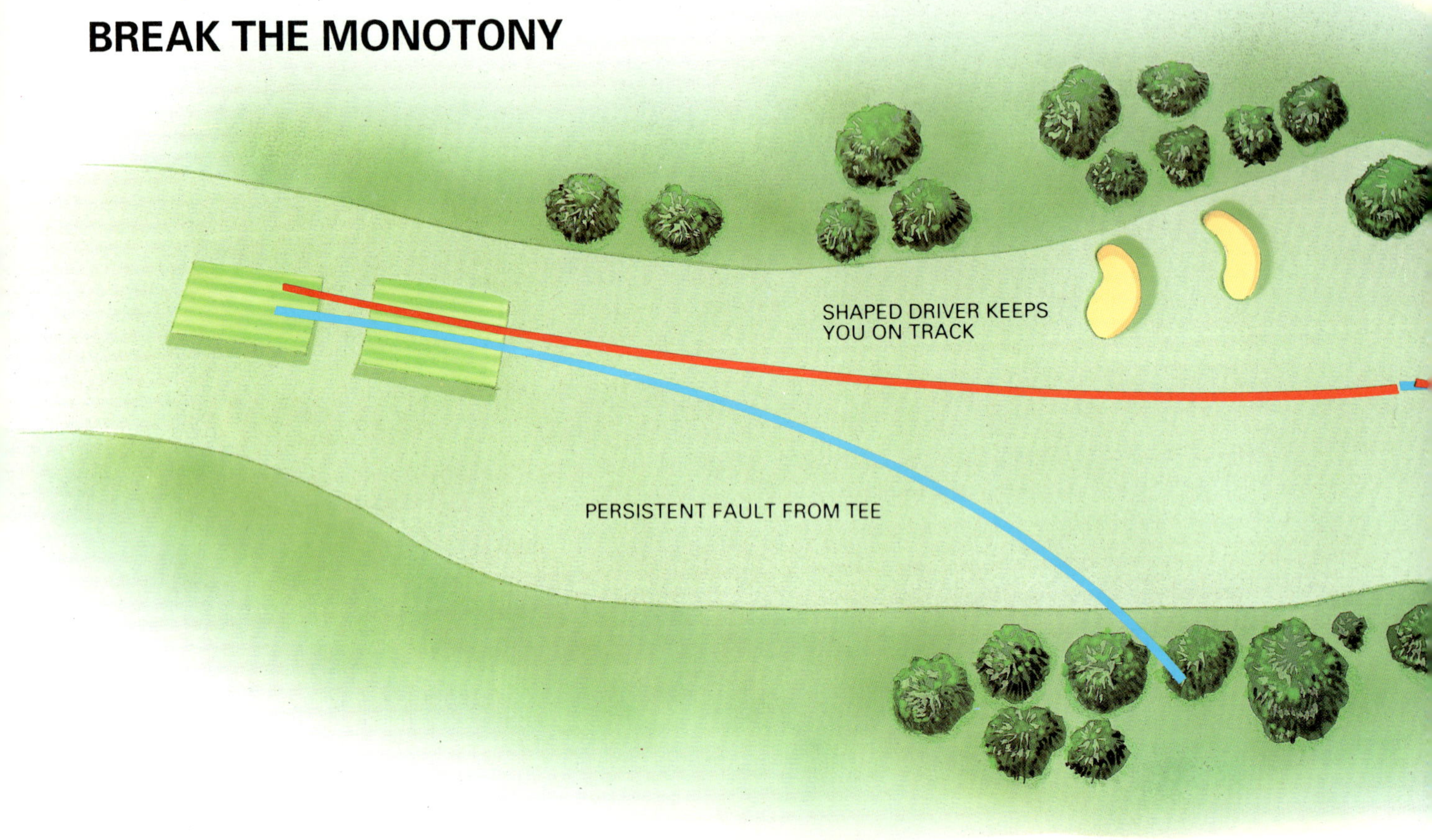

SHAPED DRIVER KEEPS YOU ON TRACK

PERSISTENT FAULT FROM TEE

DRIVER REVIVER

One of the most frustrating parts of your game – if it's off colour – is your driving. You may be striking the ball quite well but not finding the fairways. Often you have no clue as to what you're doing wrong or where the ball is going. If your shoulders slump after the tee shot, what hope have you of getting to grips with the rest of the hole?

Try something different. Shape your shots. If you are constantly hitting a slight leak out to the right, play for a draw – even if it is not your usual shape. It makes you think about your set-up and swing, rather than the result.

Move down a club or two – hit either a fairway wood or a long iron. This brings parts of the course into play that you don't often use. It makes you weigh up fresh dangers and leaves you approach shots that you rarely face.

More drastically, you could try out a new driver, as a change is refreshing. In a friendly you could also ask your playing partner if you could borrow his club.

INVIGORATING IRONS

Loss of accuracy with your irons is usually down to minor faults in your set-up or swing. By breaking your usual habits you should be able to escape the doldrums. Instead of setting up the same every time – when it is easy for a fault to creep in – experiment with your ball position and club selection.

Make sure you go behind the ball and line up properly, then address it. Place the ball differently – perhaps an inch further back in your stance for a short iron. You can also combine a variable ball position with a deliberate attempt to shape the shot. Even if there is no wind and there is little trouble around, go for a draw, fade or low punch. Hitting accurate approaches with this strategy builds confidence and enthusiasm as well.

Try playing a shot of 7 iron length with a 5 iron. This creative, conjuring stroke stimulates your mind and concentrates it on a correct swing.

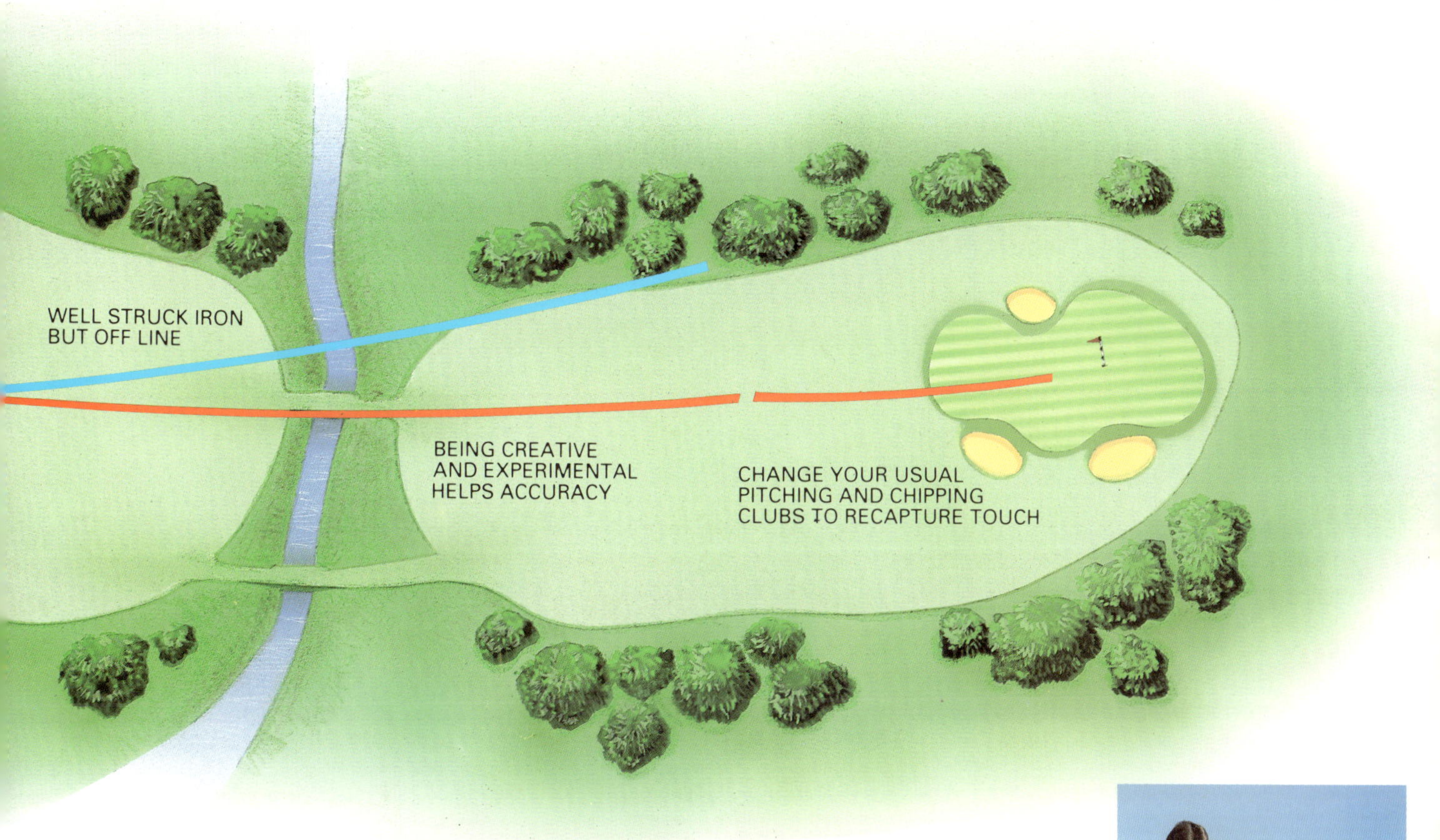

CHIP WITH RELISH

Being adept at pitching and chipping is vital to your scoring. But if your imagination has left you it's hard to roll the ball close to the flag. If you are struggling to up and down your short approaches it's probably due to an overly repetitive choice of shot.

Choosing the same club and type of shot for a situation can leave your mind cold and uninventive. Dream up different shots and play them with clubs you don't generally use around the green. Instead of hitting a sand wedge from 40yd (36m) for example, play a chip and run with an 8 iron. You have to start thinking again about your set-up and action. This should improve your touch and feel, and build confidence. It should also be more fun than plodding away with a conventional short game.

REJUVENATE YOUR PUTTING

So much enjoyment comes from holing putts that it's critical to have a fresh and effective putting game. If you're handy on the greens it can run through your whole game and have a rejuvenating effect.

If your present stroke isn't performing to the standard you expect, a slight change in your action can transform your game. Go on to the practice green and experiment with your set-up and action. Move the ball around in your stance. If you play with the ball in the middle of your feet, edge it forward slightly towards the left foot. You may find that this gives the ball a better roll. Putt with the ball both closer and further away from your feet as well – this can help you hit the ball on a better line.

Try also altering your body position. Stand slightly more upright or bend over the ball a little more to find a relaxed and comfortable posture. A trial with a new putting grip or putter can do the trick as well.

trying something different out on the course and practice ground.

To revitalize and refresh your golf, change your routine and choose different shots to play. Though you can easily alter the type of shot you hit – perhaps go for a fade rather than your usual draw – it still may not be enough to regain your momentum. Try also to vary your swing thoughts and your strategy.

Your strategies and club selections on each hole can become automatic – especially if you are too familiar with your home course – which leads to a stale mind. Change the way you play up a hole.

Where you usually hit a driver, go down to a 3 wood or long iron. Or on a reachable par 5 deliberately lay up. This leaves an approach to the green that you may not have faced for a while, stimulating your brain, and making you think of new shots to hit in.

Playing another course – preferably one you've never set foot on before – has the same effect. Learning to work your way round by looking for the dangers and hitting tactical shots to avoid them, naturally helps you escape your rut.

Practice is also essential to regain lost enthusiasm and restore faith in your abilities. But don't practise your faults. You must sort out any swing problems before you ingrain them further into your muscle memory. A quick refresher lesson with a professional has never done anyone any harm.

Since enthusiasm is such an important factor in improving your golf it's vital to find inspiration from somewhere. Watching a pro tournament live, on television or on video can help enormously. Replaying a dramatic competition – like the 1989 Ryder Cup Match – should be exciting, and make you aspire to greater heights.

masterclass

McLean refreshes his game

Mike McLean – the 10 year European Tour player from Kent – has seen both ends of the golfing spectrum. After consistently finishing in the top 40 of the Order of Merit until 1986 – with several excellent performances – the boyish McLean's fortunes took a nose-dive.

In 1987 he finished 99th, but the next year things got worse. Mike earned a mere £5,457 to come a very poor 158th on the list. His touch had deserted him as well as his confidence. He missed out at the Qualifying School and had to settle for a couple of invites in 1989. Mike's game was completely off the boil – he was stale almost beyond belief.

But 1990 proved the turning point for the likeable pro. He regained his tour card and made the most of his chance. McLean's girlfriend persuaded him that he could do it and made him enthusiastic for the game again. With renewed confidence and zest he came bouncing back to 44th on the money list, winning £91,963. And the season was brilliantly capped by a victory in the TPC Portuguese Open.

1991 has been even more productive with several top fifteen finishes and narrowly missing a Ryder Cup berth. The Boy and Youth International refreshed his golf with a mixture of mental strengthening and hard work on the practice ground.

Unorthodox

Having a pretty looking swing isn't necessarily the key to success. For a start, everyone has a different physical make-up and so a textbook action may not be easy for you. You have to learn how to use your natural build and ability to their best effect.

It doesn't matter exactly how you swing, as long as it's repeat-

LEE IN COMMAND

Laughing Lee Trevino is an enigma within the golfing world. No fellow pro deliberately slides the ball from left to right as much as he does. But he makes this huge clearing of the left side, open stance and out-to-in swing work brilliantly well.

Though it's totally unorthodox within the professional world, he has made it effective through practice. From the days as a driving range assistant in Texas until the present he has hit thousands of balls each week.

This has ingrained his swing into his muscle memory so he can repeat it consistently, even under the severe pressure of a major championship.

CONVENTION OR A STYLE OF YOUR OWN?

EAMONN THE INDIVIDUAL
One of the most enjoyable aspects of watching golf is seeing the variety of actions. Some you admire, some you laugh at, some you wonder how they get it round. Eamonn Darcy has elements of all three. But his very upright, flying right elbowed, high left knee lift action unquestionably works. He has played in the Ryder Cup four times despite having the oddest looking swing on tour. But he scores so well because his method is repetitious and natural to him, and he consistently delivers the blade square into the ball – the most vital factor in hitting shots true.

SUPER SEVE
Many people regard Severiano Ballesteros' swing to be the most fluid and natural of all time, and if there was any action to copy it would be his. If he is not showing his cavalier side – when he seems to help the ball home in on the target with body talk – he keeps perfect balance throughout the swing. The club swings on the classic plane into a superb position at the top. Seve moves into impact with ultimate control – the club attacks the ball from just the right angle. It is no wonder that he is one of the greatest performers of all time with this flowing swing, because the basics are so good.

able and controllable, and based on sound fundamentals – it is the result that counts. Just looking at the methods of some of the world's top pros backs up this theory. Most of the best golfers swing from the same mould with a few individual traits, but some have very much their own style.

UNGRACEFUL CHAMPIONS

Watching the greats such as Lee Trevino and Arnold Palmer can make an untrained eye stare in wonderment. It seems incredible that these two should have shared 13 major titles between them, using their ungainly actions.

John Daly – the 1991 USPGA champion – massively overswings on the way back, but still manages to hit the ball prodigious distances accurately. He claims: 'There is a lot of nonsense talked about the swing. It just has to be repeatable, and mine is repetitious just like Arnold's.'

But if you break down and analyse their swings, you see immense natural talent harnessed into ultimate control through the striking zone. The clubhead is deliv-

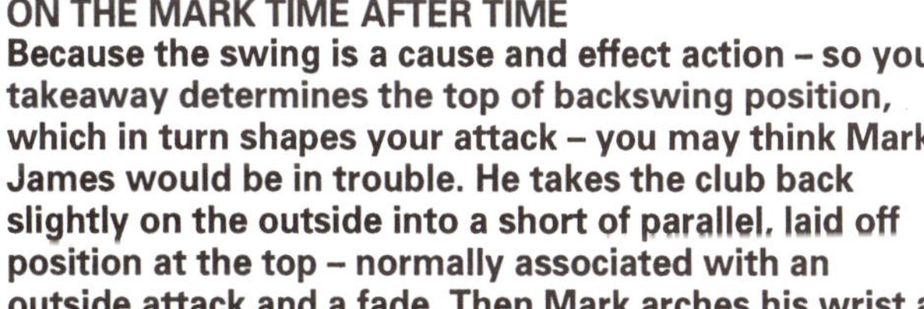

ON THE MARK TIME AFTER TIME
Because the swing is a cause and effect action – so your takeaway determines the top of backswing position, which in turn shapes your attack – you may think Mark James would be in trouble. He takes the club back slightly on the outside into a short of parallel, laid off position at the top – normally associated with an outside attack and a fade. Then Mark arches his wrist at the start of the downswing and the club points even further left of target. The clubhead swings into impact from well on the inside creating a looping effect. But Mark returns the blade square time after time because his hands control the clubhead superbly. His left side clears quite noticeably at impact, enabling him to hit shots from left to right – even with this inside attack – or a draw with a little working of the hands through the ball. Anyone less talented couldn't get away with it, but Mark found a swing that works for him and stuck to it.

A word of caution

Though individualism isn't to be discouraged there are certain elements in a swing that should be avoided. Too much overswing at the top is one such trait. When a club moves markedly past the parallel, it is very difficult to coordinate the downswing. Most often the body moves well ahead of the ball at impact, and however fast the hands and arms work they can't catch up. You lose both distance and direction.

Very few golfers have ever made an overswinging action work – but some have. Jack Nicklaus in his younger days was very full at the top but still hit the ball with immense power and control. But the best example recently is the thrilling John Daly.

Anyone wanting to emulate his prodigious hitting should not try to copy his action – he is a one-off. John only gets away with it because he has a great body action and incredibly fast hands which enable him to return the blade square.

Even if overswing seems to be your natural shape, you should think about shortening your backswing. More control is the result and you may even hit the ball a little further.

ered into the back of the ball with remarkable consistency.

Players such as this should be as much an inspiration to you as the fluent and seemingly faultless swingers like Seve Ballesteros, Nick Faldo and Ian Woosnam.

CONVENTIONAL CHANCE

There are fewer unorthodox swings around today among the young professionals than in the past because there is more importance put on coaching and practice. This has shown in a general raising of standards through all levels of the pro ranks.

This is not surprising, since basing your swing around orthodox technique undoubtedly gives you a better chance of staying in control and striking the ball sweetly and straight.

ALL ROUND PACKAGE

But scoring well isn't just a case of swinging the club decently – many other factors determine how good your game is. Your chipping and putting must also be sound, but most importantly your course management and temperament have to be balanced.

All the elite players – even though they have their moments of aberration – think their way round the course sensibly and look at each situation carefully. When the pressure is off they use these calculating skills well, but when the heat is on even the best laid plans sometimes come unstuck. That is when a honed and practised technique comes in.

Don't worry if your swing is slightly unorthodox as long as the basics are good. But you must keep working at it through practice and tuition to gain the consistency and confidence you need to tackle even the toughest courses.

Beauty isn't everything

Swinging on the classic lines with balance, poise and rhythm doesn't automatically make you a winner or set your scorecard alight. So much more goes into having the complete golf game.

You have to be mentally strong and possess good touch on and around the greens, but you also need to know what type of shot to hit and when. It's no good having the perfect shaped swing if you select the wrong stroke to play.

Being strong in all departments – with no apparent weaknesses – separates the best from the rest. US player Tom Purtzer is consistently voted as the best swinger on Tour by his fellow pros. But in 17 seasons on the circuit he has only won 5 times – including twice in 1991.

His statistics for '91 show his long game prowess – 7th for driving length and accuracy, 6th for greens in regulation – but also illustrate his weaknesses. Unfortunately Tom was 171st in the putting table averaging almost 33 putts.

Purtzer proves the point that you must have an all round game really to make an impact.

3

STAR PROFILE

Whether you are watching a golf tournament on television or are lucky enough to be there in person, you will doubtless have noticed how easy the top players make it all look. You can't help but marvel at their expertise and the scores they post. There have been many good golfers who have won events across the world, but only a handful ever achieve true greatness.

Every one of the 25 players featured here has been blessed with a rare talent all golfers are jealous of – an ability to crash arrow-straight drives down the fairways, fire in pin-splitting approaches, and hole out from almost anywhere.

Each of their very different careers is charted in detail, from the heady days of the brilliant amateur Bobby Jones – who accomplished the grand slam of the British and US Open and Amateur titles in the same year – to modern masters such as Severiano Ballesteros.

Find out how they started in the game, the turning points in their illustrious careers and even, when times were hard, how they fought their way out of a slump. These stars even impart a little of their own personal golfing experience to help you improve your game.

Isao Aoki at the 1992 Dubai Classic, held at the Emirates Golf Club.

Isao Aoki

A late developer, Isao Aoki's best performances have all come in golfing middle age. In achieving them, the Japanese player with the unorthodox swing has led his country on the international tournament stage.

The determination of Isao Aoki defied all the critics who said he would never make it in top-flight golf. He has won important tournaments worldwide.

Record breaker
When Isao Aoki finished second to Jack Nicklaus at the 1980 US Open he had given the best performance by a Japanese player in any major.

There was an unusual bonus as well. An American golf magazine offered $50,000 to the player beating the US Open record. They hadn't reckoned on paying out twice, but Aoki as well as Nicklaus left the previous mark behind.

Isao Aoki started playing golf at 15. He felt good enough to turn pro seven years later, but his unusual style caused a lot of adverse comment. The young Aoki was advised – as was Gary Player – to give up hopes of tournament success.

But perseverance paid off. After another seven years Aoki gained his first victory. By the end of 1989 he had won a massive 56 events worldwide.

WRISTY SWING

Apart from Lee Trevino, Isao Aoki is the most unorthodox of all great golfers. His shoulder turn isn't full, his leg drive is almost non-existent and his balance at the finish is not always secure. Aoki is a wristy player – overall, the impression is of a man flicking casually at daisies with a walking stick.

Perhaps the only lesson you could learn from Aoki – and it's a vital one – is that the golf swing should not look as if great force is being applied.

This relaxed swing could explain why Isao Aoki's game has lasted so well. At the end of November 1989 he won the Casio World Open in Japan. This isn't an ordinary Japanese tour event, but one of the few tournaments in that country in which a top international field competes.

At the age of 47, Aoki proved that he was still one of the world's best players. Just a handful of golfers have won important events at such an age.

◀ **As he is noted for the accuracy of his short game, a deft uphill chip proves no problem for Aoki at the Olympic Club, San Francisco during the 1987 US Open. The Championship went to Scott Simpson.**

THE RISING SUN

The toughly competitive Japan Tour grew quickly after the country's sensational 1957 World Cup win in Tokyo. Yet the tour did not boost the international reputation of Japanese golfers. Playing in Japan was highly profitable, so Japanese golfers had no incentive to compete abroad.

Isao Aoki, then the leading player in Japan, was the first to break through to international recognition with his British achievements in 1978.

First, there was the Open at St Andrews. Another Japanese, Tommy Nakajima, earned sympathy by taking shot after shot in the Road Hole bunker. In genuine contention up to that point, he ended with a 9. Aoki had no such embar-

▲ **Aoki is one of the best known and most popular Japanese players on the fairways. He has proved a consistent success in the USA and Europe, paving the way for many of his countrymen.**

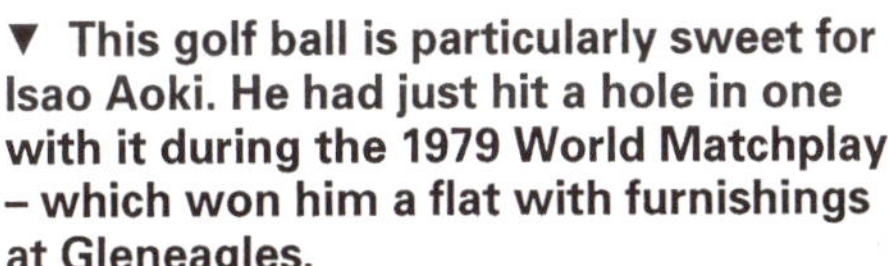

▼ **This golf ball is particularly sweet for Isao Aoki. He had just hit a hole in one with it during the 1979 World Matchplay – which won him a flat with furnishings at Gleneagles.**

rassments. He opened with a 68 for the outright lead, and had a share of the lead after both the second and third rounds. But Aoki's 1 over par 73 on the last day wasn't good enough; he finished tied for 7th place.

Although he slipped back at St Andrews, Aoki made the golfing world sit up and take notice at Wentworth in the autumn of that year. The occasion was the World Matchplay Championship.

Nobody took much notice of his first round match, when he beat Lee Elder. Next came Gary Player, who caused some surprise before their contest by announcing that Aoki was the best player in the world from 50 yards in. People began to pay heed to the Japanese

▲ **The wristy swing of Isao Aoki has been likened to 'the death throes of a cobra'. The quote remains justifiably anonymous – Aoki's record speaks for itself.**

▲ To rapt crowds, Aoki chased Jack Nicklaus right to the death in the 1980 US Open. They played so coolly that both beat the four-round Championship record.

▼ Putting has always been one of the strongest features of Aoki's game. What he lacks in distance off the tee he makes up for in deadly accuracy on the greens.

already 36 years old.

Gary Player – at the time thought the world's greatest matchplay golfer – went the way of Lee Elder. Aoki then disposed of his semi-final opponent, Raymond Floyd, shooting 8 birdies in the 16 holes played in the afternoon.

Aoki beat the New Zealander Simon Owen by 3 and 2 in the final.

His victory was seen as a prediction of Japanese success in the major championships. Yet by the beginning of the 1990s, this had still not happened. Isao Aoki came closest.

BATTLE OF BALTUSROL

Aoki's best efforts in the majors were in 1980. At the US Open, played at Baltusrol, the Japanese player hunted Jack Nicklaus right to the death.

In the third round, they played almost stroke for stroke. But the pars and birdies were achieved in very different ways – Nicklaus with his consistency into the green and Aoki with his putter.

On the par-5 17th, Aoki's 10yd (9m) putt hit the back of the hole quite hard, hopped up into the air and went in. Nicklaus had a birdie putt from about 10ft (3m) – and missed.

Aoki faltered at the start of the final round, restoring Jack's 2-shot lead. On the par-4 10th, this lead seemed certain to increase. Nicklaus was almost stone dead in 2; Aoki was on the back fringe. But the Japanese is just as effective when chipping as with his putter. Down it went.

When they arrived at the 17th tee, Aoki needed 2 birdies to draw level. He made them – but so did Nicklaus.

As Jack has said, many majors have come his way because others have failed more than he has in the cauldron of the last 9 holes. Not this time – although Jack played superbly for his 68, Aoki's 70 was equally nerveless.

Aoki also made an impression at Muirfield a few weeks later. He only just beat the 36-hole cut at the Open,

▲ Even in his late 40s, Aoki remains a powerful force. Some have suggested that his relaxed approach – seen here on the tee with his caddie – is partly responsible for his continuing success.

Aoki's short game

'A man who can putt is a match for anyone,' wrote Willie Park many years ago. Isao Aoki can certainly putt – but he has a very strange method, mainly because his first clubs were too long. He crouches low over the ball, hands about knee level. The toe of his putter sticks up at an angle in the air. Then he gives the ball a sharp rap with his right hand.

J H Taylor retorted to Willie Park: 'The man who can pitch doesn't need to putt.' Aoki is a master of pitching and chipping as well – he makes up for his lack of distance off the tee with a short game of pinpoint accuracy.

◄ During the 1978 Open, Peter Alliss said of Aoki: 'I don't think I've ever seen a worse swing from a player at this level of golf.' But while the Japanese may be unorthodox, his reliable short game always makes him a threat.

AOKI FACTFILE
Name: Isao Aoki
Born: 31 August 1942, Abiko, Chiba, Japan
Height: 6ft (1.82m)
Weight: 170lb (77kg)
Family: Wife Chie; daughter Joanne
Turned pro: 1964
Pro wins (US): 1983 Hawaiian Open
Pro wins (other): 1978 World Matchplay; 1983 European Open; 1983, 1987 Japan Open; winner of 5 Japan PGA Matchplay titles; 1992 Casio World Open
Money list (US):

Year	Position	Winnings($)
1981	88	46,420
1982	12	30,657
1983	34	146,467
1984	90	64,449
1985	84	92,659
1986	134	53,116
1987	107	82,309
1988	110	101,686
1989	135	87,516
1990	179	49,047

but he made headlines in the third round. The Japanese shot a 63 – 8 under par, a course record – which should have brought him into serious contention. But Tom Watson shot a brilliant 64, the bedrock of his third Open triumph.

ALOHA AOKI

Aoki is also the only Japanese player to have won on the US Tour. At the 1983 Hawaiian Open, he needed a birdie 4 at the last to tie Jack Renner, who was safely in the clubhouse. His chance looked gone when he hit his second shot into tall grass off the left side of the fairway.

Aoki, 128yd (117m) from the flag, took out his sand wedge and pitched his ball into the hole.

That same year, Aoki also became the first Japanese player to win a full European Tour event. (The 1978 World Matchplay was an invitation tournament.) Beginning with a 65 at Sunningdale in the European Open, Aoki led throughout and won by 2 shots.

Isao Aoki has proved that a mature player can be up there year after year with the top competitors. His place as a star of world golf is well earned.

▼ Aoki's triumph in the 1978 World Matchplay turned him into an international golfing star. He made a good defence the year after, losing to Bill Rogers in the final.

▲ Although Aoki was a long way from home at the 1980 US Open, with the galleries supporting Nicklaus, he knew he could rely on the support of at least one person in the crowd – his wife, Chie.

Ian Baker-Finch

'Just to play in it is great. To do well in it is fantastic. To win it is a dream,' says 1991 Open Champion Ian Baker-Finch. It was third time lucky for the Queenslander who tamed the beast of Birkdale.

The Open victory was made all the sweeter in view of Baker-Finch's previous near misses. 'The pain of losing before gave me the strength to win this time,' he said as he clutched the famous silver claret jug.

In 1984 the Australian almost stole the Open having led for the first three days. But his challenge drowned in the Swilcan Burn at the 1st hole of the final round and he collapsed to a 79.

'I was so apprehensive,' Ian remembers, 'I got so many over par and felt the whole of Australia had sat up all night watching me screw up. I believed I had failed. But after about a week I realized that just because you fail, it doesn't make you a failure.'

BIRDIE BLITZ

But he made no mistake in 1991. Having carded steady 71s in the first two rounds, Baker-Finch raised his game in the third round with a thrilling round of 64.

Starting the final round sharing the lead with his close friend Mark O'Meara, Ian set the course alight with five birdies in the first seven holes.

He played steady golf on the back nine with just one birdie on the 17th to win the title by 2 strokes over fellow countryman Mike Harwood.

Growing up on a small farm a couple of hours from Brisbane, Ian's nearest town only had a grocery shop and a post office. For want of anything better to do, Ian's father decided to take up golf.

Since the nearest club was 20 miles (32km) away, Baker-Finch

◄ Concentrating hard on every shot during the 1991 Open Championship, Ian Baker-Finch stayed calm despite the excited galleries and the barrage of photographers following his every move. His cool approach led to a birdie blitz and the claret jug.

The name game

Whether you call him Hyphen or the Dark Shark – as he has been – Ian Baker-Finch deserves admiration. Tabloids dubbed him Ian Baker-Flinch after his 79 on the last day of the 1984 Open Championship. But his 1991 Open victory led to a new nickname – Ian Baker-Clinch.

▼ At impact Ian's hands are absolutely square to the target which ensures that the clubface is also square. His left hand guides the club while his right adds power. The Australian keeps his head perfectly still and his shoulders parallel to the target line and clears his left side to help generate power.

senior decided to build his own course and Beerwah Golf Club duly opened for business. Ian was given a half set of clubs for his 12th birthday and was playing off 1 less than 18 months later.

JUNIOR RIVALRY

Young Norman, Harwood, Senior and Grady provided stiff junior opposition but Baker-Finch still won his age group at the Queensland Schoolboy Championship. Taking the decision to turn pro at the tender age of 15, Ian took a three year golfing apprenticeship before making his professional debut in 1979.

Progress was steady but slow. Baker-Finch celebrated his first victory at the 1983 New Zealand Open, adding the 1984 West Australian Open by the staggering margin of 13 shots.

After his crushing disappointment in the 1984 Open Championship, Ian honed his craft in the all-weather con-

ditions of the European tour. He gained some compensation by pipping Graham Marsh and Johnny Miller to win the 1985 Scandinavian Open with a closing 66.

REACH FOR THE STARS

A runner-up spot at the 1986 Scottish Open boosted Baker-Finch's credentials further. But it was victory at the 1988 Australian Masters that convinced the ambitious pro to head for America.

'You're never going to feel in your heart that you can call yourself one of the best players in the world without making it on the US Tour,' Ian says.

Armed with a handful of sponsors' invitations, Baker-Finch shared the lead after three rounds of the 1988 NEC World Series of Golf before slipping to third behind Mike Reid. But 133rd place on the money list guaranteed PGA membership for another year.

Ian's courageous decision to uproot wife Jennie and their three week old baby from their comfortable base in Europe

◀ After a superb third round 64 in the 1990 Open at St Andrews which put him on top of the leaderboard, Baker-Finch carded a disappointing 73 on the final day which dropped him to joint sixth.

Seeing red

Baker-Finch's career was almost ended in 1986. Ian was in a restaurant with his wife when a woman at another table began admiring him. Her companion – who was drunk – marched over to Ian's table and landed a punch straight between his eyes. 'I got up spitting teeth and blood,' says Ian.

Loosened teeth and a broken nose were the least of his problems. Ian's optic nerve was badly damaged, but fears that he might lose an eye later proved unfounded. However, Ian has played in glasses virtually ever since.

paid dividends with a victory at the 1989 Southwestern Bell Colonial.

Leading from gun to tape Ian had a 4 stroke lead after three rounds. Despite an impressive challenge from Tim Simpson, the Australian held his nerve to secure his first US Tour win.

Returning to Britain to compete in the 1990 Open, Ian soon made the headlines. Lying 8 shots behind joint leaders Faldo and Norman after 36 holes, Baker-Finch surged to the top of the leader board with seven birdies and an eagle in the first 12 holes.

Memories of 1984 resurfaced when Ian went out in the final pairing on Sunday afternoon. But despite returning an

▶ Ian Baker-Finch is never too proud to ask his caddie Pete Bender for advice. 'Ian finesses you to death, kills you with the putter. He's like a cobra,' says Pete. The Californian bagman has had two major successes – he also brought home the 1986 Open Champion, Baker-Finch's fellow countryman Greg Norman.

FACTS AND FIGURES

Name: Ian Baker-Finch
Born: 24th October 1960, Nambour, Australia
Height: 6ft 4in (1.9m)
Weight: 190lb (86kg)
Family: Wife Jennie, daughter Hayley
Interests: Languages, wine, tennis, all sports
Turned professional: 1979
First pro win: 1983 – New Zealand Open
Major win: 1991 – Open Championship
Australian wins: 1984 – West Australian Open, NSW Open
1985 – Queensland PGA Championship, Victoria Open
1987 – Australian Matchplay Championship
1988 – Australian Masters
1992 – Vines Classic
1993 – Australian PGA
US Tour win: 1989 – Southwestern Bell Colonial
European Tour win: 1985 – Scandinavian Open
Japanese wins: 1987 – Polaroid Cup
1988 – Pocari Sweat Open, Bridgestone Open
Team member: 1989, 1990, 1991 – Four Tours World Championship of Golf
1985 – World Cup
1985, 1986, 1987, 1988 – Australia/New Zealand Kirin Cup

Order of Merit (US)

Year	Position	Winnings ($)
1988	133	75,840
1989	53	253,309
1990	16	611,492
1991	13	649,513
1992	58	261,817
1993	114	140,621

Helping hands

Behind the mild-mannered exterior of Ian Baker-Finch lies a fierce determination to succeed. He's worked with David Leadbetter and Mitchel Spearman to increase his length off the tee. The Australian has also worked on his mental game with sports psychologist Bob Rotella.

'In 1984, I was a starry-eyed kid having a good time. Last year, I learned from the way Faldo focused on everything he did,' said the 1991 Open winner, proving that hard work always pays off.

uninspired 73, the Australian was satisfied with a share of sixth place.

Baker-Finch surged from 53rd on the US money list in 1989 to 16th in 1990 after finding new consistency in his game. He was runner-up in three events and enjoyed 12 other top 25 finishes.

Taking up where he left off, Ian was seventh behind Woosnam at the 1991 US Masters before taking second place behind Davis Love III at the MCI Heritage Classic.

PEAK PERFECTION

A week before his marvellous Open win, Ian showed he was reaching peak form with another second place. This time it was in the New England Classic after a dramatic 7 hole play-off. The Australian only lost the tournament when his opponent Bruce Fleisher holed an incredible 50ft (15m) birdie putt.

Ian Baker-Finch is just one of many successful Australian golfers – there were five in the top 10 at Royal Birkdale. 'We were all from simple beginnings. We played wherever we could, whenever we could. We started with nothing and we made it,' says Ian.

Stay on target

As one of the most consistent players on any circuit, Baker-Finch has a sure fire method for hitting fairways in regulation.

Ian imagines a pair of parallel railway lines running up and down the tee area. Positioning his feet, hips and shoulders in line with the left hand rail, Ian ensures his clubface is square to the right-hand rail, in a straight line to his target.

'Don't make the mistake of aiming yourself towards the target when your feet and body should be pointing left of it,' stresses Ian.

When he's chosen the area on the fairway he intends to hit, Ian picks a spot 10yd (9m) in front of him which the ball should travel over.

Many golfers line themselves up to markers or trees further up the fairway, or even a point on the skyline. But the drawback of using such distant targets is that a slight misjudgment often means missing the fairway.

If you're having problems finding the fairways, try Baker-Finch's method.

▶ Playing a short pitch from grassy rough during the 1989 Australian Open, Baker-Finch illustrates perfect technique. When faced with a lie in long grass you should play it like a bunker shot and take plenty of grass with the ball.

Severiano Ballesteros

Just watching Seve's game is an adventure. The most admired man on the golf circuit is Spain's most consistent and richest sportsman.

Seve was born the fifth son of a farmer-fisherman in Pedrena, near Santander in northern Spain. His three living brothers (the first died early from a wasp sting) Baldomero, Manuel and Vicente, are all golfers.

The family connection with the game stems from his uncle: Ramon Sota was the finest golfer in Spain through the 1960s, representing his country nine times in the World Cup. He also finished sixth in the 1963 British Open.

STICKS AND STONES

At seven years old, Seve was given his first club or, to be precise, part of a club. It was an old 3-iron head stuffed with sticks for the shaft. Balls were too valuable so he used stones from the beach.

At nine he was given his first 'real' club: this time a genuine 3 iron which he used for every possible shot. He was forced to learn versatility and a wide range of techniques – skills that stand him in good stead now. To this day he

▼ **Seve won his second British Open at St Andrews in 1984. His four-round total of 276 beat Tom Watson and Bernhard Langer by two strokes.**

▲ Erratic touches, from frightening mistakes to astonishing brilliance in a matter of seconds, hold the key to the Ballesteros appeal. US pro Larry Nelson says: 'Seve's a rare kind of guy. He's an excitable golfer who can concentrate`.

▲ Ballesteros captured his first British Open in 1979. Hale Irwin, who finished sixth, said: 'I cannot understand how anyone can drive so badly and still win an Open'. It was said more in disbelief than criticism – yet it sums up the Ballesteros game.

feels comfortable with a 3 iron – a club that was pressed to 'chip, putt, hook and slice and come from bunkers with'.

At 10 he played in the local caddie competition in Pedrena over nine holes. He burst into tears after a mistake at the second, but still finished fifth, in 51 strokes. At the age of 11 he shot 42 to finish second and when 12 years old he took a 79 over the full course. At 13 he says he was playing the equivalent of scratch. Against the wishes of his mother and teacher he left school – certain his future lay in golf.

GETTING NOTICED

Pedrena, his home course, was on the pros' domestic circuit. Visiting players wondered at the youngster who flailed from around his neck, hitting the ball breathtaking distances. The stories began, as did the pressure he now knows and copes with so well.

On 1 January 1974 Seve became a professional, aged 16 years and 8 months. A friend says that Seve 'went from childhood to manhood without touching life as a teenager'.

It was 1976 that witnessed the great breakthrough. He leapt to first place in the Order of Merit (OoM) with a total of £39,504, winning the Dutch Open and the Lancôme Trophy – at 19 years old.

In the British Open at Royal Birkdale that year he tied second place with Jack Nicklaus. They both finished six shots behind the American, Johnny Miller. Ken Schofield, head of the European Tour, saw how Seve always kept his rhythm and said: 'We realized we had a continental Jacklin on our hands`.

Seve gave an indication of the feats to come with one of the final shots of the Championship. His chip shot to tie Nicklaus was beautifully rolled between two bunkers as it slid up to the pin.

The following seasons saw Seve attracting huge attention as his looks and bravery gathered the crowds. In 1977 he again topped the OoM with three wins, including the French and Swiss Opens.

In 1978 he won four tournaments. He was now a truly international golfer and had won in countries as far apart as Kenya and Japan. But still the Majors eluded him.

MASTERS MAGIC

Seve captured his first British Open in 1979, becoming the youngest winner this century. Only a year later, American confidence was to take a battering from the

Back problems

Practice has brought its problems. Since childhood Seve's obsession has been to hit the ball vast distances. In doing so he has damaged his spinal discs, causing enormous pain and discomfort. Doctors advised surgery but Seve declined. 'If my back was different maybe I would not swing so good.'

For a while, he used a specially made contraption whereby he hangs, head down, and arches his back to strengthen the muscles. The trouble causes him to miss many events.

◄ Although in trouble here at the 13th at Augusta in 1989, Seve's record in the US Masters is superb. It includes two wins, two seconds, a third, a fourth and a fifth.

▼ Seve's childhood sweetheart, Carmen Botin, was at The Belfry in 1985 to share his Ryder Cup success. He married Carmen – the daughter of the President of the Bank of Santander – in November 1988.

Spaniard. At 23 he became the second foreigner and the first European to take the coveted Masters' green jacket at Augusta, Georgia.

By now, he was known as one of the longest hitters in the world game – but Augusta's narrow fairways and fearsome obstacles were lying in wait for just such a victim. Seve, however, had other ideas. No golfer can recover a wayward drive as he can and he treated the immaculate course with contempt, unleashing his tee shots in all directions yet homing in on the green with uncanny

▶ Seve's genius is recognized by Tony Jacklin, whose first victorious Ryder Cup captaincy was at The Belfry in 1985. 'To me he is one in an era, like Nicklaus, Palmer or Hogan were in theirs. He is a one-off.'

▼ Hours of childhood practice with one club taught Ballesteros the touch and feel that allows him to escape from difficult, sometimes unvisited, areas of a course.

uncanny recovery play.

Sadly, he was unsung in his native land as, on the whole, Spain is not a golfing nation. On the day he won, Spanish radio started a news bulletin with a swimming record and there was no mention of his historic US Masters win. Church bells pealed in his home village, but the rest of Spain showed scant interest.

In 1983 Seve won his second Masters' jacket and has since said that Augusta is where he most likes to win.

THE FIGHTER

Seve's fighting spirit is inherited from his father who was a former star oarsman in the Pedrena village longboat. Seve says 'If the water is rough in Santander Bay you fight harder in the boat. You do not give up'. That spirit is well instilled.

He has had his difficulties with the American touring pros who ignored him in the locker room and smiled at

him only when he lost. It is one reason he gives for declining to play there full time.

His older brother, Manuel, a moderate tournament pro, is his greatest influence and advised him not to let the Americans' hostility affect his game.

Ballesteros has made trips of several weeks to play the US circuit and has won tournaments and coveted prizes. But he has worldwide commitments and refuses to play full time on the US Tour.

Deane Beman, the US Tour Commissioner, said in November 1988 that the biggest name in golf could not play as and when he wanted. He is allowed invitations to six tournaments plus the US Open and US PGA for which his record qualifies him automatically.

THE REWARDS

In 1988, Seve bought a house in Monte Carlo, for tax purposes, though he makes regular visits to Pedrena to see his mother, Carmen. He loves the guaranteed warm weather in Monaco and the convenience of international air routes enabling him to fly anywhere at will. He is friends with Prince Rainier, who welcomes Seve's tips at the Mont Agel course where they both play and relax.

It is clear that Seve is relishing the prospect of playing the world but he is curtailed by back trouble. He regards Nicklaus' total of 20 championship wins as an unrealistic target. 'Even so I would like to win the US Open and the US PGA to complete my own Grand Slam. It is tougher to win today and that can be seen in sports other than golf.'

Solitary Seve

The source of Seve Ballesteros' greatness lies in his long hours of practice as a boy in Pedrena.

Despite his golfing pedigree, his opportunities were limited, and he received no formal golf teaching. Playing alone proved to be a big advantage. He built his own swing, without help, so he is the best person to spot the faults in his technique when shots start to go astray. Seve knows when he feels comfortable. He does not need outside advice as another pro might, because he can feel where his swing has let him down.

▶ Seve won his third British Open at Royal Lytham and St Annes in 1988 with a final round of 65. He later described it as 'the best round I ever played'.

SEVE STATISTICS

Name: Severiano Ballesteros
Born: Santander, northern Spain, 9 April 1957
Weight: 12st 9lb (80kg)
Height: 6ft (1.83m)
Interests: Cycling and fishing
First pro tournament: Pre-qualifying for Portuguese Open, Estoril. Scored 89 – and went home
First pro win: Dutch Open, 1976
Played Ryder Cup: 1979, 1983, 1985, 1987, 1989, 1991, 1993. Won 18, lost 10, halved 5
World Cup: 1975, 1976 (winner), 1977 (winner)
Dunhill Cup: 1985, 1986, 1987, 1988
Major wins: British Open 1979, 1984, 1988; US Masters 1980, 1983
Order of Merit (Europe):

Year	Position	Winnings(£s)
1974	118	2915
1975	26	4995
1976	1	39,504
1977	1	46,436
1978	1	54,348
1979	2	47,411
1980	3	52,090
1981	7	65,298
1982	10	74,617
1983	2	113,864
1984	5	142,577
1985	3	165,154
1986	1	259,275
1987	6	172,711
1988	1	502,000
1989	8	234,238
1990	18	167,674
1991	1	790,811
1992	28	248,977
1993	42	148,854

Concentration

Playing golf alone as a boy taught Seve the power of discipline and concentration. He has developed it to such an extent that, during a tournament, he is almost oblivious to outside sounds, including the applause of the gallery. He likes to imagine a crystal-clear mental picture of the shot he has to play, and that cannot be done unless he is totally absorbed.

▲ Perfect body control gives Ballesteros total balance throughout a free-flowing swing. It allows him to achieve the classical throughswing position – and an ideal shot.

Seve is not a fitness fanatic, but he takes great care to keep in shape by cycling, playing tennis and working out in the gym. He enjoys a healthy, well-managed diet. Seve follows the advice of another great champion, Gary Player, who told him that unless he was fit and strong, tiredness would disrupt his play at key moments.

He continues to be the world's most exciting golfer for one simple reason: he practises constantly. He has a strong awareness of the changing tempo and rhythm of the body. He knows that his technique must be refined to suit different conditions. For Seve, golf is an art, not a science. He keeps his movements smooth and simple, maintaining the fundamentals of a repeatable swing. Without mastery of the basics, invention is impossible.

(text ends)

Fred Couples

One of the most laid back players on the US Tour is also among the richest. 'Boom Boom' has won over $6 million in prize money despite finding more ways of blowing tournaments than any golfer before.

Fred's easy paced action is a perfect match for his personality. A smooth effortless turn flows sweetly to the top of the backswing. Creating the power with a corkscrew turn of the hips, Couples drives through impact in a blur of hands and arms, rounding off a rhythmic swing with a high, graceful finish.

'The trouble with Freddie is that he makes the game look so easy,' sighs a fellow player. Long iron accuracy, a deft short game and silky putting skills complete Couples' golf attributes. His inevitable breakthrough in the Majors came in the 1992 U.S. Masters.

Freddie was about 10 years old when he and a friend became interested in golf. The two boys would climb over the fence of the local course and play a few holes, keeping one step ahead of the course ranger. 'Those were great times,' Couples smiles.

ROOKIE HONOURS

After a successful career in junior golf young Fred went to the University of Houston and sailed through the tour school in 1980.

Progress was swift. Second to Hubert Green in the '81 Greater Hartford Open, Couples ended the year as top rookie money-winner and went on to score his first pro success at the 1983 Kemper Open. With Jan Stephenson, Couples also won the 1983 J C Penney Classic.

Fred achieved his biggest victory by holding off Trevino, Stadler and Ballesteros at the 1984 Tournament Players Championship. Delighting

◄ With his ball plugged in the face of a bunker, Couples has no choice but to play aggressively and blast the ball out. Although he can't achieve any distance from that lie he'll be satisfied that he has escaped first time.

▲ **Bouncing back to winning ways after a series of near misses, Fred Couples stormed to victory with a 2 stroke lead over the opposition to win the 1990 Los Angeles Open.**

pro tip

Improve your accuracy

Couples generates enormous power, but as every golfer knows, power without accuracy is useless. He believes the key is a full shoulder turn and a controlled takeaway which puts the club on a perfect plane.

'When I'm playing well I feel I'm brushing the club along the ground for the first 18 inches. Whenever that happens I can be sure my upper body is turning in harmony with my legs.' Freddie also knows he's resisted the temptation to snatch the takeaway.

'It's a tough discipline to master but well worth the effort if like me you're prone to tilting instead of turning,' advises Couples. Follow Fred's example – work on turning fully and see your accuracy improve.

► **In spite of the easy, fluid action, Couples' swing is enormously powerful. He earned the nickname Boom Boom because of the vast distances he can hit the ball – drives of 330yd (301m) are not unusual for the American pro.**

press and galleries alike with his charming manner, booming drives and modest victory speech, Couples was touted as the heir apparent to Watson.

But all didn't flow smoothly. Disaster followed disaster after the TPC, and the Seattle pro dropped from seventh in the '84 money list to 76th in 1986. Speculation raged over his loss of form – typically, no one was less worried than Couples.

'Freddie has always played best when he doesn't think too much about the game and just lets it happen. We call it finding the comfort zone,' said former wife Debbie. She encouraged Freddie to take advice from coach Fred Harmon, whose simple remedies did the trick. Couples made no technical changes but cut down on tournament appearances and found the comfort zone again.

In 1987 Freddie hurtled back to 19th place on the money list, aided by victory at the Byron Nelson Classic. It was a typically seesaw Couples performance – he threw away a 6 stroke lead over Mark Calcavecchia on the final day before taking the crown at the third play-off hole.

Further triumphs eluded Couples in 1988 and 1989 but earnings approaching $700,000 secured a Ryder Cup debut at The Belfry. Failing to make a birdie in the entire match, Couples partnered Lanny Wadkins to a 3 and 2 fourball defeat against Clark and James. Fred didn't get another game until his emotional singles match with Christy O'Connor jnr.

With four to play and 1 up, Freddie missed an excellent birdie chance at 15, lost the 16th, missed a short putt on the 17th to win the hole and so came to the 18th tee all square. As the excitement rose, Couples' drive flew 60yd (54m) past the Irishman's ball but O'Connor then fired a 2 iron within 3ft (90cm) of the flag. Freddie pushed a simple 9 iron wide of the green, failed to get up and down and left the green in tears.

'I've thought a lot about that game,' he reflects. 'It was the most I'd ever concentrated on golf and where did it get me? I was absolutely devastated. I couldn't get over the feeling that I'd let the whole team down. It was definitely the low point of my career.'

▲ Competing in the Bicentennial Classic at Royal Melbourne in 1988, Couples stays relaxed while he strikes down powerfully with a mid iron. He makes contact with the ball first and then takes a large divot.

BACK ON TOP

A battle hardened Couples seemed to have learned the error of his ways as he romped to victory at the 1990 LA Open. Having equalled Larry Mize's course record 62 at the Riviera CC in the third

FACTS AND FIGURES

Name: Fredrick Stephen Couples
Born: 3 October 1959; Seattle, Washington
Height: 5ft 11in (1.8m)
Weight: 185lb (83kg)
Interests: Tennis, cycling, antiques
Turned professional: 1980
First pro win: 1983 – Kemper Open
Other wins: 1983 – J C Penney Classic
1984 – Tournament Players Championship
1987 – Byron Nelson Classic
1990 – Los Angeles Open, Ronald McDonald Children's Charity Invitational, Sazale Classic
1991 – Federal Express Classic B.C. Open, Dunhill Cup
1992 – Los Angeles Open, Nestle Invitation, U.S. Masters, World Cup (with Davis Love III)
1993 – Honda Classic, Kapalua International, World Cup (with Davis Love III), Dunhill Cup
Team member: USA v Japan - 1984
Ryder Cup: 1989, 1991, 1993. Won 3, lost 6, halved 3

Order of Merit (US)

Year	Position	Winnings ($)
1981	53	78,939
1982	53	77,606
1983	19	209,733
1984	7	334,573
1985	38	171,272
1986	76	116,065
1987	19	441,025
1988	21	489,822
1989	11	693,944
1990	9	757,999
1991	3	791,749
1992	1	1,344,188
1993	19	796,579

What, me worry?

Critics have grown tired of Couples' near misses. Some suggest he lacks the killer instinct, others that he's the product of a system that rewards also rans too much, while a third group insists he just doesn't care.

Fred doesn't understand what all the fuss is about. 'People are always telling me I should do one thing or another. I should change my grip or shorten my swing. I should practise more and goof around less. I shouldn't smile on Sunday...I should...I shouldn't...I should...I shouldn't. Frankly I don't know why they worry. It's my life – and **I** don't worry.'

▶ The 1989 Ryder Cup gave Couples the worst moment of his golf career. Freddie confessed that his legs went to jelly at the thought of meeting the European side on British soil. His nervousness may have affected his play – after being beaten in the foursomes, Couples lost his singles match with Christy O'Connor jnr.

the Riviera CC in the third round, Freddie defended his 2 stroke lead and won the event.

Staying in fighting form, Couples challenged strongly for the 1990 USPGA. The tournament soon boiled down to a two horse race between Wayne Grady and the Seattle pro.

Birdies at the 3rd and 6th allowed Freddie to reach the turn level with his Australian opponent. Couples jumped into the lead at the 451yd (411m) par 4 12th, firing a 6 iron to 15ft (4.5m) and holing out for birdie.

But in his hour of need Freddie's putting stroke deserted him. He missed a 3ft (90cm) putt for par at 13, shoved a 4ft (120cm) effort wide of the hole at 14, repeated the calamity at 15 and failed to get up and down from a bunker beside the 16th green.

With that experience behind him, Couples finished third in the 1991 U.S. and British opens before finally getting his just reward – the 1992 Masters, where his scores of 69, 67, 69, 70 saw him finish the last six holes in one under par for a popular two shots win – the first American winner since Larry Mize – 1987.

Laura Davies

Laura Davies' rise to the top of the golfing scene has been meteoric. The big-hitting Surrey player looks set to add many more of the game's top prizes to her outstanding collection.

When Laura Davies won the 1987 US Women's Open at Plainfield, New Jersey, the American press insisted on comparing the British golfer's size to that of their own Joanne Carner.

Joanne's retort to their questions about height and weight was a terse 'Get lost!' But typically, Laura totally charmed her audience when she replied: 'I'm 5ft 10in [1.77m] but I've never weighed myself'.

LANGUID LAURA

Laura knows that the enormous distances she hits the ball owe as much to good timing as her general strength and stature. Much more depends on holing the putts during the pressures of the last nine holes of a tournament.

She is an excellent putter, especially in the 4-6ft (1.2-1.8m) range. When she won the US Open, she holed from 4ft (1.2m) on the 18th green to secure a place in the play-

▼ Laura enjoys bunker shots. But her enjoyment only comes from the confidence she has in her ability – gained during practice.

▲ **Winning the 1987 US Open at Plainfield, New Jersey, was a close thing. Laura was only able to raise the trophy after a tense play-off victory over Joanne Carner and Ayako Okamoto.**

off alongside Joanne Carner and Ayako Okamoto. In the play-off, she holed again from a similar distance to tie up a title which had never before been won by a Briton.

The Americans, who reacted rather badly when the French amateur, Catherine Lacoste, won their Open in 1967, could not have been more generous when it came to Laura Davies. They admired her carefree approach. The beaten Carner said: 'Long may it last'. They chuckled, too, at the fact that Davies only needed half an hour's practice a day.

SHOTS BEFORE SIX

The Americans did not realize that Laura sees tournament play as practice. She probably plays more tournaments than any of them over a year. Practice is not as important to her because she put in so much spade work in her teenage years.

Laura was introduced to golf by her

Outdriving the men
Some of the top men are threatened by Laura. In 1985 she took part in a long-driving competition at Stoke Poges, Berkshire. Her competitors included such well-known amateur stars as Peter McEvoy, Gordon Cosh and Michael Lunt.

It soon became clear that it was a 'two-man' contest between Laura and McEvoy. She did not win, but the closeness of the margin – 284yd (259m) to 293yd (267m) – was echoed in McEvoy's loud sigh of relief.

brother – he later became her caddie. When she was 14 years of age, her mother, Rita, used to drop her off at the practice ground on the way to work. She stayed there until her mother picked her up on the way back from work at 6 o'clock. 'I would experiment with a shot – and then try 60 of them,' she recalls.

She copied shots not just from her brother, but also from golfing stars she saw on the television. Her favourites were Seve Ballesteros, Jack Nicklaus and Tom Watson. As she says, these professionals have to go down as her teachers, because she has never had a formal lesson in her life.

Today she thinks she feels the same as Seve when she stands over a little chip or pitch. And when she plays a long iron, she always has a picture of Bernhard Langer's rhythm in her mind. She is convinced that copying golfing heroes is the best way to learn golf and become a better player.

► Laura's family is never far away, even during her tournament play. Brother Tony was responsible for introducing her to the game of golf and is now her regular caddie.

Driver dispute

Brother Tony is Laura's caddie – and is sometimes firm with his employer. At the 1989 Women's British Open, played at Ferndown in Dorset, he gave her strict instructions not to use her new pink driver.

Unfortunately, she only just made the halfway cut. She decided to ignore Tony's advice for the last two rounds, saying: 'The driver is coming out tomorrow. I will be pinking it and going for everything.'

GRIPPING STUFF

Like many of the golfing superstars, Laura Davies has achieved greatness without using a conventional swing. Despite the vast distances she hits the ball, she has a reduced swing arc, which normally serves to lessen, not increase, distance. This is because she takes hold of the club at the very bottom of the grip. Sometimes her forefinger and thumb actually touch the steel shaft.

Laura echoes Gary Player's theory that golfing power comes from all the big muscles of the body. She compensates for her reduced arc with her strong legs and powerful shoulders.

She first caught the eye when she won the Surrey Girls' Championship at Sunningdale in 1982. Out in 48, after six putts on one green, Laura played the back nine holes in 38. This forced a play-off with Sally Prosser, now also a professional on the European Tour.

There had been rumours about Laura's potential. As she and Sally set off down the 19th, the selectors of

◄ A hectic schedule takes Laura Davies to some of the most spectacular courses in the world. She enjoys the excitement of teeing up in new countries and tournaments, often preferring it to taking a rest.

▲ Bursting on to the European professional scene in 1985, Laura Davies won five times in her first two seasons and was top of the Order of Merit in both years.

▲ St Mellion, Cornwall, designed by Jack Nicklaus, was the testing venue for the 1987 Women's British Open. Defending champion Laura Davies finished in the pack behind Alison Nicholas.

▼ One of the biggest hitters in the women's game, Laura Davies knows that her huge length off the tee is given by a combination of her excellent timing and rhythm and her strength and power.

Laura on driving:
'As I stand on the tee, I am not saying to myself "Head steady" or "Slowly back". I am simply itching to get at the ball and my only thought is one of hitting a good shot.

'All aspiring golfers should get to grips with using a driver off the tee because, in my book, the drive is the easiest shot of all.'

▶ Family support contributes a great deal to Laura's success – she shares her ups and downs with them. Here they get together to show off her US and British Open trophies at St Mellion in 1987.

Surrey Ladies' Golf Union witnessed something which set them talking for the rest of the year. The 19th, the par-5 1st hole on Sunningdale's Old Course, measures 450yd (411m). It is a distance which normally asks for two good woods and a chip from the average low-handicap woman golfer. On that occasion, Laura caught the green with a drive and 8 iron. Then she holed for a winning eagle – an impressive performance.

DRESSING DOWN

Two years later, she represented Great Britain and Ireland at Muirfield in the two-yearly contest against the Americans, the Curtis Cup. The home side lost 9-8, but on the last afternoon, Laura beat the veteran, Anne Sander. Her performance strengthened her belief that she was ready to try her hand on the professional circuit.

Laura borrowed £1000 from her mother to get started. Two weeks later, after winning a runner's-up cheque for £4000 in the Hennessy tournament in Paris, she was able to pay her back.

Another payment she had to make out of that cheque was a £50 fine – for wearing a pair of trousers considered 'scruffy and detrimental to the tour's image'.

There was an uproar about the fine. Both the sponsor, and the winner, Jan Stephenson, said they disagreed with the judgement. Surely a quiet word from the Director of the women's tour would have been enough for a youngster who was clearly self-conscious about her size.

If she was short of suitable clothes at that early stage of her career, she could soon collect a stylish wardrobe from all corners of the world. She was top of the European Order of Merit (OoM) in both 1985 and 1986.

The Surrey golfer made it into the big money league in 1987, when she added the US Open title to the British Women's Open she had won the year before. Her already high earnings were doubled by the contracts which went hand-in-hand with two such notable titles.

She was able to buy a new sports car to go with her sponsored car. She also bought a cottage next to the family home in the Surrey countryside.

Laura on bunkers
As Laura stands over the ball in a bunker, she thinks only of where she wants it to land. If she fails to get out at the first attempt, as she failed once in the second round of her victorious US Open, she refuses to let panic set in. 'What you have got to remember,' she says, 'is that it is the panic rather than the one miscreant shot which will make the difference between a good round and bad.'

FACT AND FIGURES

Name: Laura Davies
Born: Coventry, England, 5 October 1963
Height: 5ft 10in (1.77m)
Interests: Tennis; horse and dog racing; shopping; music; cars
Amateur career: English Intermediate champion 1983; England team, Home Internationals 1983, 1984; Welsh Open strokeplay champion 1984; Curtis Cup 1984
Pro wins:
1985 – Belgian Open
1986 – McEwan's Lager Classic, Greater Manchester Open, Women's British Open
1987 – Italian Open, US Open
1988 – Italian Open, Ford Ladies' Classic, Biarritz Ladies' Classic, Tucson Open (US), Toledo Classic (US), Itoki Classic (Japan)
1989 – Laing Ladies Charity Classic, Lady Keystone Open (US)
1990 – A.G.F. Biarritz Open
1991 – Valextra Classic, Inamoura Classic (USA),
Solheim Cup: 1991
1992 – European Open, English Open, Italian Open
1993 – English Open,
Order of Merit (Europe)

Year	Position	Winnings (£)
1985	1	21,736
1986	1	37,500
1987	2	47,151
1988	8	41,871
1989	19	21,608
1990	13	36,697
1991	5	49,552
1992	1	66,333
1993	2	64,938

In 1989, Laura played mainly in the USA. She won $181,574, to finish 13th in the LPGA money list.

▼ Many spectators arrive at a tournament just to watch Laura smash balls off the tee. However, many of them become mesmerised by the feel and flair she shows on and around the greens.

▲ When Laura unveiled her new driver at the 1989 Women's British Open, played at Ferndown, Dorset, her play - unlike her club - was not in the pink. The ever-stylish Laura finished only in joint 14th place, behind Jane Geddes.

GOOD BET

Laura makes no secret of the fact that some of her money disappears each year at the various casinos she visits in the course of her travels. 'There are days when I win and days when I lose but you always finish down at the end of the year,' she says. To Laura, gambling is a form of relaxation. 'If losing worried me, I'd stop at once.'

She has a hectic schedule, as she divides her time between the USA, Europe and Japan. But she prefers it that way. 'Others may recover from a busy spell by taking a rest, but I find myself pepping up at the mere prospect of playing on a new course or in a new country.'

She is often at her most dangerous when returning to Europe after a spell in the US. In America, she finds that the par 5s often need 'two cracking woods'. She can usually reach a European par 5 with a drive and a shortish iron. 'All of a sudden all the par 5s are like par 4s. It's a great feeling.'

Laura's huge contribution to the expansion of women's golf has now been officially recognized. In 1988, at just 25, she was awarded the MBE.

Nick Faldo

Nick Faldo has built a near perfect swing. Yet it took great dedication to turn natural brilliance into championship-winning success.

A chance encounter with a new colour television set at his parents' home in Welwyn Garden City started Nick Faldo's rise to the top in golf.

It was Easter Sunday in 1971 and, for a sports-mad 13-year-old schoolboy, television held only a passing interest. Running, swimming and cycling were the activities which occupied his time.

However, on this fateful day, Faldo's eye was caught by Jack Nicklaus playing in the US Masters. Before colour television, pictures of the Masters were of just another monochrome golf course. Colour changed that – all the beauty of

▼ Nick Faldo showed his superb powers of recovery at the 1989 US Masters at Augusta. After a disastrous third round of 77 he seemed to have dropped out of the running – yet he fought back to win. Until the 1980s no European had ever won at Augusta.

▼ Faldo's first professional success was the 1978 PGA Championship at Royal Birkdale when he was 21. He lists Birkdale as one of his two favourite courses – the other is Muirfield.

the Augusta National course was there in front of him, and the youngster was transfixed.

NATURAL TALENT

From that moment on, Faldo devoted his life to golf with the dedication that has marked his career ever since. Tall and broad-shouldered, his build was not ideal for golf. It is harder for tall people to control the movements in the swing, but Faldo had aptitude. This was spotted by Ian Connelly, the professional at Welwyn Garden City private course.

Connelly saw in that raw talent a quality that cannot be taught. It was rhythm, the pace of a golfer's swing, which, in nine cases out of ten, is too fast. Faldo didn't hit *at* the ball. He swung *through* it as if it was not there.

Under Connelly's guidance, he developed rapidly. First he won local junior events, then he was selected for the Hertfordshire county colts and senior teams.

International honours followed for England Boys in the match against their Scottish counterparts. The England captain was Sandy Lyle, before he transferred his allegiance to Scotland.

Soon afterwards, Faldo played Lyle in an early round of the 1974 British Boys' Championship and Lyle was the winner. It was the first of many meetings as the two pursued their careers along parallel paths.

CROSSING THE CHASM

The climax of Faldo's amateur career came in 1975. He won the Berkshire Trophy, the British Youths' Championship and the English Amateur Championship. At 17, he was the youngest player ever to take the English Amateur title.

There were few fields left to conquer, so, early in 1976, Faldo made the decision to turn professional and join the band of hopefuls taking their first shaky steps on the PGA European Tour.

The difference between top-class amateur golf and top-class professional golf is more of a chasm than a gap and

▲ Faldo's approach play is masterful – a perfect drive at the 12th at Sunningdale in the 1988 European Open has left him with a fine chance of finishing close to the pin.

◄ Faldo's most frustrating defeat in 1988 came in the US Open at Brookline, where he lost to Curtis Strange in an 18-hole play-off. They tied on 278 after four rounds, but then Strange won by four shots.

▲ **Faldo plays cleanly out of the 18th hole fairway bunker in the last round of the 1988 European Open. Despite four rounds in the 60s at the tough Sunningdale course, he was beaten by Ian Woosnam.**

many amateurs are unable to bridge it. Faldo played steadily in his first year and in 1977 made real progress, when good performances over the season earned him Ryder Cup honours.

US EFFORTS

Faldo's goal was success in America and he began an extensive programme at the beginning of 1981. He didn't win but he certainly made an impact. He fired a second round 62 to take a share of the halfway lead in the Hawaiian Open. The next day he shot 72 and dropped ten strokes behind the new leader, Hale Irwin, who also shot 62. That showed the standard he was up against.

Unlike many British players, Faldo revelled in the brash, colourful world of the US Tour. He adapted to their ways easily, yet even the Americans were surprised by his attention to detail, his relentless practising and his sheer application.

These habits are necessary if a player is to reach the top, but there are limits. In 1983, he won three tournaments in a row and topped the money list for the first time, but he was not winning friends.

His marriage had disintegrated by the end of that year. When he flew to America with his new girlfriend, later to become his wife, he was hounded by the press. It took him years to establish a good, or at least acceptable working relationship, with them.

In 1984, he made an important breakthrough. He won the Sea Pines Heritage Classic, his first victory on the US Tour. It happened the week after the US Masters, in which he had an excellent chance to win after the first three rounds but slipped badly in the final round.

SWING SURGERY

This was to be the pattern of his play in all four Majors that year. It prompted him to undergo a radical swing change under the guidance of David Leadbetter. A Zimbabwean golf coach, resident in America, Leadbetter had achieved

Tuning his swing

David Leadbetter worked on a number of aspects of the Faldo swing. He asked his pupil to fan the blade of the club slightly at the start of the backswing, to help him achieve a flatter shoulder turn with less tilt.

Rotating his shoulders, rather than tilting them, helped Faldo to keep his right arm closer to his body at the top of the swing. It also ruled out the need for any exaggerated hip action through the ball on the downswing. The result was a much more compact swing and a more controlled movement.

▲ The rhythm and tempo of Nick Faldo's swing is as regular as clockwork – with every club in the bag. It is this consistency which helps him to overcome the tension of the final round.

◀ Coach David Leadbetter told his pupil that it would take two years to rebuild his swing to championship-winning standard. Faldo accepted the challenge.

▼ Faldo's first Major was the 1987 British Open at Muirfield. He scored 18 consecutive pars in his final round, a unique achievement in the history of the world's oldest Championship. His final score was a five under par 279.

◀ **Faldo is married to Gill and they have two children, Natalie and Matthew. After the births of each child, Faldo won the first Major he entered.**

success with players such as Mark McNulty and Nick Price.

Leadbetter told Faldo that he had a great rhythm and one of the best-looking swings in the game – but it would never stand up to the pressures of winning an important championship.

The old Faldo swing was long with a pronounced dipping action through the ball. The backswing started the club on the inside of the ball-to-target line, but the hands carried on upwards, causing the shoulders to tilt rather than turn, and placing the right elbow too far away from the body.

On the downswing, the pronounced dipping action and big hip movement was necessary to try to square the clubface to the ball. The swing contained a great deal of movement which could go awry in the heat of competition.

CATCHING UP

When the coach declared his pupil ready to test his new swing in the heat of battle, Faldo had a great deal of catching up to do. His rival Lyle had drawn ahead by winning The 1985 Open at Royal St Georges, Sandwich. He had also succeeded in America.

The first rung on the comeback ladder was climbed in 1987 when Faldo won his first tournament for three years, the Spanish Open. The victory gave him the confidence he needed. Two months later, he reached the pinnacle by winning the British Open at Muirfield.

Faldo's striking was now of such high quality that it was almost robotic. However, he had spent so much time working on his long game that his putting now suffered from neglect.

This problem was to dog him

No frills Faldo

There are few frills in Faldo's neat and compact swing. Look out for the way he swings through the ball at a measured pace – the acceleration of the club through the ball appears effortless.

Notice also how his rhythm never varies – the tempo of his swing remains the same under all types of pressure. Faldo plays golf in a cocoon of concentration and rarely talks to his fellow competitors.

Beating the best

Faldo showed his liking for the big links courses with victories in 1978 and 1980 in the PGA Championship at Royal Birkdale and Royal St George's respectively. By this time, he was established among the top five players in Europe, a Ryder Cup regular and a threat in every tournament. He did not have the flair or audacity of Ballesteros, nor did he have the awe-inspiring power of Lyle. Yet he possessed a superb putting stroke and pursued his chosen path with an intensity that left nothing to chance.

FALDO FACTFILE

Name: Nicholas Alexander Faldo
Born: Welwyn Garden City, Herts, England, 18 July 1957
Family: Wife Gill; Children: Natalie (1986), Matthew (1989)
Amateur career: England Boy and Youth International. 1975 Berkshire Trophy, British Youths' Championship, English Amateur Championship
First pro tournament: 1976 French Open (tied 38th)
First pro win: 1977 Skol Lager
Played Ryder Cup: 1977-93. 21 wins, 13 losses and 4 halved matches
Played Dunhill Cup: 1985, 1986, 1987, 1988, 1991
Harry Vardon Trophy: 1983, 1992 (top of Order of Merit)
Major wins: 1987-92 British Open, 1989-90 US Masters

Order of Merit:

Year	Position	Winnings (£)
1977	8	23,978
1978	3	37,912
1979	21	14,911
1980	4	46,054
1981	2	55,106
1982	4	68,252
1983	1	140,761
1984	12	66,169
1985	42	33,140
1886	15	92,097
1987	3	282,578
1988	2	404,708
1989	4	363,420
1990	12	237,570
1991	10	371,029
1992	1	1,220,540
1993	2	558,738

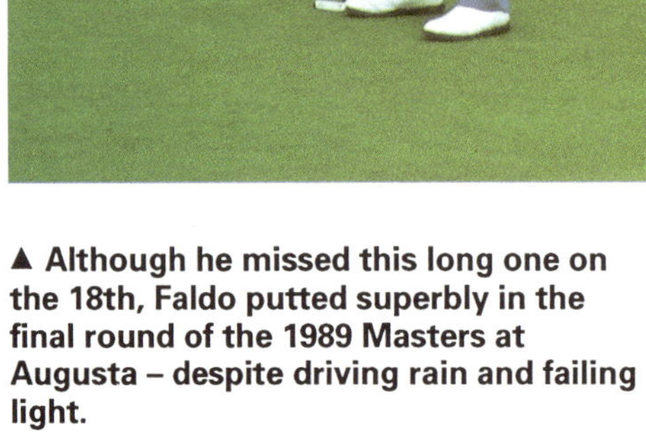

▲ Although he missed this long one on the 18th, Faldo putted superbly in the final round of the 1989 Masters at Augusta – despite driving rain and failing light.

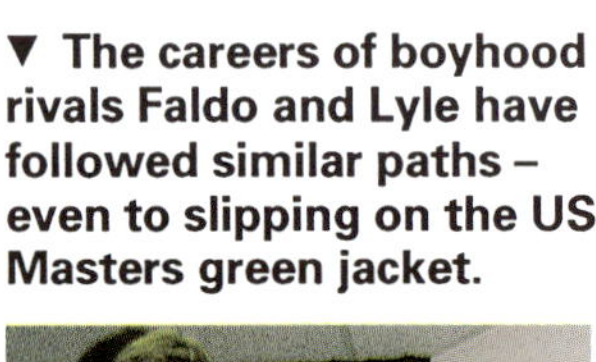

▼ The careers of boyhood rivals Faldo and Lyle have followed similar paths – even to slipping on the US Masters green jacket.

throughout 1988. He made strong challenges in three of the four Majors but failed to produce a victory.

His consolation, after eight runner-up finishes in the year, came in the final event of the season, the Volvo Masters – he defeated Ballesteros and Lyle.

FULL CIRCLE

In the 1989 US Masters it all came together. Faldo arrived at Augusta with a new putter. For the first two rounds it worked beautifully and he was tied for the lead. But in the rain-delayed third round the putter went sour on him and he changed it over the final 18.

On the first green he holed from an enormous distance and was off and running. In a nail-biting finish, he holed extremely difficult putts on the 16th and 17th to set a target that only American Scott Hoch could match.

The two players headed for the 10th tee for the sudden death play-off. Hoch missed a tiny putt for victory on that green. Faldo seized his chance and made no mistake with another long putt at the next play-off hole.

It was a sweet moment for the man who had been ridiculed for changing his swing and who had been involved in controversy throughout his career. For years he had dreamed of wearing the green jacket placed on each champion's shoulders by the last champion.

For Faldo the ceremony was extra special – the honours were carried out by none other than Sandy Lyle. Faldo went on to win a third British open – in 1992, the first Briton to do so since Henry Cotton in 1948.

Raymond Floyd

With four majors, over $5 million in prize money and the captaincy of the US Ryder Cup team to his credit, Raymond Floyd is a tenacious player now playing on the Regular and Seniors' Tours.

A gifted all round athlete, Raymond Floyd favoured baseball over golf until he won the 1960 National Jaycees Tournament when he was 18 years old. He turned professional 12 months later.

Joining the tour in 1963, Floyd quickly rose to prominence and was voted Rookie of the Year after his win in the 1963 Petersburg Open.

Floyd's career has soared the heights and plumbed the depths of golf. The peak of early success was his victory in the 1969 USPGA. He won by a single shot over Gary Player after taking a 5 stroke lead into the back nine.

Still only 27, Ray added two more tournaments to his list of winnings and was set to join Nicklaus and Player at the head of the world game when it all went disastrously wrong. It was 1975 before Floyd won another tournament – a six year period in which at times he was written off as a golfing force.

WINNING TEAM

It was no coincidence that his fight back to form came at the same time as his marriage in December 1973. As strong willed as her husband, Maria encouraged the best from Ray. The transformation in Floyd's game was extraordinary – in 1974 he tripled his earnings, and the following year came back to winning form with victory in the Kemper Open.

Acknowledged as a supreme front runner, Ray slaughtered the field in the 1976 US Masters, ending an 8 stroke winner over

▶ Floyd's characteristic finish – with the club over the top of the head instead of around his body – is a tell tale sign that he favours the fade. This type of shot gives more control, allowing him to position his strokes accurately.

▲ Captain of the 1989 US Ryder Cup team, Ray Floyd proved to be one of the most popular team leaders the side has known. His tough talking did much to raise the morale of his players and inspired them to fight back to draw with the Europeans at The Belfry. He returned to play on winning teams in 1991 and 1993.

Ben Crenshaw.

Only the fourth man ever to lead the US Masters from start to finish, the key to Floyd's success was leaving his 1 iron at home in favour of a 5 wood. The accuracy of that 5 wood was chiefly responsible for Floyd playing Augusta's fearsome par 5s in a combined total of 14 under par.

FORMIDABLE FORCE

Clearly back with a vengeance, Floyd was deprived of another major only when Dave Stockton clung on for a 1 stroke win at the 1976 USPGA on the Congressional Course in Maryland. Over the next 10 years, Floyd collected another 12 tournaments and added a second USPGA Championship in 1982.

Leading from start to finish once again, Floyd shot an opening 63 which

Risky business

During the practice round in the 1983 US Masters, Floyd and Greg Norman added a little spice to their game by inviting Tom Watson and Lanny Wadkins to a challenge match at $75 a hole. By the time they had reached the turn, the stakes had risen to $500 a man per hole; by the 18th tee, the stakes had gone up again to $1000.

Floyd struck a perfect tee shot down the middle of the 18th fairway and reached into the bag for a 7 iron. Sizing up the situation he fired his shot straight into the hole. 'I might have guessed he'd do that,' grinned a poorer Watson afterwards.

► Ray blasts out of sand at Augusta where he won the Masters in 1976. He was runner-up in 1985, 1990 and 1992.

he still describes as his best ever round of golf. He arrived on the 72nd tee at Southern Hills, Tampa needing a par 4 to beat Bobby Nichols' all time USPGA record of 271. But Floyd let his concentration lapse, pushed his approach, chipped into a bunker and could manage only a double bogey 6.

His score of 273 was still good enough for a 3 stroke victory over Lanny Wadkins. That win contributed to earnings of $386,809 in 1982 and second place in the US Order of Merit.

But by now his priorities had changed. 'My wife and children come first – there's nothing even close to being second,' Floyd admitted at the time. Unable to sustain his level of enthusiasm, Ray fell down to 68th on the money list.

Despite tying for second with Ballesteros and Strange in the 1985 US

pro tip

Headstart

Ray Floyd's head position is a model for those starting out in the game. His wide, flowing backswing pulls the left shoulder around, helping create a full shoulder turn.

Coiled to attack from the top, Floyd uses his legs to generate power. By keeping his head steady he allows his hands and arms to move down fast and strike the ball. With his head behind the ball at impact, Floyd produces a consistently powerful swing.

▲ In 1987 Floyd held a 2 shot lead after 54 holes of the USPGA but an uncharacteristic 80 put an end to his hopes of a hat trick. He won the event twice before, in 1969 and 1982.

Masters, he was being written off yet again. But an especially sweet victory was yet to come. He came storming back and won the 1986 US Open.

On the final day, eight players swapped the lead – Norman, Beck, Wadkins, Tway, Crenshaw, Sutton, Stewart and Trevino all battled it out. Then Floyd emerged from the pack with a closing 66 to become at 43 years the oldest winner of the tournament. That record stood until 1990 when 45 year old Hale Irwin won the title.

'I finally got me an Open,' said the

◄ Floyd uses an upright stance for his long putter. He works hard on his game – his attitude to practice has changed over the years. 'Golf is a healthier game now than back in the '60s – players have a better attitude towards their chosen profession. When I started out there was no such thing as practising after a round but now when you go down to the range, you can't even get on.'

jubilant champion, whose rare display of emotion was almost as remarkable as his brilliant victory.

Floyd continued his assault on the majors by leading the 1987 USPGA by 2 shots in the third round then losing the championship with a final round of 80. And he nearly took the 1988 US Masters – opening with an 80, he outscored the rest of the field over the remaining three days.

TEAM LEADER

In 1989, Floyd abandoned playing for a year to concentrate on leading the US Ryder Cup team against Europe at The Belfry. He was determined to erase the memory of successive defeats at the hands of Tony Jacklin's men.

The Americans arrived at The Belfry as slight favourites, and Floyd angered his hosts by introducing his men as 'the 12 finest golfers in the world'. Although the Europeans were far from impressed, the comment spurred them on. 'That was just the motivation we needed,' Faldo later observed.

Floyd's decision to give all his team a first day game misfired as Europe completed a clean sweep of the afternoon fourballs for a 5-3 lead. However, galvanized into action by their tough talking captain, the Americans showed

◄ Playing in strong wind, Floyd needs his immense strength to escape from a lateral water hazard. He keeps good control of the ball, guiding it surely on to the fairway.

◄ Floyd almost claimed the 1990 US Master's title until Nick Faldo snatched it from him after an exciting last round went to a play-off. 'Victory would have meant more than you can imagine – to have beaten the par-3 jinx and become the oldest winner.'

▼ Determined to conquer the hazards of Turnberry in 1977, Ray Floyd has always been a keen competitor at the Open Championship. A victory would complete his set of four majors, making him only the fifth player to achieve the feat.

FLOYD FILE

Name: Raymond Loran Floyd
Born: 4 September 1942, Fort Bragg, North Carolina, USA
Family: Wife Maria; children Raymond jnr, Robert Loran, Christina Loran
Turned professional: 1961
First pro win: 1963 – St Petersburg Open
Major victories: 1969 – USPGA
1976 – US Masters
1982 – USPGA
1986 – US Open
Total tournament wins: 22
Team member: Ryder Cup – 1969, 1975, 1977, 1981, 1983, 1985, Captain 1989, 1991, 1993. Won 12, lost 16, halved 3
US v Japan – 1982
Nissan Cup – 1985

Order of Merit (US)

Year	Position	Winnings ($)
1963	58	10,529
1964	30	21,407
1965	25	36,692
1966	32	29,712
1967	47	25,254
1968	24	63,002
1969	8	109,957
1970	24	47,632
1971	32	70,607
1972	70	35,624
1973	77	39,646
1974	18	119,385
1975	13	103,627
1976	7	178,318
1977	7	163,261
1978	30	77,595
1979	26	122,872
1980	10	192,993
1981	2	359,360
1982	2	386,809
1983	20	208,353
1984	68	102,813
1985	5	378,989
1986	9	380,508
1987	86	122,880
1988	69	169,549
1989	145	74,699
1990	55	264,078
1991	56	284,897
1992	13	741,918
1993	120	126,516

▼ 'My career wouldn't have been complete without a US Open,' Floyd admits. His name found its way on to the trophy in '86 after a brilliant final 66. Sharing his triumph are wife Maria and daughter Christina.

impressive spirit to fight back for a 14-14 tie. Floyd was such a popular leader that several of his men petitioned the USPGA to give him a second captaincy in 1991. But it was not to be.

PAST MASTER

In 1990 47 year old Ray Floyd almost made golfing history in the US Masters. After 36 holes, his name stood on top of the leaderboard, and he still remained 2 clear of the field on Sunday afternoon. But having extended his lead to 4 with a birdie at the short 12th, Floyd switched his game plan from attack to defence and paid the price.

Defending champion Nick Faldo had kept his hopes alive with a remarkable sand save from a plugged lie at the 11th. Birdies at the 13th, 15th and 16th brought him within a shot of Floyd.

Ray finally cracked by three putting on the 17th green. Suddenly the competition was level. The American who'd had victory in his sights 90 minutes earlier earned a play-off place only with a heroic par at the last after recovering from two bunkers. Nonetheless, the tide had turned in Faldo's favour, and when Floyd pulled his approach into a greenside lake at the second extra hole, it was all over.

But Floyd has no intention of bowing quietly out of golf. 'I believe I'm playing as well and consistently as I ever have... Don't write off Raymond Floyd just yet. Lots of people have done that on dozens of occasions in the past, and it's given me great pleasure to prove them wrong every time.'

▼ Floyd uses a putting grip to gain more control for this delicate chip and run. He's keen to reap the rewards of his long career and has become involved in promotion work for several companies. 'There's a lot of money out there and I mean to work my butt off to get my share,' he maintains.

Ben Hogan

Despite the interruptions of the Second World War and a car accident that all but killed him, Ben Hogan was a dominant figure in the 1940s and 1950s. He was the second man to win all four Majors.

Ben Hogan has sometimes been referred to as 'the Hawk', but all except a very few close associates call him 'Mr Hogan'.

Mr Hogan was not a natural golfer, but he was determined to create a swing which would be perfect – for him, at least. During his golfing heyday he was a very private person and expert at keeping his life hidden from view. But first and foremost he thought himself a gentleman, and expected others to do the same.

NELSON'S RIVAL

Ben Hogan was born in August 1912, at Dublin near Fort Worth in Texas. His father was a blacksmith who committed suicide when Hogan was nine years old, which forced the young boy into early maturity. At 11, Hogan was caddying at Glen Garden golf club.

His contemporaries there included Byron Nelson, who was born in Fort Worth six months earlier than Hogan. Sometimes players gave Hogan clubs, and as these were right-handed he began to hit the ball that way although he was a natural left-hander.

Ben Hogan turned professional in 1931, and Nelson did so the year after. Neither was an instant success. Nelson even joined an oil company for a time.

Meanwhile, Hogan divided his time between trying to develop his game and doing whatever he could to earn a living. Mark McCormack, the king of all sports promoters, described Hogan as the man who invented practice, and the first player to spend six hours a day on the practice ground.

Hogan married Valerie Fox in 1937, and they toured the golf circuit together. There are many stories of the hardships they endured. According to legend, they lived off oranges for a while.

In 1938, at Oakland, California,

The unforgettable Ben Hogan, in his trademark white cap, shows the style that made him a legend. Even in his late 70s he still practises and plays golf regularly.

► Hogan – widely regarded as the father of the modern golf swing – demonstrates his skill in this swing sequence. He once said, 'I know that I have had greater satisfaction than anyone who ever lived out of the hitting of golf shots.'

Smooth talker
Jimmy Demaret, a winner of 31 US events and Hogan's fourball partner, told this story: 'In a dozen matches with Ben, I've only ever heard him speak two words, but he says them on every green. The words are, "You're away".'

Following the stars
Hollywood showed its respect for Hogan's achievements by making a full-length film about his inspiring career. Called *Follow the Sun*, it's still shown.

Hogan saved parking fees by leaving his car on a vacant site. Someone jacked it up and stole the tyres – only the $380 dollars Hogan won there let him go on to the next tournament.

At 5ft 9in (1.8m) Hogan was smaller than many of his contemporaries, but he still became one of the tour's longest hitters. He used a long swing that let his hips turn round so far after contact he ended up with them left of the target, rather than square to it.

CLOSE SHAVES

No important success came until 1940, when Hogan won five tournaments and was leading money-winner with $10,655.

In 1942, having tied with Nelson for the US Masters only to lose the play-off, Hogan joined the US Army Air Corps. He served until summer 1945.

A year later, Hogan 3-putted the last green in both the Masters and the US Open – and lost each by a stroke. However, he scored his first Major win later in the year, when he beat Ed Oliver by 6 and 4 in the final of the USPGA Championship (which had a matchplay format until 1958).

◄ Putting was always Hogan's Achilles heel. When asked by Thelma Bader, wife of the fighter ace Douglas, if he would ever return to play in the Open, he replied – perhaps only half joking – 'I will when I can putt.'

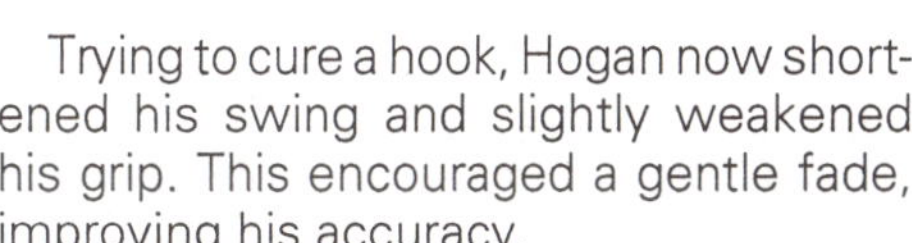

◄ Before he enlisted in the Army Air Corps in 1942, Hogan was sitting on top of his profession. He was leading money-winner in the USA in 1940, 1941 and 1942.

Sharp lesson

Ben Hogan was not considered over generous with his instruction. He is said to have dealt rather sharply with Gary Player when the South African phoned from home asking for advice.

Having established that Player wasn't using Hogan clubs, Hogan suggested he put his problem to Mr Slazenger.

▼ Hogan – showing a rare smile – poses with his wife, Valerie. He survived a horrific head-on car accident in 1949 only because he dived to protect her in the passenger seat. The steering column would almost certainly have killed him had he stayed where he was.

Trying to cure a hook, Hogan now shortened his swing and slightly weakened his grip. This encouraged a gentle fade, improving his accuracy.

On 2 February 1949, Hogan and Valerie were motoring home from Phoenix in a fog when a Greyhound bus coming in the other direction hit their car head on. Hogan avoided being crushed by the steering column because he had thrown himself across his wife to protect her. His very serious injuries included a broken pelvis – Hogan was in hospital for two months.

GRAND SLAM

Ben Hogan seemed unlikely to play golf again, but he was determined to do so. He could no longer challenge for the USPGA title – the number of rounds was too strenuous – so he concentrated on the US Open and US Masters. He succeeded brilliantly.

He won the US Open in 1950, and the

HOGAN FACTFILE
Name: Benjamin William Hogan
Born: 13 August 1912, Dublin, nr Fort Worth, Texas
Family: wife Valerie Fox
Tour wins (US): 62 – 3rd in all-time list behind Sam Snead (84) and Jack Nicklaus (71)
Major wins: US Open 1948, 1950, 1951, 1953; US Masters 1951, 1953; USPGA 1946, 1948; Open Championship 1953
Leading money-winner: 1940, 1941, 1942, 1946, 1948
Played Ryder Cup: 1947, 1949, 1951; captain 1947, 1949. Non-playing captain 1967. Won 3, lost 0, halved 0
Best years: 1946 – 13 wins; 1953 – 5 wins from 5 starts, including three Majors

Bogeyman
Ben Hogan won all four Majors – his great rival Sam Snead never captured a US Open. Yet they were involved in three play-offs together – and Snead won them all.

▼ The Open Championship claret jug was claimed by Hogan at his first – and only – attempt at Carnoustie in 1953. His steady improvement over the four rounds – 73, 71, 70, 68 – gave him a 282 and a 4-shot winning margin over Frank Stranahan, Dai Rees, Peter Thomson and Tony Cerda.

year after took the Masters as well as retaining the US Open title.

In 1953, Hogan played only five events and won all of them. They included the US Masters, and the US Open – which he won by 6 shots from Sam Snead. It was Hogan's fourth and last win in the event.

Because of these two victories, Hogan was persuaded to travel to Carnoustie for the Open. His triumph gave him the nearest thing to the legendary Grand Slam of which he was physically capable. Only Gene Sarazen had won all four events before him.

The 1953 Open was the last Major Hogan won. His final victory was the 1959 Colonial Invitational, which he had won four times before.

▲ Of his attitude to golf, Hogan wrote: 'I have proved to myself what I have always said – that a good golfer doesn't have to be born that way. He can be made. I was, and practice is what made me – practice and tough, unrelenting labour.'

Ben Hogan then began to make a fortune in business, selling clubs and equipment. He has a reputation for never accepting a first offer when a deal is suggested.

Even in his late 70s – and despite the fact that he shuns publicity – Hogan still makes an impact on golf, with his new project, the Ben Hogan Tour. A satellite circuit for players who don't have a US Tour card, the first tournaments were played in 1990.

Tony Jacklin

Tony Jacklin's fearless ability to lead from the front once made him the only world-class player in Europe. He received even greater acclaim as Europe's most successful Ryder Cup captain.

Tony Jacklin was a national hero in 1970, when he held both the British and US Open titles. When he accepted the offer to captain the 1983 European Ryder Cup team, he was soon to enjoy heroic status once again.

Previous captains of Britain and Europe have not been optimistic about winning the two-yearly battle against the Americans. Jacklin was always passionate about winning as a player. His dedicated attitude carried through to his non-playing captaincy.

The 1983 European team came very close to victory in Florida, losing by just one point. Jacklin was captain again at The Belfry in 1985, which saw the first US defeat since 1957. Two years later, the USA were favourites to win on home territory at Muirfield Village. But Europe won again, their first victory in the USA.

Jacklin received much of the credit for the European victories. He has made a lasting reputation as an inspirational captain and deserves it. Only Seve Ballesteros has received as much credit for the European Ryder Cup successes.

GOLFING DEVELOPMENT

Golf began for Jacklin when he was nine years old. A Scunthorpe neighbour asked his father out for

▼ **When Tony Jacklin won the British Open in 1969, the prize money was just £4250. But he was made for life, as endorsement contracts flowed his way.**

In gallant company
Despite the recent success of European golf, Tony Jacklin remains the only European to have won the US Open since World War Two. Only two others ever achieved the same feat – Ted Ray and the great Harry Vardon.

a game of golf and soon young Tony was joining in. He started playing with a few cut-down hickory shaft clubs.

At the age of 13, he managed to break 80 for the first time and to win the Lincolnshire Junior Championship. Two years later, he was County Champion, against a field of professionals as well as amateurs. In 1962 he turned professional, as assistant at Potters Bar Golf Club in Hertfordshire.

At this stage, Jacklin's most important characteristic was his will to win, to do more than merely make a good living from the game. He was still working on his style. His swing was too fast and relied on the top half of his body. His putting was erratic, yet he was sometimes brilliant.

HOLE IN WONDERLAND

Jacklin's first important success came in 1966 on the South African Tour. He was quickly recognized as a new British hope, and chosen to partner Peter Alliss that year in the World Cup. The following year, Jacklin's victory in the prestigious Dunlop Masters brought him enormous publicity – apart from the fact that he won. His hole in one at the 16th in the final round was the first seen live on television.

By now, Jacklin was also making a move in the USA. He became friendly with Tom Weiskopf and Bert Yancey. They were two magnificent swingers of the club who also liked to talk theory. They told Jacklin that he must learn to make far better use of his legs and lead with them in the downswing. Jacklin practised until his tempo and consistency improved.

SPECTACULAR SCORES

Quite early in the 1968 season he began to produce spectacular scores. His victory in the Jacksonville Open made him the first British player to win a full US Tour event since Henry Cotton's 1948 win at White Sulphur Springs.

His form was not impressive at the start of 1969. But his game picked up and he was given an outside chance for The Open at Royal Lytham and St Annes.

After the first round, he was well up the field with a 68. He followed with a pair of 70s and went into the final round with a two-stroke lead. He said: 'I've been nervous all week. Now I'm just bloody terrified.'

SMOOTH VICTORIES

He widened the gap to five strokes after just four holes. But his main challenger, Bob Charles, had reduced the margin to two strokes as they stood on the 18th tee. At this very difficult driving hole, Jacklin boomed a vast shot straight down the middle. Britain had her first Open Champion since Max Faulkner

Building his future
Tony Jacklin now lives in Florida and intends to start a new playing career on the U.S. Seniors' Tour following his 50th Birthday, in July 1994.

◀ In 1985, Tony Jacklin became Europe's first successful Ryder Cup captain for 28 years. Paul Way, Sam Torrance and Ian Woosnam all played a part in the win.

▶ The Scunthorpe golfer is largely self-taught. He had no coach and learnt his stylish swing by watching other players.

▼ Gritty determination to win sums up the Jacklin game. A fellow pro said: 'He was cocky, that's why he was good. I could never stand on the tee and think, who on earth is going to beat me, as Tony did.'

The will to win
Much of a player's charisma comes from great performances. At his best, Tony Jacklin showed himself to be a dynamic front runner, as in his 1970 US Open triumph. He became the first Briton since Henry Cotton to become a star of world-class ability.

His best years, from 1967 to 1972, provided his fans with stunning performances. Jacklin's long game is still impressive despite only occasional tournament appearances.

▲ Overwhelmed by emotion at the moment of Ryder Cup victory at Muirfield Village in 1987, Jacklin was unable to answer interviewers.

▼ The British and US Open winner still plays some tournaments, such as the 1988 British Open. But he says of his fortunes: 'After Muirfield in 1972, nothing ever went right for me again'.

won at Royal Portrush in 1951.

The 1970 US Open was held at Hazeltine – a very unpopular course with most of the players. After a high-scoring first round, many of them liked the course even less. With just 26 putts in a round of 71, Tony Jacklin was the only player to break par. He led the Championship by two strokes. After that, he rarely faltered and went into the final round four ahead of Dave Hill.

When he opened his locker in the clubhouse, one word faced him: 'TEMPO'. It was Weiskopf and Yancey again, reminding him to keep a smooth swing and to maintain his rhythm.

Jacklin finished in style, with a fine drive down the 18th, a good iron shot and a birdie putt from about 8yd (7m).

He now held both Open titles. Soon afterwards he was at St Andrews for the Open Championship.

OLD COURSE DOWNPOUR

His start was fantastic. He birdied the 1st, 2nd and 3rd, paused for breath, birdied the 5th and 7th and holed out his second to the 9th for an eagle 2. He was 7 under par and out in 29. Not long after, a heavy rainstorm deluged the course and play was called off for

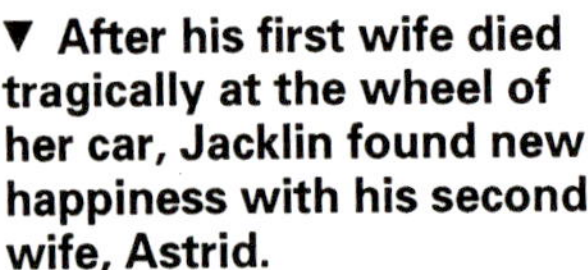

▼ After his first wife died tragically at the wheel of her car, Jacklin found new happiness with his second wife, Astrid.

the day. When play resumed, he had lost his rhythm and the round of a life time slipped away from him. In the end, Jacklin finished fifth behind Jack Nicklaus.

His 1971 season was a poor one by comparison. He did win the Benson and Hedges International and managed to finish third in the British Open, even though not in good form. In 1972, he recorded his third US Tour victory, the Jacksonville Open again.

SPICY MEXICAN CHIP

The story of the 1972 Open Championship at Muirfield was the battle Tony Jacklin fought with Lee Trevino. 'Supermex' had most of the luck that was going, including a thinned bunker shot that clattered into the flag and dropped into the hole. Going into the final round, he led Jacklin by a shot.

Though the lead did change hands, the pair played the 17th level. Trevino played his tee shot into the bunker. After playing out, he hooked into heavy rough and his approach shot ran through the green and partly up a bank. Mentally, 'Supermex' conceded the Championship at that moment.

Meanwhile, Jacklin had been playing the par 5 immaculately. He hit a long drive and a fine second which left him not far short of the green. He followed with a relatively weak pitch shot to about 5yd (4.5m).

Trevino then played a running chip into the hole for a par 5, not the seven staring him in the face. Jacklin took three putts. His opportunity had gone.

Tony Jacklin never featured in a Major again. Ten years later, though, his touch returned for a week at Hillside, when he won the 1982 PGA Championship.

His influence has been enormous. He has shown that determination and will to win are as essential as perfect technique to great success. He can also be proud of a unique boast. He was the first European to win a Major in the USA for half a century – and the only one to lead a team to the same goal.

▲ **Seve Ballesteros has enormous admiration for Jacklin's Ryder Cup leadership. The two celebrate his second victory, in 1987.**

Ruthless yet respected
As Ryder Cup captain, Jacklin was decisive and forthright. When he had made up his mind which were his strongest pairings in the fourballs and foursomes, he did not hesitate to tell players that they might only take part in the final day's singles.

If the pairings failed, he was ruthless in dropping players. This directness was the strength of his captaincy – and the proof was in the European success.

JACKLIN FACTFILE

Name: Tony Jacklin
Born: Scunthorpe, England, 7 July 1944
Height: 5ft 9in (1.75m)
Turned professional: 1962
Professional titles:
1965 – Assistants Championship
1966 – Kimberley Tournament (SA), Blaxnit Tournament (Iceland)
1967 – Forrest Products (NZ), New Zealand PGA Championship, Pringle Tournament, Dunlop Masters
1968 – Jacksonville Open (US)
1969 – Open Championship
1970 – US Open Championship, WD and HO Wills Open, Lancôme Tournament
1971 – Benson and Hedges Festival
1972 – Jacksonville Open, Viyella PGA Championship, Dunlop International (Australia)
1973 – Bogota Open, Italian Open, Dunlop Masters
1974 – Los Lagartos Open, Scandinavian Enterprise Open
1976 – Kerrygold International Classic
1979 – German Open, Venezuelan Open
1981 – Billy Butlin Jersey Open
1982 – Sun Alliance PGA Championship
Played Ryder Cup: 1967-1979 (36 matches). Won 13, lost 15, halved 8.
Captained Ryder Cup: 1983 USA 14½-13½ Europe; 1985 Europe 16½-11½ USA; 1987 USA 13-15 Europe; 1989 Europe 14-14 USA
Played World Cup: 1966, 1970, 1971, 1972
Major wins: 1969 British Open, 1970 US Open

▲ Playing brilliance brought Jacklin true worldwide success. He won in such places as Colombia, Iceland and Venezuela – as well as the main golfing venues of Europe, Australia and the US.

▼ At Muirfield in 1972, Lee Trevino snatched the British Open from Jacklin's grasp with a series of astonishingly lucky shots. Trevino admitted how unlucky his rival had been, saying 'God is a Mexican'.

Bobby Jones

Perhaps the greatest golfer of all time, Bobby Jones' competition record is unsurpassed. A modest, hardworking amateur, Jones remains a legend in the game.

There were many great men in the early days of golf, but Bobby Jones is one of the all-time giants. Winner of the Grand Slam and founder of the famous Augusta course, Robert Tyre Jones jnr was born at Atlanta, Georgia in 1902.

He was a sickly child, but improved in health when the family took summer holidays in a house beside East Lake Golf Course. The whole family took up the sport, and when a new professional, Stewart Maiden, arrived on the course, Bobby copied his easy, flowing action.

The young boy made a game of practice, hitting shots beside the house and chipping on to a nearby green. He developed such a good touch that at nine years of age he won the junior club championship.

AMATEUR STATUS

Bobby Jones was a true amateur. Instead of spending hour after hour perfecting his game, Jones concentrated on gaining a degree in mechanical engineering. He then went to Harvard and later took a law degree at Emory University. Apart from during holidays, Jones played little golf. He also enjoyed tennis, fishing and bridge.

In 1919, Jones was a fine golfer but not quite a champion. He was second in the Southern Open, the Canadian Open and the US Amateur Championship.

By 1923 championship qualities

▼ In 1927 the incomparable Bobby Jones won the Open Championship at the course he grew to love – St Andrews. During the tournament he equalled the course record by shooting a 68 in his first round.

▲ **Even when he landed in a bunker, Jones didn't ask his caddie for advice – he simply got on with playing the stroke. His determination to go for his shots made him very popular with the crowd.**

◄ **Jones first won the Open in 1926 at Royal Lytham. A plaque at the 17th marks his second shot – facing a blind shot from a bunker, he coolly nipped the ball off the sand and on to the green.**

were emerging. He beat Bobby Cruickshank to win the US Open, and from then until the autumn of 1930, when he retired, Jones was never without at least one of the big four titles.

At the same time as playing golf, Jones was a practising lawyer. In his entire golfing career, he played in only 52 tournaments – he won 23. Most of his golf was weekend fourballs.

GRAND SLAMMER

Bobby Jones' crowning year was 1930. His first success was during the Southeastern Open. He finished double bogey, par, double bogey – and still won by 13 strokes.

Bobby Jones next set sail for England and captained the US Walker Cup side at Sandwich. He helped the brilliant but erratic Dr Willing win their foursomes by 8 and 7, then went on to beat Roger Wethered 9 and 8 in his singles. Jones followed that by lifting the Golf Illustrated Gold Vase at Sunningdale by a stroke with 147, then scooped up the Amateur Championship at St Andrews with a brilliant display of skill.

In the third round of that event, Cyril Tolley faced a longish putt on the 18th to beat Jones but lost at the 19th. Bobby won the final against Roger Wethered by 7 and 6. He then equalled the course record at Hoylake during the Open Championship with a 70 on the first day. He went on to win the tournament in great style.

Bobby returned home to a ticker-tape welcome, and a week later he continued his amazing form by winning the US Open at the Interlachen Country Club.

That left just the US Amateur at Merion, the final championship of what came to be known as the Grand Slam – in those days the Slam consisted of the British and US Open and Amateur Championships. Jones swept through the field without having to go past the 14th hole in any match.

► A true amateur, Jones tailored his golf to fit in with his life. 'My wife and my children came first, then my profession. Finally, and never in life by itself, came golf,' he said.

▼ Defending his Open Championship title at St Andrews in 1927, Jones hit a mashie approach shot. He went on to win the tournament and became the darling of the crowd – they dubbed him Bonnie Bobby.

Swift striker
Jones was a quick player. He never asked his caddie for advice, and he never hesitated over club selection. He assumed his striking position instantly, without pausing to check his grip or adjust his feet.

Using the reverse overlap putting grip, he didn't spend time studying the line – he just hit the ball into the hole.

Master tactics
Jones did not use a waggle, but went straight into a takeaway. His swing was very full and slow, and the downswing seemed to follow as a continuous movement. It started with the turn of the hips, generating tension between the lower and upper parts of the body, and so producing considerable power.

JONES FACTFILE

Name: Robert Tyre Jones jnr
Born: 17 March 1902 Atlanta, Georgia, USA
Died: 18 December 1971
Family: Wife Mary, daughters Clara and Mary, son Bob
Major wins: Open Champion 1926, 1927, 1930; US Open Champion 1923, 1926, 1929, 1930; Amateur Champion 1930; US Amateur Champion 1924, 1925, 1927, 1928, 1930; Southern Amateur Champion 1917, 1920, 1922
Walker Cup player: 1922, 1924, 1926, 1928, 1930. Captain in 1928 and 1930

Paymaster

Bobby Jones is the only Open champion who's paid for the privilege of winning. During the 1926 Open at Royal Lytham, he forgot his player's badge and was refused admission. Without fuss, Jones went to the public entrance, paid 5 shillings, went in and won.

Gentleman Jones

Bobby Jones played the game strictly by the rules. During the 1925 US Open, he believed his ball moved as he addressed it. Nobody else saw, but Jones called a 2 stroke penalty on himself, tied with Willie Macfarlane, and lost the play-off.

▼ Jones hugs the claret jug after the 1927 Open. He was a popular winner and asked the Royal and Ancient Club if they could honour him by keeping the trophy in the clubhouse where it belonged.

▲ Jones tees off at the opening of his beloved Augusta, which he founded. The course gained international prestige as the home of the US Masters and remains a fitting tribute to the great golfer.

After winning all before him in 1930 – no one has ever equalled his remarkable Grand Slam feat – Jones retired and fulfilled two ambitions. He designed a set of clubs as near perfect as he could make them, and founded a dream course – Augusta National, home of the Masters.

After that, Bobby Jones became progressively more crippled by a spinal disease. He played his last game in August 1948. When asked how he coped with his painful condition, his reply belied the suffering he endured: 'Remember,' he said, 'we play the ball as it lies.'

Tom Kite

Widely regarded as one of the finest players ever, Tom Kite's consistent play still keeps him in the top league of golf.

Just as it seemed Tom Kite was to be consigned to golfing history as one of the best players never to have won a Major, his just reward came with a cherished victory in the 1992 US Open at Pebble Beach.

His win was as famous as the renowned Californian venue as it was achieved in an enthralling finish and in some of the worst weather conditions ever experienced.

So severe were the winds on the fateful last day that such seasoned campaigners as Ray Floyd and Craig Stadler took 81, as did Dr. Gil Morgan, the eye specialist who had actually led by seven strokes after seven holes at a record 12 under par in the third round.

An early last-day draw enabled the debutant Scot, Colin Montgomerie, to post a final round 70 before the storm came up, and while Jack Nicklaus felt convinced to publicly state: 'That's it, it's all over', defiant Tom Kite had other ideas.

While one by one all those around him were being swept into oblivion by the fierce gales, the biggest earner in the game but whose career was incomplete without a Major win, audaciously holed a 20 foot birdie putt on the 6th green and then chipped in for an amazing two at the terrifying short 7th, en route to a 72, being only one of five players to shoot par or better during the final round.

Tom Kite had been incredibly close to that elusive Major many times. He had finished in the top five an amazing 11 times, including twice second in the Masters and also second behind Jack Nicklaus in the British Open of 1978.

Tom had been very close to a Major before. In 1985 he stood 2 shots ahead of the Open field at Royal St George's with 9 holes to play. At the par-4 10th, Kite left a weak approach shot in an unplay-

◄ **Tom Kite, whose Majors breakthrough came in 1992 at Pebble Beach, California.**

Contented Kite

'If I got hit by a truck tomorrow and never picked up a club again, I'd still be happy with my career,' says Tom Kite.

'I've won a lot of tournaments, made enough money to support my family, and achieved far more than most of my fellow pros. Unfortunately when you're assessed at the end of your career it's majors that count, not money in the bank.'

Top gear

In the US Masters Kite was once 4 strokes behind Ballesteros with a round to go. A reporter asked him if he thought he could win.

'Well, I've as much chance as a pick-up truck of catching a Ferrari,' Kite replied. 'But sometimes even Ferraris break down, and pick-up trucks win after all. It may not happen all that often but I still believe my time will come.'

able lie between two bunkers. He finally got down in 6 and let Sandy Lyle in for victory.

'I made a bad club selection,' Kite says, 'hit a bad shot, got a bad break and another major went down the pan.'

One of the rare occasions when Kite came from behind was at the 1986 Masters. A back nine charge gave him a 10ft (3m) putt on the final hole to ake Jack Nicklaus into a play-off. 'I hit it perfectly, but it wouldn't go in,' Kite remembers sadly.

TEAM-MATE TOM

Few if any golf tournaments can match the pressure of the Ryder Cup, and Kite's outstanding record in the two-yearly event dismisses any suggestion

◄ After finding sand at the US Masters in 1989, Kite finished 18th overall. He's been unlucky at the Masters before – in 1986 he missed a putt on the 72nd that would have taken him into a play-off with eventual champion Jack Nicklaus.

▲ Kite tees off during the Ryder Cup competition at The Belfry in 1989. He was in brilliant form and beat Howard Clark 8 and 7. Kite was 7 under par for the 11 holes he played.

▶ Although Kite found heavy rough during the 1985 Open Championship, his calm approach and consistent play paid off in the end – he recovered well and finished joint 8th.

of his game buckling under pressure. A member of the American side but once since 1979, Kite has taken part in 28 foursomes, fourballs and singles matches and lost only nine.

In a classic singles encounter with Seve Ballesteros at The Belfry in 1985, Kite was 3 up with 5 to play. Then the Spaniard produced three birdies in a row to win one of the epic encounters in the history of the matches.

Two years later, Kite overcame Sandy Lyle 3 and 2, and in 1989 inflicted an embarrassing 8 and 7 win on Howard Clark. Having polished off the Yorkshire-

▶ Tom Kite emerged as a world-class player in 1981, but he already had a significant European victory under his belt having won the European Open in 1980.

man, Kite headed to the 18th green and watched in horror as successive American tee shots found their way into The Belfry lake. He missed the U.S.A's triumph at Kiawah Island in 1991, but beat Bernhard Langer 4 and 3 at The Belfry in 1993 to help retain the trophy.

RELUCTANT BEGINNER

Despite a hesitant start, Tom Kite was born to play golf. At the age of six he was handed a club by his father. He reluctantly took a few swings before heading back to the sanctuary of his sandpit. But five years later the joys of

▲ There's no doubt where this putt landed during the 1987 Ryder Cup match. Held at Muirfield Village, Ohio, the trophy went to the European team despite Kite's sound performance.

◀ Although Kite finished below the top 10 in the 1986 Open, he still enjoyed playing in the event. Unlike many American players, Kite relishes the challenge of British links courses.

the fairway had overtaken the bucket and spade, and 11-year-old Tom won his first tournament.

In 1970 Kite took second place in the US Amateur Championship, 1 stroke behind another fast-rising youngster, Lanny Wadkins. That performance was good enough to secure Kite's place in the Walker Cup side. He was also a member of the victorious team representing the USA in the Eisenhower Trophy in Madrid. Before graduating from the University of Texas, Kite shared the NCAA Trophy with another young hopeful, Ben Crenshaw.

FLYING HIGH

Kite took the decision to turn professional at the end of 1972. While other new pros found life on the circuit hard, Kite made an instant impression, capturing the

USPGA's Rookie of the Year award in 1973 with earnings of $54,270. In 1976 Kite won his first professional title, the IVB Bicentennial Golf Classic, and two years later he won the BC Open.

Kite's emergence as a world-class player began in 1981. Although he won only one title, he finished in the top ten 21 times out of the 26 tournaments he played. He ended the year with the Vardon Trophy for a stroke average of 69.8 a round. He also headed the US money list. In 1982 Kite was again awarded the Vardon Trophy and remains the only man with a stroke average better than 70 on ten occasions.

During those two remarkable years, Kite played 52 consecutive tournaments without missing the cut – a run that finally came to an end in the Canadian Open. From 1981 to 1987 Kite was the only man to win a US tour event every year. With earnings over $8 million, Tom is the highest money-earner in golf history.

► Kite has been on the US Ryder Cup team every year since 1979. His record as a team member is impressive – he's taken part in 24 foursomes, fourballs and singles matches, and has lost only four.

▼ Tom putts his way to 8th place at the 1985 Open championship. 'I love the British Open. I love the weather, the atmosphere and especially the courses because they're all unique,' he says.

Chip ace

Tom's master stroke is a chip. Like all great shots, Kite's technique is frustratingly simple. He stands further away than normal for a chip shot, widens his stance and flexes his knees, allowing the club to slide under the ball.

'I just take my normal swing and try to avoid the flatter swing plane which might make me top the ball. Getting further away means I can swing around my body, causing the ball to come out softly and stop quicker.'

FACTS AND FIGURES

Born: 9 December 1949, Texas
Height: 5ft 8in (172cm)
Weight: 154lb (70kg)
Family: wife Christie; children Stephanie, David and Paul
Turned pro: 1972
First US Tour win: 1976 IVB Bicentennial Golf Classic
Total US Tour wins: 19
Major wins: U.S. Open 1992
Played Ryder Cup: 1979, 1981, 1983, 1985, 1987 1989, 1993. Won 15, lost 9, halved 4
Order of Merit (USA):

Year	Position	Winnings ($)
1972	233	2582
1973	56	54,270
1974	26	82,055
1975	18	87,045
1976	21	116,180
1977	14	125,204
1978	11	161,370
1979	17	166,878
1980	20	152,490
1981	1	375,699
1982	3	341,081
1983	9	257,066
1984	5	348,640
1985	14	258,793
1986	7	394,164
1987	8	525,516
1988	5	760,405
1989	1	1,395,278
1990	15	658,202
1991	39	396,580
1992	6	957,445
1993	8	887,811

▼ One of the great matches of the 1985 Ryder Cup was the singles meeting between Kite and Seve Ballesteros. After some thrilling exchanges – in which the American matched the Spaniard's aggressive approach – honours were shared on the 18th.

▲ Kite chips his way out of trouble at the US Masters in 1987. Tom is renowned for this shot and can usually get down in two from around the green – a skill that all top players must have.

The key behind Tom Kite's success is consistency. Day in, day out Kite hits greens more regularly than almost any other player on the tour.

LIGHT KITE

Aware of the disadvantage of his lightweight build, Kite set out from the earliest days of his amateur career to master the short game. Greg Norman may be seen as the world's finest driver and Ben Crenshaw the best putter, but Tom Kite leaves the field behind with a pitching wedge.

Kite used his top shot effectively when he chipped over a bunker to win the 1982 Bay Hill Classic.

Bernhard Langer

Bernhard Langer is Germany's only golfer to hit the big time. His calmness, hard work and sparkling natural talent have made him one of the world's greatest players.

Langer is the youngest of three children born to Erwin Langer, a Czech who jumped a Russian train full of refugees heading for Siberia. He walked all the way to the German hamlet of Anhausen, which was best known as the birthplace of Mozart's father.

As a nine-year-old, Bernhard earned pocket money by caddying at nearby Augsburg Golf Club. The members used to let him use the practice ground and soon he announced to his slightly doubtful family that he intended to play golf for a living.

SWEET SMELL OF SUCCESS

When he left school he became assistant to Heinz Fehring in Munich. He recalls: 'There were only a few hundred members, so the possibilities for practice were endless.'

He was 90th on the European Order of Merit (OoM) at the age of 19. At 23 he was ninth, having won the Cacharel Under 25s by a huge margin of 17 shots.

The 1980 Dunlop Masters was his first big title. In 1981, he led the

▼ Bernhard Langer has three times been hit by, but later conquered, the distressing 'yips'. These happen when nerves cause the putter to be jerked back and through.

▲ **Langer is a consistent performer in The Open. At Turnberry in 1986, he was tied third behind Greg Norman, and second to Bill Rogers in 1981.**

▲ **Langer's wife Vikki and daughter Jackie were at Chepstow in 1988 to see him win the Epson Matchplay tournament. He beat Mark McNulty in the final.**

OoM and won the German Open.

The pressure on him to win it had been enormous. He had gone to Hamburg directly after finishing second in the British Open and his German fans assumed that he would lift the title easily. As it turned out, he led all the way to the 11th green on the final day – when he was caught by Tony Jacklin.

Jacklin went ahead at the 12th but, after Jacklin bogied the 14th and 15th, Langer went back into the lead by holing a 20ft (6m) putt at the 16th. Jacklin said of his rival's performance: 'It is very difficult to lead a championship in your own country and what I did to him in that last round must have been a hell of a shock to his system. He handled it coolly and calmly.'

BRANCHING OUT

At the Benson and Hedges Tournament in 1981, Langer made a name for himself when his ball landed up a tree.

He was on the point of taking a penalty stroke when suddenly he realized that if he could only reach the ball, he could knock it down on to the fairway and maybe even reach the green. To the amazement of spectators and television viewers the world over, he climbed the tree and played the shot he had in mind.

He bogied the hole – and there is now a plaque on the tree commemorating the incident. His final score of 273 secured joint second place with Ireland's Eamonn Darcy, behind Tom Weiskopf.

After leading the OoM for the second time in 1984, Langer decided to move further afield – paving the way for him to win in four continents in one year.

Following an early victory in the Australian Masters, Langer went on to win the US Masters. The Americans were fascinated by the man they jokingly called 'the only guy in Germany who can break 80'. As Langer was the first to admit, the remark was not too far from the truth. Later that year, he was asked if he would like to represent his country in the Dunhill Nations Cup. He retorted that he would have to find himself a couple of team-mates first.

Lee Trevino compared the German to Gary Player. 'Like Gary, he just loves to practise. I know, because I've played with him all around the world. He'll tee it up anywhere there's a golf course and you've got to like a chap like that.'

CLEANING UP

After Augusta, Langer promptly won the next event on the US Tour, the Sea Pines Heritage Classic. He also had back-to-back wins in Europe either side of his 28th birthday – the German Open and the European Open.

At the end of the season he had £200,000 to show for just 59 rounds on the US Tour. He finished second in the European OoM, earning £115,000, and capped it all by picking up the winner's cheque for £202,000 in the Sun City Million Dollar challenge. Yet Langer denied that he was a superstar. 'All I know,' he joked, 'is that I'm no superstar when I'm at home. The moment I go in the door my mother will throw me a drying-up cloth!'

In 1986, Langer successfully defended his German Open title in unlikely circumstances. He had to play the first round with an old set of clubs of his brother's, as his own equipment had gone missing on a return flight from the US.

He handed in a 75 which looked to

► Langer's chipping and bunker play are among his strongest suits. They have helped him to respectable scores when his putting has let him down.

▼ One of Langer's most memorable achievements of the 1981 season was to hit out from the branches of a tree short of the 17th green at Fulford.

Birthday treat

When Langer holed out at Fulford's 17th during the 1981 Benson and Hedges Tournament, after playing his famous shot from a tree, he handed over his ball to a young spectator. Unknown to Langer, the boy was celebrating his 14th birthday. The gift was mounted and is today proudly displayed at the family home in Barrnsley.

have cost him the tournament. Yet, when his own clubs were finally returned, he scored 65, 66 and 67 – good enough to take him into a play-off with Australia's Rodger Davis. Langer finally won at the fifth extra hole.

He has played in every Ryder Cup since 1981 (7), unfortunately missing the deciding putt at Kiawah Island in 1991 which would have given Europe overall victory.

YIPS AND CHIPS

It was a further measure of his character, that Bernhard came back to win his second Masters at Augusta in 1993. Significantly, two putts – a 20-footer for an eagle at the 13th and a 7-footer for a birdie at the 15th on the last day – guiding him to a four shots win.

Seve's heavy advice
Langer can thank Seve Ballesteros for bringing him out of putting doldrums in 1980. The Spaniard suggested he change his light putter for a heavier one which would almost swing itself, cutting out any tendency to a jerking, yipping action. Langer bought a putter for £5 in Clive Clark's shop at Sunningdale, and his action improved.

The quiet man
Langer's wife Vikki has shared his success since their marriage in 1986. She says: 'Bernhard never brings the game home with him. If I see something on the course I want to know about, I have to pry it out of him. He doesn't talk about golf all the time, doesn't live it 24 hours a day.'

► An important part of Langer's game is his rhythmic swing. This is especially noticeable with the long irons.

▲ In the 1985 Ryder Cup at the Belfry, Langer was a hero. When he and Ken Brown beat Wadkins and Floyd on day two, it gave his team a two-point lead for the final day.

▶ The German made a strong challenge for the 1986 French Open. He finished third, behind Seve Ballesteros. He has won the event on one occasion, in 1984.

▼ Langer's first win in a Major was the 1985 US Masters. The previous year's winner, Ben Crenshaw, presented him with the green jacket.

Agility and rhythm

Though he has a strong grip and sets himself up as if about to flight the ball right to left, Langer has enough agility to be in the perfect position at impact. Instead of coming into the ball with the slightly closed clubface suggested by his grip and set-up, he keeps the face square through the impact area. His rhythm with the long irons is legendary. His fellow professionals see this as his strongest department.

FACTS AND FIGURES

Name: Bernhard Langer
Born: Anhausen, West Germany, 27 August 1957
Height: 5ft 9in (1.74m)
Weight: 11st 2lb (71kg)
Family: wife Vikki; children Jackie (1986) and Stefan (1990)
Interests: skiing, football, tennis, dancing
Turned pro: 1972
First international pro win: 1979 Cacharel Under 25s Championship
Played Ryder Cup: 1981, 1983, 1985, 1987, 1989, 1991, 1993. Won 13, lost 11, halved 5
Played World Cup: 1976 - 1980
Major wins: 1985, 1993 US Masters
Order of Merit (Europe):

Year	Position	Winnings (£)
1976	90	2130
1977	*	691
1978	40	7006
1979	56	7972
1980	9	32,395
1981	1	95,991
1982	6	48,088
1983	3	83,605
1984	1	160,883
1985	2	163,009
1986	*	159,343
1987	5	164,821
1988	30	67,322
1989	7	231,872
1990	4	426,492
1991	3	595,444
1992	2	586,036
1993	4	469,569

* not enough counting tournaments to be placed

Wheel of fortune

US player Al Geiberger describes Langer as 'the most thorough player I've ever seen. Maybe it's his German attention to detail. We get detailed yardage charts wherever we go but Bernhard has this wheel he takes out on the course himself so that he can get his own measurements.'

▲ **Langer had his first attack of the yips at 19. He cured it by putting with his left hand below his right for putts of 20ft (6m) and less.**

It looked as if he had renewed putting problems in 1988. He won the Epson Grand Prix at St Pierre – but he used four putters and was becoming much slower over the ball. When the German Open arrived, his putting had deserted him.

It is a measure of his application that the rest of his game stayed as strong as ever. One of his biggest fans is Laura Davies, the British winner of the 1987 US Women's Open. She sees Langer as the perfect model in long iron play.

He chips immaculately, too. In 1988, the accuracy of his chipping seemed to do everything in its power to ease the effects of his putting.

Langer's overall composure saw him fight back to form in 1989. When he won the Spanish Open in fine style at El Saler, Valencia, nobody criticized such a well-deserved victory. His calmness, dedication and skill have made sure that the German remains one of the most popular names in golf.

Nancy Lopez

Nancy Lopez has the perfect image of a woman in sport. As well as being a superb role model, she has become one of the all-time greats in women's golf and the star of the LPGA tour.

In 1978 and 1979, her opening seasons as a professional, Nancy Lopez stunned the golf world by winning 17 tournaments – including a record five in a row.

In a decade, Nancy became the youngest player ever to join the elite LPGA Hall of Fame. She also resolutely played her way through marriage, divorce, remarriage and giving birth to two daughters by her second husband.

POSITIVE ATTITUDE

Nancy is widely regarded as more charming and communicative than any other top golfer, with the possible exception of Arnold Palmer.

'It is difficult to present a public face all the time and there are moments when I'd like to freak out,' she admits. 'But I find it important to retain a good image, as my image reflects on me, my husband, on my family and my life.'

Nancy's motivation partly came from her father Domingo. She also had a huge inner desire to succeed, to make her parents proud of her.

In some ways, this stemmed from her wish to pull herself out of her humble Mexican-American background. But above all Nancy Lopez had the ability to make it happen.

Taught entirely by her father, a low handicap amateur, she never had a classic swing. This was because she had rather a looping movement at the top of the backswing.

A naturally gifted putter, another of Nancy's assets has been her very slow backswing. This lets her hit with great consistency into and through the ball, so that she can rely on a repeatable, effective swing.

Practising was always a high priority for Nancy after she started the game at the age of seven. Her first club was a 4 wood given to

▼ For more than a decade the star of the LPGA tour, the exuberant Nancy Lopez takes the 1989 LPGA Championship seriously. She went on to win the event, one of the tour's majors, for the third time.

▲ In 1979, Nancy Lopez made a rare visit to Europe to play in the Colgate European Women's Open at Sunningdale. It was worth the Atlantic crossing – she won.

► There's no doubt where this putt ended up for Nancy at the World Championship of Women's Golf.

her by her father. She loved it – and was enchanted by the sound of golf spikes on tarmac.

At nine, she won a tournament by the notable margin of 110 shots. That win – and the obsessive desire to keep winning – made her want to practise even more, which she did with Domingo's encouragement.

She says, 'When you are a really positive person you can do well in sport, although there is still something different between those who win and those who don't. A lot of people want to win but can't achieve it. Because I would control my mind I was able to make it happen.'

PARENTAL SUPPORT

Nancy's father set goals for her, always giving her targets and rewards for achieving them. All of this kept her interest and turned her into a person who wanted to set records.

When she won a tournament at 17, her father presented her with a car. He protected and cosseted her very much, insisting that she was not to do the dishes at home, as it might spoil her hands for golf.

Nancy's parents saved all their money to let her compete, and she rewarded their attention with results. She won the New Mexico Women's Amateur tournament at the tender age of 12, and twice took the US Junior Girls' title. In 1976, she was a member of the US Curtis Cup team.

CLOSE SHAVES

Multiple victories came Nancy's way, but she never won the big one, the US Women's Amateur Championship. Neither has she yet taken the US

▼ When she started out, Nancy had doubts about her mental approach. 'I felt I was talented but didn't know if I could handle the pressure. But whenever I needed to make a putt, I'd make it.'

▲ Although she has never had a classic swing, Nancy shows the value of a slow backswing – it helps her to keep a regular tempo and swing through to a balanced finish.

Lopez the loner

Although Nancy Lopez is famous for being open, friendly and co-operative, one statement reveals a lot about her inner self.

'I got into the Bible study group on tour and enjoyed it, but didn't feel I belonged or could go out and have a good time with them. I don't like groups, I would prefer to be on my own or with one or two people. You have to be a loner to be successful.'

Women's Open title – though she was tied second when an amateur in 1975. She was second again in 1977 – soon after turning professional – and tantalizingly close again in 1989, when runner-up to Betsy King.

On that occasion, Nancy's father was recovering from a cancer operation, and she dearly wanted to give him the ultimate present of her victory.

STRIVING FOR VICTORY

She has been motivated in this way before. After her mother died of complications during an appendix operation, Nancy strove to win the last tournament of the 1977 season in Japan, so that she could dedicate it to her mother. She almost ended in tears as her wish was frustrated.

In February the year after – Nancy's

▼ Nancy has an assured all-round game, including powerful bunker ability. With winnings of nearly $3,000,000, she lies just a few thousand dollars behind Pat Bradley in the LPGA all-time money list.

▲ Nancy proudly displays the trophy at the only tournament she has won in Britain – the 1979 Colgate European Open, played over the tough Sunningdale course.

The Lopez swing
Nancy has a refreshingly simple attitude to her swing. 'Technique is not important to me. I need the same feel and the same swing. That is an advantage, because when you start analysing, it is confusing.'

◄ The Nabisco Dinah Shore Invitational is an important LPGA tournament – although Nancy Lopez didn't win in 1988, she claimed the title in 1981 when she shot a course record 64.

first full professional season – she dedicated her victory in the Sarasota Classic at Bent Tree to her mother.

It was the beginning of her great run of titles, which included a major – the LPGA Championship. Lopez achieved so much because she reached such an acute level of positive concentration that the shots flowed from her.

UNBEATABLE

Nancy said, 'During my winning streaks I got to the point where I thought I was never going to lose. Everything was so automatic and so easy. I was so confident, I felt no one could beat me.'

Ten years later, Nancy won again at Sarasota, and the victory guaranteed her entry into the Hall of Fame, which had always been one of her targets.

The devotion of her father – her coach and mentor – has always been in the background. Nancy is grateful for his sound advice.

'He persuaded rather than pushed me at golf,' she said. 'He always told me not to be afraid if I was behind in a tournament, that I could go out and shoot another good round. If I blew a hole he would tell me to forget it and go on to the next one, I couldn't bring it back.'

Nancy's second husband Ray Knight, a

▼ Whether she plays well or not, Nancy's on-course temperament never wavers. She says, 'People respect you more if you're shooting high scores and haven't thrown a club. If you can play badly or lose, and still be nice, that's an accomplishment.'

LOPEZ FACTFILE

Name: Nancy Lopez
Born: 6 January 1957, Torrance, California, USA
Height: 5ft 7in (1.7m)
Family: Husband Ray Knight; daughters Ashley Marie, Errin Shea
Turned pro: 1977
First pro win: 1978 Bent Tree Classic
Pro wins: 43 (to end of 1991)
Major wins: LPGA 1978, 1985, 1989; 1981 Dinah Shore Invitational
Solheim Cup: 1990
Money list (USA):

Year	Position	Winnings ($)
1977	31	23,138
1978	1	189,813
1979	1	197,488
1980	4	209,078
1981	6	165,679
1982	7	166,474
1983	15	91,477
1984	7	183,756
1985	1	416,472
1986	35	67,700
1987	7	204,823
1988	4	322,154
1989	3	487,153
1990	8	301,262
1991	26	153,772
1992	8	382,128
1993	14	304,480

▼ Nancy enjoys a joke at the 1987 Hennessy Ladies' Cup played at St Germain, near Paris. It isn't the smile of victory – the event was won by Kitrina Douglas.

▲ Nancy shows her classic throughswing position, as her weight transfers fully to her left side. Her uncomplicated approach gives her what all good swings must have – repeatability.

former baseball star, is a tremendous support and goal setter for her.

Although she admits trying too hard to be the perfect golfer, wife and mother, she is able to keep her priorities in the right order. 'Golf is not my only life, every tournament is not a life or death situation.'

She has set records and kept a balance in her life that is outstanding for a woman staying at the top of her sport for so long. It sets her apart.

Sandy Lyle

Sandy Lyle likes being first. He was the first Briton to win the Open for 16 years, and the first Briton ever to win the US Masters. He is also one of the most popular of today's golfing stars.

Lyle took the lead in the 1988 US Masters during the second round. He held it until the 12th hole on the final day. When he came to the final hole, he needed a par 4 to force a play-off with American Mark Calcavecchia.

His tee shot came to rest in a bunker 170yd (155m) from the green, leaving him in dire trouble. It was going to be difficult to make par from such a position. Most players could not even threaten the green from the bunker, especially under this sort of pressure. Lyle's match-winning temperament came to the fore.

GOLDEN WONDER

He gave himself time to calm down before lifting the ball crisply off the white sand with his 7 iron to within 10ft (3m) of the pin. It was one of the greatest single shots in the history of the sport. Lyle holed the putt and became the first player to win the Masters with a final hole birdie since Arnold Palmer in 1963.

During his career Lyle has achieved most goals a couple of

▼ Lyle has enjoyed brilliant success using a weak overlapping grip. Because his hands are bigger and stronger than those of the average player, he can use a grip which would normally cause a slice.

▲ A birdie at the last hole secured the 1988 Masters title for Lyle, letting him avoid a play-off with Mark Calcavecchia. He was only the fourth overseas player to win – and the first Briton.

◄ The ability to forget and bounce back from uninspiring performances is a Lyle trademark. He failed to make a serious impression at the 1987 US Masters – the next year he was the triumphant champion.

years ahead of his major rivals. While still a teenager he reached three of the most notable targets in the amateur game. He represented Britain and Ireland in the Walker Cup, as well as recording victories in the Berkshire and Brabazon Trophies.

At just 16 years 5 months he qualified for the third round of the 1974 Open Championship at Royal Lytham and St Annes – a record for someone so young.

Lyle turned professional in 1977.

His approach to the golf swing is as straightforward as his course strategy. In his own words, 'simplicity is the one philosophy that governs my swing and strategic play': he believes that the simpler the swing the easier it is to repeat under pressure.

Because of his enormous physical strength, Lyle swings at only 85-90% maximum speed on his drives and long irons. This allows him greater control of the ball while still hitting it vast distances. He hits 1-iron shots further than many professionals can hit with their drivers.

TRIALS AND SMILES

Bad weather poses no problems for him, either. He puts his ability to overcome and take advantage of wind down to regular playing and practising in ever-changing conditions.

In his early days as a professional, pitching was his weak point. But with constant hard work it is now one of the best parts of his game.

▼ Lyle is an assured front-runner. When he was caught at the 12th hole on the final day at Augusta in 1988, he kept his cool – despite finding some nasty hazards.

▼ Nature was generous, equipping Lyle with strong legs and powerful arms. What nature left out his father, Alex, later put in.

Such a move can produce the odd setback in even the most gifted, but Sandy took to the game without a break in stride. 'Rookie of the Year' honours – for the best newcomer – followed immediately and for the next two years he led the European Order of Merit.

THE LYLE STYLE

Much of his success came from his father's influence. Alex Lyle drummed home the importance of patience at an early age. Lyle now paces himself on the course, waiting for opportunities to come his way – unlike the aggressive games of Ballesteros and Norman.

His father also advised him to 'keep his head'. Lyle tries to maintain high spirits all the time, even after a bad shot or hole. He realizes the importance of accepting the rough along with the smooth. This relaxed attitude is always evident in Lyle's game.

▲ On the final day of the 1985 Open at Sandwich, the critical hole for Sandy Lyle was the 15th. Having birdied the 14th, an 18ft (5.5m) putt for a second birdie gave him a lead over his rivals.

Big shot

Lyle was destined to play golf. His father, Alex, was professional at Hawkstone Park in Shropshire. Legend has it that, aged three, Sandy's first shot flew 80yd (73m). By the age of 10 he had broken 80.

Lyle says, 'putting is my Achilles heel' – although it is hard to see how from the way he coped with the last three greens at the 1988 US Masters.

At the start of 1985, Lyle snr – a man whose few words are in stark contrast to the vast respect they command – suggested that his son was close to becoming the finished article. In July of that year he was proved right. At Royal St George's, Kent, Lyle became the first Briton to win the Open since Jacklin 16 years earlier – although the victory was less spectacular than that of the man who had been his inspiration.

In 1969, Jacklin played Lytham's 18th hole in textbook fashion, leaving an abiding memory of him with his arms aloft. A memory of Lyle remains of him slumped over a bank by the final green, untypically slamming a club into the ground. He had just played a poor pitch. Luckily, as it turned out, this mistake did not affect the final score.

GRITTY SANDY

The US breakthrough arrived with the 1986 Greater Greensboro' Open. Almost exactly a year later he added the Tournament Players' Championship in Florida, an event often referred to as the fifth major championship.

Professionally, events had fallen into place by 1987. Personally, they were falling to pieces. His marriage to Christine, herself a former professional golfer, had disintegrated. The effects were seen in his dramatic loss of form.

There was a chorus of opinion that wanted Lyle left out of the 1987 European Ryder Cup team. But by September Lyle had regained his purpose – and met a new girlfriend, Jolande Huurman. Lyle proudly played a major part in Europe's first victory on US soil, winning three of his four matches.

DOUBLE MASTER

1988 was a great year. An early victory in the Phoenix Open was followed by a second success in the Greensboro' Open. One week later came the Masters.

► Wentworth resident Lyle has appeared five times in the World Matchplay final, played over the West Course. He won only against Nick Faldo in 1988. In 1986, he was foiled by an outstanding Greg Norman.

Sleepy Sandy
Greg Norman calls Lyle 'Sleepy Sandy' because he often appears to be half asleep while playing the game. But his calm approach and even temperament are the secrets of his success.
Lyle believes it is important to stay relaxed between shots. His philosophy is to shut out anxiety until he is ready to play the shot. Then he concentrates on a positive attitude.

Soapy Sandy
After his 1988 Masters triumph at Augusta, a reporter asked Lyle what it felt like to be a superstar. Lyle turned a shade of puce, replying: 'Seve Ballesteros and Greg Norman are the superstars, I shall be back washing the dishes tonight at the home we have rented'.

LYLE FILE

Name: Alexander Walter Barr Lyle
Born: 9 February 1958, Shrewsbury, England
Height: 6ft 1in (1.85m)
Family: wife Yolande; children Stuart (1983), James (1986), Lonica (1993)
Weight: 13st 5lbs (85kg)
Turned professional: 1977
First pro win: 1978 Nigerian Open
European Tour wins (to end of 1993): 18
US Tour wins (to end of 1993): 5
Ryder Cup appearances: 1979, 1983, 1985 1987 and 1991; won 7, lost 9, halved 2
Major Championships: 1985 British Open, 1988 US Masters
World Matchplay: Winner – 1988, Runner-up – 1980, 1982, 1986, 1987
Order of Merit:

Year	Position	Earnings(£)
1978	49	5234
1979	1	49,233
1980	1	66,060
1981	3	51,265
1982	2	86,141
1983	5	61,020
1984	4	110,370
1985	1	254,711
1986	24	131,954
1987	12	245,355
1988	5	271,985
1989	53	49,408
1990	59	66,552
1991	22	185,510
1992	8	432,811
1993	67	79,224

▼ The Shropshire-born Scot's mastery was total in 1988. At Woburn, he added the Dunhill British Masters to the US title he had secured a few weeks before.

▲ Staying unruffled on the course is vital to the Lyle approach. When faced with a daunting shot, he never worries about the stroke until he has arrived at his ball and seen exactly how it lies.

He followed up his US Masters win with European victories in the British Masters in June and the World Matchplay Championship at Went-worth, in October. He overcame arch-rival Nick Faldo 2 and 1 in the final. Lyle ended 1988 challenged only by Ballesteros for the title of the world's best golfer.

Even though Lyle defeated the Spaniard 7 and 6 in the Wentworth semi-final the pair's respect and friendship are solid bonds. 'On his day Sandy is quite capable of destroying anyone,' said Ballesteros.

DOWNTURN

In 1989, Lyle made a brilliant start in America. He made it to a play-off for the Bob Hope Classic, but was beaten by Steve Jones. Soon after, he fought a tussle with Mark Calcavecchia for the Los Angeles Open – which the American won by a stroke. Although Lyle lost, his high finishes had him battling for top position in the US money list.

At the US Masters in April, everything started to go wrong. In defence of his title, Lyle missed the cut. From that moment, he failed to make an effective challenge in any tournament. He decided to abandon the US altogether.

In Europe, he fared no better. Although he consulted many coaches, his game was still too erratic to make headway against the best players. When captain Tony Jacklin invited him to play in the European Ryder Cup team in September, Lyle declined. Typically honest, he felt his lack of form did not justify selection. A three-year barren spell ended at the BMW International in October 1991, and his recovery continued with two more wins in 1992 when he topped £2 million in European earnings.

Jack Nicklaus

Jack Nicklaus is the most successful golfer ever. Other great players admire him as a perfectionist who knows better than anyone what his limitations are.

Jack Nicklaus birdies the 17th on his way to his 6th US Masters title in 1986. Four shots adrift at the start of the final round, he was still trailing at the 15th. An eagle there, followed by two birdies, gave him a score of 65. He beat the field by one stroke.

Perfectionists are born rather than made. Even at the age of ten, Jack Nicklaus liked to hit 300 practice shots a day – as well as playing 18 holes.

A native of Columbus (Ohio), Jack was introduced to the game by his father, Charlie. He suggested his son take a course of lessons from Jack Grout, a teaching professional, who had studied many of the world's top players.

Once he had approved his powerful pupil's grip, stance and set-up, Grout encouraged him to make a full shoulder turn and hit the ball hard.

TEENAGE CHAMPION

Within three months, Jack played nine holes of the Scioto Country Club in 51 strokes. To his dismay, he immediately 'went backwards', not scoring better than 60 for weeks afterwards.

At 12 years old, Nicklaus was breaking 80 with ease and being seen as a future champion. He had, for example, an invitation to partner one of the first female professionals, Patty Berg, in an exhibition game in 1953. By then, at 13, Jack was down to a handicap of three. But in his nine holes with Miss Berg, he scored an embarrassing 53. Only days later the family learnt that he had a mild dose of polio.

At 15, Nicklaus five times went round the Ohio State Gray Course in 63, a score he was not to match until the 1965 Australian Open. On that occasion, however, Gary Player made the achievement look meaningless by handing in a couple of 62s. In 1956, at 16, he won the junior and senior Ohio State Championship. The next year, he qualified for the US Open.

He has said that he was probably longer and stronger in his late teens and early 20s than he has ever been since. As a 21-year-old, he broke the face inserts out of nine drivers.

▼ Nicklaus plays skilfully out of a bunker at the 1986 US Masters. Early in his career, he was unhappy with his short game. To make up for it, he learnt to plot his way round a course in a manner which would make the best of the shots he already had at his disposal.

▲ In the 1977 British Open at Turnberry, Nicklaus and Tom Watson thrilled the crowds with an astonishing display. Jack finished 10 strokes clear of the next man – yet Watson won by a stroke.

▼ In 1960, Jack married Barbara Bash, a fellow student at Ohio State University. She has accompanied him around the golfing globe and seen him win all but a couple of his 20 Majors.

► Winning the US Masters in 1986, at the age of 46, was all the more satisfying as Nicklaus' son, Jackie, was carrying his bag.

The manner in which Nicklaus featured in professional tournaments, while still an amateur, suggested he would have no trouble making the switch to the professional arena. In 1960, the year he won the individual award at the World Amateur Team Championships, he finished second behind Arnold Palmer in the US Open at Denver.

TURNING PROFESSIONAL

However, turning professional did not fit in with what he had in mind. Nicklaus had been thinking about graduating from Ohio State University's college of commerce and finding a career in the insurance field.

It was only when the dean of the college asked this consistently absent pupil to leave, that Jack Nicklaus gave

Losing pounds and gaining dollars...
Nicklaus weighed 215lbs (97.5kgs) towards the end of his college days. In 1969, when he found the Ryder Cup format of 36 holes a day taking its toll, he decided to go on a diet. When he had lost 25lbs (11.3kgs) he collected two winner's cheques and a second place in three consecutive tournaments. Naturally, he redoubled his efforts. Before long he had slimmed to his best weight of 175lbs (79.3kgs).
The weight loss played its part in turning Nicklaus into a more charismatic figure. He became more conscious of his overall looks and decided to abandon his aggressively short crew-cut.

▼ Many of Nicklaus' admirers see his great length and brute force from rough as his strongest features. Nicklaus himself says that his concentration is his best weapon. His rivals agree – Ben Crenshaw said: 'Jack is simply more skilled than the rest of us at making his own breaks. He is able to put himself in an intense frame of mind, where nothing breaks his concentration and he can almost will the ball into the hole'.

▲ Nicklaus believes that most championships are lost, rather than won. After Doug Sanders had missed a short putt to win the 1970 British Open at St Andrews, Nicklaus won the play-off.

serious thought to the professional game. Mark McCormack, who was Arnold Palmer's manager, told him that in his first year he would make $100,000 from off-course activities alone. Nicklaus also began to realize that he could only develop his game to the full on the professional tour.

He made the move on 8 November 1961. In his first year, he won the US Open and finished third in the US PGA championship. Everybody marvelled at such a start. Yet Nicklaus himself describes his early time on the circuit as a 'rude awakening'.

PLAYING TO HIS LIMITS

When he compared his short game with that of other professionals, Nicklaus felt his own pitching, chipping and bunker play to be decidedly weak.

He also realized that there was more to driving than aiming down the fairway and hitting as hard as possible. He therefore turned himself into one of the best-organized pros in the game.

The other professionals recognized at once that he was in a class of his own in this area. 'A lot of us are good,' said Raymond Floyd, 'but Jack adds one intangible. I think he knows exactly what his capabilities are in any given situation. We may think we can pull off a shot, or even be pretty sure, but Jack knows.'

He also went back to work with Jack Grout. He once said of his clear-thinking coach, who died in May 1989, 'It is only when he has watched long enough and hard enough to get to the root cause

▲ **Jack Nicklaus makes a 'mental movie' of every shot. Before putting, he imagines the ball's roll towards the hole.**

▼ **Nicklaus is the best course strategist in the business. Every shot is played with the next in mind. He rarely hits flat out, usually playing for position.**

of a problem that he will proffer an opinion'.

BATTLES WITH PALMER

Early in Jack's professional career, everyone backed Arnold Palmer in their closer conflicts. The two dominated the tour in a manner unknown since the days of Sam Snead and Ben Hogan in the 40s and 50s. It was not until the 1967 US Open at Baltusrol, that the gallery finally seemed to accept him.

Five shots ahead of Palmer leaving the 17th green in the last round, Nicklaus had played into trees with his 1 iron off the 18th tee. He mishit his recovery shot to leave himself with a third of 230yd (210m) over water to the green. Jack still had enough shots in hand to play safe – yet typically, pulled out the same 1 iron which had put him in trouble off the tee. He went for the flag, the ball pulling up 20ft (6m) past to pave the way for a four.

HEROIC STATUS

Until that moment, Jack had always been the villain. Now the crowd rose to applaud its new hero. The win brought his tally of Majors to seven and a wry observation from Nicklaus: 'It's funny how such basically superficial considerations as smiling, waving and changing a hair style can affect the public's

▼ **In 1984, Jack Nicklaus was awarded an honorary doctorate by the University of St Andrews. He calls the venue 'my favourite place in golf'. Daughter Nan and wife Barbara share his delight.**

FACTS AND FIGURES
Name: Jack William Nicklaus
Born: Columbus, Ohio, USA, 21 January 1940
Height: 5ft 11in (1.8m)
Weight: 180lb (82kg)
Amateur career: US Amateur champion 1959, 1961. Walker Cup appearances 1959, 1961. US Open runner-up 1960. US Masters low amateur 1960 (13th overall) and 1961 (7th overall)
First pro tournament: 1958 Rubber City Open (finished 12th)
First pro victory: 1962 US Open at Oakmont
US Tour victories: 70
US Seniors' Tour victories: 6
Top of US Order of Merit: 1964, 1965, 1971-1976
Ryder Cup appearances: 1969, 1971, 1973, 1975, 1977, 1981. Non-playing captain 1983, 1987. Playing record: won 17, lost 8, halved 3
Major championship victories: British Open 1966, 1970, 1978. US Open 1962, 1967, 1972, 1980. US Masters 1963, 1965, 1966, 1972, 1975,

Making it happen
Tom Weiskopf's story about Jack reveals a lot. He recalls: 'Jack and I were partnering each other in the Ryder Cup at Muirfield. We both had ten footers on the last green and we needed one of those putts to win. To my astonishment, Jack told me to pick my ball up.

'He got over his own ball and, after staring at the putt long and hard, knocked it straight into the back of the cup.

'More than any other player in the game, Jack has the ability to make things happen on the golf course, especially under pressure.'

Famous amateur
Unlike most players, Jack Nicklaus was already well known before he turned professional. He had even finished second in the 1960 US Open while still an amateur. His score of 282 was an amateur record for the

impression of a fellow'.

Over the next ten years, Nicklaus continued to be the dominant force in world golf. He won Majors frequently and from 1971-76 was unchallenged in the US Order of Merit.

In 1977, Jack was second to Tom Watson in both the US Masters and the British Open. He could not have been more generous in defeat – yet the 'Golden Bear' suspected he was not the hungry golfer he had been.

It was because of this and because he wanted more time with his five children that he cut back on his schedule the next year. He promptly won the 1978 British Open at St Andrews. It gave him a new record – he had now won at least three times in each of the four Majors.

▲ Nicklaus now spends most of his time with his highly successful course design business. Yet he continues to play many tournaments, despite back trouble and the fact that he is well past his 50th Birthday.

In the 1980s, Jack became more involved with course design. He had already founded his own course, Muirfield Village, in his home state.

Just as his family have always known that they came first, so opponents from his heyday always knew where they stood. As the US player Leonard Thompson replied when asked about walking down the final fairway with the great man: 'You know he's gonna beat you, he knows he's gonna beat you and he knows you know he's gonna beat you'.

Greg Norman

From 1986 to 1990, the rankings rated Greg Norman the best player in the world, as his power and presence held the crowds spellbound. Yet bad luck left the Great White Shark with just one Major win until 1993.

A breathtaking last round of 64 he described as 'perfect' earned popular Greg Norman a second British Open title in 1993.

▲ **The Australian's massive hitting has helped him to win 14 tournaments on the European Tour.**

▲ **In 1984, Norman tied for the US Open at Winged Foot when he holed a long putt on the 18th. In his first Major play-off, he was beaten by Fuzzy Zoeller.**

Norman has often been compared to Jack Nicklaus. The two look alike, but, more importantly, many people felt that Norman was capable of repeating the tremendous feats achieved by the Golden Bear. However, Nicklaus had won 12 Majors by the time he was 34 years old. When Norman reached that age, he had only his masterful 1986 British Open triumph to his credit.

Although he realizes that Nicklaus' status is unique, Norman has always had one of the most positive outlooks in the game. 'I don't feel that I've reached my peak. I didn't hit a golf ball until I was 16 so I'm far from being burnt out. The best ten years of my life as a golfer are ahead of me.'

BAGS OF CONFIDENCE

Confidence has always been the 15th club in Greg Norman's bag. He began playing after caddying for his mother, Toini. As soon as he started, his ambition was to become the best player in the game.

Charlie Earp, Norman's coach since his apprenticeship days at Royal Queensland, said: 'He's always been so confident he has never needed pep talks from anyone. When he first came to work at Royal Queensland he was as brash as all the young guys and he told everyone he was going to be the best player in the world.'

He is a constant threat in tournaments because he is totally convinced of his own ability. Norman has no time for doubters. In the 1989 US Masters, he refused to accept that the 5 iron he struck to the 18th green was the wrong club. It landed short, and cost him a play-off spot.

Norman said that he hit a perfect shot, insisting that the driving rain knocked the ball down more quickly than he had planned. With typical determination, he declared: 'I'll get there. I'll win the Masters – I might just be older than the rest.'

HIGHS AND LOWS

Norman had trained to become a pilot in the Australian Air Force. But he soon decided that he would be better employed flying to the fairways of the world in pursuit of fame and fortune.

He has since earned millions of dollars from sponsorship deals alone. That money has given him a fabulous life-style, including a huge home in Florida and sports cars galore. Yet Norman is aware that it does not affect the golfing history books.

There have been some sad misfortunes. In the 1986 US PGA Champion-

Charity work

Despite having one of the busiest schedules in international golf, Greg Norman is building strong links with charity work.

He has organized a tournament in California to help a house programme for terminally ill children. When he won the 1988 MCI Heritage Classic at Hilton Head Island, South Carolina, his house guest was Jamie Hutton, a 17-year-old leukaemia sufferer.

ship, the fourth of the four Majors, Norman let the title slip from his grasp. He led the Championship by four strokes after three rounds, with scores of 65-68-69.

Although his form was not so good on the final day, he still looked a good bet to take the title, as he and Bob Tway came level to the 18th. But Tway holed from a bunker at the side of the 18th green, to take the Championship from under Norman's nose.

The next Major was played in April 1987, as the world's top players headed for Augusta and the US Masters. Norman played superbly, and the field was finally reduced to himself and Larry Mize, as Ballesteros fell by the wayside at the first play-off hole. At the second extra hole, Norman was safely on the green in two. Mize's second shot fell 45yd (41m) short of the pin.

As Mize prepared to play his third, Greg Norman could probably have been forgiven for thinking that lightning doesn't strike twice. Surely he could now savour the moment and start taking his measurements for the green jacket he so richly deserved. He was wrong. Mize's chip bounced and ran on – and on – into the hole. Stunned and unable to hole his putt, Norman's nightmare continued. He had to wait two years for his next chance.

▲ When Greg Norman achieved the so-called 'Saturday Grand Slam' in 1986 – he led each of the four Majors going into the final day – he won only The Open at Turnberry.

▼ Despite the worldwide demand for Norman, he still cares greatly about competing and winning in his home country. The Queenslander won his fifth Australian Masters title in 1989.

Shark and Bear

Greg Norman and Jack Nicklaus have been compared ever since they teed-up together in the Australian Open in 1976. Norman had won the week before – only his fourth professional appearance – and he topped his first drive. He scored 80 but in the locker room afterwards Nicklaus said all the right things to Norman. 'It meant a lot to me,' said the Australian.

▲ Norman is more than just a distance master. He has perfected his game in all departments, including bunker play.

▲ After three rounds of the 1986 US PGA, Norman looked to be in total command, as he had a four-stroke lead. But he was caught at the last gasp by Bob Tway.

TROON SWOON

At the start of the final day of the 1989 Open, Greg Norman did not appear to be in serious contention. Then he smashed Royal Troon into submission, shooting a course record 64.

His daring display sent blood pressures rising all over the huge crowd – as well as taking him into a four-hole play-off. Birdies at the first two holes seemed enough to give him possession of the famous claret jug for a second time.

Unfortunately, he dropped a shot at the third. His drive at the fourth play-off hole (Troon's 18th) ruined his chances. It bounced a long way up the parched fairway into a bunker. Norman played his difficult second shot into another bunker. American Mark Calcavecchia birdied the hole to snatch the title from the crowd's favourite.

Despite these reversals, Norman's record on a global basis is excellent. He has won more than 60 titles around the world. He is unhappy when people forget that. 'If you win 60 plus Championships around the world you've got to play well. I don't care who the competition is.'

NORMAN THE CONQUEROR

The golfing greats agree with him. 'He's a great player,' said Tom Watson. 'The guy could've won five or six major championships. But he's been beaten by chip shots, bunker shots. I don't understand what all the hubbub is about. I wouldn't worry about Greg Norman. He'll do lots of winning. He's still just in the middle of his career.'

Nicklaus is also a fan. 'I think Greg is a better shotmaker than Seve,' he said. Jack lives a short distance from Greg in Florida. They are good friends.

▼ 1987 was Norman's unluckiest US Masters. Before Larry Mize chipped in to steal the green jacket at the second play-off hole, the Australian had just missed a putt for outright victory on the 18th.

▲ Norman has proved himself an invaluable team member. He helped Australia to win victories in the Dunhill Cup at St Andrews in 1985 and 1986.

▼ Driving the ball great distances gives more scope to Norman's aggressive game. As he can easily reach par 5s in two shots, he can attack the pin for eagles.

Timing and subtlety

Power and accuracy are the keys to great golf. Greg Norman has huge reserves of both – yet he never resorts to brute force. The vast distances he reaches from the tee and the fairway are the result of a slow takeaway and smooth, measured swing. Every part of his body works together so that his strength is released into and through the ball. He achieves it through excellent timing.

But there is more than aggression to Norman. His chipping and putting touch is delicate and assured. It lets him take full advantage of the positive positions his power brings him.

FACTFILE
Name: Gregory John Norman
Born: Queensland, Australia, 10 February 1955
Height: 6ft 1in (1.86m)
Weight: 185lbs (83.9kg)
Family: Wife Laura; children Morgan-Leigh (born 5/10/82), Gregory (born 19/9/85)
Interests: Fishing, hunting, snooker, vintage cars
Turned professional: 1976
World Matchplay: Winner – 1980, 1983, 1986
European wins: 14 between 1977-1993
Australian Open: Winner – 1980, 1985, 1987
Australian Masters: Winner – 1981, 1983, 1984, 1987, 1989
Major wins: 1986, 1993 British Open.
Order of Merit (US Tour):

Year	Position	Earnings($)
1983	74	71,411
1984	9	310,230
1985	42	165,458
1986	1	653,296
1987	7	535,450
1988	17	514,854
1989	4	835,096
1990	1	1,165,477
1991	53	320,196
1992	18	676,443
1993	15	1,359,653

▲ Good reserves of strength have more uses than big hitting. They also help Norman to escape from stubborn bunker lies when his ball is plugged in the sand.

Jack gave him some advice at the 1986 Open at Turnberry. That year, Norman recorded the amazing 'Saturday Grand Slam' – he led each of the four Majors going into the final day.

He won only The Open at Turnberry. His second round of 63 on a grotesque day at the Scottish links is rated by Watson as 'the greatest round ever played in a tournament in which I was a competitor .

Only Ballesteros can rival Norman as the most exciting crowd pleaser in the modern game. Norman is an outgoing person, with a let's-get-up-there-and-give-it-a-rip attitude which reflects his character. The crowds follow the 'Great White Shark' in their thousands, because he plays the sort of game they adore. Norman carries an aura of excitement around with him, attracting shouts of 'Go shark, go!' as he thunders drives down the fairways.

FAMILY MAN

Despite his have-clubs-will-travel reputation, Norman loves to be at home with his family. 'They are my backbone,' he says proudly.

They added to the emotional ovation accorded him at the Royal St. Georges in 1993 when his last round 64 was heralded as one of the greatest ever as he deservedly won his second Open title.

▼ Despite his jet-setting lifestyle, Norman is first and foremost a family man. He and wife Laura have two children, Morgan-Leigh and Gregory.

▼ The Great White Shark has been labelled with the image of the bronzed, bush-whacking Australian since he burst on to the scene in the late 1970s.

José-Maria Olazabal

As soon as José-Maria Olazabal arrived on the European Tour, he established himself as one of its brightest stars. He has since proved a consistent winner and become part of Ryder Cup folklore.

When a young man from Spain carved a special place for himself in amateur golf in the early to mid 1980s, it was inevitable that many people would hail him as the second coming. After triumphing as the only golfer ever to win the British Boys, Youths and Amateur Championships, José-Maria Olazabal became the 'new Severiano Ballesteros'.

Although that was intended as a great compliment, it was something of an insult. The young Basque is not the second anyone – he is the first José-Maria Olazabal. One American player, after the 1989 Ryder Cup, said: 'He could become even better than Seve.'

▼ When he exploded on to the European golfing scene in 1986, many people compared José-Maria Olazabal to his more famous fellow Spaniard, Severiano Ballesteros. However, Olazabal's performances ever since have confirmed him as a great player in his own right.

Intensity

Like his compatriot Ballesteros, Olazabal is mainly self taught. His style is orthodox, though he sometimes swings quickly through the ball.

His intense concentration is remarkable. For example, at the 1989 Volvo Masters, a young child wandered a couple of paces behind Olazabal as he was in mid swing. Although the child must have strayed right into the centre of Olazabal's vision, the Spaniard did not even notice – he played a perfect shot.

▲ Olazabal grew up in a small village a stone's throw from the bay of San Sebastian. Seve Ballesteros' background was similar – his home was by Santander bay, not far along the coast from Olazabal's region.

▼ In the 1986 Lancôme trophy, Olazabal finished a respectable sixth. It was his first season on tour and he made an immediate impact, winning two events and claiming second spot in the money list.

Olazabal was born to play golf – literally. The day before his birth, in February 1966, his mother was still working on the new Royal San Sebastian course. In fact, the course opened its gates for play on the day José-Maria came into this world.

SEVENTH HEAVEN

His father Gaspar is still the head greenkeeper. When he isn't jetting the globe, Olazabal retires to his home opposite the 7th green.

Many of the great golfers are very solitary people. Olazabal is no exception – though he has developed a more outgoing personality. The crowd saw his skittish side when he broke into a Spanish dance across the 18th green at Muirfield Village, after the 1987 European Ryder Cup win.

However, he is not really a party-goer. Ollie, as he is affectionately called, knows when it's time to have a good time and when to be serious. He brings to his play an intensity matched only by the greatest golfers.

OLLIE FOLLY

Sometimes, Olazabal is too fanatical for his own good. In December 1988, he was practising near his home when suddenly he felt faint and giddy. The problem was diagnosed as an ulcer – a worrying condition in a man just 23 years old. The doctor told him to be as intense as he liked on the course – but to relax on the off-peak days.

Olazabal's talent was obvious early on. When the Spanish Junior Championships came to San Sebastian, Ollie, then aged just seven, won the under-nines section. He has continued to perform deeds beyond those of his own age ever since.

▲ **Years of practice around the golf course where he was brought up have provided Olazabal with one of the finest short games in the business. His smoothness from bunkers is remarkable.**

Even as a professional, his first steps were confident. The European Tour Qualifying School, at La Manga, is a frightening prospect for many young players. Olazabal went there – and won in style.

A first year on tour is a different experience altogether. The young pro has to come to terms with the constant travel and the massive leap in standard. Even the most gifted players struggle to make the grade.

As usual, the young Spaniard proved the exception to the rule. Far from struggling, he won two tournaments in his rookie year, 1986. The wins included one of the most prestigious the tour has to offer, the Ebel European Masters in Switzerland. Olazabal marched straight in at number two on the Order of Merit (OoM). A star was instantly born.

CONSISTENT WINNER

That year was no flash in the pan. Olazabal has gone on winning tournaments. Although he was pushed into second place in the 1989 European OoM by Ronan Rafferty, he could take comfort from the fact that Rafferty played in more tournaments. If he had taken part in the six extra tournaments Rafferty had played in, Olazabal would surely have finished top.

He won the first tournament of the year, the Tenerife Open. He also took the Dutch Open, beating Rafferty in a marathon 9-hole play-off. Throughout the season, he notched up 15 top-12

◄ Runner up in the 1991 US Masters highlighted Olazabal's Powers. He first played in the tournament at 19, in 1985, when he was invited as British Amateur Champion.

▼ At the age of 23, Olazabal could fill an entire room with cups and medals. The trophy room at his home in Fuenterrabia bears witness to his fabulous success.

Triple crown
Olazabal was just 18 when he beat Colin Montgomerie in the final of the British Amateur Championship. By then, he had already won the Boys title.

The year after, he won the Youths Championship. Amateur golf's triple crown – an achievement beyond everyone who came before him – had been wrapped up in a mere three years.

finishes in just 19 events – a remarkable level of consistency.

However, it is the Ryder Cup that has seen him at his best. Olazabal was introduced to its particular pressures in 1987. He had finished only 17th in the OoM, but captain Tony Jacklin knew talent when he saw it. After consulting Seve Ballesteros, he chose Ollie for the matches at Muirfield Village.

Jacklin's masterstroke was in pairing him with Ballesteros. In their first match, Olazabal was very nervous – all of the older Spaniard's experience was needed to make sure of victory.

The younger man took in the lessons. In the next match they were an equal partnership. In the third, Olazabal was the hero.

The Spaniards were 1 up on the final hole of their foursomes match (when the two players take it in turns to play the same ball) against Payne Stewart and Ben Crenshaw. Ballesteros had put them in an awful position in a greenside bunker. Ollie wasn't sure he could dig the ball out in normal circumstances, let alone under this pressure.

However, he escaped from the bunker with a near perfect shot that rolled to 10ft (3m) from the pin. The putt was downhill on a lightning fast green. As soon as he played the bunker shot, Ollie was advising his partner how to play. They had 2 shots to win the match. 'I told

▲ "Ollie" – A phenomenal talent surely destined to win Majors.

▼ When he is not playing in a tournament, Olazabal is happiest at home with his family – his father, mother, grandmother and sister.

Lonely hunter

Despite his worldwide acclaim, it is at home in Fuenterrabia where Olazabal is most at ease. He loves isolation, which he finds in the mountains near his home.

He rises at six to go hunting with his father – they look for grouse, rabbits, hares, wild pigeons and ducks, but never deer. 'I could never kill a deer,' said Olazabal. 'There is something in them that should not be killed.'

OLAZABAL FACTFILE
Name: José-Maria Olazabal
Born: 5 February 1966, Fuenterrabia, Spain
Height: 5ft 10in (1.77m)
Weight: 11st (70kg)
Interests: Music, cinema
Amateur career: 1983 British Boys Championship; 1984 British Amateur Championship; 1985 British Youths Championship
Turned pro: 1985
First pro win: 1986 Ebel European Masters
Played Ryder Cup: 1987, 1989, 1991,1993. Won 12, lost 6, halved 2
Order of Merit (Europe):

Year	Position	Winnings(£)
1986	2	155,263
1987	17	108,333
1988	3	317,910
1989	2	428,669
1990	3	434,766
1991	7	302,207
1992	6	434,353
1993	18	249,493

him he must just touch it because it was downhill; just leave it close,' he said.

If Ballesteros failed to appreciate this advice from a raw newcomer, he didn't show it. As Olazabal said later, 'It was no senior-junior relationship... It was right to remind him of the task in hand.'

SPANISH HIGHS

Ballesteros did just touch it, but the ball went as far past the hole as it had been before. Olazabal was left facing a tough 10ft (3m) putt to avoid throwing away a valuable Ryder Cup point. When Ollie's ball dropped straight into the middle, Ballesteros' ecstatic reaction said it all.

In 15 matches together over four contests, they have lost twice. Their partnership has been a cornerstone of European Ryder Cup success. When Ollie went on to beat Payne Stewart by 1 hole in the 1989 singles, he could claim the best haul of any player in that year's event – 4 points out of 5. In 1991 he lost only once in five matches.

All that remain now for the intense Spaniard are the Majors. As Olazabal admitted recently, 'I would not like to leave this world without having won at least one.' With the long career he has before him, it seems certain he will have many more than that to celebrate.

▲ The partnership between Olazabal and Ballesteros has become part of Ryder Cup legend. Beaten just twice in 15 matches between 1987 and 1993, they have formed a remarkable understanding.

▼ Olazabal's strength helps him to play out of a tricky lie in the rough. He had won 17 pro events up to the start of 1994.

Arnold Palmer

Strength and confidence were Arnold Palmer's outstanding qualities in his great years. He also triggered the growth of the American golf circuit into a multi-million dollar business.

Playing the 15th hole at Royal Birkdale during the 1961 Open Championship, Arnold Palmer sent his second shot into the rough, close to the base of a small bush. It was the kind of place from which the average golfer would be glad to sacrifice a shot to get back on the fairway.

However, Palmer chose a 6 iron. With a mighty blow, he demolished the bush and landed the ball on the green, 140yd (128m) away. He went on to win the Championship, and Royal Birkdale marked the spot of Palmer's wonder shot with a plaque. The hole is now the 16th.

BRUSHING UP HIS GAME

Arnold's father, Milfred J 'Deacon' Palmer, was the greenkeeper, and later professional, at the course in Latrobe, Pennsylvania. Arnold began playing golf when he was five years old – at 12, he could break 70.

Arnold Palmer attended Wake Forest College but left when a close friend was killed in a motor cycle accident. After three years in the

▼ A dynamic approach made Arnold Palmer one of the most popular players of his generation and brought him six Major titles. As he entered his sixties, he still enjoyed the thrill of competition.

coast guard, he returned to Wake Forest. Again, he didn't graduate, this time becoming a paint salesman.

He took plenty of time off to play golf and in 1954 won the US Amateur Championship. At the age of 25 – late by today's standards – he turned professional.

His professional start was relatively painless. He won the 1955 Canadian Open by 4 strokes, after realizing that he needed to adjust his game to suit pro conditions.

As an amateur, he had hit everything straight at the pin. His approaches were fierce, with plenty of backspin. That sort of shot tended to bounce off hard greens, so Palmer learned how to float the ball in, and how to hit a draw and a fade.

Palmer took a lot of trouble to study the Rules of Golf – a chore many pros

▲ In his glory years, the huge galleries known as 'Arnie's Army' used to gather around Palmer. The 'Army' were on hand to watch his steady first round of 71 in the 1962 Open at Troon, which he went on to win.

► His legendary strength kept Palmer in good shape on the US Senior Tour. He has won the Senior TPC, one of the Tour's Majors, on two occasions – 1984 and 1985.

Postal problems

At the height of his power, Palmer received fan mail approaching 200 letters a week. Many were requests for money, but a large proportion came from people who wanted to solve his troubles for him. In 1963, an attack of bursitis (inflamed joints) brought hundreds of remedies, suggesting everything from ultra violet ray treatment to witch hazel.

▲ **Arnold shares a moment of glory with his wife Winifred. He won the Open in 1961 at Royal Birkdale and in 1962 at Troon, and renewed international interest in the Championship. When he announced his desire to win it, others followed.**

greet without enthusiasm. In the 1958 US Masters, he hit a 6 iron over the green at the short 12th, where his ball plugged in a bank. Because the course was very soft after rain, there was a rule in force which ought to have entitled Palmer to a free drop – but the official on duty at that spot refused it. Palmer played the ball as it lay, and made 5. Next, he dropped another ball and made 3.

Then he appealed against the official's decision to the Masters chairman. While playing the 15th, Palmer heard he had won the appeal. It was an important decision because it gave him his first Major – by just 1 stroke.

ARNIE'S ARMY

'Arnie's Army' now began to gather. This huge gallery of fans followed him along every fairway and crowded around every green. What they loved above all else was his knack of 'charging' out of the pack.

A classic example occurred during the 1960 US Open at Denver. At the start of the final round Palmer was 7

▲ **Palmer is famous for his recovery play and gave a typical demonstration from the 'Church Pews' at Oakmont in the 1983 US Open. By taking part in the Championship for the 31st time, he equalled a record set by Gene Sarazen.**

Father and son

Although Arnold's father taught him to play, the two didn't approach the game the same way. Palmer's father believed in striking the ball hard – and Arnold never thought he hit it hard enough to please his father. Arnold believed in a correct grip, a compact swing, firmly placed feet and a lot of practice.

strokes behind Mike Souchak. Palmer was in determined mood on the 1st tee and drove the green, 346yd (316m) in length. Making the birdie with 2 putts was no problem. He birdied the next three holes as well and turned in 30, equalling the US Open record for nine holes. He finished with a 65, winning by 2 strokes from Jack Nicklaus.

That same year, Palmer almost repeated the charge in the Open at St Andrews. He was edged out by the popular Australian, Kel Nagle.

TOPPING PERFORMANCE

In 1961, at Royal Birkdale, Palmer achieved success in testing conditions of rain and wind which were severe enough to cause play to be abandoned on the third day.

As he wrote later, 'It was my ability to play low shots that really won me this one. I knew how to choke down on shots and hit them low ever since my father taught me how when I was a lad. I even choked down on the driver when necessary, and when I hit it many fans thought I had half topped it. In using this shot for approaches the ball would take a hop and then stop dead, aided greatly by the wet greens. My 1 iron was working especially well for this shot.'

Palmer was a spectacular 'charger' because he always took up a challenge. Before the final round of the 1962 Open at Troon his wife, Winnie, was worried. She told a reporter that 'Arn' needed something to play for because he was 5 shots ahead and likely to relax. The

▲ Over the years, Palmer has retained a strong putting technique – in his heyday, daring putts helped to create his legend. He was an aggressive putter, who hit the ball fearlessly towards the back of the cup.

► Palmer plays solidly out of a Troon greenside bunker during the 1989 Open. A great admirer of Scottish links courses, he still plays the Championship regularly.

▲ **After entering at the last minute, Palmer won the 1988 Crestar Classic. It was his first victory for three years on the Senior Tour and his biggest tournament pay cheque for 22 years.**

reporter suggested she tell him that not many people had won the title two years in a row. He shot a 69 and broke the Championship record by 2 strokes with 276.

His greatness as a links player was boosted because the conditions were so different from Birkdale. Troon was dry and fast, and Palmer had to use other skills, producing lofted shots.

Palmer tended to play down his 1-hole defeat by Peter Alliss in the 1963 Ryder Cup singles, saying he was better at strokeplay than matchplay. But in six Ryder Cup series he won more often than he lost – an extrovert and a good teammate, he has never been happy in defeat. His seven appearances in the World Cup (formerly the Canada Cup) resulted in six wins – two with Sam Snead and four with Jack Nicklaus.

Even at his best, Palmer was never a classic swinger of the golf club. His facial expressions usually suggest that he has given the ball a massive thump. He could be wild off the tee, and his chipping could be suspect. Yet self-belief and bravery brought rewards.

PALMER THE CHARMER

Rewards were not confined to the golf course, because Palmer had also become involved in the hard sell.

Back in 1950, when Wake Forest entertained William and Mary College, an ice-eyed member of the visiting team had his first look at Palmer. This young law student realized that professional golf could be exploited in ways nobody had yet thought of. His name was Mark McCormack – and all he needed was a champion with magnetic appeal.

In 1958, McCormack became Palmer's business manager. He sold his client's services for exhibition matches, golf equipment and also such unrelated items as deodorants, cars and insurance. In doing so, he raised the sights of all top golfers.

Arnold Palmer topped the US money list for the third time in 1962, with $41,448. In 1988, Curtis Strange was top of the heap with $1,184,775. Even allowing for inflation, the difference is considerable – McCormack and Palmer can claim much of the credit.

Fore!
Propositions turned down by Mark McCormack on Arnold Palmer's behalf include the promotion of a combined golf course and fallout shelter.

▼ **Success in Europe wasn't restricted to the Open Championship. Palmer twice won the World Matchplay Championship and in 1975 he took on Europe's best to win the PGA Championship at Sandwich.**

▲ **Away from the golf course, Arnold Palmer's chief passion is flying. He is a good pilot, and has owned several aircraft. His other main hobby is clubmaking and tinkering with the lie and loft of his huge collection of golf clubs.**

► **Now that his days on the week-to-week grind of the Tour are behind him, Palmer is able to spend more time at home in Florida with his wife, Winnie, and their dog Riley.**

FACTS AND FIGURES

Name: Arnold Daniel Palmer
Born: 10 September 1929, Latrobe, Pennsylvania, USA
Height: 5ft 10in (1.77m)
Weight: 178lb (81kg)
Interests: Flying, club making, tennis
Family: Wife Winifred; daughters Margaret (1956), Amy (1958)
Turned pro: 1954
First pro win: 1955 Canadian Open
US Tour wins: 60
US Seniors' Tour wins: 11
Major wins: British Open 1961, 1962. US Open 1960, US Masters 1958, 1960, 1962, 1964. Palmer has never won the USPGA title
Played Ryder Cup: 1961, 1963, 1965, 1967, 1971, 1973. Won 22, lost 8, halved 2
Other: 1954 US Amateur Champion
First player to win $1,000,000
Several wins on US Senior Tour including PGA Seniors 1980, 1984; 1981 USGA Senior Open

In the soup

Before McCormack, all the arrangements, secretarial work and financial affairs were looked after by Arnold's wife, Winnie. The daughter of a canned foods company president, she had eloped with 'Arn' in 1955. Without McCormack's shrewdness and skill, Palmer would still have made a lot of money – but may have missed out on lucrative business deals.

SENIOR SUCCESS

Towards the end of his career on the US Tour, Palmer quietened down. He was less likely to charge out of the pack, and certainly lost confidence on the greens.

His career on the Senior Tour has been consistently successful, though he doesn't play full time. He entered the 1988 Crestar Classic at Richmond, Virginia at the last minute – and even then only because the organizers asked him to strengthen the field.

It turned out to be a profitable decision. He shot 65-68-70, 13 under par, and won his first Senior PGA Tour event for more than three years. He was 59 years and 8 days old, the oldest winner on the circuit. Palmer collected $48,750, his biggest winner's cheque since September 1966, and $6000 more than he received for heading the US money list in 1958.

As senior golf gains status, all of Palmer's fellow players agree that he is the biggest draw on the tour.

He was elected to the USPGA Hall of Fame in 1980, and in 1981 the Arnold Palmer Award was created as a trophy for each year's leader on the US money list. The first winner was Tom Kite.

Gary Player

Gary Player is a complex character. Of all the qualities that combine to make up this great champion, determination to be the best dominates. He is one of just four men who have won all four Majors.

▲ South African Gary Player is the most successful foreigner to have played the US Tour. This is partly because of his positive and determined approach – especially from bunkers.

When Gary Player was 14 years old, his father, who had worked hard to earn an executive position in a goldmine, took him to play golf. Gary, a keen all-round sportsman, says he made par at each of the first 3 holes.

However, he was not hooked on the game until a few weeks later, when he went to the Virginia Park course near Johannesburg. There he met his future wife, Vivienne Verwey, the pro's daughter.

It took Gary only a few months to decide that he wanted to be a professional golfer. This was much to the dismay of his father, who would have preferred his son to go to university.

Although he was a scratch player within two years, Gary Player did not have an outstanding amateur career. When he became assistant to Jock Verwey at Virginia Park, he didn't make much impact on the professional game either.

SWING CHANGES

One reason for the lack of success was his very strong grip and upright swing. Verwey insisted Player adopt a more orthodox method.

A little later, Player moved to the Killarney Golf Club in Johannesburg where he met George Blumberg, a major benefactor of South African golf. Blumberg helped start Player's globe-trotting career by contributing towards his first trip overseas.

In 1955, Player more than doubled his finances in his first event, the Egyptian Matchplay Championship. He won the first prize of £300.

OUT OF AFRICA

Despite the Egyptian success, his early professional career was an exercise in shoestring living. Player found conditions in Great Britain and, later, the United States very

The man in black

Gary Player's most obvious features are his relatively small size and his black clothes. He believes that black helps him absorb the power of the sun – and he also admits the black clothes have become his trademark.

To hit the ball as far as the 'big boys', he has to go full out. His whole body has to work to maximum capacity. Everything must move as much as it usefully can.

Gary sometimes finishes his swing in an unusual posture, with his right foot moving ahead of his left. With such an all-action swing, anything less than perfect timing can lead to disaster.

However, around the green – where size is not vital – Player has been outstanding.

▲ Player stands steady in a strong wind, about to play a lofted iron. He is noted for the brilliance of his short game. When asked about his technique he has often said: 'The more I practise the luckier I get.'

► The US Senior Tour has brought rich pickings for Player, still one of golf's steeliest competitors. Victory at the 1988 US Senior Open increased his bank balance by $65,000.

different from those in South Africa. However, he won a British event in 1956, and finished second in the 1958 US Open.

Player has won nine of the modern Majors. The first of these was the Open at Muirfield in 1959. For this he had to qualify, by playing a round at Gullane and another at Muirfield. In the Championship itself, he was 8 strokes back going into the third round and 4 adrift after it.

Gary thought his final round of 68 was the best he had ever played, though there was an agonizing wait as he believed his double bogey 6 at the 18th had cost him the title. But Flory van Donck also finished poorly, and Player won by 2 strokes.

Gary estimated his expenses, and those of his wife and daughter, at £1500 for the week. The winner's cheque was for £1000 – but the money wasn't important.

Great though that Open Championship win was, it's likely that Player's performance in the 1960 US Masters had more overall effect on his development.

Player had already noticed that most other tournament golfers paid very little attention to their physical condition. In contrast, Player was a fitness fanatic.

He did not smoke or drink and he never had tea or coffee. He was keen on wheat germ and almost every other health-giving food. He avoided sugar, fats, red meat and fried foods. He had a punishing exercise routine, including

Player's greatest match

The 1965 World Matchplay Championship was the first of a remarkable total of five which Player won and was also the most memorable. In his semi-final against the 1964 Open Champion Tony Lema, Player was 7 down after 19 holes.

Lema – at the time one of the top half-dozen golfers in the world – played very well in the morning and took a leisurely lunch. Player had a quick snack and went to the practice ground to sort out his hook problem.

Although he hooked again at the 19th, and lost it, it was Lema who had trouble with the hook from then on. Player squared the match with a 4 at the 36th, where Lema hooked his second. Gary won after Lema did the same thing at the first play-off hole.

Player fainted after his win, but recovered to beat Australian Peter Thomson in the final, by 3 and 2. To this day, Player describes his win over Lema as his greatest match.

▲ Victory tastes good at the 1974 Open, played at Royal Lytham and St Anne's. It was Player's third and final win in the Championship.

◄ Although he didn't win on this occasion in 1980, Player has triumphed in the South African Open an incredible 13 times.

▼ **Seve Ballesteros says that being paired with Gary Player in the final round of the 1978 US Masters taught him the power of mind over matter.**

Player was 7 strokes adrift at the start of the day. With 7 birdies in the last 10 holes, he shot a course record 64 – and won by 1. Seve is convinced that Player willed himself to win.

weight training. Despite all these efforts, Gary Player found that he was still unable to reach the Augusta par 5s in 2 shots at the 1960 Masters.

He hired a trainer and consulted professional body-builders. Then he began a development programme to improve only the muscles used in golf.

The year after, Gary won the US Masters. Arnold Palmer, who needed a par 4 on the 18th to win, knocked his 2nd shot into the right-hand trap. Then he came out from a 'fried egg' lie – when the ball is half sunk – too strongly, chipped 5yd (4.5m) past the pin and missed the putt, taking 6. Before him, Player had made par from the same bunker – he won by a shot.

In 1965, Player became the first of the 'big three' – Nicklaus later joined him, but not Palmer – to win all four Majors. At Bellerive, St Louis, he was the first overseas player since Ted Ray in 1920 to win the US Open.

SAVING STROKES

Gary's preparation was meticulous. He bought a notepad, sketched the greens, paced and recorded the distances and analysed how he would play each hole in different weather conditions. He guessed that he played more than 150 holes in practice.

Consistency was the result. In the 1965 US Open at St Louis, he shot 70, 70, 71, 71. With 3 holes to go, he led the

Australian, Kel Nagle, by 3 shots. But mistakes by Player at the 16th, and a birdie by Nagle at the 17th, equalled the scores – both made par at the 18th for 282s. Next day in the play-off, Player shot another 71 to Nagle's 74.

The South African won all over the world in 1968. But it was after his success in the Open at Carnoustie that he declared: 'This is the best I've ever played, and on the hardest course there is.' His 1-over par 289 was 2 strokes better than the New Zealander Bob Charles and Jack Nicklaus.

◄ **Arnold Palmer beat Player in the semi-final of the 1964 World Matchplay, though Player won the title a record five times – 1965, 1966, 1968, 1971 and 1973.**

▲ Commitment to physical fitness is central to Player's golf philosophy. Here he shows the strength of his fingers to son Wayne and fellow pro Hal Sutton. It's a very difficult exercise.

PLAYER FACTFILE

Name: Gary Jim Player
Born: 1 November 1935, Johannesburg, South Africa
Height: 5ft 7in (1.7m)
Weight: 10st 10lb (68kg)
Family: Wife Vivienne; children Jennifer, Mark, Wayne, Michelle, Theresa, Amanda
Interests: Breeding horses
Turned pro: 1952
Pro wins (US Tour): 21
Pro wins (US Seniors'): 17
Major wins: Open Championship 1959, 1968, 1974; US Masters 1961, 1974, 1978; US Open 1965; USPGA 1962, 1972
Dunhill Cup: 1991
Other: Winner of World Matchplay Championship 1965, 1966, 1968, 1971, 1973; several wins on US Senior Tour including PGA Seniors 1986, 1988; US Senior Open 1987, 1988; 1987 Senior TPC; 1988, 1990 Seniors British Open

Strong faith

Gary Player has always been a fervent Christian, and his faith has led to some memorable sayings. One early prophecy was: 'I will win all four of the Major Championships. I have been given a message by God.'

▼ When Gary's family were younger, he sometimes took them abroad with him 'to show them how the rest of the world lives'. They enjoyed relaxing together during the 1971 Open at Birkdale.

▲ Despite his mental and physical toughness, Gary Player does sometimes need help in seeing how his ball is lying. Here his caddie is only too willing to offer assistance.

OLDEST MASTER

The final Masters win, in 1978, was one of Player's most determined successes. In the fourth round he shot a back 9 of 30, to equal the course record of 64 and win him his last Major by a stroke.

Gary said after his win that he would still be winning in the 1980s and this has come true. Three weeks after he became eligible, at 50, to play the Senior tour, he entered his first event. This was the Quadel Classic, in Florida, and he won by 3 shots. He is still winning in the 1990s.

Sam Snead

Nobody plays golf like Slammin' Sam – his natural grace and impeccable rhythm and timing make his swing one of the best the world has ever known.

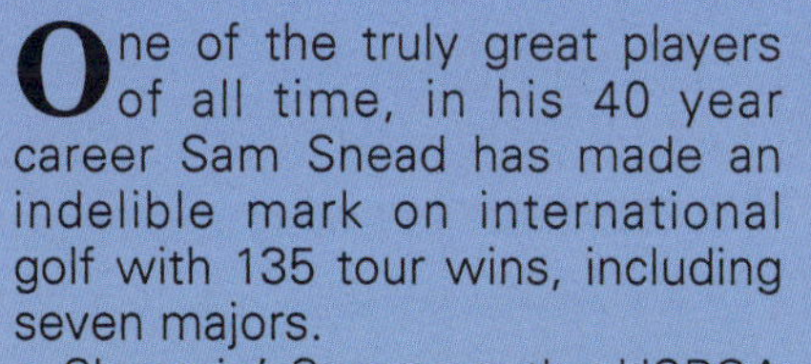

One of the truly great players of all time, in his 40 year career Sam Snead has made an indelible mark on international golf with 135 tour wins, including seven majors.

Slammin' Sam won the USPGA and the US Masters three times each and the Open Championship once. Although he was not a frequent visitor to Britain, Snead caused a stir in 1946 with a sensa-

▼ Demonstrating a unique putting stance, Snead strokes the ball firmly towards the hole. Putting problems dogged part of Sam Snead's long career. He refused to let them destroy his determination and experimented with various grips and stances, including putting side-saddle.

tional win at St Andrews. Going into the last round tied for first place, he battled through high winds to win by 4 strokes.

To his eternal disappointment this gifted golfer has never won the US Open. He was second four times, third once and fifth once.

The nearest Snead came to a US Open title was in 1939 when he came down the par 5 18th at Philadephia needing a birdie to win. But he took a disastrous 8 and lost to Byron Nelson.

SELF MADE MAN

Brought up in a poor family, Sam developed an interest in golf by picking up balls hit by brother Homer. Using a club he made from swamp maple, young Sam developed the ability to hit the ball long distances.

Snead was entirely self taught. In those early years he concentrated on making the clubhead follow as wide an arc as he could. It was this action that later gave him the nickname Slammin' Sam.

In his early days Snead's main problem was hitting the ball too low and

▲ Slammin' Sam shows perfect poise and balance while he follows the flight of the ball towards the hole. Playing at Wentworth for the 1953 Ryder Cup, Snead helped the US win the Cup.

Determined youngster
Although Sam grew to be a strong healthy man, he was a frail youngster. His attempts at caddying ended when he fainted after carrying a bag of clubs 18 holes for 50 cents. Another time he suffered frostbite after carrying a bag for 9 holes in bare feet in the snow.

► Charming the crowds at Augusta before the 1987 US Masters, Snead proves why he is considered one of the best players of all time. Well into his 70s, Sam remains supple and his swing as smooth and rhythmical as it was in his heyday.

occasionally producing a quick hook. He soon learned to weaken his grip and reduce grip pressure – this released the tension and made the swing much smoother. Although his 300yd (274m) drives seized the attention, Sam's pitching, long iron play and bunker shots were all superb.

BIG IMPACT

Snead's clubs were begged or borrowed until he was given a contract by Dunlop. In 1936 – the year before he went on the tour, such as it was, full time – Snead was paired with Sarazen in the third round of the Hershey Open.

Afterwards Sarazen remarked, 'I've just watched a kid who doesn't know anything about playing golf, and I don't want to be around when he learns how.'

Snead learned how by himself. His idea was to work on his game until his swing felt right. He believes that if he had worried overly about the more intricate mechanics of the game he would never have risen from the ranks.

The Snead theory is that if, for example, you want to pick up a pencil, you don't say to yourself, 'Elbow, bend. Fingers, contract.' You just pick up the pencil.

▲ Wearing the hat that became his trademark Sam Snead plays with authority out of a bunker. He keeps the clubface open and splashes the ball high out of the sand.

Instinctive play

Sam Snead gave Freddie Gleims – the professional where he worked in a pro shop – much of the credit for making him critic proof. In a tournament early in his career, Snead shot 68 in the first round and was leading by three when Gleims made a comment about Sam's flying right elbow. Trying to keep it in, Snead shot 80 and finished third. After that, critics soon melted away when Snead offered his standard challenge of a game with them.

▲ **Snead attacks a grassy lie on the lip, demonstrating greenside sand skill before the 1953 Ryder Cup. He breaks his wrists early to chop steeply into the back of the ball – this increases clubhead speed so that the ball travels high but not far to land softly on the green.**

And if you want the clubhead to follow a nice wide arc, you just swing it that way – the rest of the body will do what it needs to do, providing the grip and the stance are right.

Snead was a naturally gifted player, so his theory suited him. Many of today's top pros don't jeopardize a natural flow or instinctive feel for the game – but they all put in plenty of time on the practice ground.

In 1937 – his first full year on the US Tour – Snead won four events, more than any other player. The following year he won seven times and topped the money list with $19,534.

YIP ATTACK

Towards the end of 1946 Snead developed terrible putting yips. In the Los Angeles Open the following year he set a 36 hole record for the tournament with successive 69s but then the yips took over. He three putted the 14th in the third round from less than 2ft (60cm).

Snead tried various putting methods in search of a cure. After three years of problems he found a putter with a central shaft – he used this croquet style with much success in 1949, when he was named PGA Golfer of the Year.

Slammin' Sam would be included on everyone's best ever top ten list. A reserved but single minded character, for 40 years he produced some of the most magnificent golf ever to grace a course. Though approaching his 80th year Snead still delights crowds today, when he opens the US Masters with a 9 hole match against Gene Sarazen and Byron Nelson.

SNEAD FILE

Name: Samuel Jackson Snead
Born: 27 May 1912; Virginia
Family: Wife Audrey, children Sam and Terrance
Turned professional: 1934
Major wins: 1942 – USPGA Championship
1946 – Open Championship
1949 – USPGA Championship, US Masters
1951 – USPGA Championship
1952 – US Masters
1954 – US Masters
US PGA Seniors' Champion: 1964, 1965, 1967, 1970, 1972, 1973
Team member: Ryder Cup – 1937, 1947, 1949, 1951, 1953, 1955, Captain 1959, 1969 (non playing Captain) Won 10, lost 2, halved 1
World Cup – 1956, 1957, 1959, 1960, 1961, 1962

pro tip

Build your rhythm
Spend time developing a good rhythmical action. Swinging fast and hitting hard won't do you any good on the golf course. If you have a sense of timing and tempo you'll find it easy to repeat your swing.

Throughout Snead's long career he used the same unhurried action from driver to short iron. This much admired fluency paid off for Slammin' Sam – not only did he win an astonishing 135 tournaments, he's also the tour's oldest winner. In 1965, he won the Greensboro Open at the age of 52. This golfing great is still adopting the same technique in his late 70s.

Payne Stewart

Payne Stewart is the smartest dresser on the world's fairways, and now he is also one of the best players. A consistent money-winner, he had to wait until 1989 for his first Major.

Several course records and brilliant low scoring marked Payne Stewart as a player to watch in the 1980s. In 1989, he swept to the USPGA Championship to confirm his potential as a Major winner. Now, he is a leading Majors winner in the 1990s.

Some great players find major victories keep slipping through their grasp. At one time Payne Stewart was just such a player. When commentators debated who was golf's most famous bridesmaid in the 1980s, the names of Payne Stewart and Tom Kite usually came out on top.

Stewart's fellow pros didn't doubt the Missouri-born golfer's claim to the title. They even nicknamed Stewart 'Avis' (second in the US car-hire market) because he finished in the runner-up spot so often. His fame was due mainly to gaudy shirts and plus-fours.

At least Kite won events regularly, fellow players reasoned, although he did miss out on countless majors. Stewart had trouble even with tour victories. Before the 1989 season he had won nearly $3 million – but had registered just three first places. Stewart was reckoned to be a talented player

◄ Stylish Payne Stewart, who beat Scott Simpson (75-77) at Hazeltine National to win the 1991 US open.

▼ This positive style of recovery helped Stewart to a 3 and 2 win over Mark James in the 1993 Ryder Cup at The Belfry.

Top scorer
Stewart is not afraid to score well. That might sound odd, but many players become protective when they start stringing a few birdies together.

Stewart has never been like that. He wants more, and always finishes among the leaders in the tour statistics for birdies, eagles and low scoring. He is consistent too. Since 1981, he has won over $6 million on the US Tour alone.

who struggled to cope under the severest pressure.

Stewart became crisp whenever anybody mentioned the subject. 'I know how to win tournaments whether people believe it or not,' he used to say. Finally, in 1989, Stewart was as good as his word. In that year 'Avis' became a champion at last. He could now be recognized for reasons other than his dress.

BEATING THE BEST

There was a US Tour victory in April in the Heritage Classic. But Stewart's big moment came at the fourth Major of the year, the USPGA Championship.

Players such as Stewart, who win a great deal of money, are judged on how they perform in these majors. This is why his success at Kemper Lakes, Chicago, was so important. At last Payne Stewart had made it to the major league. How he did so was memorable.

From the second day to the 70th hole, the tournament was Mike Reid's. The quiet, bespectacled American looked nerveless as he holed the putts that mattered. Thunderstorms raged around Chicago and caused suspensions of play – but nothing distracted Reid.

Only Payne Stewart put Reid under pressure. It was ironic – the player who once looked suspect in such situations was now the strong one.

At the 9th hole, one of his friends asked him what it would take to win the title. Stewart replied that he would have to come home in 31 strokes if he was to stand any chance. Always a tough score for 9 holes, it was even more daunting at Kemper Lakes, Chicago, which has water everywhere.

CHARGING FROM THE PACK

It says much for Stewart's talent that he managed to do exactly what he said. In particular, he sank a tricky 10ft (3m) putt on the 18th for his fifth birdie in just 7 holes. The man from Missouri sat in the clubhouse with a 12 under par total of 276.

Yet it didn't look enough, as Mike Reid was still playing so well. Then Reid finished bogey, double bogey, par – and Stewart had won by one shot.

In his hour of glory, he remembered

► A leap of delight confirms a birdie at the 17th for Stewart in the second round of the 1989 Open. He went on to break the course record with a 65 – which was broken again by Greg Norman's 64 on the last day of the Championship.

Showing the colours
Payne Stewart's clothes are his most noticeable feature. He has been wearing plus-fours – strictly speaking they're plus-twos – since 1982.

In 1989, he signed a three-year contract worth $600,000 a year with the National Football League. Now he wears the colours of the local American football team in whatever city he happens to be playing in.

the loser – Stewart had been there too many times himself to do otherwise. 'Believe me I know how Mike feels. I have messed up a few tournaments in my time. But this makes it all worthwhile. I knew I had what it takes.'

STYLISH APPROACH

Despite his recent success, Stewart is not appreciated everywhere, partly because of his appearance.

He started to wear plus-fours in 1982, after he won his first US professional title, the Quad Cities Open. He said: 'I knew that if I could look different and play well, then I would really have something.'

And Stewart did look different. Instead of the traditional dour greys and blacks, he wore bold colours or pastels. He chewed gum as well.

Despite his showy appearance, Payne Stewart is one of the game's most sincere characters. He is honest to a fault – and generous with it.

In 1987, 'Avis' won the Hertz Bay Hill Classic, his first triumph in four years. He clutched the trophy gratefully, but the money never reached his pocket. He donated his winnings – all $108,000 of it – to a Florida hospital. This was in memory of his father, who had died of cancer.

William Stewart was the reason his son became involved in the game. 'I owe him everything,' said Payne, who won a golf scholarship to Southern Methodist University. While there he established himself as a potential star.

He won collegiate events and turned professional in 1979. Many people predicted a bright career, but things started shakily. Stewart failed to secure his card for the US Tour at the qualifying school. He decided to play the Asian Tour for two years – and it proved the

◄ A consistent money-winner, Stewart lifted over $6 million on the US Tour up to the start of 1994.

▼ The lightning-fast greens of Augusta are relished by players of Payne Stewart's quality. He is an aggressive golfer who likes to keep attacking the pin throughout a round, rather than defending a good score.

making of him. Returning to the USA two years wiser in 1981, he earned his card.

His first trophy followed a year later, as did another in 1983. Then his career seemed to stand still. Stewart picked up vast winnings, always finishing in the top 20 in the money list. But the victories dried up. Often, he moved into a position to win, only to fail each time.

SO NEAR BUT SO FAR

He nearly won the British Open in 1985 – but was pipped by Sandy Lyle. Stewart finished runner-up, an agonizing single stroke behind. His final round 68 was the best score of the day but the damage had been done in the second round. Playing in terrible conditions, Stewart had taken 75.

Stewart should have won the US Open. He was leading with 6 holes to play. Then he fluffed a chip and missed a couple of putts. Raymond Floyd, playing with Stewart, walked off with the trophy.

Sweet revenge came in 1991 when he tied Scott Simpson at 6 under par 282 on tough Hazeltine National and then won the 18 holes play-off the next day by two shots with 75.

▲ Stewart swings in a tranquil moment at the 1988 US Masters, but it turned out to be Sandy Lyle's year. It wasn't Stewart's best event of that season – he finished 25th.

▼ A birdie putt on the 18th drops to give Stewart a last round 67 and the 1989 USPGA title. After years of frustration he proved he had the temperament to beat the best.

STEWART FACTFILE

Name: William Payne Stewart
Born: 30 January 1957, Springfield, Missouri, USA
Height: 6ft 1in (1.84m)
Weight: 170lb (77kg)
Family: Wife Tracey Ferguson; children Chelsea (1985) and Aaron (1989)
Turned pro: 1979
First pro win (US Tour): 1982 Quad Cities Open
Pro wins (US Tour): 1982 Quad Cities Open; 1983 Walt Disney Open; 1987 Bay Hill Classic; 1989 Heritage Classic, USPGA Championship; 1990 Byron Nelson Classic, MCI Heritage Classic; 1991 US Open
Played Ryder Cup: 1987-91 and 1993. Won 8, lost 7, halved 1
Money list (US Tour):

Year	Position	Winnings($)
1981	157	13,400
1982	38	98,686
1983	25	178,809
1984	11	288,795
1985	19	225,729
1986	3	535,389
1987	12	511,026
1988	14	553,570
1989	2	1,201,301
1990	3	976,261
1991	31	476,971
1992	44	334,738
1993	6	982,875

▲ **Wearing team uniform, Stewart was deprived of his plus-fours for the 1987 Ryder Cup and looked unfamiliar throughout the contest. He has been allowed to wear them since.**

Stewart was clearly disappointed – but he was also defiant. 'Raymond has not seen the Taj Mahal, the Great Wall of China – or the last of me,' he warned.

He was right. Stewart's USPGA triumph assured him a place in the 1989 Ryder Cup side, of which Raymond Floyd was the captain.

He has also been in the winning teams of 1991, the 'War on the Shore' at Kiawah, winning 2 of his 3 matches in partnership with Mark Calcavecchia, and of 1993 at The Belfry where he won twice with Ray Floyd and then beat Mark James by 3 and 2 in a critical singles – point proven.

▼ **The USPGA Championship organizers have made no mistake with their labelling, as Tracey Ferguson, Stewart's wife, joins in the 1989 victory celebrations.**

Curtis Strange

Curtis Strange has earned the reputation of being a hard man who can defend a lead. He had many successful years without a big win before he made his breakthrough in the 1988 US Open.

When he retained his US Open title in 1989, Curtis Strange became the first player to achieve the feat since Ben Hogan in 1951.

▶ Although not one of the longest hitters in golf, Strange's consistently accurate driving is a hallmark of his game. While other players drive for distance, Strange's main concern is hitting the fairway.

The Strange swing
Curtis Strange's swing is technically faulty, because he has a pronounced sway away from and back to the ball. However, he keeps perfect balance throughout and his position through impact is ideal, with the left side in control. He aims to fade all his long shots.

▼ In the second round of the 1987 Dunhill Cup, Strange brought the home of golf to its knees. He shot a 10 under par 62 to better the St Andrews course record of 63 – which had been set just two days before by Australian Rodger Davis.

The great Walter Hagen once said that any good player could get lucky one week and win a national Open. But it took a great player to win two. When Curtis Strange won the 1989 US Open, he did more than that – he became the first player since Ben Hogan in 1951 to win the title for the second year in a row.

In the mid-to-late 1980s, many people in the USA called Strange the new world superstar, mainly because of his money-winning feats. The rest of the world saw no truth in this claim. Strange had not performed well outside the USA, and he had attracted most attention for losing a good lead in the 1985 US Masters. On that disastrous day, he sent 2 shots into water over the last 9 holes.

RECIPE FOR SUCCESS

However, Strange's 1989 performance at Oak Hill, New York, contained most of the ingredients to establish him as one of the world's finest players.

He came to the Championship without a win on the US Tour in 1989, but his confidence came back when he scored a 64 in the second round, 3 strokes better than anyone else managed that day. In the third round, play was very slow and Strange had 3 bogeys with no birdies. Going into the final round 3 strokes off the lead, it looked as if he would have to shoot a very low score to stand a chance.

It didn't work out like that. Strange won because he played steady golf – level par – while others, especially Tom Kite, let their chances drift away. As disasters happened to others on the course, Strange found himself with a 1-stroke lead on the 14th hole.

However, to know you have 'only' to par your way home to win is far more testing on the nerves than having to go for your shots to stand a chance. Strange's hard-man reputation was tested straightaway.

At the 15th, he had to hole a putt of 6ft (1.8m) to save par. At the next,

▼ Wife Sarah takes a keen interest in golf and watching her husband play is particularly important to her. She was on hand to see his US Open victories at Brookline and Oak Hill.

▼ His magnificent short game helped Strange to four tournament wins on the US Tour in 1988 alone. It helped him to gain top position in the money list for the third time.

▼ In the memorable tied contest for the 1989 Ryder Cup, winning his single against Ian Woosnam was Strange's only success. Strange and Paul Azinger were defeated by Sam Torrance and Gordon Brand jnr in the fourballs.

Strange gave himself room for error when he holed a good putt for birdie to go 2 shots into the lead.

Playing the last hole, he knew a bogey 5 would win the Championship – and he did just that. On the green in regulation (2 strokes), Strange used up 3 putts simply because he was making certain he didn't take 4. He wasn't interested in dramatics, just in getting the job done.

AMATEUR HIGHLIGHTS

Strange was always likely to be a huge success in professional golf. Winning at the highest level in amateur golf usually means that a player has both the skill and the nerve. Strange was college player of the year, took several regional US titles and represented the USA in both the World Amateur Team Championship and the Walker Cup.

However, success as a pro didn't come quickly or easily, as it did for Faldo and Lyle in Europe or Norman in Australia. Strange seems to have felt that tournament golf asked for something different of a player. As a result, he reckons it took him about three years before he was playing as well as during his amateur days.

The lean times came to an end when Strange won the last event of the 1979 Tour, the Pensacola Open. Since then, he has never looked back. In 1980, he earned the title 'most improved golfer', won twice and had a string of high finishes.

MONEY MAN

His reputation for consistency was to become a problem. Strange settled into a pattern of high finishes, high earnings – and no victories. In 1982, his $263,378 set a money-winning record for a player who had failed to win a tournament during the season.

Although Strange did pick up a tournament in each of the next two years, it

▼ Curtis Strange challenged strongly for the 1989 US PGA Championship, played at Kemper Lakes, Chicago, and finished joint second, behind Payne Stewart.

▲ **Rae's Creek, on the 13th fairway at Augusta, ended Strange's hopes of winning the 1985 US Masters. After playing his ball into the water, he failed to escape at the first attempt.**

was not until 1985 that he did enough to be recognized as a man whose hour had come.

For a start, Strange was leading money-winner on the US Tour. He also came close to winning his first Major – and in remarkable fashion.

He began the 1985 US Masters with an uninspiring 80, making him unlikely to beat the cut, let alone challenge for the title. Far from missing the cut, he shot a 65 to be only 5 behind the leaders. After a third-round 68, he moved up to Raymond Floyd's shoulder, 1 behind.

On the final day, Augusta's infamous back 9 holes finished off Curtis Strange. At the 13th, with a 2-shot lead, he had to decide whether to play safely short of Rae's Creek, or go for the pin. Knowing that 2 shots can change hands in moments, Strange went for the green. His ball finished in the water and he took a 6.

Much the same thing happened at the 15th. Again he went for the green and again he found water. Another 6 went down on the card, and with it the Masters – into the willing hands of Bernhard Langer.

▲ **Strange shares a joke with 1976 US Open Champion Jerry Pate, now a TV commentator for a US network. The two go back a long way, as they played together in the 1975 Walker Cup team.**

Despite the Masters reversal, Strange had far and away his best year to that date, with three Tour wins and record winnings of $542,321.

BROOKLINE BRILLIANCE

Curtis Strange topped the money list in both 1987 and 1988. In terms of his golf, it was far more important that the US Open at Brookline was one of his four wins in 1988.

He began quietly with a 72, but a second round of 67 put him 2 behind the leader. A 68 to follow gave him a

FACTS AND FIGURES
Name: Curtis Northrup Strange
Born: 30 January 1955, Norfolk, Virginia, USA
Height: 5ft 11in (1.8m)
Weight: 170lb (77kg)
Interests: Fishing, hunting
Family: Wife Sarah; children Thomas, David
Amateur career: 1974 College Player of the Year, 1974 World Amateur Team Championships; 1975 Walker Cup team
Turned pro: 1976
First pro win: 1979 Pensacola Open
US Tour wins: 17
Major wins: US Open 1988, 1989
Order of Merit (USA):

Year	Position	Winnings($)
1977	87	28,144
1978	88	29,346
1979	21	138,368
1980	3	271,888
1981	9	201,513
1982	10	263,378
1983	21	200,116
1984	14	276,773
1985	1	542,321
1986	32	237,700
1987	1	925,941
1988	1	1,147,644
1989	7	752,587
1990	53	277,172
1991	48	336,333
1992	99	150,639
1993	63	262,697

1-stroke lead into the final round. However, early bogeys meant that Nick Faldo, with whom he was playing, took over the lead for a while. They came to the last level.

Here, Faldo put his second shot on the right fringe of the green. Strange was bunkered, just short of the flag. It was a straightforward splash shot and Strange made no mistake, laying the ball 4ft (1.2m) from the hole. Faldo also got down in two shots, which meant an 18-hole play-off the next day.

Strange took a 1-stroke lead at the 3rd and gradually pulled away to win comfortably, with a 71 to Faldo's 75. The difference between the two that day was in putting – Strange was better through the green. His first-round 72 included just 22 putts, and over the first 9 holes of the play-off he needed his putter just 11 times. 'The Grinder' had his Major – as well as a reputation as the least likely player in the world to throw away a winning hand.

▲ In the play-off for the 1988 US Open, Curtis Strange needed only a steady 71 to beat Faldo's 75. After 4 rounds, they had tied on 278.

▼ When he holed out to claim the 1988 US Open trophy, Strange could reflect that he had won because his putting was better than Nick Faldo's for that round.

Lee Trevino

The classic rags-to-riches story of Lee Trevino is the stuff of which dreams are made. His career forms one of the most fascinating – and successful – stories in the history of the game.

Lee Trevino was born the illegitimate son of a Mexican gravedigger in Dallas, Texas. He grew up in extreme poverty, in a shanty town on the outskirts of the city. Racial prejudice and bigotry were an everyday part of his life.

But this harsh background was crucial to his eventual success. Poverty and prejudice gave him the hunger and drive to do well and prove himself. Like many players before him, Trevino's first involvement with golf was in trying to earn a few extra dollars as a caddie.

He left school early, and when he was old enough he joined the United States Marines. It was there he began to play golf seriously – although his standard was not very high. Fellow-Marine Orville Moody, who went on to win the 1969 US Open, was always able to beat Trevino. However, he never did anywhere near as well as Trevino in his overall professional record.

THIRSTY WORK

When he left the Marines, Trevino worked on a course and driving range in El Paso, Texas. It was here he developed one of the most unusual swings in the business as he decided what would work most efficiently for him.

It was also the schooling ground where Trevino learnt about the real meaning of pressure when he began to play games for more money than he possessed. He later talked about the tension of these contests saying: 'Pressure is playing for $100 when you've only got $10 in your pocket'.

Despite the tension and stress,

▶ The Mexican-American with the odd swing drew scorn from some in his early days – but a quarter of a century and six Majors later, he is a confirmed golfing legend.

he had huge confidence in his method. He played challenge matches using a taped fruit drink bottle as a club baseball-style and still won.

These venues for his dare-devil gambles were a far cry from the beautifully kept country clubs which played host to the touring professionals every week. Lee knew he had to play against these well turned-out golfers to realize his true worth in his profession. The spur to his ambition came when he qualified for the 1966 US Open held in San Francisco – and won $600. It was enough to encourage him to have another go a year later.

ANGLING FOR SUCCESS

It was a long way from El Paso to Baltusrol, New Jersey, where the 1967 US Open was to be played. Trevino's wife entered him for the event and had to dip into her savings to make the trip – but her faith was justified when Lee finished fifth.

He went on to win $26,000 in 1967 and

▲ ► The 1984 US PGA Championship at Shoal Creek was Trevino's sixth Major win. At the age of 44, he shot four rounds in the 60s to edge out Gary Player and Lanny Wadkins.

Tee party
If you're looking for Lee Trevino on a golf course, he normally wears a peaked cap which carries his distinctive sombrero design on the front. His highly individual swing is instantly recognizable and he usually entertains a large crowd with his banter. If you hear laughter on the course, the chances are that Trevino is not far away. Nowadays he is full time on the US Seniors' circuit – and with huge success.

was named Rookie of the Year. That was good money for those days, but it wasn't enough to cause ripples in the great pond of the US Tour – the big fish were Arnold Palmer and Jack Nicklaus.

Good results proved to Trevino that his swing, although not beautiful, was effective. His grip with the left hand was very strong. It showed three knuckles and, at the top of the backswing, the clubface was closed.

By rights, Trevino should have hooked every shot violently to the left. But he compensated by standing very open, picking the club up sharply on the backswing and driving strongly with his legs on the downswing.

Trevino became a master at controlling and flighting the ball. Every shot had a gentle fade. He used this extended push through the ball with his left hand all the time – even when putting. His control of the ball made him an ideal candidate for the tough, narrow courses normally used for the US Open.

FUNNY MAN

Lee Trevino was still unknown when he arrived at Oak Hill, Rochester, New York for the 1968 US Open. The Mexican-American with the funny swing still wasn't seen as a threat when he was only a stroke off the lead after three rounds. When he stormed to victory he became the first player to break 70 in all four rounds of the Championship. His score of 275, a 4-stroke margin over Jack Niklaus, tied the Championship record – set by Nicklaus the year before.

Trevino had crashed into the big league and the character everyone now recognizes began to emerge. The Mexican became the wise-cracking joker of the links. He gave out a constant stream of banter before every shot and the galleries loved it.

SLIPPERY CUSTOMER

Other pros were not so delighted by 'Supermex', as he came to be known. Tony Jacklin once told Trevino that he

◀ In a historic three-week period in 1971, Trevino won the US Open, Canadian Open and British Open – a feat which nobody else has achieved before or since.

▼ Trevino plays the par-3 3rd hole at Woburn on the way to victory at the 1985 Dunhill British Masters, a well-earned victory for the golfing master.

▲ Despite the on-course jokes and chatter, Trevino is a very private man. Away from the golfing world, he and his wife Claudia enjoy a quiet life.

▲ Augusta's layout is not suited to Trevino's natural fade and he has never challenged seriously for the US Masters. However, some of the old Trevino magic was on view when he topped the leaderboard after the first round in 1989.

▼ Lee enjoys sinking a putt at Troon's 18th during a fine first round at the 1989 Open. He loves the Championship – and links courses in general – and once quipped, 'I'll always play in the British Open – even if I have to swim across'.

Dry humour
In the 1960s, Trevino practised constantly, tuning his unique swing on the Texas driving range where he worked. His endless practice led to divorce. But even marital discord provided a topic for wise-cracking Lee and he delivered a memorable quip on the subject of the women in his life: 'My second wife's name is Claudia, the same as my first. I married her so I didn't have to change the monogrammed towels in the bathroom.'

◀ In 1985, the Supermex spell did not work for once, when he captained the US Ryder Cup side. He was caught napping by European captain Tony Jacklin and the USA surrendered the trophy for the first time in 28 years.

▼ Trevino's uncanny accuracy makes his game suitable for the tough, narrow courses used for the US Majors. In the 1984 US PGA at Shoal Creek he saw his way through the trees and went on to win the title.

did not want to talk during a round. 'You don't have to talk,' said Trevino cheerfully, 'just listen'. Jack Nicklaus was diplomatic about one incident just before the play-off for the 1971 US Open. Trevino produced a rubber snake on the 1st tee – and took the bite out of Nicklaus' game with a 3-stroke win.

No one could keep Trevino down during 1971. In a three-week spell, he won that US Open, the Canadian Open and the Open Championship at Royal Birkdale. He showed his mastery over British links courses, flighting the ball under the wind and conjuring neat little chip and run shots. People who had laughed at his swing were forced to think again. He was a breath of fresh air on a sometimes dour professional scene.

In 1972, the British public's appreciation of the Merry Mex was a little stretched. Two fluked chips and a holed bunker shot let him snatch The Open at Muirfield from under the nose of home favourite, Tony Jacklin. 'God is a Mexican,' Trevino declared, as the golfing world shook its head in disbelief.

ELECTRIC PERFORMANCES

Another Major win followed in 1974, when he captured the US PGA Championship. But his luck nearly ran out for good in 1975. During the Western Open in Chicago, he was struck by lightning – and he has suffered from back problems ever since.

Other strokes of misfortune followed when, after making some unwise business deals, Trevino lost most of the fortune he had collected around the world. But with true grit and determination he set out to earn another. In 1980

TREVINO FACTFILE
Name: Lee Buck Trevino
Born: 1 December 1939, Dallas, Texas
Height: 5ft 7in (1.69m)
Weight: 180lb (81kg)
Interests: Fishing
First pro win: 1968 US Open
US Tour wins (to 1989): 27
International wins: 1974 World Series of Golf; 1977 Moroccan Grand Prix; 1978 Benson and Hedges International, Lancôme Trophy; 1985 Dunhill British Masters
Major wins: 1968 US Open; 1971 US Open, British Open; 1972 British Open; 1974 US PGA; 1984 US PGA
Career winnings US Tour: $3,478,450
US Seniors' Tour: $3,868,533

Twenty great days
In June-July 1971, Trevino had the 20 most successful days in the history of golf. After his 68 to Nicklaus' 71 in the play-off for the 1971 US Open, Trevino headed north for the Canadian Open. He won after another play-off, this time dispatching Art Wall jnr at the 1st extra hole. After the prizegiving, he rushed away from Montreal to catch a plane to the British Open, with the words, 'Tell England Supermex is on his way' – he won at Royal Birkdale by a stroke on the 10th of July.

alone, he won nearly $400,000. In 1984, he won another Major, his second US PGA title.

A truly international player whose game travels well, Trevino is as popular in Sydney as he is in Sandwich. He uses jokes and chatter to relieve the pressures of tournament play. But once he decides the shot he switches off the comedy and concentrates on the matter in hand.

There are two sides to Lee Trevino. Off the course, the public nature of the joker in the pack vanishes. He is rarely seen socializing with other players in bars or restaurants. He just disappears. Keeping up the Merry Mex image all the time is too much of a strain even for the man who created it.

Nobody doubts his generosity of action and word. When he won the 1968 Hawaiian Open Trevino immediately donated $10,000 to the family of a former room mate who had died in a surfing tragedy.

▲ Since joining the Seniors' (over50s) Tour in 1989, Trevino has won more money than he did on the regular Tour in 22 years.

Tom Watson

It is rare for a golfer to be recognized as the best in the world by public, press and players alike. Tom Watson enjoyed that status from 1977 to 1984.

In 1977, Tom Watson was leading money-winner on the US Tour for the first time. He also had two other firsts which were even more important. In April, he won his first Masters and at Turnberry in July he took the Open.

In both tournaments Watson edged out Jack Nicklaus, the undisputed world number one at the time.

Soon, Seve Ballesteros became a clear rival to Watson's dominance. Yet when the Spaniard made his short victory speech at the 1984 Open at St Andrews, he declared that he was proud to have beaten 'the best player in the world, Tom Watson'.

LICKING THE LINKS

Watson came into the 1984 Open Championship as five-times winner, and holder of the title in the previous two years. He was also well on the way to becoming leading US Tour money-winner for the fifth time. However, in that defeat were perhaps the seeds of decline – and it certainly contained the most destructive shot he ever hit.

Tom Watson had fallen in love with British links golf. He used to come over early for the Open Championship and play such

Success in golf did not come quickly for the great Tom Watson. He joined the US Tour in 1971, after managing little of note in the amateur game. His most important achievement up to then was a degree in psychology from Stanford University. Once his game took off, however, there was no stopping him.

▲ In 1987, Watson came close to winning his second US Open. Early in his career, he had been called a 'choker' in the Championship. Twice he had chances to win – in 1974 and 1975 – and twice he let his chance slip away.

courses as Ballybunion in Ireland or Dornoch in north-east Scotland, because they were 'what golf courses ought to be like'.

Privately, he didn't like the way the Open courses were being prepared, because he felt they were losing their traditional quality. Greens were relatively soft. Players could fly full approach shots at the flag.

Watson thought that the Open should present a different challenge, where players have to judge the weight of shot and how the ball will run on landing.

He had shown himself to be a supreme links player. In 1984, he wanted to join Harry Vardon as the only man to have won six Opens. He could also add the icing to the cake, by winning at the home of golf, St Andrews.

However, it was not to be Watson's year. With 2 holes to play on the final day, he was level with Ballesteros. The Spaniard got his blow in first when he managed a par 4 at the 17th, the notorious Road Hole, possibly the most difficult par 4 in the world.

Playing in the final pairing, Watson then took up the challenge with the best drive of the week from the 17th tee. He had taken a line dangerously close to the out of bounds, but now he had an ideal line to the green.

It looked like a play-off as Watson weighed up his shot. Unfortunately, the 2-iron shot he decided to play moved too much, and landed on the road behind the green. His ball finished tight up against a wall, leaving him with a very restricted backswing. The 5 he took was inevitable and, after a birdie 3 from Ballesteros at the 18th, the Championship was gone.

ROADBLOCK

No single shot can ruin a career, but Watson has not been the same man since the Road Hole disaster. The year after, his confident putting stroke disappeared, and in the next five years

▲ After losing his chance in the 1975 US Open, Watson was offered help by Byron Nelson, a former giant of the game. They forged a strong partnership. Watson's all-round game improved, while his swing under pressure became more reliable.

◀ A par at Birkdale's 18th was all Watson needed to tie up his fifth Open in 1983. After a brilliant 2-iron 2nd shot and a safe putt, he enjoyed sinking this short one for victory.

he won only once.

Watson did not qualify for the Ryder Cup in 1985, 1987 or 1989, though he was captain Raymond Floyd's personal choice for the US team in 1989. This reveals the respect he still commands.

If that 2-iron at St Andrews was a disastrous shot, Tom Watson has plenty of triumphant ones to remember. He hit an outstanding 2-iron at Royal Birkdale in the 1983 Open, in a year when he did not win at all on the US Tour.

In a closely fought battle with Hale Irwin and Andy Bean, Watson came to the very long par-4 18th, needing par to win by a stroke. His drive was long and straight, although he still had about 220yd (200m) to go. With the crowd surging around him, he hit a perfect second shot, with a slight draw to hold it against the wind. That was Watson's fifth Open Championship.

However, even more memorable was a much shorter shot during the final minutes of the 1982 US Open. Watson came to the 17th needing a par 3 and a par 5 on the last to tie Jack Nicklaus. The pressure was intense. Watson wanted a US Open on his record and had thrown away strong positions before, especially early on in his career.

WATSON HOMES IN

On this occasion, his 2-iron shot wasn't perfect and his ball finished off the green in thick semi-rough, not far from the pin. With the green running fast and sloping away from him, there was no real chance of stopping the ball close to the hole. Instead, Watson holed his chip, birdied the last for good measure and won by 2 strokes.

At Turnberry in 1977, a sequence of dramatic shots gave Watson his narrow margin over Nicklaus in the Open Championship. The win took him to the position of world number one.

Playing the 15th in the final round, Jack held a 1-stroke lead, and had a good birdie opportunity after his tee shot. Watson, on the other hand, was in light rough just short of the green, about 20yd (18m) from the hole. He decided to use his putter and, improbably, holed his shot.

Power and speed

Though neither tall nor obviously powerful, Tom Watson is a very long hitter indeed. He gets most of his length from his well muscled forearms.

Tom Watson is also one of the fastest players in golf. He weighs up his shot while approaching the ball. Then there might be a very quick consultation with his caddie about choice of club. Watson takes his stance, looks at the target a couple of times, and swings.

► At the 1982 US Open, Tom Watson played one of the most famous shots in golf history. Needing a par on each of Pebble Beach's last two holes to tie Jack Nicklaus, he birdied the 17th from off the green. He also birdied the 18th for good measure, to win by 2 shots.

▼ Having played in four Ryder Cups (1977-1989), Watson led the winning 1993 US team at The Belfry as inspiring non-playing Captain.

▲ Although he didn't qualify on merit, Tom Watson was selected by Ray Floyd for the 1989 US Ryder Cup team. Watson more than justified his inclusion – when it looked as if Europe were about to win, he defeated Scotland's Sam Torrance in the singles.

► The Open Championship at Turnberry in 1977 was one of the most exciting ever played. Tom Watson and Jack Nicklaus left the rest of the field behind them and matched each other almost shot for shot over the final 36 holes. Before a huge crowd, Watson won on the 72nd.

Open strike rate
Peter Thomson, James Braid, J H Taylor and Tom Watson have all won the Open Championship five times. However, with five wins in nine years, Watson achieved the feat in the shortest timespan.

Only Harry Vardon, with six wins, has won the title more often.

WATSON FACTFILE

Name: Thomas Sturges Watson
Born: 4 September 1949, Kansas City, Missouri, USA
Height: 5ft 9in (1.74m)
Weight: 160lb (72kg)
Family: Wife Linda; children Meg, Michael
Interests: Hunting, fishing, guitar, wine, golf history
Turned pro: 1971
First pro win: 1974 Western Open
Major wins: Open Championship 1975, 1977, 1980, 1982, 1983; US Open 1982; US Masters 1977, 1981

Order of Merit (USA):

Year	Position	Winnings($)
1971	224	2185
1972	79	31,081
1973	35	74,973
1974	10	135,474
1975	7	153,795
1976	12	138,202
1977	1	310,653
1978	1	362,429
1979	1	462,636
1980	1	530,808
1981	3	347,660
1982	5	316,483
1983	12	237,519
1984	1	476,260
1985	18	226,778
1986	20	278,338
1987	5	616,351
1988	39	273,216
1989	80	185,398
1990	68	213,988
1990	68	213,988
1991	45	354,877
1992	50	299,818
1993	46	342,023

▲ Watson's wife Linda has travelled the world's fairways with him, and enjoyed his success. They have two children.

▲ Watson says that he won many tournaments because others let their game desert them. He cites one example as the Open at Troon in 1982, when Nick Price, Bobby Clampett and Hale Irwin all had excellent chances to win.

It didn't settle the Open but, as Nicklaus missed his putt, it did make the scores level. The lead came on the 17th when Watson hit a good second shot.

Watson's safety strategy on the last was carried out to perfection. He cracked a long iron straight down the middle while Nicklaus carved a driver well to the right. Jack did manage to make the green with his second, but was a long way from the hole. Watson's own second shot was almost stone dead, 2ft (60cm) from the hole.

Miraculously, Nicklaus holed his long putt to draw level, but Watson was not to be denied. He rammed home his short putt to claim the claret jug.

TROON BOON

Usually, golfers win Majors without the sort of brilliance Watson and Nicklaus displayed at Turnberry. Watson has certainly won his share because others scattered strokes to the wind.

Carnoustie, 1975, was an example. With a few holes to play, at least half a dozen players were in with a chance. Watson won that Open because his nerve held the longest – he eventually beat Jack Newton in an 18-hole play-off the next day. Of Troon, 1982, he said: 'I didn't win this Championship. I had it given to me.'

Tom Watson had the quality which only the greatest players have – he could raise his game for the shots, rounds and tournaments which really matter.

In September 1989, he was 40. The great days may be over, but he has long earned his place as one of the supreme champions of golf history.

▼ Delighted by his victory at Pebble Beach in the 1982 US Open, Watson hugs his caddie. Watson's record in the Majors is similar to Arnold Palmer's. Both have an excellent record in 3 of the 4 Majors – but neither has ever won the USPGA title.

Ian Woosnam

He may not be tall but Ian Woosnam is a big hitter, big earner and big on ambition. However, there were many lean years before the dynamic Welshman matured into one of today's outstanding stars.

As a child, Ian Woosnam was devoted to sport of all kinds. He might have become a professional footballer or even a boxer – he won a few bouts at a holiday camp in the 1960s. Instead, he became a world-class golfer, and was close to £4 million in European earnings by the start of 1994.

He first hit a golf ball when he was seven, and at the age of 13 was playing to a 6 handicap. When he wasn't practising on his father's farm, Woosnam played out of the Llanymyech Club, where 15 holes are in Wales and the other three in England.

He reckons the course is a little like himself: 'I was born in St Martins near Oswestry, just inside the English border, but I regard myself as a Welshman through and through.'

At 16 years of age, Woosnam left school to start work in Albert Min-

▼ In 1987, Ian Woosnam became the first Briton to win the World Matchplay. He won it again in 1990.

▲ A smooth, easy style is typical of every Woosnam shot. Even when the little man can only just see the pin his accuracy from bunkers is remarkable.

▲ Woosnam plays regularly on the Australasian tour. He tied for ninth place in the 1988 Australian Masters.

shall's pro shop. This was at the Hill Valley Club, Whitchurch, near his home in Shropshire. Woosnam found the job too quiet. He joined the green staff – which allowed more time for playing.

Woosnam says that playing was the real way he improved his game. Getting round in fewer strokes taught him more than constant practice.

His professional career began in 1976. He set off for the players' school at Foxhills, in Surrey, and learnt his craft there. Woosnam joined the European tour in 1978, winning the unimpressive sum of £284. That made no impact on the Order of Merit (OoM).

His apprenticeship was long and hard, but not without its funny side. He borrowed his father's old camper van,

► When Woosnam is about to tee off, huge crowds assemble to witness the vast distances he hits the ball. Here he drives towards victory in the PGA Championship at Wentworth.

gave it a coat of blue paint, and set off with a couple of other young pros to make it in the tough world of tournament golf.

LEAN TIMES

The sad fact for many golfers is that if you don't qualify for the last two rounds of a tournament, you don't eat. On many occasions, Ian Woosnam didn't dine very well. 'I ate a rather monotonous diet of crisps, soup and endless cans of baked beans. We slept, ate and dried our clothes in that old van. It became a real home from home.'

Life at the bottom end of golf is not that much fun, despite the laughs. No one, Woosnam says, would endure that kind of discomfort for long unless he was determined to succeed. The Welshman was sure he would make it in the end.

He had a long way to go before the tide turned in his favour. The next year, 1979, saw an improvement in his position. He jumped to the dizzy heights of 122nd place in the OoM (£1049) – still not enough to make a living. He had to quit the Tour for a while to make ends meet. Woosnam took all sorts of jobs from barman to golf course tree planter.

In 1980 he made £3481. This lifted him to 87th place in the OoM. In 1981,

▲ Superstar status sits easily on Woosnam's shoulders. His 1991 Masters victory has been followed by the World Cup individual title for a second time.

Shropshire lads
Ian Woosnam and Sandy Lyle, two of today's great players, were born within 20 miles (32km) and three weeks of each other in 1958. In their early days, they played a great deal together in Shropshire. After a hammering one afternoon, Ian said to Sandy: 'I'll beat you one day, Sandy Lyle.' Back came the retort: 'You'll have to grow a bit, first.' When Woosnam did win, the stakes were high. The terrier beat the gentle giant by 1 hole in the final of the 1987 World Matchplay Championship at Wentworth. The two are great friends.

▲ A birdie at the 72nd meant that Woosnam finished second in the 1989 US Open, behind Curtis Strange. His performance helped to make his face one of the best-known on the US circuit.

◀ All of Woosnam's power was displayed during the breakthrough year of 1991 when he won the US Masters and the PGA Grand Slam.

his situation got worse. He slipped 17 places in the OoM, winning only £1884. Things were becoming desperate. Woosnam was ready to quit the Tour to become a club professional. 'I was going to apply for the pro's job at Oswestry Golf Club,' he said.

CHANGING ATTITUDES

He hung on, and in 1982 a chance meeting at the practice ground on the eve of the Nigerian Open changed his attitude. A fellow pro was spraying the ball everywhere – and something clicked in Woosnam's mind. Bad shots didn't bother the other pro. He was concerned with scoring well when it mattered – not with hitting the ball consistently straight on the practice ground.

This attitude changed Woosnam. He decided to adopt the oldest saying in the game: 'It's not how, but how many.'

Woosnam went out and finished third in the Safari Tour money list. This exempted him from the qualifying school for the European Tour. It was the start of the big time.

Everything slotted into place. He won the Cacharel Under-25 Championship and the Swiss Open. He was also second in the Italian Open and totalled £48,794 in prize money to finish eighth in the OoM. Woosnam was now able to marry his childhood girlfriend, Glendryth.

TOP OF THE TREE

As the years passed, his game – and his bank balance – prospered. The camper van was gone for ever, to be replaced by fast sports cars. Woosnam soared up the OoM to finish fourth in both 1985 and 1986. He made the Ryder Cup teams of 1983, 1985, 1987 and 1989.

1987 was a great year. He led the OoM at the end of the season to claim the coveted Harry Vardon Trophy, awarded to the leading money winner on the European Tour. He could at last claim to be the best golfer in Europe.

Woosnam still had to make good on the US circuit – partly because his chances to play there had been limited. In 1987, he was angry because he did not receive an invitation to the US Masters, in spite of finishing fourth in the previous year's European money list with winnings of over £148,000.

The Welshman does not mince words. He is forthrightly honest and can be aggressive. In 1988, he said of the US Players Championship that it was 'just another golf tournament'. And of the revered US Masters: 'If a Championship is worth the name, it needs the best players in the world. I won £1,000,000 last year. That's more than anyone else. We [the Europeans] play here for the money. In five years' time the money at home may be so good that we may not even bother coming over here.'

1989 may have changed his views. At Oak Hill, New York, he put in his best

▼ In November 1988, the first golf Ashes match – based on the cricket contest – was played at the Mirage Resort, Port Douglas, Queensland. Ian Woosnam was part of the British team which triumphed over Australia.

Simple style

One of the most refreshing aspects of Ian Woosnam's game is its simplicity. He wastes no time in getting on with the game, and is a quick mover between shots.

At set-up there are no flourishes. He takes a couple of practice swings, aims the club and aligns his body. He then takes the club back and unleashes smoothly controlled power, helped by the strength of his legs. He makes a full turn of the hips, delivering a wristy crack through the ball with strong forearms to a high, elegant finish.

His power is well disguised. He does not give the ball everything he's got – the method used by another small champion, Gary Player.

WOOSNAM FACTFILE

Name: Ian Harold Woosnam
Born: 2 March 1958, Oswestry, Wales
Height: 5ft 4 in (1.64m)
Weight: 11st 7lb (67kg)
Interests: Fishing, snooker, TV westerns
Family: Wife Glendryth; children Daniel (1985), Rebecca (1988) and Amy (1991)
Turned professional: 1976
Major win: US Masters 1991
Played Ryder Cup: 1983, 1985, 1987, 1989, 1991 and 1993. Won 12, lost 10, halved 4
World Cup: 1980, 1982, 1983, 1984, 1985, 1987 (Individual winner and team winner with David Llewellyn), 1988, 1989, 1990, 1991 (Individual winner), 1992, 1993
Dunhill Cup: 1985, 1986, 1988, 1989, 1990 and 1991
Order of Merit (Europe):

Year	Position	Winnings(£s)
1978	0	284
1979	122	1049
1980	87	3481
1981	104	1884
1982	8	48,794
1983	9	48,164
1984	6	68,126
1985	4	153,605
1986	4	148,467
1987	1	439,075
1988	4	270,674
1989	6	210,101
1990	1	574,166
1991	8	257,443
1992	11	447,573
1993	3	501,353

▼ Son Daniel enjoys the spoils of victory – in this case one of golf's most impressive prizes, the World Matchplay trophy at Wentworth.

US performance. Woosnam fought hard in the US Open, before being pushed into second place by Curtis Strange. The performance made his name in the US, ensuring invitations to more tournaments there. This put the misery of his poor early American forays behind him for good.

It was no surprise to anyone when he joined the immortals of golf with a thrilling victory in the 1991 Masters at Augusta. Past trials and tribulations behind him (he had shot 81 over Augusta in 1988), he scored level par 72 in the opening round, 66 and 67 in the following rounds and any doubts about his character under pressure were triumphantly buried as he slid home a tantalising eight-footer for a concluding 72 to pip José-Maria Olazabal.

▲ Popularly known as 'Woosie', the pocket-sized Welshman has played in the last 6 Ryder Cup matches, winning 4½ points from a possible 5 in 1993.

His new-found status in golf has eaned him a living beyond belief. Where once he used to tour in a Volkswagen caravanette, he now uses his own Cessna airplane to ferry him from his homes in Jersey and his native Shropshire.

4

WORLD OF GOLF

There are many fascinating aspects to the game of golf other than just playing. The exact origins of this wonderful game are unknown, but its history is enthralling nonetheless, and so is the way the equipment and courses have evolved.

Looking back, it is hard to understand how anyone actually made it round 18 holes given the soft balls, cumbersome wooden clubs and restrictive clothing worn by the players, but somehow they did. It is interesting to consider how they would have fared on some of the fearsome courses that modern-day archictects create.

Featured in this section is a brief history of the game, an insight into how a golf course is designed and built and information on some of the gifted men who have shaped the most famous layouts around the world. Their lives and designs are traced – from the classic pen of Dr Alister Mackenzie to the devilish draughtsmanship of American Pete Dye.

You can also take a look behind the scenes to find out what it takes to keep a golf course in tip-top condition, and peep into the day-to-day running of the European Tour to discover how and why it has grown over the years to become such a dominant force in world golf.

The famous Open Championship trophy.

Yesterday's golf

No one knows exactly when or where the game of golf began, but it has an ancient and noble history. Gowf or goff was played in Scotland five centuries ago, though these early games weren't much like the golf of today.

Golf-type games have been played in different parts of the world for centuries. Nearly every civilization seems to have had some form of stick-and-ball game. There's even a claim that something a bit like golf was played in China around 200 BC.

Just which of the rudimentary games evolved into the sport we know today isn't at all clear. It's likely golf borrowed a little here, a little there, with adjustments to suit different terrains and climates.

Sometimes golf was a boisterous affair, played across country. In Holland a golf-type game was played on ice; other variations took place on formal courts. *Pele mele* was one such stick-and-ball game – the ball was hit through a hoop rather than into a hole. What was once the *pele mele* court in London is the road now known as Pall Mall.

The final target of early games

▼ Scotland is the home of golf as we know it today. At the time of this 18th-century painting, the price of the 'feathery' ball restricted the sport to the wealthy, like the Macdonalds portrayed here in their clan tartan.

▲ Mary, Queen of Scots, stayed at St Andrews in 1563 in a house that still stands. Here, she is playing the links with a court favourite. The outcome of the game isn't known, but he was later beheaded.

▼ Prime minister Lord Balfour is dressed 1909-style for the links. The game also appealed to royalty. In the 1920s-30s the Prince of Wales (later Edward VIII) and the Dukes of York (later George VI) and Kent were keen golfers. And most of the US presidents from the First World War on were enthusiasts.

wasn't always a hole – it could have been a hoop, or a landmark such as a church door. Equipment changed, too, from rough sticks to the beautifully crafted clubs made in the 19th century. The old 'feathery' – a leather ball stuffed with feathers – cost three times as much as a club of its day.

There are many legends associated with golf. For example, Charles 1, on hearing news of the Irish Rebellion of 1641, broke off a game in some relief – he was 6 shots down with 8 to play. And at the trial of Mary, Queen of Scots, it was alleged that she played golf just after the murder of her husband.

AN ANCIENT PRACTICE

Golf may have borrowed from many earlier games which gradually died out. The Romans, for example, used to play *paganica*, which we know little about except that a crooked stick or club was used to hit a leather ball.

More is known of *chole*, a game played in France and Belgium during the mid-14th century. *Chole* was played cross-country over several miles. A team had to reach a target, such as a church door, and from time to time players could hit the opponent's ball into a hazard – a hedge, long grass or ditch, perhaps, or even over a wall. A similar game, *cambuca*, was played in England at much the same time. A cross-country version of *pele mele – jeu de mail* – was played in France. A large-shafted implement was used to hit a wooden ball to a marker half a mile away.

The 'gowf', 'goff' or 'golfe' of Scotland and the 'colf' of the Low Countries were important influences on the game. There's a great deal of speculation on which came first, as there were close trading links between Scotland and Holland which stretch back as early as the 12th century.

Colf, a boisterous golf-like game, was played in the Low Countries as early as 1297. Probably a winter game, it took place on country roads and frozen lakes.

Golf was so popular in Scotland in the 15th century that it interfered with archery practice. An Act passed by James I of Scotland in 1457 banned both 'golfe' and 'fute-ball'. Two other Acts again banned golf, though in more peaceful times the kings of Scotland themselves took to the links.

The early development of golf in the

British Isles was limited to the east coast of Scotland; it didn't become popular along the west coast until the mid-19th century. In the 1880s and 90s came a great boom in its popularity.

A GROWING PASSION

Why did golf suddenly become so incredibly popular? The invention of cheap gutta-percha balls to replace the expensive 'feathery' from 1848 is often given credit. But far more important was the expansion of the railways, allowing people to get to golf courses and golfing holiday centres.

Courses spread from the links – strips of infertile land between sea and farmland – to inland heathland areas. Like linkslands, these had the advantage of a well-drained, short-turfed surface with natural hazards. When grass mowers

▲ The expansion of the railways led to a boom in golf. At one time the west side of St Andrews was flanked by railway lines. This LNER poster was designed to attract passengers to what looks like an idyllic leisure resort. For non-golfers, sea and sand beckon.

◄ This 17th-century child seems dressed to catch the eye rather than to hit the ball. In previous centuries a round of golf gave the well-off a chance to display fashionable finery.

Clubbing together

The first golf balls were struck in Australia in 1847 at Melbourne and a club was formed which lasted a few years. Golf of a sort was also played at Sydney a few years later but any real development of the game still lay several decades away. Royal Melbourne, founded in 1891, claims to be the oldest Australian club with a continuous existence. Others began before then but suffered a hiccup early on. Bothwell, in Tasmania, claims to originate from 1830.

▲ Colf, an early golf-type game, was a boisterous winter sport sometimes played on frozen lakes or rivers. Dutch landscape paintings like this 17th-century scene often showed colf being played on ice.

◄ Early golf balls weren't always round, and some burst when wet. From the left are a 'feathery', a hand-hammered guttie, a moulded guttie and a rubber core.

were invented in the late 1880s, courses sprang up on meadowlands, bringing the game of golf within easy reach of a great many people.

But the boom in golf was just one part of the general rise of interest in sport at the end of the 19th century. However, golf had – and has – two advantages: the game can be taken up at almost any age, and the handicapping system allows golfers of different ability to compete with each other.

Today, golf is one of the most widely played of the world's sports. It is now played in about 80 countries by some 30 million golfers. There are about 12,000 golf clubs, and around £200 million is spent yearly on golf equipment worldwide.

Course design

The great player Bobby Jones once described a good course as 'one that offers equal enjoyment to all standards of player'. He was talking about Augusta, but his words dictate course design today world-wide.

Designing a golf course is like trying to please all of the people all of the time, which, they say, cannot be done. In the process, courses have been designed and built on parkland, meadowland, mountains and beside the sea. Some have even been constructed in deserts.

Some courses are awash with water hazards, others abound with bunkers. Many have tree-lined fairways, others have hardly a tree in sight. A few are extremely long, others short and sharp.

WHAT MAKES A GREAT COURSE?

There are three important yardsticks of a course. The first is if you can sit down at the end of the round and instantly recall every hole. The second is if the course draws on the full range of your strokes, from controlled drives to delicate pitches. And the third is whether the holes really make you think and assess what is required before hitting each shot.

Course design as a true profession came about in the 1900s. Until then, 'new' courses were laid out using the natural features of land by the sea, and many of them were in Scotland. All the courses at that time were links. The designers, who were usually professionals such as Old Tom Morris, simply plotted a route through the sand dunes leading away from the site of the clubhouse and then mapped out a path for the return journey. No earth moving was necessary.

INLAND COURSES

The breakthrough occurred when golf moved inland with the use of the pine and heather land to the west of London in Surrey and Berkshire. This land was soon exploited as the game grew more popular, and courses such as Sunningdale and Walton Heath came into being.

The Old Course at Sunningdale was laid out at the turn of the century by Willie Park jnr, twice

▼ This dramatic hole (the 16th) at Cypress Point, California, was designed by Robert Hunter and Alister Mackenzie in the late 1920s. It is a good example of a penal hole where mistakes are severely punished.

▲ Between the end of the First World War and his death in 1934, Alister Mackenzie played a major part in the design of many, many courses around the world including Augusta (Georgia), Cypress Point (California) and St Andrews Eden Course (Fife). He attributed his ability to make a course blend in with the landscape to experience designing camouflage in the war.

Open Champion. His enchanting work features several short par 4 holes on a course which has stood the test of time and improved standards.

DESIGN IN THE USA

In the USA, course design was also taking off. Although not blessed with the natural links terrain of Britain, there was enormous potential for creating inspiring courses in magnificent settings.

The first of these was the National Golf Links on Long Island. It was designed by Charles Blair Macdonald, a native of Chicago who had attended the University of St Andrews. The National, laid out on the shore of Peconic Bay, featured many holes similar to the best at St Andrews, Prestwick, North Berwick and Royal St George's.

Other courses soon followed. Pine Valley in New Jersey is reputed to be the toughest course in the world, with fairways and greens providing the only sanctuary amid an ocean of sand and scrub. Oakmont in Pennsylvania is a parkland course of great severity and Merion, also in Pennsylvania, a marvellous example of careful planning in a small area.

The designers involved, such as George Crump (Pine Valley), the Fownes family (Oakmont) and Hugh Wilson (Merion), took the best features of the old links courses and introduced some new ones of their own. From their are

▲ Proving that with money, access to water and the will to succeed a course can be laid out anywhere – even in the desert – is the Emirates Course, Dubai. Designed by Karl Litten for Sheikh Mohammed bin Rashid Al Maktoum it has hybrid Bermuda grass watered by over 700 concealed sprinklers. They are fed by miles of pipes carrying fresh water extracted from the sea in a huge purifying plant.

◀ The famous 17th hole at Sawgrass, Florida (home of the Tournament Players Championship) is a classic example of a penal hole. Mistakes approaching the green are punished by loss of ball and a stroke to the water hazard.

▶ Nestling beside a rocky slope, is the 17th hole of the PGA West Course at Palmer Course (California). Course architects have to be very careful in their choice of vegetation, picking the grasses that provide a good playing surface and survive the weather.

Course costs
Course design is now a multi-million dollar industry. In 1975, Jack Nicklaus constructed his dream course at Muirfield Village for $2 million and moved 100,000cu yd (76,500cu m) of earth in the process. Nowadays a similar course would cost nearer $20 million – and it costs over $1 million each year to maintain Nicklaus' course in peak condition.

Player turned architect
It is now a natural progression for an accomplished player to turn his hand to course design. As well as jack Nicklaus, players involved in course projects include:

- Neil Coles
- Peter Alliss
- Peter Thomson
- Dave Thomas
- Gary Player
- Arnold Palmer
- Tom Weiskopf
- Johnny Miller

But the two outstanding architects of the modern era still remain Robert Trent Jones and Pete Dye. Jones has designed courses all over the world, while Dye is renowned for his use of huge dramatic bunkers and water hazards.

The Australian
Like most other countries, Australia owes its early golf course designs to Scotland. One of the oldest courses is the Australian in Sydney, designed by Alister Mackenzie. Links-like in feel, it shares with many of its Scottish counterparts the added challenge of strong winds blowing off the sea.

Jack Nicklaus was commisioned to design new holes in 1977 and introduced more bunkers and water hazards. He won the Australian Open on the old and the new layout.

Building St Mellion

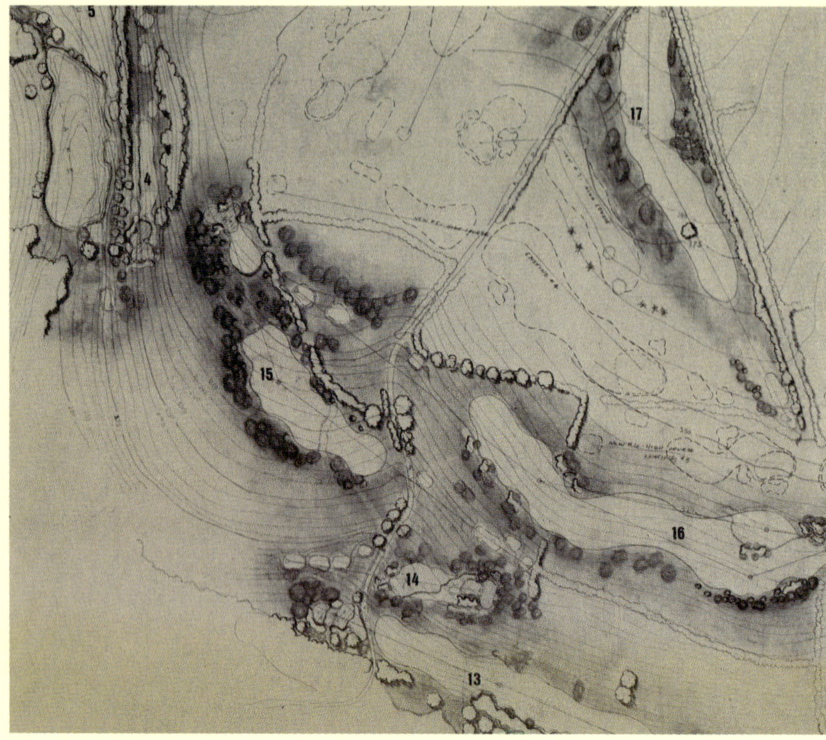

Plans for the holes

Sculpting the land

Jack Nicklaus, master designer

The finished 17th hole

work emerged two different schools of architecture – the penal and the strategic.

A penal hole gives the player no option as to the line of play he can take. The penalty for straying from the 'correct' path is far in excess of the degree of error. Strategic design offers the player a choice of routes to play a hole. It is up to the golfer to decide which one is within his ability.

GREAT AUGUSTA

The greatest influence on American design is the Augusta National Golf Club in Georgia. The course demonstrates clearly the advantages of strategic over penal design, and introduced greater subtlety in the shaping of holes.

Augusta, home of the US Masters tournament, is the inspiration of American course design. It was created by the brilliant golfer Bobby Jones and course designer Alister Mackenzie. Jones provided the knowledge of the shot-making requirements and Mackenzie interpreted them into the ultimate in strategic design – the course constantly tempts the player to bite off more than he can safely chew.

This is most evident on the last nine holes – three water holes in succession. Because of their placing in the round

After the earthmovers

Built between 1983-86, the new course at St Mellion (Cornwall), designed by Jack Nicklaus, matches the best in Europe. Following detailed plans, streams were made into features and dammed to form lakes and hillsides were carved away. In the process, over 1 million cu yd (1.1 million cu m) of soil were shifted.

The greens have grass seeded in a mix of peat and sand which provides excellent drainage. The course also has a watering system covering greens, fairways and tees.

and the psychological pressures they exert, the 11th, 12th and 13th have been dubbed Amen Corner, presumably because if a player manages them without mishap he gives a prayer of thanks.

DESIGN DEVELOPMENTS

The change from hickory to steel shafts in golf clubs and the increasing distances that golfers could hit made a radical difference to the way the game was played. Architects had to combat this, not by stretching courses to an enormous length – although some of them did – but by craft and guile.

Greens were sculpted and heavily contoured, and holes were designed to contain a tempting bait such as the chance to carry a daunting hazard. Above all, the designers of the period between the wars sought balance in their creations. One particular aspect of the game, such as driving or putting, was not emphasized at the cost of, say, long-iron play and chipping.

In recent times, the USA has led the way in course design. With sophisticated machinery it is possible to build a course on almost any terrain, provided there is enough money available.

Water is a dominant feature of design and bunkering is on a grander scale. Tees are staggered to cater for players of varying ability.

Course construction in Britain has not exploded as much as in the USA simply because of lack of space. But more courses are being built to cope with the growing demand.

BUILDING AND PLANTING

Today's architect must be part geologist, agronomist, engineer, forester – and be able to drive an earth-moving machine. It is a highly scientific profession. The importance of good drainage, the suitability of different strains of grasses, the type of sand in the bunkers, the growth patterns of trees – all these factors have to be taken into consideration.

The eventual length of a golf course depends on the land available. But as a general rule, any area of 100-125 acres (40.5-50.5 hectares) is enough.

The first stage is for the architect to do a 'feasibility study'. He finds out if the land is suitable in terms of drainage, ability to sustain grass growth and whether an attractive course can be constructed within the budget. A 100 acres (40.5 hectares) of flat arable land may not make a good course without a large amount of earth-moving to introduce slopes and contours. The best land for golf rises and falls and has a pleasing rolling aspect.

PLANNING THE HOLES

If the land is suitable, the architect walks the area and visualizes how the holes will take shape and their sequence. In an 18-hole course over 100 or more acres (40.5 hectares), the normal layout is 10 par 4s, four par 5s and four par 3s. This gives a par of 72 and a total length of 6000-7000yd (5500-6400m).

The par 5 and par 3 holes are used to break up the sequence of par 4s. Holes should be arranged so that no more than two are played in the same direction.

Par parameters

There are rules laid down for length and par of holes:

Men's pars

- Any hole up to about 250yd (228m) is a par 3.
- Any hole between 250-475yd (228-434m) is a par 4.
- Any hole longer than 475yd (434m) is a par 5.

However, these rules are now flexible if a hole is particularly difficult.

If a club committee wants to allocate pars for women on each hole, the guidelines are:

- Up to 200yd (183m) is a par 3.
- A hole 201-400yd (184-366m) is a par 4.
- Any hole longer than this is a par 5.

Grass strains

The type of grass used affects how the ball reacts from the grass when struck and how the ball lies. In Britain, fine bent grasses flourish naturally because they are not exposed to extremes of heat. In hotter climates, a broader-leaved grass, such as Bermuda or Kikuyu, has to be used to withstand the heat.

Sunshade

Care must be taken to align the holes so players don't have to play looking straight into the sun. In the northern hemisphere, this means the opening holes should not face in an easterly direction to avoid the rising sun in the morning. Similarly, the closing holes should not be directed towards the west so the setting sun dazzles the player.

▲ **Designed by the great Bobby Jones and course architect Alister Mackenzie, Augusta (Georgia) is one of the most influential courses of all. It is a course that demands strategic thinking from the golfer whatever his level of play.**

The original masterpiece
Nearly all the best-designed courses owe their fame or notoriety to a strip of land by the coast near a small Scottish fishing town.

The basic layout of the Old Course at St Andrews has remained unchanged over the centuries. Its challenges are still severe despite modern equipment and the improved physical powers of the current top players.

The legacy that the Old Course has left the game is best illustrated by three holes: the 11th (High), a short hole of 172yd (157m), the 14th (Long), at 567yd (518.5m) and the 17th – the infamous Road Hole, a par 4 of 461yd (421.5m). These holes have been major influences on golf course design, inspiring architects throughout the world.

The par 3 holes should play in different directions so that the wind varies on each one.

The prevailing wind is assessed so that on some holes it is against, some it is behind and some it is across. If possible, the course is laid out in two halves of nine holes. Then the first and 10th tees are next to the clubhouse and provide two starting points.

MAPPING THE LAND

Once the architect has planned the route for the holes, he draws up contour plans of each one showing how the land should fall plus the location of tees, bunkers and greens. If the site is so heavily wooded that a ground survey is difficult, he has to work from aerial photographs. But the best way to plot a golf course is always from ground level as that is where the game is played.

With the contour plans for each hole drawn up, the construction company is called in to start work. This may involve moving large amounts of earth. In bygone days, all earth-moving was done by hand. This created subtle undulations and contours in contrast with the deep gouging that takes place nowadays, particularly in the USA.

Great care must be taken in the construction of the greens to ensure adequate drainage. Greens are usually sand based on a gravel bed so that water flows away quickly.

When the construction is finished, seeding takes place with strains of grass that are suitable for the soil and climate. Once the course is covered with an adequate growth of grass it is ready for play. However, many stones will have been forced to the surface and these have to be cleared every now and then. It is always wiser to delay the opening of a course until the grass is well established as a mass of players in the early stages can destroy well-walked areas of the course.

Whatever and wherever, the ultimate aim is always the same – to blend the elements of the course into the surroundings, so they look as though it has always been there. Golf courses are also meant to be places of enjoyment, and not force you on an unrelenting slog through acres of grass. They should present a challenge that can be overcome if the player keeps his wits about him.

The great architects

Among the hundreds of architects who have designed the golf courses of the world, a few stand out. They were innovative and inspired and created layouts of genius.

Allan Robertson, who died in 1859, was the first known course designer. As the greatest player of his time, it was natural that he was asked to pay visits from his native St Andrews to give his opinions on the layouts of new courses. Almost no building would have been involved – he simply picked out good places for greens and a route for play.

Probably nothing remains of his work except an occasional site for a green. The exception is the Old Course at St Andrews where revolutionary changes, such as the huge double greens, came while Robertson was the resident expert.

MORRIS TRAVELLER

Old Tom Morris was the greatest name in golf following the death of Robertson and his own son, Young Tom. Where Robertson had worked only locally, Old Tom travelled the land, marking out courses for fees of up to £10.

There is a problem with Old Tom's credits however. In the records for the 1922 Open Championship for example, he is said to have designed Muirfield back in 1891. So he did: but by 1922 almost no trace of his work remained.

Even the famous idea of taking both 9th and 18th back to the clubhouse – the double loop, for which he has long been credited – was actually the work of Harry Colt in the 1920s.

Yet this doesn't in the least mean Old Tom wasn't a good designer. His layouts were originally much admired because of the skill with which he made use of naturally existing features.

However, the introduction of the

◄ ▼ **St George's Hill near Weybridge in Surrey is one of Harry Colt's classic heathland courses. He was the first to use a drawing board regularly and to prepare tree-planting plans for his layouts.**

▶ Herbert Fowler got his first chance when his brother-in-law was head of a group financing the building of Walton Heath and asked him to produce the designs. The course opened to high acclaim in the early years of the century and Fowler's services were immediately in heavy demand. He designed The Berkshire near Ascot in collaboration with Tom Simpson.

The first 'architect'
'Architect' is a surprising term to have won general acceptance for men who basically adapt the landscape to make it more suitable and testing for golf. It was introduced by Charles Blair Macdonald (1856-1939), an American who had attended the University of St Andrews and developed a passion for golf.

MacDonald produced relatively few courses, and never accepted a fee for his work. His greatest layout rejoices in the grand title The National Golf Links of America in Long Island, New York.

wound ball at the turn of the century meant layouts had to be stretched. Many courses were radically altered to accommodate the new balls. Very few courses today should be credited to Old Tom because of this stretching.

The growth of golf after the 1880s and the availability of mechanized grass cutters combined to revolutionize ideas about what kind of land could be used for golf.

On linksland with fine seaside fescues growing sideways rather than upwards, only occasional scything was needed. Inland golf had been possible only out of the grass-growing season. With demand and modest technology however, courses were built on land of all kinds, especially on under used common land.

In Britain Willie Park came quickly to the fore. Twice Open champion and with a thriving clubmaking business as well, his name was well known.

Park was in a different golf design business than earlier figures. They had simply made use of existing features already present on linksland to create greens that were not available on heath, park, moor and meadowland.

Park on the other hand had to design and build most of his greens. When producing his most famous achievement, Sunningdale Old, on rolling heathland, he used to journey back to his native Musselburgh to look again at features of greens to inspire his masterpiece.

After creating a host of courses in Britain, Park spent most of his time in North America from 1916 until his death in 1925. There his Scottish accent did him no harm at all, at a time when Scotland was the fount of all things golfing. He can truly be called the first great golf architect.

◀ ▼ Alister Mackenzie, whose practice flourished in the 1920s and '30s, is one of the most revered names in golf architecture. It is in large part because of Augusta and Cypress Point (below) in California, once described as 'the dream of an artist drunk on absinthe and sobering up on gin'. He learned much of his technique developing camouflage during World War I.

DREAM COURSE

In Britain, Harry Colt was the first amateur golfer – rather than professional – to earn a reputation as an architect. Some say he is still the greatest of them all.

His list of credits is impressive. The most famous include Muirfield, Hoylake, Portrush, Sunningdale Old (updated after Park), Lytham and St Anne's and Wentworth. He was also active around the world and especially in the USA, sometimes in partnership with either Hugh Alison or Alister Mackenzie. Pine Valley is his best known collaboration, where he helped owner George Crump create his dream course.

Colt was best known for daring to carve golf courses out of the heather and pines of central England. Swinley Forest, one of the first courses ever routed through a thick forest of trees, was among his best designs.

Equally busy over the same period in Britain was the great professional James Braid, helped by his enormous reputation as a five times Open champion.

Great players have always found it easy to secure golf architecture commissions. It is often mistakenly assumed that they will automatically be talented architects as well. Braid was the exception however, in contrast to his fellow members of the Great Triumvirate. Harry Vardon tried but never excelled in original course design and JH Taylor worked mainly as a consultant.

Braid's best works are usually considered to be the King's and Queen's courses at Gleneagles Hotel. He was very prolific and had a hand in the development of hundreds of courses in Britain and Ireland. However, being a miserable traveller he did very little work elsewhere.

MINIMAL DISTURBANCE

Among British architects, Fred Hawtree is the most prominent name since World War II. It is a sign of changing attitudes that he has been asked to do little or no work in the USA where his designs would probably have been unfashionable.

No believer in slashing millions of cubic feet of soil from the landscape, he instead tried to suit his courses to the site with as little disturbance as possible. His revision of Birkdale with JH Taylor is one of his most memorable achievements.

With the dominance of American golfers after World War I, the country's architects also came much to the fore worldwide.

▲► Prestwick is one of Old Tom Morris' best preserved creations and is the direct source for Pete Dye's use of railway sleepers as a 'traditional' material.

Some, like Jack Neville (Pebble Beach) and Hugh Wilson (Merion) produced solitary masterpieces. Others made careers of golf architecture.

Perhaps the most remarkable was the coiner of the term 'birdie', AW Tillinghast. Many a US Open has been played over his courses including Fresh Meadow, Winged Foot, Baltusrol and Inverness.

His contemporary, Donald Ross from Dornoch in Scotland, was far more prolific. Based at Pinehurst in North Carolina, where the Number 2 course was his special pride, he was involved with almost 500 courses from the early 20th century until his death in 1948. Like Hawtree, Ross believed in fitting the course to the landscape he found.

This was less true of his great successor, Robert Trent Jones, the most influential architect after 1945.

▼ Pete Dye is the best known modern designer and the darling of those who would create a fine landscape where it doesn't exist. He moved 2 million square metres of earth to create PGA West near Palm Springs, California and the 17th is its ultimate test. Tom Watson described it as 'awful, artificial, unfair and ugly'.

The great eccentric
Tom Simpson, at various times in association with Herbert Fowler, JF Abercromby and the player Molly Gourlay, was one of the most colourful British designers of the 1920s.

Simpson came from a wealthy family and had no need to attend on golf club committees cap in hand.

His arrival in a Rolls Royce, sometimes chauffeur driven, made it clear he didn't much need the fees and enabled him to have his plans more readily accepted.

He worked mainly on the continent, particularly on private estates such as those of the Rothschilds. As well as indulging his hobbies in painting and silk embroidery he became well known for his philosophical essays on golf architecture.

Problem, what problem?
Robert Trent Jones performed one of the superior examples of a put down in the history of golf architecture. Having made a stiff par 3 more difficult on a US Championship course, there was much complaining from the membership. Jones turned up one day with his clubs and went out to the offending hole with the committee. He promptly holed in one and was perfectly placed to enquire exactly what the problem was.

He first came to national prominence in the USA when Ben Hogan, having won the 1951 US Open at Oakland Hills which Jones had toughened up, announced at the victory ceremony: 'I am glad I have brought this monster to its knees'.

Jones had simply moved the fairway bunkering so that the pros could no longer fly them with the greatest of ease. He also became renowned for his dramatic use of water hazards and contouring of greens.

However he knew how to leave well enough alone, producing a superb natural links course at Ballybunion.

MOVING MOUNTAINS

The two most fashionable modern architects are Jack Nicklaus and Pete Dye. They started out together and have both come to symbolize the trend towards totally man-made courses where mountains can almost be moved to produce the perfect golf hole.

In the USA Nicklaus' flagship is Muirfield Village, used annually for his Memorial Tournament, only a notch below major championship status and venue for the 1987 Ryder Cup.

In Britain his first course was St Mellion in Cornwall, built ingeniously on a site at first unsuitable for a golf course.

One of his most demanding projects has been to build a new course at Gleneagles, probably to replace the King's as the venue for big events. Jack himself describes his design as a 'playable monster', harking back to Ben Hogan's famous remark in 1951.

Architects are usually fairly anonymous but Dye is the high profile exception, even more so after the enthralling events at Kiawah Island's Ocean Course during the 1991 Ryder Cup.

Dye, a very good amateur golfer, came into golf design having made a modest fortune selling insurance and making changes to his home course.

After doing low budget designs in the USA, he was much inspired by a visit to Scotland in the mid 1960s and thereafter incorporated traditional ideas such as pot bunkers and railway sleepers into his designs.

▼ ► Jack Nicklaus stands out from other great players turned designers of the modern era in that his name is in no way a rubber stamp on somebody else's work. Grand Cypress was an award winning design he completed in 1984.

The PGA European Tour

The tour has mightily swelled its purse and status - it attracts big names and huge crowds. Today's events now stretch from the true links at Turnberry to the desert sands of Dubai.

Golf in Europe has enjoyed phenomenal – and ever growing – success in the last decade or so. In one three month period alone, prize money doubled.

It is tempting to link the recent fortunes of European professional golf to the career of Severiano Ballesteros. But the comparison ignores the structure of the professional game before this gifted player came on to the scene, and how the idea of a tour evolved.

EARLY DAYS

At the turn of the century, the British professional was acknowledged as providing the standard for the rest of the world. This was the era of Vardon, Braid and Taylor who dominated the Open Championship, and it was Taylor who launched the Professional Golfers' Association (PGA) in 1901.

The aim of the association was to act as a kind of trade union for professionals who were employed at the clubs as servants. There were no professional tournaments – the top players of the day simply played exhibition matches where the gate money provided the purse, or perhaps a wealthy benefactor would put up a hundred guineas for a challenge match.

Commercial sponsorship of tournaments did not begin until the early 1930s, and gradually some sort of tour developed. But the main role of professionals was to serve club members. Tournaments used to end on a Thursday or Friday so the pros could carry out their duties over the weekend.

SWINGING SEVENTIES

It was not until the '70s that sponsors noticed the attractions of golf and a new kind of golf pro emerged. This was a person who, although attached to a club in name, devoted all of his time to

▼ **Mark James collects the silver trophy at the 1990 Dunhill British Masters at Woburn. With Dunhill's sponsorship the Masters is one of the top 20 richest events in Europe. Ironically smoking was banned because of fire risk.**

playing tournament golf while various assistants handled the running of his shop. Golfers like Peter Alliss, Neil Coles, Bernard Hunt and John Jacobs were the leaders of this new breed. They were responsible for creating an independent tournament-playing division of the PGA.

Although some sort of tour was in existence it was a shambles. The problem was that the PGA Committee, largely made up of club professionals, decided the policies for the tournament-playing side. The players resented being handled by golfers not playing the circuit

◄ St Andrews stages the opening ceremony of the Dunhill Cup – an event created by promoter Mark McCormack. Although not part of the main tour this world team championship has the grand title of PGA European Tour Approved Special Event.

and the club pros didn't want to lose control of their showcase.

JACOB'S GROUND RULES

Clearly something had to be done. In 1971 the then secretary of the PGA, John Bywaters, invited John Jacobs to become Director General with special responsibilities for tournaments. At that time Tony Jacklin was top of the form after his victories in the British and US Opens. But there was little continuity – prize funds were paltry and players were forced to scratch around to make a living.

As a former player, Jacobs understood these problems and set about solving them. He realized that a small country with a varying climate like Britain couldn't keep a full tournament schedule.

John Jacobs decided to expand into Europe. He set a minimum purse of £5000 – more than double the previous limit – and prevented tournament players from playing anywhere else while an event was on.

He made a rule which allowed only winners of major championships to ask for appearance money. This gave Jacklin the opportunity to resist the financial attractions in America and stay in Europe. With Jacklin on the scene, the television cameras moved in.

Within three months of taking up his appointment Jacobs doubled the prize money for the 1972 season from £220,000 in 1971 to £440,000. But a bitter power struggle followed. Finally in 1975 the tournament professionals broke away from the main body of the PGA and formed the European Tournament Players' Division – later known as the PGA European Tour.

BALLESTEROS TO THE FORE

In 1976 Ken Schofield was appointed executive director. It was to be a memorable year – the youthful talents of Seve Ballesteros were about to explode on to the European scene and provide an unexpected boost to the tour's growth.

Ballesteros was runner-up in the 1976 Open at Royal Birkdale, having led after three rounds. His first tournament win – the '76 Dutch Open – took him to the top of the European Order of Merit. More

▼ The PGA Tour's headquarters are at Wentworth in Surrey. The club has three 18 hole courses, and two prestigious tour events – the World Matchplay and the PGA Championships – are regularly held on the West Course.

▲ Stadium golf hasn't crossed the Atlantic yet – spectators at The Belfry climb high to watch the giants of the game. Lack of space was one argument in favour of moving the Ryder Cup to another venue.

▲ Seve's many wins on the PGA European Tour include the 1989 Epson Matchplay Championship at St Pierre, Chepstow. He shot to fame in 1976 when he topped the Order of Merit and made the tour an all-European affair.

JOURNEY TO THE TOUR

A professional must win a player's card to gain entry to the tour. The system is complex – there are 15 categories of card holders. These fall into three main groups, with exemption from 12 months (lower categories) to ten years (top category). Higher categories have the pick of top tournaments – if a tournament is not full players are chosen from the next available category.

PREQUALIFYING

To gain access to the tour through the Qualifying School most pros must *prequalify* in one of the six schools in England and Spain. Out of over 400 entries only 100 go forward to the Qualifying School.

▲ An inspiration for young fans, the magical play of Seve was a turning point in tour fortunes. He constantly features high in the Order of Merit and holds a record 51 for the most tour victories.

◄ The most exciting modern player to come out of Argentina, Eduardo Romero, won the 1990 Volvo Open in Florence, Italy, and the 1991 French Open at the National, Paris, and the Spanish Open at Club de Campo.

More important, Ballesteros gave the tour its first truly European flavour.

Inspired by Seve's magical performance, other players began to believe in their ability to beat the best in the world. Increased competition, created by the higher levels of prize money, attracted players such as Sandy Lyle, Bernhard Langer and Nick Faldo. Now there was no need for a player to travel the US Tour in search of the best opponents – they were in his own back yard.

Other players from further afield, such as Australia, South Africa and South America, flocked to play in Europe, making the PGA European Tour the most cosmopolitan in the world.

Unlike the US Tour, the European circuit encourages foreigners. In Europe there are generous qualification levels for overseas players.

For any pro just starting out, there is the Tour Qualifying School at the end of the year where hundreds of hopefuls battle for 50 places on the main tour.

Not an easy route by any means, and for some young pros not the only way – Irishman Ronan Rafferty actually failed the school in 1981 but qualified by an overseas tour order of merit. Unsuccessful applicants now have the chance to play on the PGA European Challenge Tour which stages prize money events on the Continent and in Great Britain.

CORPORATE IDENTITY

At the beginning of the 1980s, prize money in Europe stood at a total of £1.7 million spread over 22 events. Today the number of events has increased to 37 with the purse soaring to over £16 million. Part of the reason for this growth is that the tour has expanded from being a body which merely organizes professional golf tournaments.

The tour's operations now include course design and construction, licensing arrangements, publishing, TV and videos. All these activities have enabled the tour to promote itself on a higher level. As a result, the tour was able to negotiate a sponsorship arrangement with the Volvo car company.

The Volvo sponsorship has made

► The game attracts swelling interest throughout Europe. Golf in Sweden has a huge following – the Scandanavian Open, first held in 1973, is producing some fine Swedish golfers. Drottningholm has often staged this event.

EXEMPTIONS

The top category has the winners from the last ten years of the PGA Championship, the Open Championship and the Order of Merit. It includes top rank players such as Nick Faldo, Seve Ballesteros and Greg Norman.

Other categories include exemptions to players winning enough money on the previous year's tour. Category 11 has the top 121 from the previous year's OoM and the top five from the PGA European Challenge Tour.

QUALIFYING SCHOOL

The successful candidates join about 100 ex-card holders at the Qualifying School – at a venue in southern Europe – to contest for only 50 cards. The entry fee is high and the pressure intense – the main aim is to get a card, but a high ranking brings a bonus of more tournaments. Unsuccessful card holders must return to qualify – Ian Woosnam had to go back to the School three times.

There is still a chance for the category of players who come 51-100 in the previous year's Qualifying School – but they are unlikely to play in many tournaments.

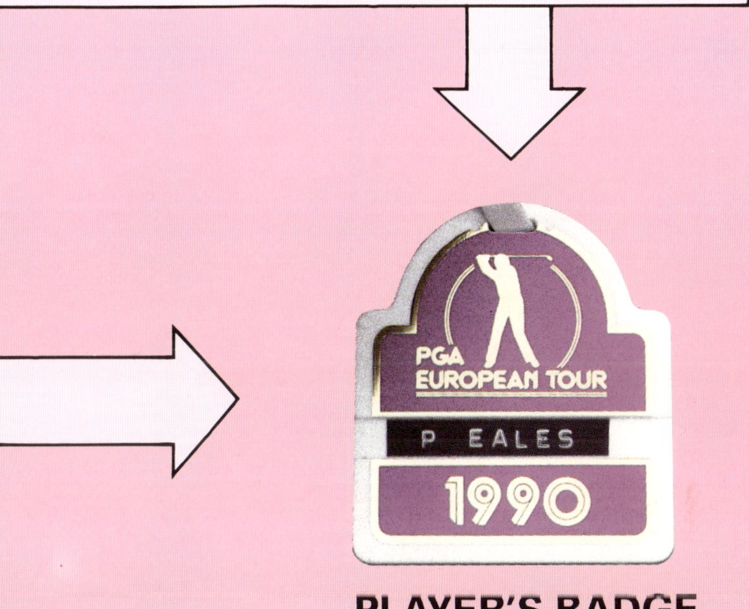

PLAYER'S BADGE

▲ Executive Director of the PGA European Tour, Ken Schofield, briefs the press on the latest Tour developments. Media coverage plays a vital role in setting up sponsorship deals which lead to bigger prize money.

▲ One-time boyhood wonder Ronan Rafferty finally came through by topping the 1989 Order of Merit.

Ryder Cup venue
There was much speculation over the venue for the 1993 Ryder Cup – a bid from Spain was popular because of Spanish players' contribution to European golf. The Belfry was picked for the third time in a row – a controversial decision that led to the resignation of PGA president Lord Derby.

standards rise even higher with better facilities for players, media and public. Such success breeds success and it's hardly surprising that the European triumphs in recent Ryder Cup matches coincide with the increased incentives.

WHEEL OF FORTUNE

One of the main reasons for the tour's success is television. Schofield negotiated long-term contracts with the BBC to cover certain tournaments. Knowing these events would be covered for up to three years, he was then able to set higher prize money from the sponsors for each event.

Mass exposure of the game contributed to the current boom. And with the arrival of satellite television every tournament on the PGA European Tour is covered.

This growth is likely to go on. Golf has more to offer than any other sport and continues to attract large sponsorship. Although Seve Ballesteros will be 43 by the year 2000 he has acted as an inspiration for a whole generation of players eager to show they can follow or even better his achievements.

There is little to prevent the tour offering somewhere between £35 and £40 million in prize money by the turn of the century – a staggering amount, unimaginable 15 years ago when the tournament players decided to control their own destiny.

▼ Media exposure covers the rough end of the game as well as moments of glory. A BBC cameraman gets to a tricky lie before Seve reaches the scene.

Greenkeeping

Pity the poor greenkeeper. He's likely to be overworked, underpaid, and has to shoulder blame for just about everything – even the weather. But things are changing to give greenstaff – and their greens – a better deal.

Though they're only just beginning to have their due share of attention, greenkeepers are responsible for golf's main asset – the courses. But all is far from well in the greenkeeping world. A combination of problems has put great strain on our golf courses – and on the men who tend them.

The average course of today has to contend with at least ten times more wear and tear than it did a few decades ago. Our greens are becoming ever more crowded, from dawn to dusk, in winter as well as summer. Golfers want to

Fallen trees present an unexpected problem for the greenkeepers. The storm of October '87 takes its toll on the World Matchplay Championship at Wentworth, Surrey.

▲ Modern machinery takes much of the drudgery out of grasscutting – it's hard to imagine that greens were once cut with 16in push mowers. But heavy machines can create problems – on certain precious courses hand mowers may still be used today.

► Greenstaff skill is apparent at the immaculate 10th hole at the Sunningdale Old Course in Berkshire. Amazingly enough, the present character of the course was originally formed from a barren and windswept landscape.

▼ A greenkeeper strategically cuts a new hole on the Brabazon Course at The Belfry for the Ryder Cup in 1989.

▲ Good husbandry sometimes involves careful use of fertilizers. A greenkeeper fills a spreader before setting to work.

▼ Storms strike again at the US Masters in 1984. A heavy downpour floods the green, creating extra work for the staff. Good drainage systems are essential for a healthy course, but the most efficient system ever devised couldn't cope with the worst excesses of weather.

▲ Greenkeeping may be a solitary occupation, though the workplace is often spectacularly beautiful. A lone greenkeeper hand waters selective areas of the green at the tranquil Desert Highlands course in Scottsdale, Arizona, USA.

enjoy year-round play on firm, fast greens and mud-free fairways – but most courses fall below these ideals.

Greenkeepers are under fire from all quarters. They are often understaffed and underfunded; many are left struggling to meet player expectation on poorly constructed courses never designed for heavy year-round play.

The level of greenstaff in Britain has remained much the same over the years – there's an average of four or five men per 18-hole course in the UK compared to about 19 in the USA. This has led to intensive management of the courses, involving frequent use of heavy machinery and water and fertilizer programmes.

► One of the greenstaff repairs a pitchmark with a mini-pitchfork. In his other hand he is holding a traditional besom, which he uses for removing leaves and twigs from the greens.

GREEN CONCERN

It's traditional for the greenkeeper to be blamed for everything, including the weather. The course may be too wet, too dry, too fast, too slow. Faced with high membership fees, players want value for money – expectation is high.

A greenkeeper may have to take unpopular decisions, perhaps to rest exhausted greens. This often leads to conflict. Should a greenkeeper give way to pressure and try to satisfy members on a particular day, or instead nurture the long-term health of the course?

Courses that stage tournaments are faced with the additional problem of professional golfers who want a course to play its best on the day – this may mean shaving the turf irrespective of weather conditions or grass species.

One of the main worries facing British greenstaff is that modern practices don't suit the tough native grasses – the fescues and bents – which can be relied on for year-round play. Springing up at an alarming rate in their place is the inferior annual meadow grass, which quickly becomes unplayable in all but the summer months.

COURSE DESIGN

Poor course construction and design add to the greenkeeper's problems.

Generally, the healthiest courses are those which are ecologically sound and make the most of the natural landscape and vegetation of the area. British courses laid down before the First World War were closely based on the links ideal, which adapted well to inland heathland courses.

Many new courses make good use of modern technology; they have superb drainage systems and a special rootzone material to absorb air and retain moisture. But on some earlier courses – particularly those badly laid out by unqualified designers on clay – a drainage system was often an unsuccessful afterthought.

With the influence of TV, the trend today is often towards a scenically attractive Augusta-style dream course, with lush green turf at all times – even in dry spells – set against a backdrop of landscaped trees and lakes.

To achieve this scenic splendour, large-scale earth-moving and the mass introduction of non-native features may be needed. Some of these courses work well, but others – especially those ill-suited to local conditions and a variable climate – are almost impossible to maintain in playable form throughout the year.

▲ A great deal of hard work is put into preparing a course for a major tournament. This greenkeeper is repairing the Hell bunker at the 14th hole for the 1990 Open at St Andrews.

▼ Home of the British Masters, Woburn Golf Club in Buckinghamshire is a splendid example of a well maintained course. This sort of peak condition is testimony to the greenkeeper's skill.

Help your greenkeeper

- Be patient – remember, the greenkeeping staff often work under difficult conditions, and have to consider the long-term state of the course.
- Greenstaff are professionals – never hesitate to ask for advice or guidance.
- Grass is a growing medium. Good conditions take time and expertise to produce. Support the greenkeepers by showing understanding.
- Take pride in the condition of your course – observe the rules and etiquette. Always repair pitch marks and footprints in bunkers and make sure divots are replaced.
- If you are an active member, ensure that the maintenance and equipment budget of your club is adequate to meet greenstaff needs.
- Show an interest in the role of your greenstaff and encourage them to play golf.

▲ A greenkeeper saves his legs by using a ride-on fertilizer machine at the 17th green in Oakland Hills, Michigan, US.

THE CHALLENGE OF CHANGE

It's essential that solutions are found which work not only now but will lead to healthy greens in the future. A new association, BIGGA – the British and International Golf Greenkeepers Association – was set up in 1987 to represent the profession.

More recently the R and A Greenkeeping Panel spoke out forcefully for radical changes to restore health to ailing greens. High on their list of priorities is greenstaff training.

► Lawrence Crampton, a 69-year-old retired Irish greenkeeper, shot to fame when he was called back to The Belfry to help out on the course for the 1989 Ryder Cup. While accompanying Gordon Brand jnr and Mark McCumber on their round, Crampton raked the bunker on the 18th hole.

As the ex-greenkeeper tried to get out of the bunker, his leg seized up from over-exertion, preventing him moving out of the way of Brand's putt. Luckily McCumber went to his aid and helped him out to rapturous applause from the gallery.

Many top greenkeepers on showcase courses came into the business straight from school. They gained their skills in the traditional way – by trial and error. This is now all changing. Britain may not yet match the US system of training – there, many superintendent greenkeepers hold degrees – but funding is being increased so that a proper training framework is possible.

The image of a greenkeeper as a person who just cuts the grass is a thing of the past. The greenstaff of today should be recognized as well qualified individuals in a skilled profession.

Training and research programmes are important initiatives. There's also a need for everyone involved in the game to work for a closer understanding. Many green committees should be restructured, with training so serving members make well informed decisions.

Relations between greenstaff and player haven't always run smoothly. Players need to be educated into a better appreciation of the problems facing a greenkeeper.

It's time to set aside grievances and misunderstandings so that everyone with a real love of the game can work together to safeguard golf's prime asset: the course.

Exercise and diet

Can you manage to walk up two or three flights of stairs without gasping for breath, or play a round of golf without your energy or concentration flagging? No? Read on.

◄ **Keep high release energy foods in your golf bag. Jack Nicklaus is one of several pros to eat bananas on the course. Glucose tablets have received the approval of the PGA – they even supply dispensers on tournament tees.**

Golfers are rarely fitness freaks. In fact W C Fields' famous line – 'Whenever I have the urge to exercise, I lie down until it passes' – could well be applied to many amateur players. But eating well and being fit can really keep your game in shape, as top professionals have shown.

Sending a golf ball consistently straight at the flag demands split second timing – a task beyond ill-conditioned bodies. You can have all the lessons you like, but unless your body is fit enough to put technique into practice the chances of playing to a high standard are almost nil.

The stars have come to realize this – mushrooming prize money and a longer season have persuaded many pros to take better care of their prize-winning apparatus: their bodies.

Bernhard Langer has invested in a home gym, Sandy Lyle tones his muscular frame with a rowing machine and Tommy Nakajima builds up endurance by running up hills. Gary Player – the ultimate fitness fanatic – has such a complex exercise programme that he needs a wallchart in his kitchen to keep track.

AVOID WEAR AND TEAR

Although lack of strenuous physical demands is one of golf's benefits – many players go on playing well into old age – muscular wear and tear does happen. Hacking divots from the ground can damage the shoulder and elbow joints. And as Nick Faldo discovered on sun-baked UK courses in 1990, fragile

► Keeping fit means you can enjoy golf well into later years. Physical exercise helped keep Arnold Palmer at the top of the tree for so long – he's still going strong as a senior. Good Open weather at Muirfield in 1980 made his morning run more enjoyable.

wrists can be jarred into injury.

Golf can have a destructive effect on vertebrae discs, while knee joints often disintegrate painfully under the strain of balancing two halves of a fast twisting body.

Taking steps to avoid these problems is a simple enough process. If you are in reasonably good health there are several exercises you can perform – and none of them requires you to invest in a singlet or leotard.

TRYING OUT EXERCISES

Concentrate on building up your back, forearms, thigh muscles and calves – these are the vital muscles you use in the swing. Your biceps and chest are less important.

Striking a dozen balls with your left arm only and hitting an old tyre – Henry Cotton's famous tip – are effective fore-arm builders. Sit-ups build the stomach area and strengthen the lower back.

Rabbit jumps are good for the legs. For these you leap high in the air from a starting position, bringing both legs under your chin. But don't ever spring into too strenuous a form of exercise. Remember to take it gently at first and always warm up properly.

FEED TO SUCCEED

If you're concerned that your weight may be affecting your golf, consider changing your diet – there's no point

▼ Chip Beck – one of the stars of the US Tour – performs some stretching exercises before a round. Toning up the muscles to avoid stiffness in the back, shoulders and legs is vital to a fluent swing and safeguards against injury.

◄ **If you want to follow Gary Player's example – the great South African golfer weighs less now than he did 30 years ago – empty your fridge of fatty bacon, red meat, eggs, coffee and cream and fill the spaces with poultry, fish, wholegrain bread, salads and cereal.**

Steer clear of fried foods, and don't eat a big meal before heading for the 1st tee – allow 90 minutes at least to digest. Eat at active times of the day – most dieticians recommend large breakfasts and lunches to give your body the chance to burn off what you consume.

caring for the engine if you don't fill up with the proper fuel.

An over generous bulk leads to poor posture. Either the player leans too far forward, or makes extra room by resting on his heels. Both positions lead to a bad strike.

Follow a healthy, balanced diet to give yourself the best chance of swinging fluently over 18 holes. And never sit down to a large meal before play. Neither the mind nor the body is agile after, say, a heavy lunch. Make sure that you finish dessert at least 90 minutes before teeing off. But don't go on to the course hungry or your energy will flag.

Gary Player's name comes up again – he cites his diet as part of the reason for his continuing success on the US Senior Tour. UK professional John Morgan has also made a study of foods suitable for golfers – apart from a well balanced diet he recommends pasta as an excellent slow release energy food. Dishes based on spaghetti or lasagna help to keep you going and aid concentration over a long period.

Diet and exercise alone won't give you the metronomic swing of Faldo or the dynamism of Ballesteros, but you may be surprised at their positive effects.

Gary Player says that the cartoon character Popeye possesses the perfect male golf physique – flat chest, narrow waist, tiny biceps and strong forearms. But bear in mind that vast amounts of spinach probably won't help you break 80. Keep your practice up as well as staying fit and eating healthily – there's no short cut to good striking.

◀ Always warm up before you play. Holding a club – a mid iron is a good idea – behind your shoulders and swivelling to the right and left promotes a full shoulder turn as well as loosening your shoulder and back muscles for the swing. Nick Faldo and Paul Way would never step cold on to the tee – neither should you. At best it causes a creaky swing – which ruins your shot and your rhythm for the round – and could lead to injury.

▶ The young Seve Ballesteros was told by Gary Player that tiredness towards the end of a round would cause him to lose concentration – and a good score. Loss of accuracy as the round wears on is usually down to leg fatigue. To combat this, try a well known skiing exercise – stand with your back against a wall and gently lower your upper body until the tops of your legs, from thigh to knee, are parallel to the ground. Hold for 15 seconds, building up to two minutes as your muscles develop.

▼ **Alcohol disturbs the natural body rhythms you need for a consistent swing – water is a much better bet to quench thirst during a round, as Bernhard Langer shows. Keep away from alcohol until you arrive at the 19th hole.**

pro tip

Avoid a pain in the neck

Keeping your head still is crucial to golfing excellence. But to turn properly, your neck muscles must be as flexible as possible. These exercises build up the trapezius area, which stretches from the back of your neck across the shoulders.

Neck rolls: lean your head towards your right shoulder, slowly rotate back and around, then lean towards your left shoulder. Repeat three times, always keeping your shoulders square.

Neck turns: similar to neck rolls, but stretching rather than turning your neck muscles. Stretch your head as far as you can over your left shoulder, return to normal, then try it over your right shoulder.

Stamina, strength, suppleness

You don't need bulging muscles or the ability to run a marathon to get the most from golf, but overall fitness leads to healthy lungs, muscles and heart – which will do both you and your game a power of good.

Specific exercises produce specific benefits – you get what you train for – though becoming fit needn't involve gain through pain at the gym. Walk up those stairs instead of taking the lift, or leave the car in the garage and cycle or walk to the station in the morning.

As a rough guide, aim for three exercise sessions of 20 minutes a week. To improve your game remember the three S points:

Stamina for staying power (cycling, running, other forms of aerobic exercise)

Strength for power when it counts (body building, circuit training, high impact workouts)

Suppleness to avoid injury and for coordination and flexible joints that turn easily (stretching exercises, low impact workouts)

Exercise benefits

The right type of exercise improves the performance of various parts of the body:

The heart becomes more effective in delivering oxygen to the working muscles.

Muscles become stronger, increasing in power and endurance.

Tendons and ligaments are strengthened, resulting in more stable, injury resistant joints.

Flexibility improves, giving supple, easy movement.

Body fat is reduced, improving overall condition.

Mental stress is lowered – certain hormones released during exercise give a feeling of well being.

5

BASIC RULES

Golf is such a complicated game to play, who needs a rule book to make life even more difficult? What happed to teeing the ball up, hitting it, playing it as it lies and adding the score up as you go? Unfortunately, golf, like life, is rarely that straightforward.

There are so many situations that can arise on a golf course and in a competition that the authorities have to have a rule to cover every eventuality. Therefore there are rules as to drop zones, immovable obstructions, loose impediments, the correct method of filling out your scorecard, the various ways of dealing with a hazard, and a bewildering number of other facts you need to know.

This section deals with the rules and decisions that a player is most likely to encounter in an everyday round of golf, and also has a good selection of the more unusual situations that players may find themselves in.

A good working knowledge of these rules and regulations will not only speed up your game, but can actually save you a few strokes. Knowing where you can drop the ball after knocking it into a lake, for example, may give you an advantage when playing your next shot.

Even though these rules provide a very good grounding, an in-depth look at the official Royal and Ancient rulebook is certainly worthwhile.

Steve Richardson drives during the 1992 Open di Firenze.

Introducing the rules

The rules of golf are there to guide you, whatever situation you find yourself in. You get much more from the game if you know how to apply them properly.

Golf began as one of the most straightforward of all games; it is now governed by the most complicated set of rules of any sport. Even those who make their living by playing the game – the tournament pros – often call for a ruling from an official when they are in doubt as to how to continue.

The most famous of modern British commentators on the game, Henry Longhurst, always maintained that the essential rules could be written on a postcard and the rest discarded, to everyone's advantage. But the detail of the rules means you can find guidance in any golfing situation, however unusual.

The rules are complex because those who make them have to legislate for a game played over vast areas of widely varying land, in all parts of the world. As soon as you start to play golf, you become aware that a long list of bizarre situations can arise – on almost all of which the rules can help you.

WHO MAKES THE RULES?

The two bodies responsible for the rules and their interpretation are the Royal and Ancient Golf Club of St Andrews (R and A) and the United States Golf Association (USGA). The USGA controls golf in North America. The R and A administers the rest of the golfing world – over 60 nations are affiliated to it.

You must come to terms with the rules if you are to play on the golf course. The code states that players may not agree to ignore a rule or a local rule or any penalty incurred. If you do disregard a rule, you are disqualified, under Rule 1-3, whether in strokeplay or matchplay.

You can refer any queries or disputes about the rules to the Rules Committee of the R and A. But they must be submitted through a club or competition secretary – individual requests would swamp an already overworked body.

COURTESY ON THE COURSE

Golf etiquette is based on common sense and consideration for others.

Slow play is one of the bugbears of modern golf – many offences against etiquette are usually involved. For instance, if you are looking for a ball, you should call through any match waiting behind you without delay. Once you have done so, you should not continue play until the players called through are out of range.

Twoball matches have precedence over three and fourball matches and are entitled to pass them. Any match playing a whole round can pass through a match playing a shorter round. If you are a single player, you have no standing on the course and must give way to a match of any kind.

If you lose a clear hole on the match in front of you, you have lost your place on the course and should invito any following match to pass.

Rules about dress on the course are nothing to do with the etiquette of golf. Where they exist, they are rules of the club concerned, and your complaints – or congratulations – should be directed accordingly.

▲ Use a pitch-mark remover to tease the turf back up after your ball has landed on the green. And once you've completed the hole, don't lean on your putter while you take the ball out.

◄ It is an essential part of etiquette to protect the course – always replace divots on the fairway.

Etiquette: Questions and Answers

Slow play

Q Last Saturday some friends and I were playing a fourball over 9 holes. We had a drink afterwards and, when the match behind reached the clubhouse, the players were clearly annoyed that we hadn't let them overtake us. They claimed that they had precedence over us because they were playing a full round. But, apart from the fact that we were being delayed by the slow match ahead of us, how could we have known that they were playing a full round?

A Many points of etiquette revolve around slow play. While it's irritating to be chivvied by a match following you, it is correct that a full-round match takes precedence over anyone playing a shorter round – even if the delay is not your fault.

As a general rule, be aware of players behind you and, if there's a bottleneck, let them know why they are being delayed. It is impossible to know whether the match behind is playing more holes than you are without asking – which is why communicating with other players is so important.

Raking bunkers

Q My opponent played from a bunker and put his ball on to the green. I then fluffed my chip from beside the bunker, which meant that my ball rolled back into the sand. When I went to play it, I found that my opponent had failed to rake the bunker, although a rake was provided, and my ball had rolled into a deep heel-mark he had made.

Section 1 of the Rules of Golf states that, before leaving a bunker, a player should carefully fill up and smooth over any holes and footprints he has made. Could I therefore have claimed the hole from my opponent in matchplay?

A No. The section on Etiquette in the Rules of Golf is a preliminary to the Rules themselves – you'll find that Rule 1 in fact comes nine pages later in the R and A approved booklet.

The section on Etiquette is highly important: note how it is placed at the beginning rather than as an appendix to the Rules. But it is a guide to how players should behave on the course, not part of the Rules of the game. Notice how this section suggests that you 'should' or 'should not' do things, while the Rules direct that you 'shall' or 'shall not' do things.

Your opponent's failure to repair the bunker was deplorable, but did not break a Rule of Golf. It is certainly not the way to win friends! Any prolonged disregard of the code of etiquette should be dealt with firmly by the Committee of the club.

Leaning on putters

Q I've seen pros on TV lean on putters when taking their ball out of the hole. Should they?

A No. Although copying the stars is excellent for improving your game, never follow their example in this area.

Noise factor

Remember that noise is distracting and puts off other players. Apart from not talking when someone's about to play a ball, never take personal stereos, radios or portable telephones on the course or any other devices that might annoy.

Parts of the course

You may feel that you know all about the different sections of a golf course. As far as the rules are concerned, there are four areas and you need to be very clear in your mind about the distinctions.

Many players immediately think of the fairway as one of the major areas of the course. But the Rules of Golf do not use the word, preferring to deal in terms such as 'closely mown areas'. There are good reasons for this – for example, the rules have to cover par-3 holes, where fairways do not normally exist.

The four areas of a golf course each have their own rules. In the order you come across them, these areas are the Teeing Ground, Through the Green, Hazards and the Putting Green.

THE TEEING GROUND

The teeing ground on a particular hole varies from day to day. It is not all of what most players call 'the tee', but a rectangle which is always two club lengths in depth. Its width varies, because it is defined by the outside limits of the two tee-markers positioned by the greenkeeper.

You must play your ball from within this rectangle. It is up to you whether or not you place it on a tee-peg. As long as your ball is correctly positioned, you may stand outside the teeing ground to play it. However, you must not move either of the markers to give yourself a clear swing.

You are penalized if you mistakenly play from outside the teeing ground. In matchplay, your opponent may make you play again if he wishes – but he will probably be content to let the shot stand if you hit a bad one! There is no other penalty.

In strokeplay, you are penalized two shots and then have to play from the proper place. Strokes played from the wrong place do not count. You must put your mistake right before you tee off on the next hole – or leave the 18th green if the error occurs there – otherwise you are disqualified.

THROUGH THE GREEN

This is the whole area of the golf course except the teeing ground of the hole being played, the putting green of the hole being played and all hazards.

The term 'through the green' dates from well back in time. Remember that it embraces all of the course, because this means that relief (permission to move the ball) given on the fairway is generally also available in the rough. For example, you can claim the same relief from casual water whether you are in the middle of the fairway or deep in the rough.

HAZARDS

There are two kinds of hazards: bunkers and water hazards. The

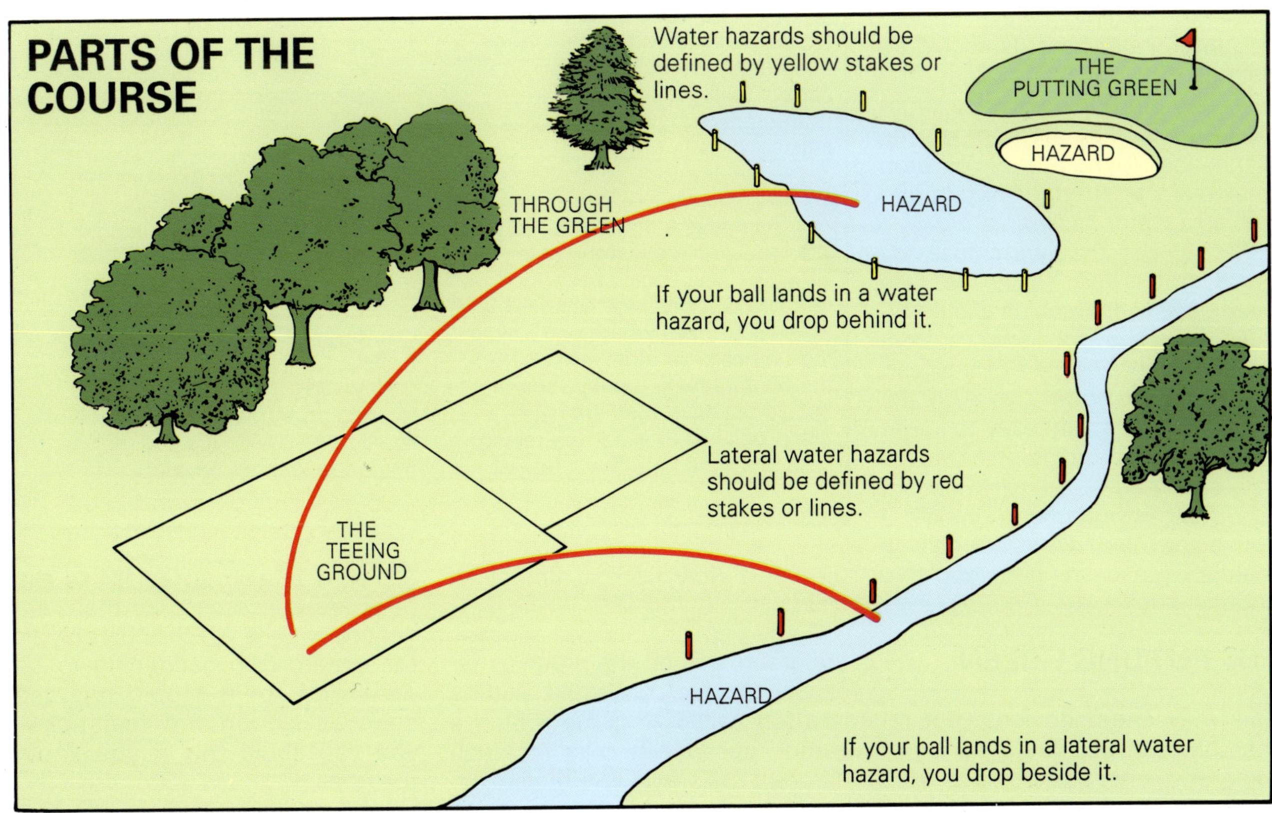

THE TEEING GROUND

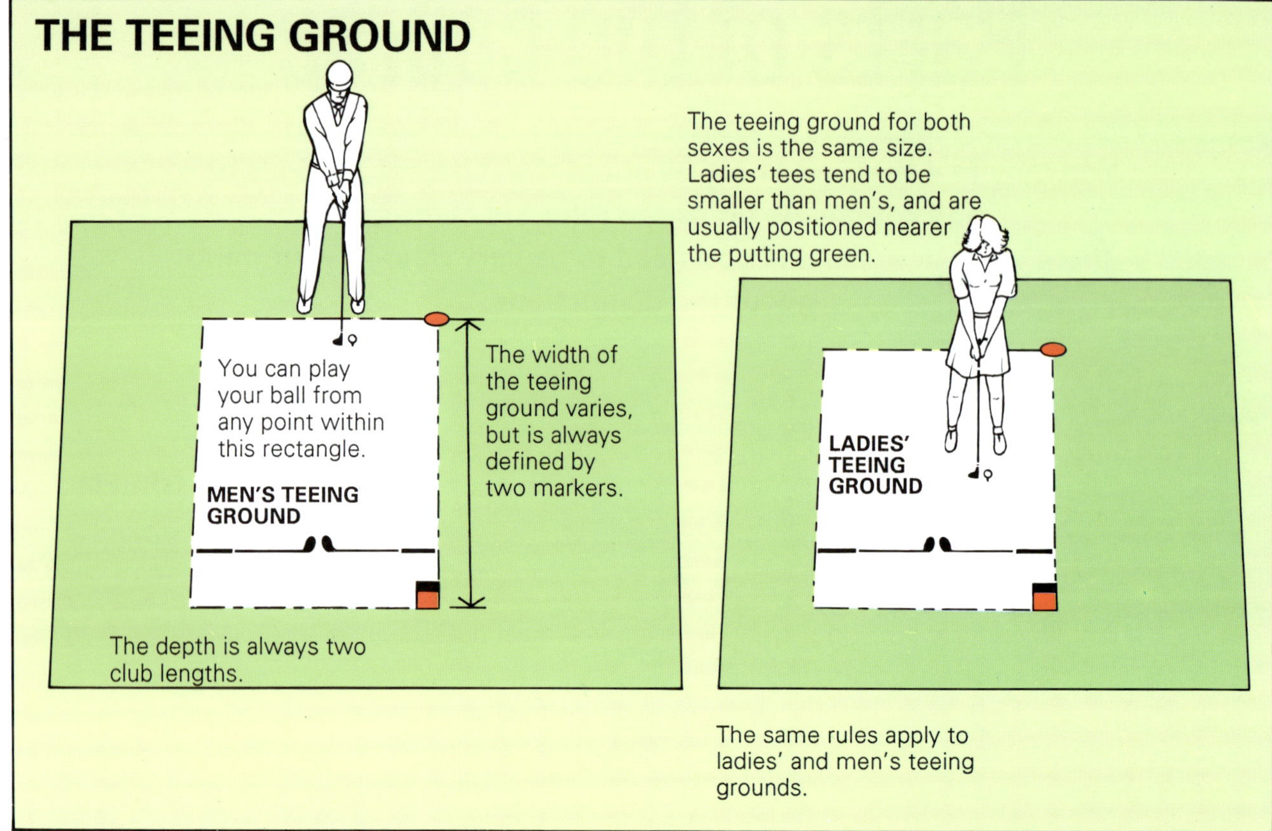

The same rules apply to ladies' and men's teeing grounds.

most vital rule to remember is not to ground your club in any kind of hazard. Grass-covered ground bordering or even within a bunker – some famous bunkers have islands of grass within them – is not part of the bunker.

Water hazards should be defined by yellow stakes or lines. These give you their limits and are themselves within the hazard.

Lateral water hazards should be defined by red stakes or lines. The rules about dropping your ball from these are slightly different, so the distinction is important. You drop *beside* a lateral water hazard and *behind* a water hazard.

Remember that water hazards need not necessarily contain water. Many on Spanish and Portuguese courses, for instance, contain water for only part of the year. But if they are defined as such, the rules apply. It's very easy to forget when perched desperately on the side of a dried-up stony ravine that you must not ground your club; if you do so, you lose the hole in matchplay and are penalized two shots in strokeplay.

Course questions and answers

Wrong teeing ground

Q I played my tee shot in a match and drove out of bounds. We then realized that I had driven from the wrong teeing ground. Obviously my opponent did not wish to recall the stroke, but we were not certain where I should play my second ball from. Eventually, I teed my ball up on the correct teeing ground and drove from there, adding a two-stroke penalty. Was I right?

A As it was a matchplay, you should have lost the hole. However, you should have dropped a ball as near as possible to the spot from where you played the first ball – in other words, from the wrong teeing ground. You should not have *teed* the ball there, because it is not the teeing ground fcr the hole being played.

Toppling off the tee-peg

Q My ball fell off the tee-peg last week when I was in the course of my downswing, and I failed to hit it at all. My opponent said I could re-tee it without penalty as I had made no contact, but I thought I had to count what had already happened as an airshot, and play my second shot without re-teeing the ball. Was I correct?

A Yes. You have to count the stroke which you made at the ball, even though you did not hit it. It does not seem very fair, but at least you avoided a hernia! And because the ball is now in play, you cannot tee it up but must play it as it lies.

However, if the ball falls off its tee-peg on the tee or is knocked off as you *address* it, you can replace it on its tee without penalty.

THE PUTTING GREEN

This may seem obvious, but remember that the fringe (apron) of the green is not part of the green – though it may be cut almost as short.

If any part of your ball touches the green, it is on the green as far as the rules are concerned. Putting is often called 'a game within a game', because it calls for such different skills from the rest of the game. It is also so as far as the rules are concerned, for there are important ones which apply only on the green. It's maddening to be penalized for a stupid mistake such as hitting the flagstick – you can avoid this if you know the rules.

Golf balls – the rules

Before beginning a match, check your golf balls carefully – they must be regulation size and easily identifiable. And to avoid penalty during play, know exactly when you can clean or change your ball.

Before a ball is used in competitive play, it must conform to the tests approved by the Royal and Ancient Golf Club (R and A) or the United States Golf Association.

Every manufacturer of golf balls could produce a ball that can fly further than the best of the current balls, but the rules would not permit its use.

It's possible to buy illegal balls because many manufacturers sell balls rejected by the R and A. These are clearly marked as rejects and are perfectly good to use whenpractising but *never* in a match. If you use an illegal ball – even innocently – you'll be disqualified.

Regulation of equipment, and balls in particular, is one of the reasons why golf courses that have been played for over a hundred years are still a challenge today.

Although the larger golf ball, with a diameter of 1.68in (4.3cm), is nearly always used these days, you may occasionally come across the smaller ball with a diameter of 1.62in (4.1cm).

Both sizes were used in British competitions during the 1970s and 1980s, but today both professional and amateur competitions require that players use the larger ball. This 1.68in ball must weigh 1.62oz (46g).

IDENTIFYING YOUR BALL

Inform your opponent or marker of the make and number of the ball you are playing before you start a round. You should also place your own identification mark on the ball. Dot or initial your ball with a permanent marker.

Marking is often ignored, but it's surprising how often balls of the same make and number surface during searches.

The responsibility for playing the proper ball rests with you alone. You may lift a ball to identify it as your own anywhere on the course, except in a hazard. If you ball lands in a bunker you may brush aside enough sand to identify the ball.

If you do lift your ball, you must first tell your opponent in matchplay or your marker or a fellow competitor in strokeplay.

You may clean the ball only enough to identify it. Once you have confirmed that it's your ball, replace it exactly where it lay. Make sure that the other player is able to watch the whole procedure.

If you don't say what you're doing or you lift the ball to identify

▼ Think twice before you lift a ball to clean it – you may fall foul of the rules. You can clean the ball before each putt or when taking relief from an unplayable lie.

WHOSE BUNKER BALL?

Beware of breaking the rules if your ball lands in a bunker

You may carefully brush aside enough sand to identify the ball but you mustn't lift it or you incur a one-stroke penalty.

You may find you still can't tell whether it's your ball – in this case you can take the shot without penalty. If it wasn't your ball the other player may place his ball where it originally lay in the bunker.

it in a hazard, you incur a penalty of one stroke.

It may be impossible to make sure you are addressing your own ball in a bunker – in this case, you can make the shot without penalty.

If it's found that the ball belongs to another player he can place it where it originally lay.

UNFIT FOR PLAY

You may change your ball at any time *between* holes whatever its condition.

If it becomes unfit for play *during* a hole, you may lift and inspect it as long as you have told your fellow players.

A ball must be visibly cracked, chipped or out of shape to qualify as unfit – superficial scratches are not reason enough to replace a ball.

If everyone agrees that the ball was damaged during the play of the hole, you may place another ball on the same spot.

It's not unusual for certain types of ball to become unfit for play. Professional golfers who use balata balls which mark easily often use eight or more balls during a round.

CLEANING YOUR BALL

There's often confusion about when you are allowed to clean your ball. Remember, to avoid penalty, it's your responsibility to know the rules.

You *may* clean your ball before each putt when you are on the green.

Out of courtesy to your fellow players make sure that you don't overdo the cleaning – once is usually enough.

You may also clean your ball when you're taking relief from an unplayable lie.

You may *not* clean your ball if you are lifting it for identification, to determine if it is unfit for play, or if it's interfering with or helping play.

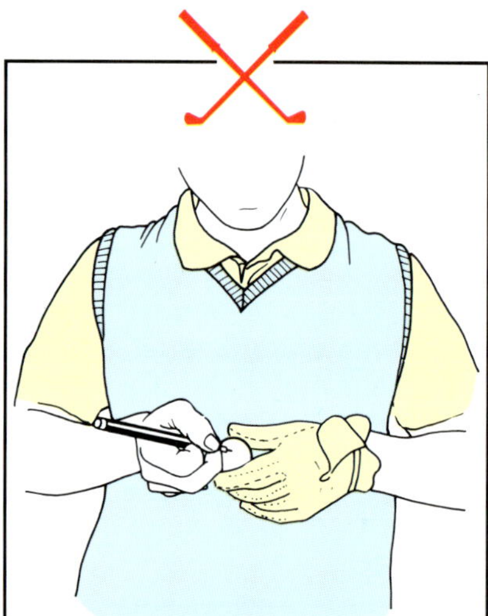

Marking your golf ball
It's important to mark your balls clearly before playing a round. A great deal of confusion is caused when identical balls appear during searches. And if you land in a bunker you can't lift a ball to identify it – you may end up playing the wrong one unless the balls are clearly marked.

Marking golf balls is a simple task – dot or initial them using a permanent marker.

Questions and Answers

Illegal ball

Q Quite unwittingly, I played a stroke with an illegal ball – one that was rejected by the R and A – in our medal competition. I substituted a correct ball as soon as my marker pointed out the error. What is the correct penalty?

A Disqualification is the penalty. If you use an illegal ball during a match, you are automatically disqualified.

To avoid an upset like this, it's essential that you check your balls carefully before playing.

Broken ball

Q When I was playing the other day with a solid ball, it split in two with part of it going out of bounds. I counted the shot, and played my next shot from where the biggest fragment lay. Was I correct?

A No, you shouldn't have continued with the shot. The stroke that broke the ball must be replayed without penalty. You should drop a ball as near as possible to the original spot.

Advice and information

The rules of golf make an important distinction between advice and information. Before playing a match, make sure you know the difference to avoid any danger of picking up a penalty.

The difference between advice and information may seem a fine point but the rules treat these two quite separately.

Advice is any suggestion which might help a player decide tactics, choose clubs or adjust a stroke. The outcome of the advice is beside the point – if you pick up a penalty it's no use arguing that the advice did no good at all or that you would have been better off without it.

Information is confined to facts which the rules accept as 'public information'. You can give information about the rules themselves, and indicate the position of features such as ditches and bunkers.

You can also show the position of the flag on the putting green. Except on the green, you can even indicate what you think is the best line of play.

But if you stand on the brow of a hill or put down any type of marker to show the best line, you must move yourself and the marker out of the way before your companion plays the stroke.

The only exception to this rule is that even while the shot is being played you may hold up the flagstick on the green to show the position of the hole.

A HELPING HAND

Certain forms of advice are allowed. For instance, you may advise your partner in a foursomes or fourball competition. And your partner or either of the caddies can advise you – the rules of golf count the members of a partnership as one in this case.

Even on the putting green your partner or caddie may point out what he thinks is the best line for your

▶ **Certain types of information or advice are allowed, but always check with the rules – you must know exactly when you can get help from a caddie or partner.**

putt – but at no time must he touch the green while doing this.

The rules also let you take a lesson between rounds of a 36-hole match without penalty. You may not receive advice, though, from anyone except your caddie during either of the 18-hole rounds.

If you are playing in a team competition without a simultaneous individual competition, the match committee may let your team appoint one person who can advise team members.

CLUB CLUE

When you see another competitor fall short of a par-3 hole, it's tempting to ask which club was used, but this is against the rules. In fact the most common form of infringement is when a player asks an opponent or fellow competitor what club was used for a particular shot.

The same rule prevents the giving as well as the receiving of advice, so don't be tempted to volunteer this sort of information yourself.

If you attend pro tournaments you sometimes see this rule broken, but you may pick up a penalty if you infringe it.

No one can stop you using your eyes, or letting your companion use his. If he's carrying a full set of irons, it's not difficult to work out which one your companion has taken. But you would be breaking the rules if you deliberately remove a towel covering his clubs to get this information.

Anecdotes about this rule abound. You hear many a tale of 2-wood covers conspicuously slipped on to 7 woods, and loud calls to caddies for 5 irons which produce 8 irons by prior arrangement. But it's as well to remember you are breaking the rules if you make a deliberately misleading statement about your club selection which is meant to be overheard by your opponent.

The penalty for all breaches is loss of the hole in matchplay and 2 strokes in strokeplay.

Line of play

The rules of golf allow you to indicate the position of features such as bunkers and ditches, and – except on the green – you can show what you think is the best line of play.

To avoid penalty make sure that any marker is removed before the shot is taken. If you stand on the brow of a hill to mark the line of play, you must move away from the marker position before the stroke is played.

The only time a marker can remain in position while a shot is being played is when the flagstick is held up on the green to indicate the hole.

Questions and answers

Permanent objects

Q Is it in order for me to ask the distance to the green from a particular tree?

A Yes – distances from permanent objects such as trees and bunkers are public information.

Ball distance

Q May I ask about the distance to the green from my ball?

A No – your ball isn't a permanent object, so you can't ask how far it is from a particular point.

Spectator help

Q In a matchplay final, I played a good shot on to the green from about 150yd (137m) out. My opponent, who was slightly nearer the green, had to decide whether to play directly over a bunker or take a safer line in the centre of the green. He called to a spectator by the green to ask how far my ball was from the hole. Was he breaking the rules?

A No, there was no infringement. Your opponent was seeking information, not advice.

After a shot

Q After my opponent played his ball on to the green, I followed and also managed to get there. I then asked my opponent what club he played. He claimed I was breaking the rules. Was I?

A No, you had already taken your shot. If you asked *before* you would be seeking advice – this is against the rules.

Sharing a caddie

Q A friend was acting as caddie to both me and my opponent. After I played my shot on to the green, my opponent asked for and was given the number of the club I played. Wasn't he breaking the rules?

A No – your opponent was entitled to ask his caddie for information. Bear this in mind when you share a caddie.

Offering advice

Q I am a beginner at golf. A fellow competitor in our medal was good enough to point out after 12 holes that I was swinging too fast. He was given a penalty. This seemed harsh.

A The decision was harsh, perhaps, but correct – the competitor was offering advice.

Before play

Q When we were waiting to play in our last monthly medal, my companion asked a player who had just completed his round what clubs he used on several holes. Should he have been penalized 2 shots?

A The rule applies during the playing of a round. There's no penalty for advice sought between rounds of a 36-hole match, or while play is suspended.

Strokeplay order of play

The competitor who is entitled to play first from the teeing ground is described as having the honour. There are clear directions as to who should play first once the ball is in play.

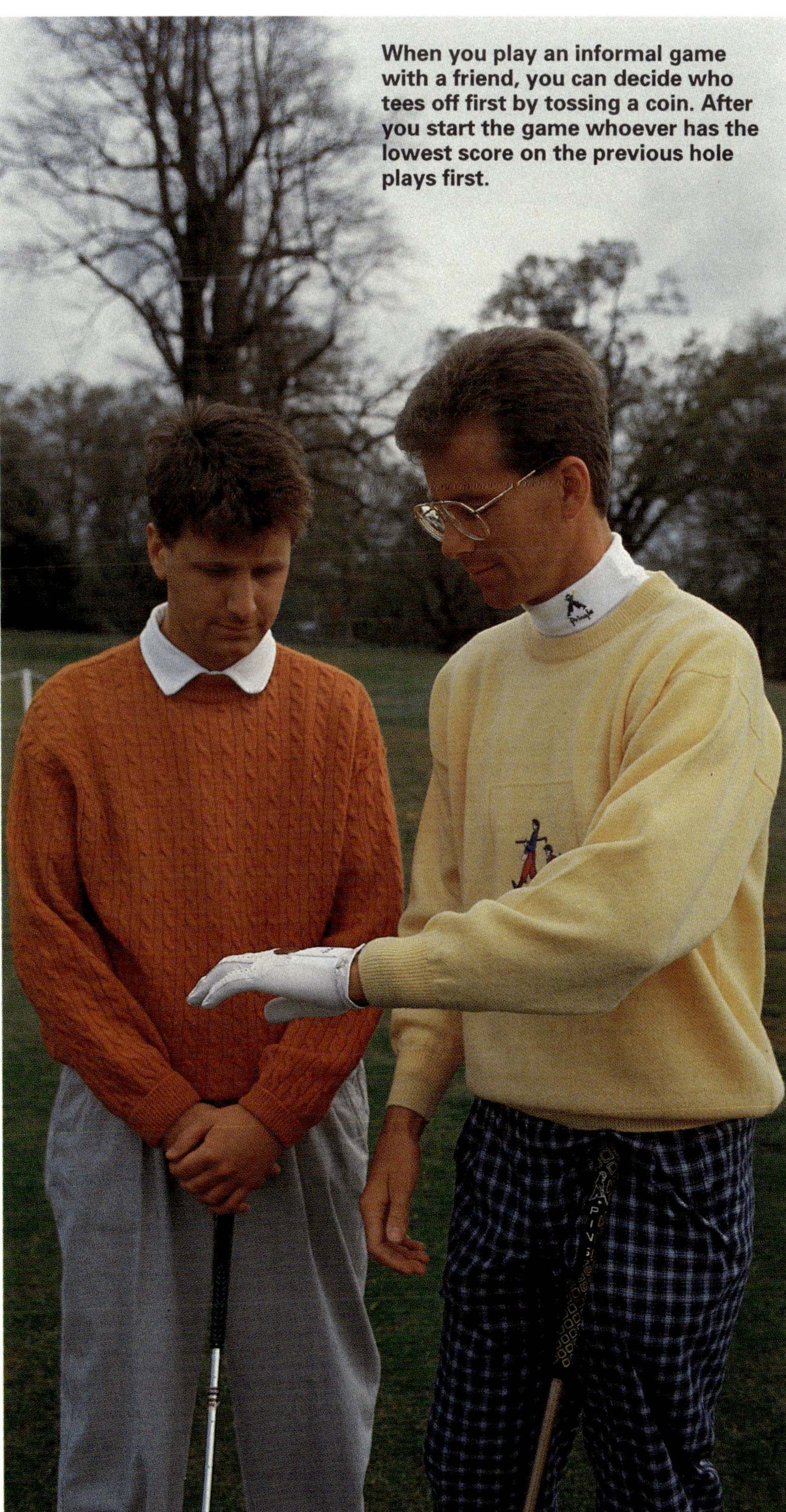

When you play an informal game with a friend, you can decide who tees off first by tossing a coin. After you start the game whoever has the lowest score on the previous hole plays first.

When there is a draw for a strokeplay competition, you begin in the order in which the names have been drawn. Where there's no draw, the order is dec-ided by lot – normally you just flip a coin.

Many people believe that the player with the lowest handicap should go first but the rules don't say so. Often this happens in friendly matches as a gesture of respect to the best player.

However, there is no penalty for playing out of turn in strokeplay unless it can be proved that you are trying to give someone an unfair advantage.

Things are quite straightforward on the other 17 tees. The competitor with the lowest score at the previous hole plays first, the one with the next lowest score follows, and so on. If two or more of you have the same score at a hole, you play in the same order as from the previous tee.

BALLS IN PLAY

Once the balls are in play, whichever of you is furthest from the hole plays first. Normally it's easy to agree on this, but if the balls are equal distances from the hole you should decide who plays first by lot.

A rare exception to this rule occurs when balls are marked. You may mark your own ball at any time when you think the ball might help someone else, or have another ball marked whenever you think it might hinder you. You may do this anywhere on the course, not just on the green. When you are asked to lift your ball in strokeplay, you may prefer to play first rather than mark your ball – even if your ball is nearer the hole.

OUT OF TURN

If it is proved that competitors have played in the wrong order to give one of them an advantage, they're likely to be disqualified.

If, for example, you decided by the 16th hole in a medal that your score was beyond redemption, you might be tempted to putt before someone else who was further from the hole than you. If he happens to be on the same line as you, he might see how much your ball turned and have an unfair advantage. For this, both of you may be disqualified.

FOURBALL

A special case arises when you play out of turn in a foursome – for example, you play the ball you are sharing when it is actually your partner's turn.

If partners play a stroke in the wrong order in a fourball, the stroke is cancelled and the side is penalized 2 strokes.

The mistake is put right by playing in the correct order from the same spot. If the side plays a stroke from the next teeing ground without correcting the error, it is disqualified.

If you play in the wrong order on the last hole of the round, you must correct the mistake by playing the hole again from the place where the error was made. You must do this before you leave the last green – if you don't, you'll be disqualified.

▼ In a more formal strokeplay game, the order of play is decided by a draw. The players swap their score cards before they play from the first tee.

Questions and Answers

Ground under repair

Q There's a large area of 'ground under repair' at our course where drainage work was recently completed. Last week both my companion and I played shots into this area and decided to take relief. I'd been further from the hole before we lifted the balls, but after we dropped them my ball was slightly nearer to the hole. Who should have played first?

A You. The order of play is determined by the positions where the balls originally came to rest.

Water hazards

Q My companion and I both put our second shots at the 18th into a lateral water hazard which runs almost alongside the green. My ball landed further from the green, but my companion's ball crossed the margin of the hazard further from the hole than mine. I thought that the ball was dead once it entered the hazard, and that he should play first. Was I right?

A No – since your ball came to rest further from the hole, you should have played first. If both balls are lost in the hazard, the decision should be by lot.

Handicaps

Q I have a much higher handicap than the friend I normally play with in strokeplay competitions. My handicap isn't deducted until the end of the round; this means that I rarely have the honour, as my gross scores are hardly ever less than my friend's. Is this correct?

A Yes. The lowest gross score on each hole is all that matters in strokeplay.

Stableford honour

Q How is the honour decided in Stableford competitions?

A The decision is made according to the best net score at each hole. This contrast with strokeplay is logical because, in Stableford, strokes are allotted to particular holes.

Out of turn

Q Last week I played out of turn in a strokeplay competition. Not realizing at the time that there was no penalty for this, I played another ball from the tee and continued the hole with that. My score with this ball was recorded on the card. Was this correct?

A No. When you played another ball from the tee, the original ball was deemed lost. You should have added 2 strokes to your score with the second ball.

Playing a provisional ball

You can play a provisional ball if you think your original ball is lost and you don't want to delay play to look for it. But be sure to follow the correct procedure.

If you think that your ball may be lost you should play a provisional ball. The only exception is in a water hazard or out of bounds.

You should tell your opponent in matchplay, or your marker or fellow competitor in strokeplay, that you intend to play a provisional ball. Play it before you or your partner looks for the lost ball.

If you don't do this, your second ball automatically becomes the ball in play and the original ball is assumed to be lost. So if you were playing a second ball from the tee, you will have played your third shot because you take a 1 stroke penalty for a lost ball.

You can continue to play strokes with your provisional ball until you reach the place where the original ball is likely to be. If you play a stroke from that place or any point nearer the hole, the provisional ball becomes the ball in play.

UNPLAYABLE LIES

If you play a provisional ball from the tee then you find your original ball in bounds but in an unplayable position, you have three options. You can find somewhere within two club lengths to take a drop, or choose a spot on the ball-to-target line – but not nearer the hole. You may also play your next shot from where the last one was played – adding a 2 shot penalty.

In this situation you're not allowed to play a provisional because the ball becomes dead as soon as you found your original ball. You must go back to the tee and play a third ball, under penalty of stroke and distance.

▼ If a shot lands in dense woodland, it saves time to play a provisional ball before you search for the lost original. Declare your ball as provisional or it becomes the ball in play.

Who plays first?
There is sometimes confusion over which partner plays a provisional ball in foursomes. If you play and think you may have lost the ball or put it out of bounds, it is your partner who plays the provisional ball, because penalty strokes do not affect the order of play.

Questions and answers: provisional balls

Visible ball

Q My opponent was driving badly. Although his ball was clearly visible not far from the tee after a bad shot on the 4th, he hit a second ball, which he declared as a provisional, in an attempt 'to play himself into form'. Was this in order?

A No – there must be a reasonable possibility that the original ball is lost or out of bounds before a provisional is allowed. Your opponent's second ball would become not a provisional but the ball in play.

Permission to search

Q At our par-3 13th hole my opponent hit his tee shot into dense scrub. He then hit a provisional ball, which came to rest very near the hole.

He walked past the area where his first ball lay, saying that he wouldn't look for it – he was happy to see it lost. Would it have been in order for me to search for his first ball, even though he did not wish to do so?

A Yes. But if your opponent walked on to the green and played a stroke at the provisional ball before you found the first one, it would become the ball in play. This is because he had played from nearer the hole than the spot where the original ball lay.

In matchplay you could recall the stroke if he had played out of turn, but that would not change the status of the original ball, which becomes lost as soon as the provisional is played from nearer the hole.

If you found the original ball before he played any further stroke, it would become the ball in play. The provisional would be a dead ball.

Search order

Q I hit my ball into rough on the right of the fairway and my opponent hit his into rough on the left. We both had caddies. My opponent's caddie went to look for his ball, while everyone else moved to look for mine.

My opponent shouted to his caddie that he should not begin to search until everyone else was ready to help. Was this in order?

A Yes – you don't search at the same time as your opponent.

Time allowed

Q I hit both my original ball and my provisional ball into deep rough. Was I allowed a total time of five minutes to search for both, or five minutes for the first and then another five minutes for the provisional?

A If the two balls are so close together that you are searching for both of them at once, you are allowed only a total of five minutes. Otherwise you are allowed five minutes for each ball.

Unannounced ball

Q I put my tee shot deep into the woods. Deciding that my second ball should be the ball in play, I did not announce it as a provisional. Could I still have had a quick look for my original ball, which was new?

A Yes, but you cannot play the original ball if you find it – and you must not unduly delay play.

pro tip

TAKING A DROP

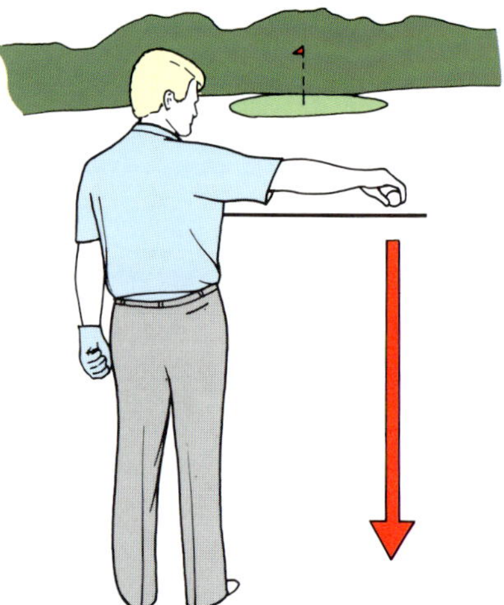

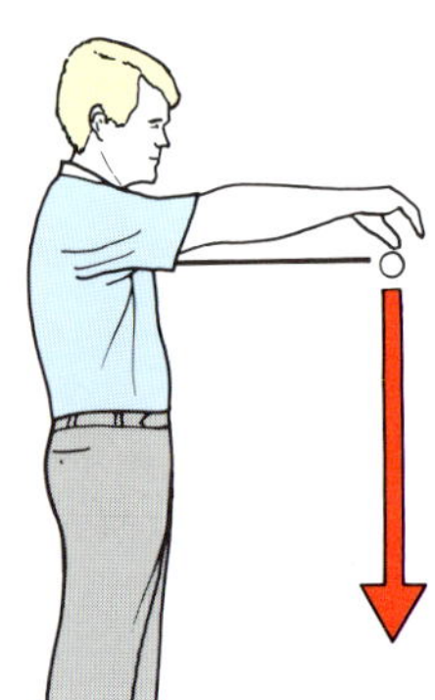

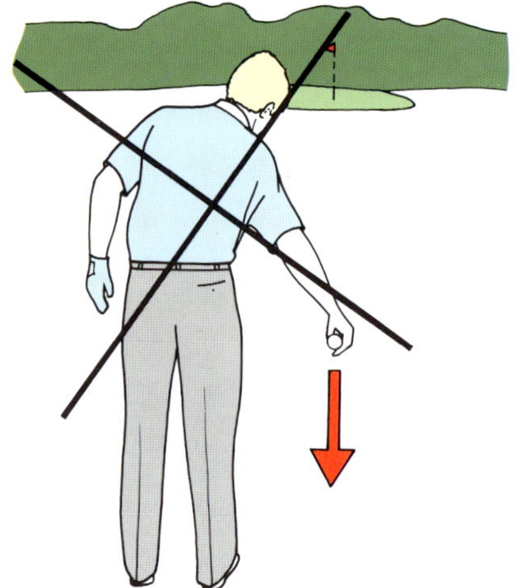

If you have to take a drop, you must drop the ball close to the place where it originally lay – but no nearer the hole.

To drop properly, stand straight and hold your arm at shoulder height. You can then drop the ball. You may extend your arm directly in front of you or to the side, whichever you prefer.

You may see a player lowering an arm and dropping the ball gently on a good lie, but while this may be acceptable in a friendly game it is illegal in competitions.

Looking for your ball

There are specific guidelines to follow when you lose your ball. If you're aware of the rules, you can avoid picking up needless penalties.

Even the best golfers have to search for a ball sometimes. You are allowed five minutes to look for your ball. The five minutes start when the search for the ball begins – not when you hit it. That means when your side – you, your partner and your caddie – start the search, not when any spectators or opponents begin to look.

Many golfers are vague about time. It's up to you to police yourself – if you haven't timed the start of your search, you should accept the view of anyone who suggests that your time is up.

Most golfers don't use the full time limit to search for a ball in friendly matches. If the competition is important enough for you to spend time searching, make sure you call other matches through when you see them waiting.

NATURAL OBSTRUCTIONS

When looking for your ball anywhere on the course, you may touch or bend long grass, heather, bushes or other natural vegetation, but only enough to find your ball and identify it as yours. You must not improve the lie of your ball, the area of your swing or your line of play.

If you cannot be sure the ball is yours, you may lift it to identify it, provided that you replace it in exactly the same lie. According to the rules, you're not necessarily entitled to see your ball when playing a shot.

If you or any member of your side moves your ball other than to find or identify it, it costs you a penalty shot. But if the ball is moved

◄ You are allowed to look for a lost ball for five minutes. If you can't find it, you must go back to where you hit the ball from and take a 1 stroke penalty.

by a member of the other side, or a fellow competitor or his caddie in strokeplay, there is no penalty. You replace the ball and play on. This applies only to searching for a ball. Touching or moving an opponent's ball leads to a 1-stroke penalty at other times.

There is no penalty for playing a wrong ball in a hazard, so you don't have to be certain that a ball is yours before you play a shot.

If your ball is covered by loose impediments or sand in a hazard, you are allowed to remove enough of this material to help you see a part of your ball. If you remove more than necessary, you must replace the material until only a part of it is visible. If you move the ball in probing or raking like this, there is no penalty, provided that you replace the ball in the same position.

In a water hazard, the rules say that there must be 'reasonable evidence' that your ball has lodged in the hazard before you can presume that it has been lost there. For instance, if the hazard is surrounded by fairway and you can't see your ball on the grass, it is reasonable to assume that it has gone into the water.

▲► **If your ball is stuck in a tree, you can use your club to dislodge it and identify it as yours. If you can't free your ball, resign yourself to a 1 stroke penalty and take a drop two club lengths from the place where the ball is lodged.**

Questions and answers

Over the limit

Q What happens if a player goes on searching for a ball longer than the five minutes which the rules allow?

A Searching for the ball after the time allowed is pointless as, even if the ball is found, it is said to be lost after the five minute period. The player is also subject to a penalty for delaying play. In matchplay this is a loss of a hole while in strokeplay it's 2 strokes. You're liable to be disqualified for repeated offences.

Declaring a ball lost

Q My companion searched for his tee shot for two minutes, then declared it lost and went back to play another ball from the tee. Before he played, I found his first ball within the five minute period allowed. He thought that he had made the original ball a lost one by his declaration and by going back to the tee, and that he therefore had to play 3 from a tee. Was he correct?

A No. This is a common misunderstanding easy to make if you've watched similar occurrences in professional tournaments on television. When you have seen a professional having to play a second ball in this situation, it is because he has exhausted his five minute search period before abandoning the ball.

A player cannot make a ball lost by declaration. As the original ball was found within the five minute search period, it remained the ball in play. If the player had actually played another ball, or even dropped one other than on the tee, it would have become the ball in play.

Unplayable ball

Q Last summer in Spain my ball lodged in a palm tree. I was able to get near enough to it to identify it as my ball, but not to retrieve it. My companion thought my ball should be deemed lost as I could not retrieve it. Was he right?

A No – as the ball was identified, it was not lost. You could declare it unplayable and carry on under that rule. Players usually choose to drop within two club lengths of the ball – taking a 1-stroke penalty. In your case you are allowed a drop within two club lengths of the spot on the ground immediately beneath where your ball was lodged.

If you could see a ball in the tree but not identify it as yours, your ball would be deemed lost. You would be allowed to shake the tree, or even throw a club at the ball, in an attempt to dislodge and then identify it.

Hidden ball

Q My ball was almost invisible in a bunker because it was covered with leaves. I knew I was not allowed to move loose impediments in hazards, but don't the rules allow me to remove enough debris to see part of the ball? When I took my stance to play my shot I couldn't see any part of the ball. Could I have removed enough leaves to let me see the ball?

A No – the ball was not invisible in the bunker, because you could see it from one angle. You are not necessarily entitled to see the ball when playing a shot. If you thought the shot was impossible, you could have taken a drop within the bunker, under penalty of 1 shot.

Improving your lie

Like it or not, you play the ball from where it stopped. But there are some exceptions where you can take relief without a penalty. It pays to be aware of them.

You usually play the ball as it lies, accepting bad luck as part of the game. If you find yourself in a divot mark or other unpleasant lie in mid fairway, you have to play the ball as it lies. You may feel this is harsh but it is part of the rules.

EXCEPTIONS

The commonest exception is the use of winter rules. These normally let you choose your lie – pick up your ball and place it on fairways and the aprons of greens. But they are not hard and fast rules because they are not part of the Rules of Golf. They are local rules made by the club committee.

Usually you can move the ball within 6in (15cm) – not nearer the hole – but the distance may vary in different golf clubs. You may also clean the ball when you lift it in these circumstances – after you have marked its position.

Sometimes clubs may continue their winter rules into spring and summer to take account of exceptional circumstances. These may include the condition of the fairways after a very dry summer.

Be careful to note when your club ends its winter rules. If you continue to choose your lie after the committee has ended the rule you lose a hole in matchplay or 2 strokes in strokeplay.

OBTAINING RELIEF

There are certain cases where you can help yourself quite legitimately under the rules. You can flatten the surface of the teeing ground of the hole you are playing in preparation for your stroke. You can lift and drop without penalty from casual water, holes made by burrowing animals and ground under repair.

You may also obtain relief without penalty from immovable obstructions, which include paths with

✗ You can't move grass and brambles.

✓ If your ball lands in a difficult position you usually must play the ball as it lies or declare it unplayable, adding a 1 stroke penalty and taking a drop. Don't flatten the surrounding ground or you are improving your lie and are liable for a 2 stroke penalty.

You are allowed to flatten the teeing ground of the hole you are about to play as part of your preparation to take a stroke.

manmade surfaces. You can drop the ball within one club length of the nearest point of relief which is not nearer the hole, except where that point puts you in a hazard or on a green. But make sure to check that there is not a local rule on the card which declares such paths 'integral parts of the course'.

If your shot from a bunker is impeded by damage caused by burrowing animals or casual water, you can take a drop but it must still be in the bunker.

There is no relief from damage by burrowing animals in a water hazard. Although this may sound odd, bear in mind that many hazards may be dry for parts of the year, leaving you the option of playing out of them.

Except in a hazard, you may remove loose impediments – stones, leaves, twigs – from around your ball, but you must be careful that the ball does not move as a result. If it does, you incur a penalty stroke and must replace the ball where it lay.

Bear in mind that you cannot remove loose impediments in bunkers. It sometimes seems quite natural to remove a leaf when you approach your ball in a bunker, but if you do so you suffer loss of hole in matchplay or 2 strokes in strokeplay. The only exception is that the rules allow you to remove enough matter to see a part of your ball.

On the green, but not elsewhere, sand and loose impediments may be removed.

Questions and answers

Folded divot

Q My ball came to rest in front of a divot which was folded over but still just attached to the ground. It clearly impeded my shot. Was I in order to remove it before playing my shot?

A No – this was not a loose impediment and removing or replacing it would have been improving your lie and line of your intended swing.

Embedded ball

Q In our last medal, I found my ball embedded in its own pitch mark on the fairway, and lifted it without penalty as the rules permit. Before dropping it, I repaired the pitch mark. My playing partner said I should not have done this, but surely I was correct?

A No – you were improving the area where your ball was to be dropped by adjusting its surface and you were subject to a 2 stroke penalty. If you had dropped the ball and it rolled back into your original pitch mark, you would have been allowed to re-drop it.

Out of bounds post

Q My partner in a foursomes matchplay competition removed a white post marking out of bounds because it was on his line of play. When our opponents pointed out that he was not allowed to do this, he replaced it carefully before playing his shot. Presumably there was no penalty?

A Yes, there was – you should have lost the hole. Your partner was in breach of the rule as soon as he moved the post and there was nothing he could do to avoid penalty.

Preparing line of play

Q My opponent was faced with a very tricky short pitch over a bunker, with the flag only 5yd (4.5m) beyond it. He went into the bunker and raked it level, just in case he was short with this delicate shot. Did this infringe the rules?

A Yes, his action was improving the line of play, which is forbidden.

Water relief

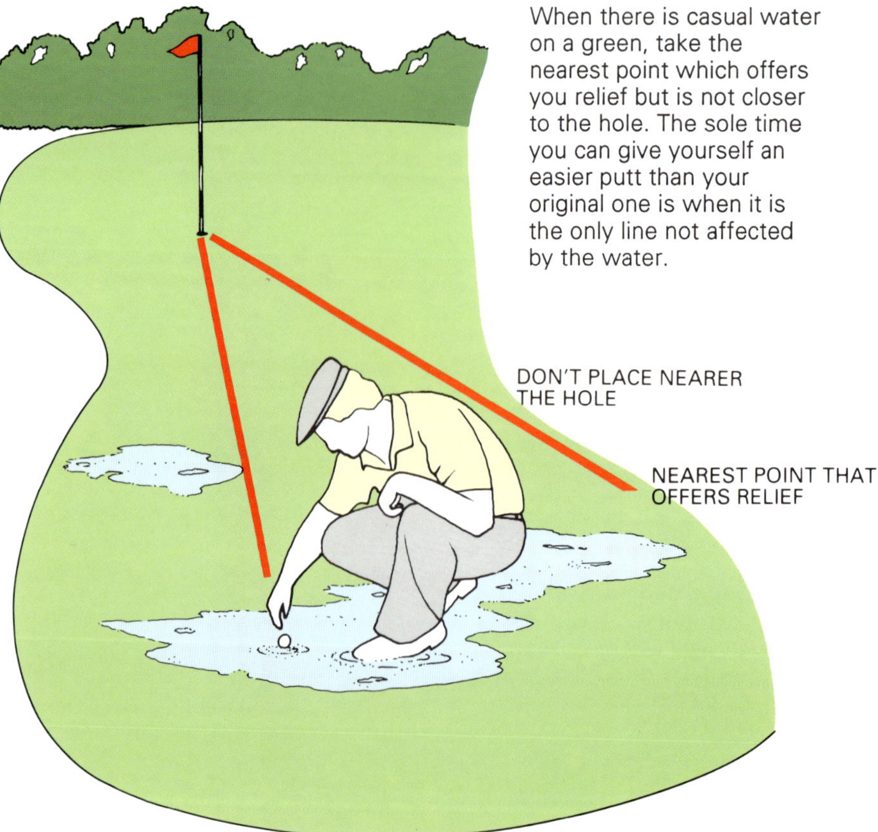

When there is casual water on a green, take the nearest point which offers you relief but is not closer to the hole. The sole time you can give yourself an easier putt than your original one is when it is the only line not affected by the water.

When a ball moves

What do you do if a dog makes off with your ball, or a sudden gust of wind moves a ball on the green? As usual, the rules are quite specific - heed them to avoid penalty.

Your ball is said to have moved if it leaves its position and comes to rest in some other place. It's important to bear this in mind because there is no penalty when the wind moves a ball or you touch it accidentally and it settles back into the same place.

If your ball is moved by an outside agency you suffer no penalty. But remember to replace the ball in its original position before you play your stroke. An outside agency is any thing or person which is not part of the match, or in strokeplay not part of your side.

For example, if a spectator, a dog or a bird moves your ball after it comes to rest, you do not suffer any penalty. You replace – not drop – your ball where it lay and carry on as if the interference never happened. You may have to place another ball if an animal disappears carrying the original.

WIND AND WATER

The rules clearly say that neither wind nor water is an outside agency. If your ball moves after you address it you are penalized a shot, even though you may feel it's not your fault. For instance, a sudden gust of wind quite often moves the ball on a green. If you have already addressed your ball you are penalized a shot.

You are said to have addressed your ball when you have taken your stance and grounded your club. This does not apply in a hazard, where you are never allowed to ground the club. Taking your stance means placing your feet into position to play a stroke.

If you think your ball is likely to move – perhaps you notice the wind making it quiver – it's wise to wait a moment before you address it. There is no penalty if it moves at that stage.

If you, or your caddie, lifts or moves your ball, except where the rules let you – for example when the ball is in casual water or on ground under repair – you take a 1 shot penalty. The same applies if your equipment or that of your partner causes your ball to move. Remember to replace your ball in its original lie before playing.

CLEARING THE WAY

Be very careful about removing loose impediments from around your ball. You are allowed to remove these except in a hazard. But if your ball moves after you have removed them there is a 1 stroke penalty. This rule applies even if you have not addressed

You pick up a penalty if your ball moves after you address it. But on the tee the ball can fall off the peg without penalty unless the stroke has been started. Jack Nicklaus developed a habit of not grounding his club to reduce the chances of picking up a penalty for a moving ball whether or not he's on the tee.

your ball and are convinced that the movement had nothing to do with whatever you removed.

If someone accidentally moves your ball in the rough while searching for it the penalty depends on who moves it. If it's you, your partner, your caddie or your equipment, there is a 1 stroke penalty. But if your ball is disturbed by an opponent, his caddie or equipment, there is no penalty. Similarly, if a fellow competitor moves your ball in strokeplay there is no penalty.

If a ball at rest is moved by another ball, replace it in its original position. This sometimes happens when a player chips on to a green and strikes a ball already there. In this case, the ball which has been struck is replaced. The ball which struck it is played as it lies without penalty.

If your ball hits an outside agency, for example a dog, there's no penalty – you replace the ball near where it was stopped and play on. If a dog or other animal runs off with your ball you place a new ball close to where the original was last in play without penalty.

Questions and answers: moving balls

Rough lie

Q My ball was lying in long grass. Before I could play it, the ball slipped vertically downwards, as had seemed likely. Had the ball moved?

A Yes – whether there was a penalty would depend on if the ball moved before or after you had addressed it, and whether you caused it to move even before you addressed it.

Grounding the club

Q When preparing to putt I usually ground my club in front of the ball to check the line, as some professionals do. Recently, my ball moved on the green after I had done this but before I had grounded my club behind the ball ready to strike.

My opponent said that I should be penalized a stroke, but I maintained that the ball had moved before I had taken my stance, so there should be no penalty. Who was right?

A Your opponent was. You are said to have taken your stance when you place your feet in position to play your stroke, and to have addressed the ball when you have then grounded the club, whether in front of or behind the ball.

Side-saddle putt

Q An elderly companion in a recent medal putted side-saddle. He stood directly behind the ball until he had aligned the clubhead and then moved to the side so as not to break the rules by straddling his putt.

Before he moved away, his ball moved. I thought he should have incurred a penalty – to my mind he had grounded the club and addressed the ball – but he maintained that he had still not addressed the ball. Should there have been a penalty?

A No – he had not addressed the ball, as he had not placed his feet into position for his stroke.

Animal interference

Q During the recent very hot summer we found my opponent's ball, which had run to the edge of a fairway on our wooded course, was lying against a coiled adder. We were not aware of its presence until it flashed into sudden life, moving away into the woods. In doing so, it moved my opponent's ball into a patch of long grass.

Was the snake an outside agency, enabling my opponent to replace his ball where it had originally been on the fairway?

A Yes, the rules are quite specific about snakes. A live snake is an outside agency and a dead one is a loose impediment – it's up to you to find out whether it's alive or dead!

Deflected balls

If your moving ball is deflected or stopped by an outside agency you have to accept it as the rub of the green. Playing the ball as it lies is often to your advantage.

The most common deflection is when a ball strikes a spectator in professional tournaments. Occasionally the ball ends in a spot worse than it would have done without the deflection, but usually it finds a better lie.

However it finishes, you must play the ball as it lies. There are just a couple of exceptions. If a ball comes to rest on an outside agency which then moves it the ball should be dropped or – on the putting green – replaced. Make the drop as near as possible to the spot where the outside agency was when the ball hit it. This includes the spectator who moves away with the ball in the hood of a duffle coat or the dog who runs off with

Be careful when there's a danger of a rebound from a bunker face. You're liable for a 2 stroke penalty in strokeplay and loss of a hole in matchplay if the ball comes back and hits you. Play out of the bunker sideways if you're in any doubt about your ability to gain the necessary height.

a ball.

If a ball putted on a green is deflected or moved by an outside agency, you should replace the ball and replay the stroke.

SIDE DEFLECTION

If your moving ball is accidentally deflected by yourself, your partner, your caddie or your equipment, you lose the hole in matchplay and are penalized 2 strokes in strokeplay.

If your ball is accidentally stopped or deflected by your opponent, his equipment or his caddie, there is no penalty. You may either count the stroke and play the ball as it lies, or cancel the stroke and replay it. If you choose to replay drop the ball as near as possible to where it lay. If it was on the tee you can tee it up again and if it lay on the green you can place it.

Care on the green

If your ball strikes another after a stroke, there's no penalty, so long as you played from off the green.

However, if you find your opponent's ball close to your line, it's best to ask him to mark and remove it while you play. If the ball is left on the green you could gain an unfair advantage by using it to stop your own ball.

The only time there is a penalty is when both balls are on the green. In strokeplay you are docked 2 strokes, in matchplay there's no penalty.

Questions and answers

Stolen ball

Q We were putting out on our 18th green when the steward's playful dog escaped and carried off my ball while it was still moving. What is the ruling in these circumstances?

A The stroke is cancelled, the ball replaced, and you putt again from the same spot, without penalty. If the ball had been deflected rather than picked up, the procedure is exactly the same, because the ball was played from on a putting green.

Hitting equipment

Q In a strokeplay competition I topped a shot badly. It hit my bag and then bounced off my caddie. I knew that I was penalized 2 shots for hitting my equipment, but my marker thought I should have been penalized 2 more for hitting my caddie as well. Was he right?

A No – 2 strokes is the penalty for this chapter of accidents. The ball is then played as it lies.

Opponent struck

Q Recently I struck my ball off the heel of the club and hit my opponent, who was standing out of bounds at the time. My ball came to rest out of bounds. My opponent said I should then be playing 3 off the tee. Was he correct?

A The fact that your opponent was out of bounds at the moment when the ball hit him does not affect the rule. You were entitled to replay the stroke without penalty.

A stroke of luck

Q My opponent took a drop clear of trees in a match, having declared his ball unplayable. I was not paying attention and I accidentally deflected his ball into a much better position, nearer the hole and clear of all trouble. I thought he should re-drop it, but he maintained that he should be allowed to play it from where it now lay. Who was right?

A He was. He had the option of re-dropping the ball or playing the ball from where it now lay.

Unlucky deflection

Q In our last monthly medal my ball struck a direction post and was diverted into deep rough. Did I have the option of replaying the stroke?

A This was a rub of the green and you had to play the ball as it lay, without penalty.

Spectator involvement

Q In a strokeplay competition the lady whose card I was marking putted on our 10th green, which is near the clubhouse. The ball struck the foot of someone not involved in the competition and was diverted into the hole. None of us knew what to do in such a case. Can you help?

A The ball should have been replaced and the stroke replayed without penalty. If the competitor did not do so before playing off the next tee, she should have been disqualified.

Dropping under penalty

There are various times in golf when you need to lift your ball under penalty. Be aware of the options when you find yourself in this situation.

You take a drop under penalty when you hit a ball out of bounds, lose a ball, or when you decide that your ball is unplayable.

If you hit your ball out of bounds or lose it from the tee, you may tee the ball up for another attempt. You don't need to play from the exact spot of your previous shot – anywhere within the teeing area is fine. Elsewhere, you must drop a ball as near as possible to where the previous one was played. You add 1 penalty stroke.

UNPLAYABLE BALL

You may declare your ball unplayable at any point on the course except in or touching a water hazard. You don't have to accept anyone else's opinion – weigh up the chances of playing the ball successfully from a particular spot. Often you see high handicap players attempting shots which professionals would probably avoid by taking a drop.

Once you have decided that your ball is unplayable, you lift it under penalty of 1 shot. You then have three options:

- As with a lost or out of bounds ball, you can play your ball as near as possible to the spot where you played the last shot from. This option is useful if there is nowhere suitable to drop a ball – for instance if you're trapped deep in the woods.
- Drop your ball within two club lengths of where it lay, but not nearer the hole. If it rolls more than two club lengths from where it strikes the ground, you drop again. If it is again outside the limit, you place the ball as near as possible to the point where it hit the ground when re-dropped.

▶ When you find yourself in an impossible lie it's often better to take a drop under penalty than to attempt to play the shot.

One of your options is to take a drop two club lengths from the ball – but not nearer the hole. Use your longest club to gauge the lengths.

Once you have measured two club lengths, drop your ball – stand straight and hold your arm out either to your side or front.

You can either take a drop two club lengths from your ball or you can walk back on the line of the ball until you find a free area to take a drop. Drop the ball on the line of your previous lie and the pin.

- Drop your ball behind the spot where it lay, keeping that point directly between the hole and the spot where you now drop it – you may go back as far as you like. This is a useful alternative to dropping within two club lengths, but sometimes it can take you deeper into trouble or beyond the bounds of the course.

If your ball lies in a bunker and you decide to declare it unplayable you can't use the options of two club lengths or going back on the ball's line. You must drop your ball in the bunker. When you lift your ball under penalty in this way, you may clean it if you want to. You can also play from where your last shot landed, under penalty.

If the ball touches you, your partner, your caddies or your equipment, whether before or after hitting the ground while you take a drop, it should be re-dropped.

Questions and answers: Drops with penalty

Drop selection

Q I declared my ball unplayable and dropped it within two club lengths as allowed under the rules. The ball rolled into an old divot mark and was again unplayable, though still within two club lengths and not nearer the hole. Could I have dropped the ball again without further penalty?

A Unfortunately not. Your ball was in play when you dropped it. You could have dropped it again, but only with a further stroke penalty. It pays to be as careful as you can in selecting the particular spot within the two club lengths where you decide to drop.

Easy way out

Q While on holiday in Scotland, I found my ball on a grassy island within a bunker. It had a horrid downhill lie, so I declared it unplayable. I took it back behind the bunker, exercising my right to take the ball back as far as I liked on a line between the hole and where my ball had been lying. My companion said that I should have dropped my ball in the bunker. Who was right?

A You were. Grass-covered ground within a bunker is not part of the bunker.

Tree lie

Q In Spain last year my ball lodged some way up in a palm tree. Though clearly visible and identifiable, it was obviously not playable, but more than two club lengths above the ground.

I went well back behind the tree to drop, keeping the spot where the ball had lodged on a line between me and the hole. Is there any way in which I could have dropped beneath the tree, where the ground was quite clear?

A Yes – you were entitled to drop a ball within two club lengths of the point on the ground immediately beneath the spot where the ball lay in the tree.

Escape from an island in a bunker by dropping on the ball's line.

Dropping without penalty

You can drop your ball without taking a penalty in certain circumstances. Make sure you know where you can take a free drop – it could make all the difference to your final score.

The most common times you can lift and drop your ball without taking a penalty are when it lands in casual water, ground under repair or holes made by burrowing animals. Many courses also have local rules requiring you to drop clear of young staked trees, without penalty.

It's not just the lie of the ball that you should consider. The rules allow you to take relief if your stance or the line of your intended swing are affected.

For instance, if you are standing in casual water to play your stroke, even though your ball itself is clear, you are entitled to relief if you want it. There doesn't have to be standing water – if it seeps up when you've taken your stance, it is said to be casual water and you can drop your ball without penalty.

ASK BEFORE LIFTING

How should you proceed when you have decided to take a free drop? You should ask your oppo-

◄ ▼ Drainage ditches are always seen as ground cover under repair and if your ball lands there you are entitled to a free drop. If the area is not defined with white lines there will be a notice in the clubhouse with details of the ground under repair.

nent in matchplay or your marker in strokeplay to confirm your right to a drop without penalty before you lift the ball. If you lift without their permission you may end up with a penalty if they dispute your right to a free drop.

You drop the ball in the same way as you would in any circumstance – standing straight, holding the ball at shoulder height and arm's length, and dropping it.

When you are taking relief without penalty, you select the nearest spot on the course which gives you relief from the situation. Drop your ball within a club length – but not nearer the hole.

Bear in mind that it may not always be a good idea to take relief, even when it is available without penalty.

For instance, if you discover your ball in ground under repair you may feel that you have a better lie than you would if you lifted and dropped your ball. In this case, you are normally free to play the ball as it lies. But sometimes a local rule makes you take relief to preserve the course.

RE-DROPPING THE BALL

When you drop the ball it may roll up to a distance of two club lengths from where it hits the ground provided it doesn't finish nearer the hole. You can re-drop if the ball is:

- nearer the hole, or has rolled into a hazard – or out of a hazard when you were taking relief within one. When you drop from a hazard, your ball must stay in it.
- on a putting green.
- out of bounds.
- back in the situation from which you are taking relief.

If it rolls into one of these situations for a second time you then place the ball on the spot where it struck the ground when re-dropped.

Questions and answers: free drops

Sly spin

Q My opponent stood erect, held the ball at shoulder height and arm's length, and prepared to drop his ball without penalty. However, in dropping it he deliberately put spin on the ball with his fingers, to try to propel the ball into the best possible lie. Is this allowed by the rules?

A No – if he lifted the ball and re-dropped it correctly there would not be a penalty. But as he dropped it incorrectly he should have taken a 1 stroke penalty.

Which club?

Q My opponent found his ball in the edge of woodland. He used his driver to measure two club lengths, but when he dropped his ball it ran into a difficult lie. Using his putter to measure, he then demonstrated that the ball had rolled outside the two club length limit, and claimed that he could therefore re-drop it. I thought that as it was still within two driver lengths he should play it from where it lay after the first drop. Was I correct?

A Yes. A player may use any club in his bag to measure his club lengths, but he must continue to use the same one he has chosen in any particular situation.

Unauthorized lift

Q My opponent marked and lifted my ball on the green without any request from me to do so. Is there a penalty for doing this?

A Yes – he may lift your ball only with your authority. He should have been penalized a stroke for lifting a ball when he was not allowed to do so.

Dropping zone

Q Behind our 18th green there is a wire netting fence which is the boundary of the course. Several times during the summer balls have come to rest against this netting. There is nowhere to drop within two club lengths, and even if it were possible to go back keeping the spot where the ball had rested in line with the hole, this would be out of bounds. Should the club create a permanent dropping zone to cope with the situation?

A Although a local rule to create a dropping zone is possible, the R and A approve of such solutions only in exceptional circumstances. The dropping zones you see on television in use at professional tournaments are temporary measures forced on the organizers because grandstands take up space. There is the option of playing again from where the previous shot was played, and adding a 1 stroke penalty.

▲ Some clubs have dropping zones behind a large area of ground under repair. You can take a free drop within two club lengths of the sign if your ball lands there.

Loose impediments

Be sure you know what objects are defined as loose impediments – the rules are very precise, and a slight misinterpretation could deny you relief or lead to a needless penalty.

The rules define loose impediments as natural objects such as stones, leaves, twigs, fallen branches and the like. They also include animal droppings, worms and insects and the casts or heaps they make. Loose impediments cannot be fixed or growing, or solidly embedded in the ground, and must not stick to the ball like, say, mud.

You may treat snow and ice as either casual water or loose impediments – the choice is yours. Treated as casual water, you can lift your ball and drop it within a club length of the nearest point of relief without penalty. Alternatively, remove the loose impediment of ice or snow, making sure that your ball does not move.

Remember that if you are playing under winter rules when you encounter snow or ice, you will be able to lift and clean your ball without penalty.

What about sand and loose soil? These are classed as loose impediments only on the green – you may remove them from the line of your putt. Elsewhere on the course you must play the ball as it lies. You may not remove sand or soil when a ball is in motion even on

If you find fallen leaves on the green – or anywhere else on the course apart from a hazard – treat them as loose impediments and move them without penalty. Loose sand or soil on the line of your putt may be moved only on the green.

pro tip

Clearing your line
When clearing leaves or other loose impediments from the line of your putt, be careful to use only your hands or a club. If you brush the loose matter away with your towel or any other piece of equipment you'll be liable for a penalty.

Unless they're in a hazard, fallen branches , twigs and leaves are loose impediments. If you find your ball beside a branch you can remove the impediment but make sure your ball doesn't move as a result. If it does you must take a penalty stroke. It's often advisable to play the ball as it lies if there is a risk of disturbance when you move the loose impediment.

the green.

Dew is not a loose impediment. Those players you may see removing dew from the line of a putt are breaking the rules.

CLAIMING RELIEF

Except in a hazard, any loose impediment may be removed without penalty. But you must make sure that your ball does not move. If it does, you incur a penalty stroke. If it moves after you, your caddie or your partner has removed a loose impediment within a club length of your ball – even though you have not addressed it – you incur a penalty stroke.

It is up to you to be careful when removing twigs, leaves and other loose impediments. If you think there is any chance of your ball moving, it's normally better not to take the risk and simply play the ball as it lies. If the ball does move in these circumstances, don't forget to replace it before you play the shot.

The only exception to this rule comes on the putting green. There, if your ball moves in the process of removing a loose impediment, you replace the ball without penalty.

There is no relief from loose impediments in a hazard. It is all too easy to forget this, and remove a leaf or twig from the top of your ball when it is lying in a bunker. You incur a 1 stroke penalty.

Questions and answers

Difficult lies

Q When we were playing golf on holiday I found my ball first under a banana skin and then against an ant hill. Were these loose impediments?

A Yes – both are defined as loose impediments in the rules and may be removed. You would have to be careful that your ball did not move.

Divot decision

Q Is a divot left by another player a loose impediment?

A If it is completely detached from the ground a divot is a loose impediment. If it is even slightly attached, you may not remove it as a loose impediment.

Helpful players

Q When playing in Spain, my opponent found his ball behind a large stone. He could not move it himself, and asked some players from a nearby fairway to help him shift it. Surely this was not allowed?

A Yes, it was. Provided it was not embedded in the ground, the stone was a loose impediment. And there is nothing in the rules to prevent a player from asking for help from others to remove it, provided this does not unduly delay play.

Fallen tree

Q Is a fallen tree a loose impediment?

A Yes – provided it is no longer attached to the ground. If it is still attached to the stump it's not a loose impediment.

Faulty fruit

Q I found my ball embedded in an orange. This was clearly not my fault – could it have been a loose impediment?

A No – whether the condition was your fault or not has nothing to do with the ruling. The orange was stuck to your ball, so it could not be a loose impediment. You should have either played the ball as it lay or declared it unplayable under penalty of a shot.

Soil clods

Q The green staff at my club had been using a machine to aerate the fairways which left behind plugs of soil. I thought these were loose impediments and could be moved. My companion pointed out that soil is not a loose impediment, and thought the plugs should not be moved. Was he right?

A No, you were right – though loose soil may not be moved on the fairway, compacted soil becomes a loose impediment.

Obstructions 1

What do you do when your ball lands under a parked car or on a bench? The ruling on movable and immovable obstructions is quite logical – find out how to gain relief.

You are normally entitled to relief without penalty from obstructions – defined as anything artificial, including the artificial surfaces and sides of roads and paths.

There are three exceptions, and for these you cannot claim relief. The first two concern **out of bounds obstructions**. There is no relief from any objects defining out of bounds, such as walls, fences, stakes and railings. And you can't claim relief from any immovable object – such as a building – which is out of bounds.

These may not seem important exceptions, but remember that you are allowed to stand out of bounds to play a ball which is just in bounds. You quite often find that an out of bounds fence, or a post outside it, prevents a swing at a ball that would otherwise be playable. In this situation it's usually best to declare the ball unplayable and drop it with a penalty of a shot.

The third exception is the one that often causes confusion. This is the clause which allows the committee to declare what would normally be an obstruction an **integral part of the course**. The most famous example of this exception is the tarmac road which runs behind the 17th green of the Old Course at St Andrews in Scotland.

Many golfers who are used to enjoying relief from roads on their own courses cannot understand why they see professionals having to play from the road at the headquarters of golf. The reason is that the committee of the club have declared this particular road to be an integral part of the course.

This rule underlines the important point that when playing at an unfamiliar course you should first check the card of the course carefully for local rules. You must know if the committee of the club has taken advantage of its powers to declare what would normally be obstructions as integral parts of the course where no relief is available.

▼ You are usually allowed relief if your ball lands on a road, but on some courses – such as the 17th at St Andrews Old – the road is declared an integral part of the course. Always check your score card before claiming relief from obstructions – if your ball lands on an integral part of the course you cannot claim relief.

MOVABLE OBSTRUCTIONS

When an obstruction is movable – a bench, for instance – you take relief from it in one of two ways. If your ball does not lie in or on the obstruction, you may remove the object. If your ball moves, there is no penalty – you simply replace it.

If your ball lies in or on the obstruction you may lift your ball without penalty, and move the object. On the green you then place your ball; anywhere else on the course you drop it. You do this so that the ball finishes as near as possible to the spot directly under where the ball lay, but not nearer the hole. You may clean your ball when you lift it.

► If your ball lands near a post defining out of bounds you cannot claim relief. You must not move the post to play your shot, even if it hampers your swing. If you do move it, you lose the hole in matchplay and 2 strokes in strokeplay.

Questions and answers

Movable decision

Q I cannot find an exact definition in the rules of golf of a movable obstruction. Can you help?

A You're quite right. The rules of golf do not give a definition of a movable obstruction, presumably because the term is thought to be self explanatory. But a decision of the R and A says that an obstruction is movable if it may be moved without undue effort, without delaying play and without damaging the property of the course.

Steep steps

Q Are wooden steps on a steep bank an obstruction?

A Yes, they are – you can take relief from these sorts of wooden steps. But if steps are simply cut into the bank and not artificially covered they are not obstructions. If your ball lies on earthen steps you must play the ball as it lies or take relief under penalty.

Parked car

Q What happens if a ball comes to rest under a parked car?

A If the car is easily movable, it should be treated as a movable obstruction – so the car should be moved and the ball played as it lies. If the car cannot readily be moved it should be treated as an immovable obstruction. Severiano Ballesteros got relief from just such a situation during his famous first Open Championship victory at Lytham in 1979.

Natural surface

Q Is a path which has been surfaced with wood chips an obstruction?

A Yes – wood chips, ash, gravel and the like are artificial surfaces just as much as concrete or tar in this context so you can take relief from them. As always you need to check the card to make sure that the committee has not exercised its right to declare such a path an integral part of the course – in which case, you cannot take relief without penalty.

Wooden planks

Q Is wood which has been made into planks an obstruction?

A Yes, planks are deemed an obstruction – unless they are a part of the course – and you can claim relief if your ball lands on or beside them.

Abandoned ball

Q In a match earlier this year my ball came to rest against an abandoned ball in the rough. I could not treat this as a loose impediment because my ball would have moved. How should I have proceeded?

A An abandoned ball is a movable obstruction. You could have moved it and dropped your ball as near as possible to where it originally lay. You could also have replaced your ball without penalty if it moved.

Obstructions 2

You are entitled to relief when an immovable obstruction interferes with your shot, but don't pick up your ball and take relief without checking the rules thoroughly.

You can claim relief from an **immovable obstruction** – something fixed and artificial such as a bridge or marker post – when your ball lies in or on the object, or so close to it that it gets in the way of your stance or the area of your swing.

There is no relief from objects which define out of bounds, or from any part of an immovable obstruction that is out of bounds. The committee can also declare any construction to be an integral part of the course – this means that there is no relief from it.

You must check the card of the course carefully to make sure that roads and buildings which would normally entitle you to relief have not been declared integral parts of the course. If they have, the information is on the card.

The fact that the obstruction is on your line of sight does not entitle you to relief. You may have seen professional golfers receiving line of sight relief from objects such as advertising hoardings, but that is an official's decision, because hoardings are temporary and abnormal additions to the course.

TAKING RELIEF

Before you claim relief from an immovable obstruction **through the green** you must find a point on the course nearest to where the ball lies without crossing over, through or under the obstruction.

Say your ball lands beside a fixed bench. You cannot measure a club length *under* the bench – you must take relief clear of the object. The point must be clear of interference, not nearer the hole, and not in a hazard or on a green. When you have found a satisfactory spot you lift the ball and drop it within a club length of this point.

▼ If your ball lands on a sprinkler head you are entitled to a free drop as the sprinkler is an immovable obstruction. Lift the ball and drop it within one club length from the obstruction but not nearer the hole or on the green.

The rule about not crossing over, through or under the obstruction does not apply to artificial surfaces of roads, or when the ball lies in or on the object. If your ball lies on a road you can bring it back across the road to find the *nearest* point of relief not nearer the hole.

To claim relief from an immovable obstruction in a **bunker** – perhaps your ball lies beside the exposed concrete wall of a man-made bunker – the ball must be dropped in the bunker.

If your ball lies in or touches a **water hazard** there is no relief without penalty from interference by an immovable obstruction.

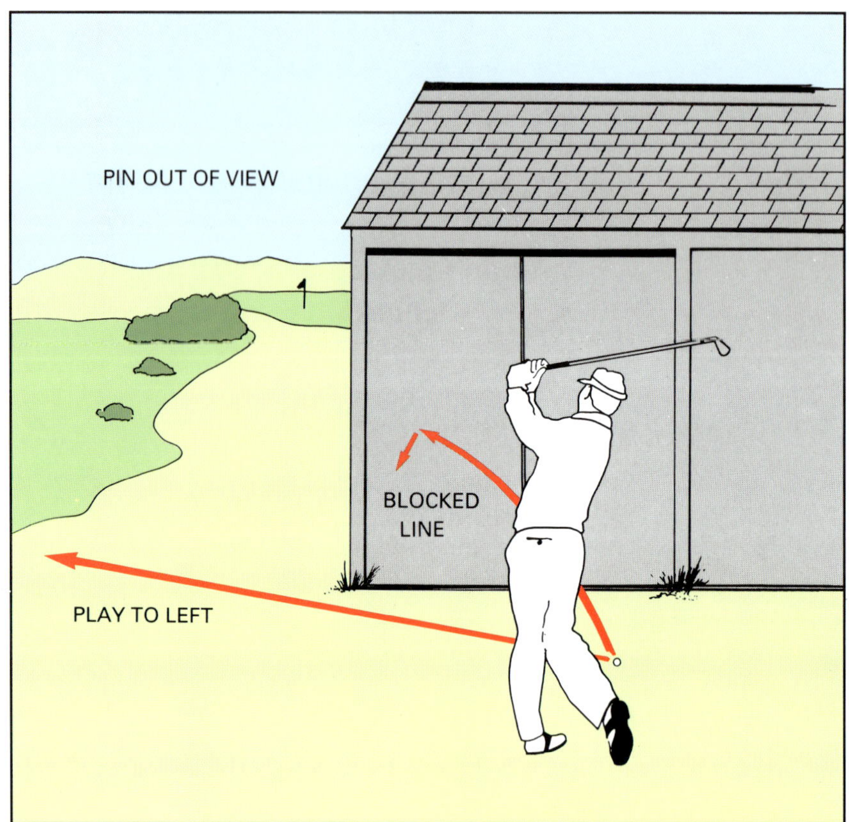

► To claim relief it has to be your stance or swing that is affected by the immovable obstruction, not your line of sight. In this case the position of the barn allows the player to swing freely so he can't take relief, despite the fact that he is unable to see his target.

Questions and answers: immovable objects

Double trouble

Q My opponent's ball was just in bounds but his shot was affected by the boundary fence, from which the rules gave him no relief. But a wall of a building near the fence interfered with his swing. He claimed that he was allowed to take relief from the immovable obstruction, even though this would also give him relief from the fence. Was he correct?

A Yes, he could claim relief. It was his good fortune that relief from the immovable obstruction also gave him a clear shot from the boundary fence.

Fairway drop

Q My opponent found his ball in the rough, with his stance impeded by an immovable obstruction. He took relief and dropped the ball in accordance with the rules, but on the fairway. Was this allowed?

A Yes – there is no distinction in the rules between fairway and rough. Both are covered by the term 'through the green'.

Swing interference

Q My ball came to rest just in bounds. I could play it by standing out of bounds, except that an immovable artificial object – a stone post – situated out of bounds interfered with my swing. Could I have claimed relief?

A No – any immovable object which is off the course is not an obstruction, and there is no relief from it.

Clubhouse chip

Q I heard of a golfer who hit his ball into the clubhouse, which had not been declared out of bounds or an integral part of the course. He then opened a window and chipped his ball on to the nearby putting green. Surely this was not in order?

A Yes, it was! The clubhouse was an immovable obstruction. But any part of it designed to be movable – such as a window or door – may be moved provided it can be done without undue delay. Even if the clubhouse has been declared an integral part of the course, the same principle applies. Similarly, a player finding his ball near a barn or shed may open the doors to play a shot through the building.

Line of sight

Q My ball came to rest behind the corner of a tractor shed which was an immovable obstruction. As this interfered with my swing, I was clearly allowed relief from it. But the shed was also on the line of sight, from which the rules allow no relief. When I dropped the ball to give myself a clear stance I also gained a clear line of sight for my shot. Was this permissible?

A Yes, you were clearly allowed relief from the immovable obstruction. The fact that this also gave you line of sight relief was simply good luck.

Outside agencies

There's no penalty if your ball is moved by an outside agency. But check the rules carefully – these agencies are strictly defined.

The rules state that an outside agency – be it human, animal or machine – is one that is not part of a match or, in strokeplay, not part of a competitor's side. So the referee, a marker, a dog or an onlooker are all classed as outside agencies. On the other hand, the rules state specifically that wind and water are not outside agencies.

This means that if the wind moves your ball on the green after you have addressed it you must take a 1 stroke penalty – even though it's not your fault. But if your ball was moved in these circumstances by an outside agency, there is no penalty provided that you replace the ball in its original spot before playing it.

The rules about interference by an outside agency while your ball is at rest are quite simple. You replace your ball as near as possible to the spot where it originally lay and play on without penalty. This applies no matter where the interference occurs on the course.

When an outside agency interferes with your ball after you have struck it the rules are more complicated. Until you reach the green, any accidental deflection or stopping of your ball by an outside agency while it is moving is the rub of the green.

▼ If a ball lands in the crowd and comes to rest in a bag or coat there is no penalty. The player must remove the obstacle and drop the ball as near as possible to where the agency picked it up.

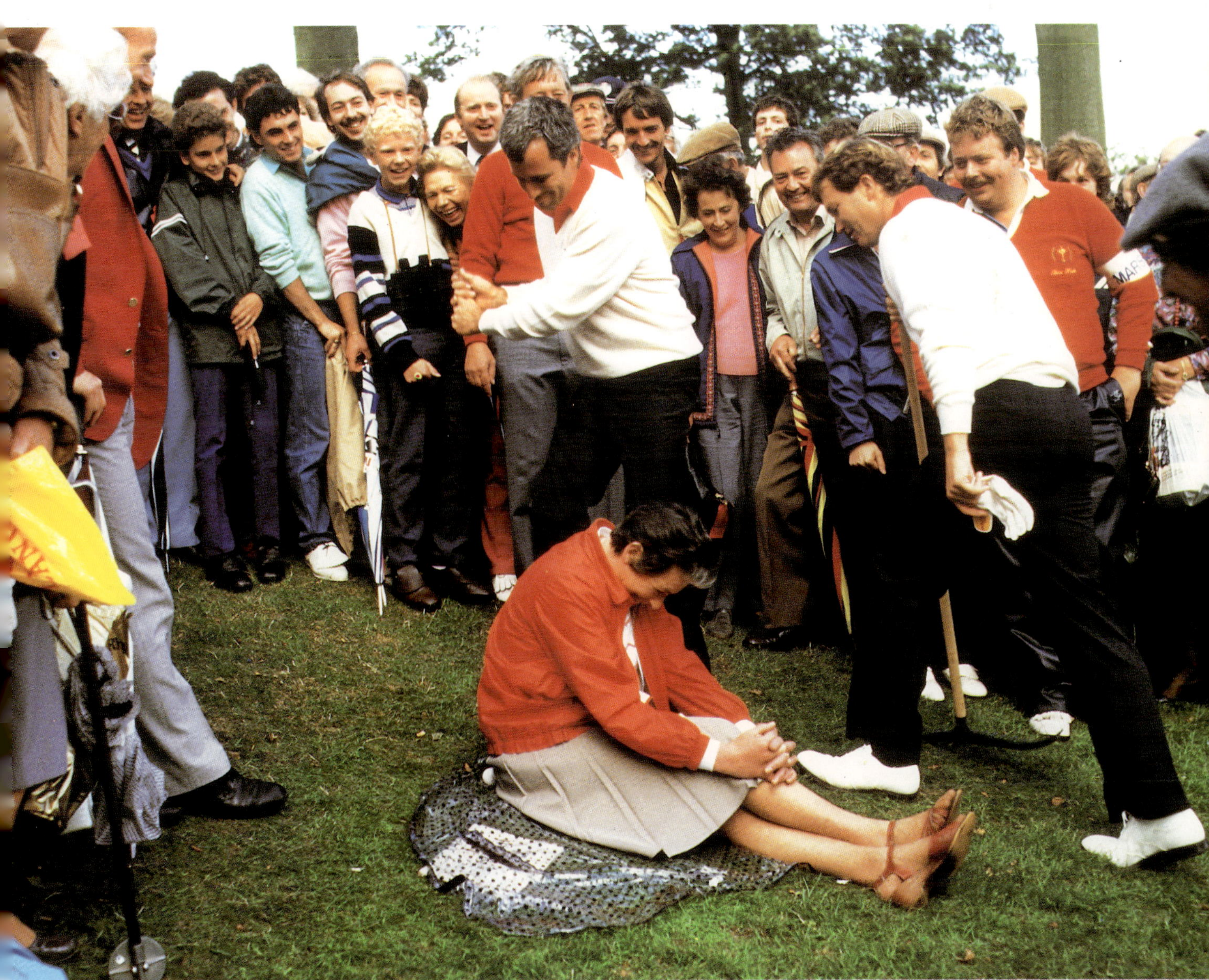

Such interference can bring you good luck or bad. In either case the procedure is the same – you must go to the place where the ball has come to rest and play it as it lies without penalty.

MOVING AGENCIES

If your ball comes to rest in or on a moving outside agency before you reach the green you drop a ball as near as possible to where the agency took it up. So if your partner's ball lands in a trailer towed across the course by a tractor he could drop a ball as near as possible to the spot where the interference took place without penalty.

When you reach the green, the procedure is different. When a ball is moving there it does not matter whether the ball is deflected by the outside agency or comes to rest in it. Whatever the interference, you replace your ball and r eplay the stroke, without penalty. If you cannot immediately recover your ball, you can substitute another one.

Questions and answers

Helpful spectator

Q The rules talk about a ball being accidentally deflected or stopped by an outside agency. I was at a professional matchplay competition some years ago when a spectator deliberately interfered with a ball by throwing it back on to the green after it had gone into the crowd. What should be the decision?

A It sounds like you're describing an incident when Nick Faldo's ball was apparently thrown or kicked back by a spectator during the 1983 Suntory World Matchplay.

In cases like these the referee makes the final decision, but there must be reasonable evidence that deliberate interference has taken place. In the case you describe both the players and the referee decided that there was not enough evidence of deliberate interference by a spectator to merit intervention. So the referee directed that the ball should be played as it lay.

Accidental interference

Q In our last monthly medal, I lifted my ball on the green. My hands were very cold, and as my companion putted my ball shot out of my hand and landed on his ball as it was moving. What was the ruling?

A Your ball was an outside agency. There was no penalty for either of you. Your companion should have replayed his putt.

Tractor deflection

Q My opponent's ball hit a greenkeeper's stationary tractor and bounced off it out of bounds. He claimed the vehicle should not have been there, and dropped another ball near thee tractor. Was he correct?

A No. The tractor was an outside agency. Had the ball been in bounds, it would have been played from wherever it had come to rest. As it went out of bounds, your opponent should have played another ball from the point where he played his last stroke, under penalty of stroke and distance.

Mystery disappearance

Q During a strokeplay competition played in threeballs, I drove from a tee on to the fairway. We could all see my ball after it had come to rest. Play was suspended because of thunder after the three of us had driven but before we left the tee. When we resumed, my ball had disappeared. We eventually found it some distance from where it had come to rest. What was the ruling?

A You were entitled to assume that the ball had been moved by an outside agency. You should have replaced your ball at the spot from which it was moved, without penalty. Had it disappeared altogether, you could have placed another ball at that spot.

▼ The 14th hole at North Berwick has a blind approach shot with a public footpath running across the fairway. Sometimes balls disappear – often picked up by passers-by who don't realize that their owners are playing the hole out of sight. In a case of interference by an outside agency like this you must have reasonable evidence that the ball has been taken, otherwise it must be treated as a lost ball.

Water hazards 1

All that glisters is not necessarily a water hazard – they can be dry ditches or vast lakes. But whatever form they take there's a certain procedure to follow if you find yourself in one.

The rules are quite specific about what is defined as a water hazard. The term includes sea, lakes, ponds, rivers and ditches. Surface drainage ditches or other open water courses – whether or not containing water – are also included in the definition. Casual water – any temporary patch of water – is not deemed a water hazard, and has its own rule.

The margin of a water hazard extends upwards and downwards, and the margin itself is counted as part of the hazard.

Margins should be clearly defined by yellow stakes or lines, since it's important that you should be able to decide whether you are in or out of the hazard. *Lateral* water hazards – like a ditch running down the side of a hole – are defined by red stakes or lines.

YOUR CHOICES

If your ball lies in a water hazard you have to take one of three options.

- You may play the ball as it lies, without penalty. You may be able to play it if the water hazard is dry – not all hazards contain water all the time. Indeed in parts of Spain and Australia it is the rule rather than the exception to find river beds dry.
- Your second option, and the one you usually have to take, is to drop a ball behind the water hazard, keeping the point where your original ball crossed the margin directly between the hole and where you drop it. You may go back as far as you like on this line – the penalty is 1 stroke.

► One of the options available to you when your ball lands in a water hazard is to play it as it lies without penalty. You need to size up the situation carefully before taking this risk – make sure the ball is visible and lying well in shallow water and play it like a bunker shot.

• Your third option is to play again from as near as possible to where your last shot was played, again adding a penalty of 1 stroke. This is proceeding as if you had lost a ball or hit out of bounds. Although you will not normally want to do this, there may be occasions when the previous options are less attractive.

If you lose a ball in a water hazard, this does not affect your score. However, there must be reasonable evidence that the ball was lost there and not elsewhere.

POINTS TO WATCH

If you opt to play your ball from within a water hazard, bear in mind that you must not remove loose impediments or touch the ground with your club before you hit the ball.

It is all too easy to forget this as you try to take a stance when perched awkwardly on the steep bank of a water hazard, but it will cost you the hole in matchplay or 2 strokes in strokeplay if you do so.

Although you may not touch the ground, there is no penalty if your club touches any obstruction – or any grass or bush – at address or on your backswing.

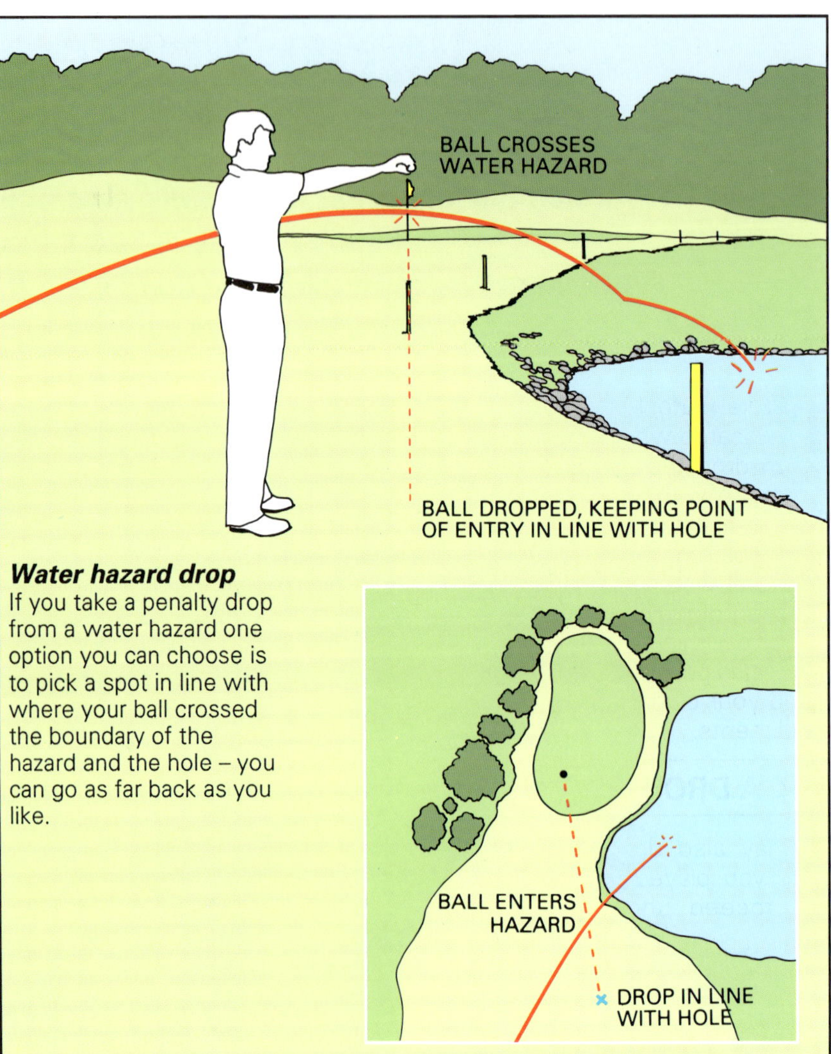

Water hazard drop
If you take a penalty drop from a water hazard one option you can choose is to pick a spot in line with where your ball crossed the boundary of the hazard and the hole – you can go as far back as you like.

Questions and answers

Which ball?

Q My opponent's ball appeared to have gone into a water hazard some 80yd (73m) ahead of us. Without saying anything he dropped a second ball and played it from the same spot. When we reached the hazard, we found that the ball had actually run through the hazard and was clear of it on the far side. Could he then have played the original ball?

A No – by dropping and playing another ball your opponent had deemed the original ball lost, and the second one was the ball in play, under penalty of stroke and distance. If he had declared the second ball provisional, he could have played the original when he found it.

Lost and found

Q In a strokeplay competition, I was unable to find my ball in a water hazard, so I dropped another one behind it under penalty of 1 stroke and played that one. Then, well within the five minute search period, I found my ball in the hazard. It was quite playable, but I was not sure of my rights. I therefore played out the hole with both balls as permitted by the rules, opting to score with my original ball in the hazard. What was the ruling?

A When you dropped the second ball behind the hazard, it became the ball in play. So that was the score which counted for that hole. Although the score with the original ball could not count since it was not the ball in play, you incurred no penalty for playing out with it.

Double trouble

Q Our 18th green has a water hazard immediately in front of it. My third shot cleared this but went through the green into the rough behind it. From there, I thinned my chip back, and was horrified to see my ball go into the water hazard from the green side. It was not playable. What were my options?

A You could have dropped the ball behind the water hazard, keeping the point where the ball entered it between you and the hole; this would mean that you returned to the tee side and played over the hazard again. Alternatively you could have dropped a ball at the point where you thinned the chip shot and played stroke and distance.

Water hazards 2

The rules for lateral water are slightly different from those covering ordinary water hazards, so make sure you're clear about how to recognize a lateral hazard and what to do if your ball lands in one.

A lateral water hazard is one that is located where it is not possible to drop the ball behind it in accordance with the normal rules for water hazards.

If your ball comes to rest or is lost in a lateral water hazard you have the option of playing your ball as it lies from within the hazard if you think that is possible. You must not ground your club or remove loose impediments.

TAKE A DROP

You may also drop another ball where you played your last shot, and proceed under the stroke and distance penalty. So far your choices are the same as when your ball lies in an ordinary water hazard.

Your third option is different. In the case of a lateral water hazard, you may drop your ball within two club lengths of either the point where the original ball last crossed the margin of the hazard or a point on the opposite margin of the hazard the same distance from the hole.

Your ball must be dropped and come to rest not nearer the hole than the point where the original ball last crossed the margin of the lateral water hazard.

As with all balls lifted and dropped from water hazards, there is a penalty of one shot. When you lift the ball under this rule, you may clean it if you wish to.

How can you be certain that what appears to you to be a lateral water hazard actually is one? Whereas

▼ The colour of the marker posts tell you which kind of hazard you're in. Red stakes indicate lateral water and yellow stakes an ordinary water hazard. Sometimes a lateral hazard can turn into an ordinary water hazard at a given point – the stakes tell you where one stops and the other begins.

water hazards are marked with yellow stakes or lines, lateral water hazards are marked with red ones.

WHICH COLOUR?

Be careful – some water hazards may be lateral for part of their length and ordinary water hazard for the rest. The colours of the stakes tell you where the change comes in such cases.

Being able to drop your ball on the green side of a lateral water hazard may sometimes have considerable advantages. Remember that when you drop within the two club lengths, the ball may roll up to another two club lengths from where you drop it provided that it finishes not nearer the hole.

▲ One option available to you if your ball lands in a lateral water hazard is to take a drop – within two club lengths from either the line where your ball entered the hazard or a point on the opposite side of the hazard the same distance from the hole.

Questions and answers

Where to drop?

Q I played recently on a course where there was a ditch on the left of a hole, marked as a water hazard. While the ditch itself was in bounds, the left hand margin was out of bounds. This meant it was impossible to drop behind the ditch. Had I no option but to play the ball as it lay in the hazard or go back and drop the ball at the spot where I had just played my last shot?

A Such a ditch was automatically a lateral water hazard – whether or not the committee had declared it so. So you could have dropped your ball within two club lengths of the point where your ball entered the ditch, on the course side of the hazard.

Lost and found

Q In a strokeplay competition, my ball went into a lateral water hazard about 150yd (137m) in front of me and I could not find it. My marker and I agreed the point where we judged it to have entered the hazard and I dropped a ball within two club lengths of this agreed point, adding the usual penalty of one shot. Before I played my next shot, a fellow competitor said that my ball had crossed the margin some 20yd (18m) further back, and in fact found my ball there for me. What was the ruling?

A Since you had dropped a ball in the wrong place you should have lifted it and dropped it in the correct place, without further penalty. You could not have played your original ball from the hazard, since this was lost the moment you put another ball into play by dropping it.

Which option?

Q We played a very pretty course on holiday. On one hole, a stream ran beside the putting green and collected many balls. Because the boundary of the course was immediately behind it, the stream was a lateral water hazard. However, at some parts of the stream, it was impossible to drop within two club lengths of the point where the ball last crossed the margin without dropping nearer to the hole. What is the procedure?

A You have to proceed under one of the other two options available to you under the rule – either playing from the lateral water hazard itself without penalty or returning to play another ball from the place of your previous stroke, under penalty of stroke and distance.

Blind shot

Q I am on the committee of my club and we have a problem with a lateral water hazard. Because of the contours of the course, most golfers are playing a blind shot over rising ground when their ball ends in this hazard. It is therefore very difficult for them to establish where a ball crossed the margin of the hazard.

Can we make a local rule allowing players to drop a ball, under penalty of 1 stroke, within two club lengths of the point on the margin opposite where the ball comes to rest in the hazard, rather than the point where it crossed the margin?

A No – a local rule cannot modify a rule of golf. The players have to agree on an honest judgment of the point where the ball is likely to have crossed the margin of the lateral water hazard.

▲ If your ball lies just outside a water hazard, you can stand in the water to play your shot without penalty. The boundary of the hazard is measured in a straight line from stake to stake.

Casual water

Most golfers are aware that they can claim relief without penalty from casual water. But there is often uncertainty about what exactly it is and how relief should be taken.

Casual water is any *temporary* accumulation of water on the course which is visible before or after you take your stance to hit a shot. It may occur anywhere on the course, except in what is already defined as a water hazard. Dew is not casual water, but you have the choice of treating snow and ice as either casual water or loose impediments.

Your ball does not have to lie in the water for you to claim relief. If the water affects your stance you may take relief even if the ball is lying clear of the pool. Once you are on the green, you are allowed relief if the water is on the line of your putt.

But what about borderline cases? What is classed as casual water? Soft, mushy turf is not casual water, unless water is visible on the surface before or after you take your stance.

That is the key point – water must be visible on the surface of the ground. Often you find that water wells up around the soles of your shoes when you take your stance, even when it wasn't previously visible. If so, you are entitled to relief. But you must take your normal stance – pressing down hard with one foot to make water appear is cheating.

On many courses water overflows from water hazards, particularly during the winter months. Players are sometimes uncertain whether this is casual water or part of the hazard. There should be no difficulty, because the limits of the

▼ The greenkeepers sweep the greens up after a downpour during the US Masters. Though heavy rain can wreak havoc, don't be tempted to clear casual water away from your line when you're on a green – you lose a hole in matchplay or 2 strokes in strokeplay. Instead, choose the nearest point of relief not nearer the hole.

Questions and answers

Out of bounds

Q My ball was just in bounds but I had to stand outside the course to play it. I found that when I took my stance I was in casual water. Was I entitled to relief?

A Relief couldn't be claimed – the definition of casual water states that it must occur on the course.

Water on the line

Q On a very wet green there was no casual water visible on the line of my putt. But when I walked forward beside the line I could see water welling up around my feet. Could I take relief?

A No – casual water must be already visible on your line or round your feet when you take your stance for you to claim relief.

Clearing the way

Q In a recent match my opponent found his ball just short of the green. He then mopped up a pool of casual water on the green before taking his shot. Was this allowed?

A This was against the rules. Your opponent should have lost the hole for improving his line of play. Even if his ball was on the green he mustn't mop up the water – though he could move his ball to get relief from water on his line.

Improving your line

Q Am I allowed to brush small amounts of casual water off the line of my putt when my ball lies on the green?

A Casual water is not a loose impediment so mustn't be removed in this way. You would lose the hole in matchplay or suffer a 2 stroke penalty in strokeplay for touching the line of your putt.

Hazard overspill

If a water hazard overflows its boundaries the water that spills outside the stakes is casual water. You can claim relief if this interferes with the lie of your ball or your stance.

water hazard are properly defined by yellow or red posts. Any overflow of water which is outside this margin is casual water, and you may take relief without penalty.

HOW TO TAKE RELIEF

For casual water **through the green** you find the nearest point which is not nearer the hole, gives relief from the water and is not in a hazard or on a green. Then you drop your ball within one club length of this point.

In a bunker you drop the ball at a spot not nearer the hole which gives relief from the water but is still in the bunker. Relief is not always possible from casual water in bunkers. If the free drop gives you nowhere reasonable to play from within the bunker, you may drop outside, under penalty of 1 stroke. You must keep the point where the ball lay directly between you and the hole.

On the green you lift your ball and place it in the *nearest position* which gives relief and is not nearer the hole or in a hazard. Remember that you must take the nearest position when pools of water lie on the green. Many players move to the line which they think gives the easiest putt, rather than taking the nearest point of relief. You may clean the ball when you lift it.

Bear in mind that you must be on the putting surface to claim relief from casual water which is on your line. If your ball comes to rest just off the green, you must tackle the problem of water between you and the hole without claiming relief.

You may lose a ball in large amounts of casual water. In that case you take relief without penalty, proceeding from the point where your ball passed the margin of the casual water. There must be reasonable evidence that your ball was lost in the water for you to claim relief. Otherwise you treat the ball as lost with the usual penalties.

Bunkers 1

It may seem obvious what a bunker is, but there are some important differences in the rules according to whether you are inside or outside a bunker.

The rules of golf define a bunker as a hazard which has had turf or soil removed and which has been filled with sand or the like.

This means that a bunker has to be deliberately created. At a seaside course, you may find yourself playing out of pure sand, even from dunes which seem like natural bunkers, but you won't be subject to the rules which govern play from hazards.

Grass-covered ground bordering, or even within, a bunker is not part of the bunker. Some courses even have small islands of grass in the middle of bunkers. All these areas must be treated exactly the same as the rest of the area through the green.

The margin of a bunker extends straight downwards, but not upwards, like that of a water hazard. So if a ball on the edge of a bunker overhangs the sand but does not touch it, it is not in the bunker.

POINTS TO WATCH

The most important point to bear in mind when playing from a bunker is not to ground your club. If you touch the sand at address or on your backswing, you lose the hole in matchplay or are penalized 2 strokes in strokeplay.

Remember also that you are not allowed to remove loose impediments. All too often, a player used to doing this on the rest of the course will remove materials such as leaves when they lie on top of

◀ Playing successfully out of bunkers isn't just down to sound technique – you must also know the rules to avoid needless penalties. Don't feel tempted to ground the club when you have addressed the ball. It's all too easy to forget this rule and allow the club to touch the sand before you play the shot, but if you do you stand to lose the hole in matchplay or take a 2 shot penalty in strokeplay.

or around his ball in a bunker.

Treat them as if they are part of the sand. If you remove loose impediments in a bunker it costs you the hole in matchplay or 2 strokes in strokeplay.

The only exception comes when your ball is completely covered, as may happen with autumn leaves. In that case, you may remove just enough matter to allow you to see part of the ball.

► **Although you can clear away twigs and leaves from your ball on the rest of the course, you cannot remove loose impediments from a bunker. If you find such material around your ball you must play it as it lies.**

Questions and answers

Unplayable ball

Q On a small course in Scotland, I found my ball lodged in a tree in a bunker. It was unplayable, but I was not sure whether I had to drop in the bunker or could go back outside the bunker and drop in line with the hole. What is the ruling?

A You could have dropped back outside the bunker on the line you suggest. Your ball was not in the bunker on two grounds – a tree, like grass, is not part of the bunker and the margin of a bunker does not extend upwards.

Accidental touch

Q Before I played my shot in a bunker, I picked up the rake and laid it beside me, so that I would be ready to rake my footprints when I had played the shot. In doing so, I touched the sand with my club. My opponent said I should lose the hole for a breach of the rules. Was he correct?

A No. Provided that you did not improve your lie and were not testing the condition of the sand, there was no penalty.

Sand spill

Q When we were playing at the seaside, I found that a lot of sand had spilled over the edge of a sloping bunker. Was this sand part of the bunker?

A No – provided that the line of the margin of the bunker was clear and the sand was outside this, it was not. If the margin is difficult to see, make sure you and your fellow-competitor agree where it is before you play your shot.

Ball on obstruction

Q The margin of a bunker does not extend upwards. If my ball comes to rest on an obstruction in a bunker, may I therefore treat it as not being in the bunker?

A No – although the margin of a bunker does not extend upwards, a ball lying on an obstruction, whether movable or immovable, is in the bunker.

Tricky lie

Q I had a very awkward lie on a steep slope, just outside a bunker. I had great difficulty in taking a stance, and I both grounded the club in the bunker and touched sand in my backswing. What was the penalty?

A Since your ball was not in or touching the bunker there was no penalty, provided that you grounded the club only lightly as the rules permit.

▲ **Sand outside a bunker is not part of a hazard.**

Bunkers 2

What do you do if your ball is deeply embedded in a bunker, or if a stone is in the way of your ball? As usual, the rules are quite specific and it pays to know them.

The state and depth of the sand in a bunker may be quite important in deciding the type of shot you choose to play. But beware – you must not test the condition of the sand in a hazard before you take your shot.

FEET PLACING

You often see players wriggling their feet before they play, sometimes so much that the sand almost reaches the tops of their shoes.

The rules allow you to place your feet firmly when you take your stance but forbid you to build a stance by deliberately packing sand under your feet. If a player gains some idea of how firm and how deep the sand is in the bunker as he takes his stance, that is his good fortune.

You are not allowed to touch loose impediments in a bunker, but you often see players removing stones from hazards without being penalized.

This is because some clubs have local rules allowing you to remove stones from bunkers on their courses. When courses have these local rules they are normally printed on the back of the card of the course.

Most clubs in Britain have a local rule regarding stones in bunkers, but be careful – there are exceptions. A leading amateur lost a hole in an important match in the 1990 English Amateur Championship because he assumed he was allowed to remove a stone in the bunker. The club in question had no such local rule.

Bunkers and water hazards provide the only opportunity for you to play a wrong ball without being penalized. It may sometimes be difficult to identify your ball in a bunker, particularly when more than one ball lands there.

You must not lift the ball to identify it in these circumstances, as you may do elsewhere on the course. Instead, play out the one you think is yours. If you then find the ball is not yours, there is no penalty. If it belongs to an opponent

▼ Gordon Brand jnr was penalized 2 strokes for smoothing out his footprints before playing his second bunker shot in the 1991 Volvo Open. Rules officials later admitted making a mistake and restored the pro to his rightful position.

or fellow competitor, you should replace the ball as near as possible to the original lie.

BURIED BALL

Sometimes your ball is completely buried in a bunker. The rules allow you to search for it, even using a club to do so. Try to expose only part of the ball. But if you accidentally expose more or dislodge the ball, there is no penalty – replace the ball and cover it with sand until just a small part is exposed to allow you to see where it is.

When a bunker has casual water in it and your ball lands there, you can lift and drop your ball without penalty. Choose the nearest spot in the bunker which gives you maximum relief and is not nearer the hole.

Sometimes you may find that the whole of a bunker is filled with water. You then have two options – you can proceed as above, dropping your ball at the point in the bunker not nearer the hole where you think the water is shallowest.

Alternatively you can drop the ball outside the bunker, keeping the point where it lay directly between you and the hole, under penalty of 1 shot.

▲ If you find casual water in a bunker you can take a free drop within the hazard. Make sure you choose a spot not nearer the hole before you drop your ball.

▶ Many courses – especially in Britain – have local rules allowing players to remove stones in a bunker. But don't throw out a stone without checking the card of the course carefully, otherwise you could be penalized.

Questions and answers: bunker play

Rake row

Q My opponent took a rake with him into a bunker so that he could smooth his footprints after he had played his shot. Before he played, he deliberately struck the handle of the rake into the sand. Was this allowed?

A No – he was testing the condition of the sand. He should have lost the hole in matchplay or been penalized 2 strokes in strokeplay. The same penalty would apply if a player pushed his umbrella into the sand.

Club choice

Q I took my stance in a fairway bunker, then decided that the club I had in my hand was too straight faced to clear the lip. I left the bunker to change the club and then took my stance again in the same place. My opponent said I was breaking the rules by testing the condition of the hazard at my first visit. Was he correct?

A No – there's nothing in the rules to stop you deciding to change your club or taking your stance twice in a bunker.

Pretend play

Q While waiting to play a bunker shot, my opponent went to another part of the hazard, took a firm stance, and simulated his bunker shot, without using his club. Was this allowed?

A No – he was breaking the rules as he was testing the sand.

Equipment in bunker

Q My opponent placed his bag of clubs in a bunker before playing his shot. Surely this was against the rules?

A No, it was quite permissible. The exceptions listed under the rules allow a player to place his or her clubs in a bunker, provided he or she does nothing to test the state of the sand or improve the lie of the ball.

Conscientious caddy

Q When I was playing in a final last year my caddie, without permission, raked the sand in a bunker before I played my second shot from the trap. Presumably as this was matchplay I should have lost the hole?

A Provided that nothing is done which improves your lie or assists you in your play of the hole afterwards, you – or your caddie – can rake a bunker before playing a second shot.

On the green

The putting green has special rules that dictate everything from the line of your putt to moving loose impediments and repairing pitch marks.

The green is the area of the golf hole especially prepared for putting. It does not include the fringe. Your ball is on the green when any part of it touches the putting surface. This can be important as different rules apply depending on whether you are just on or just off the green.

For instance, you may mark your ball, lift it and clean it once you are on the green. Elsewhere you will normally have to play the ball as it lies, unless preferred lie or winter rules are in force.

You must place a ball marker – a small coin or similar object – immediately behind the ball before you lift it. If your fellow player thinks the marker interferes with his play or stance, you can move it to one side or the other – usually one or more putter heads away to clear the path.

If your ball or ball marker is accidentally moved in the course of lifting or marking, there is no penalty, and the ball or marker should be replaced.

LINE OF PUTT

You may repair old pitch marks or old refilled holes, but nothing else. This means that you may not repair spike marks.

Removal of sand, soil or loose impediments is allowed. Do this by picking them up or by brushing them aside with your hand or club, but don't press them down.

When you measure to see which ball is nearer to the hole, or when you lift your ball, you may touch the line of the putt. Grounding the

▼ Sam Torrance was caught out by a green rule in the 1990 English Open. His ball teetered on the edge of the 10th hole and eventually fell in – but he was deemed to have waited too long, and had to add a penalty stroke. It was an important ruling, for he eventually lost the event to Mark James in a play-off.

Questions and answers

Checking the turf

Q Not being sure whether a tuft of grass was attached to the ground or not, I brushed it lightly with my hand, and found it was attached. My opponent maintained that I was in breach of the rules for trying to remove something which was not a loose impediment. Was she right?

A No – provided you restored the raised tuft to its original position before you putted, you were entitled to find out whether such a natural object on the line of your putt was loose or not.

Using equipment

Q My opponent removed loose impediments from the line of his putt by brushing them aside with his cap at one hole and with a towel at the next. Was this allowed?

A No – the rules let a player brush aside loose impediments on the line of a putt only with his hand or a club.

Touching the green

Q My opponent was preparing to putt from the apron of the green when his caddie touched the putting surface to indicate the line of his putt. Was this allowed?

A Yes – the rule about touching the green to indicate the line of play applies only when the player's ball lies on the green.

Dewy green

Q Am I allowed to brush dew from the line of my putt?

A No – dew is not a loose impediment.

Accidental breach

Q I know that a player should not step on the line of his opponent's putt. But is there a penalty if you do so by accident?

A There is no penalty for accidentally stepping on your opponent's line.

Deeply embedded

Q I found an embedded acorn on the line of my putt. I removed it, lifted it, and repaired the indentation it had left. Was this in order?

A No – you were allowed to remove the acorn as a loose impediment, since it was so solidly embedded, but you should not have repaired the indentation it had left.

Showing the way

Q When asked to attend the flag for my putt, my caddie took out the pin and rested it upright immediately behind the hole. This was because he was afraid of it sticking in the hole. My opponent claimed the hole because she maintained the green should not have been touched. Was she right?

A Yes – your caddie could have been illegally indicating the line of your putt. He is allowed to show the line only by pointing the flag at a spot.

Watch your spikes
Don't feel tempted to tap down spike marks on a green – even if you have made them yourself. A mistake of this kind will cost you 2 strokes in strokeplay or the loss of the hole in a matchplay competition.

◄ ▼ You can remove loose impediments such as sand or bits of grass from the line of your putt. But make sure to use your hand or your club to brush them away – not your towel or other equipment.

club lightly in front of the ball is also allowed when you address your putt, but you must not press anything down.

Apart from these exceptions you must not touch the line of a putt.

Either you or your partner or one of your caddies may point out what you think is the line of a putt. But you must not touch the green in the process, or place anything on the green which would help with the line of a putt.

On the other hand, if there is a leaf or similar object on the green which you think will help you with the line of a putt, there is no obligation to lift it.

Do not test the surface or speed of a green by rolling a ball or roughening the surface. If you casually knock away a putt which you have conceded, there is no penalty, provided that you were merely returning the ball to the player rather than making a deliberate attempt to test the speed of the green.

HITTING THE PUTT

Standing astride your ball to putt is forbidden. Don't stand with either foot touching the line of the putt or an extension of that line behind the ball.

What happens if your ball overhangs the lip of the hole and looks as though it might drop in at any second? You are allowed to walk up to the hole without reasonable delay, then you are allowed to wait ten seconds.

If by then the ball has not dropped, it is deemed at rest and you must tap it in. If the ball falls in after the time limit and you don't remove it and tap it in, you're penalized a stroke.

Equity

What do you do if your ball is next to a poisonous snake or a child picks up your ball and drops it in the hole? Situations like these are not covered by the rules of golf so you must decide how to proceed under equity.

Golf has the most complex set of rules of any sport. Yet situations still arise which are not covered by this elaborate code. That is why the rules say that if a point is not covered by a particular rule the decision should be made in accordance with equity.

The word equity is defined as an appeal to general principles of justice in cases not covered by the law. In a golfing context equity exists to provide justice where the rules do not lay down a procedure.

KNOW YOUR RULES

The main point you must be sure of before resorting to the concept of equity is that the situation you are dealing with is not in fact covered by the rules.

Bear in mind that a decision in accordance with equity is a rare thing, since the rules are as comprehensive as possible. It's unlikely that the situation you confront is not covered by them.

Nevertheless, there are bound to be occasions when a problem can be solved in no other way than under equity – so it pays to know what to do.

◄ The most feared hazards at the 1991 Ryder Cup in Kiawah Island were the alligator infested lakes. A ball that landed in the water was quickly abandoned.

▼ When your ball lands beside a dangerous animal, the rules allow you in equity to take a free drop rather than to risk life and limb by playing the shot as it lies.

Questions and answers

Outside interference

Q My opponent's ball was thrown back into play by a passer-by after it had gone out of bounds. Neither of us were aware of this and we played out the hole in ignorance of what had happened. What is the ruling?

A In equity there was no penalty for playing a wrong ball, as there would have been if the player had known what had happened and ignored it. If your opponent discovered what had happened before playing from the next teeing ground, he should have gone back and treated the ball as being out of bounds. If the discovery was made after this, his score with the wrong ball stood.

Acting in anger

Q My companion was almost struck by a ball driven by a player in the group behind us. In anger, he hit the ball back towards that group. Did he play a practice stroke at a wrong ball?

A No – but in equity, he incurred the general penalty of loss of a hole in matchplay or 2 strokes in strokeplay.

Practical jokers

Q At one of the par 3s on our course, most of the green and the area around it are invisible from the tee. Children often lurk around this area and pick up the balls which have come to rest. Then they place them in the hole, in the hope that players will think they have holed in one.

What is the procedure when you know this has happened but are not sure whether the ball was on the green, in a bunker, or in the surrounding area?

A The ball should be dropped in an area which is neither the most nor the least favourable of the various areas where it was possible it might have come to rest.

Watery grave

Q My ball was lost, either in a water hazard or in the casual water which had overflowed from it – we could not be sure. What was the proper procedure?

A In equity, you should have assumed the ball was in the water hazard and accepted the 1 stroke penalty involved.

Relief from danger

Q What happens if my ball comes to rest in a place which is dangerous, for instance near a bees' nest or a live snake. Do I have to play it as it lies, or declare it unplayable and drop it under penalty?

A No – it is not reasonable to expect you to play from a dangerous situation, nor fair to require you to suffer a penalty. In equity, you are permitted to drop a ball at the nearest spot not nearer the hole which is not dangerous.

Helpful opponent

Q My opponent was pulling my golf cart round the back of the green for me, but I was not aware of it as I played. My ball struck my cart. What is the ruling?

A In equity there was no penalty and you should have played the ball as it lay. Had you known what he was doing, you would have lost the hole in matchplay or suffered a 2 stroke penalty in strokeplay.

Sometimes the rules can work to your advantage. If your ball comes to rest beside an open gate, it is your good fortune that you can take your backswing and play the shot. Use your common sense in situations like these. If the gate had been shut, you would not have been allowed to open it and would have been faced with a tricky lie.

Glossary

Address
Your position in relation to the ball as you prepare to strike.

Albatross
A score of three under par on a hole.

Alignment
How your body is aligned in relation to an imagined ball-to-target line.

Birdie
A score of one under par on a hole.

Blind
A hole or shot where you can't see your target.

Bogey
Originally the expected score in which a good player was reckoned to complete a hole, but now replaced by par. Bogey has come to mean one over par.

Borrow
How much you have to aim right or left when putting to allow for the slope of the green to bring the ball back to the hole.

Bunker
A natural or artificial depression on a fairway or round the green. It is usually half-filled with sand but can be made of earth or grass.

Chip and run
A low shot that runs towards the flag played from near the green.

Clubface
The area of the club that you use to hit the ball.

Clubhead
The part of the club attached to the lower end of the shaft, and used for striking the ball.

Divot
A chunk of turf removed by the clubhead when you play a shot, usually on the fairway.

Dog-leg
A hole with a fairway that bends sharply. A hazard is often positioned at the angle of the dog-leg to put you off driving across it.

Double bogey
A score of two over par for a hole.

Drive
A shot which is played from the tee, usually with a driver (a 1 wood).

Eagle
A score of two under par on a hole.

Flagstick
Also called the pin, flag or stick, the flagstick marks the hole.

Fourball
A matchplay or strokeplay game of two players on each side, all four striking their own ball.

Foursome
A matchplay or strokeplay game between two sides of two players each, the partners striking the ball alternately.

Full set
The 14 clubs which are allowed for playing a round. A full set usually consists of three or four wooden clubs or metal woods, nine or ten irons and a putter.

Grip
The part of the club you hold, and the way you hold it.

Guttie
A ball made from gutta percha. It lost popularity when the wound ball was introduced at the beginning of the 20th century.

Half set
Either the odd or the even irons, two woods and a putter. A half set of clubs is all you need when you start playing.

Filling in a scorecard
Scorecards are used in strokeplay to record your score so your Club can work out your handicap. As you play a round, you write down the number of strokes taken for each hole and tot up the total at the end. When you have filled in four scorecards, you hand them in and are given a handicap that's your average number of strokes over par.

The par is worked out according to the length of the hole and the stroke index lists the holes in order of difficulty. This is for when you play a matchplay game: if your opponent has a handicap of, say, 10 and yours is 26 you can take 12 extra strokes – three quarters of the difference between your handicaps – on the 12 most difficult holes.

Event: MONTHLY MEDAL
Date:
STANDARD SCRATCH SCORE 70
Player: BILL JOHNSTONE
Handicap: FOR H'CAP
Strokes Recd:

Marker's Score	Hole	Yards	PAR	Stroke Index	Player's Score	Won X Lost – Half 0	Marker's Score	Hole	Yards	PAR	Stroke Index	Player's Score	Won X Lost – Half 0
5	1	293	4	13	5								
6	2	356	4	6	5			10	156	3	14	4	3
4	3	169	3	15	4			11	300	4	16	5	4
6	4	454	4	1	7			12	362	4	4	6	5
4	5	301	4	17	6			13	121	3	18	3	4
4	6	305	4	12	4			14	383	4	5	6	6
4	7	335	4	3	4			15	327	4	11	4	5
6	8	396	4	8	7			16	408	4	2	4	6
5	9	365	4	10	5			17	399	4	7	5	6
44	OUT	2974	35		47			18	479	5	9	5	5
								IN	2935	35		42	44
								OUT	2974	35		47	
								TOTAL	5909	70		89	
								HANDICAP					
								NET SCORE					

Player's Signature: Bill Johnstone
Marker's Signature: John Thomson

Strokes are taken at those holes opposite which the Stroke Index figure is equal to, or less than, the number of strokes received.

Handicap
A system devised to make play between golfers of different standards an even match. Your handicap is the number of strokes over par you average over four rounds at a golf club. For instance, if your average score is 88 on a par 72 course, you are given a handicap of 16. In strokeplay, if you play with, say, a 2 handicapper, you are allowed 14 – the difference between your handicaps – extra strokes, one on each of the most difficult 14 holes. In matchplay, the longer handicap player would receive 11 shots – three quarters of the difference.

Hazard
A bunker is a hazard. So, too, is any stream, ditch, lake or pond defined as a hazard by a club's committee.

Hole
This can mean either the actual hole that you putt into or the entire area between tee and green.

Iron
Irons are metal-headed clubs used for most shots between tee and green. Sometimes you can use them from the tee at holes where accuracy is more important than length. The sand wedge and pitching wedge are also irons.

Lie
Where the ball is in relation to the ground it is resting on. The more embedded in grass or sand the ball is, the worse the lie. Lie also refers to the angle of the sole of the clubhead to the shaft.

Loft
The angle of the clubface to the ground. The more loft a club has (indicated by how high the number is) the higher the ball goes and the shorter distance it travels.

Long game
Shots over about 180yd (164m) long, played from the tee or on the fairway with woods or low-numbered irons.

Matchplay
A game between two players or two sides which is determined by the number of holes won and lost.

Out of bounds
A ball is out of bounds if it lands anywhere prohibited for play – usually beyond the course's boundaries.

Par
The standard score for a hole, usually based on its length. Holes up to 250yd (228m) long are par 3s, up to 475yd (434m) par 4s and any longer than that are par 5s. Club committees are now authorised to vary par when a hole's difficulty warrants not sticking rigidly to the distances laid down.

Pitch
A reasonably high shot on to the green, travelling anything from a few yards to 120yd (110m). You generally use a 9 iron, a pitching wedge or a sand wedge.

Pitching wedge
A short iron with a large degree of loft, used for pitching high but short shots on to the green.

Play-off
If a competition ends with a tie, the winner is decided by playing further holes. Nowadays, the winner is usually the first competitor to win a hole, except for the US and British Opens.

Reading the green
Looking at the slope and contours of the green to decide the line and speed of your putt.

Rough
Grass left to grow so that off-line shots are made more difficult.

Sand wedge
Also called a sand iron, the shortest, most lofted iron used for playing out of bunkers and for very short pitches.

Scratch player
A golfer with a handicap of zero.

Shaft
The length of the club down to the clubhead.

Short game
Chipping, pitching, bunker play and putting on the green and around it up to a distance of 100yd (90m) away.

Square
When the clubface is placed at right angles to the imaginary ball-to-target line.

Stableford
A popular system of scoring by points for holes completed: par = 2 points; 1 under par = 3 points; 2 under par = 4 points; 1 over par = 1 point.

Stance
The position of your feet just before playing a shot.

Standard scratch score (SSS)
The score expected of a scratch player on any given course.

Strokeplay
A competition in which a player's total strokes for a round are recorded to be compared with the scores of other competitors. 'Strokeplay', the correct term, is often referred to as 'medal play'.

Stymie
A rule now abolished, where a player who was about to putt his ball into the hole, but had another one blocking its route, had to try to putt round or loft his ball over the other.

Swingweight
The weight and balance of a club. All the clubs in your set should be the same swingweight.

Takeaway
The start of the backswing.

Tee
The area of a hole from which you play the first shot.

Tee peg
You can put the ball on this device for your first shot to help raise the ball off the ground. It is then much easier to attain height.

Tempo
The timing and rhythm of your swing, which should be even and smooth throughout.

Thin
A long, low shot hit by mistake with the leading edge of the club (blade).

Top
A shot mistakenly hit with the bottom edge of the club, so that the ball is embedded in the ground before popping up, and in most cases travelling only a short distance.

Triple bogey
A score of three over par on a hole.

Wood
A club normally used for distance shots. It can be made of wood, metal or graphite.

Yardage (distance) chart
A plan of the holes on a course showing the distance from one point to another. It can be printed by the club or prepared by the golfer or his caddie.

Yips
A condition where the player is so anxious about his putting that he can't swing his putter back, and the stroke becomes a jerky jab at the ball.

Index

Page numbers in *italic* refer to illustrations
Page numbers in **bold** indicate major references

Picture credits

Photographers: Allsport 2-3, 4-5, 10, 108, 296, 313, 315, 321(t), 324(t), 335, 336(t, br), 337(bl), 338(tr), 400(b), 434(b), 435, 465, (S Bruty) 84(b), 85, 160, 342(br), 343(l), 352(r), 371(b), 383(t), 384(t), 418(b), 425, 455(t), (D Cannon) 41, 77, 83, 89, 133, 164, 172, 230(b), 234(b), 236, 276(b), 278(b), 301(t), 303-305(t), 309(t), 310-311(l), 314(b), 317, 319(t), 320(t), 323, 330(b), 331(b), 332, 334, 350(b), 354, 357(t), 364-365(t), 368-369(tl, b), 372-374, 381(bl), 382(l), 397, 403-404(b), 405(b), 408(b), 409, 411(t), 412(t), 415(b), 416(r), 422(t), 423(b), 424, 426(t), 445(b), 461(b), 468(t)-469, 471, (R Cheyne) 444(tr), 445(t), 472, (T Duffy) 364(b), (A Gatt) 459, (J Gichingi) 513, (M Hobbs) 345, (D Leah) 456(t), (B Martin) 428(br), 436(t), (S Munday) 290, (J Nicholson) 292(b), (S Powell) 299(b), 351(tr), 362(t), 408(t), (P Rondeau) 40, 306, 432(br), 433(b), (D Smith) 381(b), 384 (br), (497), (B Symes) 318(b)-319, 366(t), (Vandystadt/C Petit, 386(b), 387(b), (Vandystadt) 308(t); Associated Press 392(t), 393(b); Associated Sports Photography 45; BIGGA 461(t); Bridgeman Art Library 439, 441(b); Charles Briscoe-Knight 22, 65, 90-1, 102, 106(l), 147, 180, 253, 260-261, 312, 324(br), 325, 326(c), 327(c), 350-351(t, l), 389(t), 407, 428(bl), 449(b) 452(b), 454(t), 455(br), 457-458(t, br), 460(b), 463(t), 468(t), 479, 499, 507, 515; M Briscoe-Knight 106(r); S Carr 170; Colorsport 1, 6, 79, 93-94, 302(r), 307, 311(b), 316, 330(t), 333(b), 339, 341(r), 344(b), 352(l), 353(t), 355, 361, 367, 376(t), 402(t), 414(b), 421(tl), 426(b), 429(b), 432(t), 438, 509, 521; P Dazeley 28, 150(b), 278(t), 319(br), 341(l), 344(t), 358, 360, 375(tl), 377(t), 381(t), 387(t), 395(b), 400(c), 401(b), 416(l), 419, 433(t), 437, 450(tl), 451(t), 454(b), 455(bl), 458(bl), 460(bl), 461(c), 463(b), 473-474, 512(t), 514(t); Eaglemoss Publications Ltd (S Carr) 154(br), (P Sheldon) 9, 107, 109-125, 128-132, 136-141, 143-145, 147, 150(t), 151, 153-154(t), 155-158, 161-162(t), 163, 165-167, 169, 171, 173, 175-179, 182-192(t), 193-198, 200-203, 205-210, 212-216(t), 217-220, 222-224, 226, 228-230(cl), 231-234(t), 237-240(t), 242(t), 244-247(b), 248-252, 254-259, 262-263, 266, 273, 275, 279, 281-282(t), 283, 285, 287-289, 292(t), 293(t), 295, 481-483, 485-488, 491, 493-496, 500-501, 508(t), 516, 518, (J Suett) 247(c); Mary Evans Picture Library 440(b); Good Shot (Ludovic Aubert) 366(b); Golden Bear Inc. 446(tl); R Gould 38-39; K Hailey 17, 21, 467(t)-470, 514(c); M Harris (Golf Picture LIbrary) 1, 26, 162(b), 272, 314(t), 351(b), 452(c), 462(b), 464(t), 508(b); M Hobbs Golf Collection 66, 68, 87(l), 99, 442, 444(tl), 449(t), 450(tr, bl), 451(c); Hulton Deutsch Collection 88(t), 336(bl), 337(t, br), 338(b, tl), 346-348, 404(t), 405(t), 406; Illustrated London News Picture Library 440(t); B Morgan Golf Photography 12, 16(t), 19, 23, 35, 37, 44, 48-53, 57-58, 80-81, 95-96, 98, 101, 104-106(b), 216(b), 250(b), 297-299(tl), 300(b), 302(l), 353(b), 362(b), 363(b), 370-371(t), 395(t), 396(t), 399(r), 410(b), 417(t), 430(bl), 462(t), 504; National Railway Museum 441(t); M Newcombe 512(b), 517(t); St Mellion Golf & Country Club 446(tr), 447(tl); P Sheldon 15, 16(b), 25, 29-34, 36, 42, 46, 54, 61-62, 64, 67, 69-71, 73-76(b), 82, 84(t, c), 86, 87(r), 88(c), 134, 148, 154(bl), 168, 192(b), 274(b), 276(t), 291, 293(b), 294, 298, 300(t), 305(b), 308(b), 309(b), 320(b), 321(b), 322, 324(bl), 326(t, b), 327(t, b), 328, 340, 342(t, bl), 343(r), 356-357(b), 359, 363(r), 369(tr), 375(b), 376(b), 377(c, b), 378-380, 382(r), 383(b), 386(t), 388-389(b), 390-392(b), 393(t)-394, 411(b), 412(b), 417(b), 418(t), 420, 421(b), 422(b), 427, 430(t), 434(t), 436(b), 443-444(b), 446(br)-448, 450(br), 451(br), 466(t), 477, 498, 503, 505, (Traylen) 282(b), 318(t); Sporting Pictures UK Ltd 464(b); Swilken Golf Company 242(bl); Syndication International 375(tr), 402(b); Yours in Sport/Lawrence Levy 47-52, 59, 76(t), 100, 240(b), 241-242(br), 274(t), 277, 299(tr), 301(b), 329, 331(t), 333(t), 349, 365(b), 384(bl), 385, 396(b), 398-399(l), 401(t), 410(t), 413-414(t), 415(t), 421(tr), 423(t), 428(t), 429(t), 430(br), 431-432(bl), 451(bl), 453, 456(b), 460(t), 466(b), 467(b), 489-490, 509, 517(b); Volvo/C Briscoe-Knight 103.

Illustrators: Andrew Farmer/Strokesaver 12-15, 18-21, 24-27, 30-33, 36-39, 42-45, 48-51, 54-57, 60-63, 66-69, 72-75, 78-81, 84-87, 90-93, 96-99; Elaine Keenan 251; Kevin Jones Associates 41-142, 146-147, 152, 154, 158, 164, 173-174(tr), 183, 186, 192, 199(br), 201, 202(br), 216, 221(l), 224, 230, 233, 236, 243, 248(t), 357-258, 262, 267-271, 273, 275-277, 288-289, 475-476, 478, 480, 484, 488, 492, 494, 502, 506, 510; Chris Perfect/Egg Design 110-111, 114-115, 118, 120, 124, 132-135, 137-138, 148-149, 159-160, 166-168, 170, 172, 174(tl, b), 181, 188, 199, 202(bl), 204, 207, 210-211, 221(r), 225-227, 235, 247-248(b), 252, 264-265, 280.

Illustrations by Andrew Farmer are based on material supplied by Strokesaver, official publishers to the British Open and the European Tour.